Management

Concepts, Practices, and Skills

Management

SEVENTH
EDITION

Concepts, Practices, and Skills

R. WAYNE MONDY
McNeese State University

SHANE R. PREMEAUX
McNeese State University

PRENTICE HALL, INC.
Englewood Cliffs, New Jersey

Library of Congress Cataloging-in-Publication Data

Mondy, R. Wayne
    Management—concepts, practices, and skills /
    R. Wayne Mondy, Shane R. Premeaux—7th ed.
        p.   cm.
    Includes bibliographical references and indexes
    ISBN: 0-205-16378-5
    1. Management.   I. Premeaux, Shane R.   II. Title.
HD31.M616 1995
658—dc20   94-41368
                                            CIP

Acquisitions Editor: Natalie E. Anderson
Marketing Manager: Jo-Ann DeLuca
Production Management: GTS Graphics, Inc.
Managing Editor: Frances Russello
In-house Liaison: Penelope Linskey
Design Director: Linda Fiordilino
Interior Design: Joyce C. Weston
Copy Editor: Kathleen Smith
Proofreader: Deborah Kopka
Photo Researcher: Darcy Wilding
Buyer: Vincent Scelta
Associate Editor: Lisamarie Brassini
Editorial Assistant: Nancy Proyect
Production Assistant: Renee Pelletier
Cover Design: Rosemarie Votta
Cover Art: Phyllis Ciment

© 1995 by Prentice Hall, Inc.
A Simon & Schuster Company
Englewood Cliffs, New Jersey 07632

Printed in the United States of America
10 9 8 7 6 5 4 3 2   95 96 97

ISBN: 0-205-16378-5

Prentice-Hall International (UK) Limited, *London*
Prentice-Hall of Australia Pty. Limited, *Sydney*
Prentice-Hall Canada Inc., *Toronto*
Prentice-Hall Hispanoamericana, S.A., *Mexico*
Prentice-Hall of India Private Limited, *New Delhi*
Prentice-Hall of Japan, Inc., *Tokyo*
Simon & Schuster Asia Pte. Ltd., *Singapore*
Editoria Prentice-Hall do Brasil, Ltda., *Rio de Janeiro*

To Marianne Elizabeth, my tennis
partner and love of my life.
—*R. Wayne Mondy*

To my late grandfather,
Israel Simon, Sr. He provided wisdom
and unconditional love.
I miss you, Pa Pa.
—*Shane R. Premeaux*

Contents

PART II: DECISION MAKING AND PLANNING

PART III: ORGANIZING

7. The Organizing Process and the Informal Organization 200

Learning Objectives 200

8. Organizing Concepts and Organizational Structure 234

Learning Objectives 234

PART IV: INFLUENCING

PART V: CONTROLLING

PART VI: SPECIAL TOPICS

20. Management Information Systems 638

Preface

Like the six previous editions, the seventh edition of *Management: Concepts, Practices, and Skills* is written for an audience that expects management theory to be linked with actual management practice. Although it is essentially pragmatic in approach, the text is balanced throughout with current management theory. A common theme—a "real-world" approach to management—exists throughout the book. Each of the management functions—planning, organizing, influencing, and controlling—is discussed from the standpoint of how it interrelates to the management process. The book puts the student in touch with reality through the extensive use of real-world company examples and exercises. A major feature of the seventh edition is the further development of a theme that emphasizes how management is practiced. The following material is presented to show how management is practiced: all new extended company examples—two per chapter, many new in-text company examples, Management In Practice exercises, reality-based Ethical Dilemma exercises, Management Tips, end-of-chapter cases, and end-of-section Self-Assessment Exercises. The lead-off vignettes are new or completely updated and revised.

FEATURES OF THE CHAPTERS

• **Management: An Overview.** This chapter presents an overview of the book and shows how the management functions are integrated throughout the book to develop an effective management approach.

• **The Manager's Diverse Environment.** This chapter shows the many environmental factors that impact top-level managers. It also stresses that the environment of lower-level managers in the organization is different from that of upper-level managers. New sections that have been added include "Managing the Diverse Workforce," "The Small Business," and "The Diverse Multinational Environment."

• **Social Responsibility and Business Ethics.** The information in this chapter permits the discussion of ethics throughout the remainder of the text. Ethical

Dilemma exercises, which are based on real-life ethical problems, are presented in the remaining chapters. A new section entitled "A Change in Attitude Toward Social Responsibility?" has been added.

• **Managerial Decision Making.** The traditional decision-making topics are included in this chapter.

• **The Planning Process.** This chapter describes not only the planning process, but also includes contingency planning and a discussion of management by objectives from both a positive and negative standpoint.

• **Strategic Planning.** This chapter includes current topics in the field and the organizational aspects that impact strategic planning.

• **The Organizing Process and the Informal Organization.** This chapter discusses the organizing process, specialization of labor, departmentation, organizational differentiation, and the informal organization. A new topic, "Downsizing," has been added to the chapter.

• **Organizing Concepts and Organizational Structure.** This chapter focuses on such topics as responsibility, authority, delegation, accountability, organizing principles, centralization versus decentralization, and types of organizational structures. Also included is a section on how managers can become better at working with committees. Sections on "Reengineering" and "Job Design" have been added to the chapter.

• **Human Resource Management and the Staffing Function.** In addition to the traditional topics on this subject, a completely updated section on current laws and executive orders affecting equal employment opportunity has been provided for the seventh edition. Other topics such as the "Glass Ceiling," "Drug Testing," "Negligent Hiring and Retention," and "Sexual Harassment," have been emphasized.

• **Motivation.** The chapter focuses on philosophies of human nature, needs theory, equity theory, reinforcement theory, expectancy theory, goal setting and motivation, how managers can be better at motivating, and possible rewards a first-level manager can dispense. New topics include "Linking Pay to Performance to Achieve Workplace Diversity" and "Responding to the Needs of the Diverse Workforce."

• **Leadership.** Established topics such as the trait approach to leadership, behavioral leadership theories, and situational leadership theories are discussed in this chapter. New topics include "Leading a Diverse Workforce" and "Leadership and the Team Approach."

• **Communication.** Traditional topics such as the communication process, communication channels, barriers to communication, how managers can become better communicators, communication networks and their characteristics, barriers to effective group communication, and directing are discussed in this chapter. A new topic, "Barriers to Effective Work Team Communication," has been added.

• **Group Performance, Team Building, and Conflict.** The title of this chapter has been changed for the seventh edition to reflect the importance of teams and team building. A major focus of the chapter is on teams, as is suggested by the following chapter topics: groups and work teams, formation of effective groups and teams, development of groups into teams, factors influencing group and team effectiveness, increasing team effectiveness, work-team effectiveness, characteristics of effective teams, strategies for team building, and self-managed teams.

• **Power, Organizational Politics, and Stress.** This chapter includes such topics as power and reasons for exerting power, sources of power, how managers can increase their power, power configurations, power differences, strategies for obtaining power, significance of power to the manager, resisting intimidation, political action in organizations, and stress and burnout in organizations.

• **Corporate Culture, Change, and Development.** Traditional topics are addressed in this chapter such as factors that influence corporate culture, participative versus nonparticipative cultures, the change sequence, sources of resistance to change, approaches to reducing resistance to change, organizational development, and evidence of culture. New topics include "Diversity Training" and "Team Building."

• **The Controlling Processes and Techniques.** Topics discussed include: the controlling process, strategic control points, ways of overcoming negative reactions to controls, and disciplinary action. Topics such as budgetary control, quality control, inventory control, and network models are also discussed in this chapter. A new topic, "International Quality Standards," has been added.

• **Total Quality Management.** This chapter stresses the importance of a commitment to excellence by everyone in an organization through the TQM process. Two new topics, "Tools for Problem Solving" and "Managerial Mistakes in Implementing TQM," have been added.

• **Management in the Multinational Enterprise.** This chapter provides students with a realistic understanding of the operations of multinational companies. The chapter illustrates how different environments can affect the operation of the multinational.

- **Production and Operations Management.** Traditional topics include graphic methods, labor measurement, site selection, physical facilities layouts, maintenance control, learning curves, financial planning techniques, and simulation.

- **Management Information Systems.** Traditional topics included in this chapter are information needs of a firm, characteristics of an effective MIS, the MIS at different organizational levels, computer selection, possible information subsystems for managers, computer advancements affecting productivity, creating the MIS, guidelines for effective MIS design, and implementation of the MIS.

 ## AND, IN THE APPENDICES

- **Planning a Career in Management.** In this appendix, the student is provided with meaningful information regarding planning for a career in management. The authors stress the need for a thorough self-assessment, address the types of entry-level management positions that are available, and discuss career paths.

- **History of Management and Organizational Behavior.** In this appendix, the student is provided information that is both informative and interesting. Mistakes of the past are prone to be repeated, and therefore, students of management must understand and appreciate the history of management so they will have a better frame of reference with which to make critical decisions.

 ## FEATURES OF THE BOOK

The following features are included to promote the readability and understanding of important management concepts.

- An introductory vignette, involving management in a real company, is provided at the beginning of each chapter to set the tone for a discussion of the major topics included within the chapter. All of these cases are new or completely updated and revised.
- An "Ethical Dilemma" is provided in Chapters 4–20. These Ethical Dilemmas provide instructors with an opportunity to allow students to experience some real ethical dilemmas in a classroom setting. All Ethical Dilemmas are based upon real-world occurrences.
- Management In Practice exercises are provided in each chapter. These exercises are designed to literally put students "on the spot," to let them think through how they would react in typical management situations.
- A new "Global Perspective" is provided for each chapter. These perspectives

provide instructors with an opportunity to allow students to experience some realistic global topics.

- A new section entitled "Management Tips" is provided at the end of each chapter. These are practical tips designed to assist in the actual implementation of the subject matter.
- Two new extended examples are provided in each chapter to illustrate how the material discussed in the chapter is used in the real world.
- Two case studies involving management are provided at the end of each chapter to highlight material covered in the chapter. Half of the cases are new to the seventh edition.
- An end-of-section self-assessment exercise is provided so that students can measure their ability in such areas as ethics, decision making, organizing, leadership, time management, and cultural attitudes.
- Learning objectives are listed at the beginning of each chapter to highlight the general purpose and key concepts of the chapter.
- Review questions appear at the end of each chapter to test the student's understanding of the material.
- Key terms are listed at the end of each chapter. In addition, a key term is presented in bold print the first time it is defined or described in the chapter.
- A glossary of all key terms appears at the end of the book.
- A subject index is provided at the end of the book.
- Finally, a comprehensive list of references is provided.

IMPROVEMENTS TO THE SEVENTH EDITION

Each of the previous editions of this book has enjoyed considerable success. Many of our adopters provided us with suggestions for improving the seventh edition. Topics that have been added or have been given additional coverage are provided below.

- **The practitioner base of the book has been expanded.** The book has been thoroughly updated to include the most current management topics.

- **Multinational topics are extensively discussed throughout the book.** Opening cases that are multinational in nature include: Chapter 5—"AT&T's Mission-Centered Focus Expands into International Markets," Chapter 10— "Stylish Cars and Motivated Workers Help Nissan Overtake Honda as the Number Two Automaker in the United States," Chapter 13—"Volvo's Work Teams," and Chapter 18—"Dow: Trying to Overtake Number One DuPont." Major multinational topics are covered under the heading of "A Global Perspective" in each chapter. In addition, extended examples related to the global environment include: Chapter 2—"The North American Free Trade Agreement (NAFTA): A Nightmare for Organized Labor," Chapter 5—"Planning: A Weapon for Business Survival in Mainland China," Chapter 6—"Philips' Strategic Plan: Become Sony-Like," Chapter 6—"Global Strategy and Implementation," Chapter 7—"IBM Europe's Experiment in Decentralization," Chapter 15—"The Changing Face of Eastern Europe," Chapter 16—"JIT: No Longer Just for Japanese Manufacturers," Chapter 18—"The Face of the Global U.S. Competitor," and Chapter 19—"Effective Layout Gives Siemens a Competitive Advantage." End-of-chapter cases that relate to the global environment include: Chapter 5—"Club Med: Planning to Stay the Leader in Sun, Fun, and Fantasy," Chapter 18—"Mr. Tanaka's Plea for Respect," and "Renault: The American Adventure."

• **A major focus on work teams has been added throughout the text.** The following topics are stressed in the text: Chapter 4—Work Team and Group Methods Involved in Decision Making, Chapter 11—Leadership and the Team Approach, Chapter 12—Barriers to Effective Work Team Communication, Chapter 13—Groups and Work Teams, Chapter 13—Formation of Effective Groups and Teams, Chapter 13—Development of Groups into Teams, Chapter 13—Factors Influencing Group and Team Effectiveness, Chapter 13—Increasing Team Effectiveness, Chapter 13—Characteristics of Effective Teams, Chapter 13—Strategies for Team Building, Chapter 13—Self-Managed Teams, and Chapter 15—Team Building. In addition, Chapter 13 is entitled *Group Performance, Team Building, and Conflict,* and the front case is entitled "Volvo's Work Teams." An extended example in Chapter 13 entitled "Team Saturn" is also provided.

• **Workplace diversity is stressed throughout the text.** Chapter 2 is entitled "The Manager's Diverse Environment." Major sections related to diversity include: Chapter 2—"Managing the Diverse Workforce," Chapter 2—"The Diverse Multinational Environment," Chapter 9—"Mandating Diversity: Laws and Executive Orders Affecting Equal Employment Opportunity," Chapter 10—"Linking Pay to Performance to Achieve Workplace Diversity," Chapter 10—"Responding to the Needs of the Diverse Workforce," Chapter 11—"Leading a Diverse Workforce," and Chapter 15—"Diversity Training." Extended examples related to diversity include: Chapter 2—"Levi Strauss Values Diversity," Chapter 3—"Diverse and Socially Responsible by Design," Chapter 11—"Progress Toward Leadership Diversity," Chapter 12—"Cultural Diversity Demands New Communication Skills," Chapter 13—"The Mediation of Role-Related Diversity Problems Through Role Playing," and Chapter 15—"The Impact of Growing Diversity on Corporate Culture." In addition, an excellent video entitled *Mosaic Workplace* is available to adopters. The following segments are included in the video: (1) Why value diversity? (2) Understanding biases and assumptions. (3) Sexual harassment. (4) Managing a diverse workplace. (5) Helping new employees feel valued.

• **Emphasis is placed on small businesses throughout the text.** Small businesses are introduced in Chapter 1 in the extended example entitled, "The Allure of Becoming a Small Business Manager: Is It No Longer as Great?" In Chapter 2 a major section has been added entitled "The Small Business." A famous small business, "Wall Drug: A Badlands Small Business Success Story," is presented as the front vignette in Chapter 7. An additional small business extended example entitled "Small Businesses Shape Up by Shipping Out" is provided in Chapter 18. Further, numerous end-of-chapter cases are related to small business. End-of-chapter cases related to small business include: Chapter 1—"Pinnacle," Chapter 2—"Singing the Small Business Blues," Chapter 4—"Expansion Plans for The Toggery," Chapter 6—"Master Hardware," Chapter 7—"The Organization of Quality Control," Chapter 8—"Misco Paper Converters," Chapter 9—" 'Send Him on Down,' " Chapter 10—"A Citation for Kathy," Chapter 11—" 'You Know the Policy,' " Chapter 13—"No Cause for Concern," Chapter 14—"Threatened by a Superstar," Chapter 15—"Breaking Up the Team," Chapter 15—"Fears of Layoffs at Duncan Electric," Chapter 16—"A Problem of Shrinkage," Chapter 17—"The Faulty Cues," Chapter 19—"Materials Management at Newco," Chapter 20—" 'This Has Been a Fiasco,' " and Chapter 20—"Fort Steel Products."

• **Topics on reengineering and downsizing have been added.** New major sections are provided in Chapters 7 and 8. Chapter 7 includes a discussion of "Downsizing." An extended example entitled "Procter & Gamble Reengineers for the Future" and a discussion of "Reengineering" and "Job Design" are provided in Chapter 8.

• **A major focus has been placed on the importance of service industries to our economy.** Introductory vignettes that provide insight into the issue of service include: Chapter 2—"Subway Sandwiches Effectively Deals with the Aggressive Open Environment of the Fast-Food Industry," Chapter 3—"Social Responsibility and Business Ethics: The Least-Mentioned Wal-Mart Tradition," Chapter 5—"AT&T's Mission-Centered Focus Expands into International Markets," Chapter 6—"At GE Capital Services Performance Planning Pays Off," Chapter 7—"Wall Drug: A Badlands Small Business Success Story," and Chapter 16—"McDonald's Remains Number One Through Consistency." Extended examples related to the issue of service include: Chapter 1—"Can Keen Management Ability and Enthusiasm Overcome TWA's Problems?," Chapter 3— "Wal-Mart: Honorable Competitor or Cutthroat Retailer?" Chapter 7—"Commonwealth Edison Restructures," Chapter 11—"Liz Claiborne: Leading by Example," and

Chapter 14—"Companies Coalesce for Paramount." End-of-chapter cases that relate to the issue of service include: Chapter 1—"Wal-Mart: The Nation's Number One Retailer," Chapter 2—"Pan American's Fight Against the Environment," Chapter 5—"Club Med: Planning to Stay the Leader in Sun, Fun, and Fantasy," Chapter 5—"Planning for Effectiveness at Wendy's," Chapter 8—"Holiday Corporation: Organizing for Success," Chapter 10—"Domino's Dominoids: Motivated to Serve," Chapter 12—"Wells Fargo: From Horses to High-Tech," and Chapter 16—"Controlling 10,000 7-Eleven Stores."

• **Miscellaneous features.** Fifty percent of the introductory vignettes are new, and the remainder have been revised extensively. In addition, Management Tips are provided at the end of each chapter to give practical appreciation regarding the subject matter of each chapter.

All of these features were designed to promote and stimulate student interest. We sincerely hope that students of management derive as much pleasure from reading the book as we did in writing it.

—R. Wayne Mondy,
McNeese State University
—Shane R. Premeaux,
McNeese State University

ACKNOWLEDGMENTS

The assistance and encouragement of many people is normally required in the writing of any book. This is especially true in the writing of the seventh edition of *Management: Concepts, Practices, and Skills*. Although it would be virtually impossible to list each person who assisted in this project, we feel that certain people must be credited because of the magnitude of their contribution. Our sincere thanks go to the many members of the faculty and staff at McNeese State University. We would also like to thank Marianne Hartman and Marthanne Bello, two very competent and professional individuals who were always available to ensure that our deadlines were met. Good luck in your career, Marianne, and good luck in your future, Marthanne! We also appreciate the excellent comments of the following reviewers. They were truly valuable: Professor Marc Siegall, California State University, Chico; Professor Micah Mukahbi, Essex County Community College; Professor Vernell Walker, San Antonio College; Professor Dean Danielson, San Joaquin Delta College; Professor Lowell Lamberton, Central Oregon Community College; Professor Donna Giertz, Parkland College; Professor David Harris, Rhode Island College; Professor Dennis G. Allen, Grand Rapids Community College.

1 Management: An Overview

LEARNING OBJECTIVES

After completing this chapter students should be able to

✘ Define *management*.
✘ Explain the management functions of planning, organizing, influencing, and controlling.
✘ Describe management at different organizational levels and explain the work of managers at those levels.
✘ Discuss the importance of conceptual, technical, and human managerial skills.
✘ Explain the desirability of entering management.
✘ Define *productivity* and state why it is important to managers.

Chrysler Succeeds Under Eaton's Management

Robert "Bob" Eaton is now in charge at Chrysler, trying to fill some of the biggest shoes in the automobile industry, those of Lee Iacocca. When Iacocca assumed the presidency of Chrysler in 1979, the company had just suffered its worst one-quarter loss in history. The U.S. auto industry was beset by foreign competition, and the country was entering a lengthy recession. Interest rates were at all-time highs, depressing demand for autos and other durable consumer goods. Actual and threatened auto industry layoffs, along with wage and benefit cuts, had produced a difficult labor relations climate. Iacocca had his work cut out for him. But 14 years later, in 1992, he could look back on a remarkable career of accomplishment for both Chrysler and himself.

Throughout his career, Iacocca had an uncanny knack for sensing market needs and creating products to meet those needs. He had a reputation for getting the most out of his subordinates, for creating enthusiasm, for making difficult decisions, and for working harder than anyone around him. Iacocca lived up to, and even surpassed, his advanced billing as a miracle worker. He jawboned the union, made television commercials, and at all times maintained the appearance of a vibrant, forceful, in-charge—though kindly—executive. Dissatisfaction with Iacocca's actions was immediate, but Chrysler was on its way to recovery. The improvement was not just a flash in the pan. At Chrysler's 1987 model preview, Iacocca forecast a 15 percent share of the U.S. auto and light truck market by the 1990s. Chrysler acquired American Motors, with its popular Jeep line, in 1987, and in the same year exceeded Iacocca's 15 percent estimate. Chrysler also made the top ten on the *Fortune* 500 list, and Chrysler's stock experienced two three-for-two splits and was still trading in the mid twenties, up from $2 at the depth of the 1982 recession.

In 1992, Iacocca retired at age 68, with his company financially sound. Several so-called heir-apparents were passed over in favor of 52-year-old Robert "Bob" Eaton. Eaton, a long-time Chrysler man, was quite successful in Chrysler's

European operations, but running a division of Chrysler and managing the entire company are quite different. Eaton took over with zeal and an attitude that Chrysler management style must center around committed people and quality products. His main concern was Chrysler's product line, not his personal ability to manage Chrysler. After all, Chrysler's LH cars were referred to as the "Last Hope" for Chrysler. Eaton's decision to maintain the solid management style of his predecessor, combined with the new LH line of cars, quickly paid off. By 1993, the LH cars—the Chrysler Concorde, the Dodge Intrepid, the Eagle Vision, and the New Yorker—were hugely successful. Eaton's effective management approach resulted in Chrysler's sales rising by 26 percent, twice Ford's 13 percent increase, and over five times GM's five percent growth rate.[1]

What accounts for Chrysler's success? Most would agree that effective management plays a major role. This book is about management, which consists of getting things done through the efforts of other people. At Chrysler, management involved negotiations with government and with unions. The management process required laying off employees, closing plants, and forecasting future opportunities and preparing to take advantage of them. An executive team had to be developed. Through motivation and leadership, the company's men and women were given a boost and were made to pull together toward common, or at least compatible, goals. A complex organization had to be administered and improved. Finally, management at Chrysler involved executive succession, as Iacocca prepared Bob Eaton to take over.

Most managerial situations are not as exciting as the ones that Iacocca and Eaton faced. And not all business adventures end in success. In many of these cases, the cause of failure is ineffective management. The costs of poor management to individuals and to society are great. Not only are financial and physical resources wasted, but individuals often suffer psychological damage from business failures. Therefore, it is vitally important that effective management techniques be instilled into everyone who wishes to enter the world of business.

We live in a society of large and small organizations. Within these organizations people work together to accomplish goals that are too challenging to be achieved by a single individual. Throughout life, each person has experiences with a variety of organizations—hospitals, schools, churches, the military, businesses, colleges, government agencies, and other types of institutions. More and more it is being recognized that the most significant factor in determining the performance and success of any organization is the quality of its management.

The job of managing is likely to become even more challenging. Foreign competition, coupled with the large number of corporate takeovers and restruc-

We live in a society of large and small organizations. Within these organizations people work together to accomplish goals that are too challenging to be achieved by a single individual. Here, a group of men from various walks of life build a playground in Anne Arundel County, Maryland. Such efforts are often headed by a volunteer manager from the community. (Source: © Jim Pickerell)

turings, has resulted in new "lean and mean" organizations. Many companies like Chrysler, USX Corporation, BankAmerica, and General Electric have cut out layers of managers and made greater demands on those who remain. Similar efficiency measures were necessary at thousands of smaller firms as they tried to survive and prosper. Managers will no longer succeed because they master the bureaucracy; they must instead add real value to their organizations.

Why are some managers successful and others not? The reasons are as diverse as individual personalities. In this book, we talk about the concepts and techniques used by good managers, such as Bob Eaton. We present ideas, concepts, and practices that can aid effective management regardless of the size of the organization. We emphasize human behavior in organizations, both large and small. It is interesting to note that even though management is often discussed in relation to large business firms, in many ways, the U.S. economy is driven by smaller firms. In fact, since 1988, small businesses that employed fewer than 100 workers accounted for over 90 percent of all job growth.[2] Our primary focus is for-profit businesses; however, we include not-for-profit examples, since most of what can be said about one applies to the other.

In this first chapter, we discuss management as a concept and describe the four management functions. We then present decision making as a topic that relates to all of them. The manner in which management differs at various levels in the organization and the skills managers need come next. Then, we examine the desirability of entering management and the global perspective of management. Finally, we address the productivity challenge management faces.

❖ ❖ WHAT IS MANAGEMENT?

Unless you inherit a fortune, you will probably choose to be employed by some type of organization. Many of you will become managers, and those who do not are likely to be professional and technical employees such as engineers, salespeople, systems analysts, accountants, and marketing researchers. In any case, all of you will be managed and will likely manage others at various times in your lives. Thus, it is important to address the question: What is management?

Management is the process of getting things done through the efforts of other people. This often involves the allocation and control of money and physical resources. Eaton's position gives him extraordinary power over those with whom he works. He can hire and fire managers and employees, fund or not fund company activities, shut down plants, and carry out his purposes at Chrysler in dozens of other ways. The definition of *management* includes all of these activities. What is excluded is the action of an individual working alone. A person who is not involved in getting things done through others is not a manager. This concept will be highlighted throughout the text in the form of many company examples, Management in Practice exercises, and Ethical Dilemma exercises.

❖ ❖ THE MANAGEMENT FUNCTIONS

Management's job is to see the company as what it can become. Fulfilling such a vision requires effective planning, the first of the management functions. Basically, a **function** is a type of work activity that can be identified and distinguished from other work. By general agreement, the management process is said to consist of four functions: planning, organizing, influencing, and controlling.

How Management Is Practiced

In this text the following sections aid in understanding how management is practiced: Management in Practice exercises, Ethical Dilemmas, Management Tips, and end-of-chapter cases. All chapters contain sections entitled *Management in Practice: A Skill-Building Exercise* that permit you to make decisions about situations that could occur in the real world. These exercises are designed to put you on the spot, to let you think through how you would react in typical management situations. Chapters 4–20 contain Ethical Dilemmas that will provide you with an opportunity to experience real-world ethical dilemmas in a classroom setting. In addition, Management Tips are provided at the end of each chapter to give practical applications of the subject matter covered in each chapter. The two end-of-chapter cases provide you with the opportunity to analyze situations businesspeople might confront. Finally, an end-of-section self-assessment exercise is provided so that you can measure your ability in such areas as ethics, decision making, organizing, leadership, time management, and cultural attitudes. The purpose of these sections is to provide a practical understanding of the concepts presented in the chapter.

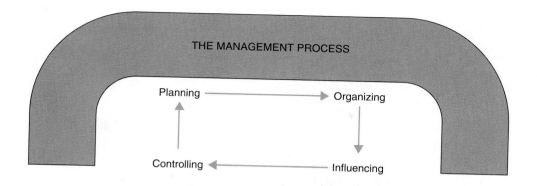

THE MANAGEMENT PROCESS

Planning → Organizing → Influencing → Controlling → Planning

❖ Figure 1.1
The management
process

Figure 1.1 illustrates the management process. The arrows connecting planning, organizing, influencing, and controlling indicate that the functions are interrelated and interdependent; a significant change in one often affects the others.

In the following example, all the functions of management must be effectively utilized if Trans World Airlines is to overcome its present difficulties.

Can Keen Management Ability and Enthusiasm Overcome TWA's Problems?

Trans World Airlines' (TWA) management team is somewhat unique, and they face an almost overwhelming goal. Their goal is to reform an airline that was known as the "backpacker's airline" because tickets were cheap and service was lousy. TWA, probably the most troubled airline that is currently flying, is being directed by a team of professional airline managers led by Co-Chief Executives Robin Wilson and Glenn R. Zander. These two individuals are part of the leadership team that devised a plan to take TWA out of bankruptcy. To accomplish this somewhat formidable task, Wilson and Zander convinced everyone in the company to embrace the plan, and they put forth maximum effort and enthusiasm to accomplish the overall goal of saving TWA. If success is based upon getting people to support organizational goals, then this team is already successful. In order to help change TWA's image, TWA pilots donated $18,000 for billboard ads, and union employees spent $30,000 to buy ads in major newspapers. Then, labor agreed to $660 million in wage and benefit concessions. It appears that TWA employees are doing their best to do whatever management needs. But, can the team led by Wilson and Zander overcome the legacy of poor service and over $900 million in debt? If enthusiasm and management ability are the keys to success, then success may well materialize at TWA.[3]

Planning

Planning is the process of determining in advance what should be accomplished and how it should be realized. Ideally, plans should be stated in specific terms in order to provide clear guidance for managers and workers. For example, when Chrysler Corporation sought to gain market share by developing new products, management had to make specific decisions about the types of new cars to produce, the number of cars to make, and the market share improvement desired. The Chrysler example is one of strategic planning—the determination of overall

Many companies send engineers to the job site to assist in planning. This allows direct observation in deciding what needs to be done and how to do it. It also improves communication, which is vital to the planning process. (Source: © Jon Feingersh/The Stock Market)

organizational purposes and objectives and how they are to be achieved—a topic that is the focus of Chapter 6.

The Chrysler story is an example of top-level planning, but the planning process is similar at all levels of an organization. For example, suppose at the beginning of the week a supervisor is given a production list for completion by Friday. Since the list tells the supervisor what should be accomplished, part of the planning has already occurred. The supervisor, however, still has to determine how the required production can be completed on time. After analyzing all available information, the supervisor may schedule one-fifth of the output for Monday, one-fifth for Tuesday, and so forth. Analyzing all information available and making decisions are major aspects of the planning process.

Planning frequently requires updating and sometimes means abandoning many aspects of the overall plan to accomplish the mission of the organization. This was the case with the year-old Euro Disney theme park, where business has recently been disappointing. Despite these difficulties, Disney's CEO Michael Eisner is planning a multibillion-dollar strategy to reinvigorate all of the theme parks with new attractions and is even planning new theme parks. Eisner's planned building spree will be expensive, but he believes it's vital to re-energize the theme parks, which have proven critical in helping to promote Disney's films and licensed merchandise.[4]

Planning is covered in greater detail in Chapters 5 and 6.

Organizing

Organizing is the process of prescribing formal relationships among people and resources to accomplish goals. The formal organization must take into account the informal organization, which is the set of evolving relationships and patterns of human interaction within the organization that are not officially prescribed. The informal organization is discussed in greater detail in Chapter 7 and more generally throughout the text.

A very important aspect of managing is ensuring that the right people with the right qualifications are available at the right places and times to accomplish the purposes of the organization. This is called *staffing,* an important human resource management topic that is covered in Chapter 9.

Influencing

Influencing is the process of determining or affecting the behavior of others. A multitude of topics is placed under this heading, including motivation, leadership, communication, group dynamics, power, politics, and corporate culture. **Motivation** is the willingness to put forth effort in pursuit of organizational goals. Motivating workers often means simply creating an environment that makes them want to work. H. Ross Perot, founder of the highly successful Electronic Data Systems Corporation, places a high premium on creating such an environment. He once went to Iran to rescue subordinates who were being held hostage. In this and other ways, Perot has served as a positive and motivating influence to those around him.

An essential element of motivation is the direction provided by the manager. Each worker may require a different means of motivation, and no manager can motivate a worker to produce if the worker chooses not to respond. Thus, the manager's challenge is to create a situation in which workers will want to be more productive (be motivated), as Lee Iacocca did, and Eaton must do at Chrysler. Motivation is the subject of Chapter 10.

Leadership is the influencing of others to do what the leader wants them to do. A good leader gets others to put forth their best efforts. Leaders depend in part on charisma and other personal attributes for their effectiveness. However, good leadership more often results from learning what motivates individual workers and using this knowledge to direct their activities. The leadership style that works best varies, depending on the characteristics of the leader, those led, and the situation. As the president of a top *Fortune* 500 firm said: "A leader must lead, not drive. People are unpredictable, different from one another, often irascible, frequently petty, sometimes vain, but always magnificent if they are properly motivated." Leadership is discussed in Chapter 11.

Communication is the transfer of information, ideas, understanding, or feelings among people. Much of a manager's day is spent communicating. Supervisors, for example, tell workers what needs to be done. They also report to managers, summarizing their units' activities, seeking support and guidance, and representing subordinates. Lack of good communication skills can hurt productivity. Communication is the subject of Chapter 12.

A **group** is two or more people who have a unifying relationship, such as common objectives or physical proximity. A work team is a group that is fully developed. We all belong to many groups—at work, in the community, and even at home (the family is a group). There are formal work groups and teams, of course, made up of managers and subordinates. There are also informal groups, which consist of two or more persons associated with one another in ways not prescribed by the formal organization. The focus of Chapter 13 is the many aspects of groups and teams that affect the management job.

Power is the ability to influence behavior. It is the ability to get things done the way one wants them to be done. **Politics** can be described as a network of interactions by which power is acquired, transferred, and exercised over others. Power and politics, which are the subjects of Chapter 14, are immensely important to managers.

The ways in which managers motivate and lead workers and communicate with superiors and subordinates affect, and are affected by, **corporate culture**—the system of shared values, beliefs, and habits in an organization that interacts with formal structure to produce behavioral norms. The culture can be one of openness and support, or it can be one of autocracy and fear. Whatever the corporate culture, it will have an impact on those in the organization. Corporate culture is discussed in Chapter 15.

MANAGEMENT IN PRACTICE

A Skill-Building Exercise: You are the personnel director for a manufacturing firm that is undergoing a major change in direction. This change involves the hiring of young, energetic workers, and you have some difficult decisions to make. The firm is building two technologically advanced plants in the state of Tennessee, and it will close four of its five old plants in Michigan and Ohio. John Morrow is a 56-year-old production worker who has been with your firm ten years. In your opinion, he is not capable of being retrained; but he is not old enough to receive any retirement benefits. You must decide whether to place John in the company's only remaining old plant or to fire him.

What would you do?

Controlling

Controlling is the process of comparing actual performance with standards and taking any necessary corrective action. Controls help ensure performance in accordance with plans. If performance is unsatisfactory, corrective action can be taken. For instance, if a company's production costs are higher than planned, management must have some means of recognizing and correcting the problem. Controls can also be applied for positive reasons. For example, when sales of Chrysler's minivans exceeded expectations, shifts were added at existing plants to meet the demand and plans were made to reopen a factory that had been closed. Controlling is discussed in Chapter 16.

An aspect of the controlling function that relates uniquely to human resources is disciplinary action taken to correct undesirable behavior. Disciplinary action can range from a verbal warning to outright dismissal, as will be discussed in Chapter 16.

❖ ❖ DECISION MAKING AND THE MANAGEMENT FUNCTIONS

Decision making is the process of generating and evaluating alternatives and making choices among them. Changes are occurring in the decision-making process because of advances in technology; information is now available to corporate executives at a moment's notice. In the past, the information that corporate executives needed for decision making was obtained from a room full of mainframe computers operated by professional computer programmers. Reasonably priced innovations such as personal computers, spreadsheet programs, Microsoft's user-friendly Windows software, electronic-mail, and local area networks linking groups of desktop computers bring even more information to the people who need it. Such free-flowing information enables corporations to flatten, and it allows teams to work across the barriers of specialty, rank, and geography to enhance the organization's strategic position.[5]

As Figure 1.2 illustrates, each management function involves decision making. In fact, management is one continuous string of decisions. Planning involves, for example, setting the company's overall direction as well as determining tomorrow's job assignments. In a similar way, organizing requires choices among basic organizational forms as well as between tight or loose reporting relationships. There are many ways to influence, and leaders must choose which approach to use in each case. Finally, choices must be made between tight and loose controls and among the many possible standards and tolerances to employ. Of course, the decisions mentioned here for each management function only begin to scratch the surface.

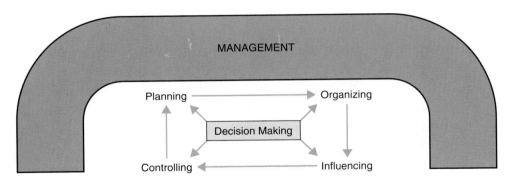

August Busch III is a corporate executive who is considered to be an effective decision maker, but one who makes decisions in unlikely ways. As chairman of Anheuser-Busch, the United States' largest brewer, Busch employs an unusual means for arriving at answers to tough, complicated decisions. He arranges debates in which managers are assigned opposing positions. Each manager is given staff support and several weeks to prepare. After listening to the debates, Busch makes the final decisions. Decision making is the topic of Chapter 4.

❖ ❖ MANAGEMENT AT DIFFERENT LEVELS

Sometimes managers are thought of as being only the top-level individuals in large organizations. But most managers do not have responsibility for an entire company. Although the distinctions are by no means clear, it is useful to think of three levels of managers, as Figure 1.3 shows.

Supervisory managers directly oversee the efforts of those who actually perform the work. Most supervisory managers have titles such as supervisor, foreman, leadman, and office manager. Department heads at universities are supervisory managers because they oversee the activities of professors, who actually do the jobs of research and teaching. At most fast-food chains, the person responsible for a particular store is a supervisory manager.

Middle managers are positioned above the supervisory level but are subordinate to the firm's most senior executives. Most major companies have a number of levels of middle managers; for example, a district manager may oversee ten sales offices. Division or area managers may be responsible for a number of district managers.

Top managers are the organization's most senior executives. They usually include the chairman of the board and the president, along with vice-presidents who are in charge of major subdivisions of the organization. Top managers are responsible for providing the overall direction of the firm. While upper-level managers are often viewed as area-specific loners, at Parametric Technology, tag-team management is being attempted. Company founder Samuel Geisberg, a

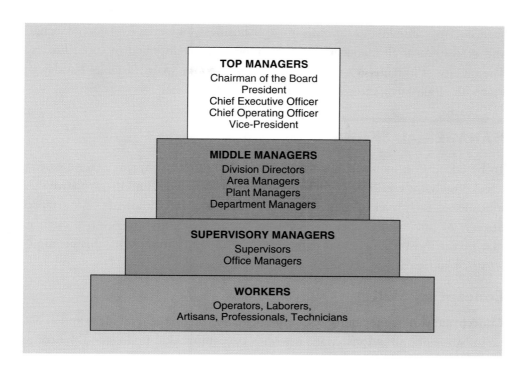

native of Russia with a Ph.D. in mathematics, is teamed with Steven Walske, a graduate of Princeton and the Harvard business school. This is an unusual sharing of power in which Walske, as president and CEO, and Geisberg, as an executive vice-president and chairman of the board, report to one another. Geisberg is the technologist, the visionary, and the product person, and Walske handles marketing and deals with the company's constituencies. According to Walske, "Here we have happily divided the world." Geisberg adds that, "We do have a very good and right sharing of the power. I consider it a cornerstone of our success." Although tag-team management may never be the norm, it is a refreshing option in a world moving toward being team centered.[6]

In sum, a manager is anyone, at any level of the organization, who gets things done through the efforts of other people. Wherever a group of people work together purposefully, a manager is usually present. School principals, meat market supervisors, and service station operators are managers, as are the presidents of Porsche, Prudential Insurance, and Bank of America. The president of the United States is a manager too. Managers set goals, plan operations, organize various resources—personnel, materials, equipment, capital—lead and motivate people to perform, evaluate results against goals, and train and develop people so the organization's goals can be met.

Unfortunately managers are often judged exclusively on short-run performance, being considered effective if a unit is earning a profit, reducing costs, or increasing the market share for the company's products—right now. Naturally, such accomplishments are important to a business; however, a major challenge and obligation of all managers is the training and development of subordinates. The quality of a manager's subordinates is perhaps the main variable that determines the long-term success and effectiveness of that manager.

❖ ❖ MANAGERIAL SKILLS

To be effective, a manager must possess and continually improve several essential skills. Figure 1.4 illustrates three categories of such skills and their relative significance at each level of management. Effective managers know the importance of each of these skills. They dare not concentrate on only one, even though it may be the most important at their level in the organization. With this in mind, let us consider each of the three categories of skills.

Conceptual Skill

Conceptual skill is the ability to comprehend abstract or general ideas and apply them to specific situations. Managers with conceptual skill understand the complexities of the overall organization, including how each unit contributes to the accomplishment of the firm's purposes. The most successful firms are good at tapping the conceptual skill of people at all management levels. All managers, and even workers, are encouraged to see their jobs in the context of the company's broader purposes. At Ford, for example, "Quality is Job 1" is a topic at every employee meeting, and signs in the factories proclaim the slogan.

Conceptual skill is especially crucial for top-level executives, who must keep the "big picture" clearly in focus. Bob Eaton, Chrysler's top executive officer, has to envision what type cars will be successful into the twenty-first century.

The farther down the organization one looks, the less need one finds for conceptual skill. Middle managers need a moderate level of conceptual skill, but

❖ **Figure 1.4**
Skills at various levels of management

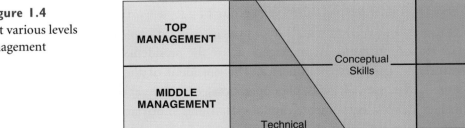

not as much as top managers. Supervisors typically have relatively less need for this skill because they usually are given fairly specific guidelines. They are concerned primarily with their own and other closely related departments, and their relationships and functions tend to be clearly defined. A fast-food restaurant manager, for example, does not have to trade off aesthetics, construction costs, and efficiency considerations to arrive at an appropriate restaurant design. That has been done at higher levels.

Technical Skill

Technical skill is the ability to use specific knowledge, methods, and techniques in performing work. This skill is important for supervisors, who must use it in training new workers and monitoring daily work activities. If corrections are needed, the technically skilled supervisor is qualified to direct them. Companies such as the Boeing Company realize the value of technically skilled employees. Many Boeing employees must read blueprints. Some assemble critical components. Others install wiring systems in airplanes. And Boeing engineers must know how to use computer-aided design (CAD) systems to make sure complex avionics systems are appropriately designed.[7]

As one moves to higher levels of management, the relative importance of technical skill usually diminishes. Mangers at those levels have less direct contact with technical operating problems and activities. Unlike supervisors, many upper-level managers generally use their technical skill only indirectly. For instance, the president of an engineering firm, although trained as an engineer, is not likely to design a new machine personally. On the other hand, some chief executives, such as Chrysler's Lee Iacocca and Bob Eaton, are highly respected by subordinates for their technical expertise. This undoubtedly makes them better managers, even though their primary organizational mission is not technical.

Human Skill

Human skill is the ability to understand, motivate, and get along with other people. Human skill is about equally important at all levels of management. Middle managers who can understand, motivate, and get along with supervisors while wielding influence with top managers are sure to be effective. The same is true of supervisors who relate well to their subordinates and superiors.

Activities requiring human skill include communication, leadership, and motivation. For example, a typical store manager must interact with workers, customers, and suppliers. And more senior executives must communicate with and influence other managers and directors in the company as well as people outside it, such as investment bankers.

The ability to under-
stand, motivate, and get
along with other people
is human skill.
(Source: © John
Coletti)

❖ ❖ THE DESIRABILITY OF ENTERING MANAGEMENT

Many students have thought about the possibility of becoming managers.
Advancement of excellent people into management is important not only to those
who are involved but also to the organization as a whole. Let us consider some
of the pros and cons of becoming a manager (see Figure 1.5).

❖ **Figure 1.5**
Pros and cons of enter-
ing management

CONS
- Not enough difference in pay
- Involvement with problems of others
- Responsibility for actions of others
- Inadequate authority
- Necessity for making tough decisions

PROS
- Higher pay and opportunity for advancement
- Respect and influence
- Special opportunities for accomplishment
- More freedom and flexibility
- Better working conditions
- Opportunity to help others

Pros Associated with Entering Management

First, an obvious reason to seek a management position is the increased salary. Although there are isolated cases where lower-level managers make no more than senior workers, a manager's pay is usually better. Even if the pay is only a little better at first, entering management may open the door to future promotions, which may involve large pay increases. Most companies prefer to promote managers from within. Even in companies that hire managers from outside, the management trainee often begins as a supervisor.

Second, many people desire the respect and influence that normally go with a managerial job. It is natural to want to have influence over others.

Third, the manager's job offers special opportunities for accomplishment. Instead of just doing mechanical or technical tasks, supervisors perform the much more complex job of managing people. Each day, they face new and different situations. Handling these situations successfully enhances their self-esteem. Accomplishing the job of managing gives a special feeling that is simply not available at the worker level.

Fourth, managers typically have greater freedom than workers. They are usually paid a salary rather than compensated on an hourly basis, and they are often allowed some flexibility in their working hours. Managers usually do not have to formally request a few hours off; they just keep their superiors advised.

Fifth, a manager's working conditions are often better than those of workers. Many have private offices and are given other advantages, such as secretarial help. Practically all managers have some control over conditions around them, including privacy and comfort.

Finally, managers have special opportunities to help people. Workers have personal problems that can sometimes be solved through counseling. These may involve conflicts with the organization. No one is in a better position than the manager to go to bat for workers or to help them understand the organization's needs. Mangers are also able to train workers and help them prepare for advancement or for additional responsibilities. Most managers find it a special thrill when a subordinate is promoted.

Cons Associated with Entering Management

Certainly, the job of a manager can be challenging and exciting. But as with anything worthwhile, there are certain trade-offs. In fact, some managers have even returned to their nonmanagerial jobs. They commonly give reasons such as: "There is just too much hassle involved." Although the negatives of management are often matters of perception rather than actuality, they have been mentioned by practicing managers as trade-offs that must be considered.

First, some managers think their pay is low in relation to that of subordinates. Workers usually just come to work, do the job, and go home. The manager, however, often is on the job before regular working hours and is still there after the workers have gone. In some instances, the difference in pay is insignificant. In fact, as suggested earlier, some beginning managers make less than their most senior subordinates.

Second, in addition to their own concerns, managers must struggle with the problems of others. Workers may bring to the job a variety of off-the-job problems. Perhaps one worker is going through a divorce and simply wants to talk. Another might be having financial problems. Workers may have the option of worrying only about their own problems. Managers do not have that choice. They have people working for them who have different personalities, aspirations, and problems. To some, this can be a burden.

Third, managers are held accountable not just for their own actions but for the actions of others. Workers need only be concerned about meeting individual quotas. Managers must make sure that members of the work group cooperate to achieve departmental goals. Daily, weekly, monthly, and even annual production standards must be met. For some, it is not easy to keep a positive attitude under such pressure.

Fourth, managers are sometimes not given enough authority to get the job done. Often they can only recommend certain actions. For instance, a supervisor may think a certain worker should be fired immediately for loafing or insubordination. But upper management may require a formal request for such a drastic measure.

Finally, some managers do not enjoy making the tough decisions that go with the job. Decisions about performance appraisals, pay raises and cuts, and layoffs are tough enough, but disciplining a worker, especially a former co-worker, is even harder. Firing someone can be traumatic. And management decisions can seldom be made intuitively; they should be systematic and rational, and the manager's reasoning often must be a matter of record.

The negative aspects described here will keep some people from wanting to enter management. For others, however, they will increase the challenge and excitement of a management career.

❖ ❖ THE PRODUCTIVITY CHALLENGE

Management knowledge is not an end in itself. Increasing the quality and quantity of goods and services produced is a major goal of most managers and of the country as a whole. **Productivity** is a measure of the relationship between inputs (labor, capital, natural resources, energy, and so forth) and the quality and quan-

The Allure of Becoming a Small Business Manager: Is It No Longer as Great?

The desirability of being a manager is often so great that individuals affiliated with organizations of all types yearn and work toward that personal goal. However, there is one facet of business where being a manager may be less desirable— that of the small business manager. To many people, the obvious advantage of being a small business manager is that they are their own boss. However, for small business managers increased salaries are never a sure thing. Many people respect managers but, at least initially, give more respect to titles, such as a vice-president for Chrysler, rather than the head of his or her own small business. The small business manager's job offers special opportunities for accomplishment, as well as failure. Although small business managers will have greater freedom of action, they typically must totally immerse themselves in the small business to help assure success. The small business manager's working conditions will probably be more hands-on and less isolated than that of mid- and large-size company managers. Finally, small business managers will have special opportunities to help people directly on a one-to-one basis. Workers' personal problems often become the small business manager's business problems. All of these challenges point to the special rigors of being a small business manager. However, capable small business managers are essential to the U.S. economy, and in all likelihood such individuals will continue to be attracted to small business management.[8]

tity of outputs (goods and services). Note from this definition that outputs must be measured in terms of both quality and quantity.

Productivity is usually expressed in terms of output per person-hour or output per employed person. What causes it to be high or low? Productivity is a result not only of the capability and motivation of workers but also of technology, capital investment, capacity utilization, scale of production, and many other factors.

In the 1980s and early 1990s some countries such as Japan pulled ahead of the United States in terms of output per hour in manufacturing. United States manufacturing firms of all types moved to alter this trend with massive restructuring and computerization. This has caused output in manufacturing to increase dramatically.[9] Specific techniques such as downsizing (Chapter 7), reengineering (Chapter 8), and Total Quality Management (Chapter 17) will be discussed as they relate to meeting the productivity challenge.

Closely related to productivity are effectiveness and efficiency. **Effectiveness** is the capability of bringing about an effect or accomplishing a purpose, sometimes without regard to the quantity of resources consumed in the process. **Efficiency** is the capability of producing desired results with a minimum of energy, time, money, materials, or other costly inputs. In general, we can say an organization is effective if it gets the job done; it is efficient to the extent that it gets the job done cheaply. For instance, prior to reorganization, the Jeep plant in Toledo, Ohio, used 5,400 workers to produce 760 cars per day in one period, an average of 7.2 employee-days per car. At the same time, the Honda plant at

---

MANAGEMENT IN PRACTICE

A Skill-Building Exercise: Peggy Turnage was excited and also a bit frightened. She worked at Saint Francis Medical Center, a large general hospital in Schenectady, New York, and had just become the new supervisor of the patient records section. Peggy had eight years' experience in patient records, five of them at another hospital. She had no experience as a supervisor. But she had recently completed a supervision course at Central State College, near the hospital. Peggy was eager to use the skills she had learned.

Peggy came to work early that morning. Sitting alone in the cafeteria, she thought about her new job. Many special cases often arise that require the supervisor's attention. For example, patients often check out earlier than expected, and these patient records must be updated. Accuracy in maintaining the records could be a matter of life or death. Imagine what could happen, she thought, if test results got into the wrong folder. When Peggy was handling the records personally, she didn't worry. But now she would be responsible for what others did.

Peggy also knew that she had been promoted over Rod Mabry, who had worked in the records office for ten years. Rod was disappointed, Peggy knew, because he felt he deserved the promotion. She also knew it would be hard for her to gain the acceptance of the other workers. Before, she had been just one of the gang, but now she was the boss. It was a thrilling feeling, but a little scary.

As Peggy was finishing her breakfast, Rod came in. "Mind if I sit down?" he asked. "Of course not. Nice to see you, Rod," said Peggy.

Rod placed his food on the table and set the tray aside. Smiling, he said: "Peggy, I want to congratulate you on the promotion. You sure deserve it. If you hadn't been here, I think I would have gotten the job. But management apparently felt you would make a better supervisor. I certainly can't question your knowledge of the job, and you seem to have a lot of patience. Anyway, what's done is done, and I'm going to try to do the best job I can."

"Thank you, Rod," Peggy said. "I was worried about how you would feel. I should have known we could work together."

Do you believe that the anxiety Peggy was experiencing is typical of many who enter management? Explain.

Marysville, Ohio, made 870 cars per day while employing 2,423 workers, an average of 2.8 employee-days per car.[10] The Jeep plant was effective but not efficient, while the Honda plant was effective and efficient. Today, the Jeep plant is both effective and efficient, something that is necessary for business survival.

❖ ❖ PURPOSES AND ORGANIZATION OF THIS TEXT

Effective management is critical for every firm's success. To be effective, managers must plan, organize, influence, and control. They should keep in mind how individuals, groups, and the entire organization are affected. Basically, managers must understand management concepts and properly apply the management functions

NAFTA: An Adventure in Advanced Capitalism

The United States, Canada, and Mexico have embarked on an adventure that will create a trading bloc of countries that will be able to compete better with the European Community, as well as with the Pacific Rim nations. The North American Free Trade Agreement (NAFTA) took effect January 1, 1994. It will eliminate many of the remaining tariffs and other trade restrictions among the three nations, and will phase out nearly all the rest over the next five to fifteen years. Since Canada and the United States already have many of these conditions in place, most of the attention is focused on Mexico. In addition to opening a very large market for American goods, this agreement will open Mexico to foreign investment, lock in rules for capital investment, and protect intellectual property rights such as patents and copyrights. NAFTA will accomplish some of what the European Community agreement accomplished: a

deregulation that aims to sweep away obstacles to the free movement of goods, services, capital, and people. Barriers will be dismantled in favor of a unified market of millions of untapped Mexican consumers. This single market should produce billions of dollars in goods and services, and should greatly benefit the United States.[11]

Over the next decade, removal of these trade barriers is expected to help revive the American economy and result in a more challenging and demanding situation for managers. As the world becomes a much smaller place, more and more businesses will be competing worldwide. Global competition, air travel, and satellite communication technology have made doing business abroad both necessary and feasible, and companies continue to establish multinational operations. When one considers that managers of mid-sized multinational companies expect their international sales to jump 15 to 20 percent a year for at least the next five years, and that

95 percent of the planet's population lives outside the United States, it becomes evident that the number of global firms will increase dramatically in the next decade.[12] Clearly, the majority of business opportunities in the future will be outside U.S. borders. American managers must learn not only to cope with the multinational environment but to thrive in it.

Unfortunately, many American managers have fallen back on their own limited management experiences and treated overseas assignments much like assignments in the United States. Some managers assume that international businesses can simply force foreign countries to conform to the companies' usual ways of operating. Fortunately, many American managers are beginning to recognize that the challenge of engaging in multinational operations is not easily met. They are finding that the managers who succeed are those who deal effectively in the assigned global environment.

to achieve organizational goals. The book is organized into six parts, as outlined in Figure 1.6, and is designed to provide you with the following:

- A greater knowledge of and insight into the art and science of managing people and other resources.
- A better understanding of the problems of directing a business organization.
- An opportunity to learn to be better decision makers.
- An understanding of basic principles of management.
- A better understanding of individual behavior and the relationship of that behavior to management.

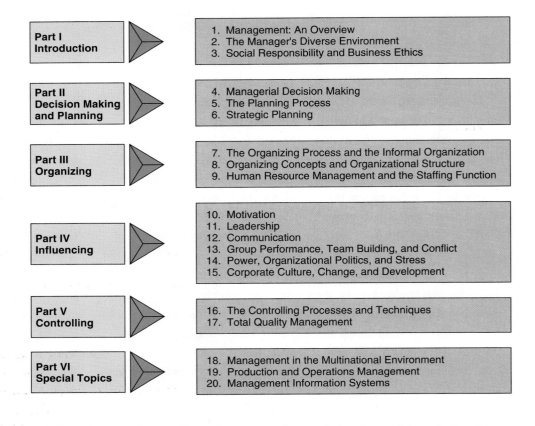

❖ **Figure 1.6**
Organization of the book

Part I Introduction
1. Management: An Overview
2. The Manager's Diverse Environment
3. Social Responsibility and Business Ethics

Part II Decision Making and Planning
4. Managerial Decision Making
5. The Planning Process
6. Strategic Planning

Part III Organizing
7. The Organizing Process and the Informal Organization
8. Organizing Concepts and Organizational Structure
9. Human Resource Management and the Staffing Function

Part IV Influencing
10. Motivation
11. Leadership
12. Communication
13. Group Performance, Team Building, and Conflict
14. Power, Organizational Politics, and Stress
15. Corporate Culture, Change, and Development

Part V Controlling
16. The Controlling Processes and Techniques
17. Total Quality Management

Part VI Special Topics
18. Management in the Multinational Environment
19. Production and Operations Management
20. Management Information Systems

- A better understanding of group and team behavior and its relationship to management.
- A better understanding of how organizations, especially business firms, behave as interactive systems.

SUMMARY

Management is the process of getting things done through the efforts of other people. This often involves the allocation and control of money and physical resources. The management process consists of four functions: planning, organizing, influencing, and controlling. Planning is the process of determining in advance what should be accomplished and how it should be realized. Organizing is the process of prescribing formal relationships among people and resources to accomplish goals. Influencing is the process of determining or affecting the behavior of others. It involves motivation, leadership, communication, group and team dynamics, power, politics, and corporate culture. Controlling is the process of comparing actual performance with standards and taking any necessary corrective action. Each management function involves and is affected by decision making, the process of generating and evaluating alternatives and making choices among them. At all three managerial levels, from supervisory to top management, managers must motivate and lead workers and communicate with superiors and subordinates.

To be effective, a manager must possess and continually develop several essential skills. Conceptual skill is the ability to comprehend abstract or general ideas and apply them to specific situations. Technical skill is the ability to use specific knowledge, methods, or techniques in performing work. The ability to understand, motivate, and get along with other people is human skill.

There are both pros and cons in becoming a manager. The pros include the following. First, an obvious reason to seek a management position is the increased salary. Second, many desire the respect and influence that normally go with a managerial job. Third, the manager's job offers special opportunities for accomplishment. Fourth, managers typically have greater freedom than workers. Fifth, a manager's working conditions are often better than those of workers. Finally, managers have special opportunities to help people.

The cons include the following. First, some managers think their salary is low in relation to that of subordinates. Second, in addition to their own concerns, managers must struggle with the problems of others. Third, managers are held accountable not just for their own actions but for the actions of others. Fourth, managers are sometimes not given enough authority to get the job done. Finally, some managers do not enjoy making the tough decisions that go with the job.

Managerial skills are developed for the purpose of increasing the quality and quantity of goods and services produced in the economy. Productivity is a measure of the relationship between inputs (labor, capital, natural resources, energy, and so forth) and the quality and quantity of outputs (goods and services). Productivity is usually expressed in terms of output per person-hour or per employed person.

Closely related to productivity are effectiveness and efficiency. Effectiveness is the capability of bringing about an effect or accomplishing a purpose, sometimes without regard to the quantity of resources consumed in the process. Efficiency is the capability of producing desired results with a minimum of energy, time, money, materials, or other costly inputs.

KEY TERMS

Management 6	Controlling 11
Function 6	Decision making 11
Planning 7	Supervisory managers 12
Organizing 9	Middle managers 12
Influencing 9	Top managers 12
Motivation 9	Conceptual skill 14
Leadership 9	Technical skill 15
Communication 10	Human skill 15
Group 10	Productivity 18
Power 10	Effectiveness 19
Politics 10	Efficiency 19
Corporate culture 10	

REVIEW QUESTIONS

1. Define management. Why does the definition exclude the action of an individual working alone?
2. List and briefly describe the functions of management.
3. Distinguish by definition and example among supervisory managers, middle managers, and top managers.
4. List and briefly define the types of skills important to managerial effectiveness.
5. Discuss the pros and cons of entering management.
6. Define productivity, effectiveness, and efficiency.

CASE STUDIES

CASE 1.1 Wal-Mart: The Nation's Number One Retailer

In 1989, with over $20 billion in sales, Wal-Mart was the nation's third largest retailer; by the end of January 1991, earnings had risen to $32.6 billion and Wal-Mart had became the nation's number one retailer. The company operated 1,650 discount department stores, 200 Sam's Wholesale Clubs, and several Discount Drug Stores and Hypermarket USA stores. A sweetheart of Wall Street, Wal-Mart stock quintupled in value in just six years, and stockholders realized nearly a 50 percent annual return in the previous decade.

Wal-Mart is headquartered in the tiny town of Bentonville, Arkansas, where the Wal-Mart saga began with a single store in the early 1960s. The man credited with Wal-Mart's success is founder Sam Walton. Walton had been successful at everything he had tried, with the exception of retirement. Until his death in 1992, Walton continued to devote about four months a year to "barnstorming the heartland," visiting Wal-Mart stores. He spent several days a week going from store to store, visiting with store managers and employees—who are called "associates"—about ways to improve the operation. Walton called this the "grassroots management style." He was frequently found greeting customers at the door of a Wal-Mart or Sam's store.

Walton always stressed participation. Not only are managers expected to interact with their people on a daily basis, but there is a mandatory meeting once a year to gather suggestions that will be passed on to top management. Portraying employees as associates is more than window dressing. It is not uncommon to see a store manager or department chief cleaning up a spill or polishing handprints off the store's glass doors, and every employee is encouraged to own stock in the company.

Although management at Wal-Mart emphasizes individual initiative and autonomy, managers are accountable for results. Every store manager must prepare a monthly financial statement listing each expenditure, from taxes and rent to paper clips and telephone charges. District managers are required to review each store manager's report and discuss ways to reduce expenses.

QUESTIONS

1. Why do you believe that Wal-Mart became the number one retailer?
2. At Wal-Mart, why do you think employees are called "associates"?

CASE 1.2 Pinnacle

Wharton Products was a New Brunswick, New Jersey, maker of valve actuators for the petrochemical industry. On her first day as president of Wharton, Gloria Phillips allowed herself a moment of nostalgia. Gloria had known that she was the likely choice for president when the previous president resigned. She had worked hard over the years and she knew she was respected for her competence in the field and for her ability to work with employees at all levels. As she sipped her coffee, her thoughts raced back over the twenty years she had been with Wharton.

Gloria had come to Wharton as a young college graduate with a degree in industrial management but no work experience. She was hired as an assistant supervisor in the air-actuated assembly area. "I don't see how I got by," she thought. "I knew so little about the operations and even less about management. It seemed that every day was filled with one brush fire after another." Thanks to procedures manuals, other technical publications, and a patient superior, Gloria was able to stay out of trouble. In fact, she was soon competent enough to handle the supervisor's job.

She did not get to do that, though. After just six months on the job, she had a chance to become assembly manager, with responsibility for three assembly areas: air-actuated, electromechanical, and hydraulic. The supervisor who had been her boss became one of her subordinates. As assistant supervisor, Gloria had been concerned mainly with daily operations. In her new job, she found it necessary to plan weeks and even months in advance. She also had to complete more reports and attend more meetings, and she found herself with less time for the technical responsibilities she had enjoyed earlier.

She chuckled as she thought about the time, just after she took over as assembly manager, when she discovered that the operating procedures manuals were grossly out-of-date and inadequate. Several new machines had been installed, and the whole hydraulic area had been added since the last revision to the manuals. It took Gloria more than a year to put the manuals in order. In the process, she learned a lot about how the assembly division fits into the overall plant operations. She also visited several other plants and discovered a number of new and better ways of doing things, which she incorporated into the procedures manuals.

Because the company was growing and because changes in the manufacturing technology Wharton used were occurring frequently, the procedures manuals had to be modified often. Soon Gloria was able to turn this work over to an assistant and spend more time on planning and on helping her subordinates do their jobs better. She also spent much time in meetings and discussions with superiors and in reviewing and completing reports.

When Gloria was 28, just five years after she had become assembly manager, Wharton lost its vice-president for planning to a competitor. Gloria applied for the job and, in competition with five others, got the promotion. Gloria had thought she was well qualified, but the complexities of her new position were overwhelming at first. It was difficult enough to forecast production requirements a year in advance, but the typical lead time for a new plant or even a new production line was several years. Also, in the new job, Gloria had to consider the interrelationships among marketing, finance, personnel, and production. The higher Gloria rose in the organization, the less she was able to depend on standard operating procedures.

From the planning job, Gloria was promoted to senior vice-president for manufacturing, and later to chief operating officer, before her advancement to president.

"Surely," thought Gloria, "at some point one begins to feel fully competent to handle any situation that might arise." Gloria knew that she had not reached that point, however; she felt nervous and apprehensive about how things would go over the next few months.

QUESTIONS

1. What specific skills will be most important to Gloria's success as president of Wharton Products? Do you believe she possesses these skills? Explain.
2. How would you imagine Gloria's managerial responsibilities changed as she progressed up the management hierarchy?

NOTES

1. This case is a composite of a number of published accounts, among them: "Chrysler Sees 1990 Sales of Over 2 Million Vehicles," *The Wall Street Journal* (September 20, 1989): B4; Joseph B. White, "Chrysler Scraps Plans to Recall 1,600 Workers," *The Wall Street Journal* (May 24, 1989): A9; Doron P. Levin, "Chrysler Net Up 90.8%, Helped by Charge in '88," *The New York Times* (May 3, 1989): D2; Edwin Diamond, "Driving Ambition: A Man with the Pedal to the Floor," *Family Weekly*, 27 (May 1984): 4–9; Michael Moritz and Barrett Seaman, *Going for Broke: The Chrysler Story* (Garden City, NY: Doubleday, 1981); James K. Glassman, "The Iacocca Mystique," *New Republic* (July 23, 1984): 20–23; Kathleen Kerwin, Larry Armstrong, and Thane Peterson, "The Big Three

Think They Smell Blood," *Business Week,* (September 28, 1992): 34–35; Ken Zino, "You've Put Us Back on Top," *Parade* (October 3, 1993): 8–9; numerous additional articles in *The Wall Street Journal;* and Chrysler Corporation, *Annual Reports* (various years).

2. Louis S. Richman, "Jobs that are Growing and Slowing," *Fortune* 128 (July 12, 1993): 53.

3. Kevin Kelly and Andrea Rothman, "Can A 'Labor of Love' End TWA's Tailspin?" *Business Week* (April 19, 1993): 80–82.

4. Ronald Grover, Stewart Toy, Gail DeGeorge, Robert Neff, "Thrills and Chills at Disney," *Business Week* (June 21, 1993): 73–74.

5. Stratford Sherman, "The New Computer Revolution," *Fortune* 127 (June 14, 1993): 56–80.

6. Andrew E. Serwer, "America's 100 Fastest Growers," *Fortune* 128 (August 9, 1993): 40–56.

7. Anthony Ramirez, "Boeing's Happy, Harrowing Times," *Fortune* 123 (July 17, 1989): 40–48.

8. James E. Ellis and Christina Del Valle, "Tall Orders for Small Business," *Business Week* (April 19, 1993): 114–120.

9. Joseph Spiers, "An End to Efficiency?" *Fortune* 128 (September 6, 1993): 12.

10. John Merwin, "A Tale of Two Worlds," *Forbes* 137 (June 16, 1986): 101–106.

11. Louis S. Richman, "How NAFTA Will Help America," *Fortune* 128 (April 19, 1993): 95.

12. Christopher Knowlton, "The New Export Entrepreneurs," *Fortune* 123 (June 6, 1988): 87.

APPENDIX I

Planning a Career in Management

A career is a general course of action a person chooses to pursue throughout his or her working life. Career planning is a process in which an individual sets career goals and identifies the means to achieve them. In this appendix, we first attempt to identify whether a person has aspirations for a career in management. Then, we offer a section on gaining insight that will allow access to true interests and abilities. We follow this section with a presentation of the types of entry-level management positions that are commonly available. We then present possible career paths, followed by a discussion of tips individuals can use in advancing their careers.

ASPIRATION TO BE IN MANAGEMENT

All of us have different aspirations, backgrounds, and experiences. Our personalities are molded, to a certain extent, by the results of our interactions with our environments. Edgar Schein's research identified five motives that account for the ways people select and prepare for a career, and he called these motives *career anchors:*

1. *Managerial competence.* The career goal of managers is to develop qualities of interpersonal, analytical, and emotional competence. People using this anchor want to manage people.

2. *Technical/functional competence.* The anchor for technicians is the continuous development of technical talent. These individuals do not seek managerial positions.

3. *Security.* The anchor for security-conscious individuals is the stabilization of their career situations. They often see themselves tied to a particular organization or geographical location.

4. *Creativity.* Creative individuals are somewhat entrepreneurial in their attitude. They want to create or build something that is entirely their own.

5. *Autonomy and independence.* The career anchor for independent people is a desire to be free from organizational constraints. They value autonomy and want to be their own boss and work at their own pace.[1a]

After considering these career anchors, you should have some notion of the desirability of a management career. For instance, if you enjoy interpersonal contacts, management may well be an appropriate career option. To determine the feasibility of a career in management, you may find it useful to gain additional insight into yourself.

GAINING INSIGHT INTO YOURSELF

Learning about oneself is referred to as *self-assessment.* Anything that could affect one's performance in a future job should be considered.[2a] Realistic self-assessment may help a person avoid mistakes that could affect the entire career progression. An individual may accept a job without considering whether it matches his or her personal interests and abilities. This approach often results in failure. A thorough self-assessment will go a long way toward matching specific qualities and objectives with the right job or profession.

Two useful tools are the strength/weakness balance sheet and the likes and dislikes survey. However, any reasonable approach that enhances self-understanding is helpful.

Strength/Weakness Balance Sheet

The self-evaluation procedure developed by Benjamin Franklin that helps people become aware of their strengths and weaknesses is called the strength/weakness balance sheet. People who understand their strengths can use them to maximum advantage. Those who recognize their weaknesses can avoid overutilizing their weaker qualities or skills. Furthermore, by recognizing their weaknesses, they will be in a good position to overcome them. This attitude is summed up by the statement: If you have a weakness, understand it and make it work for you as a strength; if you have a strength, do not abuse it to the point where it becomes a weakness. The first step in self-assessment, then, is to recognize both strengths and weaknesses.

To use a strength/weakness balance sheet, the individual lists perceived strengths and weaknesses. This perception is important because believing that a weakness exists can be the same as having a real weakness. Thus, people who believe they will make a poor first impression on meeting someone will probably do

just that. The perception of a weakness can become a self-fulfilling prophecy.

The mechanics for preparing the balance sheet are simple, although you will need to do the job several times. To begin, draw a line down the middle of a sheet of paper. Label the left side "strengths" and the right side "weaknesses." Record all perceived strengths and weaknesses. You may find it difficult to write about yourself. Remember, however, that no one else need see the results. The primary consideration is complete honesty.

Typically, weaknesses will outnumber strengths in the first few iterations. However, as the process is repeated, some items that first appeared to be weaknesses may be recognized as strengths and should be moved from one column to the other. Sufficient time should be devoted to the project to obtain a clear understanding of strengths and weaknesses. Typically, the process should take a minimum of one week. The balance sheet will not provide all the answers about a person's strengths and weaknesses, but many people have gained a better understanding of themselves by completing it.

Likes and Dislikes Survey

Individual likes and dislikes should also be a part of self-assessment. A likes and dislikes survey helps people recognize the restrictions they place on themselves. It is prepared much like the strength/weakness balance sheet. Some people aren't willing to live in certain parts of the country, and that information should be noted as a constraint. Some positions require a person to spend a considerable amount of time traveling. Thus, an estimate of the amount of time a person is willing to travel would also be helpful. The recognition of self-imposed restrictions may reduce future career problems.

Other limitations involve the size or type of firm an individual will consider working for. Some people like a major organization whose products are well known. Others prefer a smaller organization, believing that the opportunities for advancement may be greater or the environment better suited to their tastes. All factors that could affect work performance should be listed in the likes and dislikes survey.

This type of self-assessment helps people understand their basic motives, thereby setting the stage for pursuit of a management career of further technical competence. A person with little desire for management responsibilities should probably not accept a promotion to supervisor or enter management training. People who know themselves can more easily make the decisions necessary for successful career planning. Many people get sidetracked because they choose careers based on haphazard plans or the wishes of others rather than on what they believe to be best for themselves.

Getting to know oneself is a lifetime project. As individuals progress through life, their priorities change. They may think they know themselves well at one stage of life and later may begin to see themselves quite differently. Therefore, self-assessment should be viewed as a continuous process. Those who desire a career in management must realize that much of what is done in management, especially at higher levels on the career ladder, is abstract and requires ongoing personal growth and development. Career-minded managers must heed the Red Queen's admonition to Alice (in Wonderland): "It takes all the running you can do, to keep in the same place."[3a] Once you have gained insight into yourself and can appreciate the career anchors that apply to you, you may find it useful to talk to professionals in management.

TALKING TO PROFESSIONALS

People who are successful in their jobs are a valuable resource for career information. It is likely that students, their parents, or close friends know managers who would be willing to share information about careers. Most likely, these people would be willing to discuss the demands of a particular job. Before setting up an interview with such a person, identify some questions that need to be answered, for example:

1. What type of entry-level position would be available to a person with my education and experience?

2. If I didn't start off in a managerial position, how long would it take before I am promoted into management?
3. What type of training does your firm provide management trainees?
4. What is the typical salary range for a person like me starting with your firm?
5. What are the typical duties of a new employee?
6. What is the firm's policy regarding promotions from within?
7. What type of preparation or qualifications does a person need for a career with this firm?

The list could go on and on. The point is that professionals should be asked the questions that concern the student the most. The benefits are numerous. The questioner is in a position to discover if a particular job might be interesting and rewarding. The professional is not under the pressure of conducting an interview and will likely answer questions candidly. Also, valuable information that can be used in future job interviews can be gained. Confidence is also gained because the job seeker can talk intelligently about the position later on in an interview. An additional benefit of this approach is that typical salary ranges for specific positions may be obtained. This information is important because prospective employees need to be realistic about salary expectations.

COLLEGE OR UNIVERSITY TESTING CENTER

A resource that goes unused by many students is the college or university testing center. The unique feature of the testing center is that students can discover many things about themselves prior to going for an interview. They can be absolutely honest when taking a test because only they and the counselor will see the results. Since many companies give similar tests to job applicants, students may feel more relaxed if they first used the testing center. The purpose of using the testing services is to gain personal insight that may prove beneficial in seeking a job. Some of the topics students may explore in detail relate to interests, aptitudes, and personality.

Interest Tests

A large number of college students do not know what they want to do once they graduate. Interest tests, which help people identify career fields, may help. If the test interpretation supports a person's belief in what constitutes a desired career, there is a good chance that the situation has been properly assessed and the person's belief that the proper decision has been made is reinforced. On the other hand, the person may discover areas that were not initially recognized. Knowledge of these additional interests can provide the stimulus to evaluate other alternatives.

Aptitude Tests

At times, our abilities and our interests do not match up. A person may have an interest in being a brain surgeon but no aptitude for the career. Aptitude tests help individuals determine if they have the natural inclination or talent needed for a particular job. These tests are valuable in establishing the likelihood of success in a particular career.

Personality Tests

There are jobs for which certain personality types will be more successful. Personality tests help people determine if they possess the right personality for a particular job. Although it is difficult to generalize about which qualities may be beneficial in a particular job, individuals often benefit from the test result interpretations. Corporations, like individuals, have personalities. People tend to be attracted to organizations that provide the means for meeting their objectives and aspirations. A person may be a success in one firm and a failure in another merely because of personality differences.

Tests should not be expected to provide all the answers. The results should be viewed only as indicators. However, if the results suggest that an alternate career path would be warranted, it may be beneficial to reevaluate personal objectives. A conference with a respected instructor may provide some assistance. Often, individuals are pushed into careers not of their choosing because of well-intentioned but perhaps misinformed friends and associates. If at this point a management career seems appropriate, it should prove beneficial to review the possible avenues for obtaining entry-level management positions.

TYPES OF ENTRY-LEVEL MANAGEMENT POSITIONS AVAILABLE

Students need to know much more than the fact that they desire a career in management. There are a large number and many types of managerial positions. Following are four avenues for obtaining entry-level management positions.

Entry-Level Management

Sometimes a person with limited or no work experience can enter immediately into management. This is most often the case for individuals possessing a college degree. When that happens, the person typically makes decisions under the supervision of an experienced manager. These jobs offer recent graduates the opportunity to learn without the fear of making a wrong decision that could be detrimental to a career. Many of these positions are in retail management and offer titles such as assistant manager of a department.

Management Training Programs

Some entry-level management positions involve a formal management training program. In such a program, a college graduate is formally trained for a period of three months to two years in the job the person ultimately will be filling. The trainee often receives both classroom and experiential training so as to get the overall picture of the firm's operations. Along with formal training, the individual may work in production one month, marketing the next, and accounting the following month. In that way, the person is exposed to the many different aspects of the firm that could affect performance. Once the training program is completed, the individual is placed in a managerial position.

Formal management training programs are often expensive, and the firm may not receive much benefit from the employee until training is complete. Thus, it is likely that firms will use a highly competitive screening process to make sure the individual to be trained will become a productive long-term employee. Graduates who wish to enter formal programs must first convince company representatives of their potential.

From Professional to Management

Many people graduate in technical fields such as accounting, computer science, and engineering and later see their future in management.

At times, this path can be a delicate one to follow. People who have always been associated with the technical aspects of a job may have difficulty moving into management. A successful engineer or accountant may not be an effective manager. However, because many firms believe that their supervisors should be technically competent, managers often are promoted from the ranks of technical and professional staff members.

CAREER PATHS

Career paths are flexible lines of progression through which employees typically move during their tenure with a company. Customarily, the paths involve upward mobility within a particular occupation. However, their focus may depend on the organization and the nature of the jobs involved. Three types of career paths may be used: traditional, network, and dual.

Traditional Career Path

The career path by which an employee moves along in a vertical line of progression from one specific job to the next is the traditional career path. It is assumed that each job is essential preparation for the next higher level of job. Therefore, an employee must move, step by step, from one job to the next to gain experience. This type of career path is most likely to be found in clerical or production operation functions.

One of the biggest advantages of the traditional career path is its straightforwardness. The path is clearly laid out, and the employee knows the specific sequence of jobs through which to progress. Today,

however, the traditional approach has become flawed because of business trends and changes in the workforce. Some of these factors include:

- "Thinning of middle-management ranks due to mergers, downsizing, growth and ingrowth cycles.
- Extinction of paternalism and job security.
- Erosion of employee loyalty to a company.
- Fluctuations in employees' hierarchy of needs as careers are progressed.
- Predisposition to assignments that continuously challenge, educate, and encourage skill expansion.
- Turbulence in business and technology demands, with oscillations in the skill mix requirements of employers."[4a]

The certainties of yesterday's business methods and growth have vanished in many industries, and neither organizations nor individuals can be assured of ever regaining them.

Network Career Path

The career path that contains both a vertical sequence of jobs and a series of horizontal opportunities is the *network career path*. This path recognizes the interchangeability of experience at certain levels and the need to broaden experience at one level before promotion to a higher level. It is a more realistic representation of jobs in an organization than is the traditional career path. Moreover, it provides more opportunities for employee development. Because of the vertical and horizontal options in the network, the problem of a particular employee blocking the progression for other employees is lessened. One disadvantage of this type of career path is the difficulty of explaining to employees the specific route their careers may take in a given line of work.

Dual Career Path

The dual career path was originally developed to deal with the problem of technically trained employees who had no desire to move into management—the normal procedure for upward mobility in an organization. The dual career path is the career path that recognizes that technical specialists can, and should be allowed to, continue to contribute their expertise to a company without having to become managers to increase their pay. Consequently, it provides an alternate progression route for such employees as scientists and engineers. Individuals in these fields can increase their specialized knowledge, make contributions to their firm, and be rewarded for their efforts without entering management. Managers and technical people in such firms receive comparable compensation at each level.

The dual career path is becoming increasingly popular. In a high-tech world, specialized knowledge is as important as managerial skill. Rather than creating poor managers out of competent technical specialists, the dual career path permits an organization to retain both skilled managers and technical people.[5a]

NOTES

1a. Edgar Schein, "How 'Career Anchors' Hold Executives to Their Career Paths," *Personnel* (May–June 1975): 11–24.

2a. Paul Frichtl, "Keep Score," *Industrial Distribution,* 75 (August 1986): 37.

3a. Lewis Carroll, *Through the Looking Glass* (1872). (New York: Norton, 1971), p. 127.

4a. Mike Hawkins and Milan Moravec, "Career Paths Discourage Innovation and Deflate Motivation," *Personnel Administrator* 34 (October 1989): 112.

5a. Donald L. Caruth, Robert M. Noe, III, and R. Wayne Mondy, *Staffing the Contemporary Organization.* (New York: Quorum Books, 1988), pp. 253–254.

2 The Manager's Diverse Environment

LEARNING OBJECTIVES

After completing this chapter students should be able to

✘ Explain how the business system operates.

✘ Describe the major factors in the external environment that can affect an organization and how the organization responds to the external environment.

✘ Portray the diverse workforce that today's managers confront.

✘ Explain how the environment for small businesses differs from that of large businesses.

✘ Describe the major factors in the internal environment that can affect an organization.

✘ Describe the basic transformation process that may occur in any organization.

✘ Discuss the environmental differences of the multinational organization.

Subway Sandwiches Effectively Deals with the Aggressive Open Environment of the Fast-Food Industry

The fast-food industry in the United States is definitely an open environment. Managers often fail to recognize that the ramifications of operating in an open system are serious and must be dealt with effectively. Fred DeLuca, co-founder of the Subway Sandwiches and Salads chain, failed to realize that he was operating in an open system when he opened his first sandwich shop, Pete's Submarines. In fact, in the beginning DeLuca virtually ignored his environment, operating without advanced planning, with no clear strategy, and with little working knowledge of the fast-food industry. As the first store was on the brink of failure, DeLuca opened a second store. Soon, however, the Subway management team became quite aware of their environment, and they realized that the impact of the environment must be taken into account if success is to be possible. There have been a lot of changes since then. Now, as head of the world's fastest growing franchise chain, DeLuca recognizes that selling a good sandwich is not enough to make a business grow and remain profitable.

Subway must confront the same business realities as many of their competitors: labor problems, various economic pressures that specifically impact franchising, and less than totally effective management. Subway managers now work continually to deal with their environments. Colorado managers overcame the problems associated with hiring part-time employees by exercising extraordinary leadership. For instance, at 11 Colorado Subway Sandwich restaurants employee turnover was reduced to 50 percent, much less than the 300 percent experienced in most fast-food chains. Staff members were allowed to set their own hours around other priorities in their lives, and tasks were rotated to help prevent burnout.

Because economic pressures were negatively impacting the franchise operation, strategic changes were made in the franchising program. To offset the tough economic times, DeLuca reduced capital requirements for new franchisees by more than $20,000 by adding the option of leasing equipment. Additionally, the franchise fee was limited to $7,500, making it the lowest in the industry. These changes allowed Subway's sales to increase, due to franchise expansion. Subway grew by nearly 70 percent, with an average of 25 new stores opening each week. Subway began franchising in 1974, and now has more than 7,900 outlets across the country.

Thus far, DeLuca has effectively dealt with environmental problems by applying his unusual management style. His "super-highway" management style lets managers set up the highway, allowing for different speeds and exits, but it bars people from interfering with others on the highway. This style allows people to work independently, and it provides great opportunities. By properly dealing with their environment, most Subway outlets are holding on to their respectable sales levels. The future may well be extremely challenging since DeLuca's goal is to overtake McDonald's. Such a lofty goal can only be accomplished by effectively dealing with the manager's environment.[1]

It is somewhat surprising that Fred DeLuca could have succeeded even for a short period of time, since he virtually ignored his environment. The company was suddenly successful, but also became a participant in a ruthlessly competitive environment. DeLuca was now aware of the problems associated with environmental pressures and worked to deal with them as they occurred. DeLuca responded to Subway's environment so effectively that the company is profitable and striving to be even better. To help ensure success in the future, DeLuca set up an unusual management style that allows managers to work independently and provides them with great opportunities to cope with the company's ever-changing environment.

This chapter starts with an overview of the business system. Next, it describes major external environmental factors. This description is followed by a discussion of managing the diverse workforce, the small business, and the internal environment. Finally, the chapter describes the transformation process by which inputs are converted to outputs within the business system and discusses the diverse multinational environment; the chapter ends with a global perspective on how U.S. companies are better competing in the global arena.

❖ ❖ THE BUSINESS SYSTEM: AN OVERVIEW

The Subway Sandwiches story shows that management must understand the interrelationship between the firm and its environment. Middle and lower managers at Subway Sandwiches were forced to think of external environmental factors. And, in difficult straits, they had to pay renewed attention to how their units interacted inside the organization. The **systems approach** is the viewing of any organization or entity as an arrangement of interrelated parts that interact in ways that can be specified and to some extent predicted. It provides a rational means for examining interactions between a company and its environment and within the company. Use of the systems approach inevitably leads to the conclusion that every organization, indeed every system, is an open system. An **open system** is an organization or assemblage of things that affects and is affected by outside events. On the other hand, a **closed system** is an organization or assemblage of things that neither affects nor is affected by outside events. Of course, there are no completely closed systems, but rather systems that exhibit various degrees of openness. Still, some managers make the mistake of failing to consider outside events; that is, they treat their organizations as closed systems. This is what the president and CEO of Subway Sandwiches and Salads, Fred DeLuca, did when he opened his first sandwich shop, Pete's Submarines.

Figure 2.1 illustrates the business system. Note that the organization is affected by a number of forces, both external and internal. Top management has perhaps the greatest concern for external forces, while management at all levels must confront forces inside the organization. Lower-level managers face an internal environment markedly different from that of more senior managers.

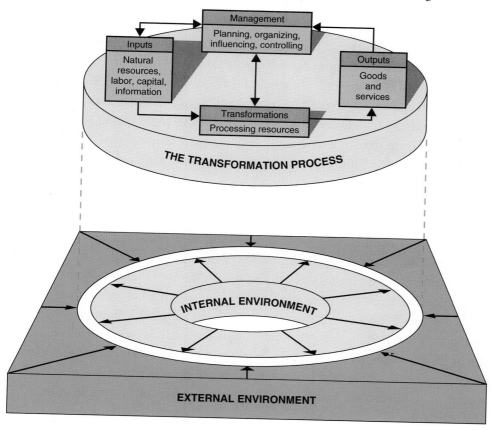

❖ **Figure 2.1**
The business system

As indicated in Chapter 1, the U.S. business system is directed more and more at providing services, as opposed to producing manufactured products. Quality is vital to the success of manufacturing companies, and it is just as important for service-oriented ones.

❖ ❖ THE EXTERNAL ENVIRONMENT

The manager's job cannot be accomplished in a vacuum within the organization. Many interacting external factors can affect managerial performance. The **external environment** consists of those factors that affect a firm from outside its organizational boundaries. The external factors include the labor force, legal considerations, society, unions, stockholders, the competition, customers, and technology. As head of Subway Sandwiches, DeLuca recognized that selling a good sandwich was not enough to make a business grow and remain profitable. Subway was confronted with the same external environmental realities as many of its competitors: labor problems and various economic pressures that specifically impact franchising.

The Labor Force

The capabilities of a firm's employees determine to a large extent how well the organization can perform its mission. Since new employees are hired from outside the firm, the labor force is considered an external environmental factor. The labor force is always changing. This inevitably causes changes in the workforce of an organization. In turn, changes in individuals within an organization affect the way management must deal with its workforce. In short, changes in the country's labor force create dynamic situations within organizations. This topic will be further discussed in this chapter under the heading "Managing the Diverse Workforce."

Legal Considerations

Managers must comply with federal, state, and local legislation and the many court decisions interpreting this legislation. A number of the laws that have had the greatest impact on business date from the 1930s and before. Among them are the Social Security Act of 1935 as amended, the National Labor Relations Act of 1935, the Pure Food and Drug Act of 1906 as amended, and the Sherman Antitrust Act of 1890. Among the laws passed in recent decades, the Civil Rights Act of 1964 as amended has probably affected business managers most extensively. This act has been largely responsible for bringing many more women and minorities into the workforce and for giving them more opportunities for advancement.

Laws that limit the actions a firm may take continue to be passed. For example, the Americans with Disabilities Act was passed in 1990, prohibiting discrimination against qualified individuals with disabilities. A new Civil Rights Act was passed in 1991. Future legislation is certain to also affect businesses. For example, if passed, President Clinton's health care reform will have a major impact on all businesses, but especially small businesses. Today, managers must be alert to the ever-changing U.S. legal environment. Likewise, when a firm's operations extend into other countries, the laws and regulations of those countries must be taken into account.

Society

Members of society may also exert pressure on management. The public no longer accepts the actions of business without question. People have learned that their voices and votes can produce changes. The large number of laws that have been passed since the early 1960s is testimony to the public's influence. The firm that is to remain acceptable to the general public must accomplish its mission within the range of societal norms.

When a firm responds effectively to societal interests, it is said to be socially responsible. **Social responsibility** is the implied, enforced, or felt obligation of managers, acting in their official capacity, to serve or protect the interests of groups other than themselves.[2] Many companies develop patterns of concern for moral issues through policy statements, practices over time, and the leadership of morally strong employees and managers. Open-door policies, grievance procedures, and employee benefit programs often stem as much from the desire to do what is right as from a concern for productivity and for the avoidance of strife.

Many firms strive to be good corporate citizens. They work cooperatively with other members of the community to control pollution, drug abuse, unemployment, and other ills. They participate in fund drives. Many executives are encouraged to be involved in civic clubs and to seek ways to support local government. Such activities enhance a firm's image in the community and in the long run may improve the firm's profitability.

A firm's workforce is part of the society the firm must accommodate. Employees serve as a conduit to the broader community and provide a source of information about society's concerns. Each employee communicates with dozens of family members and friends. If management maintains clear and honest communications with its employees, the company will be able to get its own message out more effectively. It will also know of developing problems in time to take corrective action.

Social responsibility is closely related to **ethics**—the discipline dealing with what is good and bad, or right and wrong, or with moral duty and obligation.

The North American Free Trade Agreement (NAFTA): A Nightmare for Organized Labor

NAFTA is a trade treaty among the United States, Canada, and Mexico. The creation of this free trade agreement will allow all three countries in North America to eliminate trade barriers among themselves while maintaining their own individual barriers toward nonmember nations. This agreement is expected to alter the management environment in the United States and throughout North America. Many external environmental factors are expected to be affected, but the impact of the agreement on unions is one of the most hotly debated areas. In fact, unions are so nervous about the possible repercussions of NAFTA that they are helping Mexican unions. With urgings from the United Auto Workers, some Mexican low wage earners are staging strikes at auto plants, hoping to get raises. Mexican officials claim recent strikes at two prominent auto factories were aided by U.S. unions, but thus far only financial support has been proven. The U.S. union objective is to raise production costs, making Mexican-produced cars less competitive, and thereby protecting jobs in the U.S.[3]

Social responsibility and business ethics are discussed in Chapter 3. Ethical dilemma exercises are presented in Chapters 4 through 20.

Unions

Wage levels, benefits, and working conditions for millions of employees now reflect decisions made jointly by unions and management. A **union** is a group of employees who have joined together for the purpose of dealing with their employer. Unions become essentially a third party when dealing with the company. For example, in a unionized firm, it is the union rather than individual employees that negotiates labor-related agreements with the firm.

Although unions are a fairly powerful force, union membership slipped from 33 percent in 1955 to about 16 percent today.[4] Private sector workforce union membership is presently approximately 12 percent.[5] The emphasis in the future will likely shift to a management system that deals directly with individual workers to satisfy their needs and to allow the company to compete more effectively.

Wage levels, benefits, and working conditions for millions of employees now reflect decisions made jointly by unions and managers. External forces often have an impact on these joint decisions, with the power pendulum swinging back and forth sometimes in favor of labor, and sometimes in favor of management. The North American Free Trade Agreement (NAFTA) is an external force that will affect this relationship.

Stockholders

The owners of a corporation's stock are called **stockholders,** or **shareholders.** In general, there are two types of stock: common and preferred. Typically, only the common stockholders have the right to vote, and they vote in proportion to the numbers of shares they own. The common stockholders elect directors, who make up the board of directors. The directors then elect the company's top managers and make various other decisions. As a practical matter, however, stockholders of publicly traded firms usually assign their voting rights to management or just fail to vote. Most of them see their ownership of the company as a purely financial investment.

Still, stockholders are wielding increasing influence. There are frequent stockholder lawsuits against managers and directors, claiming they failed to look out for stockholder interests. For instance, when Medco merged with Merck, unhappy shareholders filed five suits alleging the Merck deal was designed to enrich top executives at other shareholders' expense. Medco dismisses the suits as nonsense, although Martin J. Wygod, Medco's CEO, stacked the Medco Board with his pals who have made millions from generous stock options.[6]

Sometimes, takeovers and attempted takeovers occur. A group or an individual accumulates large blocks of common stock and tries to buy the rest or use its current holdings to influence management to take actions that are beneficial to shareholders.

Competition

Companies must compete with one another not only for sales but also in other areas. For example, each firm must have competent employees, and good

The modern concept of marketing requires that every manager focus on fulfilling customer needs.
(Source: © John Coletti)

employees with appropriate skills are often in short supply. An easy solution is to raise pay, but this may result in a bidding war when several competitors need people with the same skills. Besides, competition in product and service markets forces employers to keep labor costs low. Some managers often combine other benefits and working conditions to get "more bang for the buck" in terms of recruitment and retention. Probably because of such competition, pay, benefits, and working conditions tend to be comparable within an industry.

Customers

The people who use a firm's products and services are an important part of the external environment. Because sales are critical to a firm's survival, management must take care not to antagonize customers. This is nearly what happened to United Parcel Services, Inc. When executives at Eastman Kodak Company were intent on cutting the number of package carriers they used, UPS's bad attitude placed it as the number one target of cuts. But, UPS changed its attitude and assisted Terrance M. Golomb, Kodak's manager of worldwide transportation services, in cutting costs and improving services. UPS placed a full-time service representative at Kodak's Rochester (New York) headquarters. The package carrier is showing Kodak ways to cut its shipping bills. Even more astounding, UPS is offering Kodak discounts on big-volume shipments. "It's an entirely different company," say Golomb. Instead of firing UPS, he upped Kodak's business by 15 percent, to 50,000 packages a week.[7]

Technology

Change is occurring at an ever-increasing pace, and few firms operate today as they did even a decade ago. Products not even imagined only a few years ago are now being mass-produced, and new skills are continually needed to meet new technological demands. Word processing, for instance, has substantially changed the traditional role of the secretary. Many managers now keyboard and print their own letters using a word processor instead of handwriting or dictating them.

At the same time, advancements in technology have rendered some skills obsolete, requiring periodic retraining of affected employees. It has been estimated that half of all existing jobs will be substantially changed within the next decade, with 30 percent of them being eliminated because of technological advances.[8] Furthermore, by the year 2000, 75 percent of all jobs are expected to involve the use of computers.[9]

At times, the need for new technology results from changes in other environmental factors. Fast-food chains, for example, often have difficulty attracting reliable workers and have turned to automation to reduce the numbers of work-

The workplace today is often far different from that of just a few years ago. The rapid advance of information technology creates a need for employees to continually adapt. (Source: © John Coletti)

ers required. Self-service drink dispensers were installed to eliminate the need to have employees pour soft drinks.

The trend toward a service economy also affects the type and amount of technology needed. While the number of manufacturing jobs has been decreasing, the number of service industry jobs has dramatically increased. By 1993, 80 percent of the jobs in the United States were in service-related industries.[10] A major portion of Chapter 20 is devoted to the key technological advances affecting management.

The Economy

The economy of the nation and of various segments of the country is a major environmental factor affecting a manager's job. As a broad generalization, when the economy is booming, it is often more difficult to recruit qualified workers. On the other hand, when a downturn is experienced, more applicants are typically available. Remember that because economic pressures were negatively impacting the franchise operation at Subway Sandwiches, strategic changes were made in the franchising program. To offset the tough economic times, DeLuca reduced capital requirements for new franchisees by more than $20,000 by adding the option of leasing equipment. Additionally, the franchise fee was limited to $7,500, making it the lowest in the industry.

Complicating this even further is the fact that one segment of the country may be experiencing a downturn, another a slow recovery, and another a boom. Such was the situation existing in some areas of the United States in the early

1990s. While some of the northeastern states were facing a downturn, Houston, Texas was gradually recovering, and Salt Lake City was booming.[11]

❖ ❖ RESPONDING TO THE EXTERNAL ENVIRONMENT

Managers approach changes in the external environment proactively or reactively. A **proactive response** is taking action in anticipation of environmental changes. A **reactive response** is simply responding to environmental changes after they occur. For example, while the Occupational Safety and Health Act (OSHA) of 1970 was traveling its way through Congress, some companies had already implemented its anticipated provisions. Managers of these companies were being proactive. Those who waited until the law went into effect to plan the required changes were being reactive.

Organizations exhibit varying degrees of proactive and reactive behavior. When OSHA was enacted, some firms did only what the letter of the law required. Others went far beyond that and sincerely tried to create a safe and healthful environment for employees. Title VII of the Civil Rights Act of 1964 provides another illustration. Prior to passage of that law, many firms were inactive with regard to equal employment opportunity. However, many of these companies later became aggressive in promoting equal opportunity. Convinced that the national agenda was to eliminate employment discrimination based on race, color, sex, religion, or national origin, they went well beyond the explicit requirements of the law.

A firm may be either reactive or proactive in any matter, legal or otherwise. For example, reactive managers may demonstrate concern for employee welfare only after the start of a union organizing attempt. Proactive managers try to spot early signs of discontent and correct the causes of that discontent before matters get out of hand. Proactive managers also prevent customer complaints rather than "handle" them. In the markets they serve, they tend to set the prices competitors must match. They install scrubbers on exhaust stacks before environmental groups begin picketing the plant and before federal regulators file suit. In all matters, proactive managers initiate rather than react.

❖ ❖ MANAGING THE DIVERSE WORKFORCE

From McDonald's to Holiday Inn, AT&T to Levi Strauss, managers are learning to understand their "kaleidoscopic workforce" and to effectively manage diverse environments. Diversity management presents new challenges in the workplace. Not only are more businesses expanding their operations overseas, but many workers in the United States are working alongside individuals whose cultures

Levi Strauss Values Diversity

At Levi Strauss in San Francisco, "Valuing Diversity" educational programs cost the company $5 million per year, but they've helped managers and employees become more tolerant of personal differences. Levi CEO Robert Haas believes that to hire the best employees these days, companies must learn to value each individual's uniqueness, and there-fore Levi Strauss is making every effort to embrace diversity among its employees. At Ethicon in New Jersey, a subsidiary of Johnson & Johnson, a vice-president who had been through the company's diversity workshops reports that, "These days, I pay more attention to a person's competency than to whether that person fits the classical mold." The challenge for managers in the coming decades will be to recognize that people often think differently, act differently, learn differently, and communicate differently. Because every person, culture, and business situation is unique, there are no simple rules for managing diversity, but diversity experts say that employees need to develop patience, open-mindedness, acceptance, and cultural awareness. Only by such measures can productivity be maximized.[12]

differ substantially from their own, and more ethnic minorities are entering the workforce. Managers must be knowledgeable about common group characteristics in order to effectively manage diversity. **Managing diversity** is having an acute awareness of characteristics common to a culture, race, gender, age, or sexual preference, while at the same time managing employees with these characteristics as individuals.[13] This philosophy recognizes that individuals of a particular culture may indeed have unique general characteristics. However, in the work environment employees are treated as individuals, while cultural differences are taken into consideration.

By 1995, the U.S. labor force is projected to be about 129 million people, 14 percent more than the 1984 level of 114 million. Size alone, however, does not tell the whole story. The labor force now includes more women and older persons than ever before. Employees with disabilities are being included in increasing numbers. Many immigrants from developing areas, especially Southeast Asia and Latin America, are joining the labor force. In the late 1980s, immigration was proceeding at the highest rate since the 1920s.[14]

The Hudson Institute, an economics think tank, projected that there would be the following mix of new entrants into the labor force between now and the year 2000: 15 percent U.S.-born white males, 42 percent U.S.-born white females, seven percent U.S.-born nonwhite males, 13 percent U.S.-born nonwhite females, 13 percent immigrant males, and nine percent immigrant females. As is evident in Figure 2.2, a very diverse workforce has evolved in the United States.

To help resolve conflict and enhance employee effectiveness, many companies are hiring consultants or setting up their own seminars to foster better diversity awareness among employees.

❖ **Figure 2.2**

New entrants to the workforce—year 2000 (Source: Adapted from *Workforce 2000,* published by the Hudson Institute, Inc., p. 95.)

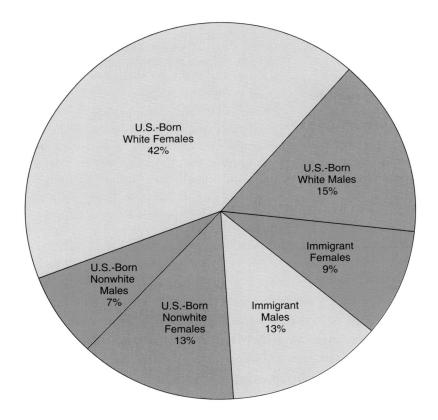

Women in Business

Today half the entry-level management positions are held by women; this is up from 15 percent 15 years ago.[15] Because of the critical mass of talent, many believe that the 1990s will be the decade that women en masse break through to upper level management. In fact, a recent survey of 400 top female executives revealed that the percentage of women who hold the title of executive vice president more than doubled over the past decade, from 4 percent to 8.7 percent.[16] The same study showed that women no longer see careers and family as mutually exclusive. Sixty-nine percent of the women polled were married and 63 percent had children.

Largely because of the number of women who are entering the workforce, there is an increasing number of nontraditional households in the United States. These households include those headed by single parents and those in which both partners work full time. Women who formerly remained at home to care for children and the household, today need and want to work outside the home. In fact, women are expected to account for over 60 percent of labor force growth during the period from 1984 to 1996.

Some executives like Marion O. Sandler, CO-CEO and president of Golden West Financial Corporation, believe that not a lot of progress has been made in terms of women moving up in business. He also believes that, "It's the power structure that doesn't allow women entry." Carleton S. Fiorina, Network Systems vice-president for strategy and market development at AT&T disagrees. Fiorina believes that her sex has not been a disadvantage. According to Fiorina, "There's a lot of discussion that men won't give adequate clout or power to women. Women share an equal burden for that. No one can expect to be handed power."[17] However, regardless of whether women have been at a disadvantage in business, it is apparent that businesses are having to adapt to employees' requirements for flexibility and innovation in child-care services, benefit plans, and work practices.

Traditionally, child-care needs were viewed as being outside the realm of the business world—a responsibility that workers had to bear and manage alone. This was particularly difficult for single parents, but even working parent couples generally cannot afford a full-time live-in housekeeper. For many workers, child care has been managed with the help of family or friends. The need for alternative arrangements is evidenced by the fact that in 1950, only 12 percent of women with children under age six were in the labor force. That figure has now risen to almost 60 percent.[18]

Today, business has begun to see that providing child-care services and workplace flexibility may influence workers' choice of employers. Many companies have begun providing day-care services for employees. Some companies located in the same building or facility provide joint day-care service. Other companies, such as IBM, provide day-care referral services. More and more companies provide paid maternity leave, and some offer paternity leave. Still other firms give time off for children's visits to doctors, which can be charged against the parents' sick leave or personal time. Managers need to be sensitive to the needs of working parents. At times, they also need to be creative in accommodating this most valuable segment of the workforce.

The increasing number of dual career couples presents both challenges and opportunities for organizations. Some firms have revised their policies against nepotism to allow both partners to work for the same company. Other firms have developed polices to assist the spouse of an employee who is transferred. When a firm wishes to transfer an employee to another location, the employee's spouse may be unwilling to give up a good position or may be unable to find an equivalent position in the new location. Some companies are offering assistance in finding a position for the spouse of a transferred employee. Overall, the trend is toward *nontraditional* households, and firms must develop programs to accommodate employees' needs.

Workers of Color

Workers of color often experience stereotypes about their group (Hispanics, African Americans, Asians, etc.). They at times encounter misunderstandings and expectations based on ethnic or cultural differences. Members of ethnic or racial groups are socialized within their particular culture. Many are socialized as members of two cultural groups—the dominant culture and their racial or ethnic culture. Ella Bell, professor of organizational behavior at MIT, refers to this dual membership as *biculturalism*. In her study of African-American women, she identifies the stress of coping with membership in two cultures simultaneously, as *bicultural stress*. She indicates that role conflict—competing roles from two cultures—and *role overload*—too many expectations to comfortably fulfill—are common characteristics of bicultural stress. Although these issues can be applied to many minority groups, they are particularly intense for women of color. This is because this group experiences dynamics affecting *both* minorities and women.[19]

Socialization in one's culture of origin can lead to misunderstandings in the workplace. This is particularly true when the manager relies solely on the cultural norms of the majority group. According to these norms, within the American culture it is acceptable—even positive—to publicly praise an individual for a job well done. However, in cultures that place primary value on group harmony and collective achievement, this method of rewarding an employee causes emotional discomfort. Employees feel that if they are praised publicly, they will "lose face" within their group.

Older Workers

The U.S. population is growing older, a trend that is expected to continue through the year 2000. Life expectancies continue to increase, and the baby boom generation (people born from the end of World War II through 1964) had only half as many children as their parents did.

The trend toward earlier retirement appears to be reversing itself. This may have been due to the 1986 amendment to the Age Discrimination in Employment Act. Firms cannot force employees to retire because of age, no matter how old they are. And many older persons do not want to retire, or even slow down. As many as one-third of retirees want to return to full- or part-time work.[20]

The "graying" of the workforce has required some adjustments. Some older workers favor less-demanding full-time jobs, others choose semiretirement, and still others prefer part-time work. Many of these individuals require retraining as they move through the various stages of their careers.

Part-Time Workers

As companies downsize and reorganize, many of them are employing part-time workers. Of course, the use of part-time workers is not without disadvantages. For example, it means more workers to do the same job. This increases the burden on management, especially in the area of communication. Part-time employees tend to be less dependent on the firm and therefore less committed to it. Remember that overcoming the disadvantages of part-time employees required Subway managers to exercise extraordinary leadership. At 11 Colorado Subway Sandwiches restaurants, employee turnover was reduced to 50 percent, much less than the 300 percent experienced in most fast-food chains. Needed training for part-timers is often hard to justify economically. The manager has only part of a work week to get a return on the training costs; besides, part-time workers tend to be less permanent than full-time ones. Some problems may be eased if part-time workers are given first shot at full-time job openings.

Temporary Employees

In the late 1980s and early 1990s many companies drastically reduced their workforce. As the economy began to recover, often full-time workers were not hired. In 1993, temporaries have filled 30 percent of all new jobs as opposed to just four percent in the previous expansion. In addition, some skilled professionals desire to work on a temporary basis. Often these individuals desire the excitement of working in a wide variety of organizations, while others like the flexibility of choosing their work schedule.

Leased Employees

Leased employees are individuals provided by an outside firm at a fixed hourly rate, similar to a rental fee, often for extended periods. Using this approach, a firm formally terminates some or most of its employees. A leasing company then hires them, usually at the same salary, and leases them back to the former employer who becomes the client. The employees continue to work as before, with the client supervising their activities. The leasing company, however, assumes all responsibilities associated with being the employer, including personnel administration.

Use of employee leasing is growing. Currently, about 75,000 employees are being leased. It is estimated that 20 percent of the 4.4 million businesses in the United States with fewer than 35 employees will be attracted to employee leasing, resulting in 10 million leased employees by the year 2000. Larger companies have also begun using employee leasing to a greater extent. It provides them with a body of well-trained, long-term employees that can expand or contract as business conditions dictate.[21]

Persons with Disabilities

The Americans with Disabilities Act (ADA) passed in 1990 prohibits discrimination against "qualified individuals with disabilities." Persons discriminated against because they have a known association or relationship with a disabled individual also are protected. The ADA defines an "individual with a disability" as a person who has, or is regarded as having, a physical or mental impairment that substantially limits one or more major life activities, and has a record of such an impairment, or is regarded as having such an impairment. The ADA prohibits discrimination in all employment practices, including job application procedures, hiring, firing, advancement, compensation, training, and other terms, conditions, and privileges of employment. It applies to recruitment, advertising, tenure, layoff, leave, fringe benefits, and all other employment-related activities. The employment provisions apply to private employers, state and local governments, employment agencies, and labor unions. Studies indicate that workers with disabilities can do as well as workers without impairments in areas such as productivity, attendance, and average tenure. In fact, in certain high-turnover occupations, disabled workers were found to have lower turnover rates.[22]

A serious barrier to effective employment of disabled persons is bias, or prejudice. Managers should examine their own biases and preconceived attitudes toward such persons. Many individuals experience anxiety around workers with disabilities, especially if the disabilities are severe. Fellow workers may show pity or feel that a disabled worker is fragile. Some even show disgust. Most disabilities affect specific parts of the body—eyes, ears, arms, legs. Except for the disorder, the affected people are usually healthy, and they should be treated accordingly. The manager can set the tone for this treatment. If someone is unsure about how to act or how much help to offer, the disabled person should be asked for

---

MANAGEMENT IN PRACTICE

A Skill-Building Exercise: Duane Roberts, a paraplegic, has just been assigned to your division as a radio dispatcher for your delivery trucks. The personnel department has given you only limited information about Duane. But you know he is 32 years old and has held similar jobs before. You are in the dis-

patching office when you see a person you assume to be Duane coming up the sidewalk in his wheelchair. You think he might have a problem getting through the double glass doors in his path, which open against his direction of travel.

How would you handle the situation?

guidance. Managers must always strive to treat employees with disabilities as they treat other employees and must hold them accountable for achievement.

Immigrants

In the 1980s, 8.7 million people immigrated to the United States. Large numbers of immigrants from Asia and Latin America have settled in many parts of the United States. Some are highly skilled and well-educated, and others are only minimally skilled and have little education. They have one thing in common— they are eager to work.[23] They have brought with them attitudes, values, and mores particular to their home-country cultures. As corporations employ more foreign nationals in this country, managers must work to understand the different cultures and languages of their employees.

Young Persons with Limited Education or Skills

Each year, thousands of young, unskilled workers are hired, especially during peak periods such as holiday buying seasons. These workers generally have limited education, sometimes even less than a high school diploma. Those who have completed high school often find that their education hardly fits the work they are expected to do. Most, for example, lack familiarity with computers. Many of these young adults and teenagers have poor work habits; they tend to be tardy or absent more often than experienced or better-educated workers.

Although the negative attributes of these workers at times seem to outweigh the positive ones, the workers are a permanent part of the workforce. There are many jobs they can do well. And more jobs can be "de-skilled," making it possible for lower-skilled workers to do them. A well-known example of de-skilling is McDonald's by substitution of pictures for numbers on its cash register keys. Managers should also look for ways to train unskilled workers and to facilitate further their formal education.

❖ ❖ THE SMALL BUSINESS

During the 1980s, small and midsized companies created 80 percent of the available jobs.[24] Every year, approximately 400,000 new businesses are established.[25] Remember from Chapter 1 that since 1988, companies that employed fewer than 100 workers accounted for over 90 percent of all job growth.[26] Every year, thousands of individuals, motivated by a desire to be their own boss, to earn a better income, and to realize the American dream, launch a new business venture. These individuals, often referred to as *entrepreneurs,* have been essential to the growth and vitality of the American free enterprise system. Entrepreneurs develop or recognize new products or business opportunities, secure the necessary capital, and organize and operate the business. Most people who start their own business get a great deal of satisfaction from owning and managing their own firm. Historically, it has been estimated that four out of five small businesses fail within five years. However, in a recent study it was found that over half survived in one form or another.[27]

Almost every large corporation began as a small business. Many small businesses are so successful that they become big businesses. For example, Steven Jobs and Steve Wozniak (the founders of Apple Computer Company) began making personal computers in Wozniak's garage. From this meager beginning, Apple Computer evolved into a major personal computer maker.

There is no commonly agreed-on definition of what constitutes a small business. The Small Business Act of 1953 defines a small business as one that is independently owned and operated and not dominant in its field. Basically, a small business is one in which the owner-operator knows each of the key personnel. In most small businesses, this key group would ordinarily not exceed 12 to 15 people. Regardless of the specific definition of a small business, it is a certainty that this category makes up the overwhelming majority of business establishments in this country.

The environment of managers in large and small businesses is often quite different. Managers in large firms may be separated from top management by numerous managerial layers. They may find it difficult to see how they fit into the overall organization. They often know managers one or two layers above them, but seldom those higher up. In some large companies, supervisors are restricted by many written guidelines, and they may feel more loyalty to their workers than to upper management.

Managers in small businesses often identify more closely with the goals of the firm. They can readily see how their efforts affect the firm's profits. In many instances, lower-level managers know the company executives personally. These supervisors know that the organization's success is closely tied to their own effectiveness on the job.

❖ ❖ THE INTERNAL ENVIRONMENT

The internal environment of an organization, as illustrated in Figure 2.3, is quite different from the external one. The **internal environment** consists of those factors inside an organization that affect the organization's management. Aspects of the internal environment include the organization's mission, corporate culture, the management style, policies, employees, the informal organization, other units of the organization, and unions.

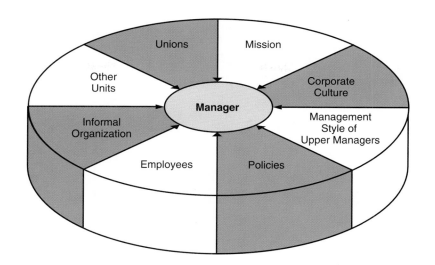

❖ **Figure 2.3**
The internal environment

Mission

A unit's continuing purpose, or reason for being, is its **mission.** Each management level should understand the overall mission of the firm. And each unit (division, plant, department) should have clearly understood objectives that coincide with the organizational mission.

Corporate Culture

The system of shared values, beliefs, and habits within an organization that interacts with the formal structure to produce behavioral norms is **corporate culture.** It is a firm's social and psychological climate. Managers can, and should, determine the kind of corporate culture they wish to work within and strive to make sure that kind of culture develops. Corporate culture will be discussed in considerable detail in Chapter 15.

Management Style

Closely related to corporate culture is the way in which the attitudes and preferences of superiors affect how a job is done. This deserves special emphasis here because of the problems that can result if the managerial style of upper-level managers differs from that of lower-level managers. In general, a lower-level manager must adapt to the style of the boss. It is hard to be open and considerate when the boss believes in just giving orders and having them followed. A lower-level manager's concern for involving employees in decision making and giving them any freedom may be seen as a lack of decisiveness. Even the company president must deal with the management style and attitudes of superiors, in this case

Effective implementation of policies often requires sending headquarters' personnel to monitor field activities. Honeywell managers spend a lot of time in customer plants, checking instrumentation the company makes and installs. Honeywell believes its process control systems give customers the tools to solidify their competitive advantage and improve financial returns. (Source: Photograph courtesy of Honeywell, Inc.)

the board of directors. The president may be a risk taker and want to be aggressive in the marketplace, but the board may prefer a more conservative approach.

Policies

A **policy** is a predetermined guide established to provide direction in decision making. Policies set limits on decisions. They are usually established formally, often in writing. Policies may concern important matters, such as the safe operation of equipment, or minor ones, such as how people dress. Managers at every level may often set policies for subordinates, but they must live within the poli-

---

MANAGEMENT IN PRACTICE

A Skill-Building Exercise: Lee Roy Howard, a supervisor in the hard surfacing department at Ampex Corporation, had just received a report from the cost accountant. It showed that his unit costs had gone up ten percent. He knew that the plant manager, Alton Williams, had also received this report.

Lee Roy expected trouble. The plant manager was the brother-in-law of company president Byron Smith. Alton had recently been assigned to the plant after many years as a "driller" in the oil field. Lee Roy knew that one

of his good friends, a supervisor in another department, had been fired by Alton for failing to get an order out on time.

Lee Roy was considering how he might explain and correct the cost increase when Shelton Lewis, one of the workers, approached him. Shelton angrily said: "Lee Roy, my machine is broken again. That's the third time this week. Do you think purchasing will get us a new one now?"

How is Lee Roy's environment different from that of top management?

cies of managers higher in the organization. Policies are discussed in greater detail in Chapter 5.

Employees

Employees differ in many areas, among them capabilities, attitudes, personal goals, and personalities. As a result, the behavior a manager finds effective with one worker may not be effective with another. In extreme cases, employees can be so different that it is virtually impossible for them to be managed as a group. In order to be effective, the manager must consider both individual and group differences. A supervisor of experienced workers, for instance, may pay little attention to the technical details of the job and more to encouraging group cooperation, while a supervisor of inexperienced workers may focus mainly on the technical aspects of the task.

Informal Organization

New managers quickly learn that there are two organizations they must deal with in the firm—one formal, the other informal. The formal organization is usually delineated by an organizational chart and job descriptions. Managers know the official reporting relationships. But alongside the formal organization exists an informal one. The **informal organization** is the set of evolving relationships and patterns of human interaction within an organization that are not officially prescribed. Such relationships are powerful. As we will discuss in Chapter 7, the informal organization can have positive effects too.

Other Units

Managers must be keenly aware of interrelationships that exist among divisions or departments, and they should use such relationships to their best advantage. Some of the possible relationships among departments are presented in Figure 2.4. The personnel department helps maintain a competent workforce; the purchasing department buys materials and parts. Because one department precedes another in the flow of work, that department's output becomes the other department's input. Most managers soon discover that cooperation with other departments is necessary if the job is to get done efficiently. Managers who make enemies of other managers may jeopardize the productivity of several departments.

Unions

Upper management typically negotiates labor-management agreements with unions, but managers throughout the organization must implement the terms of the agreements. In most instances, agreements place restrictions on the managers' actions. For example, a manager may want to shift a maintenance worker to an

❖ **Figure 2.4**
Possible relationships
with other departments

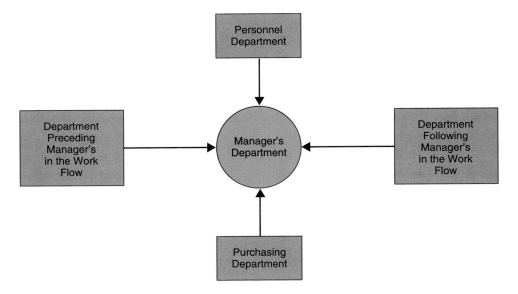

operator's job temporarily. But if the labor-management agreement specifies the tasks that can and cannot be performed in each job, the manager may not be able to make the temporary assignment.

❖ ❖ **THE TRANSFORMATION PROCESS**

In any organization, management's job is to use resources (inputs) in an efficient manner to produce desirable goods or services (outputs). Management's role in transforming inputs to outputs is illustrated in Figure 2.5.

Inputs

Just as humans cannot live long without food and water, a dynamic business system cannot survive without resources to sustain it. Managers must assure that the inputs needed to complete the transformation process exist in sufficient quantity and quality. These inputs—categorized as natural resources, labor, capital, and information—will vary according to the type of business a firm conducts and its particular goals. For example, the manufacturer of Rolex Oyster Perpetual watches emphasizes high-quality watches. The inputs needed, therefore, are likely to be highly trained workers, highly specialized equipment, and high-quality materials. A manufacturer of low-price watches will need different inputs, such as mass-production equipment and less-skilled employees.

Processing Resources

Managers are responsible for assuring that resources are properly processed. Resources (inputs) are processed (transformed) within the organization to create

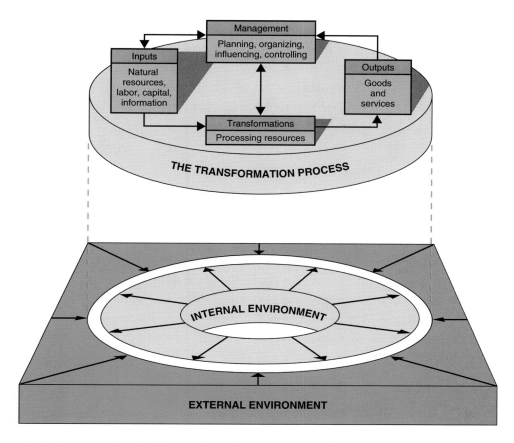

desired outputs in the form of goods or services. There are three main kinds of
production operations:

1. Inputs may be combined to form significantly different outputs, as when
   sand, gravel, and Portland cement are mixed together to make concrete.
2. Something useful may be extracted from inputs. An example of extraction
   is iron smelting, a method whereby usable iron is obtained from iron ore.
3. The form of inputs may be changed. This occurs when iron is rolled into
   sheets, logs are cut into boards, and glass is spun into fiberglass.

Processing for service industries is more difficult to describe because service firms
do not produce tangible goods. Rather, they create, produce, and distribute services. Service industries include banking, insurance, transportation, real estate,
medical care, beauty, and education. Government agencies are also considered
part of the service segment of the economy.

The fundamental process that service industries follow, however, is the same
as that for manufacturing industries. Hospitals try to convert ill patients into
healthy ones, schools try to turn uninformed students into knowledgeable ones,
and beauty salons try to transform individuals into more attractive ones.

Top management is responsible for the overall transformation process and must be concerned not only with the interrelationships among departments involved in the process but also with those among internal and external environmental factors. The foregoing analysis of the elements in Figure 2.5 suggests the complexity of the job faced by top management. In actuality, Figure 2.5 is a gross simplification designed to foster a greater understanding of the infinite complexities of the business system.

Outputs

Goods and services are the end result of the transformation process. Once inputs are converted to outputs, the products are returned to the environment. The output of IBM is largely information processing, whereas Consolidated Edison produces energy. As mentioned in Chapter 1, the capability of producing desired results with a minimum of costly inputs is efficiency; and the capability of bringing about an effect or accomplishing a purpose, sometimes without regard to the quantity of resources (inputs) consumed in the process is effectiveness. The overall objective of the manager in managing the transformation process is to obtain a high level of effectiveness and to do so efficiently.

Management

The operation of the transformation process shown in Figure 2.5 is the responsibility of those in management, who must plan, organize, influence, and control. As the arrows indicate, management receives feedback from the output of the production process and monitors the inputs and the process itself. Inputs are then controlled or changed, and the production process is adjusted to provide the desired results in the form of outputs.

❖ ❖ THE DIVERSE MULTINATIONAL ENVIRONMENT

Global competition, air travel, and satellite communication technology have made doing business abroad both necessary and feasible, and companies have responded by establishing operations overseas. American managers have recognized that the challenge of engaging in multinational operations is not easily met. This is especially true with regard to the challenges of management. Earlier in the chapter, the discussion was primarily focused on environmental factors of organizations located in the United States. However, the external environment that confronts multinational enterprises is even more diverse and complex than that confronted by domestic firms.

As illustrated in Figure 2.6, working in a multinational climate adds another layer to the external environment that management must contend with. Although

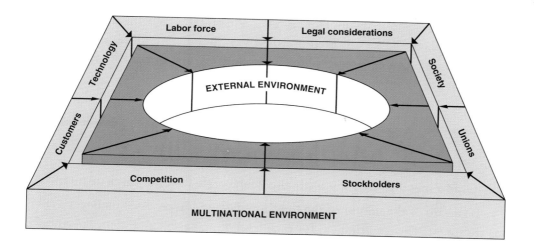

❖ **Figure 2.6**
The external environment of a multinational corporation

In the figure: Labor force, Legal considerations, Technology, Society, Customers, Unions, Competition, Stockholders, EXTERNAL ENVIRONMENT, MULTINATIONAL ENVIRONMENT

A GLOBAL PERSPECTIVE

American "Know-How" Storms the Beaches Overseas

Regardless of whether a firm operates in a domestic or global environment, management must use company resources in an efficient manner to produce desirable goods or services. Faced with the ever-increasing difficulties of global competition, managers are searching for ways to be more globally competitive. Many American companies have had problems competing with foreign competitors, especially the Japanese. However, the one area where American companies are extremely strong is in exporting "know-how." Service companies are coping with foreign competitors by coming in and becoming an integral part of an ongoing overseas project. Often they serve as problem solvers. Representatives of American companies often complain that foreign competitors do not play the game fairly, but in the case of selling know-how, the foreign customer is often in a "must-have-it" situation. In such a situation, the service company is simply the best at what it does, and it provides the service more cost effectively.

Beneath the soil of the former Soviet Republic of Uzbekistan there is a wealth of oil and gas reserves, but the terrain is so difficult that the task of extraction is challenging and often quite wasteful. In fact, with conventional extraction methods the probability of losing as much as half the oil is a real possibility. The $1.6 billion Houston-based energy and engineering consulting company, M. W. Kellogg, was asked to present a recovery solution. Kellogg scientists devised a method of extraction involving pumping pressure back into the ground so that the majority of the oil could be extracted. Kellogg is about to sign a $10 million contract to supervise the Uzbek oil extraction project. Kellogg's role is to add value to an ongoing overseas project. In addition, Kellogg plans to order about $200 million worth of American equipment for the project. According to Jack Murphy, CEO of Dresser Industries, Kellogg's parent company, "Engineering service firms are a major driver of heavy [American] industrial exports."[28] The key to exporting in the service industry is actually adding value, without actually becoming totally immersed in every aspect of the project. More than ever before, Americans are using the transformational process to produce goods with added value, and they are providing services that add value, which makes these companies more competitive in the global arena.

the basic tasks associated with management remain essentially the same, the manner in which the tasks are accomplished may be altered substantially by the multinational company's external environment. The multinational environment will be discussed at greater length in Chapter 18.

✗ Management Tips ✗

Guidelines for Dealing with the Manager's Diverse Environment

1. **Be aware of the nature of the top-, middle-, and lower-level manager's environment.** The environment for each level of management differs. Specifically, the environment faced by lower-level managers is not the same as that faced by upper management.

2. **Do not try to deal with factors beyond your control.** Upper management is responsible for company-wide matters.

3. **Familiarize yourself with the written guidelines related to your job.** You represent the company to your people and your people to the company.

4. **Know the rules that govern your workplace and enforce them.** Remember that you are in charge.

5. **Be aware of how work in your department affects work in other departments, and how their work affects yours.** The company's total productivity is what counts.

6. **Be familiar with the labor-management agreement if one exists.** Top managers approve the contract, middle managers may negotiate it, and supervisors are the main contact with the union.

7. **Understand how your boss's style of management affects your own.** Try to be compatible.

8. **Learn how to deal with the formal and informal organization.** They both can help or hinder you.

9. **Adapt to the new workforce; do not resist it.** The best approach for managers is to be constructive in managing the ever-changing workforce.

10. **Accept the challenge of engaging in multinational operations.** Global competition, air travel, and satellite communication technology have made doing business abroad both necessary and feasible.

SUMMARY

The systems approach—the viewing of any organization or entity as an arrangement of interrelated parts that interact in ways that can be specified and to some extent predicted—provides a rational means for examining these interactions. Use of the systems approach inevitably leads one to conclude that every organization, indeed every system, is an open system. An open system is an organization or assemblage of things that affects and is affected by outside events.

The business system is affected by many forces, both external and internal. Top management has perhaps the greatest concern for the external forces, while management at all levels must be concerned with the forces of the internal environment. Managers at lower levels of the organization, however, confront an internal environment that is markedly different from that encountered by management at more senior levels. Within these complex external and internal environments, the business system operates; inputs are converted to outputs through a transformation process directed and controlled by managers.

Factors that management must consider in the external environment include the labor force, legal considerations, society, unions, stockholders, competition, customers, technology, and the economy. Managers approach changes in the external environment either proactively or reactively. A proactive response is taking action in anticipation of environmental changes. A reactive response is simply responding to environmental changes after they occur. Organizations exhibit varying degrees of proactive and reactive behavior. A firm may be either reactive or proactive in any matter, legal or otherwise.

Managing diversity is having an acute awareness of characteristics common to a culture, race, gender, age, or sexual preference, while at the same time managing employees with these characteristics as individuals. This philosophy recognizes that individuals of a particular culture may have unique general characteristics. However, in the work environment employees are treated as individuals, with cultural differences taken into consideration.

During the 1980s, small and midsized companies created 80 percent of the jobs available. Every year

REVIEW QUESTIONS

1. Define systems approach. Why does a manager need to understand the systems approach?
2. Identify and describe the major external environmental factors that can affect top managers.
3. How is the workforce expected to become more diverse in the future?
4. How important is the small business to our economy?
5. What are the major internal environmental factors that can affect the jobs that managers do?
6. What are the components of an organization's transformation process?
7. How is the external environment that confronts multinational enterprises even more diverse and complex than that confronted by domestic firms?

KEY TERMS

Systems approach 34

Open system 35

Closed system 35

External environment 36

Social responsibility 37

Ethics 37

Union 38

Stockholders (shareholders) 38

Proactive response 42

Reactive response 42

Managing diversity 43

Leased employees 47

Internal environment 50

Mission 51

Corporate culture 51

Policy 52

Informal organization 53

thousands of individuals, motivated by a desire to be their own boss, to earn a better income, and to realize the American dream, launch new business ventures. These individuals, often referred to as *entrepreneurs,* have been essential to the growth and vitality of the American free enterprise system. Entrepreneurs develop or recognize new products or business opportunities, secure the necessary capital, and organize and operate the business.

Factors to be considered in the internal environment include the firm's mission, its corporate culture, management style, policies, employees, the informal organization, other units of the organization, and unions.

Management's job is to direct the transformation of resources (inputs) in an efficient manner to produce desirable goods or provide services (outputs). In the course of this process, managers plan, organize, influence, and control. They monitor the input and the transformation process and, upon analyzing feedback from the output, make the adjustments necessary in the production process to obtain the desired results.

Global competition, air travel, and satellite communication technology have made doing business abroad both necessary and feasible, and companies have responded by establishing operations overseas. American managers have recognized that the challenge of engaging in multinational operations is not easily met. This is especially true with regard to the challenges of management, in part because the external environment that confronts multinational enterprises is even more diverse and complex than that confronted by domestic firms.

CASE STUDIES

CASE 2.1 Pan American's Fight Against the Environment

Pan American World Airways, Inc. was a leader in U.S. aviation for more than fifty years. But a string of losses from 1981–1989 brought the company to its knees. And it was showing scant signs of recovery when Donald Trump bought Eastern's Washington-to-New York-to Boston shuttle. The flamboyant Trump announced plans to go head-to-head with Pan Am's shuttle, its most profitable operation. Beleaguered Pan Am managers must have thought, "What next?"

The 1978 deregulation of the airline industry had brought new challenges to all of the major airlines. At about the same time, a major recession began, and airline travel was hit particularly hard. International travel was dampened by unfavorable exchange rates. Through 1981, fuel prices, a major part of air carrier costs, continued the upward trend that had begun in 1973 with the Arab oil embargo.

The managers of Pan Am acquired National Airlines, hoping to use it to build a major domestic hub.

But stung by $700 million in losses in 1981–1982, the managers were forced to gut most of National's domestic system. Then the managers tried a new tack. They restructured the company's routes and introduced a discount fare program that undercut competition by 17 to 33 percent. To get operating cash, they sold Pan Am's Intercontinental Hotels Corporation subsidiary and some of its planes. Ten vice-presidents, 112 staff managers, and 5,000 other employees were laid off.

Pan Am was able to fly 60 percent full in 1983, but profits remained elusive. More than a third of the company's revenues were paid in foreign currencies, and foreign exchange losses were $11.5 million just for the 1984 second quarter. Another $8 million went to pay for overtime and for free drinks for passengers during air traffic control delays. Finally, 11 percent of Pan Am's second-quarter 1984 air travel represented free rides, granted under the WorldPass program. The credits were to expire on June 30 that year, so passengers rushed to use them. Still Pan Am did better than Braniff International and Continental Airlines, which both filed bankruptcy petitions. Even high-flying Delta saw losses in 1983. Eastern Airlines survived only by threatening bankruptcy, a threat it would carry out in 1989, and by paying wages partly with company stock.

In late 1984, Pam Am managers thought they had weathered the storm. But stockholders were not at all confident of the company's survival. Pan Am's stock was down to 7¼ in October 1983, a fraction of its historic value. Though the stock recovered to over 9 in 1986, it would crash to below 4 in 1989.

A number of airline-industry takeovers and mergers in 1986–1989 brought Pan Am face to face with giant carriers several times its size. Texas Air, for example, had gobbled up Eastern and People Express to become the nation's largest airline, with nearly 20 percent market share. Delta had acquired Western. Pan Am's 22,000 employees were petrified as the company's managers actively sought bids. They knew mergers invariably brought layoffs and other retrenchments. To make matters worse, OPEC agreed in 1987 to escalate oil prices to near $20 a barrel, where they would stay through 1989. And the crash of Pan Am flight 103 near Lockerbie, Scotland, in November 1988 brought the company the kind of publicity it did not need. While commercial aviation in general was surging into the 1990s, Pan Am was still trying to shake off the effects of the "dismal decade" it had just experienced. In December of 1991, Pan Am ceased to exist.

QUESTIONS

1. Describe the environmental factors affecting Pan Am.
2. Did Pan Am respond appropriately to these environmental factors? Explain.

CASE 2.2 Singing the Small Business Blues

"There seems to be a conspiracy out there to keep me from making money and to increase my stress level," said James Sharplin, the sole owner of Sharpco, Inc. James's small company manufactures steel items for heavy equipment and rebuilds the heavy tracks and related components of crawler tractors, or "dozers."

James went on to explain the elements of the conspiracy. "The workers," he said, "try to get as much pay as they can for doing as little as possible. Customers want us to repair their equipment for less than our cost. Then they bring it back a year later, expecting warranty work. Half of the customers try to pay a little late—and if I don't hound them, they'll pay a lot late, or not at all. Suppliers try to give us inferior merchandise at premium prices—everything from paint that doesn't cover to steel that has flaws.

"And government! I'd swear half of my time is spent filling out forms, worrying about income taxes, trying to keep a worker I fired for stealing from collecting unemployment compensation, meeting with the fire marshal to explain why we don't have a fire extinguisher on every column—it just goes on and on. Sometimes I think even the equipment is involved in the conspiracy. Yesterday I was just getting ready to load a rush job on a customer's truck and the crane broke down. Mother used to say, 'If it's not one thing, it's another.' I've become convinced that it's five or six others."

QUESTIONS

1. How does James's environment differ from that of a manager in a larger company?
2. Evaluate James's view of the various environmental factors to which he is subjected.

NOTES

1. "Nice Guys Finish First," *Inc.* (October 1989): 79 and CNN Pinnacle Program: Subway Sandwiches; Barbara Marsh, "FTC Inquiry into Subway Sandwich Is Widened with Survey of Franchisees," *The Wall Street Journal* (June 28, 1993): Sec B, p. 2.

2. Kenneth E. Goodpaster and John B. Matthews, Jr., "Can a Corporation Have a Conscience?" *Harvard Business Review* 60 (January–February 1982): 132–141.

3. Stephen Baker, "Free Trade Isn't Painless," *Business Week* (August 1992): 38–39.

4. Gene Koretz and Celeste Whittaker, "More Picket Lines, Fewer Rank-and-Filers," *Business Week* (May 7, 1990): 24.

5. Aaron Bernstein, "Guarded Smiles at the Union Hall," *Business Week* (December 14, 1992): 105.

6. Michael Schroeder and Joseph Weber, "Is Merck Ready for Marty Wygod?" *Business Week* (October 4, 1993): 80–84.

7. Chuck Hawkins and Patrick Oster, "After a U-Turn UPS Really Delivers," *Business Week* (May 31, 1993): 92–93.

8. Eric G. Flanholtz, Yvonne Randle, and Sonja Sackmann, "Personnel Management: The Tenor of Today," *Personnel Journal* 66 (June 1987): 64.

9. Marilyn Joyce, "Ergonomics Will Take Center Stage During '90s and into New Century," *Occupational Health and Safety* 60 (January 1991): 31.

10. Joseph Spiers, "Behind the Job Worries, Business Keeps Plodding Along," *Fortune* 128 (August 9, 1993): 19.

11. Patricia Sellers, "The Best Cities for Business," *Fortune,* 125 (October 22, 1990): 49.

12. Lee Gardenswartz and Anita Rowe, *Managing Diversity,* (San Diego: Business One Irwin/Pfeiffer & Company, 1993): 57–97; Mahalingham Subbiah, "Adding a New Dimension to the Teaching of Audience Analysis: Cultural Awareness," *IEEE Transactions on Professional Communication,* 35 (March 1992); Marcus Mabry, "Pin a Label on a Manager—and Watch What Happens," *Newsweek,* 14 (May 1990): 43.

13. Stephanie Overman, "Managing the Diverse Workforce," *HRMagazine* 36 (April 1991): 32.

14. Elizabeth Ehrlich and Susan B. Garland, "Where the Jobs Are Is Where the Skills Aren't," *Business Week* (September 19, 1989): 120.

15. Amanda Troy Segal and Wendy Zellner "Corporate Women," *Business Week* (June 8, 1992): 74.

16. "More Women Are Executive VPs," *Fortune* 128 (July 12, 1993): 16.

17. Amanda Troy Segal and Wendy Zellner, "Corporate Women," *Business Week* (June 8, 1992): 74–78.

18. Dan Cordtz, "Hire Me, Hire My Family," *Finance World* 159 (September 18, 1990): 77.

19. Ella Bell, "The Bicultural Life Experience of Career Oriented Black Women" *Journal of Organizational Behavior* 11 (November 1990): 459–478.

20. Joan L. Kelly, "Employers Must Recognize that Older People Want to Work," *Personnel Journal* 69 (January 1990): 44.

21. John Ross, "Effective Ways to Hire Contingent Personnel," *HRMagazine* 36 (February 1991): 53.

22. Susan Goff Condon, "Hiring the Handicapped Confronts Cultural Uneasiness," *Personnel Journal* 66 (April, 1987): 28.

23. Michael J. Mandel and Christopher Farrell, "The Immigrants," *Business Week* (July 13, 1992): 114.

24. Larry Light "The Job Engine Needs Fuel," *Business Week* (March 1, 1993): 78.

25. "A Surprising Finding on New-Business Mortality Rates," *Business Week* (June 14, 1993): 22.

26. Louis S. Richman, "Jobs that are Growing and Slowing," *Fortune* 128 (July 12, 1993): 53.

27. "A Surprising Finding on New-Business Mortality Rates," *Business Week* (June 14, 1993): 22.

28. Warren Cohen, "Exporting Know-How," *U.S. News & World Report* 115 (August 30/September 6, 1993): 53, 56–57.

APPENDIX 2

History of Management and Organizational Behavior

Mistakes of the past are likely to be repeated. Virtually everyone has heard this statement, but unfortunately, many ignore its message. It is important that managers understand and appreciate the history of management and organizational behavior in order to gain a better frame of reference within which to make critical decisions.

HISTORICAL PERSPECTIVES

In order to fully understand the current state of management in the world, it is useful to review the historical perspectives that dominated management thought during this century. Certain aspects of earlier viewpoints, philosophies, and schools of thought remain relevant today, and they can provide the careful observer with a great deal of valuable insight into present-day management.

Since 1900, each of a dozen major schools of thought has fallen within one of three general areas, or historical perspectives, of management thought: structural, human, and integrative. The structural perspective, which evolved around the turn of the century, encompasses the theory of scientific management, classical theory, bureaucracy theory, and decision theory. The human perspective, which first appeared in the 1920s, eventually included schools of thought focused on human relations, group dynamics, and leadership research. Since the 1960s, however, the schools of thought that have prevailed have integrated the human perspective with the structural perspective to form the third major area of organizational thought, the integrative perspective.

This appendix examines these three perspectives and their major schools of thought. Table A2-1 groups the schools into the three historical perspectives and provides a brief description of the thinking that characterized each school.

STRUCTURAL PERSPECTIVES

The earliest theorists expressed concern primarily for the structuring and the design of work within the organization.

Organizational Theory Prior to 1990

The emphasis in the book is on the current state of management and organizational behavior. However, just as political science students cannot fail to consider the history of government, management students should have at least a moderate familiarity with the history of management thought. This history obviously extends several thousand years into the past. Moses, for example, is credited with having employed the first management consultant—his father-in-law—to help design the organization through which Moses governed the Hebrews. Before the early 1900s, however, little formal business theorizing took place. Few industrial organizations of the types that exist today were around during that time, and the basic organizational models were the military and the Roman Catholic Church.

Economists such as Adam Smith sowed the seeds of later theory. In his book *An Inquiry into the Nature and Cause of the Wealth of Nations* (1776), Smith included a chapter on the division of labor that laid the groundwork for the later introduction of assembly-line processes. Smith spoke approvingly of a pin manufacturer who divided the work into a number of "branches," causing pin making to be separated into eighteen different operations. This separation of operations permitted workers to concentrate on only one task and thus radically increased the quantity of pins that could be manufactured in a day. Smith also emphasized the importance of proper machinery to facilitate labor.

Scientific Management

Not until the early twentieth century did management emerge as a concentrated field of study. Frederick W.

TABLE A2.1 Schools of Management Thought and Their Components

PERSPECTIVES AND SCHOOLS	DECADE	DESCRIPTION
Structural Perspectives		
Organizational theory prior to 1900	Before 1900	Emphasized the division of labor and the importance of machinery to facilitate labor.
Scientific management	1910s	Described management as a science, with employees having specific but different responsibilities; encouraged the scientific selection, training, and development of workers and the equal division of work between workers and management.
Classical	1910s	Listed the duties of a manager as planning, organizing, commanding employees, coordinating activities, and controlling performance; basic principles called for specialization of work, unity of command, scalar chain of command, and coordination of activities.
Bureaucracy	1940s	Emphasized order, system, rationality, uniformity, and consistency in management; led to equitable treatment of all employees by management.
Decision theory	1960s	Suggested that individuals "satisfice" when they make decisions.
Human Perspectives		
Human relations	1920s	Focused on the importance of the attitudes and feelings of workers; informal roles and norms influenced performance.
Group dynamics	1940s	Encouraged individual participation in decision making; noted the impact of the work group on performance.
Leadership	1950s	Stressed the importance of groups having both social and task leaders; differentiated between Theory X and Theory Y management.
Integrative Perspectives		
Sociotechnical	1960s	Called for considering technology and work groups in understanding a work system.
Systems theory	1970s	Represented organizations as open systems with inputs, transformations, outputs, and feedback; stated that systems strive for equilibrium and experience equifinality.
Contingency theory	1970s	Emphasized the fit between organizational processes and characteristics of the situation; called for fitting the organization's structure to various contingencies.
Management roles	1970s	Emphasized that managerial work encompasses ten roles and three focuses: interpersonal contact, informal processing, and decision making.

Taylor, who made major contributions to management thinking around the turn of the century, is often called the father of scientific management. Supported in his efforts by Henry L. Gantt, Frank and Lillian Gilbreth, and Harrington Emerson, all of whom became famous in their own right, Taylor is credited with developing the theory of scientific management.

Scientific management is the name given to the principles and practices that grew out of the work of Taylor and his followers and that are characterized by concern for efficiency and systematization in management. Taylor was convinced that the scientific method, which provides a logical framework for the analysis of problems, could be applied to the management process. The method consists of defining the problem, gathering data, analyzing the data, developing alternatives, and selecting the best alternative. Taylor believed that use of the scientific method would direct the manager to the most efficient way work could be performed. Thus, instead of abdicating responsibility for establishing standards, for example, management could scientifically study all facets of an operation and carefully set a logical and rational standard. Instead of guessing or relying solely on trial and error, management could go through the logical, though time-consuming, process of scientific research to develop answers to business problems. Taylor's philosophy is summarized as follows:

- Taylor proposed applying the scientific method to the practice of management to find the "one best way" to perform work.
- He suggested the use of scientific approaches to select employees who are best suited to perform a given job.
- He advanced the proposition that employees should be provided with scientific education, training, and development.
- He encouraged friendly interaction and cooperation between management and employees, but with a clear separation of duties between managers and workers.
- He advocated that managers take charge of all work that they are better prepared to accomplish, ending

the pattern of placing most of the work and the greater part of the responsibility on the workers.[1b]

Taylor believed that scientific management practices would benefit not only the employer, through increased output, but the workers as well, through increased income. But he stressed that scientific management would require both managers and employees to undergo a revolution in thinking.

The majority of Taylor's work was oriented toward improving the management of production operations. The classic case of the pig iron experiment at the Bethlehem Steel Company illustrates his approach.[2b] Laborers would pick up 92-pound pigs (chunks of iron) from a storage yard, walk up a plank onto a railroad car, and place the pigs in the car. Studying a group of 75 laborers, Taylor determined that the average output was about 12.5 tons per man per day. By applying the scientific method, he developed (1) an improved method of work, (2) a prescribed amount of rest on the job, (3) a specific standard of output, and (4) payment by the unit of output. After Taylor's recommendations were implemented, the average output per worker rose to 48 tons per day, and daily pay rose from $1.15 to $1.85 under the incentive system.

Taylor's dedication to the systematic planning and study of processes of all kinds pervaded his life. With a specially designed tennis racket, he played on a national doubles tennis championship team. When playing golf, he used clubs he designed individually to achieve a predictable lie; his friends reportedly refused to play with him when he used a particular putter because of its accuracy.

Frank and Lillian Gilbreth concentrated on motion study to develop more efficient ways to pour concrete, lay bricks, and perform many other repetitive tasks. After Frank's death in 1924, Lillian continued their work alone, eventually becoming a professor of management at Purdue University. Until her death in 1972, she was considered to be the first lady of management.

Henry Gantt developed a control chart that is used to this day in production operations. The Gantt chart is considered by some to have been the forerunner of modern PERT (program evaluation and review technique) analysis.

Harrington Emerson set forth "12 principles of efficiency" in his 1913 book of that title. According to these principles, a manager should carefully define objectives, use the scientific method of analysis, develop and use standardized procedures, and reward employees for good work. Emerson's book remains a recognized management classic.

General Management Theory: The Classical School

In contrast to the proponents of scientific management, Henry Fayol and Chester I. Barnard developed a broader theory of general management that is identified today as the *classical view* of organizational theory. Fayol was a French manager who wrote at about the same time as Taylor, although his works were not widely available in English until 1930. Fayol's major contribution to management literature, *General and Industrial Management*, was not translated into English until long after both Taylor and Fayol had died. Once translated, however, it became very popular in the United States. Fayol's view of management theory complemented Taylor's scientific approach in many ways. Fayol listed the duties of a manager as planning, organizing, and commanding employees, coordinating activities, and controlling performance.[3b]

Barnard's ideas, expressed in his 1938 classic, *The Functions of the Executive*, have significantly influenced the theory and practice of management.[4b] Barnard, who for years was president of New Jersey Bell Telephone, believed that the most important function of a manager is to promote cooperative effort toward realizing the goals of the organization. He believed that cooperation depends on effective communication and on a balance between rewards to, and contributions by, each employee.

Other proponents of general management, or classical, theory have identified four features of organizations. First, organizations should specialize, meaning workers should be organized according to logical groupings such as client, place of work, product, expertise, or functional area. Second, unity of command dictates that each organizational member should have only one supervisor. Third, the scalar chain of command, or the reporting relationships, should be clearly defined within a formal organizational structure, beginning with the chief administrator and extending to the least-skilled employee. Fourth, managers should coordinate activities using mechanisms that will ensure good communication among specialized groups.[5b]

A Classical Theory of Bureaucracy

Max Weber, a German sociologist, addressed the issue of organizational administration in a somewhat different fashion. He studied European organization during the late 1800s and described a prototype form of organization that emphasizes order, system, rationality, uniformity, and consistency—a bureaucracy. Weber's writings were not widely read in the United States until their English translation was published in 1947.[6b] For many people, the term bureaucracy conjures up an image of massive red tape and endless unneeded details. Weber, on the other hand, believed bureaucracy led to the equitable treatment of all employees by management.[7b] To the extent that bureaucratic organizations are impersonal and have strict rules, Weber saw these characteristics as ensuring fairness to all workers.[8b]

In a bureaucracy, each employee has specified and official areas of responsibility that are assigned on the basis of competence and expertise. Like the classical schools, bureaucracy calls for an orderly system of supervision and subordination, a unity of command that specifies a single supervisor for each subordinate. Managers in a bureaucracy use written documents extensively in managing employees. Not only do rules and regulations exist, but they are translated into detailed employment manuals. Office managers and work groups also receive extensive training in their job requirements. Within this system, management must use rules that are consistent, complete, and learnable.

Decision Theory

In the 1950s, Herbert A. Simon and James G. March introduced the decision-making framework for understanding organizational behavior.[9b] They elaborated on the bureaucratic model by emphasizing that individuals who work in rational organizations behave rationally. But their model (for which Simon won the Nobel prize for economics) added a new dimension: the idea that a human being's rationality is limited. The model suggests that individuals generally make decisions by examining a limited set of possible alternatives rather than all available options. Moreover, they do so by drawing on the rules and experience they have at hand. The model states further that individuals "satisfice"; that is, they choose adequate solutions to problems rather than seeking optimal choices.

HUMAN PERSPECTIVES

When the structural perspectives of scientific management and classical, bureaucratic, and decision theory are applied to management, many organizational problems can be solved; but much of workers' dissatisfaction and resistance to change is not addressed by these theories. Seeking answers to the remaining problems, researchers began to focus on the human side of organizations, specifically on human relations, group dynamics, and leadership theory. The classical theory of the human relations school provides some insight into solving these problems.

Human Relations School

Beginning in 1924, the Western Electric Company, in conjunction with the National Academy of Sciences, performed five studies of various work groups at Western Electric's Hawthorne plant.[10b] The first study looked at the effects of lighting on the productivity of workers in different departments of the company. In the tradition of scientific management, the study considered whether various illumination levels affected output positively or negatively. Researchers first increased the light to an extreme brightness and then decreased it until the work area was so dim that assembly materials could hardly be seen. Results showed that the workers maintained or even exceeded their normal output regardless of whether illumination in

the workplace was increased or decreased. But what explains this behavior?

Subsequent studies by Elton Mayo, Fritz (F. J.) Roethlisberger, William J. Dickson, and their colleagues examined the impact on output of pauses for rest, shorter working days and weeks, wage incentives, and the nature of supervision.[11b] They speculated that something other than the physical work environment was responsible for improved productivity among workers. By observing and interviewing the employees, the researchers discovered that the employees, by participating in experiments, felt that someone cared about them. Their morale improved and they produced more. The influence that behavioral researchers can have on the people they study become known as the *Hawthorne effect,* marking the first dramatic indication that attitudes and feelings of workers could significantly influence productivity.

On the basis of these findings, Western Electric interviewed workers regarding their feelings about work. Results of the interviews suggested even more strongly the close relationship between morale and the quality of supervision, and led to the creation of a new training program for supervisors.

In the final experiments of the Hawthorne series, researchers identified one other human feature of organizations: the tendency for workers to develop informal groups. When the researchers observed a group from the bank-wiring room, they found that the workers had established among themselves informal roles and norms (expected standards of behavior) through which they controlled and restricted their productivity level. For example, workers could be identified as leaders or followers; rate-busters—those who produced more than the level acceptable to the leaders—were ostracized by the group, as were those who produced too little.

Group Dynamics

Because of a shortage of meat during World War II, Kurt Lewin, a social psychologist at the University of Iowa, was asked to study methods of changing housewives' dietary habits to decrease meat consumption.[12b] Lewin believed that the women were expected by their families, parents, and other housewives not to serve other kinds of food; this norm created a significant barrier to change. He suggested that the way to break down the barrier was to give the housewives the opportunity to discuss and make decisions themselves about the types of foods to serve. The results of the experiments conducted by Lewin and his associates supported his ideas about participation. Housewives who joined in group discussions were ten times more likely to change their food habits than were housewives who received lectures on the subject.[13b]

Lewin's associates later extended these experiments to industrial settings. For example, Lester Coch and John R. P. French, Jr., found that employees at the Harwood pajama plant in Marion, Virginia, were much more likely to learn new work methods if they were given the opportunity to discuss the methods and to have some influence on how to apply them to their jobs.[14b] Studies such as these led to a greatly expanded awareness of the impact of the work group and spawned research on the relationship between organizational effectiveness and group formation, development, behavior, and attitudes.[15b]

Leadership

The 1950s marked the beginning of concentrated research in the area of leadership, as theorists such as Robert F. Bales and Douglas McGregor examined the roles of managers and leaders in organizations.[16b] Bales postulated the importance of groups having both task and social leaders. The task leader helps the group achieve its goals by clarifying and summarizing member comments and focusing on the group's tasks. The social leader maintains the group and helps it develop cohesiveness and collaboration by encouraging group members' involvement.

McGregor described two types of managers.[17b] Those who adhere to Theory X believe that workers have an inherent dislike of work, must be controlled and threatened with punishment if they are to put forth adequate effort, and prefer to avoid responsibility. Managers who follow Theory Y, on the other hand, believe that employees find work as natural as play or

rest, exercise self-direction toward the objectives to which they are committed (requiring less strict control), and can learn to seek responsibility. McGregor, together with other researchers, postulated that the assumptions managers hold affect the way they treat their employees and thus affect employees' overall productivity.

INTEGRATIVE PERSPECTIVES

Organizational thought in the past few decades has emphasized the integration of structural and human perspectives. More recently, contingency theory has added an emphasis on fitting organizational features to the work situation.

Sociotechnical School

In the 1950s, several theorists began studying technology and its interaction with functioning work groups. The sociotechnical school assumed that managers could exclude neither technology (representing organizational structure) nor work groups (reflecting human relations) in trying to understand a work system. The most notable members of the sociotechnical were E. L. Trist, K. W. Bamforth, A. K. Rice, and F. E. Emery.[18b]

Trist and Bamforth described a change in technology in a British coal mine where workers were used to working independently in small, self-contained units in which they organized the work themselves.[19b] When the technology for mining coal improved, management was required to increase job specialization and decrease the workers' participation in job assignments. According to scientific management and classical management traditions, greater job specialization should have increased productivity. But the coal miners hated the specialization; they much preferred working closely with one another and performing a variety of tasks.

Trist and Bamforth compared the performance of work groups whose jobs had become specialized to that of work groups that retained their original social structure when the new technology was introduced. They found that absenteeism was several times greater and productivity much lower in the specialized groups. Researchers concluded after a number of such studies that technological changes must be made in conjunction with a strong social system—that both social and technical aspects of jobs must be considered simultaneously.

Systems Theory

According to Harold Koontz, "The systems approach requires that the physical, human, and capital resources be interrelated and coordinated within the external and internal environment of an organization."[20b] Systems theory, which offers an integrated and comprehensive view of organizational functioning, evolved from economic, sociological, psychological, and natural science theories and includes human, structural, environmental, technological, and other concerns.

The general systems model described by Daniel Katz and Robert L. Kahn, among others, represents an organization as an open system, one that interacts with environmental forces and factors, much like physical systems such as the human body, a microscopic organism, or a cell.[21b] First, a system consists of a number of interdependent and interrelated subsystems; second, the organization is open and dynamic; third, it strives for equilibrium; and fourth, it has multiple purposes, objectives, and functions, some of which are in conflict.

Subsystems vary in size from the smallness of an individual cell to the largeness of a major division of an organization. To trace subsystems in organizations, the observer generally must specify significant individuals and groups and examine their interdependence. Typical subsystems include individual employees, work teams, departments, and management groups.

As described in Chapter 2, an organization as a system is also open and dynamic; that is, it continually receives new energy in the form of resources (people, materials, and money) or information (concerning strategy, environment, and history) from the environment. This new energy, called *inputs,* is then transformed into new outputs.

The key organizational components that change inputs into outputs are transformation processes. These processes include the interactions among the tasks, the individuals, the formal organizational arrangements, and the informal organization.[22b] The transformation of inputs invariably creates changes in individual, group, and organizational behaviors and attitudes.

When organizations receive new inputs or experience certain transformations, they simultaneously seek balance, or equilibrium. When organizations become unbalanced, or experience disequilibrium—for example, when changes in the environment make current staffing inadequate—they attempt to return to a steady state, which may mirror or significantly differ from the original state of equilibrium. They use information about their outputs, called *feedback,* to modify their inputs or transformations to attain the result of more desirable outcomes and equilibrium.

Assume, for example, that worker performance has declined significantly. This information cues the organization to examine the nature of its inputs and transformations for a cause. The feedback may subsequently pinpoint changes in employee training or reward systems as causes. It may also indicate which subsystems in the organization have similar goals and which have different ones.

Finally, organizations as open systems demonstrate equifinality. Equifinality suggests that organizations may employ a variety of means to achieve their desired objectives. No single structure results in a predetermined set of inputs, outputs, and transformations. Introducing a more open and participatory structure does not necessarily result in increased productivity; increasing the level of individual involvement in decision making does not necessarily change worker attitudes. Thus, organizations that survive adapt to a particular situation. They respond to changes in the environment with appropriate changes in the system.

Contingency Theory

Contingency theory asserts that there are no universal rules and that the correct management technique depends on the surrounding circumstances.[23b] It emphasizes the fit between organizational processes and characteristics of the situation.

Early contingency research looked at the fit between an organization's structure and its environment. Tom A. Burns and George Stalker described two radically different types of management systems: mechanistic (machinelike) and organic (living, human and flexible).[24b] Mechanistic systems have characteristics such as those described in the scientific and classical management traditions—for example, rigid structure and strict lines of authority. Organic systems are much more flexible and loosely structured and allow more employee influence over decisions.

Joan Woodward found that the type of structure an organization develops (and should develop) is influenced by the organization's technology, whether the technology is unit, mass-production, or continuous-process.[25b] She suggested that a mechanistic type of organization fits best with mass-production technology—producing pins, lifting pig iron, or manufacturing heavy equipment. A more organic form of organization generally responds best to a unit (craft) or continuous-process technology (for example, that of a gas refinery).

Recent thinking in organization design has reemphasized the importance of fitting organizational structure to various contingencies. Thus, contingency theory has been extended to job design, leadership, group dynamics, and power relations. (See Chapters 7, 11, 13, and 14 for discussions of these areas.)

Management Roles Approach

Harvard professor Henry Mintzberg, in studying what managers do, observed that managerial work encompasses ten roles. Three of the roles focus on interpersonal contact: (1) figurehead, (2) leader, and (3) liaison; three involve mainly information processing: (1) monitor, (2) disseminator, and (3) spokesperson; and four relate to decision making: (1) entrepreneur, (2) disturbance handler, (3) resource allocator, and (4) negotiator.[26b]

The roles that focus on interpersonal contact are described as follows:

1. *Figurehead.* The manager, acting as a symbol or representative of the organization, performs diverse ceremonial duties. By attending chamber of commerce meetings, heading the local United Way drive, or representing the president of the firm at an awards banquet, a manager performs the figurehead role.
2. *Leader.* The manager, interacting with subordinates, motivates and develops them. The supervisor who conducts annual performance interviews or selects training opportunities for subordinates performs this role.
3. *Liaison.* The manager establishes a network of contacts to gather information for the organization. Belonging to professional associations or meeting over lunch with peers in other organizations helps the manager perform the liaison role.

The roles that involve mainly information processing are described as follows:

1. *Monitor.* The manager gathers information from the environment inside and outside the organization. The manager may attend meetings with subordinates, scan company publications, or participate in companywide committees as a way of performing this role.
2. *Disseminator.* The manager transmits both factual and value information to subordinates. The manager may conduct staff meetings, send memoranda to staff members, or meet informally with staff members on a one-to-one basis to discuss current and future projects.
3. *Spokesperson.* The manager gives information to people outside the organization about the organization's performance and policies. The manager who oversees preparation of the annual report, prepares advertising copy, or speaks at community and professional meetings fulfills this role.

The roles related to decision making are described as follows:

1. *Entrepreneur.* The manager designs and initiates change in the organization. The supervisor who re-

designs the job of subordinates, introduces flextime to the workplace, or brings new technology to a job performs this role.

2. *Disturbance handler.* The manager deals with problems that arise when organizational operations break down. A manager who finds a new supplier for an out-of-stock part on short notice, replaces unexpectedly absent employees on a project, or deals with machine breakdowns performs this role.

3. *Resource allocator.* The manager controls the allocation of people, money, materials, and time by scheduling his or her own time, programming subordinates' work efforts, and authorizing all significant decisions. Preparation of a budget is a major aspect of this role.

4. *Negotiator.* The manager participates in negotiation activities. A manager who hires a new employee may negotiate work assignments or compensation with that person.

Not all managers perform every role listed here, but some diversity of role performance always occurs. The choice of roles depends on the manager's specific job description and the situation in question. An examination of the manager's work role suggests that leadership is only one of many roles, but one that is essential to effective management.

Mintzberg's view of managerial behavior offers a perspective that complements those of various organizational behavior theories, including theories of perception, attribution, motivation, communication, personal development, group dynamics, and leadership theory. The roles he identified emphasize the individual and motivation (interpersonal roles), communication (information roles), and leadership and decision making (decisional roles).

THE FUTURE: MANAGEMENT INTO THE NEXT CENTURY

While it is difficult to determine what is next for management, certain aspects are surfacing, some of which may well be history when you read this. Some of the more recent management innovations include: Total Quality Management (Chapter 17), Reengineering (Chapter 8), and Teams (Chapter 13). Total Quality Management (TQM) is a commitment to excellence by everyone in an organization that emphasizes excellence achieved by teamwork and a process of continuous improvement. TQM began in the 1930s with the pioneering work of Walter A. Shewart, who acted as a mentor to W. Edwards Deming, who later became the chief guru of TQM.

Michael Hammer is the guru of reengineering, which is the fundamental rethinking and radical redesign of business processes to achieve dramatic improvements in critical, contemporary measures of performance, such as cost, quality, service, and speed. Essentially, firms are rethinking and redesigning their business systems. Reengineering requires the organization to basically start over, and focus on processes which are the collection of tasks that people perform to get the job done.

Another management innovation is the emphasis on work teams as an officially sanctioned collection of individuals who are charged by an organization with completing a mission and who depend on one another for successful completion of work. Work teams are spreading into every aspect of organizational goal attainment.

The Virtual Corporation may well play a significant role in the future, if adaptability is the key to success. In the Virtual Corporation the most important principle is that everything is temporary, where companies come together to exploit fast-changing opportunities. Additional advantages are that companies share the costs, utilize the multiple skills of various companies, and enjoy better access to global markets.[27b]

It is quite interesting to note that none of these *innovative* management approaches are new, but are simply recombinations of management theories of the past, proving once again that history has its place in the management innovations of the future.

NOTES

1b. Frederick W. Taylor, *The Principles of Scientific Management* (New York: Harper & Bros, 1911): 36–37.

2b. Taylor, *The Principles of Scientific Management*: 41–47.

3b. Henry Fayol, *General and Industrial Management*, trans. C. Storrs (London: Pitman, 1949).

4b. Chester I. Barnard, *The Functions of the Executive* (Cambridge, MA: Harvard University Press, 1938, rev. eds. 1950, 1988).

5b. L. Gulick and L. Urwick, eds., *Papers on the Science of Administration* (New York: Columbia University Institute of Public Administration, 1937), and J. D. Mooney and A. C. Reiley, *Onward Industry* (New York: Harper & Bros., 1931), offered complementary views of management.

6b. Max Weber, *The Theory of Social and Economic Organization*, ed. and trans. A. M. Henderson and T. Parsons (New York: Oxford University Press, 1947).

7b. R. M. Weiss, "Weber on Bureaucracy: Management Consultant or Political Theorist?" *Academy of Management Review 8* (April 1983): 242–248, argues that Weber was not concerned with prescribing the characteristics of an efficient organization but rather was solely offering political theory.

8b. Max Weber, *Essays on Sociology*, ed. and trans. H. H. Gerth and C. W. Mills (New York: Oxford University Press, 1947): 196–198.

9b. Herbert A. Simon, *Administrative Behavior*, 2d ed. (New York: Macmillan, 1957); and James G. March and Herbert A. Simon, *Organizations* (New York: Wiley, 1958).

10b. C. E. Snow, "A Discussion of the Relation of Illumination Intensity to Productive Efficiency," *Tech Engineering News*, (November, 1927); cited in F. J. Roethlisberger and William J. Dickson, *Management and the Worker* (Cambridge, MA: Harvard University Press, 1939).

11b. Roethlisberger and Dickson, *Management and the Worker*.

12b. Kurt Lewin, "Forces Behind Food Habits and Methods of Change," *Bulletin of the National Research Council* 108 (1943): 403–409.

13b. M. Radke and D. Klisurich, "Experiments in Changing Food Habits," *Journal of the American Dietetics Association* 23 (1947): 403–409.

14b. Lester Coch and John R. P. French, Jr., "Overcoming Resistance to Change," *Human Relations* 1 (1948): 512–533.

15b. See C. S. Bartlem and E. A. Locke, "The Coch and French Study: A Critique and Reinterpretation," *Human Relations* 34 (July 1981): 555–566, for another view of the significance of research about participation.

16b. Robert F. Bales, "Task Roles and Social Roles in Problem Solving Groups," in *Readings in Social Psychology*, 3d ed., ed. E. Maccoby, T. M. Newcomb, and E. L. Hartley (New York: Holt, Rinehart & Winston, 1958), pp. 437–447; and Douglas McGregor, *The Human Side of Enterprise* (New York: McGraw-Hill, 1960).

17b. McGregor, *The Human Side of Enterprise*; and E. H. Schein, *The Hawthorne Group Studies Revisited: A Defense of Theory Y*, Working Paper #756-74 (Cambridge, MA.: M.I.T. Sloan School of Management, December, 1974).

18b. E. L. Trist and K. W. Bamforth, "Some Social and Psychological Consequences of the Long Wall Method of Coal Getting," *Human Relations* 4 (1951): 3–38; A. K. Rice, *The Enterprise and Its Environment* (London: Tavistock, 1963); and F. E. Emery and I. L. Trist, *Socio-Technical Systems*, vol. 2 of *Management Science: Models and Techniques* (London: Pergamon, 1960).

19b. Trist and Bamforth, "Some Social and Psychological Consequences."

20b. Harold Koontz, "The Management Theory Jungle Revisited," *Academy of Management Review* 5 (April 1980): 175.

21b. D. Katz and R. L. Kahn, *The Social Psychology of Organizations*, 2d ed. (New York: Wiley, 1978).

22b. D. A. Nadler and M. L. Tushman, "A Diagnostic Model for Organizational Behavior," in *Perspectives on Behavior in Organizations*, ed. J. R. Hackman, L. W. Porter, and E. E. Lawler III (New York: McGraw-Hill, 1977).

23b. Koontz, "The Management Theory Jungle Revisited," p. 176.

24b. T. A. Burns and G. M. Stalker, *The Management of Innovation* (London: Tavistock, 1961).

25b. J. Woodward, *Industrial Organization: Theory and Practice* (London: Oxford University Press, 1965); and P. Lawrence and J. Lorsch, *Organization and Environment* (Boston: Harvard Business School Division of Research, 1967).

26b. Henry Mintzberg, *The Nature of Managerial Work,* 2d ed. (Englewood Cliffs, N.J.: Prentice-Hall, 1979).

27b. John A. Byrne, "The Virtual Corporation," *Business Week* (July 8, 1993): 98-103.

3 Social Responsibility and Business Ethics

LEARNING OBJECTVES

After completing this chapter students should be able to

✘ Describe the concept of corporate social responsibility.

✘ Explain what is meant by stakeholder analysis and the social contact.

✘ Describe the changing values toward social responsibility and the business-government interface.

✘ Explain the concept of ethics.

✘ Describe business ethics and the social audit.

Social Responsibility and Ethical Behavior: The Least-Mentioned Wal-Mart Tradition

Wal-Mart is highly praised for many aspects of its operation, but besides being the number one retailer in the United States, it is also a leader in the field of business ethics. Wal-Mart performance is the envy of every other retailer and continues to amaze industry experts; and some experts consider Wal-Mart to be unstoppable. Wal-Mart success is the result of many things, including the company's sense of social responsibility and proper ethical behavior.

Although it is one of the least mentioned of Sam Walton's contributions to the business world, Wal-Mart's ethical behavior is exceptional. Wal-Mart ushered in the "green" era in retailing. They are looking for "Quality Products that Are Guaranteed Not to Last." Wal-Mart has challenged its manufacturers to "Improve Their Products, to Help Prevent Lasting Environmental Problems." Whenever possible, Wal-Mart provides customers with the option of purchasing environmentally improved products. Specifically, Wal-Mart is encouraging its manufacturers to: produce recyclable products or packaging; make products or packaging from recycled materials; produce packaging systems that are refillable or reusable; produce concentrated products that reduce package volume and waste; manufacture in a way that is safe for our land, air, and water; and produce products that are safe for the environment. In addition, employees are strongly encouraged to recycle.

Wal-Mart is socially responsible, and the retailer also abides by a strict code of ethics. Wal-Mart operates well above the ethical fringe, and focuses on treating others as it would like to be treated. Wal-Mart's code of ethics is part of its daily way of doing business. A few of the ways that Wal-Mart practices what it preaches are listed in its ethical code. According to this code, associates will avoid any social contact with vendors; gifts and gratuities will never be accepted; harassment of any type will not be tolerated; company supplies and property will not be used for personal gain; managers will work at all times to control expenses and to do more with less; all employees are associate-partners and will be treated as such; and associates will at all times be friendly, committed to open communication, and encourage the sharing of ideas, observations, problems, and concerns regarding the company. Wal-Mart's Annual Report echoes this sense of social responsibility and ethical correctness. The basis for their success is summed up in two words: "We care."[1]

Wal-Mart's management believes that its position is clearly enhanced by being socially responsible and ethically aware. Wal-Mart's management evidently views social responsibility and ethical behavior as good business. Most questions regarding corporate social responsibility are not clear-cut, and they are seldom answered as simply right or wrong. However, Wal-Mart makes every attempt to be clear in its approach to social responsibility and is quite definitive about its ethical expectations. Wal-Mart has behaved responsibly and managed to produce profits for stockholders, preserve jobs for employees, and provide products to consumers at everyday low prices.

This chapter examines a number of basic issues of corporate social responsibility and business ethics. First, it explains the concept of corporate social responsibility. Then, it discusses stakeholder analysis and the social contract that exists between the organization and other elements of society. Following that discussion is a description of traditional and modern views concerning the social responsibilities of business. The next three sections of the chapter discuss the business-government interface, present a model of ethics, and address the specific topic of business ethics. The last topics covered are the social audit, which is used to evaluate social performance, and a global perspective of business ethics.

❖ ❖ CORPORATE SOCIAL RESPONSIBILITY

When a corporation behaves as if it has a conscience, it is said to be socially responsible. **Social responsibility** is the implied, enforced, or felt obligation of managers, acting in their official capacity, to serve or protect the interests of groups other than themselves. Remember that Wal-Mart is encouraging its manufacturers to: produce recyclable products or packaging; make products or packaging from recycled materials; produce packaging systems that are refillable or reusable; produce concentrated products that reduce package volume and waste; manufacture in a way that is safe for our land, air, and water; and produce products that are safe for the environment.

A corporation's approach to social responsibility is usually determined by its top executives. More frequently than ever, corporate executives appear to be making decisions that closely parallel the expectations of society. One study indi-

Some companies have programs of community involvement for their employees and managers. It is important that top-level managers set the example. Here, two vice presidents of CITGO Petroleum Company lend a hand during the Jerry Lewis MDA Telethon. A major portion of charitable giving is by corporations. (Source: Photograph courtesy of CITGO Petroleum Corporation.)

cates that senior executives have begun to increase their emphasis on corporate social responsibility. The same seems to be true of boards of directors, in that "rubber-stamp boards" appear to be on the wane. Reports have unearthed a number of examples of directors correcting irresponsible decisions, firing inept and unethical CEOs, and, in general, behaving in a socially responsible manner.[2]

Many companies take action that tends to promote a corporate culture that emphasizes concern for moral issues. This is done through policy statements, practices over time, and the leadership of morally strong individuals. Some companies have programs of community involvement for their employees and managers. They cooperate with fund drives such as those of the United Way. Open-door policies, grievance procedures, and employee benefit programs often stem as much from a desire to do what is right as from a concern for productivity and avoidance of strife. In fact, some argue that a corporation itself can have a conscience, which could result in socially responsible behavior on a consistent basis.[3]

It appears that the larger the number of stockholders a corporation has, the more committed management is to a sense of social responsibility. For example, the environment service department at Allied Chemical, a major publicly held company, is charged with controlling air and water pollution and with maintaining safe and healthful working conditions for employees. The manager of that department reports directly to the company president. Koppers Company, which manufactures foam insulation and also sells tar, wood, and coke, has two committees of outside directors, one concerned with the environment and the other with human resources. At least twice a year, company management must account to these two committees about the company's efforts in the area of social responsibility. All firms do not have this sense of social responsibility. At Ben & Jerry's, the ice cream company, the rank and file hold less than one-half a percent of stock, and the company's actions have been less than socially responsible. For example, Securities and Exchange Commission filings reveal that 42 percent of Ben & Jerry's "homemade"-in-Vermont ice cream is actually made by Dreyer's in Ft. Wayne, Indiana—using Vermont milk. According to former Ben & Jerry's retailer Chuck Schiffer, "Corporately, they're absolutely vicious."[4]

It is interesting to consider how managers of many U.S. corporations like Dow Chemical, AT&T, BankAmerica, Federal Express, 3M, and Whirlpool have realized that economic and social values can at times be co-aligned. Dow Chemical invested $20 million in pollution control in a plant in Michigan. The yearly cost to run the pollution control equipment was $10.5 million. Dow claims to have recovered its costs through reduced corrosion on cooling towers and by the saving of valuable chemicals previously pumped out as waste. In three years' time, over $6 million was saved in recovery of these wasted chemicals alone. Another example of such a co-alignment involved the recycling of paper by several U.S. corporations. AT&T, BankAmerica, Federal Express, 3M, and Whirlpool are finding that recycling is good for society, saves them disposal costs, and also pulls in profits. In the future, even more corporate managers are likely to realize that responsible behavior is also good business, and they will probably search for additional ways to be socially responsible and save money.

Most Americans would not have predicted the kind of socially responsible actions described here. In fact, during the 1980s, managers and the corporations they worked for were subjected to considerable criticism, and they received low levels of approval from the public. Hardly a week passed without news headlines of corporate misconduct. Pollster Louis Harris found that 70 percent of the public believed that "business does not see to it that its executives behave legally and ethically."[5] When a Kennecott-Utah Copper plant tried to emphasize social responsibility, it was condemned by the public. The plant was ranked as the nation's fourth-largest polluter in 1987 because it reported mining emissions, which it was not required to do. Because of the extremely negative ranking, which was made based upon nonrequired information, the company stopped publishing these figures, and their ranking improved dramatically. The EPA claims that about half of the reported improvement is from reporting changes.[6]

A survey by Opinion Research Corporation found that 75 percent of the public agreed that business neglects the problems of society and 65 percent believed business executives "do everything they can to make a profit, even if it means ignoring the public's needs."[7] However, some experts believe businesses are increasingly willing to accept their societal responsibilities and that managers are becoming more ethical. They find that managers are more socially responsible and ethical than were their counterparts a generation ago. According to social theorist Archie B. Carroll, however, the demands made on business and the expectations of what is considered proper conduct have risen faster than the ability of business to raise its standards. Carroll suggests that the ethical level of "actual business practices" will continue to rise, but not as quickly as "society's expectations of business."[8] Because of this discrepancy, the public's esteem for business will probably remain low, while business actually becomes more and more socially responsible.

In order to meet the expectations of society, future managers will need to strive to be more ethical and socially responsible. DuPont management apparently acted in a socially responsible and ethical fashion when they paid $470 million to growers who claim their crops of ornamental plants and fruit were damaged by Benlate DF, a fungicide that has since been taken off the market. DuPont paid, but maintained their innocence, stating that they paid because they thought they were doing the "right thing." DuPont's efforts at social responsibility have resulted in other lawsuits filed for crop damage, and nursery owners are now complaining of health problems caused from Benlate.[9]

Today, business organizations are expected to assume broader and more diverse responsibilities to the various groups in society. However, critics argue that there is more lip service than action, more public relations programs than concrete socially responsible activities. Nevertheless, social responsibility is an area on which the modern business firm must take a stance, accompanied by appropriate policies and activities. Social responsibility can be understood in terms of the social contract that exists between a firm and its environment.

❖ ❖ STAKEHOLDER ANALYSIS AND THE SOCIAL CONTRACT

Most organizations, whether profit or nonprofit, have a large number of stakeholders. An **organizational stakeholder** is an individual or group whose interests are affected by organizational activities. Although all stakeholders are affected by the organization, managers may not acknowledge responsibility to all of them. As was mentioned earlier, corporate boards of directors increasingly hold management accountable for putting the interest of stakeholders first. In the 1970s, noted management writer Peter Drucker stated, "There is one thing all boards have in common . . . they do not function." That statement is less true today than when he uttered it. According to Kenneth A. Macke, CEO of Dayton-Hudson Corporation, boards "are thinking through the process of corporate governance— what they are responsible for—and going into more detail about it." Drucker readily admitted that boards were changing. However, he maintained that they were not responsible enough and that they worked well only "in the case of a catastrophe."[10]

❖ **Figure 3.1**
Stakeholders of Crown
Metal Products

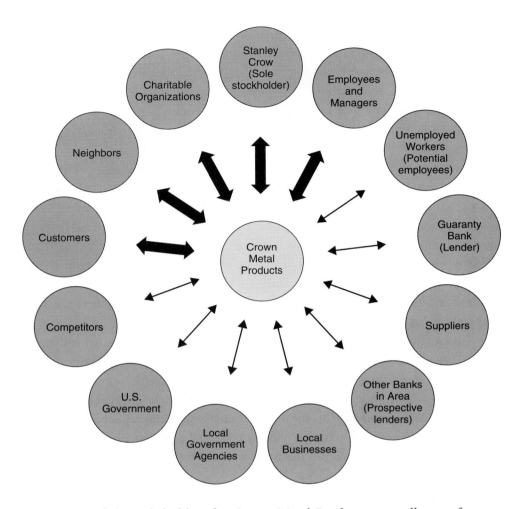

Some of the stakeholders for Crown Metal Products, a small manufacturer of metal furniture near Boise, Idaho, are shown in Figure 3.1. But only a few, identified by bold arrows, are viewed as constituencies by Crown management.

The actions of many corporate executives are designed to serve interests other than those of the common shareholder. For example, a number of managements have recently placed large amounts of company stock in employee stock ownership trusts for the purpose of avoiding takeover attempts that were clearly in the interests of common shareholders. This benefitted the employees, of course, but it also helped the managers keep their jobs. Major companies that have taken these kinds of actions to avoid takeovers include Walt Disney Productions and Martin Marietta Corporation. Other companies make gifts of company resources, often cash, to universities, churches, clubs, and so forth, knowing that any possible benefit to shareholders is remote. Some authorities favor this trend and suggest that members of the public should be placed on major corporate boards to protect the interests of nonowner stakeholders.

Protecting the diversity of stakeholder interests requires answering such questions as these: During an economic downturn, should employees be afforded continuous employment, even if this will hurt profits in the long run? Should managers try to ensure that suppliers make a reasonable profit on the items purchased from them or should managers simply buy the best inputs available at the lowest price possible? Should a company go beyond the requirements of the law in cleaning up the environment if competitors barely comply with the law?

Answering such questions is termed *stakeholder analysis*. One approach to stakeholder analysis involved consideration of the social contract. The **social contract** is the set of written and unwritten rules and assumptions about acceptable interrelationships among the various elements of society. Much of the social contract is embedded in the customs of society. For example, in integrating minorities into the workforce, society has to come to expect companies to do more than the law requires. When a company such as Wal-Mart behaves in an especially commendable way, its actions tend to increase the expectations society has concerning other companies.

Some of the "contract provisions" result from practices of the parties to the contract. Like a legal contract, the social contract often involves a quid pro quo (something exchanged for something). One party to the contract behaves in a certain way and expects a certain pattern of behavior from the other. For example, a relationship of trust may have developed between a manufacturer and the community in which it operates. Because of this, each will inform the other well in advance of any planned action that might cause harm, such as the phasing down of a plant's operations by the company. The widespread belief that such a relationship was rare prompted Congress to pass the Worker Adjustment and Retraining Notification Act. That law requires firms employing a hundred or more workers to give 60 days' notice to employees and local government officials when a plant closing or layoff affecting 50 or more employees for a 90-day period is planned.

The social contract concerns relationships with individuals, government, other organizations, and society in general as Figure 3.2 illustrates. Each of these relationships will be considered individually in the following sections.

Obligations to Individuals

Individuals often find healthy outlets for their energies through joining organizations. From the church, they expect guidance, ministerial services, and fellowship, and they devote time and money to its sustenance. From their employers, they expect a fair day's pay for a fair day's work—and perhaps much more. Many expect to be paid for time off to vote, perform jury service, and so forth. Clubs and associations provide opportunities for fellowship and for community service.

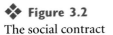

Figure 3.2
The social contract

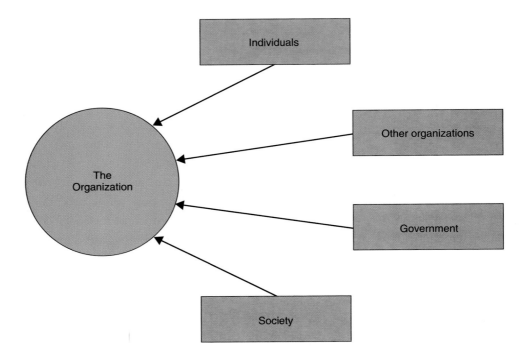

Customers expect to be catered to. To some degree, most of society still subscribes to the notion that the customer is king. To the extent that individuals' expectations are acknowledged as responsibilities by the organization, they become part of the social contract.

Organizations also have certain obligations to their employees. Reasonable ethics for employer spying seem simple. Employees have a certain right to privacy, but this right to privacy must often be infringed upon to protect the welfare of the entire organization. According to William Moroney, director of the Electronic Mail Association, "Employees have the right to expect that naked pictures of them will not be passed around the office." However, if they are "running an illegal football pool, management has the right to know about it."[11]

Obligations to Other Organizations

Managers must be concerned with relationships involving other organizations—both organizations that are like their own, such as competitors, and very different ones. Commercial businesses are expected to compete with one another on an honorable basis, without subterfuge or reckless unconcern for their mutual rights. However, some organizations appear to have a certain amount of disdain for competitors, especially when it comes to recruiting. Dr. Ferdinand Piech, chairman of Volkswagen AG, hired Jose Ignacio Lopez de Arriortua from General Motors to head manufacturing and purchasing at Volkswagen. Lopez took seven GM co-workers with him in the move. He made contact with 40 others, and may have taken trade secrets with him.[12] If this is true, it is fairly obvious

Organizations often encourage their employees to work with students in the local school system. (Source: Copyright © Tony Stone Worldwide/David Young-Wolff)

that Volkswagen AG is not competing on an honorable or ethical basis with General Motors. Charities such as the United Way expect support from business, often including the loan of executives to help with annual fund drives. At the same time, such institutions are expected to come hat in hand to business managers, requesting rather than demanding assistance.

In the traditional view of social responsibility, which we discuss later in the chapter, business best meets its obligations through pursuit of its own interests. Some companies view the social contract mainly in terms of the company's interests. For example, FMC Corporation, a major diversified manufacturer, has firm policies about how it will direct it contributions. The basic criteria FMC applies are that contributions must help areas around company facilities or where its employees live and that gifts must improve the corporation's business environment. FMC might contribute to a business college in an area where it has a plant, but it would not give gifts to distant universities.

Obligations to Government

Government is an important party to the social contract for every kind of organization. Under the auspices of government, companies have a license to do business, along with patent rights, trademarks, and so forth. Churches are often incorporated under state laws and given nonprofit status. Many quasigovernmental agencies, such as the Federal Deposit Insurance Corporation, regional planning commissions, and local school boards, have been given special missions by government.

In addition, organizations are expected to recognize the need for order rather than anarchy and to accept some government intervention in organizational affairs. On the international scene, many businesses got very disturbed

Companies like Wal-Mart carefully monitor their interactions with society. The Helen Robson Walton Award is given annually to the two most deserving Wal-Mart stores. Selections are based upon the number and quality of projects, the level of community support, and the financial success of the projects. In tiny Bentonville, Arkansas, where Wal-Mart is headquartered, a local Brownie chapter benefits from the spirit of volunteerism fostered by Wal-Mart's founder, the late Sam Walton.
(Source: Photograph courtesy of Wal-Mart Stores, Inc.)

when the move toward democratic reform in China was sidetracked. In fact, the 1989 massacre of students and other dissidents in Tiananmen Square in Beijing raised fears of civil war. But U.S. companies remain in China and are helping to resolve the problems. The market in China is so massive that businesses are willing to take considerable risk to remain there. By doing so, they certainly accept some changes due to anarchy or government intervention in their affairs.

Obligations to Society in General

The traditional view of business responsibility has been that businesses should produce and distribute goods and services in return for a profit. Businesses have performed this function effectively, giving the United States one of the highest overall standards of living in the world. A high percentage of the population has its basic needs for food, clothing, shelter, health, and education reasonably well satisfied. And most citizens are afforded some leisure time. Profitable firms are able to pay taxes to the government and make donations to charities. All this should be a matter of some pride for business owners and managers.

The main reason for the exceptional productivity of the United States is perhaps the manner in which the free enterprise economic system operates. The profit motive provides incentives to businesses to produce goods and services efficiently. Practically every firm tries to curb costs in order to keep prices low enough to attract customers and still allow for profit. Some believe this focus on profits through cost cutting causes quality to be neglected as a competitive tool.

Businesses operate by public consent with the basic purpose of satisfying the needs of society. As those needs are more fully met, society demands more of all of its institutions, particularly large business firms. Here are some of the goals businesses are expected to help society meet:

- Elimination of poverty.
- Provision of quality health care.
- Preservation of the environment by reductions in the level of pollution.
- Provision of a sufficient number of jobs and career opportunities for all members of society.
- Improvement in the quality of working life of employees.
- Provision of safe, livable communities with good housing and efficient transportation.[13]

As responsible corporate citizens, businesses should follow the spirit of the law as well as the letter. Many companies that created huge hazardous waste dumps throughout the country now defend themselves by saying that the dumps were legal when they were created. But the fact is that the laws and regulations controlling hazardous waste dumping were meant to protect public health, and the dumping of certain concentrations of substances was prohibited. In many cases, dangerous but unregulated substances and harmful (though legal) concentrations of other substances were dumped over an extended period of years. It is clear that society now considers this unacceptable.

In the sixteenth century, Sir Thomas More said, "If virtue were profitable, common sense would make us good and greed would make us saintly."[14] More knew that virtue is not profitable, so people must make hard ethical choices from time to time. Common sense hardly makes one good. Still, some social theorists continue to believe that social responsibility is just a matter of "managerial self-interest."[15] In the United States today, the consensus is clear. Corporate strategists are being held to a higher standard than just pursuing their own interests, or even those of stockholders; they must consider the interests of other groups too.

Society's broadening expectations of business are illustrated in Figure 3.3. The inner circle, Level I, represents the traditional economic function of business. The economic function remains the primary responsibility of businesses to society. Businesses produce needed goods and services, provide employment, contribute to economic growth, and earn a profit. Level II recognizes the responsibility of business to perform the economic function but with an awareness of changing social goals, values, and demands. Management must demonstrate concern for, among other things, the efficient utilization of resources, the reduction of environmental pollution, the employment and development of disadvantaged minorities and women, and the safety of employees and customers. The actions

❖ **Figure 3.3**
Primary roles of business

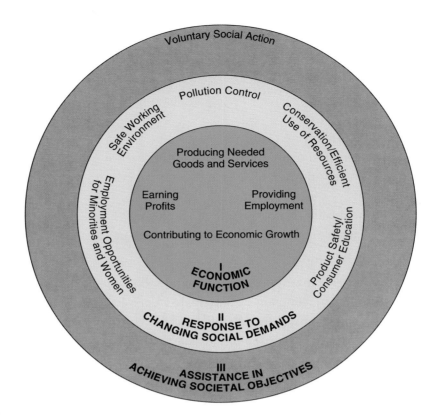

of Hershey Chocolate Company following the Three Mile Island nuclear incident provide an example of Level II concern. Located near the nuclear plant, Hershey immediately instituted a careful testing program for milk received from within 75 miles of Three Mile Island and isolated all milk coming from within ten miles. A Hershey executive said, "While we have no indication of anything wrong with any product, if we are going to err, we want to err on the safe side."[16]

Level III, the outer circle, illustrates corporate responsibility for assisting society in achieving such broad goals as the elimination of poverty and urban decay through a partnership of business, government agencies, and other private institutions. Although the responsibilities in Level III are not primary obligations, business has shown increasing interest in such voluntary social actions. By encouraging recycling, Wal-Mart went beyond simply carrying out economic functions. This is an example of Level III concerns.

❖ ❖ CHANGING VALUES AND SOCIAL RESPONSIBILITY

Numerous associations of respected business leaders, including the American Management Association and the Committee for Economic Development, have encouraged corporations and managers to become involved in socially responsible activities. In a climate of changing social values, these groups have stressed such programs as the following:

- Better jobs and promotion opportunities for minorities and women.
- Financial support for education.
- Financial and managerial help aimed at improving health and medical care.
- A safer working environment.
- Leadership and financial support for urban renewal.
- Reduction of environmental pollution.

The major arguments for the acceptance of social responsibility by business appear in Table 3.1. These arguments can be summarized by the **iron law of responsibility,** the rule, first stated by Keith Davis, that "in the long run, those who do not use power in a manner society considers responsible will tend to lose it." Thus, if business firms are to retain their social power and social role, they must be responsive to society's needs, as is Levi Strauss with regard to workforce diversity.[17]

The Traditional View of Social Responsibility

In 1776, Adam Smith published *The Wealth of Nations,* sometimes called the *capitalist manifesto.* In it, he described a system in which individuals and businesses pursued their own self-interests and government played a limited role. This system became the model for capitalism in the United States. Adam Smith wrote:

(An individual or business) generally, indeed, neither intends to promote the public interest, nor knows how much he is promoting. . . . He intends only his own gains, and he is in this, as in many other cases, led by an

TABLE 3.1 Arguments for the Acceptance of Social Responsibility

1. People expect businesses and other institutions to be socially responsible.

2. Business will benefit if it is socially responsible, so social responsibility is just a matter of enlightened self-interest.

3. Responsible businesses have better images, both as honorable corporate citizens and as desirable places to work.

4. Business should be involved in social programs because it controls the necessary resources.

5. Business exists only with the sanction of society, so it should serve society's interests.

6. If business does not respond to society's needs, the public will press for more regulation.

7. Socially responsible actions may increase profits in the long run.

Diverse and Socially Responsible by Design

The issue of diversity is one aspect of global competition. Today it would seem socially irresponsible to proclaim in an advertising brochure that "none but white women and girls are employed," but in 1908 that is just what was included in a Levi Strauss & Company brochure. In fact, today Levi Strauss has taken the moral high ground in terms of being socially responsible by developing a diverse workforce. Levi Strauss appears to be exceptionally responsible in this area, and is currently recognized as "one of the most ethnically and culturally diverse companies in the U.S., if not the world." In 1992, 56 percent of their 23,000 person U.S. workforce belonged to minority groups. Fourteen percent of Levi Strauss top managers are nonwhite and 30 percent are female. In another step up the social responsibility ladder, Levi Strauss is doing its best to eliminate the "glass ceiling" that may have prevented some qualified minorities and women from being promoted into the company's top ranks. Promoting diversity makes good business sense for Levi Strauss, and has allowed the company to design and develop merchandise for diverse markets, which it might not have understood or appreciated in the past. Levi Strauss credits the Dockers line of casual pants, now worth more than $1 billion a year, to Argentine employees. Both diversity and social responsibility are often costly and time consuming, but Levi Strauss CEO Robert B. Haas believes that harnessing diversity will continue to benefit the company well into the future. According to Levi Strauss executives, "Standing firm . . . sends an important message to employees of all races and lifestyles."[18]

invisible hand to promote an end which was no part of his intention, nor is it always the worse for society that it was no part of it. By pursuing his own interest he frequently promotes that of the society more effectively than when he really intends to promote it.[19]

This idea—that capitalism allows the serving of the public interest by individuals and businesses seeking maximization of satisfaction or profit—is considered by some to be the foundation of the U.S. economic system. Traditionally, companies were not expected to serve social goals, except indirectly. For example, until the mid-1930s, it was illegal for U.S. corporations to make charitable contributions. This was based on a precedent set in an 1883 lawsuit in Great Britain, *Hutton* v. *West Cork Railway Corporation.* The court in that case ruled that the corporation should be concerned only with the equitable distribution of its earnings to its owners. This distribution could not include corporate philanthropy, the court said.[20]

In 1935, the Federal Revenue Act provided for the tax deductibility of corporate charitable contributions. Under that provision, corporations could deduct up to five percent of net income for charitable contributions. By 1953, the right of businesses to make extensive charitable gifts was clearly established. That year, in *A. P. Smith Manufacturing Company* v. *Barlow et al.,* the New Jersey Supreme Court concluded that business support of higher education was in society's best interest.[21] Corporations today are expected to go far beyond corporate philanthropy in serving society's interests.

Economist Milton Friedman, who received a Nobel Prize in economics, called the idea of corporate social responsibility a "fundamentally subversive doctrine." Friedman said, "There is one and only one social responsibility of business—to use its resources and engage in activities designed to increase its profits so long as it stays within the rules of the game, which is to say engages in open and free competition without deception or fraud."[22]

Friedman's statement is often quoted as an example of a radical view and an excuse for corporate irresponsibility. Friedman's followers, however, say he simply subscribes to the idea that, in the long run, the public interest is served by individuals and businesses pursuing their own best interests, primarily financial well-being, through participation in a relatively free economy. It is true that Friedman sets a rather high standard when he suggests that businesses should operate within the "rules of the game," practicing neither deception nor fraud. The rules of the game obviously include accepted ethical practices, in addition to international, national, and other laws. How many corporations are willing to tell the absolute truth in their advertisements and to engage in open and fair competition, avoiding collusion, price fixing, and so forth? The fact is that few subscribe to Friedman's hard-line views today.

Organizational Constituency and Social Responsibility

Many U.S. corporate executives see themselves as legitimate servants of a variety of constituencies. In a political sense, a constituency is a body of citizens or voters who are entitled to elect a representative to a legislative or other public body. An **organizational constituency** is any identifiable group that organizational managers either have or acknowledge a responsibility to represent. The intention of political constituencies is that they will be represented by the person they elect. Unlike political constituencies, constituencies of corporate managers may or may not have the power to choose those managers.

A Change in the Attitude Toward Social Responsibility?

In recent years companies have been plagued with the thought of how they can compete in the new global environment. Companies are constantly looking for new ideas that will make them more efficient. Workforces are being trimmed. In fact, for the first eight months of 1993, an average of 2,389 American workers lost their jobs daily. Even firms that are on a rebound such as Arvin Industries, maker of the MacPherson struts, are not rehiring. Rather, they are seeking other ways to get the job done. Ray Mack, Arvin's human resources director, stated, "To remain globally competitive, we must continue to streamline operations and keep a tight rein on labor costs."[23]

In view of this new environment, some are questioning whether or not efficiency and social responsibility can be married.[24] For example, IBM once had the reputation of never laying off workers. This reputation has been shattered with the recent layoffs. In view of these layoffs, it would be reasonable to question whether or not IBM can afford to do many of the things that gained it the reputation for being socially responsible. Resource utilization may need to be thoroughly analyzed to determine if a certain "socially responsible" action actually assists the firm in remaining competitive in this ever-expanding global environment. Some firms are questioning the seventh argument for the acceptance of social responsibility ("Socially responsible actions may increase profits in the long run," see Table 3.1). They find it difficult to dwell on socially responsible actions when the survival of their firm is in doubt. Only time will tell if the concept of social responsibility survives in this new environment.

❖ ❖ THE BUSINESS–GOVERNMENT INTERFACE

The influence of business firms and other private organizations on government is understandably a matter of concern to the general public. However, the pervasive involvement of government in business activities is of more importance to most managers. The trend during the Reagan and Bush years was toward lessening regulation and reducing government interference in both business and private activities. The airline, trucking, and banking industries are now largely deregulated. It is ironic that it is the deregulated industries that tend to be the most vehement opponents of deregulation. Once companies have adapted to a regulated environment, they apparently are not sure they will be able to compete in a freely competitive one.

There is always a concern that political contributions can subvert government processes. This is especially true for contributions made by political action committees. **Political action committees (PACs)** are tax-favored organizations formed by special interest groups to accept contributions and influence government action. The growth of PACs has created an avenue through which corporations can contribute hundreds of millions of dollars to political candidates. Much of the money is obviously aimed at serving the special interests of those organizations. For example, billions of dollars in subsidies and price supports were approved for the dairy industry after PACs representing them made large contributions to key legislators.

❖ ❖ A MODEL OF ETHICS

Closely related to social responsibility, but not identical to it, is the concept of ethics. **Ethics** is the discipline dealing with what is good and bad, or right and wrong, or with moral duty and obligation. Everyone makes ethical (or unethical) decisions every day. Do you tell the clerk when you get too much change? What if your professor errs in your favor in computing your grade? You may think these

---

MANAGEMENT IN PRACTICE

A Skill-Building Exercise: Suppose for a moment that you have a goal that is critically important to you. Your friends are very supportive and are determined to assist you in the accomplishment of your goal. You later attain your goal. You then learn that your friends did some illegal things to help you. Your friends' actions did not help, and no one was hurt. You have two options: You can cover for your friends and possibly get caught, or you can turn your friends in and allow them to suffer the consequences of their actions. (This is one version of a story involving former President Richard M. Nixon and his friends, the Watergate burglars.)
What would you do?

---

minor private decisions are unimportant. But decisions in small matters tend to set a pattern for the more important ones you may make as managers.

A difficulty encountered in discussing ethics is that what is or is not ethical is so much a matter of perception. But, despite the ambiguity, ethics appears to be moving up on the corporate priority list. An increasing number of companies have codes of ethics. Remember that Wal-Mart has a strong code of ethics. Many industry associations adopt such codes, which are then recommended to members. Some consultants specialize in helping companies embed ethical principles in their corporate culture. And most business schools now teach business ethics in their courses.

A model of ethics is presented in Figure 3.4. It can be seen there that ethics consists mainly of two relationships, indicated by the bold horizontal arrows. A person or organization is ethical if these relationships are strong and positive.

The first element in the model is sources of ethical guidance. One might use a number of sources to determine what is right or wrong, good or bad, moral or immoral. These sources include the Bible, the Koran, and other holy books. They also include the "still, small voice" that many refer to as conscience. Millions believe that conscience is a gift of God or the voice of God. Others see it as

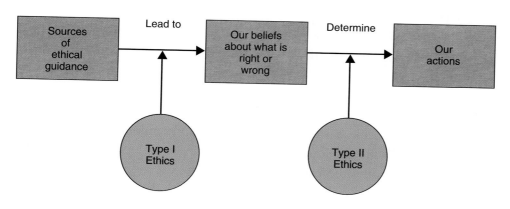

❖ **Figure 3.4**
A model of ethics

a developed response based on the internalization of societal mores. Another source of ethical guidance is the behavior and advice of the people psychologists call "significant others"—our parents, friends, and role models and members of our churches, clubs, and associations. For many professionals, there are often codes of ethics that proscribe certain behavior.

Laws also offer guides to ethical behavior, prohibiting acts that can be especially hurtful to others. If a certain behavior is illegal, most would consider it to be unethical as well. There are exceptions, of course. For example, through the 1950s, laws in most southern states relegated black persons to the backs of buses and otherwise assigned them inferior status. Martin Luther King, Jr., resisted such laws and, in fact, engaged in civil disobedience and other nonviolent forms of resistance to their enforcement. King won the Nobel Peace Prize for his efforts and is today considered by most Americans to have been a highly moral person.

Notice in Figure 3.4 that the sources of ethical guidance should lead to our beliefs or convictions about what is right or wrong. Most would agree that people have a responsibility to avail themselves of these sources of ethical guidance. In short, individuals should care about what is right and wrong and not just be concerned with what is expedient. The strength of the relationship between what an individual or an organization believes to be moral and correct and what available sources of guidance suggest is morally correct is **Type I ethics.** For example, suppose a student believes it is acceptable to copy another student's exam, despite the fact that almost everyone condemns this practice. This student is unethical, but perhaps only in a Type I sense.

Simply having strong beliefs about what is right and wrong and basing them on the proper sources may have little relationship to what one does. Figure 3.4 illustrates that **Type II ethics** is the strength of the relationship between what one believes and how one behaves. Everyone would agree that to do what one considers wrong is unethical. For example, if a student knows that it is wrong to look at another's examination answer sheet, but does so anyway, the student is being unethical in a Type II sense. If a business manager considers it wrong to damage the environment, yet dumps poisonous waste into a nearby stream, this behavior is unethical also. Generally, a person is not considered ethical unless the person possesses both types of ethics.

❖ ❖ BUSINESS ETHICS

One can usually provoke a lively discussion by simply mentioning business ethics. **Business ethics** is the application of ethical principles to business relationships and activities. Reading the newspaper or watching the evening news provides ample illustration of illegal or unethical practices of individuals in large corpo-

Wal-Mart: Honorable Competitor or Cutthroat Retailer?

Wal-Mart, the highly praised number one retailer in the United States, has always been a leader in the field of business ethics. On October 12, 1993, an Arkansas state court ruled that Wal-Mart illegally engaged in predatory pricing by selling pharmacy products at prices below cost. Naturally, Wal-Mart will appeal, but how do these actions parallel Wal-Mart's longstanding code of ethics?

If, in fact, Wal-Mart did lower prices to eliminate competition from pharmacies, then its actions may well be illegal, but also possibly unethical and socially irresponsible. On the other hand, if Wal-Mart's overall pricing strategy makes money, as it does and has for years, and if below-cost pricing is just intended to attract customers to the store so they will purchase products that are indeed profitable, then is the strategy wrong? In fact, all retailers use low-cost inducements to attract customers into their stores in the hope

of selling them a larger bag of goods. If this practice is sanctioned for other retailers, then could this practice be unacceptable for number one Wal-Mart? Ethically speaking, is Wal-Mart's policy of "meeting or beating the competition, 'without regard to cost,'" inappropriate? In the end the person hardest hit by these occurrences may well be the consumer who could be saddled with higher prices, and is that ethical and socially responsible?[25]

rations. Even Wal-Mart, which was featured in the case at the beginning of the chapter, has experienced some negative press coverage.

Deciding what is ethical is often difficult. Following are examples of business activities that are usually considered unethical:

- Falsifying information on an application blank.
- Trading stocks on the basis of inside information.
- Padding expense accounts and otherwise seeking reimbursement for questionable or nonexistent business expenses.
- Divulging confidential information or trade secrets to competitors.
- Taking company property or materials for personal use.
- Giving or receiving gifts in return for orders.
- Quitting a job without giving adequate notice.
- Firing someone without giving adequate notice.
- Stealing.
- Soliciting or offering kickbacks.

As mentioned earlier, many companies have developed specific codes of ethics. For example, Texas Instruments furnishes its managers with a handbook entitled *Ethics in the Business of TI*. The book summarizes the company's philosophy of business as follows:

It is fundamental to TI's philosophy that good ethics and good business are synonymous when viewed from moral, legal and practical standpoints. The trust and respect of all people—fellow workers, customers, consumers, stockholders, government employees, elected officials, suppliers,

A Skill-Building Exercise: Leroy Hasty was faced with a dilemma. He supervised 12 process technicians at the Indestro Chemical plant in El Dorado, Arkansas, but was being transferred to a new job. The production manager, Jack Richards, had just asked Leroy to nominate one of his subordinates as a replacement. Two possible choices immediately came to mind: Carlos Chavez and James Mitchell.

Carlos was a very capable worker. He was 24 years old and married, and he had earned his bachelor's degree in management by attending night school. His heritage was Mexican-American. He had done an excellent job on every assignment Leroy had given him. He had all the qualifications Leroy believed a good supervisor should have, including solid technical expertise. Leroy considered Carlos punctual, diligent, mature, and intelligent. A serious sort, Carlos often came to work early and stayed late and seemed to spend most of his spare time with his family.

James was a 25-year-old high school graduate. He was single, and Hasty knew he often went hunting or partying with several of the other technicians. Like most of his fellow workers, James was a WASP (white Anglo-Saxon protestant). He was a hard worker and was liked and respected by the others, including Carlos. On the basis of objective factors, Leroy believed James ran second to Carlos, although the call was a close one.

But then there was the race issue. Several times Leroy had heard fellow workers refer to Carlos as a "spic" and "wetback." Leroy believed some of the workers would prefer to have James as a supervisor, purely because of his national origin. In fact, he thought one or two of them might resist Carlos's authority to try to make him look bad. And if productivity in the section fell off because of administrative problems, Leroy knew his own record with the company might be tarnished.

At that moment, the phone rang. It was Jack Richards. "Leroy," he said, "I need to see you. Could you come to my office in a few minutes?" As Leroy hung up the phone, he thought, "I know Jack is going to want to talk about my replacement."

What decision would you recommend that Leroy make? Discuss.

competitors, neighbors, friends, the press, and the general public—are assets that cannot be purchased. They must be earned. This is why all of the business of TI must be conducted according to the highest ethical standards.[26]

In the handbook, TI sets forth many specific ethical guidelines on a wide range of issues. The areas covered include truthfulness in advertising, gifts and entertainment, improper use of corporate assets, political contributions, payments in connection with business transactions, conflicts of interest, and trade secrets and proprietary information.

There are reasons to encourage industry associations to develop and promote improved codes of ethics. It is difficult for a single firm to pioneer ethical practices if its competitors take advantage of unethical shortcuts. For example, U.S. companies must comply with the Foreign Corrupt Practices Act, which prohibits bribes of foreign government officials or business executives. Obviously, the law does not prevent foreign competitors from bribing government or business officials to get business, and such practices are common in many countries. This sometimes puts U.S. companies at a disadvantage. Several multinationals, including Switzerland's Ciba-Geigy, have encouraged other multinationals to band together and adopt policies on corrupt practices that will resemble those in U.S. law. Perhaps such voluntary codes will be effective in upgrading the standards of ethics practiced in international business.

❖ ❖ THE SOCIAL AUDIT

Many firms acknowledge responsibilities to various stakeholder groups other than corporate owners. Some even set specific objectives in social areas. Over the last two decades or so, a number of organizations have recommended that firms attempt to formally measure their contributions to various elements of society and to society as a whole. A **social audit** is a systematic assessment of a company's activities in terms of its social impact. Despite the efforts of the American Institute of Certified Public Accountants and a number of management societies, it has not been possible to do rigorous auditing in social areas. As Table 3.2 shows, there are a number of possible reasons for this failure.

Three possible types of social audits are currently being utilized: (1) simple inventory of activities, (2) compilation of socially relevant expenditures, and (3) determination of social impact. The inventory is generally a good starting place. It consists of a listing of socially oriented activities undertaken by the firm. Here

TABLE 3.2 Reasons for Not Applying Financial Auditing in Social Areas

1. The company may not have specific objectives in social areas.
2. Specific criteria or units of measurement may not be agreed upon.
3. It may be difficult to determine how an action today might affect society's interests tomorrow.
4. The business system, which previously focused on economic variables, may not have control points or measurement techniques appropriate to measuring social variables.
5. Auditing implies the collection of complete, objective, and accurate data, not usually available in social areas.

Uncompromising Ethical Behavior: Myth or Reality?

Business ethics came into sharp focus during the decade of the eighties and will become even more important in the nineties. Deciding what is ethical is often difficult, and that difficulty is compounded when the firm is competing in a multinational environment. Unfortunately, it is hard for a single multinational firm to pioneer ethical practices if its competitors undercut it by taking advantage of unethical shortcuts or socially irresponsible actions. For instance, cigarette manufacturers are attempting to eliminate all trade barriers with Japan. These barriers currently limit the manufacturers' ability to export American cigarettes to Japan. If the barriers are lifted, competitive forces will be greatly intensified, and American cigarette manufacturers will be under pressure to use promotional methods long banned in the United States, such as television advertising. Certain methods were banned because of the claim by some experts that they caused individuals to start smoking. There is no such ban in Japan; therefore Japanese cigarette manufacturers use these promotional methods.

This sort of situation raises several ethical questions: Should the United States dictate the code of ethical conduct for cigarette manufacturers headquartered in America, but operating in Japan? Should American cigarette manufacturers feel obligated to observe the U.S. promotional ban overseas, thereby forfeiting a substantial portion of the Japanese cigarette market? Can American business ethics be exported along with products? As globalized markets become a reality—with the eroding of Japanese, European, and Mexican trade barriers—the question of globalized ethical behavior must be addressed. Levi Strauss, the global denim jeans company, refuses to compromise its business ethics even if profits suffer. Levi Strauss has a set of global ethical guidelines called their "Terms of Engagement" that cover everything from safety and health to other aspects of human rights such as free association. An audit of over 600 of its overseas contractors resulted in Levi Strauss severing ties with 30 of them for ethics violations. Levi Strauss even decided to not invest in the booming Chinese market because of what they referred to as "pervasive violations of basic human rights."[27] From the standpoint of Levi Strauss, uncompromising ethical behavior is good business, regardless of where it is marketing or making its goods.

---

are some examples: (1) minority employment and training, (2) support of minority enterprises, (3) pollution control, (4) corporate giving, (5) involvement in selected community projects by executives, and (6) a hard-core unemployment program. The ideal social audit would go well beyond a simple listing and involve determining the true benefits to society of any socially oriented business activity. A social audit, conducted by Smith & Hawken, implies that Ben & Jerry's ice cream company executives ask customers to swallow a lot more than butterfat. Among its findings were that Ben and Jerry have become millionaires, while the rank and file hold less than half a percent of Ben & Jerry's stock. So executives could benefit, Ben & Jerry's modified an earlier policy that no executive in the company could make more than five times what the lowest-paid employee receives. Finally, management had to relabel its so-called low-fat Heath Bar yogurt, which is not low in fat.[28]

✘ Management Tips ✘

Guidelines for Dealing with the Manager's Diverse Environment

Pagano and Verdin developed a list of guidelines that future managers can use to resolve difficult ethical dilemmas. The guidelines are not intended to provide hard and fast answers to ethical questions, but should assist future managers in evaluating ethical dilemmas by examining their own values and those of the organization. When future managers answer the following questions they are forced to carefully consider the ethical consequences of alternate decisions.

1. **Is the problem/dilemma really what it appears to be?** If you are not sure, find out.

2. **Is the action you are considering legal? Ethical?** If you are not sure, find out.

3. **Do you understand the position of those who oppose the action you are considering? Is it reasonable?**

4. **Whom does the action benefit? Harm? How much? How long?**

5. **Would you be willing to allow everyone to do what you are considering doing?**

6. **Have you sought the opinions of others who are knowledgeable on the subject and who would be objective?**

7. **Would your actions be embarrassing to you if they were made known to your family, friends, co-workers, or superiors? Would you be comfortable defending your actions to an investigative reporter on the evening news?**

There are no absolutely correct answers to these questions. But they can help clarify ethical aspects of tough managerial decisions. Moreover, answering them is likely to improve the quality of management decisions from a purely practical standpoint.

SOURCE: Anthony M. Pagano and Jo Ann Verdin, *The External Environment of Business* (New York: Wiley, 1988), Chapter 5.

SUMMARY

Social responsibility is the implied, enforced, or felt obligation of managers, acting in their official capacity, to serve or protect the interests of groups other than themselves. Some experts believe businesses are increasingly willing to accept their societal responsibilities and that managers are becoming more ethical. They find that managers are more socially responsible and ethical than were their counterparts a generation ago.

Most organizations, whether profit or nonprofit, have a large number of stakeholders. An organizational stakeholder is an individual or group whose interests are affected by organizational activities. Although all stakeholders are affected by the corporation, managers may not acknowledge responsibility to all of them.

The social contract is the set of written and unwritten rules and assumptions about acceptable interrelationships among the various elements of society. Much of the social contract is embedded in the customs of society. Some of the "contract provisions" result from practices between parties. Like a legal contract, the social contract often involves a quid pro quo (something for something) exchange. The social contract concerns relationships with individuals, government, and other organizations, and society in general.

Numerous associations and groups of respected business leaders have encouraged corporations and managers to become involved in socially responsible activities. Their arguments for this kind of involvement can be summarized by the iron law of responsibility, first stated by Keith Davis, which says "In the long run, those who do not use power in a manner society considers responsible will tend to lose it." Thus, if business firms are to retain their social power and role, they must be responsive to society's needs. How-ever, Nobel laureate economist Milton Friedman called the idea of corporate social responsibility a "fundamentally subversive doctrine." Many U.S. corporate executives see themselves as legitimate servants of a variety of constituencies. An organizational constituency is any identifiable group that organizational managers either have or acknowledge a responsibility to represent.

There is always a concern that political contributions can subvert government processes. This is especially true for contributions made by political action committees (PACs). These committees are tax-favored organizations formed by special interest groups to accept contributions and influence governmental actions.

Closely related to social responsibility is the concept of ethics. Ethics is the discipline dealing with what is good and bad, right and wrong, or with moral duty and obligation. Business ethics is the application of ethical principles to business relationships and activities.

Over the last two decades or so, a number of organizations and individuals have recommended that firms measure the degree to which they contribute to the welfare of various elements of society and to that of society as a whole. When this effort is formalized, it is called a social audit. This audit is a systematic assessment of a company's activities in terms of their social impact.

KEY TERMS

Social responsibility 76	Political action committees (PACs) 90
Organizational stakeholder 79	Ethics 90
Social contract 81	Type I ethics 92
Iron law of responsibility 87	Type II ethics 92
	Business ethics 92
Organizational constituency 89	Social audit 95

REVIEW QUESTIONS

1. Define social responsibility. In general, how is U.S. business viewed by the public?
2. What is the social contract? Describe the various relationships involved with the social contract.
3. Contrast the traditional view of social responsibility with the current views regarding social responsibility.
4. What are political action committees?
5. What is ethics? Distinguish between Type I and Type II ethics.
6. Are the ethics of business and its managers changing? Discuss.
7. What is the purpose of the social audit?

CASE STUDIES

CASE 3.1 Turning Disaster to Advantage: The Tylenol Scare

Cyanide is a deadly poison. The ingestion of just a small amount can cause instant death. When the substance found its way into a few bottles of Extra-Strength Tylenol capsules in Chicago in September 1982, the results were disastrous: seven people died. At the time, there were more than 30 million bottles on store shelves all over the world, and many millions more in home medicine cabinets. So the incident raised an unthinkable specter: If just one percent of the bottles were poisoned, thousands of people could die.

Tylenol was made by the McNeil Consumer Products subsidiary of Johnson & Johnson (J & J). Calls began to come in from television and radio stations, pharmacies, doctors, poison control centers, and hundreds of panic-stricken consumers around the world. In the confusion of those first hours, thousands reported suspected poisonings. Practically all of the reports turned out to be false.

J & J quickly determined that the capsules were probably contaminated after they left the McNeil plant. Nevertheless, the plant was closed. Soon it was known that all of the poisoned Tylenol capsules were from one lot, which had been sold on Chicago's West Side. The danger could have been eliminated by recalling that one lot.

But company executives said the J & J credo was displayed for all to see at J & J's red brick headquarters. It declared J & J's "first responsibility" was to those who "use our products and services." Chairman James Burke prepared to recall all Extra-Strength Tylenol capsules even though the FBI opposed the recall.

Still, J & J quickly sent thousands of letters to doctors and pharmacists and orchestrated a major media campaign to get the product back. Executives said they took no chance that anyone else would be harmed. In an omission that many found remarkable for a major corporation, J & J spent almost no effort in publicizing a defense or disclaiming responsibility.

Within weeks the fear subsided, and J & J recaptured 95 percent of its earlier market share for nonaspirin, extra-strength pain relievers. But the company's former near monopoly was broken, several other drug manufacturers began national promotion of similar products, and the incident cost J & J tens of millions of dollars.

QUESTIONS

1. Based on information provided in your text, was Johnson & Johnson acting in a socially responsible manner?
2. Based on this case, whom do you believe Johnson & Johnson considered to be the major stakeholder?

CASE 3.2 "You Can't Fire Me"

Norman Blankenship came in the side door of the office at Consolidation Coal Company's Rowland mine, near Clear Creek, West Virginia. He told the mine dispatcher not to tell anyone he was there. Norman was general superintendent over the Rowland operation. He had been with Consolidation for 23 years, having started out as a mining machine operator.

Norman had heard that one of his section bosses, Tom Serinsky, had been sleeping on the job. Tom had been hired two months earlier and assigned to the Rowland mine by the regional personnel office. He had gone to work as section boss, working the midnight to 8:00 A.M. shift. Because of his age and experience, Serinsky was the senior person in the mine on his shift.

Norman took one of the battery-operated jeeps used to transport personnel and supplies in and out of the mine and proceeded to the area where Tom was assigned. Upon arriving, he saw Tom lying on an emergency stretcher. Norman stopped his jeep a few yards away from where Tom was sleeping and approached him. "Hey, you asleep?" Norman asked. Tom awakened with a start and said, "No, I wasn't sleeping."

Norman waited for Tom to collect his senses and then said, "I could tell that you *were* sleeping. But that's beside the point. You weren't at your work station. You know that I have no choice but to fire you." After Tom had left, Norman called his mine foreman, and asked him to come in and complete the remainder of Tom's shift.

The next morning, Norman had the mine personnel officer officially terminate Tom. As part of the standard procedure, the personnel officer notified the regional personnel director that Tom had been fired and gave the reasons for firing him. The regional personnel director asked the personnel officer to get Norman on the line. The regional personnel director said, "Norm, you know Tom is Eustus Frederick's brother-in-law, don't you?" Frederick was a regional vice president. "No, I didn't know that," replied Norman, "but it doesn't matter. The rules are clear. I wouldn't care if he was Frederick's son."

The next day, the regional personnel director showed up at the mine just as Norman was getting ready to make a routine tour of the mine. "I guess you know what I'm here for," said the personnel director. "Yeah, you're here to take away my authority," replied Norman. "No, I'm just here to investigate," said the personnel director.

By the time Norman returned to the mine office after his tour, the personnel director had finished his interviews. He told Norman, "I think we're going to have to put Tom back to work. If we decide to do that, can you let him work for you?" "No, absolutely not," said Norman. "In fact, if he works here, I go." A week later, Norman learned that Tom had gone to work as section boss at another Consolidation coal mine in the region.

QUESTIONS

1. What, if anything, would you do now if you were Norman?
2. Do you believe the personnel director handled the matter in an ethical manner? Explain.

NOTES

1. This is a composite of a number of published accounts, among them: John Huey, "Wal-Mart: Will It Take Over the World?" *Fortune* 124 (January 30, 1989): 52–64; Sharon Reier, "CEO of the Decade: Sam Walton," *Financial World* 158 (April 4, 1989): 56–62; Bill Saporito, "Is Wal-Mart Unstoppable?" *Fortune* 126 (May 6, 1991): 50; "Trendcheck—Wal-Mart: Starting It All," *Stores* 72 (October 1990): 69; John Huey, "America's Most Successful Merchant," *Fortune* 126 (September 23, 1991): 46–47; and the 1991 Wal-Mart Annual Report.

2. Judith H. Dobrzynski, Michael Schroeder, Gregory L. Miles, and Joseph Weber, "Taking Charge," *Business Week* (July 3, 1989): 2.

3. Kenneth E. Goodpaster and John B. Matthews, Jr., "Can a Corporation Have a Conscience?" *Harvard Business Review* 60 (January–February 1982): 132–141.

4. Carolyn Friday, "Cookies, Cream 'n' Controversy," *Newsweek* 122 (July 5, 1993): 40.

5. Louis Harris, *Inside America* (New York: Vintage Books, 1986), p. 236.

6. Mary Beth Regan, "An Embarrassment of Clean Air," *Business Week* (May 31, 1993): 34.

7. Edward L. Hennesy, Jr., "Business Ethics: Is It a Priority for Corporate America?" *FE 2* (formerly *Financial Executive*) 2 (October 1986): 14–15.

8. Archie B. Carroll, *Social Responsibility of Managers*, (Chicago: Science Research, 1984) p. 14.

9. Gail DeGeorge, Joseph Weber, and Peter Hong, "A Blight that's Eating Away at DuPont," *Business Week* (October 5, 1992): 46.

10. Archie B. Carroll, *Social Responsibility of Management*, p. 14.

11. Lee Smith, "What the Boss Knows About You," *Fortune* 128 (August 9, 1993): 88–93.

12. Alex Taylor III, "VW's Rocky Road Ahead," *Fortune* 128 (August 23, 1993): 64–68.

13. Adapted from the Committee for Economic Development and from Sandra L. Holmes, "Corporate Social Performance and Present Areas of Commitment," *Academy of Management Journal* 20 (September 1977): 435.

14. Quoted in Robert Bolt, *A Man for All Seasons* (New York: Random House, 1962).

15. William J. Byron, "In Defense of Social Responsibility," *Journal of Economics and Business* 34 (1982): 190.

16. Dennis Montgomery, "Candy Firm Monitoring Atomic Risk," *Detroit News* (April 2, 1979): 3A, 6A.

17. Keith Davis, "The Case for and Against Business Assumption of Social Responsibilities," *Academy of Management Journal* 16 (June 1973): 36.

18. Alice Cuneo, "Diverse by Design," *Business Week* (Reinventing America 1992): 72.

19. Adam Smith, *The Wealth of Nations* (1776; reprint ed., New York: Modern Library, 1937), p. 423.

20. Daniel Wren, *The Evolution of Management Thought*, 2d ed. (New York: Wiley, 1979), p. 109.

21. *Ibid.,* p. 453.

22. Milton Friedman, *Capitalism and Freedom* (Chicago: University of Chicago Press, 1962), p. 133; also see Theodore Leavitt, "The Dangers of Social Responsibility," *Harvard Business Review* 36 (September–October 1958): 41–50.

23. Louis S. Richman, "When Will the Layoffs End?" *Fortune* 128 (September 20, 1993): 54.

24. Robert J. Samuelson, "R.I.P.: The Good Corporation," *Newsweek* 122 (July 5, 1993): 41.

25. Bob Ortega, "Wal-Mart Loses Predatory-Pricing Case in Arkansas Court but Plans to Appeal" *The Wall Street Journal* XCII, No. 73 (October 13, 1993): A, A3.

26. *Ethics in the Business of TI.* (Dallas: Texas Instruments).

27. Jim Impoco, "Working for Mr. Clean Jeans: Levi's Leader Robert Haas Cares About Morals as Well as Making Money," *U.S. News & World Report* 115 (August 2, 1993): 49–50.

28. Carolyn Friday, "Cookies, Cream 'n' Controversy," *Newsweek* 122 (July 5, 1993): 40.

How Do Your Ethics Stack Up?

Are your ethical skills honed to a fine edge, or are there unanswered issues you must confront prior to facing real-world ethical situations? To assess your ethical values and better determine where you stand on the ethical plane, take the self-assessment exercise "How Do Your Ethics Stack Up?" Then, turn to page 673 to evaluate yourself.

INSTRUCTIONS: For each statement answer as follows.

Strongly Agree = **SA**   Disagree = **D**

Agree = **A**   Strongly Disagree = **SD**

SA	A	D	SD	QUESTION
❏	❏	❏	❏	1. **Employees should not be expected to inform on their peers for wrongdoings.**
❏	❏	❏	❏	2. **There are times when a manager must overlook contract and safety violations in order to get on with the job.**
❏	❏	❏	❏	3. **It is not always possible to keep accurate expense account records; therefore, it is sometimes necessary to give approximate figures.**
❏	❏	❏	❏	4. **There are times when it is necessary to withhold embarrassing information from one's superior.**
❏	❏	❏	❏	5. **We should do what our managers suggest, though we may have doubts about it being the right thing to do.**
❏	❏	❏	❏	6. **It is sometimes necessary to conduct personal business on company time.**
❏	❏	❏	❏	7. **Sometimes it is good psychology to set goals somewhat above normal if it will help to obtain a greater effort from the sales force.**
❏	❏	❏	❏	8. **I would quote a "hopeful" shipping date in order to get the order.**
❏	❏	❏	❏	9. **It is proper to use the company WATS line for personal calls as long as it's not in company use.**
❏	❏	❏	❏	10. **Management must be goal oriented; therefore, the end usually justifies the means.**

(continued on next page)

SA	A	D	SD	QUESTION
❑	❑	❑	❑	11. If it takes heavy entertainment and twisting a bit of company policy to win a large contract, I would authorize it.
❑	❑	❑	❑	12. Exceptions to company policy and procedures are a way of life.
❑	❑	❑	❑	13. Inventory controls should be designed to report "underages" rather than "overages" in goods received. (The ethical issue here is the same as that faced by someone who receives too much change from a store cashier.)
❑	❑	❑	❑	14. Occasional use of the company's copier for personal or community activities is acceptable.
❑	❑	❑	❑	15. Taking home company property (pencils, paper, tape, and so on) for personal use is an accepted fringe benefit.

Source: Lowell G. Rein, "Is Your (Ethical) Slippage Showing?" *Personnel Journal* 59 (September 1980): 743. Reprinted by permission.

4 Managerial Decision Making

LEARNING OBJECTIVES

After completing this chapter students should be able to

✗ Describe the decision-making process and identify major factors that can have an impact on managerial decision making.

✗ Describe the work team and group methods used in decision making.

✗ Explain the requirements that must be present for the decision-making process to be carried out.

✗ Describe worker participation in the decision-making process.

✗ Explain how managers can handle decision making in a crisis situation.

Coca-Cola and Goizueta "Always": Shareholders Continue to Gain into the Nineties

Coca-Cola's latest advertising slogan is "Coca-Cola Always." If Coke's CEO Roberto C. Goizueta had a slogan, it would probably be "Increase Shareholder Wealth—Always." According to Goizueta, "Management doesn't get paid to make shareholders comfortable. We get paid to make shareholders rich." Goizueta continues to reinforce his position; the value of Coke stock has surged more than eight-fold, to $55 billion, as total sales tripled, to $13.1 billion. This provides additional support for Goizueta's contention that "Increasing shareholder value over time is the bottom line of every move we make." Coca-Cola is the world's largest soft-drink company, and their Cuban-born CEO, who has been in charge since 1981, is one reason Coke remains number one. He is an admitted workaholic, who reluctantly takes only one week of vacation a year. He demands similar devotion from the other top managers at Coke, and he and his management crew take themselves very seriously.

After becoming CEO, Goizueta shook up the Coke organization. Cost cutting in every division was a continuing theme. Coke's share of the sugar-cola market had been declining for 20 years. According to Goizueta, "You can extrapolate that out and eventually you end up with zilch." The priceless Coca-Cola trademark was extended to six variations on the basic soft drink and later to clothing and other items. Classic Coke, with the old, secret formula, is still the leading soft drink.

Each decision rankled corporate conservatives, although Goizueta worked hard at building consensus. And when Goizueta decided to take on debt to acquire companies, many at Coke became even harder to convince. The company invested $2 billion to buy its biggest bottlers. Half of the stock in the bottling division was later sold to the public. Another $1.5 billion was spent on Columbia Pictures. Then, plans were announced to start buying back ten percent of Coke's common stock. Long-term debt quintupled. The Coke balance sheet had begun to look like that of many other major companies—half debt, half equity. No longer just a beverage company, Coke had become a conglomerate.

Goizueta continues to make stockholders rich. Net income was up every year from 1981–1992, as were dividends and share prices. Shareholders appear to be quite comfortable with Goizueta. As Coke emerged from its strongest decade ever, it keeps on "Increasing Shareholder Wealth—Always."[1]

The Coca-Cola story suggests the extensive need for decision making in business. **Decision making** is the process of generating and evaluating alternatives and making choices among them. As Goizueta would attest, many decisions are hard to make, especially when a manager is departing from past patterns.

A managerial decision can affect a great number of people—customers, stockholders, employees, and the general public. Coca-Cola, for example, has more than 100,000 shareholders of record and nearly that many employees. Professional managers see the results of their decisions reflected in the firm's earnings report, the welfare of employees, and the economic health of the community and the country. To survive and prosper, managers must be able to make professional decisions. Robert Allen, the CEO at AT&T, believes that decisions should be made closer to the customer than a CEO could possibly ever be, and therefore puts strong-minded decision makers beneath him. Allen keeps them focused on the company's goals and allows them to make decisions when and where solutions are needed.[2]

This chapter first discusses the decision-making process and several important factors that affect decision making. Next it describes work team and group methods of decision making. Then it presents the requirements for decision making. The final sections are devoted to how worker participation is involved in the decision-making process, how managers can handle decision making in a crisis, and the global perspective of decision making.

❖ ❖ THE DECISION-MAKING PROCESS

Companies do not want dynamic failures; they want individuals who are properly equipped to make decisions. This does not mean that managers must be right 100 percent of the time; no one is perfect. It does suggest, however, that successful managers have a higher batting average than less successful managers.

Managers are evaluated primarily on the results of their decisions. Some apparently successful executives follow an intuitive approach to decision making, basing their decisions on hunches and gut feelings. However, a more formalized approach, such as that illustrated in Figure 4.1, can usually increase a manager's batting average. Now more executives than ever are trying to put quality decision

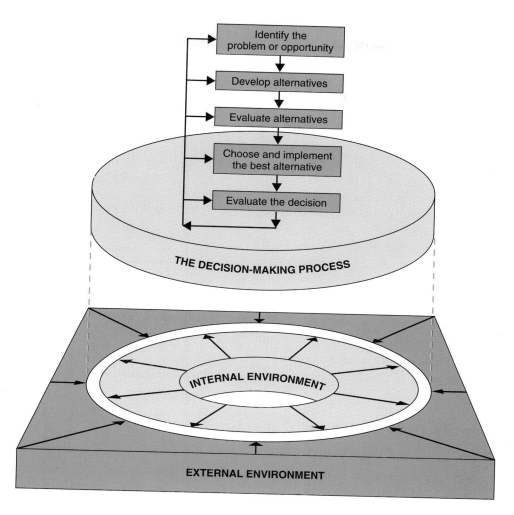

❖ **Figure 4.1**
The decision-making process

makers at every organizational level. Scott Cook, CEO of Intuit, continually communicates his vision to frontline employees, and describes his company as "A circle, with me in the middle. As we grow, my job is to push the locus of decision making out to the periphery."[3] Having quality decision makers at every organizational level will help assure a flexible and effective organization.

Environmental Factors

Decision making does not occur in a vacuum. Notice in Figure 4.1 that the elements of the organization's external and internal environment are the same as those identified in Chapter 2. Variations in any of these factors can affect decision making. For example, the success of Pepsi-Cola in gaining market share while Coca-Cola lost it helped convince Goizueta that change was needed. And price competition surely influenced his decision to cut costs. In a similar manner, the internal environment helps determine what decisions are made and who makes

Bureaucracy: A Barrier to Effective Decision Making

Certain organizations have fat, inflexible, and slow bureaucratic structures that hinder their competitiveness, when compared to lean, flexible, and fast-reacting organizations. In addition to negatively impacting competitiveness, out-of-control bureaucracy also creates a cumbersome decision-making system that often results in slow, misguided decisions. For example, at IBM, six or seven organizations were involved in decisions affecting the entire organization. Arriving at a consensus could take months, just setting up the appointments could take a month or more. On the other hand, GM executives decided that the Saturn plant's productivity must increase, but this decision adversely impacted Saturn quality. Once workers at the Saturn plant became aware that quality was suffering, they staged a slowdown during a visit by GM's CEO. With the exception of this decision-making fiasco, operational decisions that affect the Saturn plant are made by employees in the plant. The environment is so full of trust that teams even recommend cutting people in certain areas, because such a decision will be rewarded with a job elsewhere in the plant, and not termination.[4]

them. Goizueta had to overcome the resistance of conservatives at Coke as he made and implemented all of these decisions. It is fairly obvious that the internal environment of an organization and factors such as bureaucracy can also affect the decision-making process.

The steps in the decision-making process, shown in Figure 4.1, will be discussed next.

Identify the Problem or Opportunity

According to Harold Leavitt, "A business leader must have three major talents: problem solving and subsequent decision making, implementing, and visionary and entrepreneurial talents."[5] Some people view decision making only as problem solving; however, problems are usually better treated as opportunities. The first step in the decision-making process should be to look more for decision-making opportunities than for problems. Eventually, problems will make themselves evident. Opportunities, however, usually must be sought out. In purchasing Columbia Pictures, Coke was taking advantage of what seemed an opportunity. Within a few years, Coke had gotten its money back by selling stock in Columbia to the public, and it still owned about half the company. Often, however, the distinction between a problem and an opportunity is not clear.

In defining a problem (or opportunity), it is important to consider not just the problem itself but the underlying causes. For instance, the problem may be an increased number of defects coming off a production line. Untrained workers may have been assigned to the department. Maintenance people may have been doing a poor job of servicing the equipment. Or materials may have been defective because of sloppy purchasing practices. The causes of a problem must be understood before the problem can be corrected.

MANAGEMENT IN PRACTICE

A Skill-Building Exercise: Wilson Trahan had been the postmaster at Balcomville, Utah, for seven months when he received notice of a 20 percent reduction in staff, effective immediately. At first, Wilson was distressed by the news. He had only ten employees in the post office and was not sure he could do the job with eight.

However, after some thought, Wilson decided that this cutback might really be an opportunity in disguise. He had tried in the past to rearrange the work area, but to no avail. He had drawn up several alternative arrangements of the work flow. All of them would have been better than the present arrangement, but the postal workers were comfortable with the way the stamp machine, the sorting boxes, and the counters had been arranged for years. They resisted each change he tried to make.

Wilson seized on the opportunity created by the reduction in staff. He decided to let the remaining workers help him select the best work space arrangement. The workers cooperated this time, and within a few months, the post office was providing better service than ever. And Wilson, although he had already lost two people, decided that he would not hire a replacement when the next worker quit or retired.

Did Wilson encounter a problem or an opportunity? Discuss.

Often solving a problem or taking advantage of an opportunity requires working with other departments. Defining the problem in terms of what caused it, or seeing the problem as an opportunity will help identify the persons and groups who need to be involved. If a problem is due to poor maintenance, for instance, it may be necessary to involve the maintenance supervisor in deciding how to correct it.

Develop Alternatives

A problem can usually be solved in any of a number of ways. The choices that the decision maker has to decide on are **alternatives.** The only alternative that really counts is the one judged best among those considered. At this point in the decision-making process, however, it is important to consider all feasible ways by which the problem can be solved. Naturally, the number of alternatives generated is limited by the amount of time available for the decision, as well as by the importance of the decision itself. And the best alternative cannot be chosen if no one thinks of it. Finally, until all the alternatives have been evaluated, it is best not to eliminate any alternative from consideration.

Evaluate Alternatives

Usually, advantages and disadvantages can be found in every possible solution. One alternative may be clearly superior, but it may also have some weak points. It is essential that managers realistically appraise arguments for or against a particular alternative. Sometimes an idea sounds good initially, but taking time to

The only alternative that really counts is the one judged best among those considered. (Source: © John Coletti)

weigh the pros and cons of alternatives usually pays off. It prevents the manager from having to say, "I wish I had put more effort into making that decision."

There are a number of ways to evaluate alternatives. One way is to list the pros and cons of each alternative. This often results in one alternative being identified as clearly superior to the others. Care should be taken, however, not to place too much emphasis on the number of pros and cons, but rather to consider the overall importance of those relating to each alternative.

Another way to evaluate alternatives is to determine the expected payoff associated with each alternative. This "payoff relationship" (which will be discussed later in the chapter) requires consideration of both costs and benefits. It is also necessary to consider the probability of occurrence of the expected payoff. For example, an alternative that offers a 50 percent probability of a $1 million payoff generally will be chosen over one with a ten percent probability of a $2 million payoff. Mathematical techniques to calculate expected payoffs are available, but they are beyond the scope of this chapter.

Choose and Implement the Best Alternative

The ability to select the best course of action from several possible alternatives often separates successful managers from less successful ones. The alternative offering the highest promise of attaining the objective, taking into consideration the overall situation, should be selected. This step may sound easy, but for managers it is the toughest part of the job. However sophisticated the selection technique followed, a manager can never be sure that the results of a decision will be favorable.

Fear of making a wrong decision sometimes causes a manager to make no decision at all. It is no wonder that relatively high salaries are paid to managers who have reputations for having the fortitude to make decisions and for making correct ones most of the time. It is easy to be a Monday morning quarterback and criticize the coach's decisions. The coach, however, has to make decisions on the football field under pressure of time; no coach has the luxury of knowing how those decisions will turn out.

It is easy to see how managers feel a responsibility not only to make correct decisions but also to ensure that those decisions are implemented properly. Even if decision making is not done in a crisis situation, the responsibility for implementation cannot be avoided. No matter how technically correct a decision is and how faithfully a manager follows the recommended process, the decision has no value except through its implementation.

Evaluate the Decision

No decision-making process is complete until the decision has been exposed to the realities of the business environment. Evaluation requires an objective assessment of how the decision has solved the problem or has taken advantage of the problem-turned-into-opportunity. This is particularly important for firms that stress decentralized management. In these companies, lower-level managers are allowed to become more involved in decision making. This provides junior managers with decision-making experience, improving their intuition and judgment.

The implementation of a decision does not complete the decision-making process. The arrows in Figure 4.1 indicate that there is constant reevaluation of and feedback to every phase of decision making. The outcome—whether good or bad—provides information that can contribute to future decisions.

❖ ❖ FACTORS AFFECTING DECISION MAKING

Many factors can have an impact on the manager's decision-making ability. Some of the more important ones, shown in Figure 4.2, are described here. All of these factors influence managers as they make decisions, though some are more important at higher levels than at lower levels and vice versa.

Routine Versus Nonroutine Decisions

Management decisions may range from minor ones such as picking a supplier of bathroom tissue (routine decision) to major ones such as whether to build a new plant or to enter a new business (nonroutine decisions).

Routine Decisions Most managers make numerous routine decisions in the performance of their jobs. These decisions are governed by the policies, procedures, and rules of the organization, as well as by the personal habits and preferences

❖ **Figure 4.2**
Factors affecting decision making

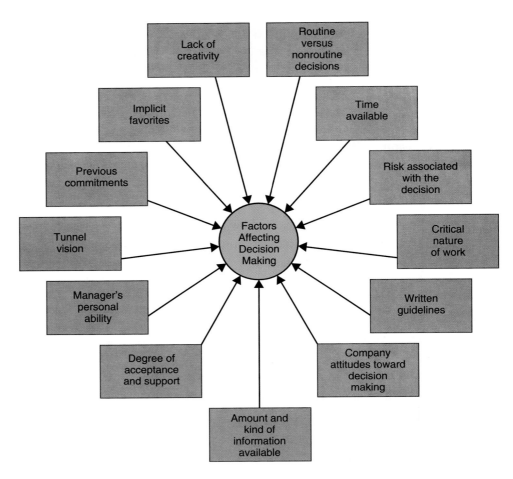

of managers. Managers certainly should not devote as much time to making routine decisions as they would to making nonroutine or more serious ones. It would be silly, for example, to follow a formal procedure in deciding whom to assign to a certain machine on a given day. Managers should be flexible in their decision making, just as in any other aspect of their job. They are little more than clerks if they simply adhere to the rule book and do not exercise some personal judgment for the betterment of all concerned.

Nonroutine Decisions Even though routine decisions may take up a considerable portion of a manager's time, individuals succeed or fail as managers on the basis of their nonroutine decisions. **Nonroutine decisions** are decisions that are designed to deal with unusual problems or situations. Whether or not to expand to foreign markets, to build a new production plant, or to buy a more advanced computer system—all are nonroutine decision situations. Nonroutine decisions are made by managers at all levels in the organization. Decisions made by a first-line supervisor might involve disciplining an employee or changing the layout or procedures in the department. But the nonroutine decisions that will result in the success or failure of the organization must be made by upper-level managers, including individuals such as the CEO, the president, or the owner.

Figure 4.3 illustrates the relationships of three levels of management and the amounts of routine and nonroutine decisions. As a manager progresses to higher levels, the number of nonroutine decisions increases. Nonroutine decisions require that managers exercise creativity and good judgment. John Bryan, Sara Lee's CEO, made a nonroutine decision to lead the company in a different direction; this decision was one that could only have been made by an upper-level manager.

Time Available

The amount of time that can be devoted to decision making is often a critical factor. Managers would prefer to have sufficient time to thoroughly evaluate and analyze all alternatives prior to making a decision, but few have this luxury. Decisions frequently must be made in time-pressure situations. As an example, assume that a customer of yours offers to make a large purchase at a low, though profitable, price. Assume further that the order must be accepted today or the buyer will go to another supplier. Even if you have good reasons to prefer taking your time with such decisions, you dare not do so.

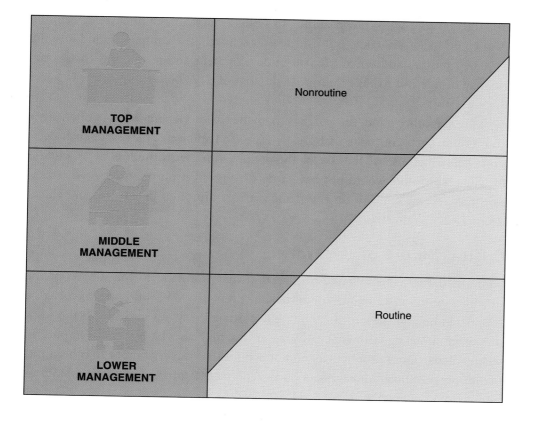

❖ **Figure 4.3**
Managerial levels and the relative amounts of routine and nonroutine decisions

New Products, New Decisions

Decision making becomes ever more complex when a company can no longer grow and gain market share in its primary business operation. Decisions relating to one business area can at times baffle even the best decision makers, but when executives accustomed to dealing with one type of business must go in a different direction they often encounter tremendous challenges.

John Bryan, Sara Lee's CEO, deliberated on his company's prospects in what had become a prolonged economic slump. He concluded that the 1990s would be tough for the mature U.S. food industry and that attracting additional market share would probably be too costly, if not impossible. As a result, Bryan decided that Sara Lee was going to take a different path into the 1990s. As Bryan put it, "We're not going to invest to grow the food business in the

'90s." Instead, Bryan decided that the company would nurture high-profile brands in packaged apparel, including everything from sweats to underwear, socks, brassieres, and hosiery. But Sara Lee was not totally stepping into new ground. The company has applied its brand-marketing know-how, using such blockbuster names as Playtex, Hanes, and Champion, to grab sales and market share. Sara Lee's market share rose to 30 percent, up from 17 percent in 1987.[6]

Risk Associated with the Decision

Decision risk is exposure to the probability that an incorrect decision will have an adverse effect on the organization. It is a factor that all managers consider, consciously or unconsciously, in decision making. For instance, Betty Harris, president of a small book publishing company, is considering paying an advance of $100,000 to a well-known author to write a book. If the book sells well, the firm could make $500,000. But if it doesn't sell well, the company could lose the $100,000 plus an additional $75,000 in development and promotion costs. Harris may decide not to take the risk if the loss of $175,000 could seriously harm the company.

On the other hand, the purchasing manager for General Motors often signs automobile parts contracts that greatly exceed $1 million. The risk in such decisions is low because of the size of the organization. Even the loss of $1 million for General Motors would not have a disastrous effect on the firm. As the decision risk increases, more time and more effort are often devoted to individual decisions.

Critical Nature of the Work

Some managers are in charge of a section that is critical to the success of the organization or to human life and health. Even where health is not involved, a mistake in one department may be quite costly or may adversely affect the work of several other departments. Adverse effects may also be especially important when a department produces a good or service that is a vital input to other units of the organization. Managers in such departments often find their operations under close scrutiny by upper-level managers.

Managers in critical areas should be especially careful and systematic in making decisions. They should, for example, document their decision-making processes, since they may be called on to explain them. A manager who is asked "Why did you do it that way?" will find it more comfortable to say, "We considered these three options and decided the first one was best on the basis of this written analysis," than to say, "It just seemed like a good idea at the time."

Written Guidelines

Some firms have extensive written guidelines covering virtually any situation. These guidelines, which are referred to as *policies, procedures, and rules,* are discussed in Chapter 5. A manager in a large organization may need only to check a written document to determine the proper course of action. A major part of the manager's decision-making effort is then constrained. Situations of this sort should not be viewed negatively, though. There is always room for creativity in areas where decisions have not been made by upper-level managers.

In a unionized firm, many of the supervisor's decisions are restricted by the labor-management agreement. For example, promotions may have to be based largely on seniority, making it hard for the supervisor to consider merit. When written disciplinary guidelines are present, disciplinary action decisions must be made in accordance with the agreement. The manager has little discretion in matters covered by the union agreement.

Company Attitudes Toward Decision Making

Some organizations encourage highly systematic decision making. Others lean toward a less formal approach. When the company's attitude is informal, a manager will probably not earn any credit by talking about the systematic decision process described early in this chapter. However, if top management follows and promotes a formal decision-making process, lower-level managers should certainly do the same. Many upper-level managers prefer to know the thought processes involved in a supervisor's decision. Given a choice, systematic decision making is usually best.

Amount and Kind of Information Available

The manager is either helped or hindered in decision making by the availability of information. Making decisions without knowing enough about the situation is risky. Certainly, simple decisions do not require exhaustive information. But specific information is necessary to decide how to handle a complex problem.

Managers can protect themselves from the problems caused by a lack of information by actively keeping up with everything related to their area of responsibility. Paying careful attention to communications of all kinds often pays off. Time spent reading technical manuals about equipment may be helpful. Discussing potential problems with workers and getting their input on possible solutions could lead to what will seem to be a stroke of genius later on. This is possibly why so many companies are becoming team oriented.

Information should be formally catalogued in some manner if it is to be available when needed. Managers cannot remember everything. Critical information should be put where it can be found quickly and easily. Of course, personal computers offer a handy way for managers to maintain ready access to a vast body of information.

Degree of Acceptance and Support by Equals and Superiors

At times, new managers are not immediately accepted. Reasons for lack of acceptance vary. Perhaps the manager is in a division where most of the other managers are much older, or perhaps the work group does not like outsiders. A similar concern may exist for a female manager who is in a male-dominated organization. If the acceptance and support by other managers is lacking, decision making will be affected, and it is up to the individual manager to overcome the problem.

A lack of acceptance on the part of subordinates can limit a manager's ability to make decisions and get them implemented. Solutions requiring close cooperation may not be feasible if subordinate acceptance is lacking. Perhaps the best way for a manager to gain acceptance is to earn subordinates' respect. Making an effort to improve communication and to involve workers in the decision-making process helps develop a feeling of mutual respect. The extremely successful Wal-Mart stores are distinguished by a top management approach that keeps employees closely informed about company plans and practices and includes them in corporate decision making. When Roberto C. Goizueta came to Coca-Cola, he gained a reputation for being a workaholic, coming to work early and staying late. It is clear that he earned respect by knowing his job and because of his willingness to put out extra effort to get work done. Any manager who wishes to gain subordinate acceptance and respect will, in all likelihood, have to work hard to get it.

The Manager's Personal Ability as a Decision Maker

Perhaps the most important factor affecting decision making is a manager's own ability and attitude. No matter how willing a manager is to make decisions and be responsible for them, it is the person's ability to make correct decisions that is essential for success. To some degree, this ability depends on following an appropriate decision-making process.

Perhaps the most important factor affecting decision making is a manager's own ability and attitude. (Source: © John Coletti)

A manager's own experiences and level of understanding also help determine the quality of decisions. Experience tends to be a good teacher. For example, many college recruiters emphasize the experience a student has gained from business and extracurricular activities. They believe the learning process for a particular job may be shortened if a student has been active in other endeavors while in college. But decision makers who rely only on their own experience may base their judgments mainly on their feel for the situation; and if they are confronted with unfamiliar situations, faulty decisions may result. Basing decisions only on experience has several obvious shortcomings, among them:

1. Learning from experience is usually random.
2. Although we may have experience, there is no guarantee that we have learned from it.
3. What we learn from experience is necessarily circumscribed by the limits of our experience.
4. Conditions change, and the past may not be a good indicator of current or future conditions.[7]

The question might be asked: Do you have 20 years of experience, or do you have one year of experience 20 times? Ralph C. Davis's classic statement summarizes the important need for a bond between experience and intellect in a professional decision maker: "A person who has nothing but background is a theorist. An individual who has nothing but practical experience is a business mechanic. A professionally trained executive is one in whom there is an effective integration of these two general types of experiences, combined with adequate intelligence regarding the types of problems with which the person must deal."[8]

Tunnel Vision

Tunnel vision is the extremely narrow viewpoint of people who have mental blinders, such as individual biases, that restrict the search for a solution to a narrow range of alternatives. For example, a male manager who has a bias against female managers may not even consider a well-qualified woman for such a job. To the extent that tunnel vision inhibits identifying additional and worthwhile alternatives, it has a detrimental effect on the decision-making process.

Previous Commitments

Decisions usually occur in sequence and therefore affect other decisions. Possibly the most difficult decision a person can make relates to choices about the fate of an entire sequence of decisions. Research indicates that people who feel personally responsible for a bad decision often tend to commit additional resources to that alternative. This escalating commitment makes it increasingly difficult to objectively evaluate other alternatives and to change the already initiated course of action.

Implicit Favorites

One researcher has shown that many people select a favorite alternative early in the decision-making process, but continue to evaluate additional solutions. Subsequent alternatives are therefore distorted perceptually—evaluated using decision criteria that emphasize the superiority of the preferred solution. The decision maker will process information in such a way that final selection of the implicit favorite is virtually guaranteed. Wal-Mart's implicit favorite decision is to always offer the best value for consumers. This decision impacts all related decisions made by Wal-Mart managers.

Lack of Creativity

Most people possess creative ability, which can be developed through training and application. **Creativity** is the ability to generate ideas that are both innovative and functional. This ability is an obvious requirement for managerial effectiveness, and is especially important in making nonroutine decisions.

Unfortunately, creativity rarely receives adequate attention in organizations. The first reason for this neglect is that organizational policies and procedures are usually designed to promote order, consistency, and uniformity, thereby limiting creativity. Second, managerial work is fast paced and action oriented, whereas creativity requires time for preparation, incubation, inspiration, and validation.[10] Finally, most individuals do not understand creativity, and therefore overlook it rather than advocating or reinforcing it.

❖ ❖ WORK TEAM AND GROUP METHODS INVOLVED IN DECISION MAKING

Up to this point, decision making has been discussed as if it were a process carried out by the individual manager. In most organizations, individuals are responsible for the outcomes of decisions under their control. Effective decisions generally combine high quality with acceptance by those affected by the decision. Groups and teams bring different resources to the decision-making task. For example, studies indicate that plants with work team systems that allow autoworkers real participation in decision making, such as General Motor's Saturn plant, produce better-quality cars more efficiently than do plants with traditional work systems. One of the most comprehensive approaches to team management and decision making is in effect at a small plant in La Porte, Texas, a subsidiary of Rohm and Haas Co., where all 67 employees are actively involved in decision making. Decisions include evaluating the performance of co-workers, hiring new employees, and even disciplining employees whose behavior they consider to be unacceptable.[11]

There are several techniques through which teams and groups can be involved in any stage of the decision-making process. Three of them are brainstorming, nominal grouping, and the Delphi technique.

Brainstorming

Brainstorming is the idea-generating technique in which a number of persons present alternatives without regard to questions of feasibility or practicality. In this technique, individuals are encouraged to identify a wide range of ideas. Usually, one individual is assigned to record the ideas on a chalkboard or writing pad. Brainstorming may be used at any stage of the decision-making process, but it is most effective at the beginning, once a problem has been stated. Sometimes, the alternatives produced through brainstorming may be rather bizarre. For example, if a brainstorming group were to consider how Coke might respond to a new Pepsi ad campaign, someone might suggest buying out PepsiCo. Building on this, another participant might suggest selling out to PepsiCo. No criticism is allowed, because the purpose of brainstorming is to come up with innovative possibilities. Evaluation can wait until later. It is not part of brainstorming.

Although brainstorming is useful for all types of decisions, it is most effective for simple, well-defined problems. It encourages enthusiasm and competitiveness among group members in generating ideas. It also prevents group members from feeling hopeless about the range of possibilities in a given situation. Brainstorming can result in many shallow and useless ideas, but it can spur members to offer terrific ideas as well. As will be noted in Chapter 17, brainstorming is an integral part of Total Quality Management.

Nominal Grouping

Nominal grouping represents an attempt to move toward a structured approach, which encourages individual creativity.[12] *Nominal* refers to the fact that members, acting independently, form a group in name only. An important feature of this technique is that it allows the members to meet face-to-face but does not restrict individual creativity, as traditional group discussions do. **Nominal grouping,** then, is the approach to decision making that involves idea generation by group members, group interaction only to clarify ideas, member rankings of ideas presented, and alternative selection by summing up the rankings. The steps, which are shown in Figure 4.4, are as follows:

1. *Statement of the problem.* After the nominal group is assembled, the group leader states the decision problem clearly and succinctly. No discussion is allowed, although group members may ask questions to clarify the problem.
2. *Idea generation.* Group members silently record and number their ideas for solving the problem.
3. *Round-robin recording.* The group members alternate in presenting their ideas while the group leader lists the ideas presented on a flip chart or chalkboard. This process continues without discussion until all of the ideas have been recorded.

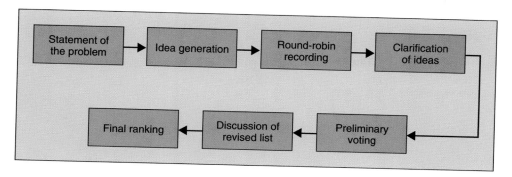

4. *Clarification of ideas.* Under the leader's guidance, group members question one another to clear up any confusion about what each idea means. No evaluation is allowed yet.

5. *Preliminary voting.* Each group member independently ranks what are considered the best of the decisions presented. The ideas that receive the lowest average ranking are eliminated from further consideration.

6. *Discussion of revised list.* Individual group members question one another to clarify the ideas that remain. The purpose is not to persuade but to understand.

7. *Final ranking.* Group members rank all of the ideas. The one with the highest total ranking is adopted.

Delphi Technique

The **Delphi technique** is the formal procedure for obtaining the consensus of a number of experts through the use of a series of questionnaires. The procedure is similar to nominal grouping, but participants do not meet. In fact, ideally, the experts do not know who else is involved. The steps in the Delphi technique, which are shown in Figure 4.5, are as follows:

1. The problem is presented to group members by means of a questionnaire that asks them to provide potential solutions.
2. Each expert completes and returns the questionnaire.
3. The results are compiled and provided to the experts, along with a revised and more specific questionnaire.
4. The experts complete the second questionnaire.
5. The process continues until a consensus emerges.

The Delphi technique prevents the individual respondents from being influenced by the personalities of the other participants and at the same time allows for the free sharing of ideas. This method of decision making was conceived by the Rand Corporation to forecast how seriously a nuclear attack would affect the United States. It is an expensive and time-consuming way to reach a consensus, which is why its use has generally been limited only to important and futuristic ideas.

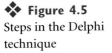

❖ **Figure 4.5**
Steps in the Delphi
technique

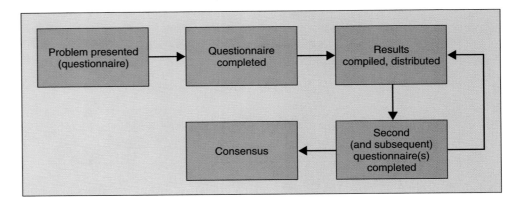

The Delphi technique is most useful in those instances where

- The problem does not lend itself to precise analytical techniques, but can benefit from subjective judgments on a collective basis.
- The individuals needed to contribute to the examination of a broad or complex problem have no history of adequate communication and may represent diverse backgrounds with respect to experience or expertise.
- More individuals are needed than can effectively interact in a face-to-face exchange.
- Time and cost make frequent group meetings infeasible.
- The efficiency of face-to-face meetings can be increased by a supplemental group communication process.
- Disagreements among individuals are so severe or politically unpalatable that the communication process must be refereed or anonymity assured.
- The heterogeneity of the participants must be preserved to assure validity of the results; that is, domination by quantity or by strength of personality ("band-wagon effect") must be avoided.[13]

❖ ❖ DECISION-MAKING REQUIREMENTS

Perhaps no other attribute so frequently distinguishes the excellent manager from mediocre ones as does the ability to make wise and innovative decisions. However, as Figure 4.6 shows, the good manager must also meet certain requirements if the decision-making process is to be carried out effectively.

Decision Maker

When Harry Truman was President of the United States, he kept on his desk a plaque that stated, "The buck stops here." He was the person responsible, and he made the final decision. The role of decision maker may be assumed by an individual or by a group of individuals, depending on how the organization is managed. The decision maker must choose from among a group of alternatives, a task

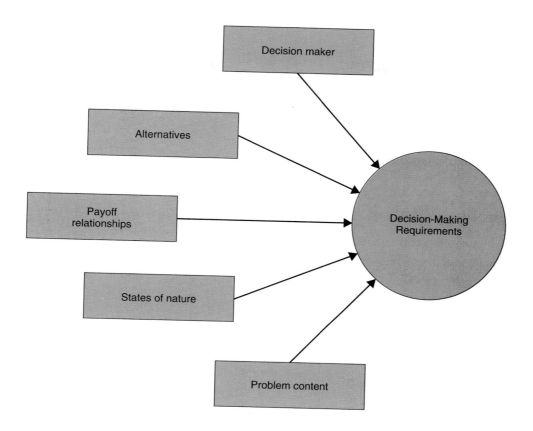

many individuals do not like. Contrary to some thinking, not everyone enjoys making decisions, even when charged with the responsibility to do so. Certainly this is not the case with Coca-Cola chief executive Robert Goizueta.

Alternatives

To have a decision problem, the decision maker must have more than one alternative to choose from. Alternatives may be many or few in number. They may merely represent the option of doing something or doing nothing. A good decision maker, however, attempts to identify and evaluate as many alternatives as possible within time and resource restrictions.

Payoff Relationships

In the **payoff relationship,** alternatives are evaluated in terms of their potential benefits or costs. Ultimately, the decision maker should attempt to choose the decision that will either maximize benefits or minimize costs. When the profits and costs associated with a particular alternative cannot be expressed in dollar amounts, the decision maker suffers. For example, decision making is much easier if one can state that a particular decision will result in a savings of $50,000, as compared with merely expressing the opinion that costs will be lowered.

States of Nature

States of nature are the various situations that could occur and the probability of each of them occurring. For example, we have all heard weather forecasters say, "There is a 20 percent chance of rain." The 20 percent chance of rain is one state of nature, and the 80 percent chance of no rain is the other. Good decision makers study situations thoroughly in the hope that their decisions will be correct more often than not. Because of the state of doubt, it is likely that decision makers will never be 100 percent correct.

Problem Content

The **problem content** includes the environment in which the problem exists, the decision maker's knowledge of that environment, and the environment that will exist after a choice is made. Because the environment is taken into consideration in decision making, a decision that may be considered proper in one organization may be improper in another. For example, managers in two firms producing similar products and presented with the same problem may make different decisions because of the internal environment each faces. One firm may encourage risk taking by managers, thereby permitting even lower-level managers to make important decisions. Another firm may want to have this type of decision approved by upper-level management. Even though a lower-level manager in the second firm might be perfectly capable of making the decision, the situation does not permit it.

A Decision-Making Problem

To understand how the components of decision making interact, imagine how a student (the decision maker) might choose a part-time job. Suppose the student needs to take a job to supplement her financial aid. She needs to analyze each element of decision making with regard to its requirements. The only available jobs are at a recently opened pizza restaurant. The two job alternatives are pizza baker and assistant manager.

The payoff for each position is different. The baker receives an hourly wage of $4.35, no matter what the level of sales. However, the assistant manager's payoff is $8 an hour for high sales, $6 an hour for average sales, and $1 an hour for low sales.

Because the restaurant is relatively new, its sales potential has not been established. However, the student, relying on her experience in the community, estimates that there is a 20 percent chance of high sales, a 50 percent chance of average sales, and a 30 percent chance of low sales. These states of nature will have a major impact on the amount of money the assistant manager will receive.

A Skill-Building Exercise: You have been put in charge of phase I of the new production process. This phase makes or breaks the rest of the production operation. If production quality and quantity standards are not met, the entire process will fail to meet the rigid time and quality restrictions placed on it by the client. You have been given two alternatives by the vice-president of operations. You can get a new semiautomated machine that will replace seven of the twelve people on your line and will assure the success of the project. The machine has allowed three of your competitors to exceed the standards you will be required to meet. Or you can keep all twelve employees on the line and attempt to retrain and motivate them to achieve the standards. These employees have never been able to meet such high standards, but they have never been formally trained either. If you fail to assure that phase I of the production process is successful, you will seriously jeopardize your career. If you get rid of seven employees, morale will be hurt, and you will be firing several people you have known for many years. **What is your decision?**

Now the student is in a position to evaluate the two alternatives. One technique for doing so is known as "determining expected value," and the computation is as follows:

Expected earnings (pizza baker) $= .2(\$4.35) + .5(\$4.35) + .3(\$4.35) = \$4.35$

Expected earnings (assistant manager) $= .2(\$8) + .5(\$6) + .3(\$1) = \$4.90$

If the student prefers the alternative with the higher expected value, she should accept the assistant manager position (expected value of $4.90 per hour, versus the $4.35 per hour guaranteed by the other position).

But one factor remains to be examined—the problem content. There may be other facts to consider before a decision is made. The student's financial situation may prevent her from taking the chance of receiving only $1 per hour if sales are poor. On the other hand, the individual may desire the status of being an assistant manager. Although numerous other considerations may also come into play, this example should provide some insight into the factors involved in decision making.

❖ ❖ WORKER PARTICIPATION AND THE DECISION-MAKING PROCESS

Although participation as a factor in corporate culture will be discussed in Chapter 15, participation as involved in the decision-making process is discussed here. **Worker participation** is the process of involving workers in the decision-making process. It is projected that worker participation in the future will go far beyond the level of participation we know today. In the future, employees will not only participate in decision making but will also be encouraged to analyze and solve problems. Most managers assume that they must be either participative or non-participative when involving workers in decision making. That is not necessarily the case, since the degree of worker participation generally differs in each step of the process.

As can be seen in Figure 4.7, worker participation may be high in some steps and low in others. In one situation, workers might participate extensively in identifying the decision-making opportunity and developing alternatives, but take almost no part in making and evaluating the decision. In other situations or with other managers, the pattern of participation might be entirely different.

Virtually every manager receives some input from employees before making important decisions. From a motivational standpoint, encouraging input is probably useful only when the employees believe they play a meaningful part in the process. The manager should be completely honest about this. If a decision has already been made, the manager should not ask employees for advice about making it. Employees should be consulted only when they have information or insight that will help managers make better decisions.

❖ **Figure 4.7**
Worker participation and the decision-making process

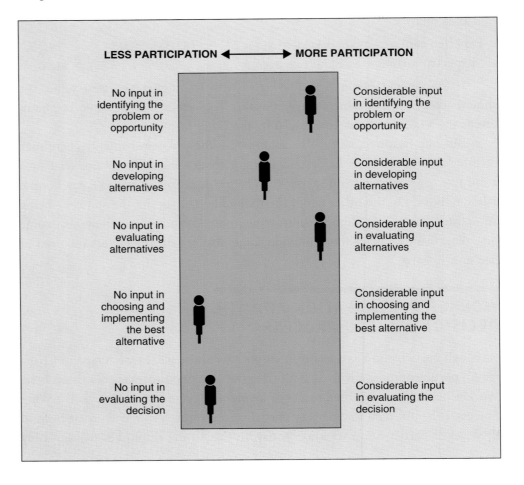

LESS PARTICIPATION ◀━━▶ **MORE PARTICIPATION**

No input in identifying the problem or opportunity — Considerable input in identifying the problem or opportunity

No input in developing alternatives — Considerable input in developing alternatives

No input in evaluating alternatives — Considerable input in evaluating alternatives

No input in choosing and implementing the best alternative — Considerable input in choosing and implementing the best alternative

No input in evaluating the decision — Considerable input in evaluating the decision

❖ ❖ HOW MANAGERS CAN HANDLE DECISION MAKING IN A CRISIS

No matter how well managers plan, they often find themselves in crisis situations. Decisions in such situations are significantly more important, urgent, and risky than usual. For instance, suppose a piece of equipment has broken down on Thursday afternoon and the manager has to get a crucial order out by Friday. Or suppose the manager has just heard that a group of senior executives is going to inspect the work area, and only one day is available to prepare. Effective managers should not be afraid of such crises. Rather, they should see them as providing opportunities to show exceptional competence. The successful handling of one crisis might earn a manager as much respect as would several years of good performance.

A few things should not be done, but often are, in a crisis situation. First, some managers pretend that nothing unusual is happening and conduct business as usual. They may prefer not to see the problem. Second, some managers overreact in crises. They take more extreme action than is needed to solve the problem. Calling everyone in on overtime when one worker would be sufficient is an example. Third, managers sometimes treat a crisis decision like any other decision. This type of decision is different, however, because of its importance, urgency, and riskiness. The manager must exert more than usual effort—perhaps

Managers must understand the nature of the market in which they compete. Considerations of both internal and external factors are important because variations in any of these factors can adversely affect decision making. These petroleum geologists study a seismic "map," which shows the density layers of the earth's crust in different colors. On a global perspective, it is equally as important for managers to consider the external environment to make the best decisions. (Source: Photograph courtesy of Atlantic Richfield Corporation.)

A GLOBAL PERSPECTIVE

Quality Business Decisions Result in Global Business Success

Decision making does not occur in a vacuum. Managers must consider both internal and external factors, because variations in any of these factors can adversely affect decision making. Operating in the multinational environment further complicates the decision-making process. It is important for managers to understand the nature of the market in which they compete. Frederick W. Smith, founder of Federal Express Corporation, lost the company millions of dollars when he expanded into the overseas market because his decisions were based on competing in the American market. For many years, Procter & Gamble (P&G) managers decided to develop products for the U.S. market and to use American-style advertising and marketing to push the products in Japan. Such decisions led to more than $200 million in losses in 16 years. Then P&G hired more Japanese, became more closely attuned to the local ways of the Japanese, and focused on doing what was necessary to capture market share from Japanese firms.[14] Both Federal Express and P&G are currently quite competitive overseas, but starting off with poor decisions is more and more risky in today's global business environment.

Experienced decision makers often sidestep such problems by making excellent decisions right from the start. Thomas Kalinske, CEO of Sega of America, epitomized what a global decision maker should be. When Kalinske became CEO in 1990, he flew to Tokyo to see Hayao Nakayama, head of parent company Sega Enterprises. He told Nakayama that the price of Sega Genesis must be cut by $50, and that he must be allowed to bundle their best software and advertise to the world that Sega is better than the competition. Nakayama was somewhat shook up, but he stood up and told him that "I hired you to make the decisions in the U.S., so do what you want to do." Kalinske has a major advantage over his competitor, Minoru Arakawa of Nintendo of America, who cannot make on-the-spot decisions. The result of Kalinske's quick and informed decisions has been to overcome Nintendo's market dominance, with Sega having nearly 52 percent of the 16-bit market.[15] This once again proves that quality and quick and informed business decisions pay off in greater market dominance.

working overtime, being more disciplined, or laying aside less urgent or less important matters.

What should be done? There are some guidelines that will help managers handle crises effectively. First, managers should be on the lookout for situations that could become critical. It may be possible to prevent a crisis from occurring. For instance, suppose a supervisor has heard that a large order is expected shortly. It might be worthwhile to alert workers about the expected overtime so they will not make other plans. Also, good machine maintenance will help prevent crises caused by breakdowns. In addition, proper attention to the needs of workers will help prevent people-related crises.

Second, managers should stay calm during crises. If the manager panics, workers may also panic. Managers can provide a calming influence. They should be careful to react appropriately, but not excessively, to any situation. Nowhere is

---

✗ Management Tips ✗

Guidelines for Decision Making

1. **Be decisive when making decisions.** Everyone respects a person who makes good decisions, communicates them effectively, and stands by them.

2. **Do not waste time regretting the failure of past decisions.** Remember that no one will ever be 100 percent accurate.

3. **Learn from the results of past decisions.** It has been said that good managers make a particular mistake only once. Others make the same mistake over and over and wonder what keeps going wrong.

4. **Keep a little levity in your attitude.** Sometimes you have to just laugh it off. It may be the best thing to do when you make a dumb mistake.

5. **Do not reinvent the wheel.** Your problems may be new to you, but others in the company have probably encountered similar ones. Ask them for advice. Most will consider this a compliment.

6. **Let the decision roll around in your mind.** Time permitting, sleep on it overnight. Then, if you still believe it is the proper decision, make it.

7. **Do not let the desire to have the decision made fast cause you to make a poor decision.** Too often, we rush a decision just to get it over with. If you need and have more time, consider this an opportunity.

8. **Do not treat all decisions the same way.** Decisions differ in their importance, urgency, and riskiness to the decision maker.

9. **Do not procrastinate.** If a decision needs to be made, make it. Making an acceptable decision in time is better than making a perfect decision too late.

10. **If time permits, get input from others.** They may suggest some alternatives that have not been considered.

---

this more important than in a hospital emergency room, where a doctor may supervise the work of several interns and nurses caring for accident victims.

Third, managers should accept the fact that in times of crisis there is additional risk. The solution to the problem may have to be an innovative one. Fear of making a mistake may prevent the manager from making the decision in time to do any good. There may not be time to go through a formal decision-making process. The manager may have to make a quick decision and live with it.

Finally, managers should remember Murphy's Law: If anything can go wrong, it will. Murphy's Law is not an excuse for pessimism. But managers who keep it in mind might be better prepared to handle the crises that inevitably occur. Managers should try to have plan B ready for the predictable crisis.

SUMMARY

Decision making is the process of generating and evaluating alternatives and making choices among them. Some people view decision making only as problem solving; however, problems are usually better treated as opportunities. Often the distinction between a problem and an opportunity is not clear. In any event, no decision-making process is complete until the decision has been exposed to the realities of the business environment. The phases of the decision-making process are: identifying the problem or opportunity, developing alternatives, evaluating alternatives, choosing and implementing the best alternative, and evaluating the decision.

Decisions may be routine or nonroutine. Many other factors may also affect a manager's decision making: the time available, the risk associated with the decision, the critical nature of the work, written guidelines, company attitudes toward decision making, the amount and kind of information available, the degree of acceptance and support by equals and superiors, the manager's personal ability as a decision maker, tunnel vision, previous commitments, implicit favorites, and lack of creativity.

Teams and groups can be involved in any stage of the decision-making process. Three ways that teams and groups may be involved in the decision making process are: brainstorming, nominal grouping, and the Delphi Technique.

There are certain decision-making requirements, including the decision maker, alternatives, payoff relationships, states of nature, and problem content. Evaluating alternatives in terms of their potential benefits or costs is the payoff relationship. States of nature are the various situations that could occur and the probability of each of them occurring. The problem content is the environment in which the problem exists, the decision maker's knowledge of it, and the environment that will exist after the choice is made.

Worker participation is the process of involving workers in the decision-making process. It is projected that worker participation will go far beyond the level of participation we know today. Most managers as-

KEY TERMS

Decision making 108	Nominal grouping 122
Alternatives 111	Delphi technique 123
Nonroutine decisions 114	Payoff relationship 125
Decision risk 116	States of nature 126
Tunnel vision 120	Problem content 126
Creativity 120	Worker participation 127
Brainstorming 122	

REVIEW QUESTIONS

1. Define <u>decision making</u> and identify the steps in the decision-making process.
2. Explain what is meant by the following statement: "The ability to select the best course of action from several possible alternatives often separates successful managers from less successful ones."
3. The text identifies several factors that affect decision making. Briefly discuss each factor.
4. Define each of the following terms:
   a. brainstorming
   b. nominal grouping
   c. Delphi technique
5. Briefly describe each of the requirements that must be present before the decision-making process can be carried out.
6. Describe how worker participation may differ in each step of the decision-making process.
7. How can managers handle decision making in a crisis situation?

sume that they must be either participative or non-participative when involving workers in decision making, but this is not always true.

No matter how well managers plan, they often find themselves in crisis situations. Decisions in such situations are significantly more important, urgent, and risky than usual. Effective managers should not be afraid of such crises. Rather, they should see them as providing opportunities to show exceptional competence. The successful handling of one crisis might earn a manager as much respect as would several years of good performance.

CASE STUDIES

CASE 4.1 Expansion Plans for The Toggery

Nan Rabinowitz, president of The Toggery, Inc., and a member of the board of directors, felt she already had two strikes against her. She knew expansion from Massachusetts into the other New England states was a good idea. But getting the mandate she needed from the rest of the board was going to be difficult. Nan thought two other members of the five-member board favored her position, but two were adamantly opposed. And Nan was unwilling to move ahead without unanimity.

The Toggery operated 14 men's clothing stores in Massachusetts. It was a family business, owned equally by Audrey and Lewis Simone and Sheila and Marc Crown. Audrey and Sheila started the business in 1980 with just one store. By 1983, they had eight stores, all profitable. That year Lewis left his job with Raytheon and joined The Toggery as vice-president and member of the board of directors. At that time, Audrey was president and Sheila was vice-president. Marc joined the board of directors that same year but continued to work full-time at BayBank Middlesex, where he was chief executive. Marc was a well-known community leader in Waltham, Massachusetts, the Boston suburb where The Toggery was headquartered. Among many other civic activities, he served as chairman of the United Way campaign in 1988 and president of the Waltham Chamber of Commerce in 1989.

Nan had worked as an executive with Filene's Department Stores for several years before joining The Toggery in 1989. She directed the company as it grew from ten stores to 14, all in Massachusetts, and took credit for doubling The Toggery's profits. Her plan in early 1993 was for the company to open four new stores that year in Vermont and to move into other states later. All The Toggery stores were rental units in neighborhood shopping centers, and that was not expected to change.

As Nan planned for the August director's meeting, she remembered a recent conversation with Marc Crown. Marc had said, "I am not willing for us to borrow any more money until we have our present operation clear of debt." Nan had argued that expansion was not possible without more borrowing, but Marc had refused to budge. Nan did not understand how a banker could feel that way, especially because The Toggery had much less debt than most similar companies. But she knew that if she could convince Marc, the others would go along.

When the meeting night arrived, Nan had prepared a very professional presentation on her proposal. After she went over it with the other directors, the following interchange occurred:

Marc: I'm still opposed. What do you think, Audrey?

Audrey: Nan has put a lot of work into this. She has a tough job trying to mediate among all of us. I think we owe her a vote of confidence.

Sheila: Marc, I usually go along with you, and I will this time. But if Lewis and Audrey are in favor, I don't think we should stand in the way.

Marc: Lewis, you and Audrey have talked about this, haven't you? Are you in agreement?

Lewis: Well, when we came here tonight, I think Audrey and I were both inclined to stay in Massachusetts. But Nan's excellent analysis has obviously changed Audrey's mind, and I could go either way.

The discussion continued for about an hour, but no decision was made. It was clear to Nan that everyone except Marc really wanted to accept her proposal, although Lewis remained equivocal.

Nan called Marc the next morning and asked if they could have lunch together. "Of course, Nan," said Marc, "I think we need to talk. The others have given me their proxies on the expansion decision, and maybe we can lay that to rest." Nan resolved that if Marc was not willing to approve her plan, she would resign and go into the business herself. She had several wealthy friends who were aware of her excellent success in managing The Toggery and would probably jump at a chance to invest in any venture she started.

QUESTIONS

1. What factors should Nan consider in deciding whether to go into business for herself?
2. Evaluate the board of director's decision-making effort.

CASE 4.2 Deere and Company: Modernizing to Survive

The farm machinery industry was failing in the mid-1980s. Massey Ferguson was threatening bankruptcy. International Harvester, the giant of the business, was in dismal shape. Of seven domestic full-line farm equipment makers in 1984, only three would survive the decade.

But even in 1984, Deere & Company, maker of the green "John Deere" tractors familiar to most Americans, was spending millions of dollars to adopt the latest manufacturing technologies. This was especially the case at Deere's complex of factories at Waterloo, Iowa. There, the company had undertaken a major capital development program that produced the following new or modernized facilities: Product Engineering Center, Engine Works, Component Works, and Tractor Works.

Even more important changes were instituted at the other three factories: the Component Works, Engine Works, and Tractor Works, the last two of which were built on so-called greenfield sites (sites in outlying rural areas). The Tractor Works was viewed by many as one of the most modern among U.S. factories: it received design awards for its computer integration from the prestigious Society of Manufacturing Engineers.

The Component Works featured a wide range of manufacturing innovations. Among the largest of the firm's factories, it housed one of the world's largest and most efficient flexible manufacturing systems (FMS). Sixteen separate computer-controlled machining centers automatically machine a large variety of castings, such as transmission cases, in random sequence. More than a dozen of these large castings moved about within this system simultaneously. The parts went from operation to operation on computer-directed carriers.

The FMS was unique among farm equipment makers in its ability to perform automatically so many functions on very large parts. The system enabled Deere to introduce new or redesigned parts into manufacturing rapidly with very little cost for retooling. It thus permitted the company to respond quickly to a changing market with new products or to act swiftly to meet customer demand for components.

The massive technology update at Waterloo, coupled with similar capital programs at other Deere factories, was designed to assure that the company would maintain a firm grip on its position as the industry's low-cost manufacturer. Not only did the advances give Deere distinct advantages over its traditional competitors, but they also brought the ability to compete on a price-and-delivery basis with so-called short-liners—companies that made only one or two farm implements on a high-volume, low-cost basis. Deere has some of the most up-to-date manufacturing facilities in the world—in any industry.

But such automated facilities were efficient only at high production levels. And in 1987 the Waterloo plant was operating below one-fourth capacity. Deere was still waiting for the resurgence it had expected in the farm economy. In contrast to the situation for less-robotized competitors, little could be saved by shutting down Deere factories. But the payroll had been slashed by 40 percent since 1980.

By 1989, solid recovery was underway. Many farmers could wait no longer to replace their equipment, which averaged twelve years old. Suddenly, Deere was buzzing, capturing 55 percent of the revitalized market. Deere's share price more than doubled from its 1986 low and analysts were shouting, "Buy! Buy!"

QUESTIONS

1. What environmental factors affected the decision-making process at Deere and Company?
2. Evaluate Deere and Company's decision to modernize its facilities.

NOTES

1. This case is a composite of a number of accounts, among them: Standard and Poor's Corporation, "Coca-Cola," *Standard NYSE Stock Reports* 56 (May 9, 1989): sec. 7; John H. Taylor, "Some Things Don't Go Better with Coke," *Forbes* 147 (March 21, 1988): 34–35; Thomas Moore, "He Put the Kick Back into Coke," *Fortune* 122 (October 26, 1987): 46–56; Peter Waldman, "Coke Enterprises Had Disappointing Fourth-Period Net," *The Wall Street Journal* (February 3, 1989): C14; Alison L. Sprout, "America's Most Admired Corporations," *Fortune* 126 (February 11, 1991): 57–58; Michael J. McCarthy, "Coca-Cola Is Facing New Pepsi Challenge: Avoiding Signs of Age," *The Wall Street Journal* (October 1, 1991): A1; Chuck Hawkins, "From Souped-Up to Bottled Gold," *Business Week* (July 19, 1993): 10; Laura Zinn, "For Coke's Peter Sealey, Hollywood Is It," *Business Week* (March 15, 1993): 84.

2. David Kirkpatrick, "Could AT&T Rule the World?" *Fortune* 127, (May 17, 1993): 54–66.

3. Andrew E. Serwer, "America's 100 Fastest Growers," *Fortune* 128 (August 9, 1993): 40–56.

4. David Woodruff, James B. Treece, Sunita Wadekar Bhargava, and Karen Lowry Miller, "Saturn," *Business Week* (August 17, 1992): 88–89; Catherine Arnst and Mark Lewyn, "Stand Back, Big Blue—And Wish Me Luck," *Business Week* (August 17, 1992): 100.

5. Jeremy Main, "B-Schools Get a Global Vision," *Fortune* 124 (July 17, 1989): 78–86.

6. Kathleen Madigan, Julia Flynn, and Joseph Weber, "Masters of the Game," *Business Week* (October 12, 1992): 110–118.

7. Adapted from Alvar O. Elbing, *Behavioral Decisions in Organizations* (Glenview, IL: Scott, Foresman, 1970), p. 14.

8. Ralph C. Davis, *The Fundamentals of Top Management* (New York: Harper & Row, 1951), p. 55.

9. Bob Ortega, "Wal-Mart Loses Predatory-Pricing Case in Arkansas Court but Plans to Appeal, *The Wall Street Journal* (October 13, 1993, Vol. XCII, No. 73): A, A3.

10. C. Patrick, *What Is Creative Thinking?* (New York: Philosophical Library, 1955).

11. D. Keith Denton, "Multi-Skilled Teams Replace Old Work Systems," *HRMagazine* 37 (September 1992): 48–56.

12. A. L. Delbecq and A. H. Van de Ven, "A Group Process Model for Problem Identification and Program Planning," *Journal of Applied Behavioral Science* 7 (1971): 466–492.

13. *Ibid.*

14. "Mr. Smith Goes Global," *Business Week* (February 13, 1989): 58, and Zachary Schiller, Ted Holden, and Mark Maremont, "P&G Global by Acting like a Global," *Business Week* (August 28, 1989): 58.

15. Nikhil Hutheesing, "Games Companies Play," *Forbes* 152 (October 25, 1993): 68–69.

5 The Planning Process

LEARNING OBJECTIVES

After completing this chapter students should be able to

✘ Describe the planning process and explain the function of a mission statement.

✘ State the importance of objectives and describe plans.

✘ Explain standing plans, explain the levels of planning, and describe the planning process for lower-level managers.

✘ Describe contingency planning.

✘ Describe management by objectives (MBO), explain the essential elements of the MBO process, and assess the overall effectiveness of MBO programs.

AT&T's Mission-Centered Focus Expands into International Markets

In seven years under the direction of CEO Robert E. Allen, AT&T more than doubled its earnings and increased revenues substantially. This is excellent performance for a company that was shocked into a top management transition when former chief executive James Olson died in 1988. Allen immediately took charge of AT&T, and in spite of his personal grief maintained the company's leadership position in the industry.

He was thrust to the helm—with only the knowledge that he must hold it steady, without a plan for the course he would steer. He had no firm plan for dealing with the sudden void that was created at AT&T, and therefore he was not ready to act immediately. However, he found the direction he needed and has been very successful. Analysts give Allen credit for changing the corporate culture to a more adaptive one and for recruiting a cadre of good, young executives, ensuring smooth management succession into the twenty-first century. A former chairman said of Allen, "He is an orderly person. He knows the business well. It is good for AT&T to have a steady person now."

Allen is indeed a steady person who plans to accomplish AT&T's number one mission: growth. This mission is not speculation, but a perfectly clear statement of what AT&T is going to do. Allen is never satisfied with the previous year's revenue increase because his focus is on growth. To achieve this mission, he recruited experienced top managers from outside the company. According to Allen, planning in the old Bell System was easy: Thick manuals provided procedures for every possible eventuality, and it didn't take a whole lot of strategy to succeed. However, today's competitive environment requires solid planning and effective management. Allen put his plan into action, hiring a few successful top managers and working with them to plan a course for the future to allow AT&T to achieve its mission of growth.

In 1993, Allen expanded his plans to accomplish his long-held mission of growth abroad. Currently, AT&T has a 20 percent stake in Canadian long-distance provider United Communications Inc.; an 80 percent stake in Poland's

Telfa; a 60 percent share in the Chinese fiber-optical venture; a 50 percent stake in Tata Telecom Ltd. in India; a 68 percent stake in Dalnya Sviaz of St. Petersburg; and a 19.5 percent stake in the design, building, and operation of the Ukraine's long-distance network. Then, with his mission firmly in focus he took the riskiest and most expensive leap abroad for AT&T, making a sweeping agreement with China to modernize their creaky phone system. With a firm commitment to planning and an unchanging mission of controlled growth, Allen continues to successfully guide AT&T.[1]

Planning is central to the success of any company, including AT&T. As the AT&T example suggests, planning in a competitive environment is much more than following well-established procedures. The mission must be clearly understood, and effective managers must be in place to accomplish it. AT&T's chairman and CEO Robert Allen has a clear picture of the company's mission of growth, which is communicated throughout the organization. Specific objectives are established in each unit, and a proven manager is in place to keep all units of the organization contributing to AT&T's overall mission.

This chapter begins with a brief overview of the planning process. Next it discusses the elements of the planning process—mission, objectives, and plans—in detail. The remainder of the chapter is devoted to the following planning topics: standing plans, the levels of planning, the planning process, contingency planning, succession planning, a global perspective of effective planning, and management by objectives.

❖ ❖ THE PLANNING PROCESS

Planning is the process of determining in advance what should be accomplished and how it should be realized. Figure 5.1 illustrates the planning process and serves as a guide for planning. The process applies to planning done by managers at all levels. As the figure indicates, planning begins with an understanding of the organizational mission. From the mission statement, specific objectives (or goals) can be established; then plans can be developed to accomplish them. Remember that AT&T's number one mission is growth. Plans are being developed to accomplish this mission. The planning process is dynamic. It must continually be evaluated and adapted to conform to the unfolding situation that management confronts. Often when companies merge, their mission statements must be reevaluated to assure that one overall vision exists for the new company. The merger of Chemical Bank and Manufacturers Hanover Corporation necessitated the formulation of a new mission statement. To arrive at the new mission statement, Walter V. Shipley and John F. McGillicuddy, the bank's two vice-chairmen, teamed up with a consultant for three days in Chemical's corporate suite at the

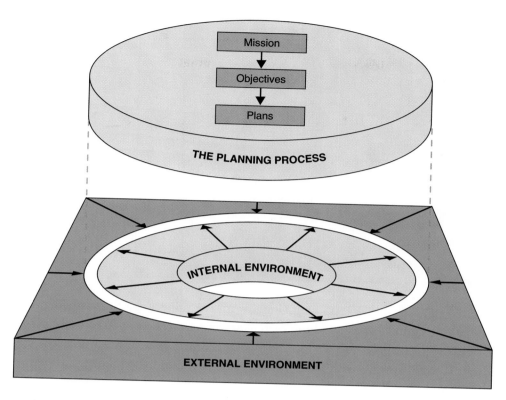

Waldorf-Astoria. These three individuals produced a clear summary description of the bank they hoped to build, and their mission statement included "developing the best broad-based financial institution, a leader in our chosen markets."[2]

Planning is vital to all firms. Effective planning can have a major impact on individual, group, and organizational productivity. Planning is becoming more and more complex as a global economy becomes a greater reality. Major U.S. companies are seeking ways to become more competitive internationally.

Planning provides direction; reduces the overall impact of change; increases productivity; and allows managers to organize, lead, control, and direct the activities necessary to accomplish organizational objectives. The need for planning exists at all levels, but is extremely important at higher levels, where the potential for impact on organizational success is greater. Top-level managers like AT&T's Robert Allen plan for the future, thereby allowing the entire organization to crystallize its strategies. Once upper-level strategies are well defined and understood, lower-level managers can plan to accomplish the objectives of their units. If one were to isolate the most significant reason for planning, it would be the fact that most studies show that managers who plan outperform nonplanners on traditional financial measures, such as profits.[3]

The elements of the organization's environment, as shown in Figure 5.1, are dynamic. For example, the Boston city government decided to dismantle an old

The need for planning is important for all managers in an organization. (Source: © Dennis Hallinan/FPG International)

elevated railway (called "The El"). Underneath the railway, traffic was being disrupted during the project, and the merchants along the street had to make plans to remain in business. A fish market owner planned to take out a loan so the business could survive with lower profits for a time. And the manager of a grocery store rearranged his store so a side entrance could be used. The external environment that organizations confront when moving into the international market is often even greater.

Planning: A Weapon for Business Survival in Mainland China

Planning reduces the overall impact of change and allows managers to organize, lead, control, and direct the activities necessary to accomplish organizational objectives. This concept is being stretched to the extreme in Hong Kong, where business tycoons are dealing with the overwhelming change of being absorbed into the empire of mainland China in 1997. The plan to colonize mainland China before Hong Kong becomes part of the empire is quite fanciful. It appears that a "free-market" China is what Hong Kong businessmen desire. Pao's Wharf Limited is involved in a project to make the industrial city Wuhan into the "Chicago of China" over the next two decades. Another target is Guangdong Province, with its cheap labor and eager workforce. Investment has poured in and so have thousands of small makers of electronics, garments, and toys. Free-market reforms are spreading from Guangdong to cities beyond the coast. Megadeals are brewing to build skyscrapers, shopping malls, and American-style suburbs. Even the Chinese leader Deng Xiaoping has embraced free-market reforms and foreign investment. Also coming are six-lane superhighways, huge amusement parks, and massive transportation terminals. The plan is to control the environment that Hong Kong tycoons and businessmen must live with in 1997, and open up countless opportunities for growth and profit. It is already beginning to succeed because "Guangdong already is looking a little too much like Hong Kong," according to *Business Week*. The plan to colonize mainland China is well underway, and the environment is seemingly under control.[4]

❖ ❖ MISSION

The **mission** is a unit's continuing purpose, or reason for being. The number one mission at AT&T is growth in the communication field. The **mission statement** is a broadly stated definition of the basic purpose and scope of a unit. A clear statement of mission serves to guide individuals, groups, and managers throughout the organization. The mission may not need to be published externally, but it should be understood by managers at all levels. A mission statement should be established for the entire company and for each department or unit in it. At Duracell, CEO Robert Kidder envisions producing batteries both domestically and internationally for portable consumer electronics for the cordless home of the future.[5] Naturally, the mission of each unit should be in agreement with the organizational mission. The question that needs to be answered to develop an appropriate mission statement is: For what reason is this unit in existence? Each unit

---

MANAGEMENT IN PRACTICE

A Skill-Building Exercise: Cecil Ross was the maintenance supervisor for Devon Products Company, a Knoxville, Tennessee, producer of plastic pipe and fittings. In early December 1994, he was told by the plant manager to make plans to refurbish the number three extruding machine. This was to be done the weekend of January 13 and 14.

The extruding machine was a vital part of Devon's operation. Cecil had been keeping a checklist of needed repairs. But making the repairs had not been possible because the machine had not been shut down for a single day since July.

Cecil stayed on the job late that evening to inspect the machine and to update his checklist. He also checked the spare parts room and the toolroom, and made up an order for additional parts and tools that would be needed for the job.

The next day, Cecil held a meeting with his maintenance workers so they would be prepared. Over the next several days, he looked at each repair item and prepared a written task assignment schedule. He assigned each task to the worker he considered most competent to do it.

Cecil knew that after the machine was shut down he would find some unexpected defects. Also, some of the jobs would not go exactly as planned. So he decided to use his best worker, Breece Gimler, as utility man. Breece would handle unexpected repairs and help the other workers when needed.

When the crew members returned from Christmas holidays, Cecil gave each person a list of that person's repair tasks for the machine. On January 11, he held a final meeting to prepare for the shutdown. Cecil worked some extra hours that weekend. But because he had planned well, the machine was back on line in good repair on Monday morning.

Was Cecil an effective planner?

of an organization has a mission that guides its direction. Organizational mission is a major focus of Chapter 6.

❖ ❖ OBJECTIVES

Once the mission is understood, specific objectives can be established. **Objectives** are the desired end results of any activity. They should be set at each managerial level in the organization; however, lower-level objectives should be consistent with upper-level objectives (see Figure 5.2). In 1985, Honda Motor Company developed a new car without clear-cut objectives. Sales representatives wanted a roomy and reliable car, the Japanese dealers wanted a sexy sporty vehicle, engineers focused on new engines, marketers were concerned with diverging tastes, and the financial people supported the practice of selling the same car in all markets. Although it was initially successful, by 1990, this approach no longer worked. Honda now accepts the conventional approach of setting clear-cut objectives. Honda produced the 1994 Accord with objectives clearly established, and thus avoided many of the last go-round's miscues.[6]

❖ **Figure 5.2**
Consistency of objectives

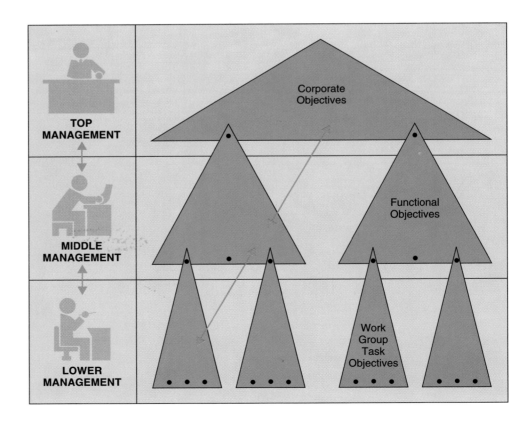

How Managers Establish Good Objectives

Objectives should have four basic characteristics: (1) They should be expressed in writing, (2) they should be measurable, (3) they should be specific as to time allotted, and (4) they should be challenging but attainable (see Figure 5.3). Placing the objectives in written form increases people's understanding of and commitment to them.

Measurability suggests that the objectives should be quantified whenever possible. It would be much better to have an objective of increasing profits by ten percent during a certain period than merely to say, "We want to increase profits." Any increase would meet the latter objective.

Objectives should be specific as to time. Individuals need and want to know when an objective should be accomplished. Also, an objective that is set without a time limit cannot be challenging. In the measurability example, are the profits to be increased by ten percent this year or by the end of the century?

Finally, an objective that is too easily accomplished provides little satisfaction when it is met. On the other hand, an unattainable objective is more likely to frustrate workers than to encourage them. Therefore, objectives should be challenging but attainable. Objectives are established at each level of management. Those set by top management should be consistent with the overall mission of the firm. And the objectives of lower-level management should be in line with those of upper-level management. The people charged with the responsibility of

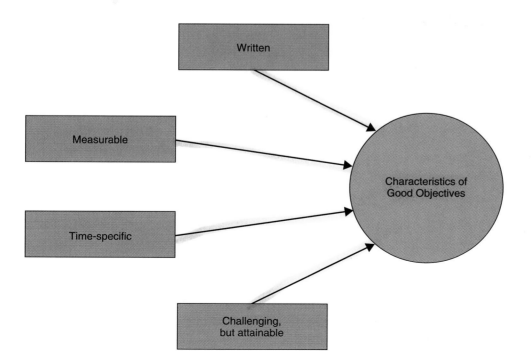

❖ Figure 5.3
Characteristics of good objectives

Objectives should be specific as to time. Individuals need and want to know when an objective should be accomplished. The creation of specific organizational and unit objectives is no simple task. Computers often assist managers to determine the best objectives. (Source: Photograph courtesy of Atari Corporation.)

establishing corporate objectives vary from business to business. At times, the president or chairman of the board provides the major thrust in objective creation. At other times, a group of top-level executives is consulted. Whatever the source, the objectives provide the course along which future energies of the firm will be directed and also serve to set the tone for objective setting throughout the organization.

Types of Objectives

The creation of specific organizational and unit objectives is no simple task. Numerous external factors exert their influence on a firm. An organization usually has a number of objectives and the emphasis each receives may change according to the impact of a particular environmental factor or group of factors. At least three main types of objectives can be identified:

- *Economic*—survival, profit, and growth.
- *Service*—creation of benefit for society.
- *Personal*—objectives of individuals and groups within the organization.

AT&T is successful, and one reason may be that the company continually attempts to achieve all three types of objectives.

Economic Objectives Survival is a basic objective of all organizations. Whether or not an organization is producing something of economic value to society seems to take second place to just staying alive. It is difficult for a firm to take into account higher social objectives when it is not known whether the next payroll can be met. As an anonymous statesman once said, "It is extremely difficult to think that your initial objective was to drain the swamp when you are up to your knees in alligators."

In order to survive, a firm must at least break even—that is, it must generate enough revenues to cover costs. But business firms want more than mere survival; they are in business to make a profit. Profit provides a vital incentive for the continued successful operation of the enterprise. An adequate profit depends primarily on the industry and the specific needs of an organization.

Growth—in sales, number of employees, or number of facilities—may also be a major objective of a firm. It may set the stage for long-term survival. A company may seek unrestricted growth, which sometimes becomes an end in itself. When this happens, the company may fail to give proper emphasis to profitability. There are, of course, certain economic advantages that come with size, and many companies see growth as a way of competing more effectively. This was certainly the case with RJR Nabisco, when the company focused on halting declining market share for Winston and Salem brands. RJR responded by an expensive promotional blitz. According to David Anderson, CFO for the tobacco unit, "We're looking at earnings as secondary to market-share performance." Clearly growth was RJR Nabisco's number one concern.[7]

Service Objectives Profit alone is often viewed as the primary motive for being in business. Although it is true that a firm cannot survive for long without making a profit, many managers also recognize an obligation to society. Even those who feel no such responsibility know that if a firm cannot consistently create economic value for society, it will not stay in business long enough to make a profit. AT&T continually strives to offer its customers value in terms of quality personal service at competitive prices. AT&T therefore consistently creates economic value for society. Many firms have gone out of existence when they ceased producing goods and services desired by society.

Personal Objectives Organizations are made of people who have different personalities, backgrounds, experiences, and objectives. Personal objectives are seldom identical to the objectives of the organization. If personal and organizational objectives are incompatible, an employee may choose to withdraw from the firm. But many employees do not feel financially able to leave their firms. A conflict between an employee's objectives and the organization's objectives can result in minimal work effort, absenteeism, and even sabotage. A conflict between group objectives and the organization's objectives can have the same negative effects. Employees are not the only ones whose objectives, when they differ from those of the organization, can affect the organization. For instance, a stockholder whose objectives conflict with the objectives of the organization could cease to provide support for the organization by selling stock.

Personal objectives also include the objectives of groups. If an organization is to survive, grow, and earn a profit, it must provide a reasonable match between its objectives and the objectives of powerful groups. Table 5.1 shows how the objectives of a business might differ from those of related groups. It is not unusual for particular groups or their members to experience actual or imagined conflict between their personal objectives and the objectives of the organization. For instance, some customers may believe that higher wages will make the price of products higher, whereas the union may believe that stockholders' profits are too high. Management has the difficult task of reconciling these conflicts, whether or not they are based on factual information.

Problems Encountered in Establishing Objectives

Conflicts among objectives can result from many sources. Three potential sources are: the existence of real objectives that are different from the stated ones, the use of multiple objectives, and the application of quantitative versus nonquantitative objectives.

Real Versus Stated Objectives The real objectives may be at odds with the stated objectives. Objectives are often the result of power plays and pressures that come from circumstances in the marketplace or from internal tensions. The personal objectives of the board of directors, outside creditors, lower-level managers, employees, stockholders, and labor unions are bound to be different. Stated objectives are often significantly altered by individuals and groups who seek to adapt the organization to their narrower purposes. Because of these differences, the stated objectives are at times different from the real objectives.

TABLE 5.1 Possible Objectives of the Organization and Related Groups

GROUPS	POSSIBLE OBJECTIVES
Organization	Maximizing profits.
Management	Promotions, higher salaries, and bonuses.
Employees	Increased wages and bonuses.
Goverment	Adherence of firm to all government laws and regulations.
Competition	Attaining a greater share of the market.
Customers	Quality product at lowest price.
Stockholders/owners	Higher dividends.
Society	Protection of the environment.
Unions	Greater influence for union members.

To determine the real objectives, one must look at the organization's day-to-day decisions and actions. A manager's actions speak louder than words. Other clues as to the actual direction of the organization may be discovered by asking these questions: What functions or groups receive the major share of the resources? What type of behavior is accorded the greatest rewards by management? The top managers of a prison may specify its major objective as being rehabilitation of prisoners. But if the prison employs only two counselors and has 500 guards, the facts contradict the stated objective.

Multiple Objectives All organizations have multiple objectives that must be recognized by management. For instance, what is the major objective of a university? Is it to provide education for students, to conduct research to advance the state of knowledge, or provide community service? In some universities, research is given the first priority in money, personnel, and privilege. In others, the teaching objective is dominant. In still others, an attempt is made to be all things to all people. Given limited funds, however, priorities must be established. One can debate the priority of objectives for such institutions as a mental hospital (therapy or confinement), a church (religion or social relationships), a prison (rehabilitation or confinement), a vocational high school (skill development, general education, or keeping young people off the streets), a medical school (training medical students for clinical practice, basic research, or academic medicine), and an aerospace firm (research information or usable hardware). Seemingly conflicting objectives may not be mutually exclusive, but choices must be made as to how much emphasis each is to receive.

Quantitative Versus Nonquantitative Objectives In general, the more quantitative an objective, the greater the attention on and pressure for its accomplishment. The feasibility of quantifying objectives varies throughout the organization. Production managers, for example, often have specific quotas and schedules. It is easy to tell if either quantity or quality declines. Human resource mangers, on the other hand, often have more subjective objectives. The fact that the human resource manager's objectives are more subjective does not mean that they are less important.

If the most important objective is also the most measurable, such as the objective of winning for a professional sports team, then little distortion will take place. But when important objectives are not so easily measured, organizations are likely to be pushed in the direction of the more quantitative, but perhaps less important, objectives. For example, in universities, research and publication are far easier to measure precisely than is excellence in teaching. Thus, the primary objective, excellence in education, may be replaced with the research emphasis.

When objectives at various levels in an organization conflict, ways must be

---

Conflicting Objectives at Saturn

General Motors (GM), the much criticized automobile manufacturer, developed its strategy for the future and called it Saturn. The strategy demanded that GM start from scratch and revolutionize how the company would build automobiles in the future. The key objective to everything that was done at the GM plant was built around the concept of "Quality." Even Saturn employees' pay was tied to quality targets, and therefore they agreed never to compromise. Saturn has since become the highest-quality American-made brand in the United States. In fact, J.D. Powers & Associates ranked Saturn behind only Lexus and Infiniti in successfully satisfying consumers. The level of employee commitment to the objective of "Quality" is extreme. Defects increased when GM executives tried to push through the conflicting objectives of increasing the number of cars produced at the Saturn plant and maintaining quality. Workers were so committed to the objective of "Quality" that they staged a slowdown when the CEO of GM visited the plant. Saturn managers backed away from the increased production objectives, and quality remained the primary objective. Saturn management decided to add a third crew to accomplish GM's objective of lifting production, and thereby maintained Saturn's goal of never compromising quality.[8]

---

found to correct the problem. This situation occurred at the General Motors Saturn plant.

❖ ❖ PLANS

The next step in the planning process is the creation of plans. **Plans** are statements of how objectives are to be accomplished. Planning is a task that every manager, whether a top-level executive or a first-line supervisor, must perform. Stating an objective does not guarantee its accomplishment. A plan must be developed to inform people about what to do in order to fulfill the objective. There is usually more than one way to accomplish an objective. The plan states which approach is to be taken. Specifically, planning should answer the following questions:

1. What activities are required to accomplish the objective?
2. When should these activities be carried out?
3. Who is responsible for doing what?
4. Where should the activities be carried out?
5. When should the action be completed?

❖ ❖ STANDING PLANS

Plans that remain roughly the same for long periods of time are **standing plans.** The most common kinds of standing plans are policies, procedures, and rules.

Policies

A **policy** is a predetermined guide established to provide direction in decision making. Policies should be based on a thorough analysis of corporate objectives. Separate policies cover each of the important areas of a firm, such as personnel, marketing, research and development, production, and finance.

To formulate a policy, the manager must have knowledge and skill in the area for which the policy is being created. However, certain generalizations apply to the establishment of policies. The most important has already been stated: Policies must be based on a thorough analysis of objectives. Several other points can help the manager create appropriate policies:

1. *Policies should be based on factual information.*
2. *Subordinate and superior policies should be complementary, not contradictory.* For instance, a policy for an individual department at AT&T should not conflict with the company's corporate policy.
3. *Policies of different divisions or departments should be coordinated.* Policies should be directed toward organizational optimization instead of toward optimizing a particular department, such as sales, engineering, purchasing, or production, to the detriment of the whole.
4. *Policies should be definite, understandable, and preferably in writing.* If a policy is to guide actions, the people concerned must be aware of its existence. This requires creating understandable directives in a definitive written form. In effect, policies are the memory of the organization, which it uses to help cope with future events.
5. *Policies should be stable and flexible.* The requirements of stability and flexibility are not contradictory. Stable policies change only in response to fundamental and basic changes in conditions. Government regulations can represent such a basic change and therefore have a major impact on a firm's policies. The higher the organizational level, the more stable the policy must be. Changing the direction of the enterprise is a much more complex and time-consuming task than changing the direction of a department or section. Armco Inc. provides an excellent example of a firm whose policies have been remarkably stable. First formulated in 1919, these policies, outlined in Table 5.2, are still applicable today.
6. *Policies should be reasonably comprehensive in scope.* Policies conserve an executive's time by making available a previously determined decision. The manager should organize the workplace in such a way that subordinates can handle the routine and predictable work in conformity with established policies while the manager's time is devoted to exceptional events and

TABLE 5.2 Armco Inc. Policies

Ethics
To do business guided and governed by the highest standards of conduct so the end result of action taken makes a good reputation an invaluable and permanent asset.

Square deal
To insist on a square deal always. To make sure people are listened to and treated fairly, so that men and women really do right for right's sake and not just to achieve a desired result. For everyone to go beyond narrowness, littleness, and selfishness in order to get the job done.

Organization
To develop and maintain an efficient, loyal, aggressive organization who believe in their company, to whom work is a challenge, and to whom extraordinary accomplishment is a personal goal.

Working conditions
To create and maintain good working conditions…to provide the best possible equipment and facilities…and plants and offices that are clean, orderly, and safe.

Quality and service
To adopt "Quality and service" as an everyday practice. Quality will be the highest attainable in products, organization, plant, property, and equipment. Service will be the best possible to customers, to shareholders, to city, state, and nation.

Opportunity
To employ people without regard to race, sex, religion, or national origin. To encourage employees to improve their skills by participating in available educational or training programs. To provide every possible opportunity for advancement so that each individual may reach his or her highest potential.

Compensation
To provide not only fair remuneration, but the best compensation for services rendered that it is possible to pay under the changing economic, commercial, and other competitive conditions that exist from time to time. It is Armco's ambition to develop an organization of such spirit, loyalty, and efficiency that can and will secure results which will make it possible for individual members to earn and receive better compensation than would be possible if performing a similar service in other fields of effort.

Incentive
To provide realistic and practical incentives as a means of encouraging the highest standard of individual performance and to assure increased quantity and quality of performance.

Cooperation
To recognize cooperation as the medium through which great accomplishments are attained. Success depends more on a spirit of helpful cooperation than on any other one factor.

Objectivity
To always consider what is right and best for the business as a whole, rather than what may be expedient in dealing with a single, separate situation.

Conflict of interest
To probihit employees from becoming financially interested in any company with which Armco does business, if such financial interest might possibly influence decisions employees must make in their areas of responsibility. The above policy does not apply to ownership in publicly owned companies. This is not considered a conflict of interest but, rather, is encouraged as part of the free enterprise system.

Citizenship
To create and maintain a working partnership between industry and community in this coutry and throughout the world. To support constructive agencies in communities where Armco people live and work in an effort to create civic conditions that respond to the highest needs of the citizens.

(Source: Used with permission from Armco Inc.)

problems. If the body of policies is reasonably comprehensive, few cases arise that are not covered by policy.

Procedures and Rules

Procedures and rules might be thought of as further restrictions on the actions of lower-level employees. They are usually established to ensure adherence to a particular policy.

Procedures A **procedure** is a series of steps for the accomplishment of some specific project or endeavor. Many organizations have extensive procedures manuals designed to provide guidelines for lower-level managers and workers. The stable body of procedures, written and unwritten, that govern an organization are called **standard operating procedures (SOPs).** For most policies, there are accompanying procedures to indicate how the policies should be carried out.

Rules A **rule** is a specific and detailed guide to action set up to direct or restrict action in a fairly narrow manner. There may be a rule that requires hard hats to be worn in a certain work area, for example. The differences among policies, procedures, and rules are shown in Table 5.3. As the table shows, procedures and rules may overlap. Taken out of sequence, a step in a procedure may become a rule.

Policies, procedures, and rules are designed to direct action toward the accomplishment of objectives. If it could be assured that people doing the work completely agreed with and understood basic objectives, there would be less need for policies, procedures, and rules. However, it is apparent that objectives at times are unclear and even controversial. Thus, all organizations need policies, procedures, and rules—which should be more definitive and understandable than the objectives on which they are based.

❖ ❖ LEVELS OF PLANNING

Planning is critical at every level in the organization. At the top-management level, the primary concern is with **strategic planning,** the process by which top management determines overall organizational purposes and objectives and how they are to be achieved. (This is the subject of Chapter 6.) Strategic plans are designed to implement the broad-based plans of top management. Strategic plans must be broken down into less generalized operating, or tactical, plans. **Tactical plans** are designed to implement the strategic plans of top management. They often relate to limited functional areas, such as sales, finance, production, and personnel. Tactical plans also encompass a shorter time frame than strategic plans. The managers who are responsible for implementing tactical plans tend to

TABLE 5.3 Examples of Policies, Procedures, and Rules

POLICY

It is the policy of the company that every employee is entitled to a safe and healthful place in which to work and that accidents should be prevented from occurring in any phase of its operation. Toward this end, the full cooperation of all employees will be required. Management will view neglect of its safety policy or program as just cause for disciplinary action.

PROCEDURE

The purpose of this procedure is to prevent injury to personnel or damage to equipment by inadvertent starting, energizing, or pressurizing equipment that has been shut down for maintenance, overhaul, lubrication, or setup.

1. Maintenance persons assigned to work on a job will lock out the machine at the proper disconnect with their own safety lock and keep the key in their possession.
2. If the job is not finished before shift change, the maintenance person will remove the lock and put a seal on the disconnect. A danger tag will be hung on the control station, stating why the equipment is shut down.
3. The maintenance person who will be coming on the following shift will place his or her lock on the disconnect along with a seal.
4. Upon completion of the repairs, the area supervisor will be notified by maintenance that work is completed.
5. The supervisor and the maintenance person will check the equipment to see that all guards and safety devices are securely in place and operable. Then the supervisor will break the seal and remove the danger tag from the machine.

RULES

The following rules are intended to promote employee safety.

1. The company and each employee are required to comply with provisions of the Occupational Safety and Health Act (OSHA). You will be informed by your supervisor of specific OSHA rules not covered here that apply to your job or area.
2. Report all accidents promptly that occur on the job or on company premises—this should be done whether or not any injury or damage resulted from the incident.

be middle- and lower-level managers, rather than top-level managers. Regardless of the type of planning involved, it is often necessary to reevaluate plans to account for changes which could impact long-term profitability.

❖ ❖ THE PLANNING PROCESS FOR LOWER-LEVEL MANAGERS

All too often, discussion of planning is limited to the benefits top management may derive from proper planning. Sometimes we forget that all effective managers engage in planning. The planning process for top-level and lower-level managers is quite similar. However, the environment of lower-level managers is mainly internal. Lower-level managers are constrained by overall company objectives and

3. Horseplay, practical jokes, wrestling, throwing things, running in the plant, and similar actions will not be tolerated, as they can cause serious accidents.

4. Observe all warning signs, such as "No Smoking," "Stop," etc. They are there for your protection.

5. Keep your mind on the work being performed.

6. Familiarize yourself with the specific safety rules and precautions that relate to your work area.

7. Approved eye protection must be worn in all factory and research lab areas during scheduled working hours or at any other time work is being performed.

8. Hearing protection is required when the noise level in an area reaches limits established by OSHA.

9. Adequate hand protection should be worn while working with solvents or other materials that might be harmful to hands.

10. Wearing rings or other jewelry that could cause injury is not allowed for persons performing work in the factory area.

11. Good housekeeping is important to accident prevention. Keep your immediate work area, machinery, and equipment clean. Keep tools and materials neatly and securely stored so that they will not cause injury to you or others.

12. Aisles, fire equipment access, and other designated "clear" areas must not be blocked.

13. Learn the correct way to lift. Get help if the material to be lifted is too heavy to be lifted alone. Avoid an effort that is likely to injure you.

14. Only authorized employees are allowed to operate forklifts and company vehicles. Passengers are not allowed on lift equipment or other material-handling equipment except as required in the performance of a job.

15. Learn the right way to do your job. If you are not sure you thoroughly understand a job, ask for assistance. This will often contribute to your job performance as well as your job safety.

16. Observe safe and courteous driving habits in the parking lot.

strategies, but the importance of planning remains. For example, no matter how grandiose AT&T's corporate planning, the company would fail without effective planning by lower-level employees throughout the organization.

The amount of time spent in the planning function at lower levels of management may not be as great as at higher levels. For instance, as compared to a corporate executive, a hotel manager may devote a much larger percentage of time to influencing or controlling than to planning. However, this does not diminish the importance of planning for the hotel manager. Also, the time frame for planning may be shorter for lower-level managers than for senior executives. To be successful, top-level management must make decisions affecting operations far into the future. But to ask a lower-level manager to plan five years ahead may be unrealistic. Daily, weekly, monthly, and yearly quotas must be met.

Strategic plans must be broken down into less generalized operating or tactical plans, which are plans designed to implement or carry out the strategic-based plans of top management. In this scene, Phillips Petroleum employees at the company's Bartlesville Research Center discuss plans for a new pilot plant to make a special resin.
(Source: Photograph courtesy of Phillips Petroleum Company.)

It is quite possible that even long-range planning for some lower-level managers may encompass a relatively short time span. However, the shorter time span does not diminish the importance of long-range planning. Consider some of the types of plans that lower-level managers typically make:

- *Production plans.* The objective might be to meet a daily, weekly, or monthly production schedule. The production plan at the supervisor's level would involve scheduling jobs and assigning workers to do them.
- *Methods improvement plans.* The objective could be to find the best way to do a certain task. The plan might consist of a simple listing of the steps necessary to obtain the improvements.
- *Absences plans.* The objective might be to ensure that the work continues to get done when some workers are absent. Scheduling vacation time is an example of this form of planning.
- *Budget plans.* A budget is a statement of desired results expressed in financial or numeric terms. Although the budget itself is a plan, the supervisor's objective might be to stay within the budget. Therefore, the lower-level manager's budget plan would describe what is considered the most effective way to expend budgeted funds.

❖ ❖ CONTINGENCY PLANNING

"The best laid plans of mice and men often go astray" (a paraphrase of a line from Robert Burns's poem "To a Mouse") is certainly applicable in today's busi-

ETHICAL DILEMMA

Your firm is one of the largest domestic subcontractors of Nintendo-type video game units. Because of the overly extreme California regulations recently implemented, the assembly plant was moved to northern Florida. The California workforce was composed primarily of individuals who needed benefits such as insurance, and who depended on overtime pay. The plant had employed over 250 employees in California, but the move to Florida allowed the employment of 300 employees who would be paid less and offered no benefits. The company gained because no overtime was required, no benefits were paid, and the group was not distracted by family problems. The town had 150 retired, well-qualified, eager workers, and the surrounding area had a large contingent of well-qualified older workers who were willing to work for minimum wages and no benefits. You promised the town's industrial board members that if they could locate another 150 retired workers who were willing to work for no benefits and minimum wages, you would give these workers permanent jobs, good working conditions, and subsidized low-cost housing. The retirees would be able to substantially increase their standard of living and quality of life by moving to the area. Your workforce subsequently grew to 300 elderly employees who enjoyed the location, their jobs, their new social relationships, and their increased income. According to your business partner, recent technological advancements would now allow each unit to be assembled at 30 to 40 percent less than with manual labor. If you purchase the new equipment and eliminate 180 workers, you could cut total assembly cost by as much as 28 percent after taxes. Your partner highly recommends that you purchase the new subassembly machine and avoid the problems associated with such a large, elderly workforce. You can take a chance that the workforce can turn a profit over the long-term or you can purchase the new machine and cut your newly hired staff by over 50 percent.

What would you do?

ness world. Events can occur so rapidly that plans may become useless before they can be fully implemented. External and internal disturbances resulting in the need for a change in plans often occur. **Contingency planning** is the development of plans to be placed in effect if certain events occur.

As Figure 5.4 shows, contingency planning is important at each level of management and for both strategic and operational planning. Even lower-level managers have a need for contingency planning. The manager of the production department undoubtedly has a contingency plan to cover breakdowns on certain pieces of equipment.

Contingency planning entails the recognition that events can alter the results of initial plans. Contingency planning makes it unnecessary for a firm to wait for a situation to occur before it prepares to respond. Naturally, not all situations can be anticipated, but the manager who tries to anticipate reasonably probable occurrences will stand a good chance of coping with future events. Separate plans

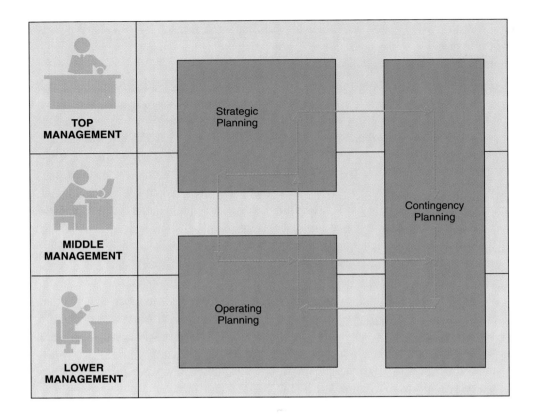

cannot be made even for all probable situations, since such situations are usually far too numerous. So it is often useful to categorize events and link each category to fairly generalized plans.

A disaster recovery plan for a computer installation is a common example of a contingency plan. Organizations that use computers become very dependent on them. This is true for practically every modern company. But what happens when the system fails? Sabotage and vandalism are human-made disasters to which computer systems may be vulnerable. Fires, floods, rainstorms, tornadoes, and hurricanes are natural threats that often disable such systems.

The plan for recovery typically involves provisions for backups, not only for the information contained in the computer but also for the functions the computer performs. The data-processing personnel for a large firm may make daily or weekly copies of master files and place them in a secure location. Contingency plans are made to obtain these files if they are needed. Some other aspects of a data-processing contingency plan might be site evaluation, damage assessment, emergency processing, and methods to keep system users informed about restoration efforts. Reciprocal emergency processing agreements between firms are often the subject of contingency plans. Because of the ever-changing external and inter-

MANAGEMENT IN PRACTICE

A Skill-Building Exercise: After several weeks of careful planning, you have set up a job rotation schedule for your crew of 21 employees. Your boss has put you in charge of the first stage of a three-stage production process to create component parts for the new ultrasound machine your company has developed. The process is very sensitive to quality variances, so you have personally trained the three production supervisors under your direc-tion. One of these individuals will be responsi-ble for quality control in each of the three stages of component part production. Two days into this production program, your boss's boss, the production manager, "borrows" five of your people, including the three production supervi-sors, to help out on a special order. You are given five replacements from the company's pool of temporary help.
How could this affect your planning?

nal conditions of many of today's businesses, contingency planning is becoming increasingly important.

❖ ❖ SUCCESSION PLANNING

Because of the tremendous changes that will confront management in the 1990s, succession planning takes on more importance than perhaps ever before. In view of these expected changes, organizations need to develop a profile of the type of individuals who will effectively lead the organization both now and in the future. Apparently many organizations are involved in their own version of succession planning. In a survey of over 400 boards of big American companies, nearly three-quarters of the firms questioned had a succession plan.[9] P. Roy Vagelos, CEO of Merck & Co., is already planning to find his successor—and he does not retire for two years.[10]

An example of an effective succession plan occurred recently at NCR when a senior vice-president of finance retired. Following his departure, nine people moved up in the organization. At the end of the chain reaction, a young college student was hired as a financial analyst.[11] The planned CEO succession at the new Chemical Bank, the merger between Chemical Banking Corporation and Manu-facturers Hanover Corporation, will help assure management stability at the new company. At the time of the merger, CEO McGillicuddy planned to depart, and the succession plan was in place to assure a smooth transition and takeover by Walter V. Shipley. McGillicuddy would really like to stay on because he loves the people and what he is doing. However, he also believes that the succession is nec-essary. According to McGillicuddy, he feels even more strongly that he has had his time. With proper succession planning, McGillicuddy believes that the best

A GLOBAL PERSPECTIVE

Effective Planning—The Key to Long-Term Global Success

Obviously, although effective planning is essential for multinational success, the key to global productivity cannot simply result from cutting jobs, lowering wages, and constantly downsizing. According to Stephen S. Roach, senior economist at Morgan Stanley & Company, if this is the plan for making America globally competitive then its " 'game over' for America." When planning for global competitiveness, America must turn to its inevitable strengths, to overcome its obvious weaknesses. The United States is still the richest nation in the world, with a superior technological base and a highly educated workforce. However, U.S. businesses are hampered by a financial system that emphasizes short-term results, whereas globally long-term results are emphasized by all major U.S. global competitors. Industrial powers, except the United States, normally have a long-term viewpoint and invest sizably in machinery, technology, infrastructure, and research and development. In fact, with the exception of the United States, these factors are emphasized to provide dramatic payoffs in terms of productivity and output. To compete in the global marketplace managers must accept the planning mindset that global competitiveness requires long-term investments that enhance global productivity. Global productivity must result in unparalleled quality and customer service at competitive prices, and it cannot be hindered by short-term thinking or planning.[12]

thing you can do is "put your hat on, say, 'Good luck, gang,' and go out and do something else."[13]

❖ ❖ PLANNING THROUGH MANAGEMENT BY OBJECTIVES

Management consultant Peter Drucker first described management by objectives (MBO) in 1954 in *The Practice of Management*.[14] During the past two decades, few other developments in the theory and practice of management have received as much attention and application as MBO. **Management by objectives (MBO)** is the philosophy of management that emphasizes the setting of agreed-on objectives by managers and their subordinates and the use of these objectives as the primary bases of motivation, evaluation, and control efforts. Above all else, MBO represents a way of thinking that concentrates on achieving results. It forces management to plan explicitly, as opposed to simply responding or reacting on the basis of guesses or hunches. It provides a systematic and rational approach to management and helps prevent "management by crisis." MBO emphasizes measurable achievements and results and may lead to improvements in organizational, group, and individual effectiveness. It depends heavily on active participation in objective setting at all levels of management.

❖ ❖ THE MBO PROCESS

The dynamics of an MBO system are illustrated in Figure 5.5. Notice that MBO requires top management support and commitment and involves five steps. These aspects of MBO are discussed in the following sections.

Top Management's Support and Commitment

An effective MBO program requires the enthusiastic support of top management. It is because of the lack of top-level commitment that many MBO programs fail. For MBO to be effective, the philosophy of top management must be consistent with its principles. MBO relies on the participative approach to management, requiring the active involvement of managers at all levels. The chief executive should trust subordinates and be personally committed to a participative style of management. Top management cannot introduce MBO by simply giving an order or a directive. Lower-level managers, too, must be convinced of the merits of the system and must want meaningful participation in the process.

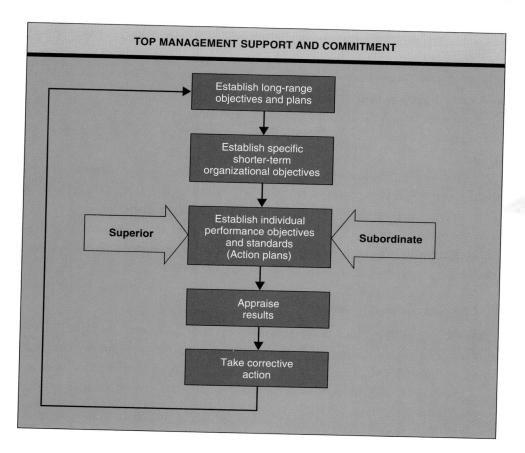

TOP MANAGEMENT SUPPORT AND COMMITMENT

Establish long-range objectives and plans

Establish specific shorter-term organizational objectives

Superior → Establish individual performance objectives and standards (Action plans) ← **Subordinate**

Appraise results

Take corrective action

❖ **Figure 5.5**
The MBO process

Establishing Long-Range Objectives and Plans

A vital element of MBO is the development of long-range objectives and plans. These plans are developed through thoughtful consideration of the basic purpose, or mission, of the organization.

Establishing Specific Shorter-Term Organizational Objectives

After long-range objectives and plans are established, management must be concerned with determining specific objectives to be attained within a shorter time period. These objectives must be supportive of the overall purpose as well as the long-range objectives and plans. Usually, shorter-term objectives are expressed as specific and quantifiable targets covering such areas as productivity, marketing, and profitability.

Establishing Individual Performance Objectives and Standards (Action Plans)

The establishment of performance objectives and standards for individuals is known as **action planning.** This crucial phase of the MBO process requires that challenging but attainable objectives and standards be established through interaction between superiors and subordinates. Individuals jointly establish objectives with their superiors, who then give the individual some latitude in how to achieve the objectives. Jointly establishing objectives makes the employee an involved part of the process. This ownership of objectives increases the likelihood that they will be met.

Action plans require clear delineation of what specifically is to be accomplished and when it is to be completed. For example, if a sales manager has a performance objective of increasing sales in his or her area by 38 percent next year, the action plan might include the employment of three experienced salespersons, six calls a week by the sales manager on major customers, and assignment of appropriate sales quotas to all the salespeople.

Appraisal Results

The next step in the MBO process is to measure and evaluate performance on the basis of progress toward objective attainment. Having specific performance objectives provides management with a basis for comparison. When objectives are agreed on by the manager and the subordinate, self-evaluation and control become possible. In fact, with MBO, performance appraisal can be a joint effort based on mutual agreement.

Taking Corrective Action

Although an MBO system provides a good management framework, it is left up to the managers to take corrective action when results are not as planned. Such action may take the form of changes in personnel, changes in the organization, or even changes in the objectives. Other forms of corrective action may include providing additional training and development of individual managers or employees to enable them to better achieve the desired results. Corrective action should not necessarily have negative connotations. Under MBO, objectives can be renegotiated downward without penalty or fear of job loss.

❖ ❖ MBO: ASSESSING ITS OVERALL EFFECTIVENESS

In a review of 185 studies, Jack N. Kondrasuk found numerous arguments relating to the effectiveness of MBO. Many organizations have adopted MBO on faith, often as a result of questionable case studies or unsubstantiated testimony. One researcher concluded, "There is relatively little empirical evidence to demonstrate the impact of MBO on any aspect of organizational or individual behavior, including job performance." According to Kondrasuk, "There are tendencies for MBO to be more effective in the short term (less than two years), in the private sector, and in organizations removed from direct contact with the customer. Basically, MBO can be effective, but questions remain about the circumstances under which it is effective."[15]

Although the evidence shows that MBO generally has not worked well as a complete system, it still provides a good model for planning. The failure of MBO is basically not due to it being a poor concept, but rather due to its improper implementation. Its central principles have been incorporated into all kinds of organizations and continue to have a major impact. These principles include specific and verifiable objectives, evaluation of performance on the basis of objective accomplishment, and integration of individual objectives with organizational objectives.

✗ Management Tips ✗

Guidelines for Dealing with Planning

1. **Make sure objectives are challenging but attainable.** Managers must not paint themselves into a corner by setting objectives that are unattainable.

2. **Become involved in objective setting with the boss.** Do not take the attitude "O.K., tell me what to do." Remember that once you have agreed to an objective, you are expected to accomplish it.

3. **Consider planning as an ongoing process.** Refer to your plan frequently to ensure that you are going in the right direction.

4. **Plan before it is time to do the activity.** Proper time management techniques are essential, regardless of the management level involved.

5. **Write down important plans.** This forces you to think through the actions included in the plan and to be more realistic.

6. **Plan with numbers.** Attempt to quantify everything in the plan.

7. **Do not forget that plans affect people.** As you develop the plan, consider your employees.

8. **Plan for results, not activities.** Say, "What needs to be accomplished in each specific time frame?"

9. **Be innovative.** Do not assume that the way it has always been done is necessarily the best way. The opposite is just as likely to be true.

10. **Plan to prevent problems rather than solve them.** It is often much easier to prevent a problem than to solve one that you helped create.

SUMMARY

Planning is the process of determining in advance what should be accomplished and how it should be realized. Planning begins with an understanding of the organizational mission—a unit's continuing purpose or reason for being. The mission statement is a broadly stated definition of the basic purpose and scope of a unit. From it, specific objectives (or goals) can be established; then plans can be developed to accomplish them. The planning process is dynamic. It should be continually evaluated and adapted to conform to the unfolding situation the organization confronts.

Objectives are the desired end results of any activity and should be set at each managerial level in the organization. Plans are statements of how objectives are to be accomplished. Those that remain roughly the same for long periods of time are standing plans. The most common kinds of standing plans are policies, procedures, and rules. All three are designed to direct action toward the accomplishment of objectives.

Planning occurs at every level in the organization. Strategic plans, relating to overall organizational purposes, are designed to implement the broader-based plans of top management. Tactical plans implement the strategic plans of top management. Those responsible for implementing tactical plans tend to be middle- and lower-level managers. Contingency planning is the development of plans to be placed in effect if certain events occur.

Management by objectives (MBO) is the philosophy of management that emphasizes the setting of agreed-on objectives by managers and their subordinates and the use of these objectives as the primary bases of motivation, evaluation, and control efforts. Above all else, MBO represents a way of thinking that concentrates on achieving results.

KEY TERMS

Planning 138

Mission 141

Mission statement 141

Objectives 142

Plans 148

Standing plans 148

Policy 149

Procedure 151

Standard operating
  procedures (SOPs) 151

Rule 151

Strategic planning 151

Tactical plans 151

Contingency planning 155

Management by objectives
  (MBO) 158

Action planning 160

REVIEW QUESTIONS

1. What are the steps involved in the planning process?
2. What is the purpose of a mission statement?
3. Describe the characteristics of good objectives. What are the three main types of objectives?
4. What are the specific questions that planning should answer?
5. Distinguish by definition among policies, procedures, and rules.
6. What is meant by the term contingency planning?
7. What is management by objectives (MBO)? Describe the basic steps in the MBO process

CASE STUDIES

CASE 5.1 Club Med: Planning to Stay the Leader in Sun, Fun, and Fantasy

Club Med markets fantasy vacations in over 100 exotic "villages" strung across the world from the Caribbean to Polynesia. Its customers have been mostly beautiful young people. The club in Huatulco, Mexico sponsored a fashion parade featuring Felicia Farrar and four other world-class designers. Skinny-dipping, kayaking, and scuba diving were part of the surrounding fun. Of course, the local manager in Huatulco had to plan more than a year in advance to get

the services of such notables. As the big day neared, there was a flurry of planning activity. One designer cancelled and another had to be substituted. All of the events were carefully scheduled. Planning concerns included everything from availability of emergency medical care to provision of adequate food and drink.

Straw hut villages on the Mediterranean provided less glitz and glamour, but solid comfort and unusual hikes and archeological tours. There was skiing in the Alps, pure luxury and entertainment in Senegal, villas in China and Mexico, and for those who found no fixed base acceptable, the Club Med I, a five-masted schooner. A fancy ship with six Burmese teak decks, pools, restaurants, a fitness center and a hair salon, it would winter in the Caribbean and summer in the Mediterranean. In each area, managers were charged with making plans to implement those from higher levels.

Fantasyland? Not for those who managed the Club Med empire for its 73 percent owner Club Mediterranee and other stockholders. Club Med's shares trade on the major world stock exchanges. Managers of the resort villages were responsible for developing their own budgets and getting them approved. They also had to insure that resources—people, money, and materials—were available and properly coordinated.

Traditionally, most Club Med managers were French, but that was rapidly changing through the 1980s. By 1990, a substantial majority would be from the Americas, Australia, Asia, and Northern Europe. Overall, Club Med expected to double in capacity every five years. One-year and three-year objectives for growth and profit were established for each country and for each resort. And cost reductions were sought through standardization and methods improvement. Club Med made plans to continue to internationalize its employees and modify the organizational structure in order to reflect that. In particular, managers in individual countries were given increasing authority.

To serve upwards of 1.7 million kaleidoscopic patrons and earn over $300 million a year in the late 1980s, the company had to continuously adjust. The Magic Isle resort in Haiti was closed because of political unrest. The Bermuda village, old and in a declining market, was put up for sale. Occupancy rates unexplainably crashed in New Caledonia. Construction chaos delayed openings in Mexico. In all these cases, local managers not only had to make plans to smoothly adjust to changes, but also to manage their own careers.

QUESTIONS

1. Evaluate the planning process at Club Med.
2. How does the external environment affect the planning process at Club Med?

CASE 5.2 Planning for Effectiveness at Wendy's

At age 12, R. David Thomas launched his fast-food career as a 25-cents-an-hour cook at a Knoxville, Tennessee lunch counter. He became a successful restaurant manager after learning all aspects of the restaurant business from his mentor Colonel Harland Sanders, of Kentucky Fried Chicken fame. While assisting Sanders, Thomas revived several chicken restaurants and helped Sanders found the Arthur Treacher's Fish and Chips chain. In 1969, Thomas opened his first Wendy's restaurant. In spite of its late entrance into the market, Wendy's was the first fast-food service chain to surpass $1 billion in annual sales within ten years. Sales tripled to $3 billion in the eighties. Even with Wendy's successes, there was a consensus among industry analysts that giant McDonald's would remain the industry leader in the foreseeable future. But with nearly 4,000 restaurants, Wendy's remained a formidable competitor.

Wendy's was able to play in the same league as McDonald's because of its solid management and productivity advantage. On the basis of labor and materials cost per hamburger, Wendy's had the most efficient production system of any quick-serve restaurant company. The hamburgers were produced on hamburger assembly lines, similar in principle to those in Detroit. Each worker had a specific job. However, the key to Wendy's success was management's emphasis on speed and efficiency. A survey indicated that on average Wendy's served customers twice as fast as its competitors.

But managers never sacrificed quality for efficiency. Thomas said, "Quality is our recipe." A number of Wendy's policies supported this motto. Wendy's used only fresh, locally purchased beef. There were no heating lamps, microwave ovens, or steam cabinets to keep food hot, and every hamburger was produced when ordered. If a meat patty was not sold within two minutes, it was put into the chili pot.

As the hamburger market became more competitive, Wendy's planned to diversify its product line, making the production process more complicated.

Managers were challenged to maintain efficiency in the face of increasing complexity. To help meet the challenge, Wendy's planned to boost its research and development expenditures to five times the 1980 level. The company invested in computerized cash registers, which compile data for sales analyses, inventory projections, cash control, and even labor scheduling. Customer-count and product mix data were rapidly communicated to regional and corporate offices so that opportunities to improve the system would not be missed. Wendy's saved millions of dollars through new building designs, resulting in better operations control and lower energy costs. With its large competitors using similar sophisticated techniques, Wendy's continually had to seek more efficient ways to make and market hamburgers and related products.

QUESTIONS

1. What is the mission statement of Wendy's?
2. Based on this case, what would be some policies and rules?

NOTES

1. This case is a composite of a number of published accounts, among them: Andrew Kupfer, "Bob Allen Rattles the Cages at AT&T," *Fortune* (June 19, 1989): 58–66; Patricia M. Fernberg, "AT&T at Centennial Plaza,"*Modern Office Technology* 34 (April 1989): 76–80; Paul B. Carol, "AT&T Reports 18% Gain in Net for 2nd Quarter," *The Wall Street Journal* (July 21, 1989): A6; Charles H. Granger, "The Hierarchy of Objectives," *Harvard Business Review* 42 (May–June 1964): 63–74; Peter Coy, "AT&T Reaches Out and Taps Some New Talent," *Business Week* (September 2, 1991): 80; Bart Ziegler, "AT&T Reaches Way Out for This One," *Business Week* (March 8, 1993): 83; Bart Ziegler, "American Telephone & Multimedia?" *Business Week* (September 6, 1993): 78–79.
2. Kelley Holland, "Why the Chemistry Is Right at Chemical," *Business Week* (June 7, 1993): 90–93.
3. Charles B. Shrader, Lew Taylor, and Dan R. Dalton, "Strategic Planning and Organizational Performance: A Critical Appraisal," *Journal of Management* 10 (Summer, 1984): 152.
4. Pete Engardio, "Mainland Mania in Hong Kong," *Business Week* (August 17, 1992): 48.
5. Julie Tilsner, "Duracell Looks Abroad for More Juice," *Business Week* (December 21, 1992): 52–56.
6. Karen Lowry Miller and Larry Armstrong, "How Honda Hammered Out Its New Accord," *Business Week* (December 21, 1992): 86.
7. Walecia Konrad, "RJR Can't Seem to Find a Spot in the Shade," *Business Week* (July 20, 1992): 70–71.
8. David Woodruff, James B. Treece, Sunita Wadekar Bhargava, and Karen Lowry Miller, "Saturn," *Business Week* (August 17, 1992): 88–89.
9. "Heirs and Races," *The Economist* 318 (March 9, 1991): 69.
10. Michael Schroeder and Joseph Weber, "Is Merck Ready for Marty Wygod?" *Business Week* (October 4, 1993): 80–84.
11. *Ibid.*
12. Michael J. Mandel and Christopher Farrell, "How to Get America Growing Again," *Business Week* (*Reinventing America 1992*): 22–23.
13. Kelley Holland, "Why the Chemistry Is Right at Chemical," *Business Week* (June 7, 1993): 90–93.
14. Peter F. Drucker, *The Practice of Management* (New York: Harper & Row, 1954).
15. Jack N. Kondrasuk, "Studies in MBO Effectiveness," *Academy of Management Review* 6 (September 1981): 419–430.

6 Strategic Planning

LEARNING OBJECTIVES

After completing this chapter students should be able to

✘ Distinguish between planning and strategic planning.

✘ State the importance of strategic planning and discuss strategic business units and the levels of strategic planning.

✘ Explain who the organizational strategists are.

✘ Explain the strategic planning and implementation processes.

✘ Describe the means of formulating corporate-level strategy.

✘ Explain the means of formulating business-level and functional-level strategy.

At GE Capital Services Performance Planning Pays Off

To reflect the diversity that is now embodied at General Electric, the company prefers not to be referred to as "General Electric," but simply as "GE." Throughout its history General Electric has been mainly identified with major appliances, electric motors, and light bulbs. In 1989, chief executive Jack F. Welch, Jr., pruned the company down to about 40 businesses. The company made jet engines, electronics items, and medical equipment, and it even provided financial services.

To accomplish the additional restructuring needed, "Neutron Jack," as Welch was known, put top managers of laggard and small-share businesses on notice: either become a dominant player or be sold or closed. The plan was to strip the corporation of its low performers and concentrate management talent and financial resources on the others. Within the individual businesses, Welch and his staff made sure resources were applied where they would do the most good. His recipe for productivity: "It has nothing to do with whips and chains and taking heads out. We're trying to unleash people to be self-confident, and so to take on more responsibility." In particular, Welch said, he wanted to "liberate" and "empower" middle managers. He shunned bureaucracy, long a curse at GE. According to Welch, "This internal focus has wasted our time, wasted our energy, frustrated us, made us so mad some nights over some bureaucratic jackass boss that we'd punch a hole in the wall."

The number one performer in the GE family is now GE Capital Services Inc. While other companies such as ITT, Xerox, and Westinghouse are retreating from the financial services business to get back to their core businesses, GE charges ahead. The CEO of GE Capital, Gary C. Wendt, is a devotee of the tough management style of his boss GE Chairman Welch. Wendt firmly subscribes to Welch's recipe for productivity and his disdain for bureaucracy. According to Wendt, "Life is staying one step ahead of the posse," and that is what he tells his managers. He does not allow bureaucracy to get in the way of success. Wendt's business managers meet four times a year at so-called "war games" to lay out three-year strategies, and operating plans are checked and adjusted, if necessary.

The Welch/Wendt approach to strategic planning assures that the organizational structure advances the achievement of organizational purposes and objectives. As the 1980s drew to a close, Welch's "grand design," adhered to by Wendt, was clear throughout GE and especially at GE Capital. Currently, GE Capital is the number one performer of GE's 13 business divisions, with a 20 percent return on equity. Welch has stated the company's goal this way: "We were a company that was identified with safety. Now it is safety with upside potential." He seems to have delivered on the promise of realizing the upside potential, particularly as it relates to Wendt's baby GE Capital.[1]

The planning process remains essentially the same at each organizational level; however, managers today have access to a number of concepts and techniques that relate specifically to strategic planning. **Strategic planning** is the process by which top management determines overall organizational purposes and objectives and how they are to be achieved. Wayne Calloway, PepsiCo's CEO, constantly preaches the essence of his strategy: Don't wait for change; stay ahead of it. "You don't wait until you're going over the cliff to change your brakes." In line with that strategy, PepsiCo's Pizza Hut isn't remaining just a sit-down pizza joint; they are actively trying to be the best "pizza distribution company" that strives to sell pizza no matter where the customer is, at the ballpark or at a desk. The strategy is not entirely new, but the implementation is very much so.[2]

General Electric has long been a leader in strategic planning. Jack Welch recognizes that GE's common stock has typically been considered a safe investment, but one with little upside potential. He expects to improve the common shareholders' opportunity for gain without decreasing the security of the stock. Part

Construction workers extend the Colorado Interstate Gas Pipeline for Coastal Corporation. Such major projects require extensive strategic planning. Unlike tactical, operational, or short-term planning, strategic planning involves an extended time frame, deployment of a substantial percentage of the resources of the organization, a wide spectrum of activities, and a major eventual impact. (Source: Photograph courtesy of The Coastal Corporation.)

of his strategic plan for doing this is to concentrate on those businesses where GE is a market leader and to eliminate weak divisions. He also embarked on a program of expansion into technology and service areas.

In this chapter, the discussion begins with the difference between planning and strategic planning. Next, the importance of strategic planning is examined. The discussion then turns to the levels of strategic planning, identification of the organizational strategists, and a brief description of the strategic planning and implementation processes. This is followed by a discussion of the formulation of corporate-level strategies, business-level strategies, and functional-level strategies, and a brief overview of global strategic perspectives.

PLANNING VERSUS STRATEGIC PLANNING

In Chapter 5, planning was defined as the process of determining in advance what should be accomplished and how it should be realized. Planning involves selecting objectives and deciding how to achieve them. Strategic planning is a type of planning. But unlike tactical, operational, or short-term planning, strategic planning involves an extended time frame, the deployment of a substantial percentage of the resources of the organization, a wide spectrum of activities, and a major impact on the organization. Basically, strategic planning is planning that is long term, wide ranging, and critical to organizational success in terms of the costs of the resources it affects and of the outcomes it envisions.

THE IMPORTANCE OF STRATEGIC PLANNING

There is an acute realization among professional managers of the importance of strategic planning to the growth and profitability of any company. It is also important to the job security and self-esteem of employees, to the welfare of communities, and to the financial security of investors. The CEO of IBM, Louis Vincent Gerstner, Jr., realizes the importance of strategic planning, and he utilizes a frontal-assault approach to strategic planning. As Gerstner explains, "I don't view the role of the CEO as some distant corporate position that blesses strategy, I get up to my eyeballs in divisional corporate strategy. I don't want it presented to me. I want to be right in it."[3] The importance of strategic planning to the growth and profitability of any company cannot be denied, as Philips Electronics has discovered.

When a firm's mission is clearly defined and its guiding principles understood, as with GE, employees and managers are likely to put forth maximum effort in pursuit of company objectives. The advantage of strategic planning is most evident as firms respond to rapidly changing environments. This fact should

---

Philips' Strategic Plan: Become Sony-Like

In 1992, Gaston Bastiens, the top executive heading up Philips Electronics, created a strategy of becoming a Sony-like company that derives much of its profits from entertainment programming, and made Philips face up to its toughest marketing challenge in its 100-year history. To meet its strategic objective, Philips must meet the challenge by convincing the world that its new Imagination Machine, known as Compact Disk-Interactive (CDI), will become the VCR of the future. CDI hooks into a television and displays programs mixing stereo sound, graphics, photos, text, and eventually video all stored on an optical disk. The software allows users to interact with programs, rather than just watch them. CDI is one of the few products that Philips is counting on to revive the Dutch giant's depressed condition. Potential rivals such as Apple and IBM are still pondering their strategies to meet this challenge.

In spite of the departure of Bastiens for a better opportunity, Philips' CDI strategy is still on. Once the strategy was established, other measures were taken to help assure success. The company was radically restructured, eliminating 45,000 jobs in fewer than three years. Philips has assembled 300 CDI titles, two-thirds from their own studios, and it is beginning to educate consumers on what CDI is, and why they need it. The strategy will either lift Philips up or relegate it to the second tier of electronics companies.[4]

---

make strategic planning even more important now as the Economic Community in Europe removes its barriers to trade, and as Asian markets, especially China's, open up even more. As the globalization of business becomes more pervasive, strategic planning may well provide a competitive edge. It allows managers in changing environments to carefully chart their courses, and it helps their organizations expand and survive.

However, strategic planning has its pitfalls too. There may be a danger of creating a bureaucracy of "planners" who lose touch with the various markets the organization is attempting to serve. Remember how GE's Welch shunned bureaucracies because of his view that bureaucracy may get in the way of success. In addition, too much emphasis on formality in strategic planning may slow down the decision-making process. Managers may seem to make rational, risk-minimizing decisions, but their efforts may limit innovation and the exploration of lucrative business possibilities. UPS is one organization that appears to be willing to accept a certain degree of risks to gain market share. In hopes of capturing more of the higher margin commercial business, UPS is moving away from the residential deliveries that had been its profit center, and is attempting to capture additional commercial business. This strategy entails a good bit of risk, but the potential gain is enormous.[5]

❖ ❖ THE LEVELS OF STRATEGIC PLANNING

It is important to consider strategic planning according to the organizational levels at which it occurs, particularly in light of the growth in recent decades of such complex organizations as GE, United Technologies, Allied Corporation, and Textron. Figure 6.1 illustrates the organizational levels of a typical complex corporation, along with the corresponding levels of strategic planning. Since each level has its own distinctive characteristics, the tools and processes that are useful in formulating strategy at the three levels differ.

If an organization produced a single product or service, then a single strategic plan would encompass everything the corporation did. However, many organizations are in diverse businesses, some of which are only vaguely related. Because so many organizations are engaged in multiple activities, it is important to understand the differences among corporate-level strategic planning, business-level strategic planning, and functional-level strategic planning. When global strategies are developed, it is important to take into consideration global diversity and to remain sensitive to those impacted by various global strategies.

Corporate-level strategic planning is the process of defining the overall

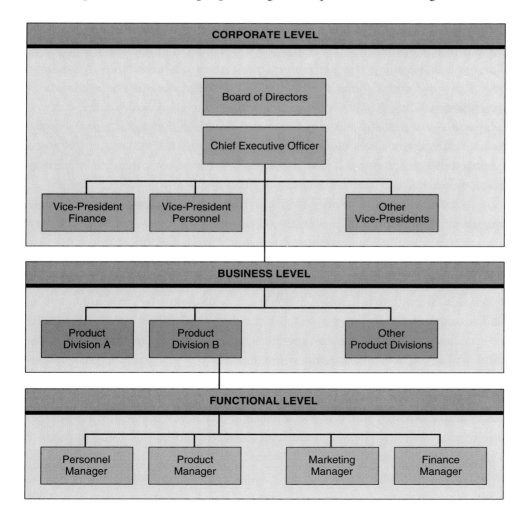

❖ **Figure 6.1**
The levels of strategic planning

character and purpose of the organization, the businesses it will enter and leave, and how the corporation's resources will be distributed among those businesses. This type of planning will determine what line of businesses the corporation should be in. Corporate-level strategy typically concerns the mix and utilization of business divisions called *strategic business units* (which will be discussed shortly). Corporate-level strategic planning addresses the actions the organization will take and determines the roles of each business in the organization's grand strategy. Corporate-level strategic planning is primarily the responsibility of the organization's top executives, like Jack Welch and his immediate subordinates at GE.

Without a carefully considered corporate-level strategic plan, corporate managers will not fulfill their objectives. Corporate strategists can make the mistake of attempting business ventures that they are not capable of operating successfully. Companies often expand without properly utilizing corporate-level strategic planning, and their expansions are often unsuccessful. According to Wayne Calloway, chairman and CEO of PepsiCo, the company's mission has been, and continues to be, to do only what it can do best. PepsiCo is no longer in the transportation business and the sporting goods business. The company is now one-third beverage businesses, one-third snack businesses, and one-third restaurants. It is number one in the chicken category, number one in the Mexican foods category, and number one in the pizza category. It is not in the hamburger business because it could not buy McDonald's and therefore could not be number one in this category. The corporate-level strategic plan takes into account all of PepsiCo's separate businesses, and business-level strategic plans are developed for each one.

Business-level strategic planning is the planning process concerned primarily with how to manage the interests and operations of a particular business. In the case of PepsiCo, different business-level plans would be appropriate for the beverage businesses, the snack businesses, and the restaurant businesses. Business-level planning determines how each of these businesses should compete, on the basis of conditions such as market variables and available resources. Since many organizations, like PepsiCo, have extensive interests in different businesses, top managers often have a difficult time organizing the complex companies and their varied activities. One approach for dealing with this problem is the creation of strategic business units, which are meant to facilitate the management of large organizations.

A **strategic business unit** (SBU) is any part of a business organization that is treated separately for strategic planning purposes. It can be a single business or a collection of related businesses. For example, PepsiCo's beverage, snack, and restaurant businesses could all be treated as separate SBUs for planning purposes. The corporate-level strategy provides the general direction, and a business-level strategy provides the direction for each SBU. The business-level strategic plan is reviewed at the corporate level, changes are made if necessary, and the final business-level strategic plan for the SBU is approved. Each SBU has a unique mission and product line and its own competitors and markets.[7]

Many companies set up SBUs as separate profit centers, sometimes giving them virtual autonomy. Other companies have tight control over their SBUs, enforcing corporate policies and standards down to very low levels in the organization. In general, SBU business-level strategic planning is the responsibility of vice-presidents or division heads.

Functional-level strategic planning is the process of determining policies and procedures for relatively narrow areas of activity that are critical to the success of the organization. Practically every large organization is divided into functional subdivisions, usually production, marketing, finance, and personnel. Military installations have supply, police, and maintenance departments, among others. Churches have preaching, education, and music ministries. Each of these functional subdivisions is vital to the success of the organization. Functional-level strategic plans conform to both corporate-level and business-level strategic plans.

❖ THE ORGANIZATIONAL STRATEGISTS

It is difficult to identify the organizational strategists for most organizations. In ancient Greece, where the concept of *strategy* originated, strategy was determined by generals. For some companies, strategy clearly comes from the top. For example, Robert Goizueta, president and chief executive officer of Coca-Cola, seems to call the shots, and GE's Jack F. Welch, Jr., appears to be firmly in control of corporate direction. One of the ultimate strategists of our time is Olive Ann Beech, who formed the Beech Aircraft company around the classic single-engine biplane created by her husband.

Many companies use in-house **strategic planning staff specialists**—individuals who assist and advise managers in strategic planning. Strategic management involves both planning and executing plans. Staff strategic management specialists are involved especially in the planning aspect.

Many organizations retain consultants to assist in designing and implementing strategy. Consultants are particularly useful in that they conduct marketing research and other kinds of research that provide an important information base for strategic decisions. Consultants can play an effective part in strategic planning, even for small firms. In fact, most small firms cannot afford full-time staff specialists. For these companies, using consultants may be the most economical approach to strategic planning.

At least to a limited extent, every manager is an organizational strategist. This is because every manager is responsible for activities related to continuing the company's business operations and to achieving vital corporate objectives. It should be recognized, however, that what may be an overwhelming matter to the human resource director—for example, the size of the annual departmental budget—may be a relatively incidental matter from the standpoint of the total organization. Whether or not a matter is important to any individual has nothing to do with whether or not it is strategic. Strategic matters are determined by answers to the question: How important is it to the organization as a whole, and to what degree does it have continuing significance? **Organizational strategists** are therefore the people who spend a large portion of their time on matters of vital or far-ranging importance to the organization as a whole. In general, they include the top two levels of management, in-house staff specialists in strategic management, and retained consultants who are experts in the areas in which strategic decisions must be made.

❖ ❖ THE STRATEGIC PLANNING AND IMPLEMENTATION PROCESSES

Strategic planning at all levels of the organization can be divided into four steps: (1) determination of the organizational mission, (2) assessment of the organization and its environment, (3) setting of specific objectives or direction, and (4) determination of strategies to accomplish those objectives (see Figure 6.2).[8]

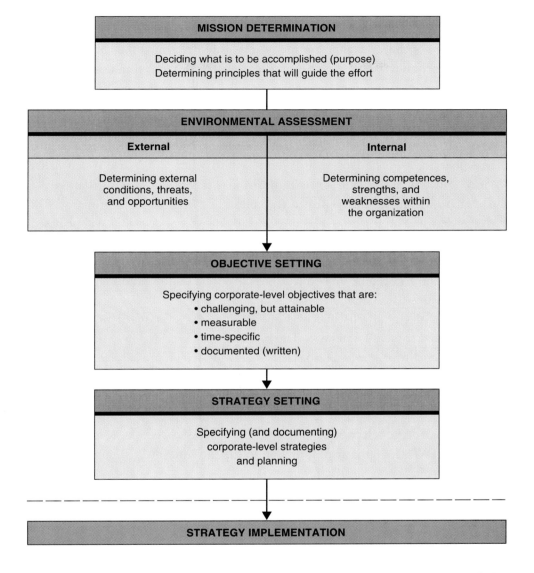

❖ Figure 6.2
Formulating strategy
and implementation

The strategic planning process described here is basically a derivative of the SWOT (strengths, weaknesses, opportunities, and threats) framework that affects organizational performance, but it is less structured. We believe the step-by-step approach just described guides the understanding of the strategic planning process.

Despite its complexity, it is useful to think of strategic planning as a sequential process. By individually examining the four steps of the strategic planning process and the final step of strategy implementation, we will now bring into focus the desirability of a systematic approach to strategic planning and implementation.

Mission Determination

The first step of the strategic planning process is to determine the corporate mission. The corporate mission is the sum total of the organization's ongoing purpose. Arriving at a mission statement should involve answering the questions: What are we in management attempting to do for whom? Should we maximize profit so shareholders will receive higher dividends or so share price will increase? Or should we emphasize stability of earnings so employees will remain secure? Remember that GE had previously emphasized what CEO Jack Welch called "safety," but organizationally, growth in earnings is more important than safety.

There are many other mission possibilities. Mission determination also requires deciding on the principles on which management decisions will be based. Will the corporation be honorable or dishonorable, ruthless or considerate, devious or forthright, in dealing with its various constituencies? The answers to these questions tend to become embedded in a corporate culture and help determine the organizational mission.

An example of a well-conceived mission is AT&T's visionary mission, which was developed some 80 years ago. The mission was described by a former chairman as "a dream of good, cheap, fast, worldwide telephone service. [This mission] . . . is not a speculation. It is a perfectly clear statement that you are going to do something."[9] In line with that mission, AT&T signed joint venture contracts with Philips, the Dutch telecommunications company, to bid together on the installation of large telephone systems in Europe, Asia, and the Middle East. It appears that AT&T's 80-year-old mission to expand into international markets is still on course.

MANAGEMENT IN PRACTICE

A Skill-Building Exercise: You are a supervisor at a company that has initiated a big push to increase productivity. The company's market share is eroding, and Japanese competitors are expected to erode it even more in the near future. Top management is concerned with holding on to the company's current customers. Its objective is not to innovate or grow but to increase internal efficiency and control to produce reliable products for its regular customers. Your boss has just reviewed the corporate-level strategic plan and has asked you and other supervisors to submit new production objectives for each unit. Your boss has indicated that "sizable increases" in production, ranging from 30 to 40 percent, are expected from each unit. Your unit has never produced more than 20 percent over established guidelines, regardless of how much you emphasized the importance of greater productivity.

What would you do?

Environment Assessment

Once the mission has been determined, the organization must be assessed for strengths and weaknesses, and the threats and opportunities in the external environment must be evaluated. Specific objectives can be established, and strategies can be developed for accomplishing those objectives.

Making strategic plans involves information flows from both the internal and the external environment. From inside comes information about organizational competencies, strengths, and weaknesses. Scanning the external environment allows organizational strategists to identify threats and opportunities, as well as constraints. In brief, the job in the planning phase is to develop strategies that take advantage of the company's strengths and minimize its weaknesses in order to grasp opportunities and avoid threats.

Objective Setting

Explicitly stating objectives and directing all activities toward their attainment is not the only approach to strategic management. It may not even be the best approach for some organizations at certain times. However, since Peter Drucker coined the term *management by objectives* in the 1950s, it has been generally accepted that the use of objectives improves the process of management. This is no less true at the corporate level of strategic management than it is for the miler who wishes to better the existing world record.

Characteristics of Strategic Objectives Objectives should be challenging but attainable. If a miler capable of running at near world record speed set an objective of a five-minute mile, the objective could be easily achieved, but the miler would probably not run at maximum speed. On the other hand, if the objective were set at three minutes, no one in the world could come close. Anyone who attempted it would be frustrated. Corporate objectives, too, should offer a reasonable opportunity for accomplishment. To avoid frustration, the probability of accomplishment should not be zero, and to avoid suboptimal performance, it should not be nearly 100 percent.

Remember, too, that objectives should be specific, preferably quantifiable, and measurable. An objective to "maximize profits" offers little specific guidance. To earn $1.2 million in profits or to increase profits by five percent over last year's level is specific. The more specific objectives are, the more definite can be the strategies designed to accomplish them.

Satisficing Herbert Simon has suggested that managers in general do not attempt to optimize or maximize corporate results.[10] He believes the term *satisficing* more correctly describes what managers do. According to Simon's theory, managers typically accept the first satisfactory outcome they are offered. For example, one who believes that ten percent is a reasonable return on invested funds is likely to approve any return on investment objective that exceeds that amount.

If Simon is right, many corporate strategists may be more concerned with establishing direction than with setting specific objectives. As long as this year's sales and profits are above last year's, that may be acceptable because the direction is upward. Many effective organizations have never set specific objectives. In fact, some have only a vague understanding of the direction in which they are headed. It appears likely, however, that any organization can improve its performance by setting objectives that are challenging but attainable and specific, preferably quantified.

Strategy Setting

Once objectives are established or direction is determined, strategies can be formulated. Many organizations limit their written strategic plans to financial budgets. And some do not even have budgets. Most authorities, however, consider it worthwhile to put strategies in writing. Whether or not strategies are written, it is the task of organizational strategists to clearly communicate how the organization tends to accomplish its goals. GE is a company that practices strategy setting.

Strategy Implementation

Once the strategic planning process is complete, the strategy must be implemented. Some people argue that strategy implementation is the most difficult and important part of strategic management. No matter how creative and well formulated the strategic plan, the organization will not benefit if it is incorrectly implemented. Strategy implementation involves several dimensions of the organization, as is illustrated in Figure 6.3. It requires changes in the organization's behavior, which can be brought about by changing one or more organizational dimensions, including management's leadership ability, organizational structure, information and control systems, production technology, and human resources. This evidently is what IBM is doing in its bid to remain a global leader in the computer industry.

Leadership A leader is able to get others to do what he or she wants them to do. Managers must influence organization members to adopt the behaviors needed for strategy implementation. Top-level managers seeking to implement a new strategy may find it useful to build coalitions and persuade middle-level managers to go along with the strategic plan and its implementation. If leaders involve other managers during strategy formulation, implementation will be easier

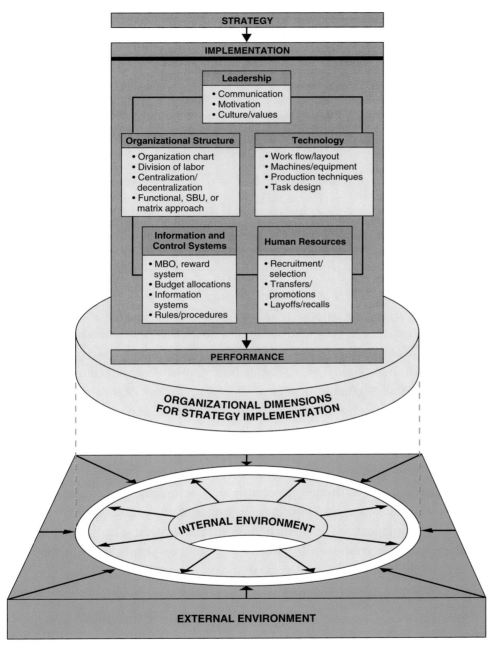

❖ **Figure 6.3**
Organizational dimensions for strategy implementation (Source: Adapted from Jay R. Galbraith and Robert K. Kazanjian, *Strategy Implementation: Structure, Systems, and Process,* 2d ed. [St. Paul, MN: West Publishing, 1986], p. 115. Used with permission.)

because managers and employees will better understand and be more fully committed to the new strategy. Basically, leadership is used to encourage employees to adopt supportive behaviors and, when necessary, to accept the required new values and attitudes.

Global Strategy and Implementation

When going global, an organization must develop a short-term entry strategy and create an expatriate policy manual to handle a range of global situations. IBM's new CEO, Lou Gerstner developed a four-part strategy for the short term to allow IBM to realign itself. First, IBM must get "right-sized" to allow IBM to get in touch with its customers, employees, and shareholders. IBM must totally reevaluate its businesses to move away from the mainframe business. Second, IBM must focus on its customers, actually becoming customer-centered. Third, IBM must figure out the handful of big strategic issues that will determine its long-term future. Finally, IBM is, for the first time in its history, cutting employees, and therefore must work on employee morale and provide morale-building incentives to those who remain.[11] Once a global strategy is developed, a comprehensive expatriate policy manual must be created that is flexible enough to handle a wide range of situations that inevitably will arise as the strategy is implemented. According to human resources experts in the area, the procedures established should involve discussions *beforehand* about the circumstances and conditions surrounding the task at hand and how implementation will be handled.[12]

Organizational Structure A company's organizational structure is typically illustrated by its organizational chart. This structure indicates individual managers' responsibilities and degrees of authority, and incorporates jobs into departments. The structure also pertains to the degree of centralization and the type of department that will be utilized. One of the earliest studies of organizational structure examined historical changes at General Motors, DuPont, Standard Oil of New Jersey, and Sears, Roebuck and Co. As these companies grew large and prosperous, they altered their structures to reflect new strategies.[13]

Information and Control Systems Among the information and control systems are reward systems; incentives; management by objectives systems; budgets for allocating resources; information systems; and the organization's rules, policies, and implementations. A proper mix of information and control systems must be developed to support the implementation of the strategic plan. Managers and employees must be rewarded for adhering to the new strategy and making it a success, or the intensity of implementation will be reduced substantially.

Technology The knowledge, tools, and equipment used to accomplish an organization's assignments are its technology. If an organization adopts a strategy of producing a new product, managers must often redesign jobs and construct new buildings and facilities. Because of its efficiency, new technology may also be required for implementing a low-cost strategy. As with other aspects of strategy implementation, the appropriate level of technology must be found for proper implementation of the strategic plan.

Human Resources The organization's human resources are its employees. The human resource function involves such tasks as recruitment, selection, training, transfers, promotions, and layoffs of employees to properly implement the strategic plan. In certain situations, existing employees simply may be incompatible with a new strategy and they may have to be replaced. The new strategy may foster resentment and resistance among both managers and employees, a matter that must be resolved quickly or it may hinder strategy implementation. In essence, a proper balance of human resources must be developed to support strategy implementation.

❖ ❖ FORMULATING CORPORATE-LEVEL STRATEGY

Corporate-level strategy typically concerns the mix and utilization of strategic business units. Executives generally define an overall strategic direction—a grand strategy—and then develop a portfolio of strategic business units to carry it out.

Several Grand Strategies

The nature of the strategic planning process has been discussed thus far in general terms. Strategic planning at the corporate level will now be considered in terms of three grand, or master, strategies that often grow out of the corporate-level strategic planning process: integration, diversification, and retrenchment.

Integration A commonly used term among organizational strategists is **integration**, the unified control of a number of successive or similar operations. The combining of companies is an example of integration. Integration also includes a company's taking over a portion of an industrial or commercial process that previously was accomplished by other firms. Integration need not involve ownership; it may include only control. Thus, supply and marketing contracts are forms of integration. Integration toward the final users of a company's goods or services, as when Tandy Corporation opened its Radio Shack stores, is **forward integration.** A company's taking control of any of the sources of its inputs, including raw materials and labor, is **backward integration.** Southland Corporation's purchase of a petroleum refinery that supplies gasoline to the company's 7-Eleven stores is an example of backward integration. Buying or taking control of competitors at the same level in the production and marketing process is **horizontal integration.** For example, when Firestone, already in the auto service business, took over J. C. Penney's auto service centers, horizontal integration occurred.

Integration can extend beyond the boundaries of the United States. AT&T's joint ventures with Italtel, an Italian telecommunications company, and Philips, a Dutch telecommunications company, are examples of backward integration.

Some convenience store companies that sell gasoline and oil have vertically integrated backward and purchased oil refineries. (Source: © Pete Saloutos 1989/The Stock Market)

These joint ventures established AT&T as a major player in the European telecommunications market.[14]

Following are some of the competitive advantages of integration:

• Improved marketing and technological intelligence.
• Superior control of the firm's economic environment.
• Product differentiation advantages.[15]

Each type of integration can be a strategy for accomplishing a different objective. For example, if the objective is to decrease the cost of inputs, a company could buy out suppliers that earn profits producing the inputs—an example of backward integration. If the objective is to increase market share, horizontal integration might be attempted. This was done when 7-Eleven's parent, Southland Corporation, bought the Pak-A-Sak convenience store chain.

Backward and forward integration are usually designed to accomplish one or both of two purposes: capturing additional profits and obtaining better control. Backward integration does this for the supply channels, and forward integration does it for the distribution channels. Obviously, if either a supplier or an intermediate customer is making exorbitant profits, vertical integration may be justified on this basis alone. Vertical integration may also be justified when a company believes it can perform the functions of suppliers or intermediate customers effectively and efficiently. But if better control of sources of supply or distribution channels is the only objective, it may be better not to buy the business. There may be better ways to ensure control, such as making franchise agreements with intermediate customers and long-term supply agreements with suppliers. Taking over customers or suppliers is costly, and it often involves the company in businesses with which its managers are unfamiliar.

Diversification Increasing the variety of goods or services made or sold is **diversification,** which may be conglomerate or concentric. **Conglomerate diversification** is the development of businesses unrelated to the firm's current businesses. **Concentric diversification** is the development of businesses related to the firm's current businesses. As a grand strategy, diversification usually has risk reduction as its purpose. A company involved in a number of businesses avoids having all its eggs in one basket. Ideally, when some of a conglomerate firm's businesses decline, others will be on the increase. Some conglomerate firms are countercyclical; that is, they tend to see increasing sales when the economy in general is declining. Such businesses are hard to find. The do-it-yourself hand-tool market is one of the rare exceptions. When times are tough, people tend to repair their own automobiles, for example, and they need tools to do so.

About the best a conglomerate firm can hope for, in general, is a group of SBUs whose valleys and peaks occur at different times in the business cycle. Of course, concentric diversification may not appear to serve the risk reduction objective as well as conglomerate diversification does; however, this type of diversification tends to be more successful in improving profitability. This is probably because the managers of concentrically diversifying firms know something about the businesses they are buying.

Diversification often occurs as a byproduct of bargain hunting by corporate strategists. Even if the preference is for a related merger candidate, corporate-level strategists may opt for acquiring an SBU in an entirely different business because it is deemed to be greatly underpriced. Diversification can also be a product of a desire for growth.

Retrenchment Another grand strategy, usually applied only when failure is imminent, is retrenchment. **Retrenchment** is the reduction of the size or scope of a firm's activities. Most corporate managements resist this strategy. Although growth is often an objective, retrenchment seldom is. When a retrenchment strategy is followed, the objective is often survival.

Prompt elimination of losing businesses has been the hallmark of a number of successful managers of large corporations. For example, Baker Hughes, Inc., is quick to "lop off weak limbs" when a loser surfaces in the corporation.[16] Of course, smaller companies also may find themselves involved in activities that are unprofitable and that appear likely to remain so. For example, Superior Printing Company, a small printing operation in Columbus, Ohio, was losing money producing standard business forms. When Superior stopped doing the unprofitable work and sold the related equipment, profits improved markedly. In addition, the owner, Jeffrey Shuman, could then pay attention to what he really knew best, limited orders for custom-printed items such as fine letterhead and direct mail circulars.

Portfolio Strategy

Once the grand strategy has been determined—that is, once the organization has established the major action by which it intends to achieve long-term objectives—a portfolio strategy is developed. **Portfolio strategy** is the process of determining how an SBU will compete in a particular line of business, with a concentration on the mix of business units and product lines that fit together in a logical way to provide maximum competitive advantage for the corporation. The technique was developed by General Electric in 1971 to integrate its many different businesses. Since then, the Boston Consulting Group (BCG) has refined the approach for use by other organizations. An organization that engages in many different businesses sometimes adopts a business portfolio approach to develop a comprehensive method for strategic planning. An individual may wish to diversify an investment portfolio with some high-risk stocks, some low-risk stocks, some growth stocks, and perhaps a few income bonds. In much the same way, corporations like to have a balanced mix of SBUs. In general, however, an SBU engages in just one line of business. The BCG matrix is probably the most popular portfolio strategy.

The BCG Matrix

Research shows that half or more of America's largest corporations practice some kind of formal business portfolio planning.[17] Most of them use a two-dimensional model to display the various attributes of their diversified group of businesses (or SBUs) in a concise way. The best-known model is the BCG matrix, illustrated in Figure 6.4. Each circle in it represents a different SBU. Although the BCG matrix greatly simplifies the strategic planning process, showing the SBUs of a complex company such as General Mills (40 SBUs) would produce a rather cluttered diagram.

Placing SBUs on the BCG Matrix The matrix shows three things about each SBU. First, the area of each circle is proportional to the sales revenue of its business. For example, SBU A is the largest in sales among those illustrated and SBU E is the smallest. Second, the relative position of a circle along the horizontal axis is determined by the SBU's market share as compared to that of the largest rival firm. Third, the vertical axis of the BCG matrix measures the market growth rate of the industry, not the growth rate in sales of the individual business. A busi-

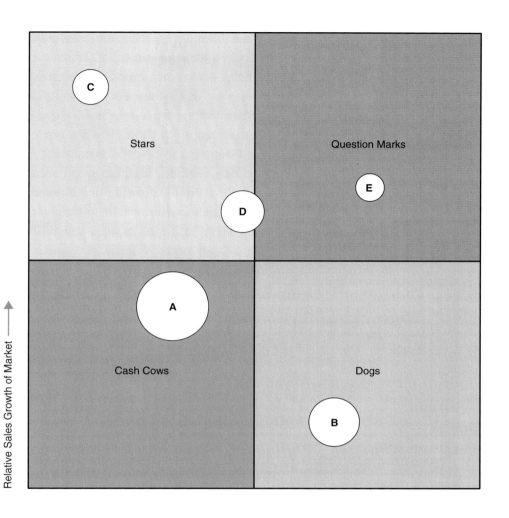

❖ **Figure 6.4**
The BCG matrix

ness that is gaining market share will show a higher growth rate than the market in general.

Stars, Question Marks, Cows, and Dogs An implicit assumption of the BCG analysis is that in a given business, market share signifies strength and market growth rate signifies opportunity. Referring again to Figure 6.4, businesses with high market shares that are also in high-growth-rate industries are given the favorable designation Stars. Theoretically, Stars offer the best profit and growth opportunities for the company. SBUs with low market shares in low-growth industries are called Dogs, because their market shares suggest competitive weakness and because the slow industry growth rates suggest approaching market saturation. The steel industry, for example, is considered by many to be saturated.

The major focus of the BCG analysis is on cash flows. SBUs that hold high market shares in low-growth-rate industries should not be rapidly expanding investment in those industries because there are better investments available. Still, these high-market-share SBUs should be allowed to earn profits. Research suggests that the profitability of such companies depends mostly on employee productivity, capital utilization, and pricing policies—not on added investment.[18] Because there is no need for added investment in the business, the profits can be used to finance the corporation's other businesses, particularly Stars. These high-market-share, low-growth-rate businesses appear in the lower left-hand quadrant of the BCG matrix and are called Cash Cows.

Usually, when a company enters a new business, it will at first have a low market share. If the new business is part of a rapidly growing industry, such as the home computer industry, the business faces an uncertain future as a new entry into the market. Thus, low-market-share businesses in high-growth industries are called Question Marks on the BCG matrix. Typically, it requires large amounts of cash to develop them into Stars. Sometimes, however, a Question Mark business grows rapidly and is so profitable that it can generate the cash flows it requires for its own growth.

Implications of the BCG Analysis The corporate-level strategist who uses the BCG approach must ask: What are the strategic implications for the corporation as a whole? What does BCG analysis say about resource allocation and about disposition of the various SBUs? First, BCG proponents argue, the corporation's overall cash flow must be balanced. There should be enough Cash Cows in the business portfolio to fund the cash needs of the Stars and Question Marks, which offer the greatest promise. Second, the positions on the BCG matrix imply certain strategies. Sale or liquidation is recommended for Dogs and perhaps for weak Cash Cows. Growth is the right path for Question Marks and Stars. Efforts should be made to get back investment funds by utilizing Cash Cows.

Some researchers believe resource allocation is an important, but often ignored, use of the BCG matrix.[19] In other words, they think BCG analysis should not be limited to buy-sell and invest-disinvest decisions, but should also be used to distribute funds within the corporation.

❖ ❖ FORMULATING BUSINESS-LEVEL STRATEGY

Strategy formulation at the business level—within the strategic business units—is concerned primarily with how to compete. The strategies of growth, stability, and retrenchment apply at the business level as well as the corporate level, but they are accomplished through competitive actions rather than by the acquisition or divestment of other business. Two frameworks in which business units formulate strategy are the adaptive strategy typology and Porter's competitive strategies.

Adaptive Strategy Typology

The *adaptive strategy typology* is based on a study of business strategies by Raymond Miles and Charles Snow.[20] The basic idea is that business-level managers seek to formulate strategies that will be harmonious with the external environment. Organizations strive to achieve a fit among internal characteristics, strategy, and external characteristics. Their strategies allow organizations to successfully adapt to the environment. The strategies based on the external environment are the prospector, defender, analyzer, and reactor strategies. These strategies, their environments, and their characteristics are summarized in Table 6.1.

Prospector The business-level strategy that involves innovation through seeking out new opportunities, taking risks, and expanding is the **prospector strategy.** This strategy is well suited to a dynamic, growing environment, where creativity is more important than efficiency. The internal organization is flexible and decentralized to facilitate innovation. United Parcel Services's computerization of its entire operation so it would be able to react quickly to changing situations is one example of prospector strategy.

Defender The defender strategy is almost the opposite of the prospector strategy in that it is concerned with stability or retrenchment rather than growth. The **defender strategy** is the business-level strategy that seeks to maintain current market share by holding on to current customers. The objective is neither to

TABLE 6.1 Miles and Snow's Adaptive Strategy Typology

STRATEGIES	EXTERNAL ENVIRONMENT	ORGANIZATIONAL CHARACTERISTICS
Prospector—Innovate. Find new market opportunities. Grow. Take risks.	Dynamic, growing	Creativity, innovation, flexibility, decentralization.
Defender—Protect turf. Retrench. Hold current market.	Stable	Tight control, centralization, production efficiency, low overhead.
Analyzer—Maintain current market. Innovate moderately.	Moderate change	Tight control, flexibility, efficient production, creativity.
Reactor—No clear strategy. React to specific conditions. Drift.	Any condition	No clear organizational approach; depends on current needs.

(Source: Based on Raymond E. Miles, Charles C. Snow, Alan D. Meyer, and Henry L. Coleman, Jr., "Organizational Strategy, Structure, and Process." *Academy of Management Review* 3 (1978): 546–562.)

One example of prospector strategy is United Parcel Service, which innovated in both services and production techniques in the rapidly changing overnight mail industry. In this promotional photograph, we see UPS's two main means of transport and get some idea of the number of countries to which the company delivers.
(Source: Photograph courtesy of United Parcel Service.)

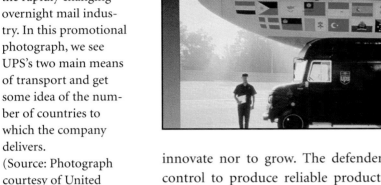

innovate nor to grow. The defender is concerned with internal efficiency and control to produce reliable products for regular customers. Defenders can be successful, especially when they exist in a declining industry or a stable environment.[21]

Analyzer Analyzers are considered to lie midway between prospectors and defenders. The **analyzer strategy** is the business-level strategy of attempting to maintain a stable business while innovating on the fringe. Some products are targeted toward stable environments with a strategy designed to retain current customers. Others are targeted toward new, more dynamic environments, where growth is possible. The analyzer attempts to balance efficient production for current lines with the creative development of new product lines. One example is Anheuser-Busch, which has a stable beer line and the innovation of offering snack foods as a complementary line.

Reactor The reactor has no strategy whatsoever. Rather than defining a strategy to suit a specific environment, reactors respond to environmental threats and opportunities in ad hoc fashion. They take whatever actions seem likely to meet their immediate needs and have no long-term plan for congruence with the external environment. Reactors exist in any environment, but may have no strategy or internal characteristics suited to that environment. A reactor strategy seems almost random because top management has not defined a plan or given the organization an explicit direction. Consequently, failing companies often are the result of reactor strategies.

Porter's Competitive Strategies

Management strategist Michael E. Porter studied a number of business organizations and proposed three effective business-level strategies: differentiation, cost leadership, and focus.[22] The organizational characteristics associated with each strategy are summarized below.

Differentiation The business-level strategy that involves an attempt to distinguish the firm's goods or services from others in the industry is the **differentiation strategy.** The organization may use such skills and resources as advertising, distinctive product features, exceptional service, and technology to achieve a product that could be perceived as unique. Successful differentiation strategy is often profitable because customers will usually be loyal and will pay high prices for the product. Examples of products that have benefitted from a differentiation strategy include Porsche automobiles and Ralph Lauren Polo clothing, both of which are perceived as distinctive in their markets.

Cost Leadership The business-level strategy in which the organization aggressively seeks efficient facilities, pursues cost reductions, and uses tight cost controls to produce products more efficiently than competitors is the **cost leadership**

A GLOBAL PERSPECTIVE

Strategic Planning: Properly Balancing Risks with Payoffs

In order to compete globally, managers must find a way to achieve their overall organizational objectives overseas. There is no doubt that global strategies often involve risks, but the payoffs for calculated risks are often tremendous. General Electric's (GE) brave new strategy involves mixing GE's future with the futures of China, India, and Mexico. This strategy is far from riskless, but the possible benefits are staggering. John F. Welch, Jr., the CEO of GE, sees the future strategy as one of shifting the company's "center of gravity" from the industrialized world to Asia and Latin America. In addition to China, India, and Mexico, GE sees possibilities in Southeast

Asia. Clearly, this strategy has political and economic risks, but with 2.5 billion people in these regions, almost ten times the population of the United States, GE is risking a few tens of millions of dollars in each, softening the blow if any one market falls through, for a projected $20 billion in revenue by the year 2000. Amazingly this could double GE's current revenues.[23]

Nike founder and CEO, Philip Knight, believes that to be the dominant athletic shoe company globally, Nike must push one product and one image. The company has no boundaries as to who must do what. Global marketing is directed from the United States, and the rest is handled in various parts of the globe. When developing their new shoe, the "Air Rage," the process started in

Oregon with development, line drawings, technical data, and a model of the shoe, which were then sent or faxed to engineers at a development center in Taiwan. The molds and cast dies were then sent to independent contractors in Asia. The shoes are stitched in Indonesia or China, and then are bound for retail outlets around the world.[24]

Strategically, many companies are opting to take the risks of going wherever the business and the resources are in order to remain competitive globally and to actually gain market share. Strategically, both GE and Nike appear to be on the correct course, even though their methods of accomplishing their objectives differ. These companies have clearly isolated their overall organizational objectives and are actively pursuing them.

strategy. A low-cost position means that the company can undercut competitors' prices and still offer comparable quality and earn a reasonable profit. Quality Inns is a low-priced alternative to lodging outlets such as Holiday Inns and Ramada Inns.

Focus The business-level strategy in which the organization concentrates on a specific regional market, product line, or buyer group is the **focus strategy.** When focusing on a single market segment, the company may use either a differentiation or a low-cost approach, but only for that narrow market. The company may be seeking either a competitive cost advantage or a perceived differentiation in the target segment.

Porter found that many businesses did not consciously adopt one of these three strategies and thus were stuck in the middle of the pack with no strategic advantage. Without a strategic advantage, the businesses earned below-average profits and therefore were not in a position to compete successfully.

There is some similarity between Porter's strategies and Miles and Snow's adaptive typology. The differentiation strategy is similar to the prospector strategy, the cost leadership strategy is similar to the defender strategy, and the focus strategy is similar to the analyzer strategy, which adopts a focus strategy appropriate for each product line. The reactor strategy, which is really not a strategy at all, is similar to what is used by the middle-of-the-pack organizations that cannot attain a competitive strategic advantage.

❖ ❖ FORMULATING FUNCTIONAL-LEVEL STRATEGY

Functional-level strategies are the action plans adopted by the major functional departments to support the execution of a business-level strategy. Major organizational functions include marketing, production, finance, human resources, and research and development. For example, strategic planning for the finance function at GE involves the establishment of budgeting, accounting, and investment policies and the allocation of SBU cash flows. In the human resource area, policies for compensation, hiring and firing, training, and human resource planning are of strategic concern.

Strategic planning is not concerned with day-to-day supervision. It is concerned mainly with providing general, longer-range direction and guidance. Most corporations are expanding their strategic planning range beyond the domestic front to the international arena. Coca-Cola, Kentucky Fried Chicken, Bausch & Lomb, Johnson & Johnson, RJR Nabisco, Seagram, and Procter & Gamble have established strategic joint partnerships with Chinese companies. Increasingly,

✘ Management Tips ✘

Guidelines for Dealing with Strategic Planning

1. **Strategic planning is important at all organizational levels.** It is not just for top-level managers.

2. **Managers at all organizational levels should base their plans on the organizational mission.** Managers must first determine what the firm desires to accomplish.

3. **The environment in which the decision is to be made must be clearly understood.** All plans should be assessed for their strengths and weaknesses and threats and opportunities.

4. **Objectives in the strategic planning process should be specific in nature.** Without them being specific, it is impossible to know if the objective has been attained.

5. **At times, it is not possible to maximize results.** Often a good decision is the best choice, given the time constraints placed on managers.

6. **No matter how good a strategic plan is, it is worthless unless properly implemented.** The organization will not benefit unless it is properly implemented.

7. **There are numerous grand strategies available in the strategic planning process.** Use the ones that best achieve your overall mission.

8. **Diversity may be necessary to achieve corporate objectives.** You may want to diversify to avoid having all your eggs in one basket.

9. **A portfolio strategy may need to be developed to determine how to compete in a particular line of business.** Use all the tools at your disposal.

10. **Be willing to expand your strategic planning range beyond the domestic front to the international arena.** Increasingly, companies are seeking potential overseas markets and making this objective part of their organizational mission.

companies are seeking potential overseas markets and making this objective part of their organizational mission.

Consider a company that has adopted a prospector strategy and is introducing new products that are expected to experience rapid growth in the early stages of their life cycle. The human resource department should adopt a strategy appropriate for growth, which means recruiting additional workers and training middle managers for movement into new positions. The marketing department should undertake test marketing, aggressive advertising campaigns, and product trials by consumers. The finance department should adopt plans to borrow money, handle large cash investments, and authorize construction of new production facilities.

A company with mature products or an analyzer strategy will have different functional strategies. The human resource department should develop strategies for retaining and developing a stable work force, including transfers, advancements, and incentives for efficiency and safety. Marketing should stress brand loyalty and the development of established, reliable distribution channels. Production should maintain long production runs, routinization, and cost reduction. Finance should focus on net cash flows and positive cash balances. Functional-level strategies should support the execution of business-level strategies by developing an effective mix of the major organizational functions.

SUMMARY

Strategic planning is the process by which top management determines organizational purposes and objectives for the company and how they are to be achieved. Corporate-level strategic planning is the process of defining the overall character and purpose of the organization, the businesses it will enter and leave, and the manner in which resources will be distributed among those businesses. Business-level strategic planning is concerned primarily with how to manage the interests and operations of a particular business. Functional-level strategic planning is the process of determining policies and procedures for relatively narrow areas of activity that are critical to the success of the organization. Many companies use in-house organizational strategists to assist and advise managers in strategic planning.

The strategic planning process is a four-step approach: (1) determining the mission, (2) assessing the organization and its environment, (3) setting objectives or direction, and (4) determining strategies to accomplish the objectives. Basically, the process is a derivative of the SWOT—strengths, weaknesses, opportunities, and threats—framework that affects organizational performance. Once the strategic plan is developed, the next step is to implement the plan.

Corporate-level strategy typically concerns the mix and utilization of strategic business units. Executives in charge of the entire corporation generally define an overall strategic direction—called a *grand strategy*—and then develop a portfolio of strategic business units to carry out the grand strategy.

The two frameworks in which business units formulate strategy are the adaptive strategy typology and Porter's competitive strategies. Functional-level strategies are the action plans adopted by major functional departments in order to support the execution of business-level strategy. Major organizational functions include marketing, production, finance, human resources, and research and development.

KEY TERMS

Strategic planning 168

Corporate-level strategic planning 171

Business-level strategic planning 173

Strategic business unit (SBU) 173

Functional-level strategic planning 173

Strategic planning staff specialists 174

Organizational strategists 174

Integration 181

Forward integration 181

Backward integration 181

Horizontal integration 181

Diversification 183

Conglomerate diversification 183

Concentric diversification 183

Retrenchment 183

Portfolio strategy 184

Prospector strategy 187

Defender strategy 187

Analyzer strategy 188

Differentiation strategy 189

Cost leadership strategy 189

Focus strategy 190

REVIEW QUESTIONS

1. Define <u>strategic planning</u>. What is a strategic business unit?
2. Distinguish among corporate-level strategic planning, business-level strategic planning, and functional-level strategic planning.
3. Who are the organizational strategists?
4. List and briefly describe each step in the strategic planning process?
5. Describe the concept of <u>satisficing</u> as suggested by Herbert Simon.
6. Identify and briefly describe the grand, or master, strategies that grow out of the strategic planning process.
7. Briefly describe the following business-level strategies:
   a. adaptive strategy typology
   b. Porter's competitive strategy

CASE STUDIES

CASE 6.1 Master Hardware

Master Hardware is a chain of 12 retail outlets located in small towns in northern Kentucky and southern Ohio. The parent corporation, Master Merchandisers, Inc., is a Kentucky-based corporation owned by the Booker family of Louisville. The Bookers, led by Beatrice, who was 85 years old in 1994, have steadfastly refused to vary from the plan that Beatrice found successful when the first Master Hardware stores were opened during the 1940s. The plan is simple: Only one store is opened in each town, and the town's population must be between 8,000 and 15,000. Inventories are tightly controlled, and no item is stocked unless it turns over at least four times a year. Each store is managed by a carefully selected local citizen, who is paid 50 percent of the profits the store generates. All purchasing is done by the central office in Louisville, although most items are shipped directly from hardware wholesalers and manufacturers to the individual stores. The store buildings are rented. After an initial infusion of capital, each store is required to pay its own way. If it does not, it is closed.

Master Merchandisers had opened no new stores for several years, although the existing stores were quite profitable. The company had never done much borrowing, so the high profits resulted in increasing cash balances, even after family members were paid director's fees, salaries, and so forth.

Until 1987, the excess funds were invested in U.S. Treasury securities, which are safe but yield low returns. That year, Beatrice Booker agreed with the board of directors—made up of two of her sons, a nephew, and a niece—that the company should go into the restaurant business. The Bookers decided that Master Merchandisers would invest $3 million and build at least five new seafood restaurants. They would feature pond-raised catfish and would be located in towns similar to those where the Master Hardware stores were.

The restaurant business was separately incorporated as Catfish Master Restaurants, Inc. By mid-1990, three Catfish Master Restaurants were opened. The system was patterned as much as possible after the Master Hardware chain. Restaurant managers were paid a percentage of the profits. Purchasing was done centrally, and each restaurant was required to support itself after the initial investment. It became clear within a year, however, that the first two restaurants would have to be closed unless additional funds were provided. The Bookers put up an additional $50,000 to help those two restaurants stay open, but both were still unprofitable two years later.

QUESTIONS

1. State what you believe to be the corporate mission of Master Merchandisers, Inc.
2. List the strategies discussed in the case that you consider business-level strategies. Explain your answer.
3. What kind of integration occurred when Master Merchandisers went into the restaurant business? Discuss.
4. Do you believe the Booker family is likely to be successful in the restaurant business? Explain.

CASE 6.2 NutraSweet: Developing a Strategy

G. D. Searle and Company has spent millions annually on research and development—$200 million on drug research alone in one year. But the company's most exciting product, NutraSweet, was discovered by accident. The Searle scientist who is credited with developing NutraSweet in 1965 was working on a product for ulcer treatment.

NutraSweet was introduced nationally in 1982 and accounted for about half of Searle's billion-dollar revenues in 1984. For the rest of the decade the product was the sweetener of choice for most artificially sweetened products. NutraSweet sales were $746 million in 1988 and recently topped $1 billion. Customers ranged from Coca-Cola and Pepsi, General Foods, Procter & Gamble, Heinz, and Wrigley to the millions of consumers who made the NutraSweet-based diet sweetener Equal an instant best-seller.

The path from the development of the product in 1965 to its domination of the artificial sweetener market was not an easy one. Exceptional management skill and a great deal of strategic planning were required. First, the Food and Drug Administration (FDA) had to be convinced that the product was safe. Partial FDA approval came in 1981, 16 years after the product was developed. It was not until 1983 that the government allowed carbonated soft drinks to be sweetened with NutraSweet. Despite FDA approval, some groups continue to question NutraSweet's safety.

Searle created a new division for NutraSweet in 1983. Donald Rumsfeld, Searle's chief executive, chose Robert Shapiro, the company's general counsel, to head this division. The multimillion dollar marketing effort Shapiro initiated was aimed mainly at consumers, although NutraSweet was not sold to them directly. Because of the exceptional success of the advertising program, Shapiro faced another challenge. How could the company produce 3,000,000 pounds and be ready for growth that was sure to come? While Shapiro was fighting off adverse publicity related to NutraSweet safety, he had to build a new organization involving thousands of workers and hundreds of managers and sales personnel. Two European companies were engaged to help make NutraSweet. Despite having a new $160 million plant in Augusta, Georgia, demand outstripped supply, and new customers were refused.

Competitors in West Germany and the United States had already patented innovative new sweeteners, and others were on the verge of doing so. So

Shapiro had to intensify research and development efforts.

Also, Shapiro knew that at $90 a pound, Nutra-Sweet, which is 200 times sweeter than sugar, would face continued cost pressure compared to $4 a pound for saccharin, which is 300 times sweeter than sugar. Productivity had to be increased at the NutraSweet plants in Illinois, Michigan, and Georgia. Monsanto Corporation paid $2.8 billion for Searle—and Shapiro had access to the expert manufacturing help that was lacking inside Searle.

The overall NutraSweet strategy worked. Nutra-Sweet is still producing roughly 20 cents profit on every sales dollar. However, when the exclusive patent rights are eliminated, the cost pressure will intensify even more. NutraSweet's strategy for continued success is to take advantage of its brand recognition and customer insistence, to continue its aggressive promotional campaigns, and to make every attempt to become more price competitive. Hopefully, this strategy will assure that NutraSweet remains an ingredient in over 4,000 products. Brand insistence and aggressive promotional campaigns are nothing new, but price competitiveness is a strategic element that may add the little extra needed to keep the strategy effective. Can this strategy make NutraSweet competitive with producers of the less-expensive sweetening ingredient in NutraSweet, aspartame? Will this strategy assure that NutraSweet continues to enjoy the sweet taste of success? Well, the strategy is in place, the previously successful management team is poised for action, and the future is now.

QUESTIONS

1. On the basis of the information provided in this case, what do you believe the mission statement is for NutraSweet?
2. Who are the organizational strategists at Nutra-Sweet?

NOTES

1. This discussion is a composite from a number of sources, among them: Stratford P. Sherman, "Inside the Mind of Jack Welch," *Fortune* 124 (March 27, 1989): 39–50; John A. Byrne, "Is Your Company Too Big?" *Business Week* (March 27, 1989): 84–94; Edwin A. Finn, Jr., "General Eclectic," *Forbes* 148 (March 23, 1989): 74–80; Howard Banks, "General Electric—Going with the Winners," *Forbes* 143 (March 1984): 97–106; N. Nelson-Horchtes, "GE Builds a High-Tech Arsenal," *Industry Week* 3 (October 1983): 49–50; N. Snyderman, "GE Is Doing the Things the U.S. Must Do to Be Competitive," *Electronic News,* suppl. B, 3 (October 1983).
2. Seth Lubove, "We Have a Big Pond to Play in," *Forbes* 152 (September 13, 1993): 216–224.
3. Patricia Sellers with David Kirkpatrick, "Can This Man Save IBM?" *Fortune* 127 (April 19, 1993): 63–67.
4. Jonathan B. Levine, Catherine Arnst, and Neil Gross, "Will Philips Sell the World on the VCR of the Future?" *Business Week* (August 17, 1992): 44–45.
5. Chuck Hawkins and Patrick Oster, "After a U-Turn, UPS Really Delivers," *Business Week* (May 31, 1993): 92–93.
6. Ann Hagedorn, "Colgate Still Seeking to Placate Critics of Its Darkie Brand," *The Wall Street Journal* (April 18, 1988): 36–37.
7. Frederick Gluck, Stephen Kaufman, and A. Steven Walleck, "The Four Phases of Strategic Management," *Journal of Business Strategy* 2 (Winter 1982): 11–12.
8. Ian Wilson, "The Strategic Management Technology: Corporate Fad or Strategic Necessity," *Long-Range Planning* 19 (1986): 21–22.
9. Quoted in Charles H. Granger, "The Hierarchy of Objectives," *Harvard Business Review* 42 (May–June 1964): 63–74.
10. Herbert A. Simon, *The New Science of Management Decision* (New York: Harper & Row, 1960).
11. David Kirkpatrick, "Lou Gerstner's First 30 Days," *Fortune* 127 (May 31, 1993): 57–62.

12. Stephenie Overman, "International Waters," *HR-Magazine* 38 (September 1993): 46–49.

13. Alfred V. Chandler, *Strategies and Structures* (Cambridge, MA: M.I.T. Press, 1962).

14. Harris Collingwood, "In Business This Week," *Business Week* (February 13, 1989): 38.

15. Kathryn Rudie Harrigan, "A Framework for Looking at Vertical Integration," *Journal of Business Strategy* 3 (Winter 1983): 30–37.

16. Todd Vogel, "Baker Hughes Lops Off a Weak Limb," *Business Week* (May 19, 1989): 34.

17. Philippe Haspeslagh, "Portfolio Planning: Uses and Limits," *Harvard Business Review* 60 (January–February 1982): 58–73.

18. Ian C. MacMillan, Donald C. Hambrick, and Diana L. Day, "The Product Portfolio and Profitability: A PIMS-Based Analysis of Industrial-Product Businesses," *Academy of Management Journal* 25 (December 1982): 733–755.

19. Frederick Gluck, "The Dilemmas of Resource Allocation," *Journal of Business Strategy* 2 (Fall 1981): 67–71.

20. Raymond E. Miles and Charles C. Snow, *Organizational Strategy, Structure, and Process* (New York: McGraw-Hill, 1978).

21. Donald C. Hambrick, "Some Tests of the Effectiveness and Functional Attributes of Miles and Snow's Strategic Types," *Academy of Management Journal* 26 (1983): 5–26.

22. Michael E. Porter, *Competitive Strategy* (New York: Free Press, 1980), pp. 36–46.

23. Tim Smart, Pete Engardio, and Geri Smith, "GE's Brave New World," *Business Week* (November 8, 1993): 64–70.

24. Jim Impoco and Warren Cohen, "Nike Goes to the Full-Court Press," *U.S. News & World Report* 114 (April 19, 1993): 48–50.

Are You a Good Decision Maker?

Since effective decision making is so important in business, it is essential that you develop, and continually fine-tune, your decision-making skills. To assess your decision-making ability, take the self-assessment exercise "Are You a Good Decision Maker?" Then, turn to page 673 to evaluate yourself.

INSTRUCTIONS: For each statement answer either yes or no.

YES	NO	QUESTION
❑ Yes	❑ No	1. Do you often try to avoid or delay making important decisions and even hope that problems will go away?
❑ Yes	❑ No	2. When required to make a decision fairly promptly, do you become flustered and fail to function at your best?
❑ Yes	❑ No	3. Would you consider it demeaning to consult your subordinates regarding a problem with which they have experience?
❑ Yes	❑ No	4. In deciding a complicated problem where strong arguments exist for either side, would you trust your "gut reaction"?
❑ Yes	❑ No	5. Do you often wish that you didn't have to make any decisions?
❑ Yes	❑ No	6. When faced with a serious decision, are your sleep and appetite usually adversely affected?
❑ Yes	❑ No	7. Do you secretly dislike making decisions because you lack self-confidence?
❑ Yes	❑ No	8. Are you uneasy even when required to make unimportant decisions?
❑ Yes	❑ No	9. Would you fire a friend if his continued employment was against the welfare of the enterprise in which you held a high position?
❑ Yes	❑ No	10. When baffled by a problem within your jurisdiction, would you try to pass it off to others?
❑ Yes	❑ No	11. At home, do you participate in all or most of the important decisions?
❑ Yes	❑ No	12. Are you usually edgy both before and after making important decisions?

Source: Adapted from Walter Duckat, "Check Your Decisionmaking Skills," *Supervision* 41 (February 1979): 3. Reprinted with permission from *Supervision.* Copyright © 1979 by The National Research Bureau, Inc., 424 North Third Street, Burlington, Iowa 52601.

7 The Organizing Process and the Informal Organization

LEARNING OBJECTIVES

After completing this chapter students should be able to

✗ Describe what an organization is and explain the organizing process.
✗ Define *specialization of labor* and identify its benefits and limits.
✗ Identify and describe the primary means of departmentation.
✗ Describe organizational differentiation.
✗ Describe the concept of *downsizing*.
✗ Describe the informal organization and explain its benefits and costs.

Wall Drug: A Badlands Small Business Success Story

Success began for Wall Drug with a 12- × 36-inch board that read: "Get a Soda/Get a Root Beer/Turn Next Corner/Just as Near/To Highway 16 and 14/Free Ice Water/Wall Drug." This sign, particularly the part about "Free Ice Water," combined with the hot prairie of South Dakota, brought in customers to a business barely holding on in 1936. As the customers came to sample the "free ice water," they bought other items as well—medicines, combs, and facial tissues. Shelves were no sooner filled than they were empty again. The owners, the Husteads, expanded their line of merchandise and increased the size of the store every few years. Until 1971, they remained cautious, adding inventories and floor space only when the funds to pay for them were in sight. By that time, Wall Drug included a gasoline station, a coffee shop, an art gallery, and a hodgepodge of other attractions. Today, if you take the exit to the little town of Wall, near the Badlands of South Dakota, you will find a lot more than a drugstore, and much more to do than drink ice water. In fact, Wall Drug is more than a store, it's a service station, a place of amusement, a family entertainment center, a gallery of South Dakota history, and a Western heritage museum. In 1972, the Husteads borrowed $250,000 to build what they called "the Mall," and sales jumped 20 percent the next year. The mall is patterned after the main street of a typical Western town, the small shop buildings constructed of native timber and old brick. The street surface is made of rock hauled from the nearby Cheyenne River. Wall Drug is the largest drugstore in the world, but Wall Drug is definitely the right size, even though it is located in a town of only 800 people.

With about $5 million in sales and seasonal employment as high as 200, Wall Drug Company may be the most widely known small business in the world. The company takes out small ads in such unlikely places as the *Village Voice* (in New York City) and the *International Herald Tribune.* Articles about Wall Drug have appeared in *The New York Times, Redbook* magazine, *Time,* and *Reader's Digest.* Posters that mimic the Wall Drug Company highway signs have been seen in Manhattan's Greenwich Village and all over Europe.

Wall Drug is a perfect example of a formal organization that functions more like an informal organization. The set of relationships at Wall Drug are continually evolving, even though the pattern of human interactions are officially prescribed and change very little. The affiliates of Wall Drug joined together to satisfy customer needs. The organization is continuously changing, and even though there is a recognized pecking order, the employees at various organizational levels all work together and are extremely productive.

Because of factors such as the close proximity in which people work, the frequent interaction of group members, and the long time periods employees spend working together, there will always be informal groups and an informal organization at Wall Drug. Managers at Wall Drug deal with the informal organization quite effectively and that spells success at Wall Drug.[1]

The organizing process as it evolved at Wall Drug is similar to that of many other firms, whether small or large, domestic or international, service or manufacturing. In this chapter, the organizing process is discussed first. Then, specialization of labor is presented, followed by a discussion of departmentation. Next, organizational differentiation, which becomes necessary as an organization grows, is presented, followed by a discussion of downsizing. In conclusion, the informal organization and its benefits and costs are addressed and a global perspective is presented.

❖ ❖ WHAT IS AN ORGANIZATION?

The word *organization* is used widely. Most of us are reminded of it each day when we read newspapers, walk around campus, watch television programs, or listen to the radio. When some of us hear the word, we envision large companies such as Wal-Mart and General Motors. But few of us think of the local grocery store, service station, fast-food restaurant, or nursery school. Each of these, however, is an organization. Certainly Wall Drug is an organization.

Organizations, large or small, have at least three characteristics:

1. They are composed of people.
2. They exist to achieve objectives.
3. They require some degree of limitation on member behavior.

Thus, an **organization** is two or more people working together in a coordinated manner to achieve group results. Because most people spend a considerable part of their lives working in organizations, it is important to understand how organizations function and how they can be managed effectively. To be effective, a manager must be capable of organizing human resources, physical factors, and functions such as production, marketing, and finance, in a manner designed to ensure the achievement of the objectives of the firm. This process is crucial to the success of every organization where people work together as a group or a team. In global organizations it is even more essential that managers correctly organize human resources, physical factors, and organizational functions. Many organizations like Chrysler, IBM, and Nike are modifying their organizations by making them lean and flexible to better accomplish organizational objectives.[2]

❖ ❖ THE ORGANIZING PROCESS

Organizing is the process of prescribing formal relationships among people and resources to accomplish objectives. It is vitally important that executive-level managers be comfortable with the organizing process and understand the process and its desired functions. At Motorola, almost every top executive is a trained engineer, each of whom is very comfortable with technology, the backbone of Motorola's business. Motorola is dominated by what cellular chief Edward Staiano, president and general manager of the General Systems sector, calls engineering entrepreneurs. These engineers are heavily into the business of technology, and they all understand and support the organizing process.[3]

The organizing process, as is illustrated in Figure 7.1, takes place within the constraints of the organization's external and internal environments. First, it is necessary to consider the organizational objectives and to determine the kind of organizing needed to accomplish those objectives. Next, the types of functions, or work activities, that will be required to meet company objectives must be determined. Finally, activities that are similar must be grouped together. A number of departments or otherwise separate organizational units need to be set up, each designed to carry out a different function or group of functions.

❖ ❖ THE EXTERNAL ENVIRONMENT

In Chapter 2, we saw how the external environment affects the management of corporations. The external environment also affects the organizing process. For instance, laws and public concern about clean water and air may create a need for a manufacturer to add personnel to monitor any possibly toxic substances that may be discharged. The necessity of dealing with a wide range of suppliers and of buying in large volumes requires a sophisticated purchasing department at company headquarters. Differences in legislation from state to state require that someone be responsible for helping individual managers stay within the law.

More now than in the past, rapidly changing technological factors have an influence on the organizing process. For example, new automotive technology

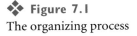

Figure 7.1
The organizing process

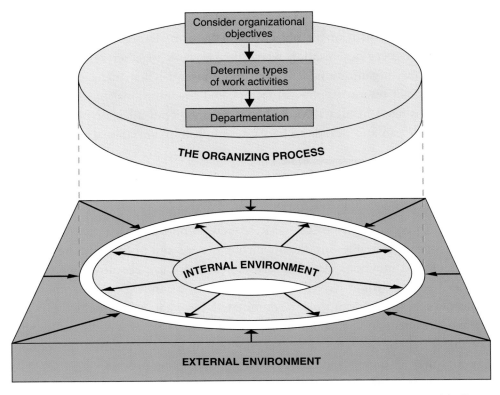

required U.S. automobile manufacturers to make major changes in assembly lines, which had changed little from those developed by Henry Ford before 1920. Robots often do repetitive tasks previously done by humans. In some plants, cars are assembled at work stations rather than on mile-long assembly lines. Rapid technological change is occurring in virtually every industry sector. As changes in the manufacturing process occur, organizations must be able to respond with new and more flexible ways of assigning persons and machines to jobs.

At the General Motors Saturn Plant in northern Tennessee, Japanese methods and machines are used to help produce the new compact model. The Japanese method of cooperation between employees and management is the norm at the Saturn plant. Union members work alongside managers in activities ranging from job-related matters to strategic planning.

❖ ❖ THE INTERNAL ENVIRONMENT

The organizing process is also influenced by the internal environment that individual managers face. The approach to organizing that a manager uses must be compatible with the internal environment. For example, a company's procedures manual may specify the manner in which machinery can be rearranged, and personnel regulations may restrict the reassignment of workers.

New automotive technology, mainly introduced by Japanese producers, has forced U.S. automobile manufacturers to make major changes in assembly lines, which had changed little from those developed by Henry Ford before 1920. Robots, such as the automated welding system shown here, now do many of the repetitive tasks previously done by humans. (Source: © Jim Pickerell)

The boss's view of the company's strategic and operating plans will limit the way a lower-level manager can organize resources to carry out those plans. At Wal-Mart, it is well known that the company places emphasis on individual initiative and autonomy and holds managers accountable for results, whereas at Wall Drug there is a recognized pecking order, and everyone working for the company exercises very little initiative or autonomy.

❖ CONSIDERING ORGANIZATIONAL OBJECTIVES

Everything the manager does should be directed toward accomplishment of objectives, and organizing is no exception. Organizing should have as its purpose arranging people and resources in the best way possible to support the organization's objectives. It is important that every phase of the organizing sequence be directed at accomplishment of objectives. Wall Drug's objective is to satisfy customer needs. Organizing for Wall Drug therefore involves arranging people and resources in the best way possible to achieve that objective.

❖ DETERMINING TYPES OF WORK ACTIVITIES

Once objectives and the kind of organizing needed to accomplish them are established, it is possible to determine the kinds of work activities that should be involved. On a typical baseball team, players perform the tasks of fielding, hitting, and pitching. A good team must develop competent specialists in each of these activities. Pitching can be further broken down into starting, long relieving, and short relieving. Fielding involves playing the infield and the outfield. And playing second base requires talents that are different from those needed to do the other infield jobs.

Similarly, the work activities required to accomplish the objectives of business firms can be identified. In a manufacturing concern, raw materials must be procured and the product must be made and sold. Each of these major phases involves hiring and supervising people, processing paperwork, and numerous other activities. So all these types of activities must be distinguished from one another before the organizing process can proceed. An important concept in specifying different kinds of tasks is specialization of labor.

❖ ❖ SPECIALIZATION OF LABOR

In *The Wealth of Nations* (1776), Adam Smith explained how he was able to increase the productivity of a group of pin makers more than a thousandfold through the specialization (division) of labor. **Specialization of labor** is the division of a complex job into simpler tasks so that one person or group may carry out only identical or related activities. One purpose of organizing, like everything else a manager does, is to improve productivity. Through specialization of labor, it is possible for members of the organization to concentrate on a single area,

---

MANAGEMENT IN PRACTICE

A Skill-Building Exercise: Jim Beck was the drawbench crew chief at Jamestown Tube Corporation's West Monroe, Louisiana, stainless steel tubing facility. The drawbench pulls, or draws, the welded tubing down to smaller sizes. Jim supervised six workers and often lent a hand himself, particularly when maintenance or adjustment was required.

In early 1994, the plant manager, Ken Kincaid, told Jim an additional drawbench was soon to be added. "Jim," said Ken, "we have approval to add six more workers for the new drawbench. But I want you to study the operation and see if we can cut that to five. It seems to me that with the two drawbenches right beside each other, we may be able to cut some of the labor costs." Jim said, "I'm sure we can, Ken. I'll see if I can find a way to do it." Jim continued, "I'm a little worried about supervising 11 people. I think that I can do it,

but it's going to be kind of tough."

As Jim left the office, he thought about how things were always changing in the plant. Just two years earlier, when the plant was opened, he had helped plan the operation of the drawbench. Since Jim had two years' experience, he felt it would be easier the second time. As Jim approached the drawbench, Mike Robinson saw him and said, "Jim, Ed is going to have to be off this afternoon to take his baby to the doctor. That will leave us one operator short." "Okay, Mike," replied Jim. "Do you remember when I had you and Ed switch places a while back? I did that so you could learn each other's job. You can take up the slack when Ed is gone. We'll have to slow down the drawbench a little, but you can handle it."

Did Jim properly determine the types of work activities? Explain.

High Specialization	Moderate Specialization	Low Specialization
Each employee performs a few routine operations such as putting on the knobs for volume control.	Each employee assembles one component of the radio.	Each employee assembles the entire radio.

❖ **Figure 7.2**
Degrees of specialization associated with the job of producing small transistor radios

thereby increasing output. To achieve efficiency, specialization is especially essential in mass-production industries. But in fact, most work activities in nearly all organizations are of a specialized nature.

Organizations have endless options as to the degree of specialization for each job. For instance, if a company produces small transistor radios, several different approaches might be available (see Figure 7.2).

Advantages of Specialization

As Figure 7.3 shows, there are five specific advantages of specialization. First, specialization often increases productivity. A worker who is allowed to concentrate skill and effort on just a small number of tasks can usually achieve a higher level of output. In the manufacture of electronic components, output per worker tends to be much higher in situations where employees perform highly specialized work

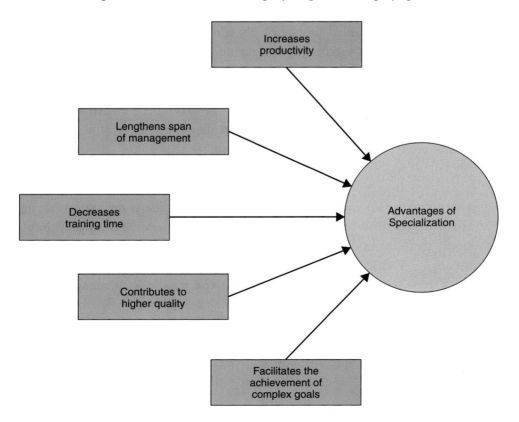

❖ **Figure 7.3**
Advantages of specialization

activities. The same thing applies to many fast-food restaurants. At McDonald's, employees efficiently perform such specialized functions as cooking hamburgers or french fries. This specialization contrasts with the work in more traditional restaurants, where employees may perform a wide variety of jobs.

Second, specialization permits managers to efficiently supervise a large number of employees. A manager may be able to supervise 30 workers who are performing the same specialized tasks. If workers are performing a number of diverse tasks, the number of employees a manager can effectively supervise will be much lower.

Third, specialization decreases training time. A more specialized job can be learned more quickly than a job that entails numerous different work activities. When training time is reduced, workers become productive more quickly. For instance, the time required to train a worker to cook french fries or prepare shakes is minimal compared with the time required for an employee to learn all the jobs performed in a fast-food restaurant.

Fourth, specialization contributes to consistently higher-quality goods and services. It has been said that we live in an age of specialization, one in which most people are employed as specialists. Many students who pursue a degree in business administration specialize in accounting, finance, management, or marketing. Few professions better demonstrate the move to specialization than does medicine. As more is learned about each phase of medicine, entire careers emerge, with concentrations on specific parts of the body or specific symptoms. Forty or fifty years ago, most doctors treated all of the ailments of all members of the family. Now, most physicians specialize, becoming gynecologists, pediatricians, cardiologists, ophthalmologists, and so forth. By specializing in a narrow range of medicine, a physician is able to offer the best diagnosis and treatment medical research and technology have available.

Finally, specialization can facilitate the achievement of highly complex objectives. Complex projects usually require large numbers of specialists. The U.S. space program would not have been possible without the contributions of the thousands of specialists assembled by the National Aeronautics and Space Administration. Teams of specialists, each knowledgeable in a particular phase of the project, contributed to its success. Similarly, the design and construction of airplanes and of large buildings require the contributions of many different specialists.

Disadvantages of Specialization

Despite its advantages, specialization of labor is not always desirable. In some organizations, too much specialization has caused certain jobs to become over-simplified, leading to boredom and fatigue among employees. For example, some people find it very boring to tighten a thousand bolts every day. Typically, the highest degree of specialization is found in this kind of assembly-line work, and the result is often a high level of employee turnover and absenteeism and a deteriorating quality of output. These negative consequences may offset the advantages and increase the costs of specialization.

A number of companies have established programs to overcome the disadvantages of specialization. Others have reduced the degree of specialization. General Motors is using work teams and team monitors assigned on a rotating basis. This gives each worker a feeling of involvement in the company's efforts to increase the quality and quantity of output. Shaklee Corporation has a unique management philosophy for its plant in Norman, Oklahoma. There, small teams of employees make, inspect, and package a diverse array of products. The teams establish their own production schedules and working hours. They select new workers from a pool approved by the personnel department and can even initiate discharges.[4]

DEPARTMENTATION

Departmentation is the process of grouping related work activities into manageable units. The purpose of departmentation is to contribute to more effective and efficient use of organizational resources. This section first discusses the ways functions should be grouped in an organization. Then, it describes common types of departments.

Functional Similarity

Ideally, each department or division in the organization should be made up of people performing similar tasks. This is the concept of *functional similarity,* a guiding principle in the creation of sections, departments, and divisions. Jobs with similar objectives and requirements are grouped to form a section, and the person with the background necessary to supervise these functions effectively is assigned as the manager. For example, a construction company might employ a plumbing crew, an electrical crew, and so forth. Each different crew performs a group of related functions. The achievement of functional similarity depends on a number of factors, several of which are shown in Figure 7.4 and discussed here.

Volume of Work Sometimes the volume of work does not allow for specialization. In small firms, people have to cope with a wide assortment of jobs. For example, at a full-service gas station, workers have to do a variety of tasks ranging from pumping gas to fixing flat tires. But with increases in volume, the concept of functional similarity can be applied more rigorously. For example, compare the operations of a small grocery store with those of a large supermarket. In the

❖ **Figure 7.4**
Factors affecting functional similarity

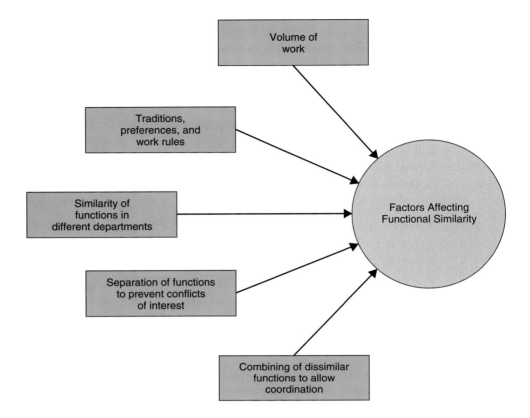

small store, one person may perform such functions as setting out produce, stocking shelves, and checking out and bagging groceries. In the large supermarket, each worker may specialize in one or only a few of the basic functions. It is common for one manager to oversee the produce section, another the stocking, and another the checking out and bagging functions.

Traditions, Preferences, and Work Rules Although two tasks may be similar, traditions, personal preferences, and work rules may prevent their assignment to one individual. For example, the function of installing electrical conduit (the steel pipe that protects electrical wire) is similar to the function of running water piping. However, few plumbers would be willing to run conduit, and electricians would usually object to installing water pipes. This is because individuals associate a set of behavioral expectations, duties, and responsibilities with a given position.

Similarity of Functions in Different Departments Another complicating factor is that a particular function often occurs in different departments. For example, inventory control would appear to fit logically in the purchasing department, which buys materials and thus has the need for records of inventory levels. However, the production department uses the same materials and, in scheduling, must work with the same inventory records. Inventory control could be placed in either department.

Separation of Functions to Prevent Conflicts of Interest Sometimes similar functions are not combined because doing so might create conflicts of interest. Quality control is intimately involved in production; inspectors frequently work side by side with production employees. Inspectors, however, should not be unduly influenced by the production manager. Thus, inspection, although similar to production, should be separate from production to protect its independence.

Combining of Dissimilar Functions to Allow Coordination Finally, there are occasions when two dissimilar functions must be combined for purposes of effective action and control. In a factory, purchasing is clearly differentiated from selling. But in department stores, buying and selling are so interdependent that one person is often made responsible for both. The theory is that a well-bought dress or hat is already half-sold.

Kinds of Departments

There is no standard way to divide an organization. Even companies in the same industry often have vastly different kinds of departments. It is possible, however, to identify five bases on which departmentation normally occurs: (1) function, (2) product, (3) customer, (4) geographic territory, and (5) project. Additionally, a combination approach may be used.

Departmentation by Function Departmentation by function is perhaps the most common means of dividing an organization. Under this approach, departments are formed on the basis of specialized activities such as finance, marketing, production, engineering, and personnel (see Figure 7.5). Grouped together, specialists become more efficient. Departmentation by function is especially useful in stable environments where technical efficiency and quality are important. Undoubtedly, functional specialists also feel more comfortable working with others of similar background and experience.

Departmentation by function has several advantages and disadvantages. As mentioned, it is advantageous in a stable environment. In addition, it fosters the development of expertise, allows specialization, and requires little coordination and few interpersonal skills. By and large, the advantages of functional specialization outweigh the disadvantages, but certain disadvantages are important.

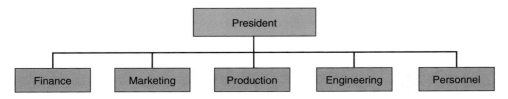

❖ **Figure 7.5**
Departmentation by function

❖ **Figure 7.6**
Departmentation by
product

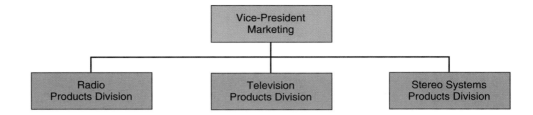

Employees in a specialized department may become more concerned with their own department than with the overall company. Because of the sometimes conflicting purposes of various departments, upper management must ensure that an effective means of coordination exists. Functional departmentation may also result in a slow response time in large organizations. Bottlenecks may occur when sequential tasks are performed. And functional departmentation may not encourage innovation, could foster conflict over product priorities, and may limit the development of general managers.

Departmentation by Product Product departmentation is concerned with organizing according to the type of product being produced or sold by the firm. This method, through which efficiency is enhanced by the application of specialized knowledge of particular goods or services, is often used by large, diversified companies. Figure 7.6 shows the organization of a large electronics firm divided into three product divisions. Firms manufacturing and selling technologically complex products are often set up this way.

Departmentation by Customer Departmentation by type of customer is used by organizations that need to provide different services to different types of customers. As Figure 7.7 illustrates, a diversified manufacturing company may have industrial, government, and consumer sales divisions. A USX salesperson who obtains government contracts simply maintains good relations with purchasing agencies and makes sure that USX has opportunities to bid. Selling to industrial customers, in contrast, requires greater emphasis on personal persuasion and longstanding relationships. It is possible that a person who does well in one area may be a failure in the other. Banks also use departmentation along customer lines. For example, commercial loan officers deal only with business customers, and consumer-lending specialists make personal loans. When client satisfaction

❖ **Figure 7.7**
Departmentation by
customer

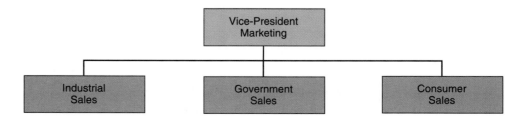

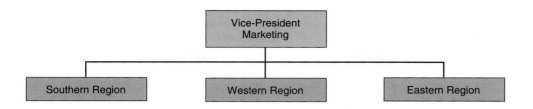

is the main competitive issue, especially in an uncertain environment, customer departmentation is often appropriate.

Departmentation by product and customer has several advantages and disadvantages. The advantages are that it enables people to cope with fast change, it allows high product visibility, it allows full-time concentration on the tasks, it clearly defines responsibilities, it permits the processing of multiple tasks, and it facilitates the training of general managers. The disadvantages are that it fosters politicking for resource allocation, it may not encourage coordination of activities among divisions, it could encourage neglect of long-term priorities, it may permit a decline in competencies, and it can create conflicts between divisional and corporate tasks.

Departmentation by Geographic Territory Grouping activities according to geographic territory is a method used by organizations with physically dispersed or noninterdependent operations or markets. For example, the marketing function of a company may be organized into southern, western, and eastern regional divisions (see Figure 7.8). Geographic departmentation offers the advantages of better service with local or regional personnel, often at less cost. Division by geography is the single most common scheme for international companies. For example, when Wendy's expanded into Europe, the company faced a competitive and legal environment very different from that in the United States, and therefore a separate division for the European operations was established. Geographic departmentation is most effective when the corporation's activities are widespread and there are few product lines. Often, however, the advantages of geographic departmentation are outweighed by the advantages of functional, product, and customer departmentation.

Departmentation by Project When the work of an organization consists of a continuing series of major projects, departmentation by project normally occurs. This type of departmentation is especially common in the construction industry. Figure 7.9 shows how a typical construction operation might be departmentalized. In this example, each project superintendent, under the direction of the general superintendent, is responsible for a separate contract. Such an organization changes frequently as projects are completed and new ones are started. The superintendent in charge of Project A may transfer to a new project or back to

❖ **Figure 7.9**
Departmentation by
project

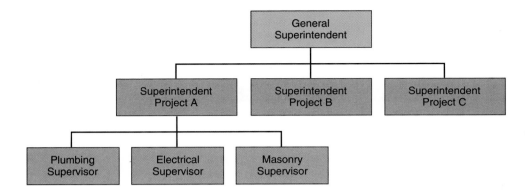

headquarters or be laid off when Project A is finished. In addition, the plumbing supervisor currently working on Project A may move to Project C when the plumbing on Project A is complete. **Matrix departmentation** is the form of departmentation that occurs when project departmentation takes on a permanent status designed to achieve specific results by using teams of specialists from different functional areas of the organization.

Departmentation by project and matrix has several advantages and disadvantages. The advantages are that it offers increased flexibility and greater interdisciplinary cooperation, it involves and challenges people, it develops employee skills, it frees top management for planning, it motivates employees to identify with the end product, and it allows experts to be moved to crucial areas as needed. The disadvantages are that it may create a risk of anarchy, it can encourage power struggles, it may result in too much discussion and not enough activity,

ETHICAL DILEMMA

The external environment often has a major impact on business dealings. The external environment can reduce profits to nearly nothing if such factors are not properly addressed. The insurance industry has been hard hit by disasters, including recent floods in the Midwest, fires in California, and riots in Los Angeles. Such external occurrences are placing great pressure on insurance companies to guard their profits carefully. All insurance companies, including Allstate Insurance Company, are doing whatever is in their power to limit risk in their day-to-day operations to better cope with such external disasters. Allstate is now accused of discrimi-nating against low-income households and minorities to lower their risks of loss. Low-income and minority homeowners were refused coverage for a variety of reasons, such as Allstate no longer insures homes with flat roofs or any home worth less than $55,000. Even though substandard coverage was usually offered, it was at much higher rates than those charged to upper-income locations.[5] If you were the CEO of Allstate, would you insure these high-risk groups, or would you follow Allstate's current insurability strategy?

What would you do?

IBM Europe's Experiment in Decentralization

IBM Europe, like IBM America, is looking for dramatic ways to change its organization. IBM Europe Chairman Renato Riverso completed a year-long effort to slice the Continent into 200 autonomous business units. Each of these autonomous business units has its own profit plan, employee incentives, and consumer focus. According to Riverso, "We used to manage from the top, like an army. Now we are trying to create entities that drive themselves." The drive for autonomy is causing great pain in IBM's European operations. The autonomous movement began with the elimination of 10,000 jobs. If profit does not result in these autonomous units within a year, then the cutting ax will fall again. IBM Europe's top management see, no other alternatives with profits dropping steadily. With the cash-making mainframe business in a probable permanent downslide, other areas of IBM Europe must make up the difference. The first test of the new autonomous division has resulted in a three percent higher margin for shipments of PCs, IBM's first independent European operation. In addition, PC sales shot up about 35 percent in the first quarter of the year. The freedom to negotiate for the products and services that will best satisfy consumers, combined with the ability to react to changing market conditions, as only an autonomous unit can, may well spell success for IBM Europe. If Riverso succeeds with IBM Europe, it may well become the model for IBM worldwide.[6]

it requires interpersonal skills, it is costly to implement, it may cause duplication of effort by project teams, and it probably will affect morale negatively when people are reassigned.[7]

Departmentation: A Combination Approach Unless the organization is quite small, it is likely that several different bases for departmentation will be used in combination. No one form of departmentation can meet the needs of most firms, particularly of large companies like General Motors, GE, and Exxon. Figure 7.10 shows an organizational chart of a manufacturing company that uses three forms of departmentation: functional (engineering, production, marketing, finance, and

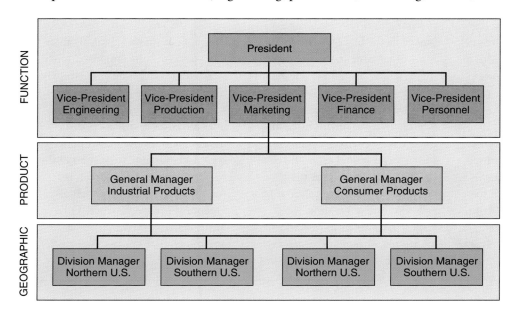

❖ **Figure 7.10**
Organization chart: A combination approach to departmentation

personnel), product (industrial and consumer), and geographic (northern and southern parts of the United States). The precise forms of departmentation a firm chooses must be based on its own needs, as with IBM Europe.

❖ ❖ ORGANIZATIONAL DIFFERENTIATION

In a newly formed small organization, a single owner-manager performs all the major functions of the business, such as financing, procuring materials, designing the product, and making and selling the product. This was the case with Woodrow Shepherd of Freeport Firestone when he opened his service station. But such simplicity did not last long.

The evolution of the organization at Freeport Firestone is typical of that at many other firms. As the volume of business grows, the work required increases beyond the capacities of one person. When Woodrow Shepherd decided to hire Joe Gross, he had to describe the tasks that Gross would perform; that is, he had to differentiate them from the other tasks of the organization. Gross was to pump gas and fix flats, among other duties. A new level in the organization had been

---

Freeport Firestone

Freeport, Maine, is well known as the home of L. L. Bean, Inc., the famous catalog merchandiser of sporting goods and clothing. L. L. Bean also operates a 50,000 square-foot retail store in Freeport. The store is open day and night and attracts celebrities and others from all over the world.

Woodrow Shepherd, the owner of Freeport Firestone, started out as an L. L. Bean employee in 1969. Shepherd quit his job with L. L. Bean in 1974 and invested his life savings, plus $20,000 he borrowed, in a service station. At first, he worked from daylight to dark six days a week. He employed only one helper, Joe Gross, who pumped gas, fixed flats, and did whatever else Woodrow needed him to do. As

Freeport grew over the next ten years, Shepherd's business did also. It was not long before the bookkeeping was too much for him, so he asked his wife to start coming in half-days to take care of that.

Shepherd added on to his service station and in 1976 got the Firestone tire franchise. The tire business was especially profitable, so he spent most of his time in the tire department, selling, installing, and repairing tires. By that time, Joe Gross had become a seasoned and dependable attendant, so Shepherd hired another man to help Gross take care of the service island. He also hired a helper in the tire department.

By 1980, Shepherd found it necessary to hire a full-time bookkeeper. He also employed an additional worker and a supervisor in the tire department. Until 1981,

Shepherd called the place simply Shepherd's Gulf Station. That year, he had a nice sign painted and changed the name to Freeport Firestone. In 1984, he installed another service island and added a tire and battery showroom next to the tire service bays. He hired a night manager in 1986 to keep the service island open until midnight. By then, Freeport Firestone employed fourteen persons full time and two part time.

The town of Freeport had grown to about 35,000, and Shepherd thought about opening a smaller service station and tire center at the opposite end of Main Street. In August 1993, the new branch of Freeport Firestone opened. Obviously, many new challenges lay ahead.

created, even though Freeport Firestone was only a two-person firm (see Section A of Figure 7.11). The employment of additional people requires vertical and horizontal differentiation.

The process of creating additional levels in the organization is **vertical differentiation.** Initially, there are just two levels, managerial and operative, but managers such as Woodrow Shepherd usually do not assign all the operative work to a subordinate. Shepherd continued to wait on customers and often worked alongside Joe Gross, in addition to supervising him. In the early stages of organizational growth, functions that are considered vital to success and that require special expertise, such as sales and finance, often continue to be done by the manager. This was evidently the case at Wall Drug.

As the volume of business continues to grow, additional employees will be added and more operative functions will be differentiated and allocated. The process of forming additional units at the same level in the organization is called **horizontal differentiation.** The result is shown in Section B of Figure 7.11. For Freeport Firestone, this process occurred when Shepherd hired a person to help

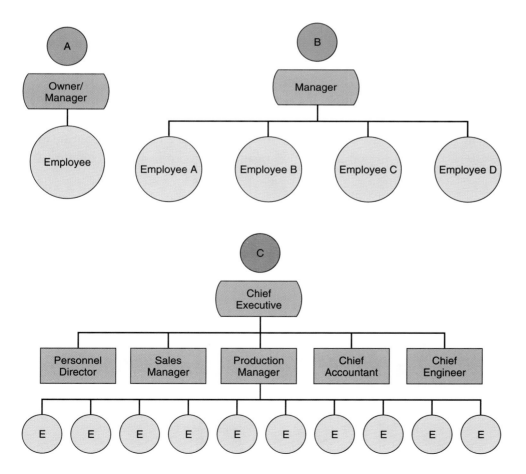

❖ **Figure 7.11**
Functional differentiation downward and outward

Gross on the service island and a helper for the tire department. Although Shepherd continued to do operative work for a time, he knew that the management job would soon take most of his time.

Woodrow Shepherd employed horizontal differentiation because the workload became too great. There is another reason for adding additional workers or departments at a given level. The original manager may find that certain functions can be more effectively and economically performed by a specialist. For example, a manager may find sales a weak area, because of ineffective or inadequate training programs. Therefore, a sales trainer would be employed to take over that phase of the business, so the manager could devote more time to other areas. As in the case of Freeport Firestone, horizontal growth usually occurs at lower levels as additional workers are required. When the number of workers becomes too large for one manager to supervise, additional supervisors must be added. As the organization grows, horizontal differentiation usually results in the splitting off of functions that are the most complex and least similar to other functions of the firm.

As is shown in Section C of Figure 7.11, horizontal differentiation usually results in the creation of several functional departments. If the organization continues to grow, further differentiation will be needed, both horizontal and vertical. Figure 7.12 shows how personnel, production, and engineering might be further subdivided, resulting in an additional level of managers.

When differentiation occurs, coordination is required. **Coordination** is the process of ensuring that persons who perform interdependent activities work together in a way that contributes to overall objective attainment. Coordination assumes a greater importance as the organization becomes more complex. For

❖ **Figure 7.12**
Horizontal differentiation of functional departments

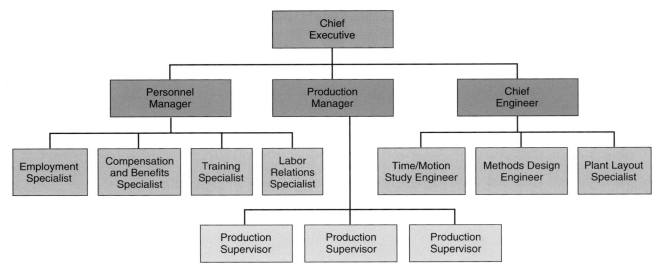

example, the manager of the company illustrated in Figure 7.12 would have to be much more concerned with coordination than was Woodrow Shepherd when his only employee was Joe Gross. For large, multibusiness companies, separate business units are often set up. Usually, the more diverse the products such a company makes, the more authority will be decentralized.[8]

❖ ❖ DOWNSIZING

The previous section dealt with how companies grow; this section discusses how companies shrink. **Downsizing**, also known as *restructuring* and *rightsizing,* is essentially the reverse and suggests a one-time change in the organization and the number of people who are employed by a firm. Typically, both the organization and the number of people in the organization shrink. The trend among many companies in the 1980s and early 1990s was to cut staff and downsize. This has certainly been the case with utility companies such as Commonwealth Edison.

Downsizing is often unsuccessful, however. The reason is that the companies have not been able to solve the fundamental causes of the problem. They have not developed an appropriate strategy for growth, but rather have focused on reducing costs, which is merely a symptom of the problem. Downsizing at such firms as American Express, Westinghouse, and Sears Roebuck has not achieved the expected success.[9]

One result of downsizing is that many layers are often pulled out of the

---

Commonwealth Edison Restructures

Utility companies traditionally have been able to survive by assigning rate increases when times got tough. When the price of coal or natural gas increased, then the utility company usually got to pass the increase on to the consumer; after all, the increase was not their fault, right? However, with utility companies investing in the unproven area of nuclear power generators, state regulators began to more closely scrutinize their management actions. If utility managers made bad decisions in this area, then it was an inappropriate management decision and not some external factor causing profitability problems. Commonwealth Edison made this mistake, but it was not alone; Cincinnati Gas & Electric made similar management errors, and Houston Lighting & Power Company was also caught in the no-rate-increase pinch. Since regulators appear to be worried about ratepayer rebellion and recession, these and other utility companies have no choice but to cut costs. Commonwealth Edison turned to restructuring and its inevitable personnel cuts. Often restructuring is unsuccessful, but at Commonwealth Edison the individuals who are most responsible for such mistakes, managers, are the ones paying the price. So far, 1,250 managers have been cut, an additional 1,200 managers may be cut, and other cuts may be on the block. Cincinnati Gas & Electric announced that it would eliminate 800 jobs, and Houston Lighting & Power Company cut staff positions by 17 percent. Naturally, other changes are being made in all of these restructurings, but the one common thread that runs through all restructuring is that personnel cuts are inevitable.[10]

organization, making it more difficult for individuals to advance in the organization. In addition, often when one firm downsizes, others must follow if they are to remain competitive. Thus, more and more individuals are finding themselves plateaued in the same job until they retire. To reinvigorate demoralized workers, some firms are providing additional training, lateral moves, short sabbaticals, and compensation based on a person's contribution, not title.[11] Some firms are gaining enthusiasm from their employees by providing raises based on additional skills they acquire and use.

Historically, firms have downsized in difficult times and rehired when times got better. Today, with firms competing globally, managers are rethinking their automatic rehiring strategies. For instance, Arvin Industries, a manufacturer of automotive components, had cut its workforce by ten percent to just under 16,000 since 1990, but by 1993 the company had rebounded with profits estimated to grow at an annual rate of 20 percent through 1995. Even with enhanced business success, Arvin is not rehiring and is trying to further trim its staff. According to Arvin's human resources director, Ray Mack, "To remain globally competitive, we must continue to streamline operations and keep a tight rein on labor costs."[12]

❖ ❖ THE INFORMAL ORGANIZATION

It is possible to identify many groups, of varying size, within a typical firm. Naturally, a number of these groups have a place in the formal organization. The groups also have a place in the informal organization. In fact, all the groups blend together to form the **informal organization**—the set of evolving relationships and patterns of human interaction within an organization that are not officially prescribed.

In the formal organization, managers establish what employees should do through formal organization charts and manuals that detail the duties and responsibilities associated with jobs. Traditional managers tend to emphasize the values of organizational and personal loyalty. Many will tolerate incompetence more readily than disloyalty. The formal organization represents management's attempt to specify the way things should be done in the various sections, departments, and divisions of the firm. But the official organizational structure is only part of the story. Another structure exists alongside the formal one, which consists of informal relations created not by officially designated managers, but by organization members at every level. Wall Drug certainly had an informal organization within its formal organization.

Because of the impact of the informal organization, an increasing number of firms are training their managers to cope with it. The director of corporate

The official organizational structure is only part of the story. There emerges another structure, existing alongside the formal one, which consists of informal relationships created not by officially designated managers, but by organizational members at every level. Here a group of Conagra employees from various levels in the company enjoy a fundraising activity to help children's charities.
(Source: Photograph courtesy of Geldermann, Inc.)

personnel for a large insurance company says, "We teach our managers/supervisors to be alert to the formation of 'informal work groups' and that such groups can be either a positive or a negative influence on a department or company objective."

The informal organization has the following definable characteristics:

• *Its members are joined together to satisfy needs.* They may have completely different reasons for developing informal relationships. One worker may want to make friends, and another may be seeking advancement. Progress toward either of these objectives might be furthered through interactions with the informal organization.

• *It is continuously changing.* The informal organization is dynamic. Relationships that exist one day may be gone the next.

• *It involves members of various organizational levels.* The informal organization does not abide by the boundaries established by the formal organization. A worker in one area may have close ties to a supervisor in another.

• *It is affected by relationships outside the firm.* Two workers might associate with each other because they are Masons or members of the Moose Lodge.

• *It has a pecking order.* Certain people are assigned greater importance than others by the informal group. Once workers adhere to group norms, their status within the informal organization tends to increase.

Because of factors such as the close proximity in which people work, the frequent interaction of group members, and the long time periods employees spend working together, there will always be informal groups and an informal organization. How managers deal with it can affect the productivity of their work unit.

Although an informal organization cannot be placed into a formal organization chart, it does have its own structure. Like the formally structured organization, the informal organization may have a chain of command, which is sometimes charted after the fact by management. Managers should recognize that informal work groups exist at all levels of the organization. A formal organization chart can be misleading in terms of who has real authority and influence.

The nature of the informal structure is dynamic and constantly changing. As different members enter and exit the group, the structure is modified. The structure is based heavily on the communication patterns that develop among group members. If many people attempt to gain the advice of one individual, this individual is often the informal leader around whom the structure develops. Just as formal organizations have vice-presidents, the informal group may have an equivalent counterpart. The informal structure evolves rather than being formally laid out, yet it is often as rigid as the formal structure. The informal organization enhances the productivity of the workplace, and therefore is vital to workforce productivity and to a certain degree cohesiveness. For all the seriousness of personal rights issues such as sexual harassment protection, it would be a great pity if men and women got to the point of giving up on workplace friendships altogether and tearing apart the informal organization. Unfortunately this is a point that some men say privately they've already reached. Remember Rob, Buddy, and Sally on the old Dick Van Dyke Show? Okay, it was way back in the supposedly benighted early Sixties, but those three were a great professional team, and they were pals. For men and women in corporate America, there could be

---

MANAGEMENT IN PRACTICE

A Skill-Building Exercise: John Higgins has recently taken over the accounting and finance department. He had been the number two person in the department for over five years. He has all the qualifications for the job, and that is why you selected him to take over from Thomas Magnum, the former head of the department.

As John's superior, you have received a memo from John about the behavior of a secretary who has been with the company for 16 years. According to this memo, she is leaking information from John's department—and has been doing so for many years. She has most recently given out some informal information to the unit heads to allow them to begin their budgeting activities. When John took her to task about the leaks, she claimed that the information she gives out is really not confidential. Furthermore, she said that the unit heads need the information early because the formal reports come out too late to allow them to budget adequately. At the end of the memo, John noted, "Either she straightens up, or she has to go; I need your support." John has just walked in.

What would you do?

far worse role models. It will be a sad day for both the organization and the employees when people are too nervous to ask a pal out for a drink.[13]

The organizational structure of the informal work group may be studied by means of a contact chart. A **contact chart** is a diagram showing various individuals in the organization and the number of interactions they have with others. These charts are developed to identify the connections an individual has with other members of the organization. As can be seen from the contact chart in Figure 7.13, not all contacts follow the formal organization chart. In various instances, certain levels of management are bypassed; other instances show cross-contact from one chain of command to another. On the basis of the number of contacts in Figure 7.13, individual 19 appears to be very popular.

One difficulty with a contact chart is that it does not show the reasons for relationships. Also, it is never clear whether the contacts shown will work for or against the organization. Individual 19 could be helping other employees accomplish their tasks. On the other hand, this individual could be badmouthing the organization and promoting disharmony among company employees. Once managers have identified the major contact points, they are in a position to either encourage or discourage the individual within the work group.

❖ ❖ BENEFITS AND COSTS OF THE INFORMAL ORGANIZATION

Managers often have mixed emotions about the informal organization. Although it is capable of contributing to greater organizational effectiveness, it is not without its costs. But if management is properly trained to understand and work with

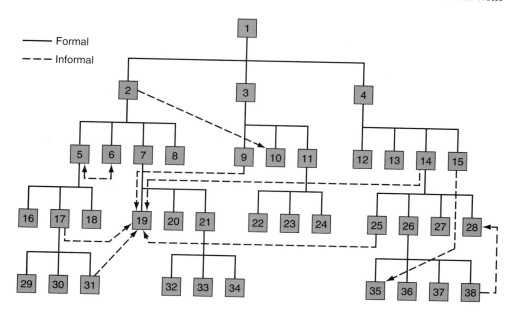

❖ **Figure 7.13**
A contact chart

the informal organization, the benefits should exceed the costs, as Figure 7.14 suggests. However, if management is not careful, the reverse may be true.

Benefits of the Informal Organization

It is fortunate that managers cannot destroy the informal organization, because it is capable of contributing in significant ways to an organization's effectiveness. Following are several of the means by which the informal organization can benefit the work group.

Assists in Accomplishing Work For managers to be effective, their subordinates must be permitted a certain degree of flexibility in accomplishing assigned tasks. Monitoring subordinates' every move is detrimental to their achieving success. If employees acted only when they were told to act, following standard instructions to the letter at all times and contacting others only when duly authorized, the business would have to cease operations. Still, there are traditionalists who tend to rely more heavily on formal decisions based on the scientific study of business problems.

There are also decision-making situations in which the formal command is inadequate, even wrong. If the atmosphere is heavily traditional, subordinates may exhibit malicious obedience by executing commands faithfully despite personal knowledge that their actions will ultimately result in failure, or greater

❖ **Figure 7.14**
Benefits and costs of the informal organization

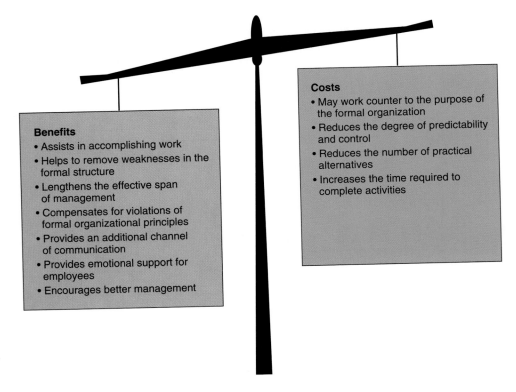

Benefits
- Assists in accomplishing work
- Helps to remove weaknesses in the formal structure
- Lengthens the effective span of management
- Compensates for violations of formal organizational principles
- Provides an additional channel of communication
- Provides emotional support for employees
- Encourages better management

Costs
- May work counter to the purpose of the formal organization
- Reduces the degree of predictability and control
- Reduces the number of practical alternatives
- Increases the time required to complete activities

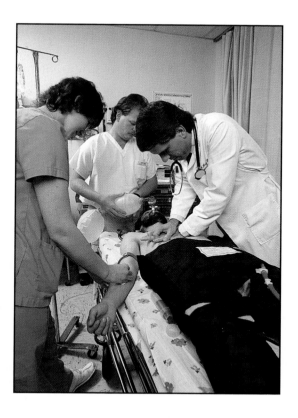

For managers to be effective, their subordinates must be permitted a certain degree of flexibility in performing their required tasks. It might very well be detrimental, for example, for the emergency-room physician shown here to attempt detailed direction of the professionals who assist him. (Source: © Jim Pickerell)

problems. Many managers have discovered that a subordinate can agree with them all day, follow every directive to the letter, and yet fail miserably. When managers place more faith in informal relationships, subordinates may voluntarily adapt the formal order to the requirements of the situation. Loosely structured groups are often more effective in achieving organizational objectives.

Helps to Remove Weaknesses in the Formal Structure The formal organization often has a number of gaps that the informal group can fill. Consider a person who is promoted to a position that exceeds that individual's current capabilities. This is not an unusual occurrence in the armed services, for instance, where young officers may be appointed unit commanders. Without the advice and assistance of experienced sergeants, these officers might not survive their first assignments. In fact, most likely there are many officers who are unsuccessful in the military because they fail to recognize the power of the informal organization. Formal orders and regulations may state that someone is the commander, with particular responsibilities and a certain amount of authority. But in reality, that person may be deficient. By admitting temporary weaknesses, the commander might be able to obtain help from other officers and enlisted personnel. In such a case, deficiencies in the formal structure are overcome by shared decision making. In time, the informal organization may conform to the formal one more closely.

Lengthens the Effective Span of Management The number of direct subordinates reporting to any manager is referred to as the **span of management.** As individuals and small groups learn to interact effectively and are permitted to do so by their supervisors, the manager should be able to devote less time to each worker. This may allow the manager's effective span of management to grow.

Compensates for Violations of Formal Organizational Principles Informal relationships can compensate for the ineffectiveness of certain traditional principles of formal organizations. For example, even though authority should equal responsibility, the principle is frequently violated. As a result, managers often try to develop informal contacts with people over whom they have no formal authority. As favors are traded and friendships are formed, one quickly learns that the formal prescription of authority often is not sufficient. This does not negate the desirability of authority equaling responsibility. We discuss this organizing principle further in Chapter 8.

Provides an Additional Channel of Communication The informal means by which information is transmitted in an organization is the **grapevine.** To some managers, the grapevine constitutes an obstacle to be destroyed. They seek to channel and control most, if not all, communications through the official chain of command. However, the grapevine can add to organizational effectiveness if the manager uses it. The grapevine is fast and usually accurate in the information it transmits.

Use of the grapevine does not decrease the importance of maintaining an official channel of communication and command. Although the grapevine can spread much information in a short time, it cannot provide the authority necessary to ensure that action will take place. The grapevine is discussed in greater detail in Chapter 12.

Provides Emotional Support for Employees Over half of all voluntary resignations in many organizations occur within the first six months of employment. These are often the result of little help being provided the new employee in joining and being accepted by the group. Friendships, or at least speaking acquaintances, are essential to a satisfactory working environment for most people. In one hospital where the turnover rate of janitorial personnel was high, the formation of cleanup teams reduced turnover considerably. The janitors had felt isolated and uncomfortable working alone among physicians, nurses, and patients.

Encourages Better Management Awareness of the nature and impact of the informal organization often leads to better management decisions. The acceptance of the fact that formal relationships will not ensure full accomplishment of organizational tasks should stimulate management to seek other means of increasing motivation. Managers should seek to improve their knowledge of the nature of the people in general and subordinates in particular. They should realize that organizational performance can be enhanced by workers' cooperation and enthusiasm. Means other than formal authority must be sought to develop attitudes that support effective performance.

Cost of the Informal Organization

The informal organization is not without its drawbacks. Here are some of the possible detrimental effects of the informal organization.

May Work Counter to the Purposes of the Formal Organization It is apparent to most managers that individuals in informal groups can and sometimes do work against the formal objectives of an enterprise. Few would object to the

---

A GLOBAL PERSPECTIVE

International Strategic Alliance: A Global Competitive Advantage

An international alliance is an organization of sorts. Organizations bring people together in a coordinated manner to achieve group results. An effective organization is designed to ensure the achievement of the firm's objectives. Similarly, an effective international alliance is designed to ensure and support achievement of the firm's common objectives. Specifically, an international alliance is a collaboration between two or more multinational companies that is developed to let them jointly pursue a common objective.

According to Fortune magazine, U.S. companies entered into some 2,000 alliances with European companies alone in the decade of the eighties. Most ma-

jor multinational companies maintain numerous international cooperative arrangements. GE has formed eight alliances with companies in Europe, Japan, and South Korea, and is currently expanding with such alliances into China, Mexico, and India.[14] Corning, Inc., maintains more than a dozen joint ventures with multinational companies in Europe, Australia, China, Japan, and South Korea. General Motors has entered into separate partnerships with Toyota, Isuzu, Suzuki, and Daewoo. AT&T also has over 20 such major alliances throughout the world.

International strategic alliances make it possible for companies to share the costs and risks of doing business. Strategic alliances were somewhat rare at one time, but in the global environment, correctly structured alliances are seen as

essential. AT&T could actually rule the world's communications networks; going from country to country and forming strategic alliances would allow them to enter and control communication networks throughout the world.[15] Strategic alliances enable companies to share financial resources, technology, production facilities, marketing know-how, and human resources. The major driving force behind many international alliances is the rapid development of technology and the globalization of markets and products. International alliances have become a competitive necessity for any firm that aspires to become a global player. In a sense, what an effective organization is to a domestic company, an international alliance is to a successful global firm.[16]

existence of the informal organization if its objectives could always be the same as those of the formal organization. However, informal groups sometimes pressure workers to exhibit disinterest in company requirements, disloyalty, and insubordination, or to engage in unauthorized actions that may work at cross-purposes with the organization.

Reduces the Degree of Predictability and Control An objective of most organizations is to ensure predictability and control of behavior so individuals will work effectively toward organizational objectives. This objective depends, however, on people interpreting and following the formal guidelines. If managers recognize and accept the possibility of a good outcome from permitted flexibility, they must also accept the risks that accompany this lesser degree of control. Informal relationships can and do add much to an organization's effectiveness; they also have a similar effect on the degree of uncertainty.

Reduces the Number of Practical Alternatives A study of the U.S. Army during World War II concluded that the natural unit of personal commitment is the informal group, not the formal organization.[17] For example, the soldiers reported that one of the major reasons for moving forward in combat was to avoid letting the other fellows down. In all organizations, business or military, the solidarity of the informal group can be a major constraint on management actions.

This solidarity may create problems in the reassigning of personnel. If informal groups are broken up by the moving of individual members, the members may feel insecure and show decreased motivation and cooperation. This may suggest that management should think in terms of moving whole groups, rather than individuals. If management wishes to capitalize on the considerable value of informal relationships in work groups, it must be willing to accept some loss of flexibility in decision making.

Increases the Time Required to Complete Activities If the cooperative efforts of informal work groups can be aligned with the objectives of the firm, management has the best of both worlds. The collective power generated can be phenomenal. But informal work group activities such as gossiping, betting pools, long coffee breaks and general horseplay are time-consuming and may be detrimental to efficient operations. These acts often tax the patience of managers. However, if effective work groups are to be established, some of these activities will have to be permitted, and possibly even encouraged. Managers must realize that despite their concern for accomplishing objectives, they must allow the group time and opportunity to maintain itself in good working order. People can usually sustain action for a longer period of time in an informal atmosphere than they can when the situation is rigid, controlled, and formal.

✗ Management Tips ✗

Guidelines for Dealing with the Organizing Process and the Informal Organization

1. **All managers, from supervisors to top-level managers, are involved in the organizing process.** Understand it and use it to your benefit.

2. **Only reorganize when it helps you achieve your objective better.** Don't just reorganize because you want to seem busy. Your time can be better spent.

3. **Get the maximum benefit from worker specialization.** Attempt to assign related work to each job.

4. **Organize so that each worker has a full-time job.** Unequal workloads are unfair to workers and result in reduced output.

5. **Do not be afraid to reorganize.** Situations change and the best organization of yesterday may not be the same for today.

6. **Do not try to eliminate the informal organization.** You cannot do it. Besides, the informal organization can be useful to you.

7. **Remember that the grapevine often transmits information told in absolute confidence.** Most people find secrets hard to keep. When you have told one person, you have no control over where the message goes.

8. **Know when directives violate informal group norms.** There is no need to make an order harder to obey than it needs to be.

9. **Do not try to be a buddy and a boss.** Make your informal position agree with your formal position as much as possible.

10. **Make a conscious attempt to understand the informal organization.** Notice who talks to whom and about what.

SUMMARY

An organization is two or more people working together in a coordinated manner to achieve group results. Organizing is the process of prescribing formal relationships among people and resources to accomplish objectives. It is affected by both the external environment of the firm and the internal environment that individual managers face. Organizing should be directed toward accomplishment of objectives; once objectives are established, work activities can be determined. Complex objectives are often achieved through specialization of labor, which offers a number of benefits, including increased productivity. Negative consequences of specialization may offset its advantages and increase costs.

The process of grouping related work activities into manageable units is *departmentation*. Ideally, each department should be made up of people performing similar tasks. This is the concept of *functional similarity*. In addition to function, there are four other ways to divide an organization: by product, by customer, by geographic territory, and by project. Unless the organization is quite small, it is likely that several different bases for departmentation will be used.

Additional levels in the organization are created through vertical differentiation. Additional units at the same level are created through horizontal differentiation. Coordination ensures that persons who perform interdependent activities work together in a way that contributes to overall objective attainment.

Downsizing, also known as *restructuring* and *rightsizing*, is essentially the reverse of expansion, and suggests a one-time change in the organization and the number of people who are employed by a firm. Typically, both the organization and the number of people in the organization shrink. One result of downsizing is that many layers of the organization are eliminated, making progression in the organization much more difficult.

The informal organization is the set of evolving relationships and patterns of human interaction within an organization that are not officially prescribed. It has a number of definable characteristics and may be studied by means of a contact chart, a diagram showing various individuals in the organization and the number of interactions they have with others.

Managers often have mixed emotions about the informal organization. Although it is capable of contributing to greater organizational effectiveness, there are certain costs. But if management is properly trained to understand and work with the informal organization, the benefits should exceed the costs.

KEY TERMS

Organization 202
Organizing 203
Specialization of labor 206
Departmentation 209
Matrix departmentation 214
Vertical differentiation 217
Horizontal differentiation 217

Coordination 218
Downsizing 219
Informal organization 220
Contact chart 223
Span of management 226
Grapevine 226

REVIEW QUESTIONS

1. Define <u>organization</u>. What are the three common characteristics of an organization?
2. Describe the process of organizing. What tasks must managers perform in the organizing process?
3. In terms of the organizing process, what types of work activities are needed on a baseball team?
4. Define <u>specialization of labor</u>. What are its advantages and disadvantages?
5. What guidelines should be used in grouping work activities?
6. What are the primary means of departmentation?
7. Distinguish between vertical and horizontal differentiation.
8. What does the term <u>downsizing</u> mean?
9. What is the purpose of a contact chart?
10. Describe the benefits and costs that may be attributed to the informal organization.

CASE 7.1 The Organization of Quality Control

Shelton Lewis holds the position of production manager at Memorand, Inc., a maker of small components for the hydraulics industry. Shel, as his employees call him, came to Memorand eight years ago as a production foreman. He believes the company has been good to him, and he has chosen not to leave, even though he has had a number of offers of better-paying jobs with competing firms.

Gloria Honeycutt is in charge of the quality control section of Memorand and reports directly to Shelton. Gloria started out as Shelton's secretary five years ago. With his encouragement, she attended college and got a degree in industrial management with a concentration in quality control. She then was reassigned to the quality control job, but she continued to report directly to Shelton.

One day recently, a delicate situation arose, creating a strain on the usually excellent relationship between Shelton and Gloria. The problem began with the following conversation.

Gloria: Shel, I'm finding too many flaws in the cylinders we're making for Ingersol Rand. I know you're facing a deadline, but I believe we should slow down and inspect all the cylinder parts before they're assembled.

Shelton: Have you found more than the standard number of defectives?

Gloria: No, but a number of cylinders barely passed the leakage tests, and many of the mounting holes are just within specs. If you don't slow down, we may miss a chance at future orders from Ingersol Rand. You know how quality-conscious they are.

Shelton: If we do slow down, we won't make the scheduled delivery date. If we don't do that, Memorand may not even be considered for future contracts. I don't expect you, of all people, to stand in the way of getting the order out on time.

Gloria didn't know what to do, so she just left the office. She still felt she was right. The contract with Ingersol Rand was a lucrative one, and it had been given to Memorand only because Shelton had guaranteed quick delivery. Pleasing Ingersol Rand could easily result in a ten percent sales increase for the company as a whole. Ingersol Rand has a reputation for selecting suppliers carefully and sticking with them as long as delivery and quality are up to par.

QUESTIONS

1. Is there anything amiss with the organizational relationship between Gloria and Shelton? If so, what? How would you change it? Defend your answer.
2. What do you believe Gloria should do at this point? Explain.

CASE 7.2 Derek Garments: The Informal Group at Barnwell

Derek Garment Company's Barnwell, South Carolina facility was one of hundreds of small nonunion garment factories throughout the South that paid low, piece-rate wages and kept extreme pressure on costs. Even unionized garment workers averaged only $7.00 to $7.75 an hour in the early 1990s. And the nonunion factories paid much less.

Linda Watson quit her job at the Barnwell factory in October 1993. The human resources director, Mavis Wilson, conducted an exit interview, at which Linda told her story. Linda said she had been excited to get a job at Derek several months earlier. She explained that she had been looking for a job for nearly six months at that time, and her unemployment pay had run out. She said she was especially pleased to be paid a piece rate for production above standard. Mavis asked why incentive pay had been so important. "Wherever I have worked before I did more than most other people for the same pay," replied Linda.

Linda told how she became attached to a group of new friends soon after being hired. During coffee breaks and lunch periods, she said, they chatted about their husbands or ex-husbands, their children, and the problems of being working women. Linda said she had learned a lot from her new friends about Derek Garments, things that had not been covered during orientation. Among the items she mentioned were Mavis's reputation for protecting workers from the operations manager, who was thought to be quite ruthless, and the fact that several of the plant manager's relatives, including two sons-in-law, had cushy jobs with Derek. Finally, she gave other workers credit for answering her frequent questions about the medical plan, sick leave, and so forth.

Within two weeks Linda had exceeded the production standard. Her third paycheck included a piece-rate bonus of nearly $50. Linda said she was barely making ends meet and needed the extra money. She told of a conversation she had with Charissa Gorman, one of the more experienced workers: "I was happy about my bonus and told Charissa so. But Charissa said, 'A bonus would be handy for any of us. But if you keep it up, they will just change the standard, and we will all be worse off.' Charissa also said I was making the rest of them look bad."

Though admittedly aware of Charissa's disapproval, Linda said she had continued to work faster. But she said she soon noticed a definite coolness toward her. "No one would come and sit with me in the lunch room," she explained, "And when I joined a table with other people, I felt a strain. You know, they had been talking and the conversation would end when I got close." Linda said when she finally confronted one of the women about freezing her out she was told, "If you don't stop trying to show off, you're not going to have a friend left around here."

Linda said she slowed down the next week to just a little above standard and things got better. "But I was between a rock and a hard place," said Linda, "Janice [Linda's supervisor] told me to come see her the next day. I know she was going to ask why I slowed down and put pressure on me." When Mavis asked if there was any single event that caused her to decide to quit when she did, Linda replied, "Well, I was already pretty upset at having to go see Janice and when I got ready to go home I had a flat tire. The personnel office had the closest phone to the parking lot, so I tried to call my husband from there to come fix the flat. Some clerk told me to use the phone at the plant. I would have quit anyway, but that really did it for me."

QUESTIONS

1. How did the informal work group affect the operations at Derek Garments?
2. Why do you believe that "things got better" when Linda slowed down her level of productivity?

NOTES

1. This story is a composite from a number of sources, including: James D. Taylor, Robert L. Johnson, and C. Philip Fisher, "Wall Drug Store 1983," in Arthur Sharplin, *Strategic Management* (New York: McGraw-Hill, 1985); "American Scene in South Dakota—Buffalo Burgers at Wall Drug," *Time* 31 (August 1983): 8; "Wall and Water," *Guide Post Magazine* (July 1982): 34; David Grogan, "Main Street," *People Weekly* 5 (March 5, 1986): 74–76.

2. Shawn Tully, "The Modular Corporation," *Fortune* 128 (February 8, 1993): 106–115.

3. Gary Slutsker, "The Company that Likes to Obsolete Itself," *Forbes* 152 (September 13, 1993): 139–144.

4. "The New Industrial Relations," *Business Week* (January 30, 1984): 45.

5. Adapted from Albert R. Karr, "Advocacy Group Accuses Allstate of Bias in Low-Income and Minority Markets," *The Wall Street Journal* (September 1, 1993): A4.

6. Jonathan B. Levine, "For IBM Europe 'This Is the Year of Truth'," *Business Week* (April 19, 1993): 45–46.

7. Harold Kerzner, "Matrix Implementation: Obstacles, Problems, Questions, and Answers," in David McCleland, ed., *Matrix Management System Handbook* (New York: Van Nostrand Reinhold, 1984): 307–329.

8. Vijay Govindaragan, "Decentralization, Strategy, and Effectiveness of Strategic Business Units in Multibusiness Organizations," *Academy of Management Review* 29 (October 1986): 844–856.

9. Elizabeth Lesly and Larry Light, "When Layoffs Alone Don't Turn the Tide," *Business Week* (December 7, 1992): 100–101.

10. Kevin Kelly, "Why Commonwealth Edison Is Feeling the Heat," *Business Week* (August 17, 1992): 59.

11. Jaclyn Fierman, "Beating the Midlife Career Crisis," *Fortune* 128 (September 6, 1993): 53.

12. Louis S. Richman, "When Will the Layoffs End?" *Fortune* 128 (September 20, 1993): 54.

13. Anne B. Fisher, "Sexual Harassment: What to Do," *Fortune* 128 (August 23, 1993): 84–88.

14. Tim Smart, Pete Engardio, and Geri Smith, "GE's Brave New World," *Business Week* (November 8, 1993): 64–70.

15. David Kirkpatrick, "Could AT&T Rule the World?" *Fortune* 127 (May 17, 1993): 55, 57, 62–65, 66.

16. Wayne F. Cascio and Manuel G. Serapio, Jr., "Human Resources Systems in an International Alliance: The Undoing of a Done Deal?" *Organizational Dynamics* 19 (Winter 1991): 63–66; and Leigh Bruce and Jack Burton, "Strained Alliances," *International Management* 45 (May 1990): 29.

17. Vijay Govindaragan, "Decentralization, Strategy, and Effectiveness of Strategic Business Units in Multibusiness Organizations," *Academy of Management Review* 29 (October 1986): 844–856.

8 Organizing Concepts and Organizational Structure

LEARNING OBJECTIVES

After completing this chapter students should be able to

✘ Describe the concepts of responsibility and authority.

✘ Explain delegation and accountability.

✘ Describe several important organizing principles.

✘ Contrast centralization and decentralization.

✘ Describe the basic types of organizational structures.

✘ Describe the concepts of reengineering and job design.

✘ Explain how managers can become better at working with committees.

The Focused and Innovative Reorganization of Texaco Continues to Pay Off

In 1993, Alfred C. DeCrane, Jr., was named the new CEO of Texaco to replace James W. Kinnear. Kinnear's successes include bringing Texaco back from bankruptcy after Pennzoil won a $10 billion judgment against them for their interference with the Getty takeover by Pennzoil. In the ensuing two years, Texaco settled with Pennzoil for $3 billion, sold $7 billion worth of plants and other assets, restructured itself, and avoided a takeover bid by Carl Icahn. Even in the midst of this desperate situation, chief executive James W. Kinnear addressed the worldwide staff of Texaco and predicted that "Texaco would ultimately emerge as one of the most admired companies in the world."

By 1990, Texaco had emerged from bankruptcy and bought off Icahn. Kinnear continued the job of reorganizing with the avowed goal of enhancing shareholder value. Kinnear cut 10,965 employees from the payroll and pegged salaries to performance. Then, he violated Texaco's tradition of promoting from within and brought in some "new blood." The 26 exploration and production divisions became 12 independent profit centers, each operating like a small company, and two layers of management were eliminated. Decision-making authority was pushed down in the organization. Union-management work groups, which cut across organizational lines, were set up at selected plants.

The idea of submitting to the will of shareholders was new at Texaco. The 1987 proxy statement issued by the board of directors had imperiously said, "The Company strongly supports the role of corporate democracy and the right of stockholders to have their views submitted to, and considered by, the company." A student of Texaco's history wrote, "Concern for shareholders' happiness is a marked reversal of attitude at Texaco, where haughty autocratic leaders once ran the business however they pleased . . . "

Kinnear preached the gospel of organizational transformation, and it appears that DeCrane will adhere to Kinnear's vision. DeCrane also dislikes the "ozone layer" of corporate bureaucracy and advises employees to "just say no" when bosses assign make-work duties. He also encourages them to "take risks" as if they were entrepreneurs, to eliminate red tape. And what about Kinnear's prediction of Texaco being "one of the most admired companies in the world?" Well, Texaco appears to be well on its way. Texaco has since been ranked as one of the most-improved companies in the annual *Fortune* poll. DeCrane's adherence to Kinnear's strategy may well lead to Texaco soon being one of the most admired companies in the world.[1]

In Chapter 7, the organizing process and the informal organization were discussed. Here, we take up organizing concepts and structure. The structure at Texaco was traditionally quite rigid, with many levels of management bound by strict rules. Chief executive Kinnear changed all that, and it looks like DeCrane will continue in his footsteps. Like many reorganizing attempts, Texaco's resulted largely from external pressure.

In this chapter we first discuss four important management concepts: responsibility, authority, delegation, and accountability. Then, we review several organizing principles. Next, we discuss the trade-off between the needs of centralization and those of decentralization. Then, we describe common types of organizational structures and describe reengineering and job design. In the final section of the chapter, we present a global perspective and the means by which managers can become better at working with committees.

❖ ❖ RESPONSIBILITY

In accepting a job, a person takes responsibility for performing the tasks involved in it. **Responsibility** is the obligation to perform work activities. Texaco's former CEO James W. Kinnear was obviously responsible for everything that went on within the company. But he made those lower in the organization responsible for their units. Layers of management were slashed and decision-making authority was pushed down in the organization. The degree to which a manager feels the obligation to perform is enhanced if responsibilities are clearly defined. Nothing is more frustrating to a manager or a worker than being confused about the nature, scope, and details of specific job responsibilities. For instance, suppose Susan James, a first-line supervisor for Texaco, has the following conversation with her boss, Phil Williams:

Susan: Am I responsible for processing the new drilling policies, or should Joe Davis's unit handle them?

Phil: I don't think it really matters too much which unit handles these policies so long as it's done correctly and thoroughly.

Susan: But what do you expect me to do?

Phil: I'll get back to you later on this—I'm busy at the moment.

Obviously, Phil's comments leave Susan unsure of her responsibility. In fact, in cases such as this, managers often assume that someone else will do what needs to be done. Therefore, Phil should not be surprised if the new policies do not get processed at all. When he finds out that nothing has been done, he may be upset with Susan, but the real fault is his own.

❖ ❖ AUTHORITY

A common complaint of managers is that although they have unlimited responsibility, their authority is often inadequate. **Authority** is the right to decide, to direct others to take action, or to perform certain duties in achieving organizational objectives. The definition of authority suggests that it has at least three key characteristics:

1. Authority is a right.
2. Exercising authority involves making decisions, taking actions, or performing duties.
3. Authority is granted for the purpose of achieving organizational objectives.

Every manager must have some authority in order to organize and direct the use of resources to attain the objectives of the organization. For example, a supervisor

MANAGEMENT IN PRACTICE

A Skill-Building Exercise: You have been promoted to supervisor over the newly created third shift. The competition was intense for the job, but you were the one promoted. The departmental manager told you that the third shift is essential for the success of the entire restructuring of the manufacturing operation. He also said that he is counting on you to make sure that the third shift is every bit as good as the other two shifts. He specifically said, "It is your responsibility; that's the reason I selected you."

You will have 12 people working for you, and they will be performing three sequential assembly operations. You are to choose six people from the other two shifts. You must also train six new employees. The first person you thought of was your old buddy, John. He has worked all three assembly-line positions and could help you train the new employees for your line. Your former supervisor agreed to allow you to "draft" John for your shift, but the assistant manager of the department said that you cannot have John. The assistant manager normally has to approve all personnel changes. It may be just coincidence, but the assistant manager wanted someone else promoted to the supervisor's position. You really need John to complete your assignment.

What action would you take?

made responsible for staffing a department may have the authority to do so at any of the levels of authority shown in Figure 8.1. At the lowest level, the supervisor will believe he or she lacks the authority to staff the department adequately. Various sources and types of authority will be discussed later.

❖ ❖ DELEGATION

Delegation is the process of assigning responsibility along with the needed authority. Delegation is one of the most significant concepts affecting a manager's ability to get the job done. It creates a risk for managers, however, because the success or failure of an operation is ultimately their responsibility. When a manager delegates a responsibility to a subordinate, the relationship between the two is based on an obligation. Managers should remember an important point: One cannot relieve oneself of any portion of the original responsibility; delegation only allows for someone else to do the work. Some managers attempt to reduce risk by avoiding delegation and doing everything themselves.

Since Texaco cut several layers of management, it is quite likely that the managers who remain must be capable of delegating if they are to survive. Delegation of responsibility and authority is essential if managers are to provide opportunities for the development of their people. Also, few managers have the capability of personally performing all the duties for which they are responsible. A frequent cause of operational failure is the unwillingness or inability of some managers to delegate responsibility and authority.

❖ **Figure 8.1**
Degrees of authority in staffing a department

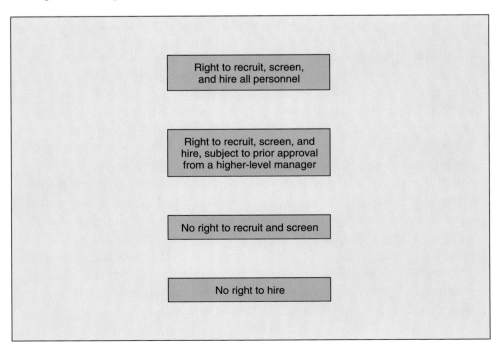

Delegation is one of the most significant concepts affecting a manager's ability to get the job done. It creates a risk for managers, however, because the success or failure of an operation is ultimately their responsibility. In this typical construction scene, a great deal of authority has been delegated to the project superintendent, shown speaking. But managers at company headquarters are still responsible for the outcome. (Source: © Jim Pickerell)

Some of the more significant reasons that delegation is important are illustrated in Figure 8.2. First, delegation of authority often leads to quicker action and faster, better decisions. Action can be taken much faster if people can avoid going to a higher level in the organization for a decision.

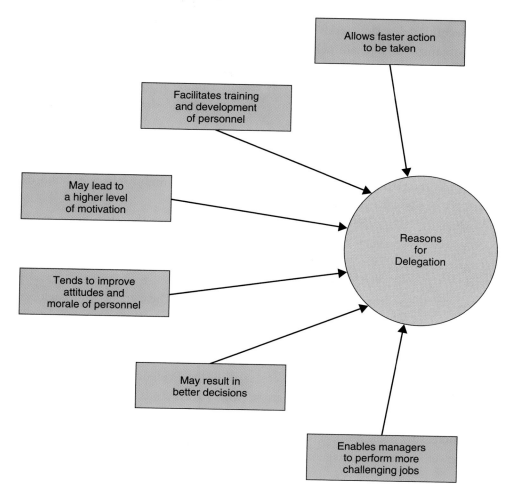

Allows faster action to be taken

Facilitates training and development of personnel

May lead to a higher level of motivation

Tends to improve attitudes and morale of personnel

May result in better decisions

Enables managers to perform more challenging jobs

Reasons for Delegation

❖ **Figure 8.2**
Reasons for delegation

Managers should delegate with finality. Workers should know that they are expected to do the jobs assigned and should know when completetion is expected.
(Source: © John Coletti)

Second, delegation tends to be an important factor in training and developing organizational personnel. Managers cannot learn to perform a certain function or make decisions unless they are given the opportunity to do so. Delegation of responsibility and authority is essential if the firm is concerned about developing personnel to assume more challenging and demanding jobs in the future.

Third, delegation may lead to a higher level of motivation. People who are given authority and responsibility by their superiors often see this as a reflection of trust in their abilities. This may become a self-fulfilling prophecy as subordinates try to live up to that trust.

Fourth, closely related to improved motivation are the attitudes and the morale of employees. People who are given responsibility and authority tend to have better attitudes toward their superiors. They are often easier to manage and more cooperative, and their morale is higher.

Fifth, delegation may result in better decisions. The person who is closest to the job being done is often the one who knows how to do it best.

Finally, it is through delegation that managers are able to perform especially challenging jobs, such as putting a man on the moon. Delegation can be thought of as a way of extending the manager's capabilities. Evidence suggests that managers recognize this. A study of graduating MBAs and practicing managers revealed that the ability to perform a wide variety of tasks tends to be associated with increasing delegation.[2] Organizations are now flatter, meaning that they will have fewer layers of management between the chief executive and the supervi-

Entrenched Bureaucracy Doesn't Work in the PC Business

The trend away from traditional bureaucratic structures continues into the nineties. One organization that is known for its entrenched bureaucracy is IBM. IBM took a major step to break with bureaucratic tradition by setting up its personal computer (PC) business loosely. This freedom will hopefully give IBM's PC division a better shot at fending off clones and reversing its slide in the PC industry. According to James A. Cannavino, general manager of IBM's $11 billion Personal Systems Division, personal computer makers like IBM must be lean, flexible, aggressive, and lightning-fast in order to be competitive. Dell Computer and Compaq Computer are structured in a competitive fashion, but IBM is not, so IBM sliced its personal computer hardware development and manufacturing division off from the giant bureaucracy, and began focusing specifically on personal computer hardware. With the elimination of IBM's bureaucratic yoke, the new personal computer division is being streamlined, so they can cut prices often, roll out new products several times a year, sell through any kind of retail outlet, and provide consumers with any type of software they want, even non-IBM software. The competition never worries about anything except personal computer hardware, and that is what IBM's personal computer division must be allowed to do. The IBM bureaucracy is slow and fat, but the PC business is fast and lean, and companies that are not fast and lean are part of the past, not the future.[3]

sory level. Span of management is necessarily widened. Today's manager could oversee the efforts of as many as 300 people rather than 30. This is evidently what is occurring at Texaco, as well as at IBM.

Despite these and other advantages of delegation, managers should consider certain limitations or potential problems of delegation. Table 8.1 mentions four such limitations.

Certain general guidelines should be followed in delegating. First, managers should not fail to delegate just because they personally enjoy doing a particular job. Many managers were specialists before they were promoted. Some continue doing some of the tasks they particularly enjoyed. If a subordinate can satisfactorily perform the job, it should probably be delegated, no matter how much fun it is.

Second, managers should not be afraid to delegate the dirty work. They

TABLE 8.1 Limitations or Potential Problems with Delegation

- If improper feedback is provided, the manager may lose control and may not have the time to correct the situation if a problem occurs.
- Delegation can fail if the level of responsibility and authority is not clearly defined and understood.
- If the delegatee does not possess the ability, skills, and experience to accomplish the job or to make decisions, delegation can prove disastrous.
- Problems can result if an employee is given responsibility but insufficient authority to perform the task.

should recognize that at times less than desirable assignments have to be given out. Some managers feel guilty about assigning undesirable jobs and instead do the jobs themselves. This is not an efficient use of time. Both pleasant and unpleasant tasks should be considered for delegation.

Third, the manager's ability to perform a task better and faster than workers in the unit is not a reason to fail to delegate. Most managers are better at doing certain tasks than the average worker and can get the job done faster themselves. But they could have accomplished more by spending time on their main responsibility—supervising others. Besides, there are not enough hours in a day to perform tasks that others should be doing.

Finally, managers should delegate with finality. Delegate and let workers know that you expect them to do the job you assign and to complete it by a certain time. Workers should not believe that they can bring jobs back at the first sign of trouble. Some workers are very good at managing their manager.

❖ ❖ **ACCOUNTABILITY**

No organization can function effectively without a system of accountability. **Accountability** is any means of ensuring that the person who is supposed to perform a task actually performs it and does so correctly. Situations can rapidly get out of control when people are not held accountable. By setting up 12 independent profit centers, Texaco's former CEO Kinnear was making the managers in charge accountable. As organizations become flatter and span of management is broadened, managers have more responsibility and corresponding authority. Therefore, it is appropriate to hold managers accountable. When managers are given the resources necessary to accomplish assigned tasks, they will have to bear the inevitable burden of accountability.

Before a manager can be held accountable for results, certain conditions should be present, as Figure 8.3 shows. First, responsibilities must be thoroughly and clearly described. An individual who is unaware of what is expected cannot be properly held accountable. Second, the person must be qualified and capable of fulfilling the obligation. It would be inconceivable to assign the responsibility and authority for performing engineering or accounting functions to individuals having no educational background or experience in these areas. Finally, sufficient authority to accomplish the task must be delegated. Assigning a manager the total profit responsibility for a department, but no authority to hire or fire employees might mean that insufficient authority has been delegated. The manager probably would object to being held accountable for these results.

Because a manager's accountability is so closely related to responsibility, it cannot be delegated to someone else. Managers are usually accountable not only

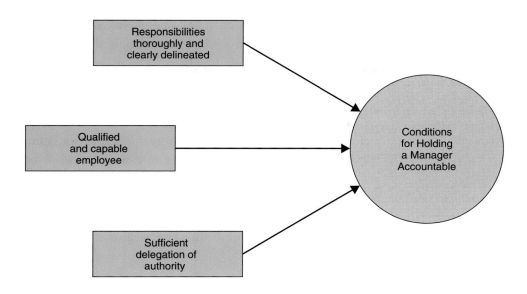

❖ **Figure 8.3**
Conditions for holding
a manager accountable

for their own actions and decisions but also for the actions of their subordinates. In navy tradition, the captain should go down with the ship, but this is an extreme case.

Accountability can be established in several ways. The first method is through personal inspection by the manager. After assigning a person to do the task, the manager checks to see that it is done properly. The second method is to have the subordinate complete reports and give them to the manager. It is likely that each of the profit center managers at Texaco will submit reports to DeCrane. However, because it is human nature to want to be seen in the best possible light, such reports might be biased in favor of the subordinate. A third method is through reporting done by others. A quality control inspector might report the number of defective units for each worker to the manager. Customers may report poor service or faulty products. This method of accountability is out of the hands of the person held accountable and is therefore reasonably free of bias. Finally, accountability may be obtained through a machine with a counter or some other measuring device. In a supermarket, a cash register tape of all sales serves this purpose. Most modern retailers, like Wal-Mart, use point-of-sale accounting systems, under which most mistakes are immediately logged for correction.

❖ ORGANIZING PRINCIPLES

To accomplish organizational objectives, organizations may follow any or all of a number of important organizing principles. The future may well be ruled by the Virtual Corporation, where adaptability is the key to success. In the Virtual Corporation the most important organizing principle is that everything is temporary, and companies come together to exploit fast-changing opportunities. Additional advantages are that companies share the costs, utilize the multiple skills of various companies, and enjoy better access to global markets.[4] The principles briefly discussed here are summarized in Table 8.2.

Unity of Command

The belief that each person should answer to only one immediate superior is the **unity of command principle.** That is, each employee has only one boss. Unity of command allows better coordination and understanding of what is required and improves discipline. However, even though this principle is valid in theory, it is almost universally violated in practice. An important problem caused by its violation is that an employee with two or more bosses can receive contradictory orders.

TABLE 8.2 Organizing Principles

PRINCIPAL	DEFINITION OF	REASON FOR	POSSIBLE CAUSES OF VIOLATION	POSSIBLE RESULTS OF VIOLATION
Unity of command	A person should report to only one boss.	Clarity and understanding, to ensure unity of effort and direction and to avoid conflicts.	Unclear definition of authority.	Dissatisfaction or frustration of employees and perhaps lower efficiency.
Equal authority and responsibility	The amount of authority and responsibility should be equal.	Work accomplished more efficiently, people developed, and frustration reduced.	Fear on the part of some managers that subordinates might take over.	Waste of energies and dissatisfaction of employees, resulting in reduced effectiveness.
Scalar principle	There should be a clear definition of authority in the organization (going through channels).	Clarity of relationship avoids confusion and improves decision making and performance.	Uncertainty on the part of the employee or a direct effort by the employee to avoid the chain of command.	Poor performance, confusion, or dissatisfaction.
Span of management	There is a limit to the number of employees a manager can effectively supervise.	Increased effectiveness in direction and control of a manager.	Overloading of a manager because of growth in the number of employees.	Lack of efficiency and control, resulting in poor performance.

Equal Authority and Responsibility

An important principle of management is that the degree of authority should equal the degree of responsibility. Following this principle ensures that work will be performed efficiently and with a minimum amount of frustration. If an adequate amount of authority is not delegated, energies and resources are wasted, and employee dissatisfaction often results. Unfortunately, many managers continue to give their subordinates more responsibility than authority.

Scalar Principle and Chain of Command

The philosophy that authority and responsibility should flow from top management downward in a clear, unbroken line is the **scalar principle.** If this principle is followed, there is a clear chain of command for every person in the organization. The **chain of command** is the line along which authority flows from the top of the organization to any individual. A clear chain of command clarifies relationships, avoids confusion, and tends to improve decision making, thus often leading to more effective performance. When the scalar principle is followed, superiors and subordinates communicate by going through channels.

Span of Management

The number of direct subordinates reporting to any manager is the **span of management (control).** Although the span of management may vary greatly, there is a maximum number of employees a manager can effectively supervise in a given circumstance. Efficient use of managerial talent also dictates that there be a minimum number of subordinates assigned to each manager. The maximum effective span of management is determined to a large extent by the sophistication of reporting technology such as computerized reports, electronic mail, facsimile transmission of documents, and other technological advancements.

Accepted spans of management have historically been relatively narrow, usually ranging from six to 15 employees. Narrow spans of management permit closer supervision of personnel but tend to create tall organizational structures—structures with a large number of levels. This may cause difficulties in communication and result in managers and workers at lower levels feeling isolated. Wide spans result in relatively fewer levels, or flat organization structures, and greater latitude for the individual employee.

A number of factors affect the span of management:

1. In general, the more complex the work, the shorter the optimal span of management.
2. The span can be longer if the manager is supervising employees performing similar jobs.

3. If jobs are closely interlocked and interdependent, the manager may have greater problems with coordination, creating the need for a rather limited span of management.

4. If the organization is operating in an unstable environment, a narrow span may prove to be more effective.

5. The establishment of numerous standards increases predictability and provides the basis for effective control, thereby resulting in a wider effective span.

6. Managers and employees who are highly skilled, experienced, and motivated can operate with wider spans of management and less supervision.

7. Where high commitment to the organization is as important as technical efficiency, such commitment can be enhanced through wider spans of management.[5]

In addition, it has been proven that technology can have a significant impact on the span of management. Joan Woodward, a British researcher, conducted studies in 100 English manufacturing firms. This led to her discovery that the type of production technology used in business organizations affected their span of management. Woodward classified production technology on the basis of the following categories:

- Unit or small-batch processing (for example, made-to-order goods such as custom-tailored clothing).
- Mass production (assembly-line operations).
- Process production with continuous long runs of a standardized product such as oil, chemicals, or pharmaceuticals.

She discovered that spans of management were widest in firms using mass-production technology. The jobs in a mass-production situation tend to be more routine and similar to one another, thereby leading to wider appropriate spans of management.[6] On the other hand, unit and process production were marked by narrower spans of management.

❖ ❖ CENTRALIZATION VERSUS DECENTRALIZATION

It is important that management determine the appropriate levels of responsibility and authority to be delegated. **Centralization** is the degree to which authority is retained by higher-level managers in an organization rather than being delegated. If a limited amount of authority is delegated, the organization is usually characterized as being centralized. **Decentralization** is the condition that exists when a significant amount of authority is delegated to lower levels in the enterprise. According to Wayland Hicks, a Xerox executive vice-president, the business world is headed toward more decentralization, with offices, factories, and suppliers spread throughout the world.[7] There are many degrees of centralization, but today the real question is not whether a company should decentralize but what degree of decentralization is appropriate.

In a highly centralized structure, individual managers and workers at lower levels in the organization have a rather narrow range of decisions or actions they can initiate. By contrast, the scope of authority to make decisions and take actions is rather broad for lower-level managers and employees in decentralized organizations. In a highly centralized organizational structure, upper management makes all decisions regarding the hiring or firing of personnel, the approval of equipment and supply purchases, and similar activities. In a decentralized structure, lower-level management may make these decisions.

Decentralization is advocated by many who believe that a greater share in management decision making should be given to lower organizational levels. Decentralization tends to create a climate for more rapid growth and development of personnel. Decentralization also tends to be favored by informal people who are achievement oriented. Engineers tend to be informal people, and because engineers run Motorola, informality is a hallmark of Motorola. If Motorola Chairman George Fisher has a question, he may well pick up the phone and talk to the engineer directly involved, instead of contacting that person's boss. Decisions and solutions are made as close as possible to the problem, making for quick and effective decisions and a more productive organization.[8] If virtually all decisions and orders come from one central source, organization members tend to act like robots and unthinking executors of someone else's commands. On the other hand, there are exceptionally competent managers in high positions—such as former chief executive James W. Kinnear at Texaco and current Texaco CEO Alfred C. DeCrane, Jr.—who are better able to make valid decisions than are their subordinates. When this is the case, a reasonable tendency is to lean toward centralization. In addition, many employees and lower-level managers do not wish to be involved at high levels in the organization.

In addition to the human behavior implications of decentralization and centralization, several other factors affect a manager's decision in this regard. Centralization

1. Produces uniformity of policy and action.
2. Results in few risks of errors by subordinates who lack either information or skill.
3. Utilizes the skills of central and specialized experts.
4. Allows close control of operations.

On the other hand, decentralization

1. Tends to make for speedier decisions and actions on the spot without the need to consult higher levels.
2. Results in decisions that are more likely to be adapted to local conditions.
3. Results in greater interest and enthusiasm on the part of the subordinate to whom the authority has been entrusted. These expanded jobs provide excellent training experience for possible promotion to higher levels.
4. Allows top management to use its time for more study and consideration of the basic objectives, plans, and policies of the enterprise.

The following sections discuss several factors that may account for differing decisions about the amount of centralization that is appropriate.

Size and Complexity of the Organization

The larger the enterprise, the more authority the central manager is forced to delegate. The globalization of business that is occurring will definitely increase the size and complexity of organizations. If a firm is engaged in many separate businesses, the limitations of expertise usually lead to decentralization. Authority is delegated to the heads of the various units. Each major product group is likely to have different product problems, customers, and marketing channels. If speed and adaptability to change are necessary for success, decentralization is a must.

Dispersion of the Organization

When the difficulties of size are compounded by geographic dispersion, it is evident that a greater degree of decentralization must occur. Not every decision or

The widespread use of computers in business gives managers more flexibility in deciding whether to centralize. (Source: Photograph courtesy of Lockheed Corporation.)

every function must be decentralized, however. Control of operations may have to be pushed down to lower levels in the organization, even though control of financing may still be centralized. Because of the increasing complexity of federal and state legislation affecting employment practices and unionization, centralization of labor relations is often established for purposes of uniformity throughout the company.

Competence of Available Personnel

A major limiting factor in centralization is the degree of competence of personnel. If an enterprise has grown up under centralized decision making and control, subordinates are often poorly equipped to start making major decisions. They were hired and trained to be followers, not leaders and decision makers. In some convenience store chains, this has developed into a major problem. Store managers are promoted to supervisor, not because of their decision-making ability but because they are experienced in basic store functions and can ensure that the new store managers follow standard operating procedures. In such situations, people who eventually make it to the top may not be equipped to cope with all the necessary decision-making requirements that are not based on established practices and procedures. Those inclined toward more independent thought and action may be driven away from the centralized firm.

Adequacy of the Communication System

Greater size, increased complexity, and geographic dispersion lead to the delegation of larger amounts of authority for decision making to lower levels in the organization. Unwanted decentralization can be avoided through the development of a communication system that will provide for the speed, accuracy, and sufficiency of information top management needs to exercise centralized control. In effect, although large size and geographic dispersion may preclude one's being on the spot, one can control subordinates by detailing standards of performance and by ensuring that information flows quickly and accurately to the person with central authority.

❖ ❖ TYPES OF ORGANIZATIONAL STRUCTURES

The formal relationships among groups and individuals in the organization are the **organizational structure.** This structure provides guidelines essential for effective employee performance and overall organizational success. It should clarify and communicate the lines of responsibility and authority within the firm and assist management in coordinating the overall operation.

It is common to think only of large companies when organizational structures are discussed, but every firm, large or small, has a structure of some kind. It may or may not have an organizational chart. Small businesses may have structures that are simple and easy to understand. In fact, the organizational structure may be informal and highly changeable in small, uncomplicated businesses. By contrast, large, diverse, and complex organizations usually have a highly formalized structure. But that should not mean the structure is so rigid that it does not change, perhaps even frequently. Determining the most appropriate organizational design or structure is not a simple matter if one must consider frequency of reorganization as a factor. Newly formed high-technology companies are most likely to restructure or reorganize frequently, but even some of the largest *Fortune* 500 industrial firms often experience major reorganizations. When organizations reorganize, some employers are required to provide workers with 60 days' notice before shutdown. However, the General Accounting Office has concluded that most employers who closed plants did so without giving notice either to workers or to the proper state agencies.[10]

Many variations of organizational structures are used today. The most common types of structures, the ones from which variations are developed, are line, line and staff, functional authority, project, and matrix.

Line Organizational Structure

Organizations that have only direct, vertical relationships between different levels in the firm are **line organizations.** These organizations consist of only **line departments**—departments directly involved in accomplishing the primary purpose of the organization. In a typical company, line departments include production and marketing. In a line organization, authority follows the chain of command. Figure 8.4 is an illustration of a simple line organizational structure.

Several advantages are often associated with pure line organizational structure.

1. A line structure tends to simplify and clarify responsibility, authority, and accountability relationships in the organization. The levels of responsibility and authority in a line organization are likely to be very precise and easily understandable.
2. A line structure promotes fast decision making and allows the organization to change direction rapidly because there are few people to consult when problems arise.
3. Because pure line organizations are small, there is greater closeness of management and employees, and everyone usually has an opportunity to know what is going on in the firm.

There are also certain disadvantages to the line structure. The major disadvantage is that as the firm grows larger, there is an increasing lack of effectiveness. At some point, improved speed and flexibility do not offset the lack of specialized knowledge and skills. In other words, a line structure may reduce the effectiveness of managers by forcing them to be experts in too many fields. In a line organization, firms tend to become overly dependent on the few key people who can perform numerous jobs. If the organization is to remain purely line, management can create additional levels to share the managerial load. This, however, will result in a longer chain of command and consequent loss of some of the speed, flexibility, and centralized control. Therefore, there are few pure line organizations of any substantial size.

Line and Staff Organizational Structure

Most large organizations are of the line and staff type. **Line and staff organizations** have direct, vertical relationships between different levels and also specialists

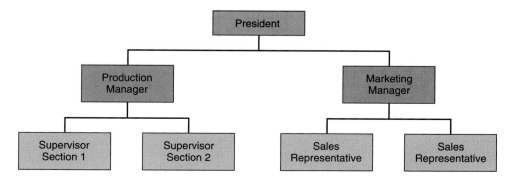

❖ Figure 8.4
A line organizational structure

responsible for advising and assisting other managers. Such organizations have both line and staff departments. **Staff departments** provide line people with advice and assistance in specialized areas.

As the line and staff organization chart in Figure 8.5 shows, staff functions under the president typically include personnel, quality control, research, and accounting. The line functions are marketing and production. Each staff manager is responsible to people at every level of the organization. For simplicity, however, only the staff relationships between the personnel director and people in the production department are shown. Notice the dotted lines from personnel to superintendents, supervisors, and workers. The personnel director, however, also has staff responsibilities to the other department heads. Personnel, quality control, research, and accounting are separate, specialized staff functions, but the managers of these functions have a direct line reporting relationship to the president.

Three separate types of specialized staffs can be identified: (1) advisory, (2) service, and (3) control. It is possible, though, for one unit to perform all three functions. For example, the personnel manager advises line managers on labor relations topics. The personnel department simultaneously provides a service by procuring and training needed production and sales personnel. A control orientation enters when the personnel manager audits people's salaries to ensure conformity to line-approved pay ranges. Some staffs perform only one function. For example, a staff economist advises on the establishment of long-range plans, and a quality control staff unit enforces authorized product standards. It is apparent that the potential for conflicts in coordination between line and staff tends to grow as one moves from advice to service to control. One can possibly ignore advice, but service is needed, and control is often unavoidable.

The line and staff organizational structure offers both advantages and disadvantages. The primary advantage is the organization's use of the expertise of

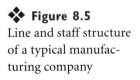
❖ **Figure 8.5**
Line and staff structure of a typical manufacturing company

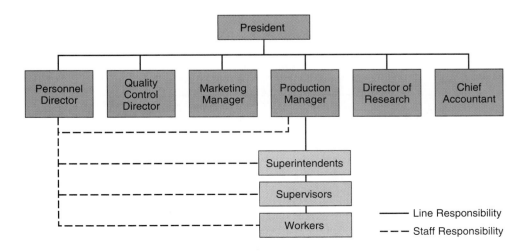

staff specialists. Their concentrated and skillful analysis of business problems allows managers to be more scientific. In addition, managers' effective span of management can be lengthened; that is, once relieved of technical details, managers can supervise more people. Some staff people even operate as extensions of managers and assist in coordination and control.

Despite the fact that a line and staff structure allows for increased flexibility and specialization, it may create conflicts. When specialists are introduced into the organization, line managers may feel that they have lost authority over certain specialized functions. These managers do not want staff specialists telling them what to do or how to do it, even though they recognize the specialists' knowledge and expertise. It is important to use staff personnel without destroying unity of command. The authority of line managers should be preserved while their ability to produce is enhanced. Some staff people have difficulty adjusting to the role, especially if line managers are reluctant to accept advice. Staff people may also resent their lack of authority, and this may cause line and staff conflict.

There is a tendency for specialists to seek to enlarge personal influence by assuming line authority in their specialty. The tendency is compounded by the realization that the fundamental purpose of all staff is to produce greater economy and effectiveness of operation. This means that staff must attempt to introduce changes that result in more efficiency. These changes will not always be welcomed by line personnel. Thus, the introduction of specialists into what was once a fairly simple organizational structure often complicates relationships.

Functional Authority Organizational Structure

Organizations whose staff departments have authority over line personnel in narrow areas of specialization (a modification of line and staff organizations) are **functional authority organizations.** In a pure line organization, there is limited use of specialist by management. In the line and staff organization, specialization of particular functions characterizes the structure, but the specialists only advise and assist. In the functional authority organizational structure, however, specialists are given **functional authority**—the right of staff specialists to issue orders in their own names in designated areas.

The principle of unity of command (having one boss) is violated when functional authority exists. Even though few organizations give all of their staff managers functional authority, it is quite common for one or two specialists to have such authority. If a function is considered to be of crucial importance, it may be necessary for the specialist to exercise direct rather than advisory authority. Then, the violation of unity of command is intentional, and the possible losses resulting from confusion and conflicting orders from multiple sources may be more than offset by increased effectiveness.

Examples of specialists often given functional authority are the managers of

quality control, safety, and labor relations. Figure 8.6 shows a functional authority organizational structure. Notice that this structure is quite similar to the line
and staff organizational structure shown in Figure 8.5, except for the nature of
the relationship between the staff specialist and other managers. Quality control
is a very important function in most manufacturing firms, and its level of authority and status has increased over the years. A traditional staff department would
merely advise. Because of the critical nature of its work, however, a quality control department often directs as well as advises.

Safety and labor relations specialists may exercise functional authority over
personnel in other areas throughout the organization, but only in relation to their
specific specialties. A safety manager may issue compliance guidelines and give
direct interpretations of the Occupational Safety and Health Act throughout the
organization. The labor relations specialist often will have complete authority in
contract negotiations with the union.

In each of these illustrations—quality control, safety, and labor relations—
the traditional chain of command has been split. As long as the splitting process
is restricted, coordination and unity of action are not in excessive danger. Many
organizations that utilize functional authority relationships attempt to confine the
impact to managerial rather than operative levels. Thus, a department supervisor may have to account to more than one boss, but the supervisor's employees
are protected from this possible confusion.

The major disadvantages of a functional authority organizational structure
are (1) the potential conflicts resulting from the violation of the principle of unity
of command and (2) the tendency to keep authority centralized at higher levels
in the organization. If the functional authority organizational structure is used
extensively, there may be a tendency for the line department supervisor to become
little more than a figurehead. The structure can become very complicated when
functional specialists exist at various levels of the organization.

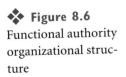

❖ **Figure 8.6**
Functional authority
organizational struc-
ture

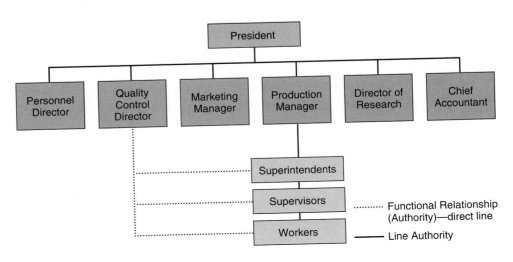

Project and Matrix Organizational Structures

The line, line and staff, and functional authority organizational structures have been the traditional approaches to organization. The primary objective of these forms of organizing has been the establishment and distribution of authority to coordinate and control the firm by an emphasis on vertical, rather than horizontal relationships. In major aerospace projects such as the Space Shuttle Project, however, work processes flowed horizontally, diagonally, up, or down. The direction of work flow depends on the distribution of talents and abilities in the organization and the need to apply them to the problem that exists. The organizations that have emerged to cope with this challenge have been referred to as project and matrix organizations.

Project Organizations A **project organization** is a temporary organization designed to achieve specific results by using teams of specialists from different functional areas in the organization. The team focuses all of its energies and skills on the assigned project. Once the project has been completed, the team is broken up, and its members are reassigned to their regular positions in the organization or to other projects. Many business organizations and government agencies make use of project teams or task forces to concentrate efforts on specific project assignments, such as the development of a new product or technology or the construction of a new plant.

As Table 8.3 shows, there are times when the project organizational structure is the most valuable type of structure. Figure 8.7 illustrates a highly simplified project structure attached to an existing organization. Personnel are assigned to the project from the existing permanent organization and are under the direction and control of the project manager. The project manager specifies what effort is needed and when work will be performed, whereas the concerned department managers may decide who in their unit is to do the work and how it is to be accomplished. Home base for these project members is the existing department—human resources, engineering, quality control, and production.

TABLE 8.3 When the Project Organizational Structure Is Most Valuable

- Work is definable in terms of a specific objective and target date for completion.
- Work is unique and unfamiliar to the existing organization.
- Work is complex with respect to the interdependence of activities and specialized skills necessary for accomplishment.
- Work is critical in terms of possible gain or loss.
- Work is temporary with respect to the duration of need.

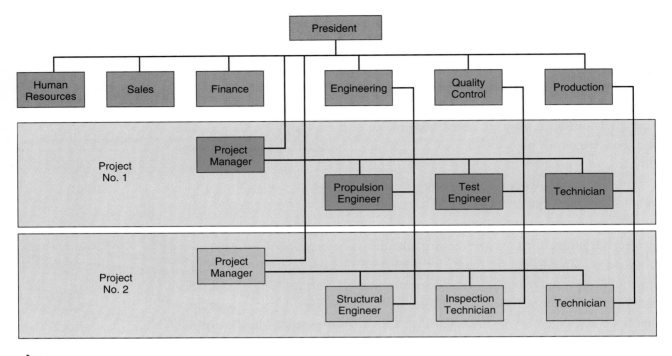

❖ **Figure 8.7**

Project structure

The authority over each of the three project members is shared by the project manager and the respective function managers in the permanent organization. The four specialists are on loan on a temporary basis and spend only a portion of their time on the project assignment. It is apparent that authority is one of the crucial questions of the project structure. A deliberate conflict has been established between the project manager and the other managers in the organization. The authority relationships are overlapping, presumably in the interest of ensuring that all problems will be covered.

Project managers and department heads are often forced to use means other than formal authority to achieve results. Informal relationships become more important than formal prescriptions of authority. In the event of conflict and dispute, discussion and consensus are required, rather than the forcing of compliance by threat or punishment. Full and free communication, regardless of formal rank, is required among those working on the project. More attention is allocated to roles and competencies in relation to the project than to formal levels of authority. The National Aeronautics and Space Administration (NASA) provides the most widely known example of the use of the project organization.

Matrix Organization   A **matrix organization** is a permanent organization designed to achieve specific results by using teams of specialists from different functional areas in the organization. This type of organization is often used when it is essential for the firm to be highly responsive to a rapidly changing external environment. For example, an electronics firm might find that the matrix structure facilitates the company's quick response to its environment. Matrix organizational structures have been used successfully in such industries as banking, chemicals, computers, and electronics. However, they require an effective coordinating mechanism to offset the negative effect of dual authority.

In matrix organizations, there are functional managers and product (or project) managers. Functional managers are in charge of specialized resources such as production, quality control, inventories, scheduling, and selling. Product managers are in charge of one or more products, and are authorized to prepare product strategies and call on the various functional managers for the necessary resources. When a firm moves into a matrix structure, functional managers must realize that they will lose some of their authority and will have to take some direction from the product managers, who have the budgets to purchase internal resources. In fact, true matrix organizations imply that project and line managers will have roughly equivalent power.[11]

Despite their limitations, project and matrix management concepts demonstrate that people can work for two or more managers and that managers can effectively influence those over whom they have only partial authority. There is the possibility of conflict and frustration, but the opportunity for prompt, efficient accomplishment is great.

❖ ❖ REENGINEERING

When business problems occur, workers are often blamed, even though the real obstacle lies in process design. Unfortunately, many managers believe that the manner in which an operation is accomplished is unchangeable. Rather than looking for process problems, managers often focus on worker deficiencies, at least initially. This is true even though the design of the process may be causing problems. If process is the problem, it can often be reengineered for a substantial improvement in productivity, as Procter & Gamble discovered.

Reengineering is "the fundamental rethinking and radical redesign of business processes to achieve dramatic improvements in critical, contemporary measures of performance, such as cost, quality, service, and speed."[12] Reengineering emphasizes the radical redesign of work in which companies organize around process instead of by functional departments. It is not incremental changes that are desired, but radical changes that alter entire operations with the stroke of pens. Essentially, the firm must rethink and redesign its business system. Reengineering focuses on the overall aspects of job designs, organizational structures, and management systems. It stresses that work should be organized around outcomes as opposed to tasks or functions. Reengineering should never be confused with restructuring (discussed in Chapter 7), even though a workforce reduction may result.[13]

The reengineering approach championed by consultant Michael Hammer, president of Hammer & Company in Cambridge, has impressed some experts so much that they believe it will displace TQM at many companies.[14] In a recent survey of senior executives, reengineering comprised a major focus of the agenda of most corporate plans.[15] Some firms such as Eastman Kodak Company and American Express have gone so far as to appoint senior officers for reengineering.

As an example of how reengineering might work in a university environment, let us think about the process of student registration. Consider the various units on a typical college campus that are involved in registration: the registrar's office, the housing office, campus security, the bookstore, and certainly many more. The process of registration has changed little in many years, with the exception of telephone registration, which often causes more problems than it cures. With reengineering, this process would be analyzed as if it were being done for the first time. Tradition would be thrown out of the window, and the result might be a quick and efficient process for registering students. However, please do not count on this occurring while you are in school.

In the language of reengineering, a term that is often used is *process manager*. As opposed to being a functional manager such as a production manager, a marketing manager, a finance manager, and so forth, a process manager is responsible for accomplishing all operations associated with a specific process. It is similar in nature to the matrix organization discussed previously in this chapter. For example, there would likely be a process manager for student registration.

❖ ❖ JOB DESIGN

The previous section focused on processes and the concept of reengineering, which requires a certain degree of job design or redesign to occur. In fact, many organizations do not need to reengineer, but rather to change job designs. **Job design** is the process of determining the specific tasks to be performed, the methods used in performing these tasks, and the way the job relates to other work in the organization. Several concepts related to job design including job enrichment, job enlargement, and employee-centered work redesign will be discussed next.

Job Enrichment

In the past two decades, there has been considerable interest in and application of job enrichment in a wide variety of organizations. Strongly advocated by Frederick Herzberg, **job enrichment** involves basic changes in the content and level of responsibility of a job so as to provide greater challenge to the worker. Job enrichment provides a vertical expansion of responsibilities. The worker has the oppor-

Procter & Gamble Reengineers for the Future

Reengineering essentially involves a firm rethinking and redesigning its business system to become more competitive. Procter & Gamble (P&G) Chairman Edwin L. Artzt has been preaching a strategy of good value since 1991, and has since launched sweeping changes in the way that P&G markets its products. Now, P&G has gone far beyond just a strategy change. It is currently involved in a far-ranging self-appraisal aimed at streamlining the organization. P&G must be streamlined because a decade of acquisition and foreign expansion has resulted in an unwieldy organization, with costs running out of control. Overhead has risen two percent in only three years. P&G's solution to the problem is to "bottom-up reengineer" to cut costs in sales, research, and administration. Ten teams are determining how to streamline the company. Basically, at P&G "You've got people checking people," to determine who to cut, and how many to cut, and how to improve the basic areas of sales, research, and administration. The key to this reengineering effort is that real contributors will remain at P&G. According to Artzt, "Real contributors don't have to worry (about these cuts)." One place where cuts are a must is in the area of overlapping staffs in the United States, where bureaucracy is thickest. P&G has been trying to boost performance for years in the areas of marketing, sales, and logistics, but with only limited success. Artzt believes that reengineering is the answer.[16]

tunity to derive a feeling of achievement, recognition, responsibility, and personal growth in performing the job. Although job enrichment programs do not always achieve positive results, they have often brought about improvements in job performance and in the level of satisfaction of workers in many organizations.

According to Herzberg, five principles should be followed when implementing job enrichment:

1. *Increasing job demands:* The job should be changed in such a way as to increase the level of difficulty and responsibility.
2. *Increasing the worker's accountability:* More individual control and authority over the work should be allowed, while the manager retains ultimate accountability.
3. *Providing work scheduling freedom:* Within limits, individual workers should be allowed to schedule their own work.
4. *Providing feedback:* Timely periodic reports on performance should be made directly to workers rather than to their supervisors.
5. *Providing new learning experiences:* Work situations should encourage opportunities for new experiences and personal growth.[17]

Job Enlargement

Many people have attempted to differentiate between job enrichment and job enlargement. **Job enlargement** involves the changes in the scope of a job so as to provide greater variety to the worker. Job enlargement attempts to provide a horizontal expansion of duties. For example, instead being responsibile for operating only one machine, a person is taught to operate two or even three machines; however, no higher level of responsibility is provided. On the other hand, job enrichment entails providing a person with additional responsibilities. There may be other tasks to perform, but responsibility is given along with the tasks. For instance, the worker may be given the responsibility of scheduling the operation of the three machines. Increased responsibility means providing the worker with increased freedom to do the job, including making decisions and exercising more self-control over work.

Employee-Centered Work Redesign[18]

A concept designed to link the mission of the company with the job satisfaction needs of employees is **employee-centered work redesign**. Employees are encouraged to become involved in redesigning their work to benefit both the organization and themselves. Workers can propose changes in their job design to make their jobs more satisfying, but they must also show how these changes better accomplish the goals of the entire unit. With this approach, the contribution of each employee is recognized, while at the same time, the focus remains on effective accomplishment of the organizational mission.

A GLOBAL PERSPECTIVE

Decentralization, Not Necessarily a Global Solution

Global organizational structures must always ensure a tie-in between profits and operational aspects of the business such as productivity enhancement, staffing, research, and development. When an organization goes global it often creates problems for managers and employees alike. Effective international management requires an organizational structure that assists in the accomplishment of organizational objectives. Global companies like Dow Chemical must often learn to develop the correct organizational structure by making costly mistakes. Dow's organizational structure was developed not by product line, but by global area. This decentralized organizational structure was intended to allow managers in each region to be as close as possible to the problems in each area of the world, and to empower them to make quick and informed decisions as close as possible to the operational area of concern. However, global distance and managerial independence got out of hand, and similar business units in different parts of the globe ended up competing with one another, to the detriment of the entire Dow organization.

The solution to this time and distance problem was to reorganize Dow into four global business units including plastics, chemicals, hydrocarbons, and new business ventures. Now, spending on plants and productivity levels are determined by the needs of the global business unit involved rather than by the individual area where a certain operation is located. Plants in a certain global business unit are built, closed, or modernized based on the overall operating efficiencies of the entire global business unit and not just on the concerns of an individual plant or region. The new organizational structure has promoted accountability, managerial, and employee focus, and quicker and better decisions. Basically, Dow is getting "more bang for the bucks they're investing," and other companies probably can do the same.[19]

❖ ❖ HOW MANAGERS CAN BECOME BETTER AT WORKING WITH COMMITTEES

Committees have been the brunt of many harsh jokes. For example, it has been said that a camel is a horse designed by a committee. A **committee** is a group of people assigned to work together to do something not included in their regular jobs. Other names used to designate committees include *boards*, *councils*, and *task forces*. A permanent committee is referred to as a standing committee. Committees are necessary for several reasons. They can bring together experts from various areas to handle difficult problems. At least in theory, two heads are better

✗ Management Tips ✗

Guidelines for Dealing with the Organizing Concepts and Organizational Structure

1. **Be sure that authority equals responsibility.** It is difficult for workers to do a job right if they have responsibility without authority.

2. **Put people where they fit best.** If you have given a worker responsibility for a task and it is not done well, you may have assigned the task to the wrong person. This individual may fit better in another assignment.

3. **Be willing to delegate.** Many managers believe they must do everything themselves. There are not that many hours in a day. The task of the manager is to get things done through the efforts of others.

4. **Consider the human element when organizing.** Some people work much better together than others.

5. **Be flexible.** What worked well yesterday may not be best for today. Be open to new approaches.

6. **Hold workers accountable for what they do.** This is your basic means of maintaining control.

7. **Know what needs to be done.** Organizing should be directed toward accomplishing goals.

8. **Most individuals work best when they have one immediate superior.** At times this is not possible, but it is difficult for workers to operate effectively when they receive contradictory orders.

9. **Supervise only as many workers as you can effectively handle.** Understand your limitations.

10. **Work with the staff people in your organization.** They are there to assist you.

than one. Even if the decisions that committees make are technically no better than those made by individuals, such decisions are often more readily accepted. In fact, it is common practice to make sure that people who are likely to oppose an expected decision are placed on the committee responsible for making it.

Committees also have weaknesses. Often, the decision process is slow. One person can make decisions faster than a group can. Committees are also costly. If five people are on a committee and the average cost of each worker is $25 an hour, it costs $250 to have a two-hour meeting. Another weakness of committees is that they encourage compromise, even though the best decision may be at one extreme or the other.

The shortcomings of committees can be minimized if a few simple rules are followed.

1. The purpose of the committee should be clearly stated in writing.
2. The size of the committee should be just adequate to obtain the representation and intellectual input required.
3. There should be an odd number of members so the committee will not deadlock on important issues.
4. Every committee meeting should have a specific written agenda.
5. The committee should be immediately disbanded when it has accomplished its purpose.

SUMMARY

Responsibility is the obligation to perform work activities. Authority is the right to decide, to direct others, and to perform certain duties. Delegation is the process of assigning responsibility along with the needed authority. Accountability is any means of ensuring that the person who is supposed to perform a task actually performs it and does so correctly.

These concepts are basic to the organizing process. In addition, managers follow certain guidelines in performing the organizing function. The unity of command principle is the belief that each person should answer to only one immediate superior. Another important principle is that authority should equal responsibility. The scalar principle is the philosophy that authority and responsibility should flow from top management downward in a clear, unbroken line, called the chain of command. A clear chain of command clarifies relationships, avoids confusion, and tends to improve decision making. The number of subordinates reporting directly to any manager is referred to as the span of management (control).

Management must determine appropriate levels of responsibility and authority to be delegated. Centralization is the degree to which authority is retained by higher-level managers. If a significant amount of authority is delegated to lower levels, the enterprise is described as being decentralized.

The organizational structure is the formal relationships among groups and individuals in the organization. Line organizations have direct, vertical relationships between different levels in the firm. They include only line departments—the departments directly involved in accomplishing organizational objectives. Line and staff organizations also have direct, vertical relationships, but they also include specialists responsible for advising and assisting other managers. The functional authority organization is a modification of the line and staff organization. Staff departments have authority over line personnel in narrow areas of specialization. A project organization is a temporary organization designed to achieve specific results, using teams of specialists from different functional areas in the organization. A matrix organization is the same as a project organization, except that it is permanent rather than temporary.

Reengineering is defined as the fundamental rethinking and radical redesign of business processes to achieve dramatic improvements in critical, contemporary measures of performance, such as cost, quality, service, and speed. Reengineering emphasizes the radical redesign of work in which companies organize around process instead of by functional departments. It is not incremental changes that are desired, but radical changes that alter entire operations at the same time. Job design is the process of determining the specific tasks to be performed, the methods used in performing these tasks, and the way the job relates to other work in the organization. Several concepts related to job design include job enrichment, job enlargement, and employee-centered work redesign.

Committees are groups of people working together to do something not included in their regular jobs. They bring together experts from various areas to handle difficult problems. Managers can overcome the shortcomings of committees and be better at working with them if they follow the guidelines provided in the chapter.

KEY TERMS

Responsibility 236
Authority 237
Delegation 238
Accountability 242
Unity of command
   principle 244
Scalar principle 245
Chain of command 245
Span of management
   (control) 245
Centralization 246
Decentralization 246
Organizational structure 249
Line organizations 250
Line departments 250

Line and staff
   organizations 251
Staff departments 252
Functional authority
   organizations 253
Functional authority 253
Project organization 255
Matrix organization 256
Reengineering 257
Job design 258
Job enrichment 258
Job enlargement 259
Employee-centered work
   redesign 260
Committee 261

REVIEW QUESTIONS

1. Distinguish by definition among the following terms:
   a. responsibility
   b. authority
   c. delegation
   d. accountability
2. Describe each of the following organizing principles:
   a. unity of command
   b. equal authority and responsibility
   c. scalar principle
3. Distinguish between centralization and decentralization. Briefly describe the primary factors to be considered in determining the degree of centralization that is appropriate for an organization.
4. What are the basic types of organizational structures? Briefly describe each type.
5. Under what circumstances are project and matrix structures the most appropriate?
6. When would it be appropriate to use reengineering?
7. Define the following terms:
   a. Job design
   b. Job enrichment
   c. Job enlargement
   d. Employee-centered work design
8. Discuss the merits of this statement: A camel is a horse designed by a committee.

CASE STUDIES

CASE 8.1 Holiday Corporation: Organizing for Success

Holiday Corporation is the "Nation's Innkeeper." With almost 2,000 hotels in 53 countries, a more apt title is the "World's Innkeeper." Holiday Corporation did not attain its position of supremacy by standing still. Kemmons Wilson, the founder, was well known for his devotion to effective organizing, and it is that devotion that accounts for much of Holiday Corporation's success. Holiday Corporation expanded beyond providing simple lodging services, billing itself as the "world's largest hospitality company." In addition to its flagship chain of Holiday Inn hotels, the company operates three new hotel chains: one to appeal to upscale business travelers, a suite-type hotel chain aimed at persons who planned to stay several days in one location, and another directed at economy-minded travelers. Holiday Corporation expanded its gaming business to include Harrahs Casinos in Las Vegas, Lake Tahoe, Reno, and Atlantic City.

Although involved in a number of businesses, Holiday Corporation management recognizes the company's reliance on its traditional main business: lodging. They made efforts to upgrade the Holiday Inns chain and determined how many hotels would close and how many new ones would be built. Specific goals based upon the frequency of guests' complaints were set and they emphasized the human aspect of Holiday Inns' business. Confident of success, Holiday Inns' management offered a remarkable guarantee, "Your room will be right . . . or we'll make it right . . . or you stay the night free."

New areas for planning soon emerged because the entire industry suffered from overcapacity, due to a proliferation of new chains. Holiday embarked on a continuing program to divest less-desirable hotels and to maintain occupancy at others.

QUESTIONS

1. How have environmental factors affected the organizing process at Holiday Corporation?

2. Would you consider Holiday Corporation centralized or decentralized? Explain.

CASE 8.2 Misco Paper Converters

When Dick Valladao and George Smeltzer, owners of Misco Paper Converters, began their business, it was only a part-time operation. The operation involved buying rolls of brown kraft paper, such as that used for grocery bags, cutting the paper into various shapes and sizes, bundling the sheets together, and shipping the bundles to industrial customers. The pieces of paper were used for various purposes: as vapor barriers in electronic equipment, to place between glass or china plates and bowls prior to shipping, and as a protective wrapping for many small manufactured items.

As the business grew and became more profitable, Dick and George decided to leave their jobs and work at Misco full time. They had been doing the work in a small building behind George's house; but when they went into business full time, they rented a 6,000-square-foot warehouse. They also purchased a shear press and a stripper to complement the press and stripper they already owned, as well as a truck to pick up the raw paper at the paper mill and make some deliveries. Most of the bundles of paper, however, were shipped to customers by common carrier.

Dick and George had to hire six workers to help with the operation. The paper was fed off the large rolls through a stripper, which cut it to the appropriate width and clipped these strips off every 50 feet or so. These strips were then stacked onto a set of rollers that allowed them to be fed back into one of the shear presses, which clipped them to the appropriate length. The resulting rectangular stacks of brown paper were tied with twine and stacked onto shipping pallets. When a pallet was full, it was set aside to wait for shipment.

At first, George and Dick worked with the operators as a team, with each worker doing whatever needed to be done. Each person soon learned to operate the forklift, the strippers, and the shear presses and to tie bundles as well. Dick and George saw themselves as equals, so neither attempted to exercise authority over the other. As time went on, however, Dick began to think that the whole operation could be accomplished more efficiently if some kind of structure were imposed.

QUESTIONS

1. Do you believe that anything is to be gained at Misco by establishing an organizational structure, including specialization and lines of authority and responsibility? Explain your answer.

2. Assuming that George and Dick decide to set up a typical kind of organization, how should they decide who is to be chief executive? Should they have to decide that at all? Explain.

NOTES

1. This case is a composite of a number of published accounts, among them: Allanna Sullivan, "Texaco Alters Exploration and Production," *The Wall Street Journal* (March 8, 1989): A4; Mark Ivey, "Jim Kinnear Is Pumping New Life into Texaco," *Business Week* (April 17, 1989): 50–52; Randolph B. Smith and David B. Helder, "Icahn Sells Stake in Texaco, Inc. in Surprise Move," *The Wall Street Journal* (June, 2. 1989): A3; "He's Baaaack, with $2 Billion," *Time* (June 12, 1989): 51; Stratford P. Sherman, "Who's in Charge at Texaco Now?" *Fortune* 123 (January 16, 1989): 69–72; Alison L. Sprout, "American's Most Admired Corporations," *Fortune* 126 (February 11, 1991): 60; and Standard & Poor's Corporation, "Texaco Inc., *Standard NYSE Stock Reports* 56, no. 93 (May 15, 1989): sec. 20; "Personals," *Oil & Gas Journal* 91 (January 18, 1993): 72.

2. J. D. Ford and W. H. Hegarty, "Decision Makers' Beliefs About the Causes and Effects of Structures: An Exploratory Study," *Academy of Management Journal* 27 (June 1984): 281.

3. Catherine Arnst and Mark Lewyn, "Stand Back, Big Blue—And Wish Me Luck," *Business Week* (August 17, 1992): 23.

4. John A. Byrne, "The Virtual Corporation," *Business Week* (July 8, 1993): 98–103.

5. L. W. Fry and J. W. Slocum, Jr., "Technology, Structure, and Workgroup Effectiveness: A Test of a Contingency Model," *Academy of Management Journal* 27 (June 1984): 236.

6. Joan Woodward, *Industrial Organization: Theory and Practice* (London: Oxford University Press, 1965), pp. 52–62.

7. Brian Dumaine, "What the Leaders of Tomorrow See," *Fortune* (July 3, 1989): 48–62.

8. Gary Slutsker, "The Company that Likes to Obsolete Itself," *Forbes* 152 (September 13, 1993): 139–144.

9. Adapted from a case represented in Karen Berney's article, "Finding the Ethical Edge," *Nation's Business* 75 (August 1987): 24.

10. Kevin G. Salwen, "Most Firms Fail to Warn Workers Of Plant Closings," *The Wall Street Journal* (February 23, 1993): A2, A6.

11. William F. Joyce, "Matrix Organization: A Social Experiment," *Academy of Management Journal,* 29 (September 1986): 537.

12. Michael Hammer and James Champy. *Reengineering the Corporation: A Manifesto for Business Revolution* (New York: HarperCollins Publishers, Inc., 1993), p. 32.

13. "The Malapropian 'R' Word," *Industry Forum* prepared by the American Management Association (September 1993): 1.

14. Otis Port, John Carey, Kevin Kelly, and Stephanie Anderson, "Quality: Small and Midsize Companies Seize the Challenge—Not a Moment Too Soon," *Business Week* (November 13, 1992): 72.

15. "The Malapropian 'R' Word," *Industry Forum* prepared by the American Management Association (September 1993): 1.

16. Zachary Schiller, "A Nervous P&G Picks Up the Cost-Cutting Ax," *Business Week* (April 19, 1993): 28.

17. Frederick Herzberg, "One More Time: How Do You Motivate Employees?" *Harvard Business Review* 65 (Sept–Oct 1987): 109–120.

18. Stephen L. Perlman, "Employees Redesign Their Jobs," *Personnel Journal* 69 (November 1990): 37–40.

19. Seth Lubove, "Dow's Downer," *Forbes* 151 (June 21, 1993): 58–59, 64.

9 Human Resource Management and the Staffing Function

LEARNING OBJECTIVES

After completing this chapter, students should be able to

✘ Identify and briefly describe the basic human resource functions.

✘ Describe the predominant laws and executive orders that affect equal employment opportunity.

✘ Explain the staffing process, job analysis, human resource planning, and recruitment.

✘ Explain each phase of the selection process.

✘ Describe the factors involved in internal staffing administration.

✘ State some special considerations involved in selecting managerial personnel.

PepsiCo: Closing In on Number One Coca-Cola

PepsiCo has long been one of *Fortune's* "Most Admired Corporations," often ranking first among beverage companies. Chief executive D. Wayne Calloway is one reason that PepsiCo continues to be ranked among the best. According to Calloway, the reason for Pepsi's success is "We have a great team spirit. Our people want to be the marines. We hire eagles and teach them to fly in formation." Throughout the late 1980s, PepsiCo earned large profits in all its main businesses, soft drinks (Pepsi-Cola, Slice, Seven-Up, Mountain Dew), snack foods (Frito-Lay), and restaurants (Pizza Hut, Kentucky Fried Chicken, Taco Bell). PepsiCo is now one-third beverages, one-third snacks, and one-third restaurants. They are number one in the chicken category, number one in the Mexican category, and number one in the pizza category. If they could buy number one McDonald's, they would be in the hamburger business. Being number one is critically important to Calloway, and he will accept nothing less than the top spot in an area.

Calloway claims to spend 40 percent of his time on people issues. "People, people, people" are his "three Ps" of good management. PepsiCo continually attracts and develops good people. But PepsiCo is not a "touchy-feely" company, employees are driven to perform. However, being driven has its rewards, especially with the implementation of SharePower, a plan that cuts 120,000 PepsiCo workers in on the Pepsi profit pie, allowing these individuals to buy stock options valued at ten percent of their previous year's compensation. The environment at PepsiCo will never be warm and cuddly, but it will be profitable for those who produce. Managers usually work 60 hours a week. At annual performance reviews, bosses make subordinates justify themselves on the basis of meeting sales targets, making useful innovations, and other objective measures. According to the Frito-Lay chief, "Nothing is ever good enough." When goals are met one year, they are upped for the next. Failure to meet goals brings quick help, but if failure continues, it brings discharge. Pepsi-Cola, the company's $6 billion flagship division, is moving to eliminate an entire layer of management. If it is not profitable, then it goes. Employees justify their affiliation with PepsiCo by reaping benefits for themselves and the company.

There is a feedback program that involves confidential performance reports by each manager's subordinates. Personnel managers, especially, get rotated. "We expect our personnel people to be in the business up to their eyeballs—to know sales, profits, and margins," said Calloway. A new personnel manager usually spends time in a line job right away, perhaps driving a delivery truck or selling. Since graduates of top business schools are seldom willing to start out in menial jobs, PepsiCo often recruits from second-tier schools.

Workers see similar pressures and rewards. Calloway said, "It's been part of our whole culture to say 'you are important.'" The goals PepsiCo sets for workers are to build team spirit, increase identification with the company and its work, encourage longevity, and increase productivity.[1]

Human resource management (HRM) is the wide range of organizational activities involved in staffing, training and development, compensation, health and safety, employee and labor relations, and human resource research. The main HRM principles at PepsiCo seem to be: hire good people, train them well, demand that they perform, evaluate them thoughtfully, and reward those who make the grade. A company's human resource management policies and practices must be integrated into a sound overall administrative system.

In Chapter 7, we said that organizations, large or small, have these three characteristics:

1. The are composed of people.
2. They exist to achieve objectives.
3. They require some degree of limitation on member behavior.

Thus, a major focus of the organizing function is the people who work together in pursuit of organizational objectives. In this chapter, we will first define the basic human resource management functions. Then, we will describe the primary legislation affecting equal employment opportunity. We will devote the next and largest part of the chapter to the elements of the staffing process: job analysis, human resource planning, recruitment, and selection; then, internal staffing administration will be discussed. In the concluding sections, we will discuss special considerations involved in selecting managerial personnel and the global perspective of human resource management.

❖ ❖ HUMAN RESOURCE MANAGEMENT FUNCTIONS

As we discussed in Chapter 2, the labor force is constantly changing. In the midst of these changes, every successful organization must attract, select, train, and retain qualified people. Just having adequate numbers of people is not enough; they must also be qualified or the organization will have problems obtaining its objectives. The six basic human resource management functions are illustrated in Figure 9.1. They are staffing, training and development, compensation, health and safety, employee and labor relations, and human resource research.[2]

Staffing

Staffing is the formal process of ensuring that the organization has qualified workers available at all levels to meet its short- and long-term business objectives.[3] The staffing process involves job analysis, human resource planning, recruitment, selection, and internal staffing administration. These topics will be covered in greater detail later in the chapter.

Training and Development

Training and development programs are formal efforts to help employees learn new skills, improve existing skills, or otherwise improve their ability to perform in the organization. Training and development is needed in part because people, jobs, and organizations are always changing. Training can help ease management

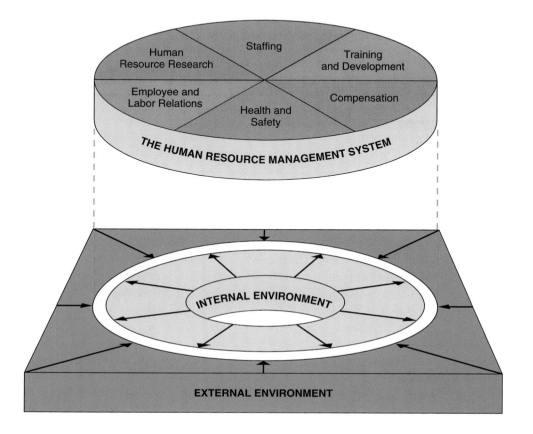

❖ **Figure 9.1**
The human resource management system (Source: Reprinted by permission from R. Wayne Mondy and Robert M. Noe III, *Human Resource Management,* 5th ed. [Boston, MA: Allyn and Bacon, 1993], p. 7.)

Training and develop-
ment (T&D) programs
are formal efforts to
help employees learn
new skills, improve ex-
isting skills, or other-
wise improve their
ability to perform in
the organization. T&D
is needed in part be-
cause people, jobs, and
organizations are al-
ways changing. Amoco
designed this mock
tanker trailer to allow
firefighting and emer-
gency personnel from
any community to gain
actual training in a sim-
ulated accident.
(Source: Photograph
courtesy of Amoco.)

resistance to change, as it did at UPS. Because the company offered advanced
training, the headquarters-driven overhaul of the corporate culture to focus on
customers has met with little resistance from managers and supervisors in the
field. More than 500 managers were sent to Michigan State University's business
school for week-long seminars in which professors coached employees to think
in terms of customer service.[4] Training and development should begin when individuals join the firm and should continue throughout their careers. It often
includes classroom instruction, on-the-job training, and various forms of counseling, such as career planning. New methods to help employees be better at what
they do are constantly being developed, but the initial costs are often staggering.

Performance appraisal systems may be used to identify training and development needs and to measure progress in the area. PepsiCo is well known for
using performance appraisal in this way. **Organizational development (OD),** a
special kind of training and development, is a planned and systematic attempt to
change the organization typically to a more behavioral environment.

A Virtual Reality System of Training

The Electric Power Research Institute has teamed up with MITRE
Corporation to develop a Virtual
Reality (VR) mock-up of a power
plant utilizing stereo projection displays to be used in training plant
operators. Traditional training
rooms for fossil-fuel plants cost up
to $1 million, whereas VR systems
could cost as little as $100,000.

According to Hugh W. Ryan, director for Arthur Anderson Consulting,
VR environments will also be used
to simulate business interactions
such as sales negotiations and general management problems. VR systems could replace some of today's
very expensive seminars and training classes. Boeing Company's project manager, Keith Butler, sees VR
systems as valuable for training
workers in flexible manufacturing.
Butler is developing techniques to

project job instructions onto see-
through goggles worn by assembly
workers or onto the work space in
front of them. It is possible that
with such systems "workers might
assemble wing flaps, then switch to
noise cones on the same day with
little loss of productivity." VR could
really lessen the time and money invested in training and development
in the not-too-distant future.[5]

Compensation

The question of what constitutes a fair day's pay has been a major concern of managers for centuries. Employees must be provided with adequate and equitable rewards for their contributions to the achievement of organizational objectives. **Compensation** is all rewards individuals receive as a result of their employment. As such, it is more than monetary income. The rewards may include one or any combination of the following:

- *Pay*—the money a person receives for performing a job.
- *Benefits*—economic rewards other than pay, such as paid holidays, medical insurance, and retirement programs.
- *Nonfinancial rewards*—noneconomic rewards, such as job satisfaction and a pleasant working environment.

Senior executives often receive stock options—the right to purchase company stock at a set price during a specified period. The set price is usually near the market price of the company's stock at the time the option is granted. Holders of stock options can wait until the stock goes up and then purchase it at the lower, fixed price.

Health and Safety

Health is the condition of being physically and emotionally able to perform vital functions normally or properly. It includes general physical and mental

---

Out-of-this-World Plant Marshals in a Shocking Union/ Management Relationship

The out-of-this-world plant is GM's Saturn plant. The revolutionary labor agreement has created a partnership between Saturn's blue- and white-collar workers. Everyone is given the authority to raise and solve quality problems. In this environment, line workers who encounter defective parts can and often do phone the supplier with recommendations on how to remedy the problem. According to a Saturn team member, Gregory L.

Arthur, a 20-year GM veteran, "You can trust the people you're working with. So if I come up with an idea (that eliminates my job), I won't be out of a job." Anthony Mills, UAW business unit coordinator, views his role as dramatically different at the Saturn plant. He actually has a great deal of input on business and personnel issues. Formerly, when he represented a union member, he did so whether the individual was innocent or guilty. At Saturn, everyone is accountable for his or her actions, and when something is wrong, it is fixed for the benefit of everyone in the company. Milton Fletcher,

human resources advisor, was "initially shocked" when he sat alongside UAW representatives to conduct performance reviews of managers. The 19-year veteran was somewhat surprised when the talk of partnership was more than just lip service. The out-of-this-world Saturn plant appears to really have an out-of-this-world Union/Management relationship. Saturn's Union/Management relationship really works, and has resulted in Saturn becoming the highest-quality American-made brand automobile in the United States, second only to Lexus and Infiniti.[6]

well-being. **Safety** is freedom from danger. Most managers believe employees who enjoy good health and who work in a safe environment are more likely to be efficient. Beyond that, however, many companies believe it is their social responsibility to provide safe and healthy working conditions. Federal legislation, especially the Occupational Safety and Health Act (OSHA), has forced all organizations to be concerned with their employees' safety and health.

Employee and Labor Relations

In 1991, union membership slipped to 16.1 percent, and the unionized share of the private workforce had shrunk to less than 12 percent.[7] According to a study conducted by the National Bureau of Economic Research, union membership in the private sector could drop below five percent by the year 2000, if present trends continue.[8] Even so, a business firm is required by law to recognize unions and to bargain with them in good faith if employees vote to be represented by them. There are many different forms of labor management agreements; one unusual example is at work at the General Motor's Saturn plant.

Human Resource Research

Human resource research has become increasingly important, and the trend is likely to continue. The human resource researcher's laboratory is the entire work environment, and studies may involve every HRM function. For instance, a study of recruitment may suggest the types of workers who are most likely to succeed

---

ETHICAL DILEMMA

Effectively staffing the organization is essential to corporate success. Organizations must seek out the most qualified workers available at all levels, because failure to do so will usually limit overall productivity over the long-term. Michelin has had business problems in the past that were usually associated with poor timing. The company ran up heavy debts and losses as it proceeded to build new factories at the rate of two per year in the late 1970s. A few years later the oil shock deflated the tire market, but fortunately the company bounced back. Michelin has survived because it is continually willing to sacrifice short-term concerns for its long-term objectives of quality and market share. To become a stronger company, Michelin even produces almost all materials, including the steel belting and the synthetic rubber used in its tires. However, its long-term outlook appears not to extend into the personnel area. The most qualified employees are sought out as long as they are not union members. Hoping to avoid unions, Michelin prefers to build plants in the southern United States.[9] Is it appropriate for Michelin to build plants in the southern United States, not because the workers are more qualified or as qualified as elsewhere, but because Michelin does not want any unionized workers?

What would you do?

in a particular firm. Or research on job safety may identify the causes of certain work-related accidents.

The causes of problems such as excessive absenteeism and too many grievances may not be readily apparent. When such problems occur and the reasons are not evident, human resource research can fill the knowledge void. In Sweden, the labor force is highly educated and well trained. But the country's high income tax rates reduce the motivational power of pay, even incentive-type pay. Research at Sweden's Volvo auto factory revealed that the Swedes objected to the dinginess and grime of the typical automobile factory. Close supervision and machine pacing of work on the assembly lines were also sore points. So Volvo built more pleasant and colorful factories where teams of workers are allowed to largely manage themselves. Each team assembles a substantial portion of the car, which is moved from area to area. In the new Volvo plants, morale and productivity are better and absenteeism is lower than in the older factories.[10] Human resource research is clearly an important key to developing the most productive and satisfied workforce possible.

Interrelationships of HRM Functions

The functional areas of HRM are not separate and distinct; they are highly interrelated. Management must recognize that decisions in one area will impact other areas—and they must predict what those impacts are likely to be. For instance, a firm that emphasizes recruiting and training of a sales force while neglecting to provide adequate compensation is wasting time, effort, and money. In addition, if management is truly concerned about employee welfare, it must ensure a safe and healthy work environment. An added benefit may be keeping the firm union-free. An understanding of the interrelationships among the six HRM functional areas is very important.

MANAGEMENT IN PRACTICE

A Skill-Building Exercise: Allen Fender is personnel manager for ML Plastics, a small injection molding company near Wichita, Kansas. ML has been experiencing some worker unrest, and there have been hints of a unionizing attempt. As Allen rounded the corner in the mixing department one day, he heard Judy Morgan reprimanding one of her operators. Several other workers were watching the episode. Allen quickly figured out that the operator had spilled some oil near his machine and had failed to clean it up. The operator was obviously embarrassed and was trying to put oil absorbent on the spill. But Judy continued to press the issue. She said, "When you risk other people's safety around here, you are risking your job."

What should Allen do?

❖ ❖ MANDATING DIVERSITY: LAWS AND EXECUTIVE ORDERS AFFECTING EQUAL EMPLOYMENT OPPORTUNITY

Numerous federal laws and executive orders are concerned with providing equal employment opportunity. In general, the regulations reflect changing public attitudes toward the employment practices of business. As society and the workforce become even more diverse, more regulatory changes will probably be forthcoming. Managers must be aware of ever-changing regulations to properly deal with regulatory mandates. The most significant of these laws and one executive order are briefly described in the following sections.

Civil Rights Acts of 1866 and 1871

The Civil Rights Act of 1866 forbids racial discrimination in making and enforcing contracts, which has been taken to include hiring and promotion agreements. This act applies to private employers, unions, and employment agencies. The Civil Rights Act of 1871 invalidates state and local laws that violate civil rights protected by federal law. There is virtually no effective statute of limitations for either of these acts, so cases can be brought under them long after any alleged offense.[11]

Equal Pay Act of 1963

The Equal Pay Act of 1963 (an amendment to the Fair Labor Standards Act of 1938) prohibits discrimination in pay on the basis of sex for certain employees. A 1972 amendment expanded the act to cover employees in executive, administrative, professional, and outside sales force categories, as well as employees in most state and local governments, hospitals, and schools.

The Equal Pay Act requires equal pay for equal work, but advocates of comparable worth prefer a broader interpretation: equal pay for comparable work. **Comparable worth** is the concept that requires the value for dissimilar jobs to be compared under some form of job evaluation and pay rates to be assigned according to their evaluated worth. The basic premise behind comparable worth is that jobs traditionally held by women are paid less than those traditionally held by men even though both types may make equal contributions to the organization's objectives.[12]

Title VII of the Civil Rights Act of 1964—Amended 1972

One law that has had an extensive influence on human resource management is Title VII of the 1964 Civil Rights Act, as amended by the Equal Employment Opportunity Act of 1972. This legislation prohibits discrimination based on race, color, sex, religion, or national origin. Title VII covers employers in industries affecting interstate commerce that have 15 or more employees for at least 20 calendar weeks in the year in which a charge is filed or the year preceding the filing of a charge. Included in the definition of employers are state and local governments, schools, colleges, unions, and employment agencies. The act created the Equal Employment Opportunity Commission (EEOC), which is responsible for its enforcement.

Age Discrimination in Employment Act of 1967— Amended in 1978 and 1986

As originally enacted, the Age Discrimination in Employment Act (ADEA) prohibited employers from discriminating against individuals who were at least 40 but less than 65 years old. The 1978 amendment changed the upper age limit to 70. In 1986, President Reagan signed into law an amendment to the ADEA making it illegal for employers to discriminate against anyone over the age of 40 because of age. The latest amendment prohibits employers from firing anyone on the basis of age, with no maximum age limit.[13] The act pertains to employers that have 20 or more employees for 20 or more calendar weeks in either the current or the preceding calendar year. It also applies to unions of 25 or more members; employment agencies; and federal, state, and local government units. The EEOC is charged with administering the act.

Pregnancy Discrimination Act of 1978

Passed as an amendment to Title VII of the Civil Rights Act, the Pregnancy Discrimination Act extends the protection of that law to pregnancy, childbirth, and related medical conditions. A woman is protected against such penalties as being fired or refused a job or promotion merely because she is pregnant or has had an abortion. Also, she usually cannot be forced to take a leave of absence solely on the basis of her pregnancy. And after pregnancy-related leave, she must be allowed to return to work under the same rules that govern other employees who have been on disability leave.

The same principle applies in the benefits area, including disability benefits, sick leave, and health insurance. A woman unable to work for pregnancy-related reasons is entitled to disability benefits or sick leave on the same basis as employees unable to work for other medical reasons. Also, any health insurance must cover expenses for pregnancy-related conditions on the same basis as expenses for other medical conditions.

The Americans with Disabilities Act (ADA)

Passed in 1990, the ADA prohibits discrimination against "qualified individuals with disabilities." Persons discriminated against because they have a known association or relationship with a disabled individual also are protected. The ADA defines an "individual with a disability" as a person who: has a physical or mental impairment that substantially limits one or more major life activities, has a record of such an impairment, or is regarded as having such an impairment. The ADA prohibits discrimination in all employment practices, including job application procedures; hiring; firing; advancement; compensation; training; and other terms, conditions, and privileges of employment. It applies to recruitment, advertising, tenure, layoff, leave, fringe benefits, and all other employment-related activities.

The employment provisions apply to private employers, state and local governments, employment agencies, labor unions, and employers with 15 or more employees.[14] The full impact of this new law is yet to be determined, but some believe that obesity may emerge as a condition that is protected under the act.[15] In fact, a lower court ruling in December of 1993 stated that *uncontrollable obesity* is protected under ADA.

Civil Rights Act (CRA) of 1991

The CRA of 1991 amended the Civil Rights Act of 1964 and had the following purposes:

1. To provide appropriate remedies for intentional discrimination and unlawful harassment in the workplace.
2. To codify the concepts of "business necessity" and "job related" pronounced by the Supreme Court in *Griggs* v. *Duke Power Co.,* and the other Supreme Court decisions prior to *Wards Cove Packing Co.* v. *Atonio.*
3. To confirm statutory authority and provide statutory guidelines for the adjudication of disparate impacts under Title VII of the Civil Rights Act of 1964.
4. To respond to recent decisions of the Supreme Court by expanding the scope of relevant civil rights statutes in order to provide adequate protection to victims of discrimination.

Under this Act, a complaining party may recover punitive damages if the complaining party demonstrates that the company engaged in a discriminatory practice with malice or with reckless indifference to the law. However, the following limits were placed on the amount of the award:

1. Between 15 and 100 employees—$50,000
2. Between 101 and 200 employees—$100,000
3. Between 201 and 500 employees—$200,000
4. Greater than 500 employees—$300,000

In each case, employees must be with the firm for 20 or more calendar weeks in the current or preceding calendar year.

With regard to burden of proof in disparate impact cases, an unlawful employment practice passed on disparate impact is established under this title only if a complaining party demonstrates that a respondent uses a particular employment practice that causes a disparate impact on the basis of race, color, religion, sex, or national origin and the company fails to demonstrate that the challenged practice is job related for the position in question and consistent with business necessity. The Act also extends the coverage of the Civil Rights Act of 1964 to extraterritorial employment. However, the Act does not apply to United States companies operating in another country if it would violate the law of the foreign country. Further, the Act reverses the following Supreme Court decisions: *Patterson* v. *McLean Credit Union, Martin* v. *Wilks,* and *Wards Cove Packing Co.* v. *Atonio.*

The Act mandates the establishment of the Equal Employment Opportunity Commission's Technical Assistance Training Institute (TATI) and enhances Title VII's provisions regarding education and outreach. The TATI provides technical assistance and training regarding the laws and regulations enforced by the Commission. The Commission is charged with carrying out educational and outreach activities (including dissemination of information in languages other than English) targeted to individuals who historically have been victims of discrimination and have not been equitably served by the Commission. The Act also extends the nondiscrimination principles to Congress and other government agencies such as the General Accounting Office and the Government Printing Office.

Also included in the CRA of 1991 is the Glass Ceiling Act. The purpose of this Act is to establish a Glass Ceiling Commission to study: the manner in which businesses fill management and decision-making positions, the developmental and skill-enhancing practices used to foster the necessary qualifications for advancement into such positions, and the compensation programs and reward structures currently utilized in the workplace. It also established an annual award for excellence in promoting a more diverse skilled workforce at the management and decision-making levels in business.

Glass Ceiling

A phrase that has been used in recent years is the **glass ceiling**, meaning the invisible barrier in organizations that prevents many women from achieving top-level management positions. Companies have discovered that the courts are being forceful in eliminating such barriers. In one instance, a highly rated female supervisor was denied a promotion because her boss said it would be easier for employees to work with a man who was their "chum." The employer reasoned that when it came to working long hours, the staff would work better with the male worker who was promoted. The courts disagreed and called this action unlawful discrimination.[16]

The situation may have changed in recent years. As was mentioned in

Chapter 2, half of today's entry-level managers are women; this is up from 15 percent 15 years ago.[17] Because of the critical mass of talent, many believe that the 1990s will be the decade that women break through to upper-level management. In fact, in a recent survey of 400 top female executives it was found that the percentage of women who hold the title of executive vice president more than doubled over the past decade, from 4 percent to 8.7 percent.[18]

Executive Order 11246, as Amended by Executive Order 11375

Executive Orders are directives issued by the President that have the force and effect of laws enacted by Congress. In 1965, President Lyndon B. Johnson signed Executive Order 11246. This order made it the policy of the government of the United States to provide equal opportunity in federal employment for all qualified persons. It prohibits discrimination in employment because of race, creed, color, or national origin. It also requires promoting the full realization of equal employment opportunity through a positive, continuing program in each executive department and agency. The policy of equal opportunity applies to every aspect of federal employment policy and practice.

A major provision of Executive Order 11246 is that every executive department and agency that administers a program involving federal financial assistance will require adherence to a policy of nondiscrimination in employment as a condition for the approval of grants, contracts, loans, insurance, and guarantees. During the performance of a contract, contractors agree not to discriminate in employment because of race, creed, color, or national origin. **Affirmative action,** which is a major part of Executive Order 11246, is performance required to ensure that applicants are employed, and that employees are treated appropriately during employment, without regard to race, creed, color, or national origin. The human resource practices covered relate to employment, upgrading, demotion, transfer, recruitment and recruitment advertising, layoffs and firings, rates of pay and other forms of compensation, and selection for training, including apprenticeships. In 1968, Executive Order 11246 was amended by Executive Order 11375, which changed the word *creed* to *religion* and added sexual discrimination to the other prohibited items.

❖ ❖ THE STAFFING PROCESS

Staffing, defined earlier in the chapter, is a major component of human resource management. Staffing is concerned not only with hiring people but also with keeping them. There are several components of the staffing process, each closely linked to the others. Figure 9.2 illustrates these basic components.

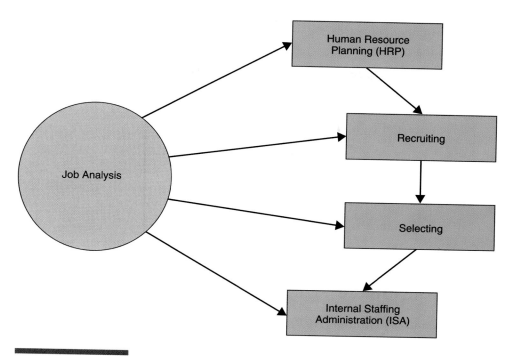

❖ ❖ JOB ANALYSIS

Job analysis is the systematic process of determining the skills and knowledge required for performing jobs in the organization. Facts about the job are gathered, recorded, and analyzed. Areas of interest here include job duties, working conditions, and relationships to other jobs. Referring again to Figure 9.2, notice that job analysis affects all of the components of staffing. It is also vital to the other human resource management functions.

Some of the techniques used in conducting job analyses are:

• Observing the work.
• Interviewing workers and supervisors.
• Having workers and their supervisors complete questionnaires.
• Having workers and their supervisors keep job diaries.
• Having job information evaluated by experts.

Information obtained through job analyses is used in developing job descriptions. The **job description** is a document that describes the tasks and responsibilities of a job and its relationships to other jobs. Job descriptions should be both relevant and accurate. They should clearly answer the questions: What is to be done? When? Where? And how? Among the items often included in a job description are the following:

• Major duties.
• Percentage of time devoted to each duty.

- Performance standards.
- Working conditions.
- Possible hazards.
- Number of persons working on each job.
- Reporting relationships.
- Machines and equipment used.

Another item often included in the job description is the **job specification**—a statement of the minimum acceptable qualifications a person should possess to perform a particular job. Job specifications may include standards for education, experience, physical abilities, and sometimes, personality.

❖ ❖ HUMAN RESOURCE PLANNING

Human resource planning (HRP) is the development of strategies and tactics to ensure that the required number of employees with the required skills are on the job when they are needed. There is a growing mismatch between emerging jobs and qualified people available to fill them. There are two main aspects to human resource planning: requirements and availability. Forecasting human resource requirements involves determining the number of employees needed at each location and the qualifications they must have. Availability refers to both internal sources (current employees) and external sources (the labor market). If a mismatch between requirements and availability is projected, action should be taken right away. Any surplus may be eliminated through restricted hiring, reduced hours, early retirement, or layoffs. Shortages can be prevented through any combination of training and transferring present employees and hiring new ones.

Human resource planning should have the following objectives, among others:

- To avoid or correct human resource management problems before they become serious.
- To forecast recruitment needs, in terms of both the numbers of employees required and the skills they should have.
- To identify and evaluate sources of new employees and to focus recruitment efforts on the best sources.
- To identify replacements, from inside or outside the organization, for key managers and workers.
- To integrate human resource plans with financial plans and forecasts.

❖ ❖ RECRUITMENT

Recruitment is the process of attracting individuals—in sufficient numbers and with appropriate qualifications—and encouraging them to apply for jobs with the organization. In most large organizations, this process begins with an employment requisition. An **employment requisition** is a form issued to activate the recruitment process, typically including such information as the job title, starting date, and pay scale and a brief summary of principal duties. Recruitment can range from locating qualified individuals within the firm to a sophisticated and extensive search for a new president.

The usual means of internal recruiting is through the use of a job bidding and posting system. The purpose of job posting is to communicate the fact that job openings exist. Job bidding permits individuals in the organization who believe they possess the required qualifications to apply (bid) for the job. At PepsiCo, for example, an attempt is made to fill every job above the entry level from within. So job posting and bidding is an integral part of PepsiCo's recruitment program. Internal recruitment, or promotion from within, is an important source of workers for positions above the entry level. Here are several potential advantages of promotion from within:

1. It may improve morale.
2. It may improve the quality of selection, since the strengths and weaknesses of internal applicants are usually better known than those of external ones.
3. It may motivate employees to prepare for more responsible positions.
4. It may allow the attraction of better external applicants, since it ensures better promotion prospects.
5. It may assure that existing employees are more fully utilized.

A firm policy of promotion from within can also have its disadvantages. Here are two that are frequently mentioned:

1. An adequate supply of qualified applicants may not be available inside the organization.
2. Internal sources may lead to the inbreeding of ideas. (That is, current employees may lack new ideas on how to do a job more effectively.)

Some well-known companies that practice promotion from within are Delta Airlines, Lincoln Electric, and Hewlett-Packard.

Even if a company is committed to promotion from within, external recruitment is required just to maintain a stable workforce. It is particularly necessary when organizations change and grow. Common sources of new employees include competitors, other business firms and government agencies, high schools, vocational schools, community colleges, other colleges and universities, and pools of applicants at state employment offices. Recruitment methods include ads in newspapers and other media, employment agencies, recruiters, and employee referrals. The recruiter must first determine where the right kind of applicants are likely to be found and then select the best method to get them to apply.

❖ ❖ THE SELECTION PROCESS

Of course, recruitment at any company is designed to attract the individuals who are most capable of meeting the requirements of the job. **Selection** is the process of choosing from a group of applicants the individual best suited for a particular position. Companies with guaranteed employment and promotion from within must pay special attention to selecting good employees. The selection process is shown in Figure 9.3. Its elements are discussed in the sections that follow.

Preliminary Interview

The **preliminary interview** is used to eliminate any obviously unqualified job applicant. This type of interview may be conducted before or after an application form is completed. Reasons for elimination may include excessive salary requirements, inadequate training or education, or lack of job-related experience.

Evaluation of Application Blank

The next step in the selection process is to evaluate each applicant on the basis of the completed application. The specific type of information requested in an application blank may vary from firm to firm and by positions within the organization. Separate sections of an application typically relate to education, work experience, and other job-related information.

An application blank must supply the firm's information needs while meeting legal requirements. Only questions that have job relevance should be included. Questions related to sex, national origin, religion, color, and race should not be asked. Questions regarding criminal convictions should be considered only if they are job-related. For jobs requiring licenses, such as pilot positions, the application blank may ask about the license.

Testing

Traditionally, testing was an integral component of the selection process. Tests have been used to screen applicants in terms of skills, abilities, aptitudes, interests, personality, and attitudes. The Civil Rights Act of 1964 and various federal

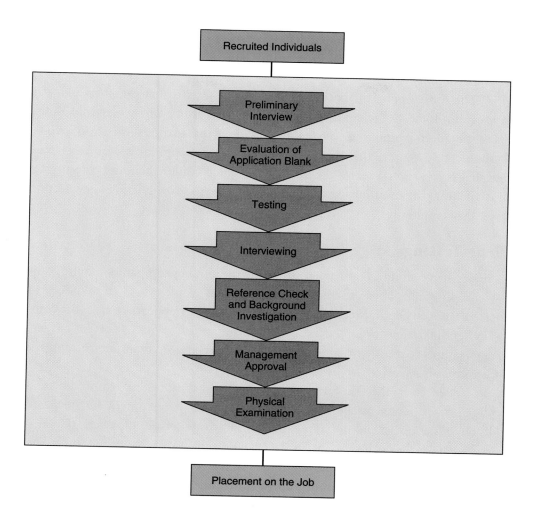

❖ **Figure 9.3**
The selection process

court rulings have discouraged the use of selection tests, however. For instance, in the 1973 *Griggs* v. *Duke Power Company* decision, the U.S. Supreme Court ruled that preemployment requirements, including tests, must be job-related. It has proved to be very difficult to design tests consisting totally of job-related items.

Certain conditions should be met if tests are to be used for employee selection. First, the tests should be reliable; that is, they should provide consistent results. If a person takes the same test a number of times, the scores should be similar. Second, tests should be valid; they should measure what they are designed to measure. If a test is designed to predict job performance, prospective employees who score well on the test should prove to be good performers. Third, tests should be objective. When different scorers interpreting the results of the same test arrive at similar interpretations, the test is said to be objective. Finally, tests should be standardized. This requires them to be administered under standard conditions to a large group of persons who are representative of the individuals for whom the tests are intended. The purpose of standardization is to obtain norms, so specific test scores will be meaningful when compared to other scores in the group.

The most important criterion for selection tests is that they be valid. If a test cannot indicate the ability to perform the job, it must not be used. Validity has always been a proper concern of organizations that use tests. If testing is done, it should help achieve the most efficient matching of applicants with jobs. Testing that is job-related serves the objective of equal employment opportunity. So it is vital that organizations have a thoughtful process for validating any selection tests they employ.

Drug Testing

A major survey found that 23 percent of the responding companies require some type of substance abuse testing as a condition of employment. In addition, 11 percent are considering requiring testing. Drug testing appears to be most common in utility, transportation, and communication firms, with 73 percent of these organizations requiring or considering tests. Overall, more than one-third of the organizations surveyed are in this category.[19]

In two cases, the U.S. Supreme Court upheld drug testing required by federal agencies. These cases stemmed from Fourth Amendment challenges.[20] Although these cases did not apply directly to private sector employers, the decisions are nevertheless important. First, it can be anticipated that drug testing conducted by private sector employers under similar circumstances will be upheld. If drug testing can pass rigorous Fourth Amendment scrutiny, it should also be defensible under normal invasion-of-privacy claims. In addition, federal rules, regulations, and programs tend to become models for private sector behavior.[21]

Interviewing

The interview is the most widely used method of assessing the qualifications of job applicants, and many interviewers consider it to be highly valid. The subjective judgments made during employment interviews, however, may reduce their reliability. In addition, giving too much weight to interview results certainly risks discrimination against persons who are unlike the interviewers. However, interviews can accomplish the following purposes:

1. They allow interviewers to get information not included on the application forms and to clarify any questionable information.
2. They allow applicants to obtain additional information about the prospective employer and job.

The interview is the most widely used method of assessing job applicants. But giving too much weight to subjective interview results risks discrimination against persons who are unlike the interviewer. (Source: © Frank Sitemann 1990.)

3. They allow interviewers to transmit a favorable impression of the organization to applicants.

4. They allow applicants to "sell" themselves to the interviewer.

Interviews are often classified according to how structured they are. Probing, open-ended questions are asked in what are called *nondirective interviews*. Usually, the interviewers who use the nondirective technique are highly trained because it requires a subjective appraisal of the job candidate. The *patterned interview*, on the other hand, consists of standardized questions that are asked of all applicants for certain jobs. Standardization permits easy comparison of candidates. It also helps in achieving and proving validity. Of course, no interview can be completely nondirective, and it is hard to conceive of one that is totally patterned.

Interviews also differ according to how many interviewers and applicants are involved. Normally, job applicants meet with interviewers one-on-one, but in the *group interview*, several applicants are questioned together by one or more interviewers. In a *board interview*, one candidate is interviewed by several representatives of the firm.

Most interviewers try to place applicants at ease. The opposite is true in the *stress interview*. Here, the applicant is intentionally placed on the defensive by being criticized or ridiculed by the interviewer. The purpose is to observe the interviewee's reaction to stress and tension. This type of interview may be used in hiring for intelligence-type positions (for example, with the Central Intelligence Agency or the Federal Bureau of Investigation) or, less commonly, for certain sales or management jobs.

Over the years, many have questioned whether interview results predict success on the job. Interviews can certainly be instruments of unlawful discrimination. For these reasons, among others, they have received close scrutiny by the

EEOC in recent years. Such attention has led to an increase in the use of patterned interviews. It is easier to control the content of patterned interviews than of nondirective ones to prevent bias. Patterned interviews are also easier to defend when they are criticized, since their content can be objectively determined. Of course, this does not necessarily mean patterned interviews are better in predicting job success; they are just safer.

Reference Check and Background Investigation

Once applicants successfully clear the interview hurdle, reference checks and background investigations are often conducted. The reference check has a major weakness as a screening device: Job applicants normally provide their own references, often selected because they are likely to make favorable comments about the applicant. A provision of the Federal Privacy Act of 1974 further increases the likelihood of bias in comments by references. That act gives employees of the federal government the right to see those comments, although the right may be waived.

Background investigations may be similarly unreliable, unless done carefully and at great expense. For example, a prime source of background information is the applicant's previous employers. But the only information many organizations are willing to provide about former employees is dates of employment and salary ranges. Some require the former employees' written authorization to do even this. Further, if comments are provided, they may represent a "whitewash job," because negative remarks are often avoided, even for employees who were fired.[22]

Some companies dispense with reference checks because they are concerned that the practice might be discriminatory or be perceived as an invasion of privacy. A study conducted by the National Consumers League found that about 80 percent of the job-seeker respondents stated that the firms they wanted to join intruded into their private lives by asking inappropriate questions.[23]

Sometimes, the expense of doing a thorough background investigation is justified. It has been found that between seven and ten percent of job applicants are not what they present themselves to be.[24] One area of particular concern is credentials fraud, which has increased in recent years. Professors, stockbrokers, and even doctors have claimed credentials they did not have in attempting to get a new position.

The polygraph, or lie detector, test has often been used in efforts to verify background information. However, the validity of such tests is questionable. In 1988, the Employee Polygraph Protection Act was passed. This act makes it unlawful for any employer engaged in or affecting interstate commerce to test job applicants using the polygraph.

Negligent Hiring and Retention

An employer can be held responsible for an employee's unlawful acts if it does not reasonably investigate the employee's background, and then assigns the person to a position where he or she can inflict harm. A firm can't go overboard with the investigation, however, since invasion of privacy is a possibility. Negligent retention involves keeping dangerous workers on the payroll.

Employers are being held responsible for actions outside the scope of the employee's duties. For example, if an employer hired a manager of an apartment complex without investigating the person's background and the individual later assaulted a tenant, the employer could be held responsible for the action if it were discovered that the manager had a history of assault. Employers are required by law to provide employees a safe place to work. This duty has been extended to providing safe employees because the courts have reasoned that a dangerous worker is comparable to a defective machine.

The primary consideration in negligent hiring is whether the risk of harm from a dangerous employee is reasonably foreseeable. The nature of the job also has a critical bearing on the employer's obligation. If the job gives employees access to homes or property, as in the case of security guards or exterminators, the hiring firm may be found to have an obligation to make a reasonable investigation into the person's background. Industries that have a greater responsibility for safe hiring include landlord-tenant relationships, common carriers, hospitals and other patient-care facilities, and taxi services.[25]

A case in point is a Fort Worth cab company. One of its drivers picked up a young mother and her daughters at a bus station and took them to a deserted area, where he raped and robbed the mother. The young woman sued the cab company and won a judgment of $4,500,000 for negligent hiring.[26] It was determined that a reasonable background investigation would have made it quite clear that the cab driver should not have been hired. He had previously been convicted of robbery and forgery and, before that, had been arrested and charged with using a hammer to assault a woman. To avoid cases of this sort, employers should consider how employees are exposed to customers. They should also make reasonable background investigations and keep written records of them.

Management Approval

In large organizations, the human resource department performs many of the selection functions. However, the final hiring decision is usually reserved for the person who will be the immediate superior of the new employee. This person normally reviews all the available information about the applicant and conducts

The EEOC has issued interpretive guidelines which state that employees have an affirmative duty to maintain a workplace free from sexual harassment. (Source: © Mugshots 1994/The Stock Market)

a final interview. Sometimes, the decision is made on the spot and communicated to the applicant. At other times, the superior consults with the human resource department or with other managers before deciding.

Physical Examination

Typically, job offers are contingent on the applicant's passing a physical examination. Physicals screen out individuals who have contagious diseases. They may also help spot physical deficiencies that can limit the person's ability to do the work. An often ignored purpose of a physical examination is to develop a record of the employee's condition at the time of employment. This can protect the company and its insurer against claims for previously existing medical conditions.

❖ ❖ SEXUAL HARASSMENT

In one survey, 42 percent of the women and 15 percent of the men reported that they had been sexually harassed on the job.[27] Perhaps because of the publicity caused by the Navy's Tailhook incident and the testimony of Anita Hill and Clarence Thomas, one of the most fervently pursued civil rights issues today relates to sexual harassment.[28] In fact, from 1987 to 1992 the number of sexual harassment complaints filed with the Equal Employment Opportunity Commission has nearly doubled to 10,532.[29] Research has shown that 90 percent of *Fortune* 500 companies have dealt with sexual harassment complaints and a third have been sued at least once. As we previously mentioned, Title VII of the Civil Rights Act generally prohibits discrimination on the basis of gender in employment. The EEOC has also issued interpretative guidelines that state that employers have an affirmative duty to maintain a workplace free from sexual harassment. The Office of Federal Contract Compliance Programs has similar guidelines. Managers in both for-profit and not-for-profit organizations should be particularly alert to the issue of sexual harassment, as the EEOC believes that sexual harassment continues to be a widespread problem. Table 9.1 contains the EEOC's definition of sexual harassment.

According to the guidelines, employers are totally liable for the acts of their supervisors, regardless of whether the employer is aware of the sexual harassment act. Where co-workers are concerned, the employer is responsible for such acts if the employer knew, or should have known, about them. The employer is not responsible if it can show that it took immediate and appropriate corrective action as soon as it learned of the problem.

Another important aspect of these guidelines is that employers may be liable for acts committed by nonemployees in the workplace if the employer knew, or should have known, of the conduct and failed to take appropriate action. Firms are responsible for developing programs to prevent sexual harassment in the workplace. They must also investigate all formal and informal complaints alleging sexual harassment. After investigating, a firm must take immediate and appropriate action to correct the situation. Failure to do so constitutes a violation of Title VII, as interpreted by the EEOC.

TABLE 9.1 EEOC Definition of Sexual Harassment

Unwelcome sexual advances, requests for sexual favors, and other verbal or physical conduct of a sexual nature that occur under any of the following situations:

1. When submission to such conduct is made either explicitly or implicitly a term or condition of an individual's employment.
2. When submission to or rejection of such conduct by an individual is used as the basis for employment decisions affecting such individual.
3. When such conduct has the purpose or effect of unreasonably interfering with an individual's work performance or creating an intimidating, hostile, or offensive working environment.

There have been numerous sexual harassment court cases. In *Miller v. Bank of America,* a U.S. Circuit Court of Appeals held an employer liable for the sexually harassing acts of its supervisors, even though the company had a policy prohibiting such conduct and even though the victim did not formally notify the employer of the problem. Another U.S. Circuit Court of Appeals ruled that sexual harassment, in and of itself, is a violation of Title VII. The court ruled that the law does not require the victim to prove that she resisted harassment and was penalized for that resistance. The first sexual harassment case to reach the U.S. Supreme Court was the case of *Meritor Savings Bank* v. *Vinson.* The Vinson decision was the first time the Supreme Court recognized that Title VII could be used for offensive environment claims.[30] However, only recently has a hostile environment been defined as a workplace atmosphere or behavior that a reasonable woman would find offensive.[31]

❖ ❖ INTERNAL STAFFING ADMINISTRATION

Staffing encompasses much more than planning, recruitment, and selection. It is also concerned with employees after they are hired. Internal staffing administration involves providing advice and assistance in the following areas:

- Employee orientation.
- Employee assistance programs.
- Performance appraisal.
- Employee status changes, such as promotions, transfers, demotions, resignations, discharges, outplacements, layoffs, and retirements.

Employee Orientation

New workers bring with them fears and anxieties about the job. They worry about their ability to handle the work or whether they will be accepted by their co-workers. They are also anxious to learn as much as possible about their employer. **Employee orientation** is the formal process of helping new employees adjust to the organization, job, and work group. It has three main purposes:

1. To provide specific information.
2. To ease the adjustment process.
3. To enhance new employees' impressions of the organization.

The specific information an employee needs first usually relates to the job. How is the job to be done? What results are expected? How is the job related to others? It is important that the new hire become productive as rapidly as possible.

And although being thrown into a job to sink or swim may build character, it probably does not build productivity. Therefore, job-related information should be provided early and in as specific terms as possible. In addition, reporting relationships need to be clear. Orientation also involves a great deal of information only indirectly related to the job. Where is the infirmary? How do benefit programs work? What are the rules and regulations of employment? Many such questions are often answered in an employee handbook.

The second concern in orientation is adjustment. The new hire's relationship to the formal organization can be easily and quickly spelled out. But relationships with the informal organization must be worked out over time. The first days on a new job are thus often lonely and anxious. To make matters worse, new employees are not always greeted with open arms. There may be a certain amount of hazing and kidding by "old hands." Such problems can hurt a new employee's productivity or even cause the person to quit. To reduce the anxiety new employees may have, attempts should be made to help them build informal relationships. A sympathetic and knowledgeable superior can speed this process. Perhaps a peer will accept responsibility for showing the new person the ropes. But above all, the need to integrate new employees into the social structure of the organization should be taken seriously.

The final purpose of orientation is to enhance the impression the new employee has of the organization and its work. The flow of information to job applicants is somewhat controlled during the hiring process. But as an insider, the employee is able to see the organization's bad points. It is important to continue the selling job that started with recruitment.

Effective orientation is particularly important for employees with disabilities. There is no reason to think these employees are less adaptable than others, but disabilities often make the adaptation process somewhat different. For example, a person with a hearing loss may not be able to understand all that is said in a group presentation. For this person especially, thorough written orientation material or individual briefings may be appropriate. In addition, other employees may not know how to act around a disabled person. Managers can lead the way here. No one should act as if the disability does not exist. Also, it is important to remember that most workers with disabilities want to be as independent as possible. Such a desire should be respected. A manager may have to stop other employees form "helping" the person. A good way to handle questions about whether to do this or that for a person with disabilities is just to ask the person. Insofar as possible, disabled people should be treated like everyone else. Employee assistance programs are an important way of dealing with special needs of disabled employees.

Employee Assistance Programs

An **employee assistance program** is a coordinated effort by an organization to help employees deal with special problems and needs. The kinds of problems specifically covered by the program may include stress and burnout, alcohol and drug abuse, and depression. AIDS (acquired immune deficiency syndrome) is an increasingly serious problem for employers, and some assistance programs are being expanded to deal with this issue. Among the needs employee assistance programs often address are those for child care and for transportation to and from work.

Most programs focus on problems related to substance abuse, emotional problems, and personal situations that produce emotional stress. Such problems are a proper concern of employers because they may affect productivity as well as employee well-being. A particular program may provide for in-house professional counselors or for the referral of employees to an appropriate outside agency or professional. Typically, most or all of the costs are borne by the employer, up to a predetermined amount. The trend is toward providing the same consideration for people with emotional problems as for those with physical illnesses.

Employee assistance programs should actively promote health improvement and disease prevention. Treatment only after a problem affects productivity is the common practice. But there is evidence that preventing alcohol and drug abuse, at least, may be more cost-effective than treatment.

Performance Appraisal

Performance appraisal is the formal and systematic measurement and evaluation of job performance. It involves observing workers' behavior and measuring that behavior in accordance with certain standards. Performance appraisal is central to the staffing function. It provides feedback needed to evaluate the effectiveness of recruitment and selection. It also identifies individuals who are trainable and those who already have the skills to meet current and future job requirements.

However, the main contribution of the performance appraisal process may be in helping to create work environments in which managers and subordinates set objectives, monitor results, and formally evaluate success against predetermined standards. A good performance appraisal process ensures improved communication throughout the organization; however, it is vital that managers realize employee evaluation is a continuous process rather than an event that happens once a year.

MANAGEMENT IN PRACTICE

A Skill-Building Exercise: "There, at last it's finished," thought Tom Baker, as he laid aside the last of 12 performance appraisal forms. It had been a busy week for Tom, who supervised a road maintenance crew for the Georgia Department of Highways.

The governor, in passing through Tom's district a few days earlier, had complained to the area superintendent that repairs were needed on several of the highways. Because of this, the superintendent assigned Tom's crew an unusually heavy workload. In addition, Tom received a call from the personnel office that week telling him that the performance appraisals were late. Tom explained his predicament, but the personnel specialist insisted that the forms be completed right away.

Looking over the appraisals again, Tom thought about several of the workers. The performance appraisal form had places for marking quantity of work, quality of work, and co-operativeness. For each characteristic, the worker could be graded outstanding, good, average, below average, or unsatisfactory. Since Tom's crew had completed all of the extra work assigned for that week, he marked every worker outstanding in quantity of work. He

marked Joe Blum average in cooperativeness because Joe had questioned one of his decisions that week. Tom had decided to patch a pothole in one of the roads, and Joe thought the small section of road surface ought to be broken out and replaced. Tom didn't include this in the remarks section of the form, though. As a matter of fact, he wrote no remarks on any of the forms.

Tom felt a twinge of guilt as he thought about Roger Short. He knew that Roger had been sloughing off and the other workers had been carrying him for quite some time. He also knew that Roger would be upset if he found that he had been marked lower than the other workers. So he marked Roger the same to avoid a confrontation. "Anyway," Tom thought, "these things are a pain in the neck, and I really shouldn't have to bother with them."

As Tom folded up the performance appraisals and put them in the envelope for mailing, he smiled. He was glad he would not have to think about performance appraisals for another six months.

What weaknesses do you see in Tom's performance appraisals?

Employee Status Changes

Few employees remain in the same job, with the same company, throughout a career. According to Robert J. Samuelson, stable jobs have vanished, and even the status quo among men is changing. The status quo for the typical male employee between the ages of 45 and 54 had been to remain with his present employer for 12 years, with about a third of the group having been with the same employer for 20 years or more. As more women aggressively pursue careers, their job tenure is actually increasing, but what is gone for both these groups is a sense of confidence and faith that their careers are permanent. Although the anxiety may exaggerate the reality to those involved, it is keenly felt.[32] Most people experience one or more of the following types of status changes:

- *Promotion*—advancement to a more responsible job in the organization.
- *Lateral move*—transfer to another job at the same level of responsibility.
- *Demotion*—assignment within the organization to a job with less responsibility.
- *Resignation*—voluntary termination of employment initiated by the employee.
- *Discharge*—involuntary termination of employment initiated by the employer.
- *Outplacement*—placement of a person in another company with the active assistance of the former employer.
- *Layoff*—involuntary termination of employment that is viewed as temporary.
- *Retirement*—withdrawal from active employment with a certain organization, usually with some form of pension.
- *Reduction in force*—systematic process of reducing the size of the workforce, initiated by the employer.

To ensure the highest level of productivity, better-managed firms strive to achieve a proper match between individuals and jobs. Careless or random selection of employees can seriously impair the ultimate ability of the company to survive.

❖ ❖ SPECIAL CONSIDERATIONS IN SELECTING MANAGERIAL PERSONNEL

The effect on the organization of a poor or excellent choice of a manager is typically greater than that of a worker. Also, more subjective judgment is commonly involved. Here are some of the characteristics managers might be expected to have:

- Good planner.
- Good communicator.
- Good decision maker.
- Good organizer.
- Good motivator.
- Good leader.
- Good conceptualizer.

• Adaptable to change.
• Self-confident.
• Aggressive.
• Empathic.

Of course, no one is outstanding in all these talents. For this reason, among others, it is hard to say just who should be groomed for a management job.

A GLOBAL PERSPECTIVE

Women Managers, an Essential Addition to the Global Labor Pool

In the global job market, human resource managers are facing a growing mismatch between new jobs requiring higher-level skills and the people available to fill them. In addition, many potential and highly skilled managers are overlooked because they are women. In the case of American multinationals, human resource management is becoming an even greater challenge because, according to the Commission on Workforce Quality and Labor Market Efficiency, "unless government and business undertake a vast increase in their investment in human capital, U.S. companies will not be able to hire the types of workers they need to compete in international markets."[33] To compound the problem even more, managers affiliated with some companies—for example, General Motors—are learning the techniques for improving the quality of production, but are not learning the management

attitudes that make operations such as GM's joint venture with Toyota (NUMMI) successful.[34]

In addition, women managers are often overlooked for global assignments; this further reduces the global labor pool and may result in less effective global managers. As with any other assignment, the best qualified person should get the job. The three aspects that have limited global assignments for women include the perceptions that: women do not want to be international managers, companies refuse to send women abroad, and foreigners are prejudiced against women managers. According to a survey conducted by McGill University professor, Nancy J. Adler, women do want overseas assignments as much as their male counterparts, but four times as many firms are reluctant to select women for international assignments. Finally, even though few overseas management assignments are currently given to women, 97 percent of the women who have had overseas assign-

ments were successful. Even in Japan, a professional woman is viewed as a professional manager.[35]

Coping with human resource problems in the global environment is very complex. American human resource managers must find a way to educate, or reeducate, much of the American labor force to give the United States a competitive workforce; they must carefully review the human resource situation in host countries; and they must plan to cope with the limitations of the labor situation and take advantage of the strengths of the host countries' labor forces. Human resource professionals cannot afford to overlook qualified women for overseas assignments. Whether it will take more progressive attitudes toward managing the country's labor force, a more progressive attitude about global women managers, or some other approach, effective human resource management is essential for success in the global environment.

The *assessment center* provides for the systematic evaluation of the potential of individuals for future management positions. In the typical assessment center, a series of activities is designed to test the potential manager's skills, abilities, attitudes, and judgment. The activities are similar to those the manager might be expected to do in an actual job. They include in-basket exercises, management games, leaderless group discussions, mock interviews, and tests. Assessors observe the participants and study written results of the exercises.

A typical business game might involve computer simulation of several firms in an industry. Teams of participants, in competition with each other, are required

---

✗ Management Tips ✗

Guidelines for Dealing with Human Resource Management and the Staffing Function

1. **Be Selective.** Employing people who are qualified to do the work will make your job easier.

2. **Do not be too gullible.** Realize that not everyone tells the truth in an interview.

3. **Devote time and effort to the selection process.** Good workers make a good unit.

4. **Follow company policies and procedures in hiring.** They are established for your benefit.

5. **Learn the government regulations affecting selection.** Remember, ignorance of the law is no excuse.

6. **Stay on the lookout for good potential employees.** Look both inside and outside the company.

7. **Assume personal responsibility for orienting new workers on the job.** Be systematic so that no important aspects are left out.

8. **Use the personnel department.** It is there to advise and assist you.

9. **Know what to look for in workers.** Hire people who are capable of doing the job.

10. **Strive to achieve a proper match between individuals and jobs.** Careless or random selection of employees can seriously impair the ultimate ability of the company to survive.

to decide how much to expend each period on, for example, advertising, research and development, and maintenance. They also may be asked to establish target production and inventory levels. The computer program is usually designed to provide financial statements reflecting the results of all the decisions, as if the firms were real. Leaderless group discussions may be employed to see how effectively participants take the lead in discussion, influence others, mediate arguments, speak, and summarize or classify issues.

SUMMARY

If organizational objectives are to be accomplished, firms must attract, select, train, and retain qualified people. To meet the firm's human resource needs, six basic functions of human resource management must be accomplished: staffing, training and development, compensation, health and safety, employee and labor relations, and human resource research. The functional areas of HRM are not separate and distinct, but are highly interrelated.

Numerous national laws and executive orders are concerned with providing equal employment opportunity, thus signifying an attitude in the general population that changes should be made in employment practices. The most significant are the Civil Rights Acts of 1866 and 1871, the Equal Pay Act of 1963, Title VII of the 1964 Civil Rights Act and its 1972 amendment, the Age Discrimination in Employment Act of 1967 and its 1978 and 1986 amendments, the Pregnancy Discrimination Act of 1978, the Americans with Disabilities Act of 1990, the Civil Rights Act of 1991 and Executive Order 11246, as amended by Executive Order 11375. The so-called "glass ceiling," which is an invisible barrier in organizations that prevents many women from achieving top-level management positions is a problem that must be addressed by HRM professionals. With negligent hiring, employers can be held responsible for an employee's unlawful acts if it does not conduct a reasonable background investigation and then assigns the person to a position where he or she can inflict harm.

Staffing is an integral part of human resource management. The basic elements of the staffing process are job analysis, human resource planning, recruitment, and selection. Job analysis is the systematic process of determining the skills and knowledge required to perform jobs in the organization. Developing strategies and tactics to ensure that the required numbers of employees with the required skills are on the job when they are needed is human resource planning. The ultimate objective of recruitment is to attract the

KEY TERMS

Human resource
    management (HRM) 268
Staffing 269
Training and development
    programs 269
Organizational development
    (OD) 270
Compensation 271
Health 271
Safety 272
Comparable worth 274
Glass ceiling 277
Executive Orders 278
Affirmative action 278

Job analysis 279
Job description 279
Job specification 280
Human resource planning
    (HRP) 280
Recruitment 281
Employment requisition
    281
Selection 282
Preliminary interview 282
Employee orientation 290
Employee assistance
    program 292
Performance appraisal 292

individuals who are most capable of meeting the requirements of the job. Selection is the process of choosing from a group of applicants the individual best suited for a particular position. Steps in the selection process typically include the preliminary interview, evaluation of the application blank, testing, interviewing, reference checking and background investigation, management approval, and physical examinations. One of the most fervently pursued civil rights issues relates to sexual harassment. The EEOC has issued interpretative guidelines that state that employers have an affirmative duty to maintain a workplace free from sexual harassment.

Internal staffing administration includes orientation, employee assistance programs, and performance appraisals, among other activities. In recruiting and selecting managerial personnel, more subjective than objective judgment is often required, focusing on an evaluation of skills, abilities, attitudes, and characteristics, many of which are intangible.

REVIEW QUESTIONS

1. Briefly define each of the basic functions of human resource management.
2. Describe the major federal laws and executive orders affecting equal employment opportunity.
3. Distinguish between a job description and a job specification.
4. Describe the advantages and disadvantages of promotion from within.
5. What steps are involved in the personnel selection process?
6. Describe the two basic types of employment interviews.
7. List the various types of employee status changes.
8. Discuss the purpose of assessment centers.

CASE STUDIES

CASE 9.1 "Send Him on Down"

Jack Stephens was production manager for Thompson Manufacturing Company, a Seattle, Washington, maker of electrical enclosures. Jack had to approve the hiring of any new supervisors in the plant. The human resource manager performed the initial screening.

One Friday afternoon, Jack got a call from Pete Schneider, Thompson's human resource director. "Jack," Pete said, "I've just spoken to a young man who may be just who you're looking for to fill that supervisor job you asked me about. He has some good work experience and it seems his head is screwed on straight." Jack replied, "Great, Pete, I look forward to seeing him." Pete continued, "He's here right now, Jack, if you could possibly talk with him." Jack hesitated a moment before answering. "Gee, Pete," he said,

"I'm certainly busy today but I'll try to squeeze him in. Send him on down."

A moment later Allen Guthrie, the new applicant, arrived at Jack's office and introduced himself. "Come on in, Allen," said Jack. "I'll be right with you after I make a few phone calls." Fifteen minutes later, Jack finished the calls and began talking with Allen. Jack was quite impressed. After a few minutes, Jack's door opened and a supervisor yelled, "We have a small problem on line number one and need your help."

"Sure," Jack replied. "Excuse me a minute, Allen." Ten minutes later, Jack returned and the conversation continued for at least ten more minutes before a series of phone calls again interrupted them.

The same pattern of interruptions continued for the next hour. Finally, Allen looked at his watch and said, "I'm sorry, Mr. Stephens, but I have to pick up my wife."

"Sure thing, Allen," Jack said as the phone rang again. "Call me later this week."

QUESTIONS

1. What specific policies might a company follow to avoid interviews like this one?
2. Explain why Jack, not Pete, should make the selection decision.

CASE 9.2 Human Resource Management at Nucor Steel

As steel producers went during the 1980s, Nucor Steel was a high flyer. While giants such as USX Corporation (formerly U.S. Steel) and Bethlehem Steel suffered huge losses in the early 1980s, Nucor stayed prosperous. More than 100,000 steel workers remained out of work in 1987, but Nucor had not laid off a single hourly employee. Near the end of the decade, Nucor stock sold at 19 times earnings, compared to 11 for USX Corporation, five for Bethlehem Steel, and eight for Armco.

Things were not always so rosy for this relatively small (if $1 billion in sales can be called small) steel producer. Nucor started off during the Great Depression as Reo Motors, Inc., a spinoff from the R. E. Olds Company. In 1938, the company filed for reorganization under the bankruptcy laws. It was briefly revived by World War II and then lingered until 1954, when liquidation seemed to have ended its suffering.

The only remnant that survived was Nuclear Corporation of America, the shares of which had been distributed to the former shareholders of Reo Motors. Nuclear Corporation was a hodgepodge of small, unrelated businesses, one of which was a steel bar joist maker. Bar joists are light steel beams made of angle iron and rods. They are used mainly to support elevated floors and roofs in commercial buildings.

Nuclear Corporation struggled along until 1965, posting a $2.2 million loss in that year alone. In the depths of Nuclear's despair, Kenneth Iverson took over as president and chief executive officer. Things began to change. By 1971, sales were $64.8 million and profits $2.7 million, healthy in comparison with the past. By 1980, sales had climbed to $482.4 million. Profits had increased even more markedly to $45.1 million. When the recession of the early 1980s decimated the rest of the steel industry, Nucor barely flinched. And the company remained continuously profitable through the last half of the decade.

What accounts for the success of Nucor while the rest of the steel industry stagnated? Opinions differ, but there are a number of possibilities. First, the company produces a narrow product line, using modern and highly efficient mini mills to melt scrap steel and shape it into angles, channels, and bars. Large, integrated producers such as those mentioned earlier mine iron ore and try to make every kind of steel plate and shape.

Probably the most significant factor in Nucor's success is the productivity of its workforce. Nucor located its mini mills in rural areas where the work ethic was strong and there was little pro-union sentiment. This facilitated the company's use of certain innovative personnel policies designed to enhance worker productivity.

Iverson said two things are very important to most people: What am I going to be paid, and am I going to have a job tomorrow? Two fundamental Nucor policies grew out of this line of thinking. First, compensation is based on individual and group productivity and company profitability. Second, Nucor does not lay off hourly employees. Nucor also emphasizes communication with employees. There are only three layers of management.

QUESTIONS

1. Evaluate the human resource management policies at Nucor Steel.
2. What are the environmental factors that affect human resource management at Nucor Steel?

NOTES

1. This case is a composite of a number of published accounts, among them: Jolie Solomon, "Pepsi Offers Stock Options to All, Not Just Honchos," *The Wall Street Journal* (June 28, 1989): B1; Michael J. McCarthy, "PepsiCo's Net Income in Second Quarter Rose 21% Due in Part to Special Gains," *The Wall Street Journal* (July 27, 1989): A4; Carol Davenport, "America's Most Admired Corporations," *Fortune* 124 (January 30, 1989): 68–94; Walter Guzzardi, "Wisdom from the Giants of Business," *Fortune* 124 (July 3, 1989): 78–88; Alison L. Sprout, "America's Most Admired Corporations," *Fortune* 126 (February 11, 1991): 57–58; Standard and Poor's Corporation, "PepsiCo," *Standard NYSE Stock Reports* 56, no. 95 (May 17, 1989): sec. 18; Laura Zinn, "Pepsi's Future Becomes Clear," *Business Week* (February 1, 1993): 74–75; Grace M. Kang, "More Workers Are Getting a Stake—For Now," *Business Week* (April 12, 1993): 30.

2. R. Wayne Mondy and Robert M. Noe III, *Human Resource Management,* 5th ed. (Boston, MA: Allyn and Bacon, 1993): 5–10.

3. R. Wayne Mondy, Robert M. Noe III, and Robert E. Edwards, "What the Staffing Function Entails," *Personnel* 63 (April 1986): 55.

4. Chuck Hawkins and Patrick Oster, "After a U-Turn, UPS Really Delivers," *Business Week* (May 31, 1993): 92–93.

5. Joan Hamilton, Emily T. Smith, Gary McWilliams, Evan I. Schwartz, and John Carey, "Virtual Reality," *Business Week* (October 5, 1992): 100.

6. David Woodruff, James B. Treece, Sunita Wadekar Bhargava, and Karen Lowry Miller, "Saturn," *Business Week* (August 17, 1992): 88–89.

7. Barry T. Hirsch and David A Macpherson, "Union Membership and Coverage Files from the Current Population Surveys: Note," *Industrial & Labor Relations Review* 46 (April 1993): 577.

8. Gene Koretz and Celeste Whittaker, "More Picket Lines, Fewer Rank-and-Filers," *Business Week* (May 7, 1990): 24.

9. Adapted from E. S. Browning, "On a Roll: Long-Term Thinking and Paternalistic Ways Carry Michelin to Top," *The Wall Street Journal* (January 5, 1990): 1 and A8 (Col 4).

10. Jonathan Kapstein and John Hoerr, "Volvo's Radically New Plant: 'The Death of the Assembly Line?' " *Business Week* (August 28, 1989): 92–93.

11. Howard C. Lockwood, "Equal Employment Opportunities," in Dale Yoder and Herbert G. Heneman, eds., *Staffing Policies and Strategies* (Washington, D.C.: Bureau of National Affairs, 1979): 4–252.

12. Doug Grider and Mike Shurden, "The Gathering Storm of Comparable Worth," *Business Horizons* 30 (July–August 1987): 81–82.

13. Michael R. Carrell and Frank E. Kuzmits, "Amended ADEA's Effects on HR Strategies Remain Dubious," *Personnel Journal* 66 (May 1987): 112.

14. *The Americans with Disabilities Act: Questions and Answers* (U.S. Government Printing Office, 1991): 1.

15. Christine D. Keen, "Lifestyle Disabilities Could Become a Civil Rights Frontier," *HRNews* 9 (October 1990): 7.

16. Jack Raisner, "When Workplace Relationships Cause Discrimination," *HRMagazine* 36 (January 1991): 75.

17. Amanda Troy Segal and Wendy Zellner, "Corporate Women," *Business Week* (June 8, 1992): 74.

18. "More Women Are Executive VPs," *Fortune* 128 (July 12, 1993): 16.

19. Joseph E. McKendrick, Jr., "Latest AMS Foundation Survey Finds: One-Third of Nation's Employers Have or Are Considering Drug Testing," *Management World* 19 (March–April 1990): 3.

20. The Fourth Amendment prohibits the government from conducting unreasonable searches or seizures.

21. Gerard P. Panaro, *Employment Law Manual* (Boston: Warren, Gorham & Lamont, 1990): 4–28.

22. Brad D. Smart, "Progressive Approaches for Hiring the Best People," *Training and Development Journal* 41 (September 1987): 51.

23. Arthur Bragg, "Checking References," *Sales and Marketing Management* 142 (November 1990): 68.

24. Scott T. Rickard, "Effective Staff Selection," *Personnel Journal* 60 (June 1981): 477.

25. James W. Fenton, Jr., "Negligent Hiring/Retention Adds to Human Resources Woes," *Personnel Journal* 69 (April 1990): 62; and Stephanie Overman, "A Delicate Balance Protects Everyone's Rights," *HRMagazine* 35 (November 1990): 36–39.

26. Caleb S. Atwood and James M. Neel, "New Lawsuits Expand Employer Liability," *HRMagazine* 35 (October 1990): 74.

27. Kely Flynn, "Preventive Medicine for Sexual Harassment," *Personnel* 68 (March 1991): 17.

28. Michele Galen, "Ending Sexual Harassment: Business Is Getting the Message," *Business Week* (March 18, 1991): 98.

29. Anne B. Fisher, "Sexual Harassment: What to Do," *Fortune* 128 August (23, 1993): 84.

30. Stacey J. Garvin, "Employer Liability for Sexual Harassment," *HRMagazine* 36 (June 1991): 107.

31. Troy Segal, "Sexual Harassment: The Age of Anxiety," *Business Week* (July 6, 1992): 16.

32. Robert J. Samuelson, "R.I.P.: The Good Corporation," *Newsweek* 122 (July 5, 1993): 41.

33. Stephen B. Wildstrom, "A Failing Grade for the American Workforce," *Business Week* (September 11, 1989): 22.

34. Dean Foust, "A Tough Look at General Motors," *Business Week* (September 11, 1989): 22.

35. Nancy J. Adler, "Women Managers in a Global Economy," *HRMagazine* 36 (September 1993): 52-55.

How Well Would You Fit in a Bureaucracy?

Since you will probably work for an organization one day, it is important for you to appreciate the differences among types of bureaucratic organizations. Some individuals prefer highly bureaucratic organizations, whereas others prefer less bureaucratic organizations. Since your happiness as an employee may be affected by the bureaucratic orientation of the firm you work for, you should evaluate your preference prior to selecting a firm. To assess your degree of bureaucratic orientation, take the self-assessment exercise "How Well Would You Fit in a Bureaucracy?" Then, turn to page 674 to evaluate yourself.

INSTRUCTIONS: Check either "mostly agree" or "mostly disagree."

MOSTLY AGREE	MOSTLY DISAGREE	QUESTION
❑	❑	1. I value stability in my job.
❑	❑	2. I like a predictable organization.
❑	❑	3. The best job for me would be one in which the future is uncertain.
❑	❑	4. The U.S. Army would be a nice place to work.
❑	❑	5. Rules, policies, and procedures tend to frustrate me.
❑	❑	6. I would enjoy working for a company that employed 85,000 people worldwide.
❑	❑	7. Being self-employed would involve more risk than I'm willing to take.
❑	❑	8. Before accepting a job, I would like to see an exact job description.
❑	❑	9. I would prefer a job as a freelance house painter to one as a clerk for the Department of Motor Vehicles.
❑	❑	10. Seniority should be as important as performance in determining pay increases and promotion.
❑	❑	11. It would give me a feeling of pride to work for the largest and most successful company in its field.

(continued on next page)

MOSTLY AGREE	MOSTLY DISAGREE	QUESTION
❑	❑	12. Given a choice, I would prefer to make $30,000 a year as a vice-president in a small company to $35,000 as a staff specialist in a large company.
❑	❑	13. I would regard wearing an employee badge with a number on it as a degrading experience.
❑	❑	14. Parking spaces in a company lot should be assigned on the basis of job level.
❑	❑	15. An accountant who works for a large organization cannot be a true professional.
❑	❑	16. Before accepting a job (given a choice), I would want to make sure that the company had a very fine program of employee benefits.
❑	❑	17. A company will probably not be successful unless it establishes a clear set of rules and procedures.
❑	❑	18. Regular working hours and vacations are more important to me than finding thrills on the job.
❑	❑	19. You should respect people according to their rank.
❑	❑	20. Rules are meant to be broken.

Source: Adapted from Andrew J. DuBrin, *Human Relations: A Job Oriented Approach*, © 1978, pp. 667–688. Reprinted with permission of Reston Publishing Co., a Prentice-Hall Co., 11480 Sunset Hills Road, Reston, VA 22090.

10 Motivation

LEARNING OBJECTIVES

After completing this chapter students should be able to

✘ Describe some philosophies of human nature.

✘ Describe needs theories, equity theory, and reinforcement theory.

✘ Explain expectancy theory and motivation and the reward system.

✘ Describe how linking pay to performance can help to achieve workplace diversity and how managers can be better at motivating.

✘ Discuss how managers are responding to the needs of the diverse workforce, and describe the possible rewards a first-level manager can dispense.

Stylish Cars and Motivated Workers Help Nissan Overtake Honda as the Number Two Automaker in the United States

In early 1992, 82-year-old Yutaka Katayama, the man who brought Nissan to the United States and made Datsun a household name in the 1960s, was very disappointed with Nissan USA. According to Katayama "Nissan has lost its spirit." Nissan appeared to be in a constant, unstoppable downward spiral. Nissan's main problem was the lack of stylish cars and not focusing on customer desires. CEO and president Tom Mignanelli decided to overtake number two Honda and aim for number one Toyota. Mignanelli was supported by a motivated workforce ready to execute his new strategic direction. Nissan's Smyrna Tennessee plant was just the foundation Mignanelli needed to make his goal of overtaking Honda a reality. Nissan cars were redesigned in the mold of the Altima, the "new image of Nissan reliability and quality," and then the motivated workforce at Nissan's Smyrna plant did their magic. According to AutoPacific market researcher, Christopher W. Cedergren, "We are seeing . . . the beginning of a renaissance at Nissan."

The workforce at Nissan's Smyrna plant is a very select group. When the Smyrna plant opened, there were 180,000 applicants for 3,000 jobs, and area unemployment was 13 percent. Nissan did not promise lifetime employment, but pledged to do everything possible to preserve jobs. Certain auxiliary functions such as security and grounds and maintenance were contracted out, so that contract personnel could be released and those jobs filled with Nissan employees if sales dropped.

At Nissan, employees participate in all decisions affecting their jobs. "Technicians," as Nissan calls its production workers, work in teams, rotate jobs, and punch no time clocks. Turnover is extremely low, even though the work is fast-paced. Nissan's wage structure compares favorably with U.S. auto industry averages, with bonuses paid to especially productive employees. The current movement appears to be toward a bonus plan more closely connected to quality, productivity, and other such factors.

The Smyrna plant remains technologically advanced, with robots doing many repetitive jobs, and state-of-the-art computers controlling much of the manufacturing process. Workers learn multiple skills because Nissan managers claim that multiskilled workers are more productive and contented than traditional assembly-line workers. The combination of a technologically advanced plant, and a motivated, well-trained workforce appears to have paid off. Robert J. Thomas, the new president and CEO of Nissan's U.S. sales arm, believes that this combination offers a rare opportunity for Nissan to "pull ahead." In June 1993, Nissan Motor Company finally ousted Honda Motor Company from its long-held perch as the number two import manufacturer in the United States, behind Toyota Motor Corporation. In addition, Nissan USA was the only Japanese automaker to gain market share during that period.[1]

Technicians at Nissan's Smyrna plant appear to be motivated by bonuses that are associated with productivity, as well as multiskilled training. Also there is a movement toward a bonus plan even more closely connected to quality, productivity, and other such factors. Some managers motivate employees through the use of various types of rewards, as does Nissan USA, while other managers use punishment and formal authority to motivate. **Motivation** is the desire to put forth effort in pursuit of organizational goals. Managers can always improve their understanding of the forces that energize employees. There is enormous energy within every person, and managers certainly should not prevent its release.

In this chapter, we first discuss three philosophies of human nature. Then, we describe four major motivation theories: needs theories, equity theory, reinforcement theory, and expectancy theory. Next, we review how motivation relates to the reward system and how linking pay to performance helps achieve workplace diversity. We follow this with a discussion of how managers can be better at motivating and how managers are responding to the needs of the diverse workforce. In the final sections, we present ideas that relate to possible rewards a first-level manager can dispense, and then provide a global perspective of motivation.

❖ ❖ PHILOSOPHIES OF HUMAN NATURE

A manager's philosophy of human nature helps determine the motivational techniques the manager will employ. According to George Fisher, Motorola's CEO, goading and coaxing people to seek to achieve the seemingly unachievable is a necessary part of management. Fisher sees motivation as people being "challenged to achieve what on a day-to-day basis they might have thought was unachievable."[2] Early in this century, Frederick Taylor and Elton Mayo proposed what many consider to be contrasting philosophies. Taylor was convinced that the scientific method, which provides a logical framework for the analysis of problems, could be applied to the management process. He believed that use of the scientific method would direct the manager to the most efficient way of doing work. Individuals were components of the process but had to be guided by rationality. When they performed most efficiently, Taylor said, both they and the organization would gain. The organization would have increased profits, and workers would make more money. Taylor believed in benchmarks, and so does Eastman Kodak CEO, Christopher J. Steffen, who builds cost-consciousness into the culture by benchmarking against the world's best companies. Steffen believes that "You motivate people to change by judging them against a benchmark. Then it becomes pride. Then it becomes a cultural change."[3]

Elton Mayo and his associates conducted their famous Hawthorne studies in the 1920s and 1930s at Western Electric's Hawthorne facility, on Chicago's West Side. Their research demonstrated that the attitudes and feelings of workers significantly influence productivity. This "illogic of sentiments" turned out to be just as important as Taylor's "logic of efficiency." The studies also revealed the Hawthorne effect—the fact that the presence of researchers influences the behavior of the people being studied and, therefore, biases the results. Never again could human behavior be seen as determined by simple, or even completely discoverable, cause-and-effect rules.

Modern managers tend to take a balanced view, giving attention to both logical and sentimental aspects of behavior. At many U.S. companies, employees work in teams that are frequently self-managing, including responsibility for problem solving.

McGregor's Theory X and Theory Y

Douglas McGregor stressed the importance of understanding the relationships between motivation and the manager's philosophy of human nature. He believed most managers of his day tended to make a certain set of assumptions about employees. He labeled this traditional view **Theory X**—the assumption that people dislike work and responsibility, lack ambition and creative ability, and mainly want security and money. McGregor pointed out that managers who hold such a view think they must coerce, control, and threaten employees in order to motivate them. McGregor proposed an alternate philosophy of human nature, which he considered more realistic. He called it **Theory Y**—the assumption that expending physical and mental effort is natural; that people can be self-directed if achievement brings rewards; and that most can exercise imagination, ingenuity, and creativity and learn to seek responsibility. Thus, McGregor believed employees do not require coercion or excessive control to perform effectively.[4]

Today many companies are unable to reward with raises and promotions as

Prodigamente
Profusamente

lavishly as before, and therefore some in corporate America are embracing the new career enhancement doctrines. Chevron's head of personnel development, Sarah Clemens, states that Chevron is "working to help people revitalize their jobs in a way that will benefit them and the company." Beverly Kaye, an "inplacement consultant," worked with Chevron for three years to set up its program. According to Kaye, "What you want is for employees to be *productively plateaued. . . .* They may not be moving up in an organization, but if they feel stuck, productivity suffers and absenteeism soars."[5]

The Theory X and Theory Y assumptions are shown in Table 10.1. The Theory Y assumptions suggest a high degree of faith in the capacity and potential of people. Here are some managerial practices Theory Y managers may follow: (1) abandonment of time clocks, (2) flexible work hours, (3) job enrichment,

TABLE 10.1 A Comparison of McGregor's Theory X and Theory Y Assumptions

THEORY X	THEORY Y
The average person inherently dislikes work and will avoid it if possible.	The expenditure of physical and mental effort in work is as natural as play or rest.
Because of the dislike of work, most people must be coerced, controlled, directed, and threatened with punishment to get them to perform effectively.	People will exercise self-direction and self-control in the service of objectives to which they are committed.
The average person lacks ambition, avoids responsibility, and seeks security and economic rewards above all else.	Commitment to objectives is a function of the rewards associated with achievement.
Most people lack creative ability and are resistant to change.	The average person learns, under proper conditions, not only to accept but to seek responsibility.
Since most people are self-centered, they are not concerned with the objectives of the organization.	The capacity to exercise a relatively high degree of imagination, ingenuity, and creativity in the solution of organizational problems is widely, not narrowly, distributed in the population.

(Source: Based on material in Douglas McGregor, *The Human Side of Enterprise* (New York: McGraw-Hill, 1960.)

and (4) participative decision making. All are based on the beliefs that abilities are widely, not narrowly, distributed in the population and that each person can be trusted to behave responsibly. If Theory Y is correct, management need only create an environment that permits workers to be motivated and realize their potential. Remember that Nissan's Smyrna workers did not have time clocks and that they participated in all decisions affecting their jobs. Since tangible rewards are also important, those who were especially productive were paid additional bonuses.

Theory Y does provide a basis for improved management and organizational performance, but it is not a panacea for all managerial problems. Simply assuming people are creative, responsible, and so forth may not always make them so. And McGregor himself said most managers made Theory X assumptions. Surely, some of those Theory X managers were effective.

Argyris's Maturity Theory

The research of Chris Argyris helped explain an important dimension of human behavior in organizations. Argyris believed healthy individuals develop along a continuum from immaturity to maturity. Mature people, he said, tend to be active, not passive; independent, not dependent; and self-aware and self-controlled, rather than unaware and controlled by others. Argyris saw a fundamental conflict between the demands of a mature personality and those of typical organizations. He described the ways in which four attributes of formal structure inhibit maturation:

- Specialization of labor limits initiative and self-expression and allows few of one's abilities to be used.
- Chain of command limits self-control and makes individuals passive and dependent on the leader.
- Unity of direction (or unity of command) puts the path to the objective under the control of one leader, which creates problems when employees are not able to use a wide range of abilities and to define their own objectives on the basis of inner needs.
- Span of control (or span of management) decreases self-control and shortens the time perspective of lower-level employees.

In an organization where these characteristics are embedded in rigid rules and procedures, Argyris believed, employees could not grow to maturity. He said this is true for the following reasons:

1. They have little control over their workaday world.
2. They are expected to be passive, dependent, and subordinate.

3. They are expected to have a short time perspective.
4. They are induced to perfect and value the frequent use of only a few shallow abilities.
5. They are expected to produce under conditions that will lead to psychological failure.[6]

Argyris argued that when mature employees encounter such conditions, three reactions are possible:

1. *Escape*. An employee may escape by quitting, being absent, or attempting to climb to higher levels in the firm where the structure is less rigid.
2. *Fight*. A person can fight the system by exerting pressure on the organization by means of informal groups or through formally organized labor unions.
3. *Adapt*. The most typical reaction by employees, Argyris found, is to adapt by developing an attitude of apathy or indifference. The employee plays the game, and pay becomes the compensation for the penalty of working.

Of the three responses, Argyris considered adaptation most contrary to good mental health. At many companies, the need for adaptation is diminished by letting workers participate in decisions that affect them.

Criticisms of McGregor and Argyris

Managers cannot assume that all employees are mature, as defined by Argyris, or Theory Y types, as defined by McGregor. Security may mean more than a challenging job to some individuals. And some workers may thrive on doing highly structured and repetitive tasks that may be boring to others.

Argyris argued that a highly structured environment will cause employees to act immaturely. One could argue as well that maturity involves the ability to adapt to any kind of environment, structured or not. Many people can and do adjust to tightly regimented work situations. One need only observe workers on a well-functioning assembly line to recognize this. In addition, workers who prefer challenges can find them. In U.S. business, only a fraction of jobs are of the highly structured, totally controlled type. To the degree that an open job market operates efficiently, there will be a matching of various human needs and organizational demands.

The ideas of McGregor and Argyris have great relevance to the practice of management, of course. Managers probably have tended to make Theory X-type assumptions about their subordinates, and the modern organization does restrict behavior somewhat. However, to suggest that either McGregor or Argyris has provided an adequate guide for managers in all situations is erroneous.

The Self-Fulfilling Prophecy

The **self-fulfilling prophecy** is the idea that the manager's positive or negative expectations will have a significant influence on employee motivation and performance. This concept is very important in management. According to J. Sterling Livingston:

- A manager's expectations of employees and the way the manager treats employees largely determine their performance and career progress.
- A unique characteristic of superior managers is their ability to create high performance expectations that subordinates fulfill.
- Less effective managers fail to develop high performance expectations, and as a consequence, the productivity of their subordinates suffers.
- More often than not, subordinates appear to do what they believe they are expected to do.[7]

High performance expectations tend to be self-fulfilling prophecies. A manager communicates expectations through both verbal and nonverbal means. The manager's facial expressions, eye contact, body posture, or tone of voice can indicate high approval and high expectations or the reverse.

Numerous studies support the notion of the self-fulfilling prophecy. In one study, 18 elementary school teachers were informed that certain of their students were "intellectual bloomers." The supposedly exceptional students had been chosen at random and so did not differ in intelligence or abilities from the rest of

High performance expectations tend to be self-fulfilling prophecies. The manager's facial expressions, eye contact, body posture, or tone of voice can indicate high approval and high expectations, or the reverse. This manager seems to be communicating a sense of confidence in the computer operator and vice versa. (Source: © Jim Pickerell)

the students. During the school year, the chosen students actually did make significantly greater progress. Thus, the teachers' high expectations apparently became self-fulfilling prophecies.

Similar results have been achieved by managers. More often than not, if managers communicate high expectations to their employees, the employees will perform well. To illustrate: David McNeill was the manager of the computer center at a state university in Louisiana. While McNeill was working late one night, George Johnson, who was employed as a janitor, talked with him about learning to operate computers. McNeill became convinced that Johnson had the necessary potential, although none of his experience or education seemed to qualify him. At McNeill's suggestion, Johnson enrolled in a training program. He became not only an operator but eventually a trainer as well.

The self-fulfilling prophecy can be an important element in developing managers internally. And no company has an excess of truly exceptional managers. The greatest impact of high expectations may be on younger employees, whose self-image may not be well formed. But anyone is likely to strive harder and develop faster if expected to do that. A superior's confidence in a subordinate can build the subordinate's self-confidence and spark efforts aimed at self-development and advancement.

Of course, a negative prophecy can be self-fulfilling as surely as can an affirmative one. Therefore, managers who wish their units to achieve excellence must guard against expecting too little. Managers who expect little of employees tend to create organizational cultures marked by low employee motivation and performance. Working in such cultures can damage employees' self-esteem or self-image, as well as their careers.[8]

MANAGEMENT IN PRACTICE

A Skill-Building Exercise: One of your employees, Bob Edison, spends every free minute that he's off the job—and most of his earnings—on bowling. Bob belongs to three leagues and bowls in a tournament every weekend. He has won numerous trophies. His name constantly appears on the sports page of the local paper.

You have observed that Bob does only enough to keep his job. You made the following comments on Bob's latest performance report: "Gets along well with everyone. Does not disrupt anyone else's work. But seems to live for quitting time, his paycheck, and bowling." Upon reading this, Bob said it was true. He just shrugged when you told him you expected him to improve. It is three weeks later, and one of Bob's co-workers has just complained that she has been having to do most of Bob's work, because he keeps sloughing off.

What would you do?

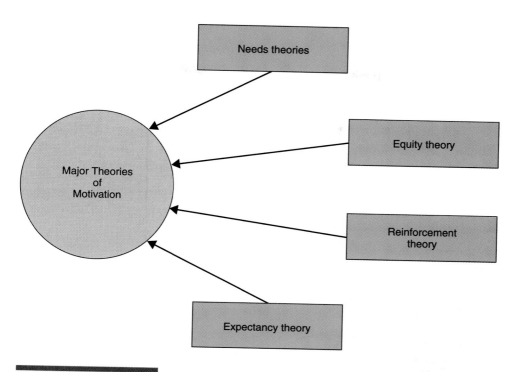

❖ **Figure 10.1**
Major types of motivation theories

❖ ❖ NEEDS THEORIES

Figure 10.1 illustrates four major types of motivation theories. The first is needs theories. As the name implies, such theories are based on the proposition that motivation can be best explained in terms of needs fulfillment. Four of the most popular needs theories are discussed in this section: (1) Maslow's hierarchy of needs theory, (2) Herzberg's motivator-hygiene (two-factor) theory, (3) Alderfer's ERG theory, and (4) McClelland's needs theory. As Table 10.2 indicates, the categories of needs associated with each differ somewhat. The theories also differ as

TABLE 10.2 Comparison of Needs in Four Theories of Motivation

MASLOW'S	HERZBERG'S	ALDERFER'S	McCLELLAND'S
Physiological	Hygiene	Existence	
Safety and security	Hygiene	Existence	
Belongingness and love		Relatedness	Need for affiliation
Self-esteem	Motivators	Growth	Need for achievement
Self-actualization	Motivators	Growth	Need for power

to how unfulfilled needs influence motivation. The other major types of motivation theories—equity theory, reinforcement theory, and expectancy theory—are discussed later in the chapter.

Maslow's Hierarchy of Needs

Many psychologists believe that there are certain patterns, or configurations, of human needs, although there obviously are individual differences. A common approach to establishing a pattern of needs is that of developing a universal needs hierarchy. Psychologist Abraham Maslow proposed one widely known pattern (see Figure 10.2). Examples of how an organization might help to satisfy these basic needs are also presented here.

Maslow stated that individuals are motivated to satisfy certain unsatisfied needs. His theory of human motivation is based on the following assumptions:

· Unsatisfied needs motivate or influence behavior.
· Satisfied needs do not motivate behavior.
· Needs are arranged in a hierarchy.
· Needs at any level of the hierarchy emerge as a significant motivator only when the lower-level needs are reasonably well satisfied.[9]

According to Maslow, the needs hierarchy extends from physiological needs

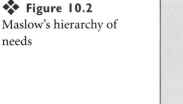

❖ **Figure 10.2**
Maslow's hierarchy of needs

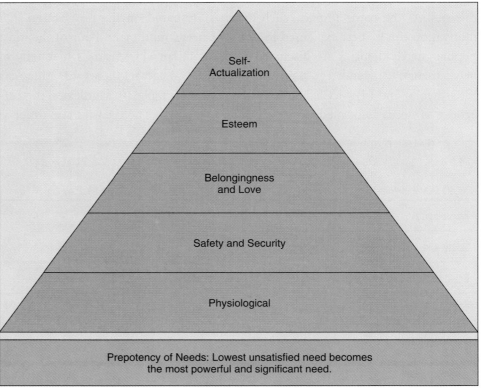

at the bottom to the need for self-actualization at the top. Until physiological needs are reasonably well satisfied, he believed, higher-level needs will not significantly influence behavior. Maslow acknowledged that a person is never completely satisfied on any need level. But he said a type of need can be prepotent (have exceptional power to influence behavior) only when those below it in the hierarchy are largely fulfilled.

Maslow's advice to managers was to focus their motivational efforts on the lowest-level category of needs that is substantially unsatisfied. He said an average person might be 85 percent satisfied in physiological needs, 70 percent in safety and security needs, 50 percent in belongingness and love needs, 40 percent in esteem needs, and ten percent in self-actualization needs. Thus, Maslow's theory implies that the manager of the average person should pay attention to the belongingness and esteem needs. Physiological and safety needs are viewed as weak motivators in this instance because they are, respectively, 85 and 70 percent satisfied. And although self-actualization needs are only ten percent satisfied, they are seen as weak motivators too. They cannot come into play, according to Maslow's theory, until something is done about the needs for belongingness and esteem. There were early predictions that Nissan's U.S. plant would fail because of the firm's reliance on stable employment as a motivator. Job security fulfills a safety need, and it was reasoned that U.S. workers were higher on the Maslow hierarchy than Japanese workers and thus were less concerned with the need for safety. Apparently, however, job security has been an important component in Nissan's successful motivational approach.

Maslow's theory is widely known and is used as a guide by many practicing managers. But some researchers have called it into question.[10] Certain studies suggest needs fall into only two or three distinct categories, not five. In addition, some critics say the order of need fulfillment may not always be the same. These authorities admit that considerable importance should be placed on physiological needs if they have not been satisfied. A person has to eat, for example. But once physiological needs are satisfied, there appears to be no clear-cut order in which higher-level needs become prepotent.

Herzberg's Motivation-Hygiene Theory

In his classic study in the 1950s, Frederick Herzberg asked his research sample, a group of professionals, to tell of a time when they felt especially good or bad about their job. Such an approach is often called "critical incident" research, because respondents are expected to describe a particular event that seems important. From responses to the initial question and follow-ups, Herzberg identified two distant classes of factors that he said were important to behavior on the job. He called these classes *hygiene factors* and *motivators*.[11]

Hygiene factors, he said, were capable of creating dissatisfaction but not

Hygiene factors relate to the job context, the interrelated conditions in which the job is done. Herzberg concluded that hygiene factors cannot promote motivation, but that they can cause dissatisfaction. Thus, a neat, well-organized office, such as the one shown here, may be vital to preventing worker dissatisfaction. But workers in such an office will not necessarily be highly motivated. (Source: © Jim Pickerell)

positive motivation. As Figure 10.3 shows, they relate to the *job context*—the interrelated conditions in which the job is done. These factors include pay and benefits as well as working conditions, interpersonal relations, and other elements. When Herzberg's subjects told of times when they felt particularly bad about their jobs, they mentioned these factors.

Herzberg concluded that hygiene factors cannot promote motivation but can cause dissatisfaction. He believed hygiene factors maintain an employee, in the way dental hygiene maintains the teeth and gums. But hygiene can only prevent problems; it does not create a high level of well-being. Herzberg suggested that an organization that meets only the hygiene needs of its employees will eliminate dissatisfaction but will not get superior performance.

❖ **Figure 10.3**
Hygiene and motivator factors

HERZBERG'S TWO-FACTOR THEORY

Hygiene Factors			Motivators		
Dissatisfaction	The Environment	No Dissatisfaction	No Job Satisfaction	The Job	Job Satisfaction

• Pay
• Status
• Security
• Working conditions
• Fringe benefits
• Policies and administrative practices
• Interpersonal relations

• Meaningful and challenging work
• Recognition for accomplishment
• Feeling of achievement
• Increased responsibility
• Opportunities for growth and advancement
• The job itself

Motivators, on the other hand, produced high levels of satisfaction, which Herzberg treated as synonymous with motivation. As Figure 10.3 shows, motivators include challenging work, recognition for accomplishment, and the feeling of achievement. Herzberg's motivators are concerned mainly with the job content (whereas hygiene factors relate mostly to the job context). That is, motivators tend to be internal to the job. When Herzberg's subjects described times when they felt especially good about their jobs, they mentioned these factors. Both hygiene factors and motivators are associated with the work environment at Nissan's Smyrna plant.

Criticisms of Herzberg's theory include the following:

1. The analysis of critical incident–type responses is highly subjective.
2. The theory is most applicable to managers, engineers, accountants, and other professionals. Studies show less relevance to blue-collar workers.
3. Herzberg's study focused on level of satisfaction, not performance per se. Satisfaction and performance are not synonymous.

Herzberg's motivators are closely related to the esteem and self-actualization needs of Maslow's hierarchy. His hygiene factors closely correspond to Maslow's physiological, safety, and social needs (see Figure 10.4).

Herzberg contended that most managers give inadequate attention to the motivators, focusing instead on employee pay, benefits, and working conditions. But hygiene factors, Herzberg said, cannot produce positive motivation. To achieve excellence, he believed, organizations must satisfy the needs related to both hygiene factors and motivators. The obvious implication is that management should show relatively more concern for providing challenging work, increased responsibility, recognition, and other motivators.

Alderfer's Erg Theory

Clayton Alderfer reorganized Maslow's needs hierarchy into three levels of needs: (1) *existence needs,* (2) *relatedness needs,* and (3) *growth needs* (ERG).[12] The Alderfer model is illustrated in Figure 10.5. *Existence needs* relate to physical well-being and roughly correspond to Maslow's physiological and safety needs. *Relatedness needs* relate to interpersonal relationships—Maslow's belongingness needs. Alderfer's *growth needs* incorporate both self-esteem and self-actualization, the higher-order needs in the Maslow hierarchy.

The Mechanism of Needs Satisfaction Alderfer agreed with Maslow that unsatisfied needs motivate individuals. For example, he believed workers with unsatisfied relatedness needs will be motivated to produce if peers and superiors affirm and encourage efforts to increase productivity. Alderfer also agreed that individuals, in satisfying their needs, generally move up the hierarchy; that is, they satisfy lower-order before higher-order needs. Like Maslow, he believed that as

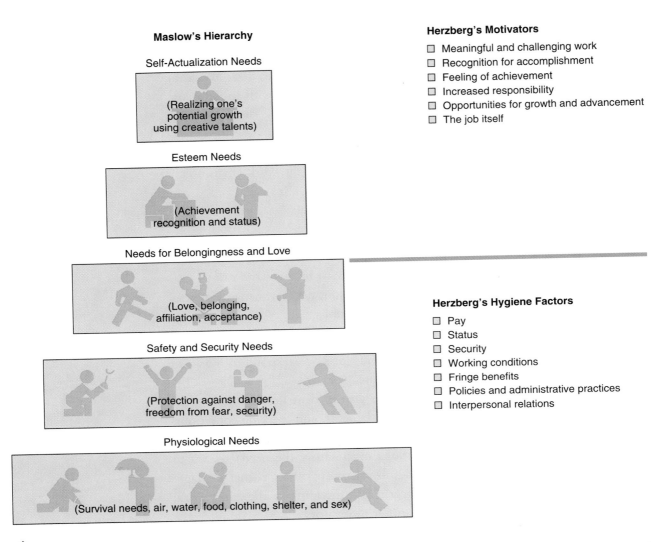

Maslow's Hierarchy

Self-Actualization Needs

(Realizing one's potential growth using creative talents)

Esteem Needs

(Achievement recognition and status)

Needs for Belongingness and Love

(Love, belonging, affiliation, acceptance)

Safety and Security Needs

(Protection against danger, freedom from fear, security)

Physiological Needs

(Survival needs, air, water, food, clothing, shelter, and sex)

Herzberg's Motivators

☐ Meaningful and challenging work
☐ Recognition for accomplishment
☐ Feeling of achievement
☐ Increased responsibility
☐ Opportunities for growth and advancement
☐ The job itself

Herzberg's Hygiene Factors

☐ Pay
☐ Status
☐ Security
☐ Working conditions
☐ Fringe benefits
☐ Policies and administrative practices
☐ Interpersonal relations

❖ **Figure 10.4**
Maslow and Herzberg related

lower-order needs are satisfied, they become less important. But he also believed that as higher-order needs are satisfied, they become more important. Under some circumstances, however, individuals might return to a lower-level need. An employee frustrated in the effort to satisfy growth needs, for example, might be motivated to satisfy the lower-level relatedness needs.

Consider the employee who earns a good salary, has a reasonably high standard of living, and has made many friends at work. According to Maslow and Alderfer, this person is probably motivated to satisfy growth needs. However, what if the individual is continually frustrated in attempts to get more autonomy and responsibility—features of a job that generally encourage individual growth? When asked, the employee reports that having friends at work and getting together with them outside of work are most important. Frustration in satisfying a higher-level (growth) need has resulted in regression to a lower level of (relatedness) needs.

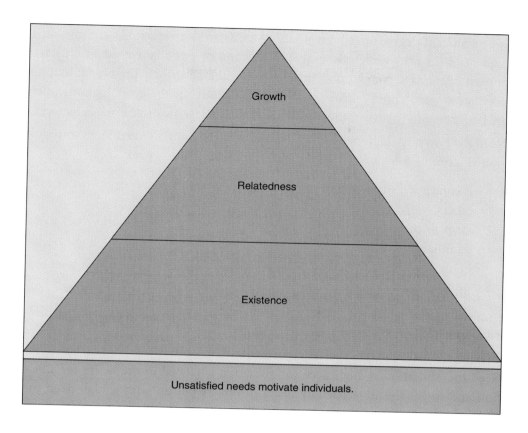

❖ **Figure 10.5**
Alderfer's hierarchy of needs

McClelland's Needs Theory

The research of David McClelland emphasizes that certain needs are learned and socially acquired as the individual interacts with the environment. McClelland's needs theory is concerned with how individual needs and environmental factors combine to form three basic human motives (needs): the need for achievement (*n Ach*), the need for power (*n Pow*), and the need for affiliation (*n Aff*). Motives explain behavior. McClelland conducted numerous studies attempting to define and measure basic human motives.

Need for Achievement A person with a high need for achievement is one who

- Wants to take personal responsibility for finding solutions to problems.
- Is objective oriented.
- Seeks a challenge—and establishes moderate, realistic, and attainable objectives that involve risk but are not impossible to attain.
- Desires concrete feedback on performance.
- Has a high level of energy and is willing to work hard.

People exhibiting a high need for achievement find this pattern of behavior personally rewarding. For these people, the value of objective accomplishment is enhanced if the objectives are at least moderately difficult to achieve and if there is a significant degree of risk involved.[13] McClelland's research has shown that a high need for achievement is probably a strong or dominant need in only ten percent of the U.S. population. Persons high in the need for achievement tend to gravitate toward entrepreneurial and sales positions. In these occupations, they are better able to "manage" themselves and satisfy the basic drive for achievement.

Need for Power A high need for power means that an individual seeks to influence or control others. Such an individual tends to be one who

- Is concerned with acquiring, exercising, or retaining power or influence over others.
- Likes to compete with others in situations that will allow him or her to be dominant.
- Enjoys confrontations with others.

McClelland says power can be positive or negative. Positive use of power is essential if a manager is to accomplish objectives through the efforts of others. The negative side of power is seen in an individual who seeks power for personal benefit, which may prove detrimental to the organization.[14]

Need for Affiliation A high need for affiliation is related to the desire for affection and for establishing friendly relationships. A person with a high need for affiliation tends to be one who

- Seeks to establish and maintain friendships and close emotional relationships with others.
- Wants to be liked by others.
- Enjoys parties and social activities.
- Seeks a sense of belonging by joining groups or organizations.

To varying degrees, each person possesses all three needs; however, one of the needs tends to be more characteristic of the individual than the other two.[15] People in a given culture may have the same needs, but the relative strength of those needs differs. For example, the strength of Japanese workers' need for affiliation may be stronger than that of U.S. workers.

Each of McClelland's three motives evokes a different type of satisfaction. For example, the achievement motive tends to evoke a sense of accomplishment. A manager whose prevalent motive is to obtain power may experience satisfaction by being in control of or influencing others.

According to McClelland's theory, the probability that an individual will perform a job effectively and efficiently depends on a combination of

- The strength of the motive, or need, relative to other needs.
- The possibility of success in performing the task.
- The strength value of the incentive or reward for performance.

The most effective mixture of these three motives depends on the situation. In studies of over 500 managers, it was concluded that the most effective managers have a high need for power, a moderate need for achievement, and a low need for affiliation. These managers tend to use their power in a participative manner for the good of the organization. The best managers have a moderate need for achievement, one not strong enough to interfere with the management process. Persons with high needs for both power and achievement have high managerial motivation, but they may not make the best managers.[16] After all, managing means getting work done through the efforts of others, not overpowering them.

Outstanding salespeople tend to be high in the need for achievement and moderately high in the need for power. Entrepreneurs who develop ideas and promote specific enterprises tend to be high in achievement motivation. They delight in personally solving problems and getting immediate feedback on the degree of success. Entrepreneurs sometimes are unable to make the transition to top-level management positions because their need for personal achievement gets in the way of the requirements for effectively influencing the organization's employees.

❖ ❖ EQUITY THEORY

The second type of motivation theory—equity theory—is generally credited to J. Stacy Adams.[17] It evolved from social comparison theory—the theory that individuals must assess and know their degree of performance and the "correctness" of their attitudes in a situation. Lacking objective measures of performance or correct attitudes, they compare their performance and attitudes to those of others. **Equity theory** is the motivation theory in which people assess their performance and attitudes by comparing both their contribution to work and the benefits they derive from it to the contributions and benefits of "comparison others" whom they select—and who in reality may be like or unlike them.

Determination of Equity

Equity theory further states that a person is motivated in proportion to the perceived fairness of the rewards received for a certain amount of effort as compared to what others receive.[18] Someone might say, "I'm going to stop working so hard—I work harder than Susan and she gets all the bonuses." This individual has compared his effort and the rewards he received to the effort exerted and the rewards received by Susan. In fact, no actual inequity may exist, but the perception of inequity influences subsequent actions. Nissan's wage structure compares favorably with U.S. auto industry averages and is therefore perceived by most as fair. The purpose of Nissan's bonus plan is to build on quality-based productivity. Equity dictates that everyone who is especially productive in this regard should receive bonuses; and that is exactly what Nissan does to help assure equity.

According to equity theory, individuals are motivated to reduce any perceived inequity. They strive to make the ratios of outcomes to inputs equal. When inequity exists, the person making the comparison strives to make the ratios equal by changing either the outcomes or the inputs.

Determining Equity in the Workplace

When inequity exists in an organization, individuals react in a variety of ways, some of which have been described earlier. Some people adjust their inputs; for example, they may decide to exert less effort. Others change the outcomes; they request pay increases or more vacation time. Still others adjust their perception of their own or others' inputs and outcomes; they might revalue their own or others' effort, experience, or education. Some workers leave the situation entirely. The remaining people choose a different comparison person. Thus, when high absenteeism, low productivity, high turnover, or other such symptoms exist, the following questions can be asked of each person to determine whether inequity exists:

1. What contributions, or inputs, does the person make to the situation? What is the person's level of education, effort, or experience?

ETHICAL DILEMMA

Motivation is the desire to put forth effort in pursuit of organizational goals. Managers at all levels must motivate workers if they are to maximize productivity. Individuals are motivated by many factors, including a friendly workplace. Automobile company workplaces are normally unfriendly, and therefore do not help motivate workers. Usually, employees adapt to the workplace, specifically the equipment, not vice versa. In such an environment, employees must do a lot of unnecessary bending and stretching, which can be unhealthy over the long-term. Ford slightly changed work surface heights, moved handles to more accessible spots, and even leaned a parts bin in a particular way to make the workplace more accessible. At Ford, even UAW members feel better on the job, quality has increased, and employees are more motivated and productive.[19] However, because of the cost of these improvements, Ford's "everybody-wins-situation" is not accepted at other similar plants. Your company has the capital necessary to create a more friendly workplace that is more beneficial to the health and productivity of your employees, and you must decide to invest substantially and reduce profits over the short-term or to continue to subject employees to an unfriendly work environment.

What would you do?

2. What benefits, or outcomes, does the person receive? What is the level of job complexity, pay, or status of that person?

3. What is the ratio of inputs to outcomes? (Some quantification of both inputs and outcomes should occur. These can then be compared in ratio form. If the inputs or outcomes cannot be quantified, the ratio must be determined qualitatively.)

4. Is the ratio the same as, greater than, or less than the ratio of comparison others?

Answers to the first three questions must also be obtained for the relevant others. The resulting ratios can then be compared.

Equity theory does not negate needs theory. Rather, it provides another perspective for analyzing motivational problems and predicting individuals' behaviors and attitudes.

❖ ❖ REINFORCEMENT THEORY

Reinforcement theory is based primarily on the research of B. F. Skinner. **Reinforcement theory** is the idea that human behavior can be explained in terms of the previous positive or negative outcomes of that behavior. People tend to repeat behaviors that they have learned will produce pleasant outcomes. Behavior that is reinforced will be repeated; behavior that is not reinforced will not be repeated.

Skinner contends that people's behavior can be controlled and shaped by rewarding (reinforcing) desired behavior while ignoring undesirable actions. Over time, the reinforced behavior will tend to be repeated, whereas the unrewarded behavior will tend to be extinguished and disappear. Punishment of undesired behavior is to be avoided, since it may contribute to feelings of restraint and actions of rebellion. Over a period of years, one can control the behavior of another without that person being aware of it. In his book, *Beyond Freedom and Dignity,* Skinner says people can be controlled and shaped while at the same time feeling free.[20] Skinner's theory of shaping behavior is useful to managers, although one should not assume that human behavior is simple to understand or to modify. The primary technique suggested by Skinner is organizational behavior modification.

Organizational behavior modification is the application of Skinner's reinforcement theory to organizational change efforts. It is based on two fundamental concepts: (1) people act in ways they find most rewarding personally, and (2) behavior can be shaped and determined by controlling the rewards. The rewards are termed *reinforcers* because the objective is to stimulate the continuation of the rewarded behavior. The particular reinforcers that work in motivating people are determined by trial and error and experience. What is successful with one employee may not work with another because needs and wants differ. Praise is used most frequently because it is most readily available. However, praise becomes less effective whenever it becomes predictable or is continuously applied. Often, however, managers do not understand the importance of praise and recognition as motivators. Money is also used, as are public or private letters of commendation, time off, and increased status.

Punishment is rejected as a reinforcer because although it suppresses the undesired behavior, it stimulates anger, hostility, aggression, and rebellion. Also, at times it is difficult to identify the punishment. In one instance, placing prisoners in solitary confinement on bread and water turned out to be a status symbol and led to the repetition of offenses. When the bread and water were changed to baby food, the status symbol disappeared, leading to a significant reduction in the number of undesirable acts. When undesired behavior is not rewarded, it tends to disappear over time.

When reinforcing desired behavior in a positive fashion, it is important to allocate the rewards soon after the behavior occurs so the person perceives a clear and immediate linkage. Fast and accurate feedback of information to the performer in itself constitutes reinforcement.

For the manager who desires to use organizational behavior modification, the following actions are necessary:

- Identifying the desired performance in specific terms—for example, improving attendance rates or answering questions within one hour.
- Identifying the rewards that will reinforce the desired behavior—for example, praise, money, and time off.
- Making the reward a direct consequence of the behavior.
- Selecting the optimum reinforcement schedule.

Despite the successes achieved by behavior modification, it has been criticized as being a manipulative and autocratic approach to the management of people. People are conditioned to change their behavior in the direction required by management and the organization. Some critics argue that organizational behavior modification is not consistent with the theories of such behavioral scientists as Maslow, Argyris, and McGregor. The assumption underlying these theories is that people are motivated by their own internal needs and are capable of a degree of self-control. On the other hand, behavior modification assumes that the causes of human behavior are in the environment and are therefore external to the individual.

❖ ❖ EXPECTANCY THEORIES OF MOTIVATION

One of the more popular theories of motivation has been expectancy theory.[21] The approaches to motivation developed by Maslow, Herzberg, and McClelland do not adequately account for differences in individual employees or explain why people behave in certain ways. Victor Vroom developed **expectancy theory**—the approach to motivation that attempts to explain behavior in terms of an individual's goals and choices and the expectations of achieving the objectives.[22] The theory assumes that people can determine which outcomes they prefer and can make realistic estimates of their chances of obtaining them. Expectancy theory offers a comprehensive view of motivation and integrates many of the elements of the needs, equity, and reinforcement theories.

Vroom's model states that motivation is a function of expectancy, valence, and instrumentality.[23] In other words:

$$\text{Motivation} = E \times V \times I$$

Expectancy (E) refers to a person's perception of the probability that effort will lead to performance. For example, a person who perceives that he or she will produce more by working harder has a high expectancy that hard work leads to productivity. A person who perceives that he or she will be ostracized by other workers by working harder has a high expectancy that effort leads to exclusion. A person who sees no link between effort and performance will have zero

Expectancy theory assumes that people can determine which outcomes they prefer and can make realistic estimates of their chances of obtaining them. The person receiving this award evidently wanted the award and believed there was a good chance of obtaining it. (Source: © John Coletti)

expectancy about this relationship. If expectancy is zero, then motivation will be lower than if expectancy is positive.

Valence (V) refers to a person's perception of the value of the projected outcomes—that is, how much the person likes or dislikes receiving those outcomes. An individual with high esteem needs generally will attach a high valence to a new job title or a promotion. An individual with strong security needs will value pension and retirement programs or the awarding of tenure. An individual with growth or self-actualization needs will view challenging jobs or increased responsibility as motivating because of their high valence. When valence is high, motivation is likely to be higher than when valence is low or negative.

Instrumentality (I) refers to a person's perception of the probability that certain outcomes, positive or negative, will be attached to performance. For example, a person who perceives that he or she will receive greater pay or benefits for producing well has high instrumentality. A person who sees no link between performance and pay has zero instrumentality. Motivation is a function of the value of instrumentality.

Barry Staw, among others, introduced a revised expectancy theory.[24] Rather than limiting his model to **extrinsic motivation** (motivation by factors outside the job, such as pay, job title, and tenure),[25] Staw also considers **intrinsic motivation** (motivation by factors within the job, such as creativity, autonomy, and responsibility).[26] In short, performing a task has intrinsic and extrinsic valence, both of which enter into the calculation of motivation. It is possible that intrinsic factors are sometimes more important than extrinsic factors, meaning that managers should avoid the so-called *Motivation Trap*.

The Motivation Trap

Motivation is the desire to put forth effort in pursuit of organizational goals. Some managers often fall into what is referred to as the "Motivation Trap" when they only attempt to motivate employees with pay raises and promotions. Often this approach backfires and actually decreases employee motivation. According to John J. Hudy, a research psychologist with Acumen International, "Managers can learn to effectively motivate co-workers without pay raises by using a simple model based on co-workers traits and orientations—'what they are like on the inside.'" While most experts agree that motivation energizes, maintains, and guides behavior, they do not agree on how to motivate or what factors affect any given person's motivation to work and to perform most efficiently and effectively. Hudy believes that managers should motivate by seeking people who want to be a part of the organization, by encouraging these individuals to be dependable and committed, and by creating an environment where people are creative, spontaneous, and innovative at work. Managers must also help people adapt to and use new technology. If one accepts the notion that "By themselves, merit-pay plans, raises and promotions won't motivate employees," then what can managers do to make motivational efforts successful? According to Hudy, "management must focus on intrinsic factors—rewards that come directly from performing the task itself—instead of extrinsic factors—rewards that are given for performing a task."[27]

In this model, motivation is reduced if an individual does not value either the intrinsic or the extrinsic outcomes, or if the person perceives that the intrinsic or extrinsic performance-to-outcome expectancies (rewards) are low. For example, a worker's motivation will be reduced if (1) the person does not like doing certain tasks, or (2) the person does not receive the rewards desired for performing them. A manager can increase extrinsic motivation either by depriving a worker of a valued outcome or by giving the worker the extrinsic rewards valued most; the manager can also ensure that rewards accompany task performance. Managers can increase intrinsic motivation by changing the characteristics of work activities, such as by redesigning jobs.

Expectancy theory has dominated research on motivation since the early 1970s, principally because it has provided three factors useful to managers in their efforts to increase employee motivation: expectancy, valence, and instrumentality. Its emphasis on the individual and its ability to highlight individual differences can also be useful to the practicing manager. Expectancy theory, more than any other presented so far, offers a comprehensive guide for understanding motivation.

❖ ❖ MOTIVATION AND THE REWARD SYSTEM

Money is undoubtedly a motivator to many, and fear may well alter behavior; but more long-term motivators, such as a comprehensive and applicable reward system, should be sought. Thus, pay based on performance is one of the best means for motivating people and encouraging increased productivity, but more money is simply a short-term motivator. Nissan USA management agrees that at least a portion of pay should be based on performance, but as may be seen in the situation described below, managers differ in their interpretation of what it takes to motivate employees to be more productive.

The Relationship Between Motivation and Productivity

According to Arlie C. Skory, director of human resource management for Enprotech Mechanical Services Inc., the key motivational factor that affects employee productivity is the correct incentive plan. Henry L. Tebbe, regional director of human resources of the New Orleans Omni Royal Orleans Hotel agrees, but Pat V. Agudow, second vice-president of Cologne Life Reinsurance Company, agrees only to a point. Agudow believes that compensation is important, but that involvement is the real key to motivating people to maximize productivity. Donald Davis, vice-president of human resources for Health Alliance Plan, agrees that employee empowerment is the key to motivating for maximum productivity, and Billy Anderson, manager of employee relations for Florida Power and Light Company, concurs. These human resource professionals may disagree somewhat on the key to motivating for maximum productivity, but it appears evident that all of these individuals believe that there is a relationship between motivation and productivity.[28]

Edward Lawler has concluded that five factors influence the degree of satisfaction gained from rewards. First, satisfaction depends on the amount received and the amount the individual thinks should be received. Typically, the larger the reward, whether extrinsic (such as pay) or intrinsic (such as job challenge), the more satisfied people feel. However, the feeling is moderated somewhat by the perception of whether the reward is justified. Some people feel uneasy if they receive a disproportionately large reward, particularly for the amount of effort they exert or in comparison to the rewards of co-workers whom they perceive as similar.

Second, comparison to what happens to others influences people's feelings of satisfaction. If an employee believes she is being over- or underrewarded in comparison to other employees whom she views as similar to herself, she probably feels less satisfied than if she believes she is being treated equitably.

Third, an employee's satisfaction with both the intrinsic and extrinsic rewards received affects overall job satisfaction.

Fourth, people differ widely in the rewards they desire and in the value they attach to each. For instance, some individuals are willing to trade off flexible working hours for increased compensation. Others choose benefits (sick leave, medical insurance, pension contributions) over salary increases.

Finally, many extrinsic rewards satisfy only because they lead to other rewards. For example, increased pay may satisfy because it results in more recreational opportunities or increased status for an employee.[29]

These observations suggest the need for a diverse reward system. Lawler's observations also suggest that a comprehensive reward system demands a complete analysis of the organization's members and their work situation before rewards are chosen and allocated. They emphasize the nature and consistency of rewards while not ignoring the individual members and their specific needs.

An effective reward system ties rewards to performance. Individuals who work harder, produce more, or produce better-quality outputs should receive greater rewards than poorer performers. Reward systems should also offer a sufficient number and diversity of rewards.

The criteria for the allocation of rewards must be clear and complete. Individual members of the organization should know whether they will receive rewards for level or quality of performance, attendance, innovativeness, or effort, for example. The criteria for achieving specific wages, benefits, and incentives must be clearly defined. But different individuals should be treated differently when appropriate. Workers who perform at different levels or who have different needs often should not receive the same rewards. At the same time, management must ensure that workers perceive the distribution of rewards as equitable. Finally, organizational rewards should compare favorably with rewards in similar organizations. For organizations to attract, motivate, and retain qualified and competent employees, they must offer rewards comparable to those of their competitors.

❖ ❖ LINKING PAY TO PERFORMANCE TO ACHIEVE WORKPLACE DIVERSITY

Many companies today are concerned about getting their workforce to value diversity. They must determine whether or not the managers responsible and accountable for achieving workplace diversity are succeeding in getting the job done. In Chapter 8 the concept of accountability was described as any means of ensuring that the person who is supposed to perform a task actually performs it and does so correctly. Clearly, if a company establishes a goal of achieving diversity, there must be some means of holding managers accountable for achieving these results.

Certain companies such as Colgate-Palmolive are linking pay to the process of achieving cultural diversity in their workplace. Colgate-Palmolive uses its Executive Incentive Compensation Plan to link pay and diversity. In their plan, for managers in operating units, two-thirds of their annual award is based on financial results and one-third is based on four to six individual objectives. One of these individual objectives is focused upon achieving cultural diversity primarily with regard to women, African-Americans, and Hispanics.[30] Achieving

---

Progress Toward Leadership Diversity

Future leaders will probably be less frequently white male and much more often ethnically and culturally diverse. Kenneth Chenault, president of American Express Consumer Card Group, USA and one of the top African-American senior executives in the country believes that "The 21st Century leader must succeed in a world ruled by cultural diversity and collaboration." In the mid-'60s, people of diversity began to join the corporate mainstream, but far too few have broken through the glass ceiling and taken leadership positions. Future leaders must be diverse high performers who have been mentored and welcomed into key leadership roles. According to John Sculley, former CEO of Apple Computer, Inc., "Adults and young people must realize that this is going to be a multicultural society, with equal opportunities for men and women. We must have a society that uses strengths of all people." Reuben Mark, CEO of Colgate-Palmolive Company, believes that to succeed, companies must be "committed to bringing women and minorities into the workforce, and especially in leadership positions." Finally, only 15 percent of incoming workers in the year 2000 will be white males; the balance will be females and minorities. Jerry R. Junkins, CEO of Texas Instruments, believes that "women and minorities are the raw material for future leaders, and therefore we'd better begin right away to prepare them to lead in the next century." Although there are obstacles for members of a diverse workforce to overcome in gaining leadership roles, there appear to be many more opportunities for women and diverse peoples to advance in the future.[31]

workforce diversity where team members put aside prejudices, honor differences, and respect all people regardless of gender, race, or creed is the ideal that will hopefully define the future for employees and leaders.

❖ ❖ HOW MANAGERS CAN BE BETTER AT MOTIVATING

One of the primary objectives of managers is to achieve higher worker productivity. A prime means of accomplishing this task is through creation of a motivated workforce. For a worker to achieve higher productivity, the following three elements must be correctly isolated and combined into a package tailored to motivate each individual worker: specific employee desires, the probability of satisfying these desires, and the time frame for satisfying the desires.[32]

Specific Employee Desires

A worker must have a personal desire for something in order to be motivated. Factors that motivate one person may have no effect on another. One worker may strongly desire additional money, whereas another may want a promotion. Some workers prefer status symbols to money; others hope for praise. It is likely that many of the technicians at Nissan's Smyrna plant are motivated because of the excellent work environment and the bonus plan that is in place.

For some workers, nothing related to the job or the job environment serves to motivate. Work is merely a means to pay the bills and put food on the table—something unpleasant that must be endured. Perhaps the only factor that could possibly increase productivity among these individuals is the fear of being fired.

Understandably, workers want to know: What's in it for me? Managers must first attempt to determine the specific desires of each worker and then, when possible, create an environment in which the worker can satisfy personal needs through increased performance.

Probability of Satisfying Employee Desires

The identification of personal needs is only one factor in increasing productivity. Workers want to know their chances of getting what they want if they produce more. Therefore, employee rewards must be directly tied to the desired result—increased productivity—so workers can connect their efforts with the possible rewards. When technicians at Nissan's Smyrna plant achieve higher productivity levels, they receive bonuses. Although the bonuses are not guaranteed to all members of the workforce, those who are highly productive will receive them. An employee's perception of the manager's past actions significantly influences motivation. Suppose a manager frequently says, "If you don't get moving, I'm going to fire you!" but never does. Workers probably will attach a low probability to the enforcement of his threats. If the manager always follows through on oral statements, workers are likely to respond.

Motivation requires a relatively high likelihood that the worker's needs will be fulfilled—that the offer of money will yield a raise or that the threat of disciplinary action will result in that action. At times, however, the manager may be able to identify a need but have no control over fulfilling it. For example, some managers cannot grant pay raises or promotions themselves but can still use these rewards as motivators if they have a reputation of getting their recommendations approved. Realistically, a manager who cannot satisfy a strong need may not be able to obtain higher productivity.

Time Frame Involved in Satisfying Desires

The closer the reward is to the expenditure of effort, the greater the likelihood that the worker will put forth that effort. And the degree of effort will increase when the reward and the expenditure of effort occur within a limited time frame. The worker who desires more money may be highly motivated if the money is to be received in the next paycheck, but enthusiasm may wane if the possible pay increase is a year away.

How the Factors Are Related

In practice, employee desires, probability, and timing all combine to produce motivation. All three factors must be correctly isolated and combined into a

---

MANAGEMENT IN PRACTICE

A Skill-Building Exercise: Mary Martin was assistant for planning at Diamond Technologies Corporation in Dallas, Texas. She had just completed a report, and she smiled as she handed it to the boss, administrative vice-president Jim Newberg. Mary knew she had done an excellent job on the report and that he would be impressed. "I have all my work caught up," Mary said. "Would you like me to do that budget workup on the new copy machine you mentioned last week?"

"It has to be in by the middle of next week if we're going to get the machine," Jim said with a smile. "Do you think you can do it that fast?"

"Yes, sir," Mary replied. "I may have to work a few extra hours, but it'll be on your desk Tuesday."

Mary had a pleasant feeling as she left Jim's office. Everyone knew that he was being promoted to executive vice-president within a couple of months and that he would select his own replacement. Mary believed she was definitely in the running. Doing a good job on this project might clinch it. As she walked eagerly back to her desk, she thought, "I'd better call Harry and let him know that I'll be working late tonight."

Can Mary be considered a motivated employee? Explain.

package so each worker will be motivated. Incorrectly identifying or misrepresenting any of these three factors could substantially reduce a manager's motivation efforts. The better the manager is at identifying employee desires, the greater the likelihood of inducing increased performance. But identification of a specific desire is not enough; the manager must be able to satisfy that desire or it is useless as a motivator. Then the time frame must be structured so the reward is forthcoming soon after the expenditure of effort. The glue that holds this entire relationship together is the credibility of the manager. The manager's behavior must be related directly to the promises or threats made.

❖ ❖ RESPONDING TO THE NEEDS OF THE DIVERSE WORKFORCE

Several concepts are available to assist managers in coping with the job requirements and personal demands of a diversified workforce. These concepts include flextime, the compressed work week, and job sharing.

Flextime

Flextime is the practice of permitting employees to choose, with certain limitations, their own working hours. In a survey involving companies of all sizes, from all industries, and from every region of the United States and Canada, flextime was being used by 30 percent of the responding firms.[33] In another study, it was found that employers who used flexible time and family-leave polices had, on average, 50 percent less absenteeism than for the workforce as a whole.[34]

In a flextime system, employees work the same number of hours per day as they do on a standard schedule. However, they are permitted to work these hours within what is called a *band width*, which is the maximum length of the workday. That part of the day when all employees must be present is the *core time*. The time period within which employees may vary their schedules is *flexible time*. A typical schedule permits employees to begin work between 6:00 A.M. and 9:00 A.M. and to complete their workday between 3:00 P.M. and 6:00 P.M. Perhaps flextime's most important feature is that it allows employees to schedule their time to minimize conflicts between personal needs and job requirements. Flextime also permits employees to work the hours during which they believe they function best.

Compressed Workweek

A **compressed workweek** is any arrangement of work hours that permits employees to fulfill their work obligation in fewer days than the typical five-day workweek. The most common approach to the compressed workweek has been four

A GLOBAL PERSPECTIVE

Global Motivators Depend on the Makeup of the Global Workforce

In order to create an environment conducive to a high level of employee motivation, global managers must understand some basic philosophies of human nature in the host country. They must have a thorough appreciation of the characteristics of the workforce and of any cultural or social elements that could affect motivation. Multinational managers must encourage the development of subordinates in ways that contribute to their performance, career development, and personal satisfaction. They must also realize that motivating employees globally is a complex job. Individuals in different countries are often motivated differently, and managers must realize the various differences. At the American NUMMI automobile plant, team members are motivated by a formal agreement between management and employees that assures the workers that if the team concept works and productivity increases, no one will lose a job.[35] Similar motivators exist at GM's Saturn plant, where the overwhelming motivation for these employees is job security.

Motivational factors in other countries may vary from those in the United States. In Sweden, the labor force is highly educated and well trained, but people do not like to work in factories, so Swedish automaker Volvo has built more pleasant factories and allows teams to largely manage themselves as a means of keeping workers on the job and productive.[36] In Japan, quality of life and salaries are quite important, and therefore motivating Japanese workers requires higher-order motivators. Eastern Europeans are in need of everything, much of which is taken for granted in most industrialized countries. These individuals will in all likelihood be motivated by money for quite sometime. Basically, as incomes rise, the motivators that are needed to enhance productivity are of a higher order, such as factors that impact self-esteem and self-actualization needs.[37] Basically, motivating in the global environment requires that managers develop a system that will cause employees to want to put forth effort in the pursuit of organizational objectives.

ten-hour days. Working under this arrangement, some employees have reported an increase in job satisfaction. In addition, the compressed workweek offers them the potential for better use of leisure time for family life, personal business, and recreation. Some employers have cited advantages such as increased productivity and reduced turnover and absenteeism.

On the other hand, problems have been encountered in the areas of work scheduling and employee fatigue. In some cases, these problems have resulted in lower-quality products and reduced customer service. Some firms have therefore reverted to the conventional five-day week. It seems clear that overall, acceptance of the compressed workweek is not as clear-cut as acceptance of flextime.

Job Sharing

A relatively new approach to work—job sharing—is attractive to people who wish to work fewer than 40 hours per week. **Job sharing** is two part-time people splitting the duties of one job in some agreed-on manner and being paid according to their contributions. From the employer's viewpoint, compensation is paid for only one job, but creativity is obtained from two employees. Job sharing may be especially attractive to individuals who have substantial family responsibilities and to older workers who wish to move gradually into retirement.

❖ ❖ HOW FIRST-LEVEL MANAGERS CAN DISPENSE REWARDS

It has already been said that different individuals are motivated by different things. The effective first-level manager attempts to satisfy needs in order to increase productivity. Some of the rewards the manager might control are

- Formal recognition, such as letters of appreciation.
- Invitations to coffee or lunch.
- Recommendations for pay increases and promotions.
- Time off.
- Desirable work assignments.

✘ Management Tips ✘

Guidelines for Dealing with Motivation

1. **Do not assume that everyone is motivated by the same thing.** Just because you are "turned on" by the prospect of getting extra money does not mean that all workers will be.
2. **Know that workers are individuals.** A worker's background, experience, goals, and aspirations provide some indication of his or her needs.
3. **Do not mistake high morale for motivation.** People can be happy and cheerful and still not be motivated to increase work productivity.
4. **Develop predictability in the workplace.** Make sure workers know the connection between performance and reward.
5. **Let the rewards and penalties be applied as soon as possible after they are earned.** The further away the rewards or penalties are from behavior, the more difficult it is to use them as motivators.
6. **Reinforce desired behavior.** Reward workers for doing what you want them to do.
7. **Do not issue idle threats.** Your actions speak louder than words.
8. **Make the work interesting.** Dull jobs are not likely to motivate workers.
9. **Listen to workers.** Very often they will tell you what motivates them.
10. **Realize that different individuals are motivated by different things.** The effective manager attempts to satisfy actual needs in order to increase productivity.

Perseguimiento
Acosamiento
seguimiento
disposicion

SUMMARY

Motivation is the willingness to put forth effort in the pursuit of organizational objectives. To create an environment conducive to a high level of motivation, managers must understand some philosophies of human nature, such as McGregor's Theory X and Theory Y, Argyris's maturity theory, and the self-fulfilling prophecy.

Four popular needs theories are (1) Maslow's hierarchy of needs theory, (2) Herzberg's motivator-hygiene (two-factor) theory, (3) Alderfer's ERG theory, and (4) McClelland's needs theory. Maslow stated that individuals have a hierarchy of five needs, from the most basic level of physiological needs to the highest level of self-actualization needs. Herzberg suggests that motivators—features of a job's content, such as responsibility—satisfy higher-order needs, motivate a person to exert more effort, and encourage better performance. Hygiene factors, which meet physiological, security, or social needs, satisfy lower-order needs and prevent dissatisfaction. Alderfer reorganized Maslow's needs hierarchy into three needs levels: (1) existence, (2) relatedness, and (3) growth. McClelland focused on needs similar to the higher-order needs identified by Maslow—needs for achievement, affiliation, and power.

Equity theory suggests that people assess their performance and attitudes by comparing their contribution to work and the benefits they derive from it to those of "comparison others." In reinforcement theory, human behavior is explained in terms of the previous positive or negative outcomes of that behavior. Vroom's expectancy theory states that motivation is a function of expectancy, valence, and instrumentality.

KEY TERMS

Motivation 308	Expectancy theory 327
Theory X 309	Extrinsic motivation 328
Theory Y 309	Intrinsic motivation 328
Self-fulfilling prophecy 313	Flextime 334
Equity theory 323	Compressed workweek 334
Reinforcement theory 325	Job sharing 335
Organizational behavior modification 325	

REVIEW QUESTIONS

1. Define <u>motivation</u>.
2. Compare and contrast McGregor's Theory X and Theory Y. What are some examples of managerial practices that are consistent with a Theory Y philosophy of human nature?
3. What is Argyris's maturity theory?
4. Relate Herzberg's theory of motivation to the needs theory developed by Maslow.
5. Describe McClelland's theory of human motives. How does it relate to motivation, and what are the basic characteristics of individuals described by the theory?
6. Define <u>equity theory</u> and describe it as it relates to motivation.
7. Briefly describe reinforcement theory.
8. What is expectancy theory?
9. How can linking pay to performance help achieve workplace diversity?
10. What are the factors that Edward Lawler has concluded influence satisfaction with a reward?
11. Explain how managers can be better at motivating.
12. Define the following terms:
    a. flextime
    b. compressed workweek
    c. job sharing

Money is undoubtedly a motivator to many, and fear may well alter behavior; but more long-term motivators, such as a comprehensive and applicable reward system, should be sought. Pay based on performance is one of the best means for motivating people and encouraging increased productivity.

Many companies today are concerned about getting their workforce to value diversity. They confront the problem of actually determining whether or not their efforts are succeeding and whether managers who are responsible for achieving workplace diversity are also to be held accountable for getting the job done. Clearly, if a company establishes a goal of achieving diversity, there must be some means of holding managers accountable for achieving these results.

One of the primary objectives of managers is to achieve higher worker productivity. A prime means of accomplishing this task is through creation of a motivated workforce. For a worker to achieve higher productivity, three elements must be correctly isolated and combined into a package tailored to motivate each individual worker. These three elements include specific employee desires, the probability of satisfying these desires, and the time frame for satisfying the desires.

Several concepts are available to assist managers in coping with the job requirements and personal demands of a diverse workforce. The practice of permitting employees to choose, with certain limitations, their own working hours is flextime. Any arrangement of work hours that permits employees to fulfill their work obligation in fewer days than the typical five-day workweek is the compressed workweek. In job sharing, two part-time people split the duties of one job in some agreed-on manner and are paid according to their contributions.

Lower-level managers may be able to recommend only certain rewards, such as pay and promotion. But these rewards can still be motivators, particularly for managers who have a reputation for getting their recommendations approved.

CASE STUDIES

CASE 10.1: A Citation for Kathy

Bob Rosen could hardly wait to get back to work Monday morning. He was excited about his chance to get a large bonus. Bob was a machine operator with Ram Manufacturing Company, a Wichita, Kansas, maker of electric motors. He operated an armature-winding machine. The machine wound copper wire onto metal cores to make the rotating elements for electric motors.

Ram paid machine operators on a graduated piece-rate basis; operators got a certain amount for each part made, plus a bonus for producing above standard. A worker who produced ten percent above standard for a certain month received a ten percent bonus. For 20 percent above standard, the bonus was 20 percent. Bob realized that he had a good chance of earning a 20 percent bonus that month. That would be $287.

Bob had a special use for the extra money. His wife's birthday was just three weeks away. He was hoping to get her a new Chevrolet. He had already saved $450, but the down payment on the Chevrolet was $700. The bonus would enable him to buy the car.

Bob arrived at work at seven o'clock that morning, although his shift did not begin until eight. He went to his work station and checked the supply of blank cores and copper wire. Finding that only one spool of wire was on hand, he asked the fork truck driver to bring another. Then he asked the operator who was working the graveyard shift, "Sam, do you mind if I grease the machine while you work?"

"No," Sam said, "that won't bother me a bit."

After greasing the machine, Bob stood and watched

Sam. He thought of ways to simplify the motions involved in loading, winding, and unloading the armatures. As Bob took over the machine after the eight o'clock whistle, he thought, "I hope I can pull this off. I know the car will make Kathy happy. She won't be stuck at home while I'm at work."

QUESTIONS

1. What are the advantages and disadvantages of a graduated piece-rate pay system such as that at Ram?
2. Explain Bob's high level of motivation in terms of needs theory, reinforcement theory, and expectancy theory.

CASE 10.2 Domino's Dominoids: Motivated to Serve

As the decade of the 1990s began, Domino's Pizza was the world's largest pizza chain. Domino's main strategy: "fast service." Delivery was guaranteed in 30 minutes, but it averaged only 23 minutes. Drivers were motivated by getting to keep their tips and being paid so much for each delivery. Young restaurant workers sometimes jumped at the chance to deliver. But motivated driving has its downside. In 1989, Domino's admitted that primarily its younger drivers had been involved in 20 fatal accidents within the year. To rectify this situation, the company agreed to terminate or reassign drivers who were under 18.

Tom Monaghan, the former chief executive of privately owned Domino's, called his employees "Dominoids" and insisted they focus on customer satisfaction. "Mystery customers," 10,000 of them, were paid to sample pizzas throughout the year and report on service and quality; store managers' pay was adjusted based on the results. Each restaurant rated the service and ingredient quality provided by distribution employees, whose pay was determined in part by these scores. The district offices evaluated the headquarters staff. Mrs. Monaghan, who was payroll chief, considered those ratings in setting monthly bonus amounts for home office employees. It is fairly obvious that Monaghan viewed money as an extrinsic motivator that would enhance customer service and keep Domino's the world's largest pizza chain.

Seventy percent of Domino's 5,000 units were owned by franchisees, entrepreneurs who adopted the standardized system and paid the franchisor part of their income. Domino's clay-animated "Noid" figure became popular through the company's ads, and 3,000,000 units of Noid merchandise were sold in two years. Overall, Monaghan said, his franchisees were "happy." Many of them had also gotten rich.

However, competitors were creeping up on Domino's fast delivery times. Monaghan welcomed the challenge, especially from industry giant Pizza Hut. But his viewpoint changed quickly. The new national ad campaign said "Nobody delivers better." Shortly after the new ads began running, Monaghan announced he wanted to deliver Domino's itself into new hands. But within two years, Monaghan was back. Currently, Domino's sales are up, and Domino's share of the delivery market is still the largest.

QUESTIONS

1. Using the section in your text entitled "How Managers Can Be Better at Motivating," relate the text to motivation at Domino's.
2. Given the environment existing at Domino's, does the company have a motivated workforce?

NOTES

1. This article is a composite from a number of published accounts, among them: Gregory A. Patterson, "Labor Showdown: The UAW's Chances at Japanese Plants Hinge on Nissan Vote," *The Wall Street Journal* (July 25, 1989): A1, A8; "Nissan Workers Reject UAW Representation," Associated Press Newswire, Smyrna, Tennessee, July 27, 1989; Louis Kraar, "Japan's Gung-Ho U.S. Car Plants," *Fortune* 124 (January 30, 1989): 98–108; Karen L. Miller, Larry Armstrong, and James B. Treece, "Will Nissan Get It Right This Time?" *Business Week* (April 20, 1992): 82–86; Larry Armstrong, "Altima's Secret: The Right Kind of Sticker Shock," *Business Week* (January 18, 1993): 37; Jacqueline Mitchell, "Nissan's Metamorphosis from Stodgy to Stylish Works Magic on Car Buyers," *The Wall Street Journal* (August 2, 1993): B1 and B3.

2. Gary Slutsker, "The Company that Likes to Obsolete Itself," *Forbes* 152 (September 13, 1993): 139–144.

3. Mark Maremont and Elizabeth Lesly, "Getting the Picture," *Business Week* (February 1, 1993): 24–26.

4. Douglas McGregor, *The Human Side of Enterprise* (New York: McGraw-Hill, 1960) pp. 15–60.

5. Jaclyn Fierman, "Beating the Midlife Career Crisis," *Fortune* 128 (September 6, 1993): 52–62.

6. Chris Argyris, *Personality and Organization* (New York: Harper & Row, 1957) pp. 31–42.

7. John L. Single, "The Power of Expectations: Productivity and the Self-Fulfilling Prophecy," *Management World* 9 (November, 1980): 19, 37–38.

8. *Ibid.*

9. Abraham Maslow, *The Human Side of Enterprise* (New York: Harper, 1954) pp. 16–23.

10. Clayton P. Alderfer, "A Critique of Salancik and Pfeffer's Examination of Need-Satisfaction Theories," *Administrative Science Quarterly* 22 (December 1977): 658–672.

11. Frederick Herzberg, *Work and the Nature of Man* (Cleveland: World, 1966) pp. 91–106.

12. Clayton P. Alderfer, *Existence, Relatedness, and Growth: Human Needs in Organizational Settings* (New York: Free Press, 1972) pp. 29–51.

13. S. M. Klein and R. R. Ritti, *Understanding Organizational Behavior* (Boston: Kent Publishing, 1984) p. 257.

14. David C. McClelland and David H. Burnham, "Power Is the Great Motivator," *Harvard Business Review* 54 (March-April 1976): 103.

15. David R. Hampton, Charles E. Summer, and Ross A. Webber, *Organizational Behavior and the Practice of Management* (Glenview, IL.: Scott, Foresman, 1978) pp. 11–15.

16. M. J. Stahl, "Achievement Power and Managerial Motivation: Selecting Managerial Talent with the Job Choice Exercise," *Personnel Psychology* 36 (Winter 1983): 786.

17. J. S. Adams, "Toward an Understanding of Inequity," *Journal of Abnormal and Social Psychology* 67 (November 1963): 422–436.

18. J. S. Adams, "Inequity in Social Exchange," *Advances in Experimental Social Psychology,* ed. Leonard Berkowitz (Washington, D.C.: Academic Press, 1965) pp. 267–300.

19. Business Week (March 10, 1986): 67; *Manufacturing Systems* (March 1988): 18–20 and *Automation* (March 1988): 24–26.

20. B. F. Skinner, *Beyond Freedom and Dignity* (New York: Knopf, 1971) pp. 60–100.

21. Adrian Harrell and Michael Stahl, "Additive Information Processing and the Relationship Between Expectancy of Success and Motivational Force," *Academy of Management Journal* 29 (June 1986): 424–425.

22. Victor Vroom, *Work and Motivation* (New York: Wiley, 1964): 38–62.

23. *Ibid.*

24. B. M. Staw, *Intrinsic and Extrinsic Motivation,* (Morristown, N.J.: General Learning Press, 1976) pp. 13–29.

25. See S. Koch, "Behavior as 'Intrinsically' Regulated: Work Notes Towards a Pretheory of Phenomena Called Motivation," in M. R. Jones, ed., *Nebraska Symposium on Motivation* (Lincoln: University of Nebraska Press, 1956) pp. 68–81.

26. K. C. Montgomery, "The Role of the Exploratory Drive in Learning," *Journal of Comparative Physiological Psychology* 47 (February 1954): 60–64.

27. John J. Hudy, "The Motivation Trap," *HRMagazine* 37 (December 1992): 63–67.

28. Carrie A. Miles and Jean M. McCloskey, "People: The Key to Productivity," *HRMagazine* 38 (February 1993): 40–45.

29. E. E. Lawler, III, "Reward Systems," in J. R. Hackman and J. L. Suttle, eds., *Improving Life at Work* (Santa Monica, CA: Goodyear, 1977).

30. Stephenie Overman, "A Measure of Success," *HR-Magazine* 37 (December 1992): 38.

31. Lynne Joy McFarland, Larry E. Senn, and John R. Childress, *21st Century Leadership* (New York: The Leadership Press, 1993) pp. 227–232.

32. Portions of this section were adapted from R. Wayne Mondy, Shane R. Premeaux, and Arthur Sharplin, "Motivation in Practice," *Manage* 39 (Second Quarter, 1986): 13, 22–23.

33. Joseph E. McKendrick, Jr., "Stretching Time in '89," *Management World* 18 (July–August 1989): 10.

34. Michele Galen, Ann Therese Palmer, Alice Cuneo, and Mark Maremont, "Work & Family," *Business Week* (June 28, 1993): 82.

35. Dean Foust, "A Tough Look at General Motors," *Business Week* (September 18, 1989): 17.

36. Jonathan Kapstein and John Hoerr, "Volvo's Radical New Plant: 'The Death of the Assembly Line?'" *Business Week* (August 28, 1989): 92–93.

37. Bill Saporito, "Where the Global Action Is," *Fortune* 128 (Autumn/Winter 1993): 63–65.

11 Leadership

LEARNING OBJECTIVES

After completing this chapter students should be able to

✘ Define *leadership*.

✘ Describe the trait approach to the study of leadership.

✘ Identify and describe the major behavioral leadership theories.

✘ Describe the major situational leadership theories and the concepts involved in leading a diverse workforce.

✘ Explain leadership and the team approach and the importance of leading through example.

IBM'S New Leader Louis V. Gerstner Rethinks IBM

IBM has had one extraordinary leader after another for nearly 80 years. Founder Thomas J. Watson turned the reins over to his son, Thomas, Jr., who was followed by T. Vincent Learson, Frank Cary, John Opel, and then John Akers. More than any other factor, the leadership of these men is credited with keeping IBM number one in the computer business. Then came the era of change in the computer industry, and with it came a new type of leader, CEO Louis V. Gerstner. Thomas Watson, Jr., became chief executive of IBM in 1955. Watson described himself as "perhaps innovative, certainly highly motivated, and not cautious at all." In his time, Thomas Watson, Jr., was exactly what IBM needed to become the strong giant it is now, but in the decade of the nineties, a different type leader is needed, possibly a leader like Louis V. Gerstner.

When Gerstner took over as CEO of IBM, he had his work cut out for him. He set about changing IBM's three major weaknesses: "towering cost, a preoccupation with internal processes, and slowness." IBM had lost money for the past three quarters, and to turn things around Gerstner had to convince 250,000 employees in 140 countries to change the way they think and act. Many experts agree that this is the "toughest leadership job in Corporate America."

Gerstner is a hands-on leader who personally talks to customers about helping them run their businesses better. When he needs to see someone he walks the halls of IBM headquarters and finds them, which is far removed from summoning employees to the corner executive office. Gerstner is personally determined to lead IBM into a new era where "bureaucracy (does not) run amok."

Gerstner altered the basic corporate culture of IBM, focusing on "expectations of performance, not (bureaucratic) rules of behavior." He also mandated that the focus is always on solving consumer problems, coordinating IBM's technological advancements, cutting cost to the tune of 35,000 additional layoffs, and trimming $1.75 billion in overhead costs. He brought in two outsiders, Jerome York as CFO and Gerald Czarnecki as vice-president for human resources and administration, and then created a new management structure designed to give each division more input into the companywide decision-making process. Finally, he set up a compensation system that rewards top management for companywide performance rather than the performance of their individual units. Under Gerstner's leadership, everyone in the company was productive or they were gone. He leads by example, making tough decisions, putting in six and one-half day weeks, working 16 to 18 hour days. He was so sure of his leadership ability that he spent $772,250 on 17,500 shares of stock. The leadership legacy at IBM, especially prior to Akers, is virtually unmatched by any other corporation, but can IBM magic be regained?[1]

What does it take to be a good leader? And what is the most effective leadership style? These questions have perplexed and challenged managers for generations. Literally thousands of research studies have focused on them. But the research has not identified any set of traits or qualities that are consistently related to effective leadership. The main conclusion that can be drawn from this is that there is no single most effective leadership style.

We do know that effective leadership is essential to the survival and growth of every organization. Despite high salaries and excellent opportunities in large corporations, there continues to be a shortage of competent managers. The shortage is not confined to business but also exists in government, churches, schools, and all other types of organizations. The problem is not a lack of people who would like to be leaders or managers but rather a scarcity of people who have developed the ability to lead effectively.

The primary challenge of leadership and management is to guide an organization toward the accomplishment of objectives. The leader does so by influencing and encouraging employees to attain high levels of performance within the limitations of available resources, skills, and technology. Although IBM has immense resources, skills, and technology, can they be led to their former greatness? Although we do not have all the answers, a more complete understanding of the skills, attitudes, and values related to effective leadership should greatly improve our ability to select, train, and develop effective managers.

In this chapter, we first define *leadership* and distinguish it from the related term *management*. Then we discuss three perspectives that have been used to develop leadership theories: (1) trait, (2) behavioral, and (3) situational perspectives. Next, we address the difficult question of how managers lead a diverse workforce, and we explain leadership and the team approach. We end the chapter with a discussion of leading through example and provide a global perspective of leadership.

❖ ❖ LEADERSHIP DEFINED

Leadership, or **leading,** involves influencing others to do what the leader wants them to do. It is only one of the many things that a manager does. Highly regarded companies often have a history of excellent leadership. For example, for 75 years, IBM has had one extraordinary leader after another. More than any other factor, this leadership is credited with keeping IBM a force in the computer business. Currently, Louis Gerstner is the individual leading IBM into the future. Thanks to the current rage for outsiders, top executives, who are effective leaders, are more and more willing to jump from company to company. "This is not unlike star players switching teams," says Jeffrey Heilpern of Delta Consulting Group Inc. "We're starting to have the equivalent of a free-agency system [for leaders]. People are realizing that their [leadership] capabilities are portable."[2]

In Chapter 1, we defined *management* as the process of getting things done through the efforts of other people. Obviously, this definition overlaps with that of *leadership*. Managers get all sorts of things done through the efforts of other people, so they must lead. The main distinction between the two terms is one of focus. *Leadership* focuses on human interactions—influencing others. According to Judy B. Rosener, author of "The Ways Women Lead," women and men use very different leadership styles, and women lead "behaving like women." Her study of 456 successful female executives revealed that men generally prefer a "command and control" style in dealing with subordinates—relying on orders, appeals to self-interest, rational decision making, and rewards. On the other hand, women prefer to work "interactively," sharing power and information, motivating by appeals to organizational goals, and promoting empowerment.[3] *Management* is more concerned with procedure and results—the process of getting things done.

Autocratic leadership is not recommended where building long-term relationships is important to success. (Source: © Spencer Grant 1993/FPG International)

Also, *management* suggests more formality. *Manager* often refers to a position in an organization. On the other hand, a leader may have no formal title at all, and may rely on personal traits and style to influence followers. These shades of meaning will grow clearer as we discuss leadership style.

Four basic leadership styles have been identified: autocratic, participative, democratic, and laissez-faire (see Table 11.1). An **autocratic leader** tells subordinates what to do and expects to be obeyed without question. This style is typical of a person who accepts McGregor's Theory X assumptions, described in Chapter 10. Research suggests that autocratic leadership is most effective where the task is simple and fairly repetitive and where the leader has only short-term relationships with subordinates. For example, some construction managers hire a new crew of laborers for each project and treat them autocratically. But this approach begins to break down as the task becomes more involved and requires more talented and experienced employees. And it fails where building long-term relationships is important to success.

A **participative leader** involves subordinates in decision making but may retain the final authority. Prior to his death in 1992 Sam Walton, the flamboyant founder of Wal-Mart stores, established a management team that keeps employees closely informed about company plans and practices, and he included employees in corporate decision making. Walton prided himself on being a participative leader.

A **democratic leader** tries to do what the majority of subordinates desire. Participative and democratic leaders tend to be those who make Theory Y assumptions. Democratic leaders are becoming more and more important as the use of the team approach to management increases.

Russell A. Nagel, general manager of Westinghouse Furniture Systems, evidently is a democratic leader. He has supported the existence of an elaborate system of committees and ad hoc task forces to discuss issues ranging from business strategy to the constant redesign of work areas for product innovation. This high degree of worker participation has been accompanied by a 74 percent increase in productivity.[4]

TABLE 11.1　Leadership Styles and Their Relation to Types of Workers

AUTOCRATIC STYLE	PARTICIPATIVE STYLE	DEMOCRATIC STYLE	LAISSEZ-FAIRE STYLE
Leader tells workers what to do.	Leader allows and expects worker participation.	Leader seeks majority rule from workers.	Leader lets group members make all decisions.
McGregor's Theory X workers	McGregor's Theory Y workers		Expert-specialist workers

The **laissez-faire leader** is uninvolved in the work of the unit. It is difficult to defend this leadership style unless the leader's subordinates are expert and well-motivated specialists, such as scientists. In fact, practically every leader who has attained recognition for effectiveness—from Mahatma Gandhi in India to John Akers at IBM—has done so by being deeply involved and active.

With this understanding of the definition of leadership and the four basic leadership styles, let us now turn to the trait, behavioral, and situational theories of leadership.

❖ ❖ THE TRAIT APPROACH TO LEADERSHIP

The leader has always occupied a central role in management theory. Most of the early research on leadership attempted to either compare the traits of people who became leaders with those who did not or identify characteristics and traits possessed by effective leaders. The **trait approach to leadership** is the evaluation and selection of leaders on the basis of their physical, mental, social, and psychological characteristics. Research studies comparing the traits of leaders and nonleaders have found that leaders tend to be somewhat taller, more outgoing, more self-confident, and more intelligent than nonleaders. Even within an organization, leaders often have far different traits, depending in part on the type of work they supervise. But a specific combination of traits that can differentiate leaders

---

MANAGEMENT IN PRACTICE

A Skill-Building Exercise: Marian Lillie, general project manager at Prodyne Corporation's Los Alamos, New Mexico, plant, was studying progress reports when she heard a tap at her door. "Got a minute, Marian?" asked Scotty Needham, a project director.

"Sure, come on in," said Marian. "What've you got?"

"You know that new manager the boss sent over, Brit Salvo?"

"Yes," answered Marian. "I approved hiring him."

"Well," Scotty continued, "you know he's a retired military officer. Wanted to start a second career. I thought it was a good idea, because we have that tank fire control project.

But Brit sure is creating problems."

"What kind of problems?" asked Marian.

Scotty was obviously trying hard to stay calm. He spoke slowly. "I put him on the team with Chuck Talley. But Chuck claims Brit acts like he's the team leader, and Chuck is. I talked to Brit about it, but he bristled and said something about working with a bunch of wimps. I told him two of the team members are Ph.D.'s. I remember his exact words: 'Any organization needs strong leadership, no matter who's in it.' I didn't know what to say, so I just ended the conversation."

How would you respond if you were Marian?

Democratic leaders are becoming more and more important as the use of the team approach to management increases. Nowhere is this more prevalent than in the computer industry. In this photograph, a research team at Atari Corporation discusses new software developments. (Source: Photograph courtesy of Atari Corporation.)

or potential leaders from followers has not been found. Clearly, it is difficult to identify a leader from an initial impression. Still, some leaders seem to be readily identifiable even at a young age. Eminent national consultant Frederick W. Gluck was described by a close longtime personal friend as "one little kid who was obviously running the whole show."[5]

Aggressiveness, ambition, decisiveness, dominance, initiative, intelligence, physical characteristics (looks, height, and weight), self-assurance, and other factors have been studied to determine if they were related to effective leadership. The major question is: Could traits differentiate effective from ineffective leaders? Perhaps the underlying assumption of some trait research has been that leaders are born, not made. Some people still believe there are certain inborn or acquired traits that make a person a good leader. Clearly, physical traits have not been shown to distinguish effective from ineffective leaders.[6]

The trait approach to the study of leadership is not dead, however. Edwin Ghiselli has tried to identify personality and motivational traits related to effective leadership. Ghiselli has identified 13 traits, the six most significant of which are as follows:

1. *Supervisory ability*—the performance of the basic functions of management, including planning, organizing, influencing, and controlling the work of others.
2. *Need for occupational achievement*—the seeking of responsibility and the desire for success.
3. *Intelligence*—creative and verbal ability, including judgment, reasoning, and thinking capacity.
4. *Decisiveness*—the ability to make decisions and solve problems capably and competently.
5. *Self-assurance*—the extent to which the individual views himself or herself as capable of coping with problems.

6. *Initiative*—the ability to act independently and to develop courses of action not readily apparent to other people; to self-start and find new, innovative ways of doing things.[7]

Most of the "traits" Ghiselli has defined are subsets of a broader trait we might call "leadership ability" and are, of course, related to it. For example, supervisory ability, intelligence, and decisiveness surely make one a better leader.

In this same vein, though with the use of the word *trait*, Warren Bennis offers the following "protocol" for effective leadership:

1. Leaders must develop the vision and strength to call the shots.
2. Leaders must be conceptualists (not just tinkering with the nuts and bolts).
3. Leaders must have a sense of continuity and significance in order to see the present in the past and the future in the present.
4. Leaders must get their heads above the grass and risk the possibility of getting hit by a rock.
5. Leaders must get at the truth and learn how to filter the unwieldy flow of information into coherent patterns.
6. Leaders must be social architects who study and shape what is called "the culture of work."
7. To lead others, leaders must first know themselves.[8]

Individuals can cultivate these qualities as the basis for building leadership effectiveness. And, of course, people differ from birth in their capacity for learning, including learning related to leading. Still, there are few shortcomings that cannot be overcome through effort—and there are few strengths that cannot be frittered away or misdirected.

A recent revival of trait theory emphasizes the importance of charisma. Robert House has proposed a "theory of charismatic leadership" that suggests great leaders employ four personal characteristics—dominance, self-confidence, a need for influence, and conviction of moral righteousness—to increase their effectiveness. The terms House has used imply that leaders with these traits are more charismatic than others.[9]

Leadership is never more vital than during periods of sweeping organizational change, such as turnarounds and Chapter 11 bankruptcy reorganizations. A person who has the special ability to lead an organization through major strategic change is a **transformational leader**. Such a leader can modify the mission, structure, and human resource management system and continue to guide the organization toward its objectives. Often marked by charisma, this type of leader must inspire followers. Followers are told how essential their performance is, how confident the leader is in them, how exceptional they are, and how the leader expects their group's performance to break records.[10]

Lee Iacocca, former chairman of Chrysler Corporation, assumed a transformational leadership role when he took over Chrysler and brought it back from the brink of financial ruin in the early 1980s. He shared his vision of success with employees—and, through television advertisements in which he starred, with America at large. He was able to mobilize thousands of workers to enact their respective visions, which resulted in record profits and high levels of employee morale and productivity.[11] Recall the discussion of motivation in Chapter 10. It was noted there that individuals work to satisfy certain needs and to achieve desired outcomes. A manager who is a transformational leader often motivates subordinates to do better than they expected—in three ways. The leader (1) raises employee consciousness about the importance of certain outcomes, such as high productivity or efficiency; (2) shows the value of concentrating on team success rather than on individual interests; and (3) rearranges the workers' need structure to increase the value given to challenges, responsibility, and growth.[12]

Many leaders find it useful to assume a developmental role in relation to subordinates. According to behaviorist Judith Gordon, such a role involves elevating employee potential, setting examples, assigning tasks on an individual basis, increasing subordinate responsibilities, delegating challenging work, serving as a role model, keeping subordinates informed, providing intellectual stimulation, seeking ways of acting, and being proactive (acting in anticipation of change).[13]

The trait approach leaves many unanswered questions about what is required for effective leadership. A major limitation of trait theory is that traits associated with leadership success in one situation may not relate to achievement in another.[14] This has led to a continuing search for an appropriate leadership style.

❖ ❖ BEHAVIORAL LEADERSHIP THEORIES

Dissatisfaction with the trait approach led most leadership researchers to focus on how leaders should behave rather than on traits or characteristics they might possess. In general, the behavioral theories discussed in this section provide greater insight into appropriate leadership principles than does trait theory.

Ohio State Leadership Studies

Beginning in 1945, researchers in the Bureau of Business Research at Ohio State University made a series of in-depth studies of the behavior of leaders in a wide variety of organizations. The key concern of the Ohio State leadership studies was the leader's behavior in directing the efforts of others toward group objectives. After a considerable number of studies had been completed, two important dimensions of leader behavior were identified: initiating structure and consideration. **Initiating structure** is the extent to which leaders establish objectives and structure their roles and the roles of subordinates toward the attainment of the objectives. **Consideration** is the extent to which leaders' relationships with subordinates are characterized by mutual trust and respect for employees' ideas and feelings. H. Ross Perot has great consideration for his employees' ideas and feelings, as well as for their physical welfare. He once even put together a commando team and sent them across the Turkish-Iranian border to rescue two of his employees who had been trapped by political turmoil in Iran.[15]

Initiating structure and consideration are separate and distinct dimensions of leadership behavior. Figure 11.1 illustrates four leadership styles representing different combinations of the two dimensions. A manager can be high in both consideration and initiating structure, low in both, or high in one and low in the other. The Ohio State researchers did not suggest a single most effective combination of initiating structure and consideration. Rather, they found that the right combination depended on the demands of the situation.

University of Michigan Studies

Rensis Likert and his colleagues at the University of Michigan Institute for Social Research were conducting leadership studies at about the same time as the Ohio State research. The Michigan researchers chose two leadership orientations as the

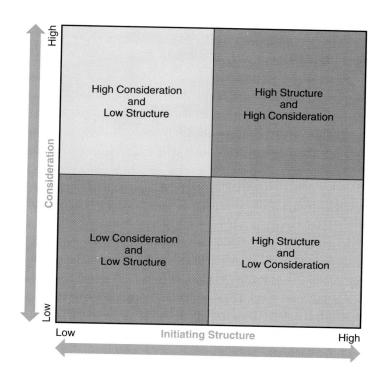

❖ **Figure 11.1**
Ohio State leadership model

focal point for their experiments: the employee orientation and the production orientation. These orientations are similar to the dimensions used at Ohio State. The results were also similar.[16] Productivity differences among work groups were checked against differences in supervisor behavior. It was found that supervisors of highly productive groups spent more time planning departmental work and supervising employees and spent less time working alongside subordinates and performing the same task. They also tended to be employee oriented.[17]

Leadership Grid® (Formerly the Managerial Grid)

One of the most widely known leadership theories is that based on the Managerial Grid.[18] The **Managerial Grid**—or as it is labeled in its latest form, the Leadership Grid (Blake & McCanse, 1991)—is the three-dimensional matrix developed by Robert Blake and Jane Mouton that shows concern for people on the vertical axis, concern for production on the horizontal axis, and underlying motivations on the third axis. Seven leadership styles are noted that represent varying degrees of concern for people and production:

- 1,1 *Impoverished management*. The manager has little concern for either people or production.
- 9,1 *Authority-compliance*. The manager stresses operating efficiently through controls in situations where human elements cannot interfere.
- 1,9 *Country club management*. The manager is thoughtful, comfortable, and friendly, and has little concern for output.
- 5,5 *Middle of the road management*. The manager attempts to balance and trade off concern for work in exchange for a satisfactory level of morale—a compromiser.
- 9+9 *Paternalist "father knows best" management*. This manager promises reward for compliance and punishment for noncompliance.
- Opp *Opportunistic "what's in it for me" management*. This manager uses the style that the leader feels will return him or her the greatest self-benefit.
- 9,9 *Team management*. The manager seeks high output through committed people, achieved through mutual trust, respect, and a realization of interdependence.[19]

According to Blake and Mouton, the first six styles listed are not the most effective. The Managerial Grid is illustrated in Figure 11.2. They suggest the 9,9 team management style, maximum concern for both output and people, is the most effective style. Blake and McCanse say their studies prove this approach will result in improved performance, lower employee turnover and absenteeism, and greater employee satisfaction. Grid organizational development technology is used to strengthen organizational effectiveness. The Managerial Grid concept has

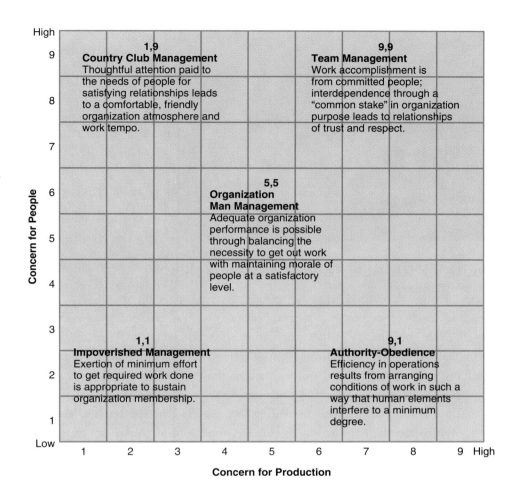

been introduced to thousands of practicing managers since its development in the early 1960s. Blake and McCanse and their adherents have conducted grid training seminars around the world.

Now let us turn from the Grid, which promotes one leadership style, to a group of theories that assume there is no single best way to lead.

SITUATIONAL LEADERSHIP THEORIES

Situational, or contingency, leadership theories start out with the assumption that appropriate behavior depends on the circumstances at a given time. The more prominent of these theories are House's path-goal theory, Tannenbaum and Schmidt's leadership continuum, Fiedler's contingency leadership theory, Vroom and Yetton's normative theory, and Hersey and Blanchard's situational leadership theory.

A supportive manager is friendly with employees and shows interest in them. Young workers, like the women in this photograph, need support from their superiors. But we never outgrow the need for supportive leadership. (Source: © Jim Pickerell)

House's Path-Goal Theory of Leadership

Robert House developed what he termed the path-goal theory of leadership,[20] which is closely related to the expectancy theory of motivation discussed in Chapter 10. **Path-goal theory** is the proposition that managers can facilitate job performance by showing employees how their performance directly affects their receiving desired rewards. In other words, a manager's behavior causes or contributes to employee satisfaction and acceptance of the manager if it increases goal attainment by employees. According to the path-goal approach, effective job performance results if the manager clearly defines the job, provides training for the employee, assists the employee in performing the job effectively, and rewards the employee for effective performance.

Leadership style facilitates accomplishing a particular objective by clarifying the path to that objective in subordinates' minds. The following four distinct leadership behaviors are associated with the path-goal approach:

- *Directive.* The manager tells the subordinate what to do and when to do it (no employee participation in decision making). Some historians view Henry Ford, founder of the Ford Motor Company, as a directive manager, because he tended to view his employees as factors of production, like raw materials and capital. Such individuals tend to chart their own course and go ahead regardless of the obstacles. It may be appropriate for CEOs to practice directive leadership under certain circumstances.
- *Supportive.* The manager is friendly with employees and shows interest in them. Ross Perot seems to be a supportive leader.
- *Participative.* The manager seeks suggestions and involves employees in decision making. The late Sam Walton, founder of the Wal-Mart and Sam's stores, always got his employees involved in decision making. During his tenure, employee suggestions were forwarded to the Wal-Mart main office, where they were rewarded by management.

- *Achievement oriented.* The manager establishes challenging goals and demonstrates confidence that employees can achieve them. Robert M. Kavner, AT&T's chief financial officer, was brought in to run AT&T's computer division. He initiated achievement-oriented leadership in his group, focusing on the capabilities of his "very able team."[21]

Following the path-goal theory, a manager may use all four of the behaviors in different situations. For instance, a manager may use directive behavior toward a new employee and supportive behavior toward an experienced one who is aware of the goals to be attained.

Two sets of contingency factors influence the nature of the leadership situation, according to path-goal theory. The first set, subordinates' characteristics, includes such factors as authoritarianism of the subordinate, locus of control (an individual's perception of how much control she or he has), and ability. The second set is environmental factors, which include the nature of the task, the formal authority system, and the primary work group. The characteristics of subordinates influence both job satisfaction and the subordinates' acceptance of the leader. Environmental factors affect the motivational behavior of the subordinates. Utilizing the appropriate leadership style and properly accounting for the two groups of contingency factors can increase employee motivation and job satisfaction by clarifying performance objectives and the path to achieve them.[22]

Tannenbaum and Schmidt's Leadership Continuum

The **leadership continuum,** developed by Robert Tannenbaum and Warren H. Schmidt, is the graphical representation of the trade-off between a manager's use of authority and the freedom that subordinates experience as the leadership style varies from boss-centered to subordinate-centered. Tannenbaum and Schmidt described several factors they thought should influence a manager's choice of leadership style. They advocated a continuum of leadership behavior, based on the notion that the choice of an effective leadership style depends on the demands of the situation.

The boss-centered and employee-centered dimensions are similar to initiating structure and consideration, discussed earlier. Here are the factors Tannenbaum and Schmidt believed should determine the appropriate leadership style:

- *Characteristics of the manager*—background, education, experience, values, knowledge, objectives, and expectations.
- *Characteristics of the employees*—background, education, experience, values, knowledge, objectives, and expectations.
- *Requirements of the situation*—size, complexity, objectives, structure, and climate of the organization, as well as technology, time pressure, and nature of the work.

According to the Tannenbaum and Schmidt leadership continuum, a manager may engage in a more participative leadership style when subordinates

- Seek independence and freedom of action.
- Are well educated and experienced in performing the jobs.
- Seek responsibility for decision making.
- Expect a participative style of leadership.
- Understand and are committed to the goals of the organization.

If these conditions do not exist, the manager may need to adopt a more autocratic, or "boss-centered," leadership style. Thus, in essence, managers must be able to diagnose the situations confronting them and then choose a leadership style that will improve their chances of effectiveness. The most effective leaders are flexible enough to select a leadership style that fits their needs as well as the needs of their subordinates and the situation.

Fiedler's Contingency Leadership Theory

The contingency theory of leadership developed by Fred E. Fiedler has received considerable acceptance.[23] Like all situational theorists, Fiedler believes there is no single most effective style that is appropriate to every situation. The Fiedler framework, illustrated in Table 11.2, involves eight situations and two basic leadership orientations. Three major elements are said to determine whether a given situation is favorable to a leader:

- *Leader-member relations*—the degree to which the leader feels accepted by

TABLE 11.2 Framework of Fiedler's Contingency Leadership Model

SITUATION	DEGREE OF FAVORABLENESS OF SITUATION TO LEADER	LEADER-MEMBER RELATIONS	TASK STRUCTURE	POWER POSITION OF LEADER
1	Favorable	Good	Structured	High
2	Favorable	Good	Structured	Low
3	Favorable	Good	Unstructured	High
4	Moderately favorable	Good	Unstructured	Low
5	Moderately favorable	Poor	Structured	High
6	Moderately favorable	Poor	Structured	Low
7	Moderately favorable	Poor	Unstructured	High
8	Unfavorable	Poor	Unstructured	Low

subordinates. The atmosphere may be friendly or unfriendly, relaxed or tense, and threatening or supportive.

- *Task structure*—clearly defined objectives, decisions, and solutions to problems.
- *Position power of the leader*—the degree of influence over rewards and punishments, determined mainly by the official authority the leader has.

The eight situations in Table 11.2 vary in degree of favorableness for the leader, which determines the leader's influence and control over the group. A leader has maximum influence in situation 1 and minimum influence in situation 8. Fiedler's research indicates that a task-oriented, controlling leader will be most effective when the situations are either very favorable or very unfavorable to the leader.[24] According to Fiedler, the more permissive, considerate leader performs best in intermediate situations, those moderately favorable to the leader.

Figure 11.3 illustrates Fiedler's framework in another way. The task-oriented leader is more effective in situations 1, 2, 3, and 8, whereas the relations-oriented leader is more effective in situations 4, 5, 6, and 7. Obviously, Gerstner leads by example and is largely task focused. He expects results.

Vroom and Yetton's Normative Theory

Victor Vroom and Philip Yetton finalized their normative theory of leadership and decision making in 1973.[25] It attempts to show to what extent leaders should involve subordinates in decision making. Managers always have some freedom to make decisions that affect subordinates. According to the Vroom-Yetton model, managers can choose one of five procedures for involving subordinates in decision making. The processes are on a continuum—from solving the problem alone, using available information, to delegating the problem-solving responsibility. A similar set of choices exists for group problems: The leader can make the decision alone, using available information; solve the problem with information or ideas from subordinates; or solve the problem together with subordinates.

Selecting the appropriate decision process involves assessing the characteristics of the particular problem. The aim of using the correct one is to improve one or more of the following elements:

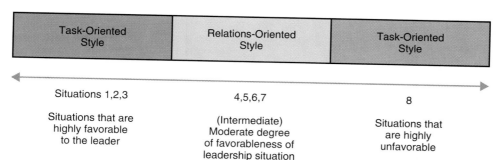

❖ **Figure 11.3**
Appropriateness of leadership styles to situation

1. "The quality or rationality of the decision."
2. "The acceptance or commitment of the subordinates to execute the decision effectively."
3. "The amount of time required to make the decision."[26]

For example, assume you must decide which of three subordinates to promote next week. You would prefer to approach this problem in a way that ensures (1) a high-quality decision and (2) one that subordinates will accept and to which they will be committed. But (3) you would not like to waste time making the decision.

A manager's view of a situation as a crisis, a challenging problem, or a minor issue may affect the choice of a decision process. The degree of urgency may also determine the appropriate leader-subordinate interaction.

Hersey and Blanchard's Situational Leadership Theory

Paul Hersey and Kenneth Blanchard have developed a situational leadership theory that has attracted considerable attention.[27] Hersey and Blanchard's theory is based on the notion that the most effective leadership style varies according to the level of readiness of the followers and the demands of the situation. Their model uses two dimensions—task behavior and relationship behavior. These dimensions are similar to the classifications used in the leadership models developed by the Ohio State researchers and in the Managerial Grid. Hersey and Blanchard argue that an effective leader is one who can both diagnose the demands of the situation and the level of readiness of the followers, and choose a leadership style that is appropriate. Their theory is based on the relationship of these factors:

ETHICAL DILEMMA

The rewards of effective managerial leadership are many. Managers who are effective leaders are held in high esteem in the business community, and are usually quite well paid. However, the leadership responsibilities can be quite overwhelming at times. Managers are human, and therefore make mistakes; even effective leaders make mistakes. Commonwealth Edison Co., the nation's largest nuclear utility company, is definitely the leader in the nuclear power generation industry. In anticipation of the extreme need for reasonably priced electri-cal power in the future, Commonwealth Edison dramatically overbuilt. It now appears that the overbuilding was massive and Commonwealth Edison's management mistake was passed on to consumers in terms of higher rates. It also appears that managers did not exercise proper leadership in their monitoring of the construction of Braidwood nuclear plant, resulting in hundreds of millions of dollars of cost overruns.[28] Are consumer refunds due?

What would you do?

1. The amount of task behavior the leader exhibits (providing direction and emphasis on getting the job done).
2. The amount of relationship behavior the leader provides (consideration of people and emotional support for them).
3. The level of task-relevant readiness followers exhibit toward the specific objective, task, or function that the leader wants accomplished.

The key concept of Hersey and Blanchard's leadership theory is the level of task-relevant readiness of the followers. *Readiness* is defined not as age or psychological stability but as the following:

- A desire for achievement—level of achievement motivation based on the need to set high but attainable objectives.
- The willingness and ability to accept responsibility.
- Education or experience and skills relevant to the particular task.

A leader should consider the level of readiness of followers only in relation to the work to be performed. Certainly, employees are "ready" on some tasks when they have the experience and skills as well as the desire to achieve and the capability of assuming responsibility. For example, Dianne Crawford, an accountant, is "ready" to prepare accurate quarterly IRS tax reports, but not to prepare written audits of the company's operations. She needs little task-related direction from her manager in preparing the tax reports, but may require considerably closer supervision and more direction in preparing and writing audits. Dianne may not currently have the skills or motivation to prepare audits; but with proper training, direction, and encouragement from her manager, she can assume greater responsibility in this area.

As Figure 11.4 illustrates, the appropriate leadership style used by a manager varies according to the readiness level (represented by R1 through R4) of the followers. Four leadership styles are appropriate, given different levels of readiness. As the task-relevant readiness level of followers increases, the manager should reduce task behavior and increase relationship behavior. The four styles can be classified as follows:

S1—Telling	High-task, low-relationship behavior
S2—Selling	High-task, high-relationship behavior
S3—Participating	High-relationship, low-task behavior
S4—Delegating	Low-relationship, low-task behavior

With the S1 (telling) high-task, low-relationship leadership style, the leader uses one-way communication, defining the objectives and roles of employees and telling employees what, how, when, and where to do the work. This style is appropriate for managers dealing with subordinates who lack task-relevant readiness—for example, those who are relatively new and inexperienced.

❖ **Figure 11.4**
Hersey and Blanchard's situational leadership® theory
(Source: Paul Hersey and Kenneth Blanchard, Center for Leadership Studies, 1989. Used with permission of Leadership Studies, Inc.)

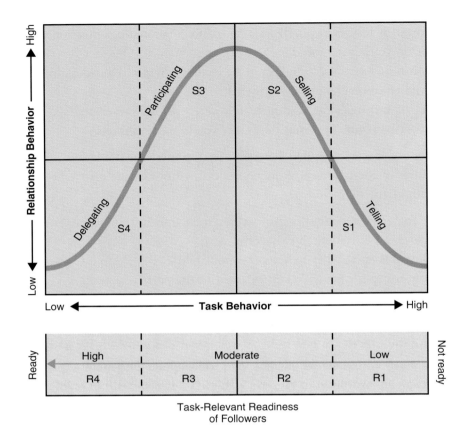

As employees learn their jobs, a manager can begin to use an S2 (selling) leadership style. There is still a need for a high level of task behavior, however, since the employees do not yet have the experience or skills to assume more responsibility. But the manager must also provide a high level of emotional support—high-relationship behavior—to encourage the employees and demonstrate trust and confidence in them.

As employees exhibit an increase in task-relevant readiness—as they become more experienced and skilled, as well as more achievement-motivated and more willing to assume responsibility—the leader should reduce the amount of task behavior but continue the high level of emotional support and consideration. Continuing a high level of relationship behavior is the manager's way of reinforcing the employees' responsible performance. Thus, S3 (participating) high-relationship and low-task behavior becomes the appropriate leadership style.

The S4 (delegating) low-relationship, low-task leadership style goes with the highest level of follower readiness. In this stage, the employees are at a high level of task-relevant readiness. They are skilled and experienced, possess a high level of achievement motivation, and are capable of exercising self-control. At this point, they no longer need or expect a high level of task behavior from their leader.

We should not conclude from this discussion that Hersey and Blanchard consider it simple to determine the appropriate leadership style. The ability to diagnose the readiness level of the followers, as well as the specific needs of the situation, is complex. The leader must have insight into the abilities, needs, demands, and expectations of followers and must be aware that these elements can and do change over time.

Also, managers must recognize that they need to adapt or change their style of leadership whenever there is a change in the level of readiness of followers, for whatever reason—a change in jobs, personal or family problems, or change in the complexity of the job caused by new technology. For example, Bill Woodall, a sales manager, has been using an S4 leadership style in supervising John Chriswell, who normally is a highly productive sales representative. John's pending divorce, however, has recently been adversely affecting his performance. In this situation, Bill might increase the level of both task and relationship behavior in order to provide John with the direction, support, and confidence he may need to cope with his problems and improve his performance.

Hersey and Blanchard's theory provides a useful and understandable framework for situational leadership. In essence, it suggests that there is no single best leadership style to meet the needs of all situations. Rather, a manager's leadership style must be adaptable and flexible enough to meet the changing needs of employees and situations. Evidence indicates that a given individual might respond differently to a certain leadership strategy at different times.[29] The effective manager is one who can change styles as employees develop and change, or as required by the situation.

❖ ❖ LEADING A DIVERSE WORKFORCE

The discussion of leadership theories may seem to imply that managers merely decide which leadership style to use, sometimes changing styles to adapt to different situations. Even when the situation the leader must cope with is known, the appropriate leadership style may not be obvious. But three important factors should be considered in determining a leadership style for the diverse workforce of the future: those related to the manager, to the worker, and to the situation.

Factors Related to the Manager

Self-knowledge is important to effective leadership. Leaders have different abilities and objectives. They also have had different experiences. Through those experiences, they develop basic beliefs about people. Some think people must be threatened to make them work. Others believe in encouraging workers and rewarding them for performance. Although managers should be flexible in the choice of a leadership style, they usually perform better if they use a style consistent with their personal beliefs.

The manager's professional and technical competence also affects leadership style. Not only are competent managers more confident, but workers are less likely to challenge or question them. This would seem to allow the manager to be more autocratic. Actually, though, it gives managers more flexibility in leadership styles. Thus, a particular manager can be gentle and supportive in certain situations and a stern disciplinarian in others.

Factors Related to the Workers

The diverse workforce was discussed in Chapter 2. Because of this diverse workforce, characteristics of subordinates should also be taken into account when deciding on a leadership style. One important consideration is the work ethic of subordinates. Some workers feel that work is, in and of itself, satisfying, pleasurable, and fulfilling. Such workers are easy to lead. Others see work as an unpleasant way to get money. Perhaps rewards and punishments are the only effective motivators for these workers. Workers' attitudes toward authority must also be considered. Some believe that the job of the manager is to tell them what to do. They do not want to help make decisions. Others wish to make all the decisions; they resist any exercise of authority by the leader.

The maturity level of the subordinates is another influence on leadership style. Some workers are mature in the way they approach their work. They exercise initiative not only in doing their job but also in self-development. Others may have to be watched quite closely if even minimum performance is to be obtained. Workers may handle one aspect of their job maturely yet be quite immature in other aspects.

Another factor is the experience level and skill of subordinates. The leadership style used with a trainee will be different from that used with an experienced craftsperson. A more directive style may prove best for the trainee, while the craftsperson may need no direction at all.

For some employees an autocratic style will work best. This may be particularly true in extremely favorable or extremely unfavorable situations. Studies have shown, however, that workers with a very wide range of characteristics generally respond more favorably to a participative approach.[30] Even at companies with a strong authority structure, such as IBM, workers tend to be more highly motivated if they take part in the decision-making process.

Factors Related to the Situation

Many situational factors affect the manager's leadership style. Following are some of the major ones:

1. *Number of people in the work group.* Managers can give more individualized attention in smaller work groups. As group size increases, management by exception may tend to be used.

2. *Kinds of tasks.* Jobs involving simple repetition may permit the manager to be more autocratic. Workers with creative or complex jobs require more freedom.

3. *Situational stress.* Managers often shift to a more autocratic style when the going gets tough. The firm may be in financial difficulties, a manager may be experiencing unusual pressure to increase output. However, the manager should be careful in changing leadership styles and should not do so purely as a reflex action.

4. *Objectives of the unit.* The specific objectives the manager is expected to accomplish affect leadership style. If the only objective is to get the job done immediately, the use of strong authority may be justified, even though it may make workers unhappy. When there is an important rush project, subordinates are more likely to accept simply being told what to do.

5. *Leadership style of the manager's boss.* Managers tend to lead as they are led. If the manager's boss is autocratic, the manager may lean toward this leadership style.

6. *Relationship of the manager with subordinates.* If the manager-subordinate relationship is one of mutual respect, the manager will usually let workers

Progress Toward Leadership Diversity

Achieving workforce diversity where team members put aside prejudices, honor differences, and respect all people regardless of gender, race, or creed is the ideal that will hopefully define the future. Future leaders will probably be much less often white male and much more ethnically and culturally diverse. Kenneth Chenault, president of American Express Consumer Card Group, USA, and one of the top African-American senior executives in the country, believes that "The 21st Century leader must succeed in a world ruled by cultural diversity and collaboration." In the mid-sixties people of diversity began to join the corporate mainstream, but far too few have broken through the glass ceiling and are in leadership positions. Future leaders must be diverse high performers who have been mentored and welcomed into key leadership roles. According to John Sculley, former CEO of Apple Computer Inc., "Adults and young people must realize that this is going to be a multicultural society, with equal opportunities for men and women. We must have a society that uses strengths of all people." Reuben Mark, CEO of Colgate-Palmolive Company, believes that to succeed companies must be "committed to bringing women and minorities into the workforce, and especially in leadership positions." Finally, only 15 percent of incoming workers in the year 2000 will be white males; the balance will be females and minorities. Jerry R. Junkins, CEO of Texas Instruments, believes that women and minorities are the raw material for future leaders, and therefore we'd better begin right away to prepare them to lead in the next century." Although there are obstacles to overcome for members of a diverse workforce to gain leadership roles, there appear to be much greater opportunities for women and diverse peoples to advance in the future.[31]

A Skill-Building Exercise: "Phil is a great leader," said Jim Hollis, the plant manager, as he looked out over the factory floor from the production manager's office.

"Yes," said the production manager, "I believe those carpenters would follow him off the end of the Earth."

Phil Granger is the carpentry supervisor in the shipping department at Jacobs Castings Company. Phil and his crew of six make wooden boxes for packaging the several hundred custom-made castings that Jacobs ships every day. The work requires little skill, but is vital to the plant.

Jim has said that before Phil took over, the carpentry division was a bottleneck. Shipments were often delayed for days because the carpentry work just did not get done. Turnover in the department had been high. And Jim has noted that the carpenters had more personal problems than other workers in the plant.

According to Jim, everything changed almost immediately after Phil took over. The work was caught up within a few days, and castings no longer have to wait for more than a day to be shipped. The carpenters are happier because Phil leads by example and does not expect more from his people than he is willing to do. During the first two months that Phil was in charge, there was not a single complaint, and only one day was lost because of absenteeism.

One day, Jim came by as Phil was determining how the boxes were to be made the next morning. "Phil," he said, "I thought you would be home with the kids by now." "I sure would like to go home a little early today," Phil replied, "but I want the others to know I'm trying as hard as they are. Anyway, I need to finish these sketches so I'll have time to help with the boxes in the morning. I also want to check with Brad before he leaves today. Since I took him around and showed him how our work affected the rest of the plant, he sure has done a great job."

Would you consider Phil a good leader? Explain.

take part in managing themselves. Workers, too, are likely to contribute more when they are respected and liked by their supervisor.

This list does not, unfortunately, answer the question: What leadership style should be used? In fact, there is no absolute answer. In the 1990s, organizations will be flatter and more decentralized. This has increased, not decreased, the need for interdependence, collaboration, and communication—for flexibility in leadership style. Thus, the leader must recognize the subordinate as a major situational determinant. This recognition involves not only careful observation of subordinates' behavior but the ability to interpret that behavior in a meaningful way.

The best we can suggest is that managers thoroughly evaluate themselves, their subordinates, and the situation and then choose an appropriate style. The style may change as the manager leads a more diverse workforce.

A GLOBAL PERSPECTIVE

Global Success Through Open and Aggressive Leadership

Although leading is only one of the many things a manager does, it is one of the most distinguishing factors separating effective managers from ineffective ones. The most appropriate leadership style depends on many factors, and a style that is appropriate in one firm or country may be inappropriate in others. This makes the concept of effective global leadership quite complex.

Some individuals have already surfaced as effective multinational leaders, and some leaders truly distinguish themselves in the business world. The leader of AT&T, CEO Robert Allen, hopes to make AT&T "Rule the World." Through Allen's aggressive leadership, AT&T has modernized management globally, by creating an organization that is neither slow nor lethargic nor bureaucratic. AT&T is what all successful global companies must be: quick to react, flexible, and nonbureaucratic. The one major problem area in the AT&T organization was the Global Business Communications System unit that makes office phones and equipment. Enter Jerre Stead, a somewhat different type of leader, but definitely a successful leader, to solve the problem. After Stead solved the problems at the Global Business Communications System unit, Allen was so impressed that he promoted Stead to run NCR. Stead, like Allen, is an open leader. In fact, Stead doesn't shut his door; he even had his door lock removed. He insists that employees call him "coach." Stead is militant and aggressive, an individual who has a disdain for meetings unless they are accomplishing something for customers or focusing on how to effectively deal with competitors. Under the open and aggressive leadership style of Allen and Stead, AT&T is thriving worldwide, with the fourth largest market value in the world, behind only Nippon Telegraph, Exxon, and GE.[32]

❖ ❖ LEADERSHIP AND THE TEAM APPROACH

In the last few years the management world has been rethinking many concepts. The team approach is being stressed in organizations throughout the world. Work teams are being given responsibility formerly held by managers. As we attempt to sort out our thinking, some management experts have begun to question the degree of focus that should be placed on leadership. The reasoning goes that if we indeed want all team members to be empowered to make more decisions and take on more responsibility, then the focus should be on one leader or the team. If this reasoning is proper, today's managers must relinquish some of their leadership power and allow their workers to assume alternating roles as leaders in teams.[33] According to Charles F. Hendricks, author of *The Rightsizing Remedy*, "So, managers, throw out your script. Your role is changing. Get out of the way of your people. Lead for once by following their advice, facilitating their movement, and franchising their futures."[34]

❖ ❖ LEADING THROUGH EXAMPLE

Workers often look to their managers as examples of what to do and what not to do. Managers who want their people to be on time should come to work a little early and stay a few minutes late. The way managers behave in the community will also be noticed by workers. If they see the manager drinking and carousing, they will assume that this is acceptable conduct. Louis Gerstner of IBM leads by example, making tough decisions, putting in six and one-half day weeks, working 16 to 18 hour days. Wellfleet Communications CEO, Paul Severino, also leads

✗ Management Tips ✗

Guidelines for Dealing with Leadership

1. **Gather influence.** Harsh as this statement may sound, the amount of influence managers have over subordinates is largely determined by the manager's influence outside the unit.

2. **Lead through example.** This is particularly important to the working manager. Employees often use the manager as a role model in deciding what is right and wrong.

3. **Be specific.** Make sure that your people know what you want done.

4. **Be competent, then confident.** Once you know the job well, you will have confidence. Acting confident without knowing the job is cockiness.

5. **Look like a leader.** Dress appropriately as a manager in your organization. This standard is different from company to company.

6. **Sound like a leader.** When you issue an order, say what you mean and mean what you say.

7. **Be goal-oriented.** Lead your workers in the right direction.

8. **Do not pass on a directive from upper management with an apology.** Some managers accept a directive from upper management without question and then criticize the directive while transmitting it to subordinates. Remember that to your workers, you are management. The spirit in which the manager passes on a directive will have a major impact on how the job is done.

9. **Do not blindly follow directives that you know are incorrect.** Question them. If you believe that someone will be hurt because of the directive, refuse to take action. In either case, remember that you have an obligation to take it up with the next higher level of management.

10. **Remember that self-knowledge is important to effective leadership.** Leaders have different abilities and objectives.

Liz Claiborne: Leading by Example

Elisabeth [Liz] Claiborne has built America's top-selling women's clothing label by giving women the fashions they want to wear. Liz's fashions are simple, straightforward garments for career-oriented women. Claiborne was not only a leader in the industry, but she was also a leader to her employees. Claiborne and her husband decided from the start that employees should feel part of the company. To foster team spirit, she spent a part of each day working with a different division. Her leadership and upbeat manner shaped positive relationships with her employees. Claiborne offered her employees both credit and responsibility for the tasks they performed. They took responsibility for mistakes, learned, and then went forward. Claiborne led by teaching her designers, not by doing the designing for them. She let them know, however, that she could do it as well as they could, or better, she lead by example. In 1989, Liz Claiborne and Arthur Ortenberg turned over the reins of the $2 billion-plus fashion empire to Jerome Chazen, an original partner in the firm, and the leadership she instilled in everyone continued. The years of leading, teaching, correcting, and guiding have paid off because Liz Claiborne's leadership style continues to make the company successful.[35]

by example. According to Severino, "We all live by the same rules here . . . When I go on vacation I fill out a request form."[36]

All managers can set an example by showing enthusiasm for and seriousness about the work. Another aspect of leading by example is the way the manager deals with superiors. Lower-level managers who are not honest with upper management cannot expect workers to be honest with them. Managers who want their subordinates to trust them must be seen by the workers as being trustworthy. Many managers try to stay in clear view of their subordinates. Liz Claiborne certainly leads by example.

SUMMARY

Leadership (or *leading*) is influencing others to do what the leader wants them to do. Four basic leadership styles have been identified. Autocratic leaders tell subordinates what to do and expect to be obeyed without question. Participative leaders involve subordinates in decision making but may retain final authority. Democratic leaders try to do what the majority of subordinates desire. And laissez-faire leaders are uninvolved in the work of the unit.

The trait approach to leadership is the evaluation and selection of leaders on the basis on their physical, mental, social, and psychological characteristics. Dissatisfaction with the trait approach has caused most leadership researchers to focus attention instead on how leaders should behave. In studies conducted by researchers at Ohio State University, the key concern was the leader's behavior in directing the efforts of others toward group objectives. These studies identified two important dimensions of behavior: initiating structure and consideration. A series of leadership studies at the University of Michigan related differences in high-productivity and low-productivity work groups to differences in supervisors' behavior. The Managerial Grid, a two-dimensional matrix developed by Robert Blake and Jane Mouton, depicts seven leadership styles, each representing a different degree of concern for people and for production.

Contingency, or situational, leadership theories assert that no single way of behaving works in all situations. Robert House's path-goal theory proposes that managers can facilitate job performance by showing employees how their performance directly affects their receiving desired rewards. The leadership continuum, developed by Robert Tannenbaum and Warren Schmidt, shows the tradeoff between a manager's use of authority and the freedom that subordinates experience as the leadership style varies from boss-centered to subordinate-centered. Fred Fiedler developed the contingency leadership theory that states that the most effective leadership style depends on the nature of the situation. Victor Vroom and Philip Yetton introduced a normative theory of leadership and decision making in which managers determine the extent to which they should involve subordinates in the decision-making process. In Paul Hersey and Kenneth Blanchard's situational leadership theory, effective leadership depends on the level of readiness of the followers and the demands of the situation.

There are certain practical aspects of leading a diverse workforce. Self-knowledge is important to effective leadership in a diverse environment. Leaders have different abilities and objectives; they also have had different experiences. Through those experiences, they develop basic beliefs about people. Characteristics of subordinates should also be taken into account when deciding on a leadership style. Many situational factors, too, affect the manager's leadership style. Finally, workers often look to their managers as examples of what to do and what not to do.

In the last few years the management world has been rethinking many concepts. The team approach is being stressed in organizations throughout the world. Work teams are being given responsibility that formerly only managers had.

KEY TERMS

Leadership (leading) 345	Transformational leader 349
Autocratic leader 346	Initiating structure 351
Participative leader 346	Consideration 351
Democratic leader 346	Managerial Grid 352
Laissez-faire leader 347	Path-goal theory 354
Trait approach to leadership 347	Leadership continuum 355

REVIEW QUESTIONS

1. Define leadership. What are the basic leadership styles?

2. Distinguish between leadership and management.

3. Discuss the trait approach to leadership.

4. List and briefly describe the various behavioral leadership theories.

5. Describe each of the following situational leadership theories:
   a. House's path-goal theory of leadership
   b. Tannenbaum and Schmidt's leadership continuum
   c. Fiedler's contingency theory of leadership
   d. Vroom and Yetton's normative theory of leadership and decision making
   e. Hersey and Blanchard's situational leadership theory

6. What are ways that managers can become better at leading a diverse workforce?

7. Why is it important to lead by example?

CASE STUDIES

CASE 11.1 "You Know the Policy"

Dwayne Alexander was the Dallas-area supervisor for Quik-Stop, a chain of convenience stores. There were seven Quik-Stop stores in Dallas, and Dwayne had full responsibility for managing them. Each store operated with only one person on duty at a time. Although several of the stores stayed open all night, every night, the Center Street store was open all night Monday through Thursday but only from 6:00 A.M. to 10:00 P.M. Friday through Sunday. Because the store was open fewer hours during the weekend, money from sales was kept in the store safe until Monday. Therefore, the time it took to complete a money count on Monday was greater than normal.

The company had a policy that when the safe was being emptied, the manager had to be with the employee on duty, and the employee had to place each $1,000 in a brown bag, mark the bag, and leave the bag on the floor next to the safe until the manager verified the amount in each bag.

Bill Catron worked the Sunday night shift at the Center Street store and was trying to save the manager time by counting the money prior to his arrival. The store got very busy, and, while bagging a customer's groceries, Bill mistook one of the money bags for a bag containing three sandwiches and put the money bag in with the groceries. Twenty minutes later, the manager arrived, and both men began to search for the money. While they were searching, the customer came back with the bag of money. The company has a policy that anyone violating the money-counting procedure must be fired immediately.

Bill was very upset. "I really need this job," Bill exclaimed. "With the new baby and all the medical expenses we've had, I sure can't stand to be out of a job."

"You knew about the policy, Bill," said Dwayne.

"Yes, I did, Dwayne," said Bill, "and I really don't have any excuse. If you don't fire me, though, I promise you that I'll be the best store manager you've got."

While Bill waited on a customer, Dwayne called his boss at the home office in Houston. With the boss's approval, Dwayne decided not to fire Bill.

QUESTIONS

1. Discuss Dwayne's leadership style in terms of the Managerial Grid.
2. Evaluate the action Dwayne took. Take particular note of how the events in the case might affect other store managers.

CASE 11.2 Sanford Sigoloff: Tough Leader for Tough Jobs

In the corporate turnaround story of the century, the mammoth Wickes Companies, a marketer of building products, went from a $258 million loss in 1982 to a modest profit in the 1983–1984 fiscal year. From 1987–1989 Wickes was not only solidly in the black, but was in an expansive mode. Wickes paid over $1 billion for a Gulf + Western Corporation division and made millions in attempts to take over other companies. The success continued until a buyout of the company in 1989.

Most authorities give the credit for Wickes's recovery to Sanford Sigoloff. When Sigoloff took over at Wickes in 1982, losses had totaled over $400 million in just 15 months. The corporate treasury was hemorrhaging cash. Shelves and showrooms in thousands of Wickes stores were bare or stocked with inferior goods, and customers were staying away in droves. Needless to say, many employees were discouraged and lethargic.

Sigoloff—"Flash Gordon" or "Ming the Merciless," depending on whom you ask—had earned his reputation turning around disabled companies. In Wickes, the former nuclear physicist, then 52, faced his greatest test. He accepted what he called "a very, very tough challenge" because he couldn't resist it.

The Sigoloff stamp meant total commitment

throughout the organization. Sigoloff expected 14-hour days out of his corporate staff. Almost the entire financial department quit when they learned this. Many other employees left involuntarily as he expelled nearly a fourth of Wickes' 40,000-member workforce. The managers who chose and were permitted to remain with Wickes were supplemented with Sigoloff lieutenants who had worked with him in the past.

Sigoloff practiced a team approach to problem solving. He demanded personal loyalty from top executives and their help in making difficult decisions, but he readily admitted reserving the right to make all "terminal" decisions, those that could not be revisited. His frequent trips to farflung stores and offices inspired workers and managers at every level. His concept was to share the wealth and promote the dignity of the individual, and practice an inviolate open-door policy. Those who came to know Sigoloff during the turnaround recall his snappy stride, his neat, trim appearance, his ready smile, and his reputation for personal integrity. He was criticized, though, for failing to delegate enough responsibility, even to his top people.

Early in his turnaround effort at Wickes, Sigoloff chose to seek protection under Chapter 11 of the U.S. Bankruptcy Code. This held creditors off and gave time to regroup. But it also discouraged employees and customers, many of whom knew that most companies never successfully emerge from Chapter 11. Sigoloff had to convince all of them that Wickes would survive. In conjunction with his efforts inside the company to refurbish stores and restore optimism, Sigoloff launched a national TV ad campaign, with the serious-looking chairman in front of the camera personally guaranteeing Wickes' products and services.

QUESTIONS

1. What leadership style did Sigoloff exhibit? Explain.
2. Do you believe that Sigoloff, or a person like Sigoloff, would be as successful in a research and development environment that requires creative thinking? Explain.

NOTES

1. This case is a composite of a number of published accounts, among them: Joel Dreyfuss, "Reinventing IBM," *Fortune* 124 (August 14, 1989): 31–39; "The Greatest Capitalist in History," *Fortune* 122 (August 31, 1987): 24–35; Joanne Lipman, "Wells Rich's New IBM Campaign Presents Firm as User-Friendly," *The Wall Street Journal* (April 13, 1989): B6; Paul B. Carroll, "IBM Names Jack Kuehler President, Recognizing His Role in Technology," *The Wall Street Journal* (May 31, 1989): A3; John W. Verity, "A Bold Move in Mainframes," *Business Week* (May 29, 1989): 72–78; Geoff Lewis, Anne R. Field, John J. Keller, and John W. Verity, "Big Changes at Big Blue," *Business Week* (February 15, 1988): 92; Rick Whiting and Hugh Willett, "IBM at the Crossroads," *Electronic Business* 17 (September 9, 1991): 36–46; Thomas McCarroll, "The Humbling of a Computer Colossus," *Time* 137 (May 20, 1991): 41–44; Judith H.

Dobrzynski, "Rethinking IBM," *Business Week* (October 4, 1993): 86–97.
2. Elizabeth Lesly, Zachary Schiller, Stephen Baker, and Geoffrey Smith, "CEOs with the Outside Edge," *Business Week* (October 11, 1993): 60–62.
3. Barbara Presley Noble, "The Debate over la Difference," *The New York Times* (August 15, 1993): B1.
4. John Hoerr, "Getting Man and Machine to Live Happily Ever After," *Business Week* (April 20, 1987): 61.
5. John A. Byrne, "What's a Guy like This Doing at McKinsey's Helm?" *Business Week* (June 13, 1988): 82–84.
6. Dorwin Cartwright and Alvin Zander, eds., *Group Dynamics,* 3d ed. (New York: Harper & Row, 1968).
7. Edwin Ghiselli, *Explorations in Managerial Talent* (Pacific Palisades, CA: Goodyear, 1971).
8. W. Bennis, "Leadership: A Beleaguered Species?" *Organizational Dynamics* 5 (1976): 13–14.

9. R. J. House, "A 1976 Theory of Charismatic Leadership," in *Leadership: The Cutting Edge,* ed. J. G. Hunt and L. L. Larson (Carbondale: Southern Illinois University Press, 1977): pp. 205, 207.

10. B. M. Bass, "Leadership: Good, Better, Best," *Organizational Dynamics* 13 (Winter 1985): 26–40.

11. Judith R. Gordon, *A Diagnostic Approach to Organizational Behavior,* 2d ed. (Boston: Allyn and Bacon, 1987) pp. 425–426.

12. *Ibid.*

13. *Ibid.*

14. R. M. Stogdill, "Personal Factors Associated with Leadership: A Survey of the Literature," *Journal of Psychology* 25 (1948): 35–71.

15. Walter Guzzardi, "Wisdoms from the Giants of Business," *Fortune* 124 (July 3, 1989): 78–88.

16. E. Fleishman, E. F. Harris, and R. D. Burtt, *Leadership and Supervision in Industry* (Columbus: Ohio State University Press, 1955); and E. Fleishman and E. F. Harris, "Patterns of Leadership Behavior Related to Employee Grievances and Turnover," *Personnel Psychology* 1 (1959): 45–53.

17. R. L. Kahn and D. Katz, "Leadership Practices in Relation to Productivity and Morale," in D. Cartwright and A. Zander, eds., *Group Dynamics* (Evanston, IL: Row, Peterson, 1953) pp. 585–611.

18. Robert R. Blake and Anne Adams McCanse. *Leadership Dilemmas—Grid Solutions* (Houston: Gulf Publishing Company, 1991).

19. Robert R. Blake and Jane Srygley Mouton, *The Managerial Grid III: The Key to Leadership Excellence,* 3d ed. (Houston: Gulf Publishing Company, 1985).

20. Robert House, "A Path-Goal Theory of Leadership Effectiveness," *Administrative Science Quarterly* 16 (September 1971): 321–338.

21. John J. Keller, "Has the AT&T-Olivetti Romance Lost Its Magic?" *Business Week* (May 9, 1988): 46.

22. Alan C. Filley, Robert House, and Steven Kerr, *Managerial Process and Organizational Behavior* (Glenview, IL.: Scott, Foresman, 1976) pp. 256–260.

23. Fred E. Fiedler, *A Theory of Leadership Effectiveness* (New York: McGraw-Hill, 1967).

24. *Ibid.*

25. V. H. Vroom and P. W. Yetton, *Leadership and Decision-Making* (Pittsburgh, PA: University of Pittsburgh Press, 1973).

26. V. H. Vroom and A. J. Jago, "Decision-Making as a Social Process: Normative and Descriptive Models of Leader Behavior," *Decision Sciences* 5 (October 1974): 743–769.

27. See Paul Hersey and Kenneth Blanchard, "So You Want to Know Your Leadership Style?" *Training and Development Journal,* (February 1974): 22–32. This article contains the Leader Adaptability and Style Inventory (LASI), an instrument that can be used to examine leadership behavior, style adaptability, and effectiveness. Since this article was published, the LASI has been renamed as the Leader Effectiveness and Adaptability Description (LEAD). Information, LEAD inventories, and training materials may be obtained from the Center for Leadership Studies, 17253 Caminito Canasto, Rancho Bernardo, San Diego, CA 92127.

28. Adapted from Thomas M. Burton, "Commonwealth Edison Offers Refund Rate Cut to Settle Nuclear Litigation," *The Wall Street Journal* (September 28, 1993): A3.

29. S. D. Malik and Kenneth N. Wexley, "Improving the Owner/Manager's Handling of Subordinate Resistance to Unpopular Decisions," *Journal of Small Business Management* 24 (July 1986): 27.

30. M. E. Heilman, H. A. Hornstein, J. H. Cage, and J. K. Herschdag, "Reactions to Prescribed Leader Behavior as a Function of Role Perspective: The Case of the Vroom-Yetton Model," *Journal of Applied Psychology* 69 (February 1984): 50.

31. Lynne Joy McFarland, Larry E. Senn, and John R. Childress, *21st Century Leadership* (New York: The Leadership Press, 1993) pp. 227–232.

32. David Kirkpatrick, "Could AT&T Rule the World?" *Fortune* 127 (October 1992): 55–57, 62–64, 66.

33. John A. Byrne, "Management's New Gurus," *Business Week* (August 31, 1992): 44–51.

34. Charles F. Hendricks, "Rightsizing Remedy," *HRMagazine* 37 (June 1992): 13.

35. Andrew E. Serwer, "America's 100 Fastest Growers," *Fortune* 128 (August 9, 1993): 40–56.

36. Joan E. Rigdon, "Using Lateral Moves to Spur Employees," *The Wall Street Journal* (May 26, 1992): B1, B9.

12 Communication

LEARNING OBJECTIVES

After completing this chapter students should be able to

✘ Describe the basic components of the communication process and state what should be communicated to workers.

✘ Explain the two basic forms of communication channels.

✘ Describe communication networks and their characteristics.

✘ Identify the barriers to individual communication and discuss the barriers to effective work team behavior.

✘ Describe how managers can become better communicators and explain the concept of directing.

Communication Helps the PPG Blueprint Work

PPG's new CEO, Jerry E. Dempsey, considers communication essential for the success of PPG's *Blueprint for the Decade*. Former CEO Vincent A. Sarni, named "Outstanding Chemical Executive of the Year in 1992," created the *Blueprint for the Decade* and also viewed communication as essential for its successful implementation. The Pittsburgh glass, paint, and chemical maker, normally referred to as PPG Industries, was always considered to be dull and bureaucratic until Sarni took over in 1984. Sarni shattered the old company's culture and remolded PPG into a model of modern management. The company that he inherited was reasonably successful and technically competent, but it suffered through each economic downturn and sleepily responded to recoveries. The *Blueprint for the Decade* changed all that. The *Blueprint* is an eight-page pamphlet developed in 1984 that contains PPG's mission statement, corporate objectives, and performance goals. The virtues of the *Blueprint* were communicated to each plant, and then the plan went into action.

Implementation of the *Blueprint for the Decade* required a revision of PPG's organization to assure that everyone was pulling in the same direction and to afford everyone an opportunity to grow. Under the organizational section of the pamphlet is an explanation of how PPG's strategy will be carried out and how the goals of making PPG more profitable and as recession proof as possible will be achieved. Management, staffing, and information for decision making are the elements of the PPG organization essential for goal attainment. The focal point of the PPG organization is effective communication, which is vital to corporate success.

PPG's *Blueprint for the Decade* mandates that "management communicate openly and challenge people to be creative and entrepreneurial, with the aim of deepening the understanding of each other's point of view and rallying everyone to the pursuit of excellence." In relation to staffing, PPG employees must have the appropriate technical skills, but it is also imperative that they have effective communication skills. Finally, PPG's blueprint specified that information for decision making must "provide information across the company so that people can communicate more fully with each other, and provide and maintain state-of-the-art systems for information handling." Actions by PPG such as the creation of "Mythbusters" underscored their concern for effective communication in their plants. Mythbusters are quality action teams assembled for the purpose of recommending to management effective ways of communicating timely information to employees.

Through effective communication and by following the essence of PPG's blueprint, PPG earned record sales and earnings. The company's return on investment also increased to a modern high. Experts insist that under Dempsey, "the company won't skip a beat," mainly because he appears to be willing to subscribe to Sarni's formula that has prepared PPG for just about anything.[1]

Perhaps the worst criticism that managers can receive from their peers, superiors, and subordinates is that they cannot communicate effectively. PPG is acutely aware of the importance of effective communication. Communication could be a costly, productivity-affecting component of any organization, but at PPG it is cost effective, enhances productivity, and has a positive effect on the company's bottom line.

In Chapter 1, *management* was defined as the process of getting things done through the efforts of other people. In order for employees to achieve the objectives identified by the manager, they must have a clear understanding of those objectives. The statement of a frustrated manager—"You did what you thought I meant very effectively; unfortunately, that was not what I wanted you to do"— reveals that effective communication did not take place. Effective communication

---

Twenty-First Century Communication

At Mars candy company, communication takes a front seat, manifesting itself in a unique office layout where managers are engaged in effective communication at all levels. The typical Mars office layout puts the boss in the center of a large room with no walls, but surrounded by subordinates. Frills like private offices are rare, and anything that could interfere with communication is eliminated. Communication was one of the factors at center stage when General Motors was creating the Saturn plant. General Motors started from scratch when they designed the Saturn plant, and carefully selected employees who were considered to be quite adaptable and able to work in teams. The last, and possibly the most important skill was the ability of each Saturn employee to communicate effectively. Virtually all companies are becoming acutely aware that effective communication means "[putting aside] prejudices, honoring differences, and respecting all people regardless of gender, race, or creed." According to Lynne Joy McFarland, Larry E. Senn, and John R. Childress, authors of the book *21st Century Leadership*, "The new leader asks more questions, empathetically listens, openly shares perspectives and invites ideas."[2] In other words, the new leader effectively communicates.

should be considered not an end in itself but a means of achieving company objectives. The most encouraging feature of communication is that it is learned. Individuals who desire to improve their ability to communicate can do so by giving proper attention to the task.

This chapter begins with a discussion of the communication process and of what should be communicated. Next, it presents the various channels of communication, which are followed by a discussion of communication networks and their characteristics. Then, the chapter reviews the barriers to both individual and work team communication. Finally, it discusses the means by which managers can become better communicators, explains the concept of directing, and provides a global perspective on communication.

❖ ❖ THE COMMUNICATION PROCESS

Communication is such a complex concept that one researcher uncovered over 95 definitions, none of which were widely accepted.[3] We define **communication** as the transfer of information, ideas, understanding, or feelings among people. It is hard to conceive of an organizational objective that could be accomplished without communication. Effective communication is fundamental to success in every organization, now and well into the 21st century.

The manner in which plans are to be implemented and actions coordinated to achieve a particular objective must be communicated to the individuals who

Effective communication should not be considered an end in itself, but a means of achieving company objectives. (Source: © John Coletti)

must accomplish the task. In fact, managers spend a considerable portion of their time communicating. Communication provides the means by which members of the firm may be stimulated to implement organizational plans willingly and enthusiastically.

Communication must have a recipient. Shouting for help on a desert island is not communication. Similarly, if a professor lectures and no one listens or understands, there is no communication. The basic elements of the communication process are shown in Figure 12.1. Each step in the sequence is critical to suc-

❖ **Figure 12.1**
The communication process
(Source: Adapted from H. Joseph Reitz, *Behavior in Organizations* Third Edition [Homewood, IL: Richard D. Irwin, 1987], p. 304. Copyright ©1987 by Richard D. Irwin, Inc. Used with permission.)

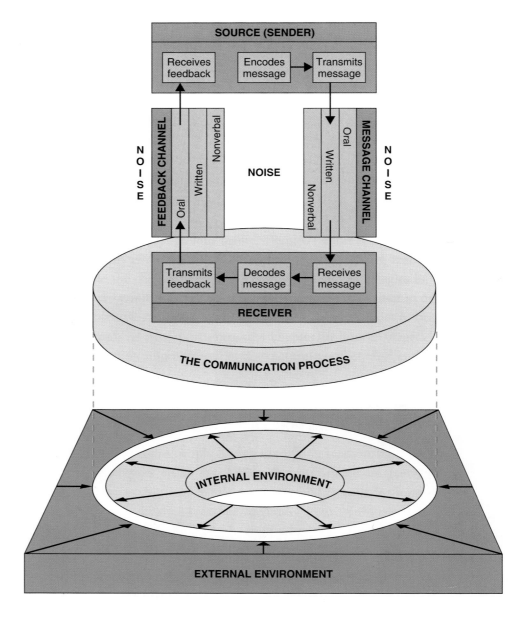

cess. The **source** (or **sender**) is the person who has an idea or message to communicate to another person or persons. A problem that often affects the communication process is that people have different backgrounds, experiences, and objectives. As the first step on the communication process, the sender must *encode* the message or idea—put it into a set of symbols that the receiver will understand. Words on this page are symbols to the reader. The sound of a car's horn on a busy freeway often means the likelihood of an accident. Thus, the blast of a horn becomes a symbol of danger.

When communication is attempted, messages are transmitted through such means as speaking, writing, acting, and drawing. A number of communication channels may be used to transmit any message. **Communication channels** are the means by which information is transmitted in organizations. Words can be communicated orally through such methods as face-to-face conversations, telephone conversations, radio, and television. Books, articles, and letters can serve as written channels. The senses of touch, smell, and taste are nonverbal channels (although for a blind person reading braille, touch is a verbal channel). Much meaningful communication takes place without a word being spoken.

Continuing to the lower part of Figure 12.1, the receiver must *decode* the message—convert the symbols into meaning. Like senders, receivers have diverse backgrounds, experiences, and aspirations. When the receiver's decoding matches the sender's encoding, communication is likely to be effective. The receiver acts in response to the communication. This action can be to ignore the message, to perform some task, to store the information for future use, or something else. The receiver also usually provides feedback so the sender will know if the message was accurately received and the proper action was taken. An unavoidable part of communication is *noise*—any interference that occurs during the communication process.

In business, communication is vital to success. If communication break-

---

MANAGEMENT IN PRACTICE

A Skill-Building Exercise: One of your oldest and most trusted employees has just taken you aside and said: "It's all over the plant about you and the boss's secretary. I always thought you were a fine, respectable person. Your wife and I have been friends since grade school. Everyone around here admired you in the past. I am really disappointed. I just can't believe you'd do such a thing!" You are stunned because you do not know what she is talking about.

How would you respond?

downs occur, costly mistakes may result. At PPG, the establishment of the quality action teams called "Mythbusters" illustrated that the company wanted to communicate effectively with all employees.

❖ ❖ WHAT SHOULD BE COMMUNICATED?

Henry Mintzberg and others have estimated that individual managers spend about 80 percent of their time communicating.[4] Some managers limit their communication with subordinates to the issuance of orders. But communication should take on a much larger scope. Communication with employees is a critical requirement of good management and of the performance of various managerial roles.

Mintzberg has described the manager's job in terms of three types of roles—interpersonal, informational, and decision-making—and communication is vital to the performance of each role. In their *interpersonal roles*, managers act as figureheads and leaders of their organizations. Mintzberg indicates that managers spend 45 percent of their time with peers, about 45 percent with people outside their company, and ten percent with superiors. In their *informational roles*, managers exchange information about jobs and responsibilities with peers, subordinates, and other personal contacts. They also provide information to others, such as suppliers, peers outside the organization, and other outside groups. Finally, in their *decision-making roles*, managers implement new projects, handle problems, and allocate resources. Even private decisions that managers make will be based on information provided to the managers by others. The managers will then communicate their decisions to others for implementation.[5] Accomplishing all of these roles is not easy, but without effective communication it is virtually impossible.

Today's managers face a complex environment. The acceleration of technology both expedites and complicates communication. Digital technology may be the greatest leap forward in communications since the invention of the transistor. This could accelerate the information available to managers, whether at home or at the office. According to Gerald M. Levin, chairman of Time Warner Inc., "It's a grand vision, and one that lends itself to grandiloquence: 'When I turn on my television, I'll be able to switch to anything, anywhere.' " This type of communication network could really connect the office and the home and allow the manager to draw on an endless flow of information.[6] When a corporation is in a state of flux, an even greater burden is placed on the communication process.

Behavioral scientists have demonstrated that worker motivation is impossible without effective communication. Research has also underscored the need for

TABLE 12.1 Information Employees Want to Know

- **How their jobs should be performed.** Most workers want to do a good job. In order to be effective, they must be told the proper way to do it.
- **How effectively they are performing their jobs.** Workers need and want to know how their superiors view their performance. Problems cannot be corrected if workers do not know what needs to be changed.
- **How much they will be paid.** Pay is a sensitive subject. Workers need to have a clear understanding of how much they will receive and how their pay is calculated.
- **Changes in conditions within the firm that might affect them.** Workers want to know what is going on. If management does not tell them the real story, they may get inaccurate information through informal sources.
- **Company policies and rules that directly affect their jobs.**

subordinates to be heard and understood by their supervisors. The globalization of the business environment complicates the communication process and acts as a barrier to effective communication. The need for an effective communication system to advance the objectives of the organization is obvious. The responsibility to maintain a good communication climate clearly falls to management.

Determining the specific topics to be communicated is often difficult. The manager who believes that everything is suitable for transmission will not only clog the channels with insignificant trivia but may harm operations by releasing wrong information. To sustain employee cooperation in the pursuit of organizational objectives, the manager must consider employee needs and must communicate how those needs will be addressed. As Table 12.1 indicates, employees want to know certain types of things.

CHANNELS OF COMMUNICATION

As Figure 12.2 shows, organizations provide many communication channels. The channels can be formal or informal. **Formal communication channels** are officially recognized by the organization. Instructions and information are passed downward along these channels, and information flows upward. Information also travels through informal channels. **Informal communication channels** are ways of transmitting information within an organization that bypass formal channels. The informal channels shown in Figure 12.2 will be discussed later in the chapter.

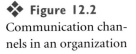

❖ **Figure 12.2**

Communication channels in an organization

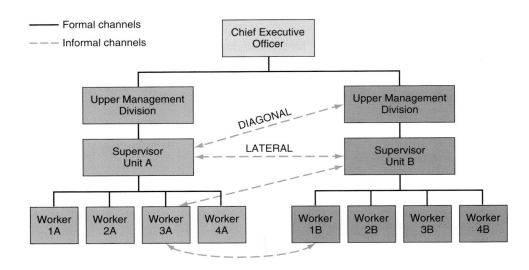

Formal Downward Channels

Many managers emphasize the importance of downward channels of communication. They are aware of the need to convey upper-level management's orders and viewpoints to subordinates, although they may be unaware of how subordinates will perceive the communicated information. The managers believe that the logic of the orders will stimulate desired action. Some of the formal channels available to carry the information downward are the chain of command, posters and bulletin boards, the house organ, letters and pay inserts, employee handbooks and pamphlets, annual reports, and loudspeaker systems.

Chain of Command Orders and information can be given personally or in writing and can be transmitted from one level to another through the chain of command (the line along which authority flows from the top of the organization to any individual). This is the most frequently used formal channel and is appropriate on either an individual or a group basis. The most common way in which communication flows downward is face-to-face interaction. Therefore, the subordinate, whether manager or worker, should become a good listener. The junior person can usually ask questions to clarify the message.

Written documents also provide a major means of downward communication. Letters and memorandums should be written with consideration for how they will be understood. Incorrect interpretations are frequent, however. Lower- and middle-level managers may not have originated the confusing communication, but they can help subordinates understand any from upper management. The directive may require some translation into the language of subordinates.

Written communications should be used for matters that are extremely important to either the manager or the company. Relatively permanent information such as policies, procedures, and rules should also be written. Additionally, managers should write communications that they suspect might otherwise be misunderstood.

Posters and Bulletin Boards Information of concern to company employees is often communicated on posters and bulletin boards. Some workers may not read them, however. This is especially true when the information is not kept current. Materials often remain long after their usefulness has passed. Thus, this channel may be considered only a supplementary device.

The House Organ Many firms have company newsletters or newspapers, often referred to as house organs. A great deal of information regarding the organization can be communicated this way. Newsletters often contain information about new products, about how well the company is doing, and even about policies. Readership is increased if some space is allocated to items of personal interest to employees. For instance, scores of the company bowling team or an award to a long-term employee might be mentioned.

Letters and Pay Inserts Direct mail may be used when top management wants to communicate matters of importance. Since letters are sent directly to employees from the company, there is a reasonable chance they will be read. Inserting a note with the paycheck may also encourage readership. It at least ensures that each worker will receive a copy. Also, workers may be in a mood to read the insert because it is payday. Letters also help stimulate interest in company matters by spouses of employees.

Employee Handbooks and Pamphlets Handbooks frequently are used during the hiring and orientation process as an introduction to the organization. Too often, however, they are unread, even when the firm demands a signed statement that the employee is acquainted with their contents. When a special system is being introduced, such as a pension plan or a job evaluation system, a concise, well-illustrated pamphlet about the subject may facilitate understanding and stimulate acceptance.

Annual Reports Annual reports are increasingly being written not only for stockholders but also for employees. A worker may be able to obtain information about the firm in this way. Information about new plants, new products, and company finances is often included.

Loudspeaker Systems The loudspeaker system is used not only for paging but also to make announcements while they are "hot." Such systems can also be misused, as in the case of a vacationing company president who thoughtlessly sent greetings from his cool mountain retreat to the hot, sweaty workers on the production floor.

Formal Upward Channels

Advocates of participative management emphasize the establishment of upward channels of communication. These channels are necessary not only to determine if subordinates have understood the information sent downward but also to satisfy the need of subordinates to be involved. An upward flow of information is also necessary if management is to coordinate the various activities of the organization. Among the many channels from which to choose for the upward flow of information are an open-door policy, suggestion systems, questionnaires, the grievance procedure, an ombudsperson, and special meetings.

Open-Door Policy An established guideline that allows workers to bypass immediate supervisors in regard to substantive matters without fear of reprisal is an **open-door policy.** This communication channel can go a long way toward reducing tension among subordinates and improving trust. It is important that employees know of the open-door policy and believe management is sincere about it. At Rubbermaid Inc., the former chairman and chief executive officer, Stanley C. Gault, took the open-door policy one step further by strolling through the factories and talking directly with workers.[7]

The advantages of an open-door policy are well known, but the disadvantages should also be recognized. Managers often feel insecure when they know that subordinates can take complaints directly to upper-level managers. At times, a supervisor first finds out a problem exists when an upset upper-level manager calls. Also, an open-door policy may cost management time. Feeling obligated to stop work any time a worker shows up at the door may make it hard to complete administrative tasks.

Suggestion Systems Many companies have formal suggestion systems. Some have suggestion boxes; others have suggestion forms that workers are encouraged to complete. When a suggestion system is used, every suggestion should receive careful consideration. Workers should be promptly informed of the results of the decision on each suggestion.

Questionnaires Anonymous questionnaires sometimes are given to workers in an attempt to identify problem areas in the organization. When a large number of workers rate the firm low in a given area, management should search for solutions. For instance, if a significant number of workers indicate dissatisfaction with pay, an investigation is certainly warranted. Pay may actually be too low, or the workers may just be unaware of what other firms are paying. Whatever the case, the company should take some action, or workers' faith in the use of the questionnaires may be lost.

The Grievance Procedure A systematic process through which employees complain about matters affecting them is a **grievance procedure.** This procedure is a mechanism that gives subordinates the opportunity of settling disputes within the organization. Most unions have negotiated formal grievance procedures. When employees do not have avenues to voice their complaints, even small gripes may grow into major problems. Some managers believe a formal grievance procedure weakens their authority. Others see the grievance procedure as a way of keeping minor problems from becoming serious.

Ombudsperson In nonunion organizations, the ombudsperson provides a means of resolving grievances. An **ombudsperson** is a complaint officer with access to top management who hears employee complaints, investigates them, and recommends appropriate action. This form of grievance resolution has been used for some time in Europe, and the practice is becoming more popular in the United States. Ombudspersons act as top management's eyes and ears. Because of their access to top management, ombudspersons can often resolve problems swiftly. In many cases, they simply help employees find people who can solve their problems. Sometimes they recommend specific action to managers.

Ombudspersons have even assumed the additional duty of helping management uncover scandals in their organizations. Workers for large defense contractors, such as McDonnell Douglas and General Electric, who believe that a company problem exists can bypass their supervisors and gain an audience with the ombudsperson. To prevail in court, companies must have clear procedures for handling sexual harassment complaints. Typically, employers choose an impartial ombudsperson, usually in the human resources department, to hear and investigate charges before lawyers get involved. If the sexual harassment complaint appears legitimate, the company must take "immediate and appropriate action" as established in the pivotal 1986 case, *Hunter* v. *Allis-Chalmers.*[8] An impartial ombudsperson is essential for the resolution of these types of organizational problems.

Special Meetings Special employee meetings to discuss particular policies or procedures are sometimes scheduled by management to obtain employee feedback. The keystone of teamwork in the Pitney Bowes Company, for example, is monthly departmental meetings of all employees. In addition, a central employee council of 13 employee representatives meets monthly with top executives. Employees on the council are elected for two-year terms and devote time to investigating company problems and improving communication processes.

Informal Communication Channels

The formal organization structure does not include informal communication channels. If a manager has a problem that is affected by another department, the two managers involved may get together informally over coffee. Informal communication may be either lateral or diagonal (see Figure 12.2). Communication by managers at the same organizational level is **lateral communication**. This form of communication benefits from established personal relationships and mutual trust. The development of lateral communication often takes time, but if it is effective, it can improve the productivity of both departments.

Diagonal communication also bypasses the formal chain of command. **Diagonal communication** is the exchange of information with people who are higher or lower in the organization but who are not directly in the formal chain of command. Again, this is not an automatic process; trust must first develop. Care must be taken in using diagonal communication because immediate supervisors might take offense. Used effectively, diagonal communication can be an important source of information for managers.

As discussed in Chapter 7, the grapevine is the organization's informal communication system. It exists within the organization, but it may also extend beyond it (see Figure 12.3). The grapevine does not respect formal lines of authority. It reaches into every unit and level of an organization. However, most of the information it transmits is derived from the formal organization. The grapevine usually transmits information more rapidly than the formal system does, although sometimes not as accurately. Employees generally consider the grapevine one of the primary sources of current information.

The grapevine has four basic characteristics:

1. It transmits information throughout the organization in every direction. Information on the grapevine can go down, up, laterally, and diagonally, all at the same time. The grapevine can connect organizational units that have only indirect formal relationships.

❖ **Figure 12.3**
The grapevine

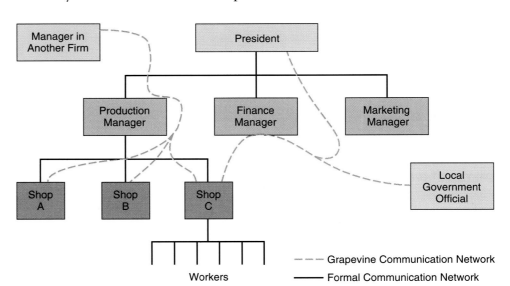

Informal communication may be either lateral or diagonal. Managers involved may get together over coffee or lunch and discuss problems of mutual interest. The relaxed atmosphere of this informal meeting undoubtedly contributes to openness in communication. (Source: © Jim Pickerell)

2. The grapevine transmits information rapidly. It is not restricted by formal policies and procedures. The chain of command does not have to be followed. Once a message gets into the grapevine, it can move almost instantaneously to any point in the organization.

3. The grapevine is selective in regard to who receives the information. Some people are tuned in to it and others are not. There are certain people to whom even gossips do not talk. Consequently, some managers are not even aware of the grapevine.

4. The grapevine extends beyond the formal organization. Considerable communication about the firm occurs off the job. Workers at a party may pass on or receive information about the company. Figure 12.3 shows the grapevine connecting to a manager in another company as well as to a government official. There are usually hundreds or even thousands of such connections.

Managers should not ignore the grapevine, because it cannot be eliminated. Wise managers attempt to remain tuned in to the grapevine. Not only will they obtain useful information, but they will be able to replace incorrect messages with accurate ones. The grapevine is an important part of the communication process, even for enlightened companies that try to make the formal communication system as effective as possible.

❖ ❖ COMMUNICATION NETWORKS

Organizations are made up of individuals in certain positions or roles. The relatively permanent role arrangements in a group describe in part the group's structural configuration, or group structure. Group structure may also be described by the enduring patterns of communication among the role holders.

The pathways through which messages between and among people in organizations flow are **communication networks.** Figure 12.4 illustrates five such networks.

The wheel network consists of a single person who communicates with all the others in the work group. The Y network (particularly if it is inverted) and the chain network resemble the chain of command in a formal communication channel. Communication flows up and down a hierarchy, with little skipping of levels of communication outside the hierarchy. The circle resembles the chain except that the communication loop is closed. For example, the lowest-level member of a group may have a top manager as a mentor and may communicate with that person. In the completely connected network, all group members regularly communicate with all other members.

Of course, a single network does not precisely describe the communication in any one group. Rather, a group's communication may be typified by one network, or the group may use variants of one or more networks. Identifying the predominant structural configuration, however, helps explain or predict the performance and satisfaction of the group and its members.

In the wheel configuration, information is exchanged relatively quickly between the center position and peripheral ones. Information flows somewhat slower between two spoke positions because it must pass through a third position, the center, which acts as an intermediary. Compare this speed of information exchange with the speed between two positions in the chain. Obviously, passing information through two positions requires less time than moving it through three.

In the wheel, accuracy of information is high, because little filtering occurs; only one person, the central person, can pass information on to others. Contrast this to the chain or Y network, where distortions increase as information passes

❖ **Figure 12.4**
The characteristics of
five communication
networks
(Source: Based on
A. Bavelas, "Communication Patterns in Task-Oriented Groups,"
*Journal of the Acoustical
Society of America* 22
[1950]: 725–730.)

Network:	Wheel	Y	Chain	Circle	Completely connected
Characteristics of Information Exchange:					
Speed	Fast	Slow	Slow	Slow	Fast-Slow
Accuracy*	Good	Fair	Fair	Poor	Good
Saturation	Low	Low	Moderate	High	High
Characteristics of Members:					
Overall satisfaction	Low	Low	Low	High	High
Leadership emergence	Yes	Yes	Yes	No	No
Centralization	Yes	Yes	Moderate	No	No

through several positions. The links of the wheel, chain, and Y receive less information than the links of the circle and the completely connected network.

In the circle and completely connected network, the greater opportunity for feedback seems to be associated with greater member satisfaction. This satisfaction may also be due to sharing of the leadership responsibility and decentralization of decision making.

The effectiveness of the structural configuration selected will vary among groups and at different times within the same group. For example, when a group is newly formed, a wheel configuration may be best, so a large quantity of information can be conveyed as rapidly as possible to the new members. But in an established group whose members must identify and evaluate alternatives, discussion is more essential than information conveyance; and a completely connected network may therefore be more appropriate. Effectiveness exists when the network, the group members, and the task characteristics fit together well.

❖ ❖ BARRIERS TO COMMUNICATION

For communication to be effective, the receiver must correctly interpret the sender's message. Often, however, communication is ineffective because of breakdowns that can occur at any stage in the communication process. If a manager tells an employee to "produce a few more parts," and the employee makes two but the manager wanted 200, a breakdown in communication certainly took place. If managers are to develop their ability to communicate, they must understand the ways in which communication breakdowns occur. At times, even communication aids that are intended to assist the communication effort actually interfere with it, because the focus is on the communication aid. Louis V. Gerstner, IBM CEO, says, "I have never seen foils [slides] like in this company. There must be a manual that says every foil must have 4 circles, 2 squares, 2 triangles, 16 arrows, and as many of them as possible should be three dimensional—with shading—and at least 4 colors." Gerstner deemphasized this aid, and reemphasized effective communication.[9]

As Figure 12.5 shows, successful management decisions must pass through the barriers to communication if organizational objectives are to be achieved. If the barriers are excessive, communication may be reduced to the point where the firm's objectives simply cannot be met. Barriers are classified as technical, language, and psychological.

Technical Barriers

Environmental barriers to communication are referred to as *technical barriers*. Timing, information overload, and cultural differences are three such barriers.

❖ **Figure 12.5**
Communication
barriers

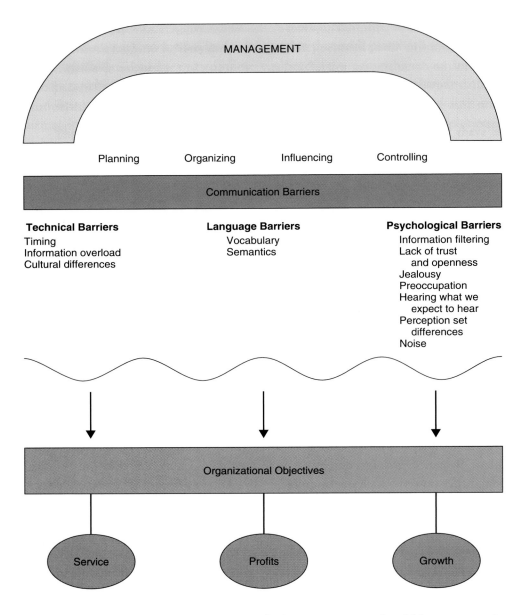

Timing Timing is the determination of when a message should be communicated. It is often important for a manager to determine the most appropriate time to transmit a message. For instance, a manager who must reprimand a worker for excessive tardiness will want to speak to the worker as soon as possible after the event. If, say, six months pass before the reprimand is made, the worker will likely have forgotten the event.

Information Overload Information overload is the condition that exists when an individual is presented with too much information in too short a time. With the many channels and media available, as well as the desire of organizations to share more information than in the past, it is little wonder that information overload occurs. A person can absorb only so many facts and figures at any one time. When excessive information is provided, a major breakdown in communication can occur.

As a professor, one of the authors contributed to information overload in a classroom. The course was a statistics class that met one day a week for four hours. In the first hour, students were eager to take notes. By the fourth hour, few students could repeat what the instructor had said. Information overload had occurred. Some students have discovered that their grades suffer when they attempt to take all of their classes on Monday, Wednesday, and Friday or on Tuesday and Thursday. By the end of the last class, many of the students have no idea what the instructor said.

Cultural Differences Breakdowns in communication can also be caused by cultural differences. In the United States, time is a valuable commodity, and a deadline suggests urgency. But in the Middle East, giving another person a deadline is considered rude, and the deadline is likely to be ignored. If a client is kept waiting in the outer office for 30 minutes in the United States, the delay may mean that the client is perceived to have low status. In Latin America, a 30-minute wait is common. If a contract offer in this country has not been acted on over a period of several months or a year, an American might conclude that the other party has lost interest. In Japan, long delays mean no slackening of interest, and delay is often a negotiation tactic, known to be effective in dealing with impatient Americans.

Americans conduct most business at an interpersonal distance of five to eight feet; a distance of one to three feet suggests more personal or intimate undertakings. The normal business distance in Latin America is closer to the personal distance in the United States. This cultural difference results in some interesting communication difficulties. Consider the backpedaling North American as his or her Latin American counterpart presses ever closer. Regarding status symbols, consider a manager's office in the United States. Spacious, well furnished, and located on the top floor, it conveys an aura of prestige. In the Middle East, size and decor of office mean little or nothing; and in France, managers are likely to be located in the midst of their subordinates in order to control them.

Language Barriers

Language problems can result from the vocabulary used and from different meanings applied to the same word (semantics).

Vocabulary A manager must understand the type of audience being addressed. Statisticians, skilled mechanics, and unskilled laborers likely have different vocabulary sets. Words that the statistician might fully understand have little meaning to the unskilled laborer. Breakdowns in communication often occur when the sender does not tailor the message to match the knowledge base of the receiver. This problem is most severe when someone deliberately uses fancy words just to seem more knowledgeable.

Certain words are part of practically every person's vocabulary. Figure 12.6 calls them the *common vocabulary base.* Arbitrarily selected difficulty levels from 0 to 4 on a scale of 10 are used to determine the level of difficulty of a word. If a speaker used words of level 4 or less, both the statistician and the unskilled laborer will understand. As the speaker progresses above this base level, more and more people will be unable to comprehend the message. If the statistician uses words above the level of 6, communication with the skilled mechanic is lost. Naturally, there will be times when higher-level words must be used to communicate a technical concept, but if managers can concentrate their messages in the common vocabulary base, they have a much better chance of being understood.

Semantics When a sender transmits words to which a receiver attaches meanings different from those intended, a semantic (relating to the meaning of words) communication breakdown will likely occur. A major difficulty with the English language is that multiple meanings may be attached to a single word. Take, for instance, the word *charge.* A manager may place an employee *in charge* of a section. A company *charges* for its services. A person gets a *charge* out of a humorous story. Jargon also creates barriers to communication.

Jargon is a special language that group members use in their daily interaction. Virtually every industry develops a jargon that is used in everyday business. So do groups within an industry. The statistician, computer programmer, word processor, and unskilled laborer are likely to use the jargon associated with their jobs. When one person in a trade speaks to another not associated with the trade—and therefore unfamiliar with the jargon—a breakdown in communica-

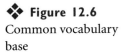

❖ **Figure 12.6**
Common vocabulary base

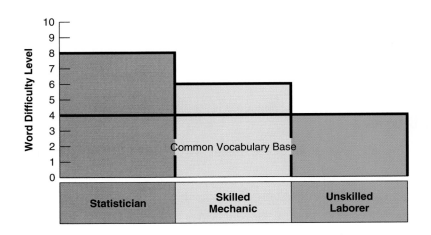

tion may occur. For this reason, many firms provide new employees with a list of definitions of terms associated with the particular industry.

Psychological Barriers

Technical factors and semantic differences cause many breakdowns in communication, but psychological barriers tend to be the major cause for miscommunication. These barriers include various forms of distortion and problems involving interpersonal relationships.

Information Filtering Information **filtering** is the process by which a message is altered through the elimination of certain data as the communication moves up from person to person in the organization. As subordinates communicate, they know the information will be used for at least two purposes: (1) to help management control and direct the firm (and therefore the worker), and (2) to evaluate the worth of their performance. Managers often discover that information that has been provided to them by subordinates has been filtered. Managers at all levels are also tempted to filter information as it progresses through the chain of command. Even the president may filter information before it goes to the board of directors or is communicated to subordinates.

There have been many managerial attempts to reduce the levels of authority that clog organizational communication channels. Decentralization is one means of reducing the number of levels of authority in the organization. One organization reduced the number of managerial levels from eight to four, with a consequent speeding up of the communication process.

Lack of Trust and Openness Trust and openness on the part of both managers and employees must exist if orderly changes in the organization are to occur. There are no such barriers at PPG. According to PPG's *Blueprint for the Decade*, it is mandated that "management communicate openly and challenge people to be creative and entrepreneurial, with the aim of deepening understanding of each other's point of view and rallying everyone to the pursuit of excellence."

Managers who are open and receptive to employees' ideas encourage employee feedback. Managers need this feedback to do their job. If managers give the impression that their orders should never be questioned, communication tends to be stifled.

A major factor in the success of Japanese business is that Japanese managers trust their peers and superiors as well as their workers. This attitude results in a simpler organizational structure. Japanese firms assume that people at all levels of the company are trustworthy, and they do not have to employ highly paid executives to review the work of other highly paid executives.

Jealousy Not everyone may be pleased by a manager's successful performance.

Openness and trust must exist if orderly changes in the organization are to occur. When employees feel that openness and trust do not exist, barriers to communication are present. (Source: © John Coletti)

In fact, a manager's competence may actually be viewed by peers and superiors as a threat to their security. They may even try to minimize the manager's accomplishments in the eyes of upper management. Because of the jealousy of peers, the effectiveness of communication between the manager and upper management may be severely reduced.

Preoccupation Some people are so preoccupied with themselves that they do not hear the message they are listening to. Preoccupation causes people to respond in certain predictable though inappropriate ways. A columnist tells the story of attending a party at the home of a socialite. The socialite was famous for being so preoccupied with making a favorable impression on his guests that he did not listen to what the guests said. The columnist decided to play a trick on the person. He deliberately arrived late. As he entered, he gave this explanation: "I'm sorry to be late, but I killed my wife this evening and had a difficult time stuffing her body into the trunk of my car." The host responded, "Well, the important thing is that you've arrived; now the party can really begin."

Hearing What We Expect to Hear Most of us are conditioned to hear what we expect to hear, not what is actually said. Because of past experiences, we develop preconceptions of what is being said. Sometimes we hear what we want to hear. An employee who has been reprimanded quite a few times by a certain supervisor may even interpret a compliment by that supervisor as a negative statement.

Perception Set Differences A **perception set** is a fixed tendency to interpret information in a certain way. Differences in past experiences, educational back-

Often with the passage of time, clearly communicated business deals become rather fuzzy and vague. Organizations protect themselves from future misunderstandings by signing contracts with their constituents. However, at times, solutions to public relations problems go well beyond mere contract enforcement. You are the public relations manager for the J. L. Shiely Company, a St. Paul mining concern. Your company has always coexisted harmoniously with the community in which it is located. Suddenly, however, the town turns against your company. A new town board views digging for profit as immoral, and in order to punish your company, the new company passes an ordinance to take 15 acres of your property without payment. In 1955 Shiely had given the town permission to use the park, with a provision that the firm could eventually reclaim it for mining. You could probably win a lawsuit against the town, but that would sour the relationship even further. You can either take the town to court, or you can lobby residents to intervene to make the town start treating your company fairly.[10]

What would you do?

ground, emotions, values, beliefs, and many other factors affect each person's perception of a message or of words. The word *management*, for example, may provoke an entirely different image in the minds of two different people. The parents of one person may have been business managers, while the parents of the other may have been labor union organizers. Perception set differences even affect the meanings of words such as *chair, pencil,* and *hat,* which represent tangible objects. The impact is much greater for such intangibles as *liberal* and *conservative.*

Noise Noise is anything that interferes with the accurate transmission or reception of messages. It is the principal source of error in communications, and it can occur at several or all points in the communication process. Although it cannot be completely eliminated from the communication process, its negative impacts can be lessened.

❖ ❖ BARRIERS TO EFFECTIVE WORK TEAM COMMUNICATION

Barriers to communication also affect work teams. Additionally, work team attitudes toward collaboration and competition can create barriers. Parties with a competitive attitude

- Define conflict as win-lose.
- Pursue only their own objectives.
- Understand their own needs but publicly disguise them.
- Expand their power.
- Use threats to get submission.
- Overemphasize their own needs, goals, and position.

- Adopt an attitude of exploiting the other party whenever possible.
- Emphasize only differences in positions and the superiority of their own position.
- Isolate the other person or team.[11]

This "we-they" perspective is a major barrier to interteam communication. It polarizes the interacting teams, and it causes communications to take on an aura of bargaining, rather than transmitting facts or solving problems.

❖ ❖ HOW MANAGERS CAN BECOME BETTER COMMUNICATORS

When breakdowns in communication occur, the result is often lowered productivity. Sometimes, managers believe they have told a worker to do one thing, and the worker perceives it as a directive to do something else. In this case, the manager not only may lose the worker's time, but also may discover that harm was done when the worker performed the wrong task. Thus, learning how to communicate effectively can significantly improve productivity. The main thing to remember is that communication skills can be learned. Empathy, listening, reading skills, observation, word choice, body language, and actions are all involved in improving communication.

Empathy

Empathy is the ability to identify with the feelings and thoughts of another person. It does not mean you necessarily agree with the other person, but you understand why that person speaks and acts in a certain way. If someone is bitter, an empathic person is able to "feel" the bitterness. Managers should take the time to understand as much as possible about the people they work with daily. By being empathic, they can more easily get to the heart of many workers' problems.

Listening

To facilitate communication, one of the most effective tools managers have at their disposal is the ability to listen. Constant talking interferes with listening and learning. Listening skills help managers discover problems and determine solutions.

Communication cannot take place unless messages are received and understood. It has been observed that the average speaking speed is about 120 words per minute. The speed at which most people are able to comprehend words is more than four times the speed at which the words are spoken. The question therefore arises: What does the listener do with the free time that results from this difference in speeds?

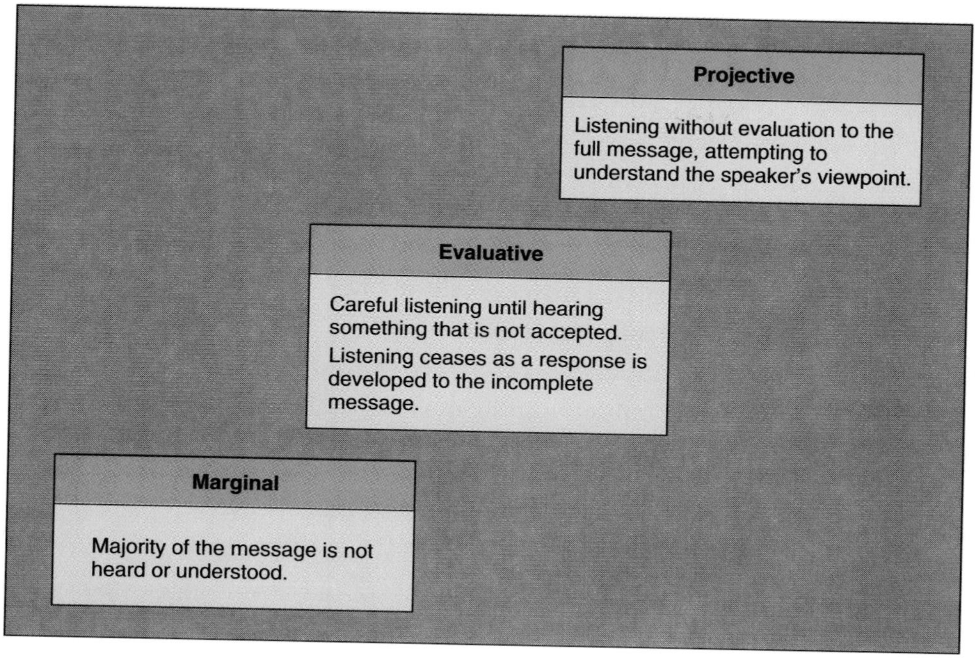
Projective
Listening without evaluation to the full message, attempting to understand the speaker's viewpoint.
Evaluative
Careful listening until hearing something that is not accepted.
Listening ceases as a response is developed to the incomplete message.
Marginal
Majority of the message is not heard or understood.

Figure 12.7 Levels of listening

As Figure 12.7 shows, at least three types of listening have been identified: marginal, evaluative, and projective. The slower speed of the speaker provides the listener with an opportunity for marginal listening—letting the mind stray while someone is talking. This can lead to misunderstanding and even insult. Most of us have experienced a conversation in which we realize that the other person's mind is "a million miles away." The person may have heard a few words, but most of the message was not understood.

Evaluative listening occurs when any free time is devoted to evaluating the speaker's remarks. As soon as the sender says something that is not accepted, communication ceases, as the receiver begins to develop a response. Instead of one idea being transmitted and held by two people, two ideas develop, neither of which is really communicated. If the listener allocates too much time to disapproving or approving of what is heard, there may not be time to understand it fully. This is particularly true when the remarks are loaded with emotion or threats to the security or status of the receiver.

Projective listening holds the greatest potential for effective communication. To fully utilize their time, listeners attempt to project themselves into the position of the speaker and to understand what is being said from the speaker's viewpoint. Effective listening should precede evaluation. After understanding what has been said, individuals are better able to evaluate it. Carl Rogers has suggested a rule to follow to ensure some degree of projective listening: "Each person can speak for himself only *after* he has related the ideas and feelings of the previous speaker accurately and to that speaker's satisfaction."[12] There is no need to agree with the statements, but there is a need to understand them as the speaker intended. Only in this way is it possible to frame a reply that will actually respond to the speaker's remarks. Effective listening is empathic listening. It requires an ability to listen for feeling as well as for words. The listener attempts to "stand in the shoes" of the other person.

Reading Skills

The amount of written material managers must cover has increased significantly in recent years, and some attempt should be made to consolidate and reduce it. Particularly in larger organizations, the ability to read rapidly and with understanding is an essential communication skill. It has been found that through training, reading speeds can be doubled and tripled with little or no loss in comprehension.

Observation

Most people have heard of police reports of traffic accidents where there were many witnesses. When the witnesses are questioned by the police, they come up with many different versions of what occurred. "The blue car went through the stop light," says one witness. "No, that is not correct," says another. "The light was green." Most people miss a great deal by failing to carefully observe important elements in the environment. We mentioned earlier how some managers are adept at assessing the atmosphere of an organization merely by strolling through its workplace. Observation of furnishings, housekeeping, clothing, and activities can provide much information. Using our powers of observation to supplement listening and reading adds immeasurably to our understanding of what is going on.

Word Choice

There is a certain base of words that virtually everyone can understand (refer back to Figure 12.6). Managers who want to communicate effectively must choose their words carefully. The words transmitted by the sender should be in the vocabulary set of the receiver. Generally, for effective communication, simple or common words are best.

Body Language

Research has shown that 90 percent of first impressions are based on nonverbal communication and only 10 percent on verbal communications.[13] Because it is the manager's job to get things done through the efforts of other people, it is important for managers to be aware of how they are communicating nonverbally. **Body language** is the nonverbal method of communication in which physical actions such as motions, gestures, and facial expressions convey thoughts and emotions.

An infinite variety of body positions are available to the receiver at any one moment. The manager will find it useful to know the language of body position and to use it correctly. Although body language is highly individualized, some generalizations, used cautiously, may be helpful. Crossed legs or ankles and folded arms may indicate a defensive posture or a dislike of the situation. A more open position may indicate the opposite, as may leaning forward or backward in a relaxed manner. A worker facing away from the manager, or putting hands in pockets, may be adopting a negative posture.

Many people almost literally talk with their hands. Usually, the meaning of hand gestures is readily understandable. As part of the total message, the importance of these gestures should not be ignored by the manager. Free use of hand gesturing is likely to indicate one of two contrasting psychic states—highly emotional and animated or relaxed and relatively carefree. If the emotional zeal of the first state develops into stress, gesturing becomes more restricted. The really tense individual is likely to hold the body rigid and use limited hand movement.

While free use of hand gestures generally reflects a positive attitude toward the other person, it sometimes can indicate other states. Nervousness, discomfort, or an unfavorable attitude may be reflected by such things as clenching the fists; drumming the fingers; twiddling the thumbs; and tugging at the nose, ear, or chin. The more neutral stance of thinking or evaluating may be indicated by stroking or rubbing the chin or forehead.

Cultural Diversity Demands New Communication Skills

Managers in companies such as AT&T, Levi Strauss, and McDonald's are beginning to better understand and manage their diversified workforce. In a culturally diverse environment, communication problems often have as much to do with cultural norms and expectations as with language barriers. In a culturally diverse workforce, inappropriate verbal and nonverbal messages may well cause communication problems. Communication problems could lead to embarrassment, confusion, and an offending environment. Probably nonverbal signals have the potential to cause the greatest communication problems. The degree of eye contact, the type of hand gestures, the level of formality, and the degree of physical contact and distance could negatively impact work team effectiveness. Since every individual, culture, and business situation is unique, there are no simple rules for communication in a diverse work team. The one rule for effectively communicating in a diverse workplace is for all team members to have an acute awareness of characteristics common to a culture, race, gender, age or sexual preference. Individuals with common characteristics have a fixed tendency to interpret information in a certain way, and this must be taken into consideration when communicating. Effective communication in a diverse work environment demands that team members develop patience, open-mindedness, acceptance, and cultural awareness. Only by such measures can work team effectiveness be assured and communication enhanced.[14]

Facial expressions are usually readily understood. By observing a person's face, we can often distinguish among such emotions as anger, interest, happiness, disgust, contempt, surprise, fear, and love. Facial expressions may indicate true feelings more reliably than verbal messages. In fact, when these two types of messages are contradictory, the receiver is more likely to believe the facial expression. For most people, it is more difficult to communicate false information through facial expression than through any speaking or writing.

Effective managers appreciate the importance of body language in the communication process. All people give off physical signals in attempting to communicate. These signals provide significant insight into the exact meaning of the message. Managers, particularly, must be aware of the signals they are presenting. Employees grasp at these small signals to determine what the boss really means. A frown may cause words that are positive in nature to be perceived as negative. A sarcastic smile along with the words "you did a good job" will likely

A GLOBAL PERSPECTIVE

Learning and Linking: Essential for Effective Global Communication

In the global environment, communication problems are intensified by language barriers and poor communication systems. Faced with the ongoing globalization of business, an increasing number of U.S. executives are learning a second language. For instance, du Pont chief executive Edgar S. Woolard, Jr., learned Japanese. Other du Pont managers are cramming for second languages as well. Their counterparts at Eastman Kodak, Citicorp, General Electric's Medical Systems division, and other corporations are doing the same thing.[15] Most big companies sign up with 111-year-old Berlitz International to teach executives to speak another language. Berlitz is the leading language school worldwide, operating 267 centers in 25 countries and teaching 50 languages. Recently there has been a steady increase in the company's corporate clients. Enrollment in the company's corporate-oriented total language immersion program and other classes has increased more than 50 percent. French and German are among the most popular languages for Americans attending Berlitz classes, with Japanese picking up fast.[16] Because many international companies have declared English as their official language, English classes account for 64 percent of Berlitz's business internationally. Since language proficiency tends to make employees more effective communicators, the trend toward learning a second language is likely to continue.[17]

Once language proficiency is achieved, the problem of linking individuals must be overcome. In many parts of the world, this is a very challenging problem. Motorola is determined to make direct, flawlessly clear individual communication a reality throughout the world. Motorola is buying up radio frequencies throughout the world, and has conceived the ambitious Iridium project, which uses 66 satellites to connect calls anywhere in the world. This system will be a godsend to electronically backward nations like Russia, where individuals may really have to wait a week for a dial tone. With language proficiency achieved and a communication system established to link proficient individuals, effective individual communication can begin and business success is possible.

be interpreted to mean that the worker actually did not do a good job. A blank stare may signify to the employee that the manager is not interested.

A manager must also be aware of the signals that a subordinate may be giving off. Sweaty hands or nail biting may mean that the worker feels ill at ease. Managers need to recognize these signs and be prepared to adjust their actions. Most nonverbal signals are given subconsciously. Hence, it may take great effort to change them. In the diverse workforce we encounter today, nonverbal signals are quite important.

Actions

The manager must also recognize that one communicates by what one does or does not do. If a man comes to work one day and finds his desk moved from a location in a private office to one in an open area, communication of a sort has taken place. If no verbal explanation accompanies the action, people will interpret it their own way; the missing symbol or signal will be supplied by the observer. And despite any verbal statement to the contrary, such a move will likely be interpreted as a demotion.

MANAGEMENT IN PRACTICE

A Skill-Building Exercise: As accounting supervisor Dave Roberts started walking toward accounting clerk Brad Stewart to give him some paperwork on an order, he saw that Brad was on the phone. When he got within earshot, he heard Brad say, "I really need 24 months on this because I don't want the monthly payments to take too much of my paycheck." Not wanting to seem too nosy about Brad's personal business, Dave went back to his office.

Thirty minutes later, Dave returned with the same papers, only to find Brad away from his desk and involved in a conversation with two of the other accounting clerks. Dave decided to interrupt what seemed to be a social conversation and give Brad the papers. As they walked back to Brad's desk together, Dave explained, "This is that Osborn order that the boss was so excited about." At about that time,

Brad's phone rang. He answered it and said, "My supervisor is here right now. Can I call you back in a few minutes?" Dave said, "That's okay. Just come to my office when you have time to talk."

As Dave returned to his office, he thought about how Brad had changed. He had been an excellent worker. But now he was spending a lot of his time visiting and chatting with the other workers in the office. He also seemed to have "telephonitis." Brad's work was still satisfactory, but Dave didn't like the idea of his spending so much time on nonproductive activities. "I don't know what I can do," thought Dave. "Brad does have a good record here, and as long as he does his job I suppose I can't really say much about it."

What action should Dave take to help return Brad to his former level of productivity?

In one company, management had introduced a change in procedure for a small crew of employees. The new method was timed, and standards were established. The workers all produced less than half the standard, and they all filed grievances protesting the unfairness of the standard. Management tried everything it could think of to correct the problem, from all-day time studies to providing each employee with a private instructor in the new method. A check on similar jobs in other companies revealed that the standard was in line. Thus, management concluded that the workers were deliberately restricting their output.

✘ Management Tips ✘

Guidelines for Dealing with Communication

1. **Have a plan.** Think of why you want to communicate this particular idea. Then consider the best way to get the message across.

2. **Get organized.** Merely having a general idea of what you want to communicate is not sufficient. A logical thought process should be followed.

3. **Develop the message from the receiver's viewpoint.** Do not try to impress the receiver with big words and long phrases. Remember, if the message is not understood, effective communication has not taken place.

4. **Select the best way to communicate the message.** At times, a verbal exchange is best. At other times, a written memorandum will prove superior. Sometimes you may best communicate by saying nothing.

5. **Look for feedback.** Communication is not complete until you know that your message is clearly understood. A mere nod may be satisfactory. However, it is best to ask, "What do you think I mean?" rather than merely, "Do you understand?"

6. **Follow up.** Even if the message is accurately received, the desired action may not occur. Your priority may not correspond to that of the receiver. You may need to check to see if what you wanted done has actually taken place.

7. **Do not assume too much.** Sometimes, matters that seem obvious to you are not so obvious to your workers.

8. **Be a good listener.** Listening is more than just hearing.

9. **Use language that others can understand.** It is not what you say that counts; it is what the receiver hears.

10. **Observe nonverbal cues.** This form of communication may be a more accurate indication of what is meant than merely the words spoken.

The next move was one of communication by action. An engineer was sent to the production department, and he proceeded to measure various angles and spaces on the floor. He volunteered no information to the group. Finally, one man's curiosity got the best of him, and he asked the engineer what he was doing. The engineer indicated that management wanted to see if there was sufficient room to locate certain machinery that could do the work of this crew. He continued about his business of measuring. The next day, all work crew members were producing amounts well above the established standard.

❖ ❖ DIRECTING

Directing is the process of telling a person what to do. Naturally, much of a manager's work is associated with directing. After giving a directive, the manager should ensure that the subordinate knows:

- What to do.
- How to do it.
- When to do it.
- Why to do it.
- That it is a directive.

It is not being suggested that a manager should tell a worker each of these items every time an order is given. The manager should consider whether the worker already knows the elements. If not, the worker should be told. Difficulties often arise because the manager assumes the worker has the information. A good rule of thumb is to provide the information when you're unsure.

When a directive or order is particularly important, do not simply ask the worker, "Do you understand?" Instead, ask the worker to describe the action to be taken.

SUMMARY

Communication is the transfer of information, ideas, understanding, or feelings among people. Through communication, organizational objectives may be accomplished. Each step in the communication process is critical to success. In the communication process, a sender encodes a message into a set of symbols that the receiver will understand. Messages are transmitted through such means as speaking, writing, acting, and drawing. The receiver decodes the message by converting the symbols into meaning. Communication is effective to the extent that the receiver's decoding matches the sender's encoding. The receiver can ignore the message, perform some task, store the information, or do something else. Through feedback, the sender knows whether the message was accurately received and the proper action taken.

Communication channels, the means by which information is transmitted in organizations, may be formal or informal. Formal channels are those that are officially recognized by the organization. Instructions and information are passed downward, and information flows upward. Information also travels through informal channels, which bypass formal channels. The grapevine is an informal communication system that extends in every direction throughout an organization and even beyond it.

Messages flow along communication networks, such as the wheel and chain configurations. In a group or team, communication may be through one type of network, or the members may use variants of one or more networks. Identifying the predominant structural configuration, however, helps explain or predict the performance and satisfaction of the group or team and its members.

Communication breakdowns often occur when messages are not interpreted correctly. Barriers to communication may be technical, language, or psychological. Environmental barriers such as timing, information overload, and cultural differences are referred to as *technical breakdowns*.

Language problems can result from vocabulary and semantics. A manager must understand the type of audience being addressed. When a sender sends words to which a receiver attaches different meanings than those intended by the sender, a semantic (relating to the meaning of words) communication breakdown has occurred.

Psychological barriers tend to be the major cause of miscommunication. These barriers include various forms of distortion and problems involving interpersonal relations. With information filtering, for example, messages are altered through the elimination of certain data as the communication moves from person to person in the group, team, or organization. Openness and trust must exist if orderly changes are to occur. Jealousy is often a barrier to communication, as are self-preoccupation and the tendency to interpret information in a certain way. Differences in past experiences, emotions, and beliefs affect each person's perception of a message.

When teams take a competitive stance, a "we-they" attitude is projected. This attitude polarizes the interacting teams and thus establishes a communication barrier between them.

KEY TERMS

Communication 375	Diagonal communication 384
Source (sender) 377	Communication networks 386
Communication channels 377	Timing 388
Formal communication channels 379	Information overload 388
	Jargon 390
Informal communication channels 379	Information filtering 391
	Perception set 392
Open-door policy 382	Noise 393
Grievance procedure 383	Empathy 394
Ombudsperson 383	Body language 396
Lateral communication 384	Directing 401

REVIEW QUESTIONS

1. Define <u>communication</u>. Describe the basic communication process.
2. Distinguish by definition between formal and informal channels of communication. Provide examples of both types of channels.
3. Distinguish among technical, language, and psychological barriers to communication.
4. Describe the most common barriers to effective work team communication.
5. List some of the factors that have the ability to improve communication.
6. Define <u>empathy</u>. Explain why empathy is important to a manager.

Empathy, listening, reading, observation, word choice, body language, and actions all facilitate communication, and are all skills that can be learned. Body language is a nonverbal method of communication. Physical actions such as motions, gestures, and facial expressions convey thoughts and emotions. An infinite variety of body positions are available to the receiver at any one moment. The manager will find it useful to know the language of body position and how to use it correctly.

The process of telling a person what to do is directing. Naturally, much of a manager's work is associated with directing. After giving a directive, the manager should ensure that the subordinate knows what to do, how to do it, when to do it, why to do it, and that it is a directive.

CASE STUDIES

CASE 12.1 Wells Fargo: From Horses to High-Tech

The recipe for effective communication is quite interesting at Wells Fargo. Information represents a huge cost for modern banks. Financial institutions recently accounted for 35 percent of U.S. information technology purchases—computers, fax machines, telephones, and other devices. Commercial banks alone spent $12 billion. In the late 1980s, Wells Fargo was considered the leader among major banks in applying such technology to its operation. It was also the undisputed cost leader overall.

Carl Reichardt, Chairman of Wells Fargo and Company, was famous for his use of symbolism, as well as for blunt language. His chief financial officer, Clyde Ostler, told how Reichardt handled subordinates who applied for capital funds during a cost-cutting campaign. Applicants would arrive to see Reichardt sitting in a ragged upholstered chair. Sometimes he would pick at the stuffing while hearing their presentation.

It is easy to think Reichardt could have been friends with William G. Fargo. Fargo began his career as a horseback messenger in the 1830s. He later joined Henry Wells to form their famous overland mail and express company, delivering mail by pony and stagecoach. Wells Fargo tied the far West together and connected it with the East throughout the 19th century. After the transcontinental railway took most of the express business, Wells Fargo began to emphasize its banking arm, which had arisen in Nevada to handle gold transactions. Eventually, the company became what it is today, a major bank holding company.

The modern Wells Fargo company makes full use of automated teller machines, networks of computers, and other proven systems. Wells Fargo was much more interested in reliability than being on the leading edge. Inside Wells Fargo, electronic purchasing and inventory accounting allowed the company to cut its sources of office supplies from 150 to just several. And those few provide just-in-time delivery, all but eliminating what had been a six-month inventory at most offices. The company's 6,600 employees interchange 15,000 to 20,000 messages on the electronic mail (E-mail) system. Wells Fargo was on a roll as it looked forward to the 1990s. Earnings per share had risen 25 percent a year from 1983 on. Share price had quadrupled.

QUESTIONS

1. Evaluate the communication system at Wells Fargo.
2. In this case give an example of how communication was achieved without a word being spoken.

CASE 12.2 Open the Door!

Barney Cline, the new human resource manager for Ampex Utilities, was just getting settled in his office. He had recently moved from another firm to take over his new job. Barney had been selected over several in-house candidates and numerous other applicants because he had a good reputation for working with people to get the job accomplished.

Just then his phone rang. The person on the other end of the line said, "Mr. Cline, could I set up an appointment to talk with you?" "Certainly," Barney said. "When do you want to get together?" "How about after work? It might be bad if certain people saw me speaking to anyone in management."

Barney was a bit puzzled, but he set up an appointment for 5:30 P.M., when nearly everyone would be gone. At the designated time, there was a knock on his door. It was Mark Johnson, a senior maintenance worker who had been with the firm for more than ten years.

After the initial welcome, Mark began talking. "Mr. Cline, several of the workers asked me to talk to you. The grapevine has it that you're a fair person. The company says it has an open-door policy. We're afraid

to use it. Roy Edwards, one of the best maintenance men in our section, tried it several months ago. They hassled him so much that he quit only last week. We just don't know what to do to get any problems settled. There has been talk of organizing a union. We really don't want that, but something has to give."

Barney thanked Mark for his honesty and promised not to reveal the conversation. In the weeks following the conversation with Mark, Barney was able to verify that the situation was just as Mark had described it. There was considerable mistrust between managers and workers.

QUESTIONS

1. What types of communication breakdowns had occurred in the company?
2. Discuss the impact of the grapevine on the resolution of this problem.

NOTES

1. This case is a composite of a number of published accounts, among them: Bill Saporito, "PPG: Shiny, Not Dull," *Fortune* 124 (July 17, 1989): 107; Jack Keough and Christine Forbes, "Welcome to Vendor City," *Industrial Distribution* 80 (May 1991): 32; Jack Keough and Christine Forbes, "Selling Innovation," *Industrial Distribution* 80 (May 1991): 38–40; Vincent A. Sarni, *Blueprint for the Decade* (Pittsburgh, 1984): 1–8; and William J. Storck, "PPG Industries Works on Ways to Dampen Business Cycle Effects," *Chemical and Engineering News* 67 (May 29, 1989): 9–10; Richard Ringer, "PPG Selects an Outsider as New Chief," *The New York Times* (July 16, 1993): D4; Erle Norton, "PPG Industries Taps Jerry E. Dempsey as First Outsider to Be Chairman, Chief," *The Wall Street Journal* (July 16, 1993): B3.

2. David Woodruff, James B. Treece, Sunita Wadekar Bhargava, and Karen Lowry Miller, "Saturn," *Business Week* (August 17, 1992): 88–89; "Quality Control from Mars," *The Wall Street Journal* (January 27, 1992): A10; *Fortune* 123 (September 26, 1988): 98–104; Lynne Joy McFarland, Larry E. Senn, and John R. Childress, *21st*

Century Leadership* (New York: The Leadership Press, 1993): 247.

3. F. E. X. Dance, "The 'Concept' of Communication," *Journal of Communication* 20 (June 1970): 201–210.

4. Henry Mintzberg, *The Nature of Managerial Work* (New York: Harper & Row, 1973).

5. Henry Mintzberg, "The Manager's Job: Folklore and Fact," *Harvard Business Review* 53 (July–August 1975): 49–61.

6. Mark Landler, Ronald Grover, Bart Ziergler, and Chuck Hawkins, "Media Mania," *Business Week* (July 12, 1993): 110–119.

7. Christy Marshall, "Rubbermaid Yes, Plastic," *Business Week* (December 1988): 37.

8. Anne B. Fisher, "Sexual Harassment: What to Do," *Fortune* 128 (August 23, 1993): 84–88.

9. Judith Dobrzynski, "Rethinking IBM," *Business Week* (October 4, 1993): 86–97.

10. Adapted from a case presented in Karen Berney's article, "Finding the Ethical Edge," *Nation's Business* 75 (August 1987): 24.

11. D. W. Johnson and F. P. Johnson, *Joining Together: Group Theory and Group Skills* (Englewood Cliffs, NJ: Prentice-Hall, 1975).

12. Carl R. Rogers and F. J. Roethlisberger, "Barriers and Gateways to Communication," *Harvard Business Review* 30 (July–August 1952): 57–58.

13. Murray Mizock, "What You Aren't Saying May Be Everything," *Data Management* 24 (September 1986): 33.

14. Lee Gardenswartz and Anita Rowe, *Managing Diversity,* (San Diego: Business One Irwin/Pfeiffer & Company, 1993), pp. 57–97; Mahalingham Subbiah, "Adding a New Dimension to the Teaching of Audience Analysis: Cultural Awareness," *IEEE Transactions on Professional Communication* 35 (March 1992).

15. Richard S. Teitelbaum, "Language: One Way to Think Globally," *Fortune* 124 (December 4, 1989): 11.

16. *Ibid.*

17. *Ibid.*, p. 12.

13 Group Performance, Team Building, and Conflict

LEARNING OBJECTIVES

After completing this chapter students should be able to

✘ Describe groups and work teams, the formation of effective groups and teams, and the development of groups into teams.

✘ Explain the factors influencing group and team effectiveness and the means of increasing team effectiveness.

✘ State the characteristics of effective teams, strategies for team building, and self-managed teams.

✘ Define *conflict* and explain its potential causes.

✘ Explain how conflict becomes apparent.

✘ Describe how managers can become better at managing interpersonal and structural conflict.

Volvo's Work Teams

At Volvo's two radically innovative factories, a fixed rather than moving assembly line is the norm. Gone are the days of the moving assembly line introduced by Henry Ford three-quarters of a century ago. In Sweden, the close supervision and machine-pacing of work on the assembly lines were major sore points with employees. At Volvo's newer plants, "work teams build cars much like doctors operate on a patient. Each car frame sits on its individual rotating holder while assembly crews attach the pieces. Instead of foreman and engineers, ordinary workers manage the shop floor." This radical change was brought about because Sweden's highly educated and well-trained labor force does not like to work in conventional factories.

This factory environment is conducive to so-called self-management. Volvo gives workers 16 weeks' training before they are allowed to get close to a car, and 16 months more of on-the-job orientation. In Sweden, at two Volvo plants, functional work teams assemble entire cars and assist in certain management activities. The work teams at these two innovative Volvo automobile plants assemble large units of a car without much supervision from managers. At the Kalmar plant, 15 or 20 people are grouped into teams that build cars without a moving assembly line. Each team builds a large section of a car, with a work cycle of 30 minutes. According to Volvo management, productivity is higher at Kalmar than at the large, conventional assembly plant at Gothenburg. Uddevalla goes much farther with functional work teams. The Uddevalla facility is divided into six assembly plants, each of which has eight teams. Teams basically manage themselves, handling scheduling, quality control, hiring, and other duties normally performed by supervisors. There are no first-line supervisors and only two tiers of management. Each team has a spokesperson who reports to one of the six plant managers. These six individuals report directly to the company president.

In Sweden, as in many countries, the move toward utilization of functional work teams is increasing. Basically, in Sweden the "old way" of running automakers and other large industrial companies is outmoded. However, this approach to automobile manufacturing is not perfect. Problems have occurred with some assembly teams. Workers have reported "friction" and disagreements among team members that have created a certain degree of conflict. Still, few wish to go back to the old way, with supervisors making all the decisions. In Sweden, as in all countries, the environment surrounding the workforce is extremely important and must be designed to encourage employees to put forth effort in the pursuit of organizational goals. The combination of motivated work teams and aggressive marketing has allowed Volvo to be more profitable in the United States as well as in the rest of the world.[1]

Group behavior, team building, and conflict are part of the realities of today's business world, and the problems associated with these factors are often intensified by the teamwork movement. At Volvo, individuals are brought together as teams for the purpose of transforming certain inputs into a Volvo automobile. Functional team members interact with one another on a daily basis to facilitate accomplishment of Volvo's organizational objectives. Conflict has resulted at times, but most employees agree that this approach is better than the alternative.

In this chapter, we first describe *groups* and *work teams* and discuss the formation of effective groups and teams. Next, we review the significant aspects of the development of groups into teams. Then, we address the factors influencing group and team effectiveness and the means of increasing team effectiveness. Next, we state the characteristics of effectiveness teams, strategies for team building, and describe self-managed teams. Then, we discuss conflict in organizations, including potential causes of conflict and the need for conflict to become apparent. We devote the final portion of the chapter to how managers can become better at managing interpersonal and structural conflict, and end with a global perspective.

❖ ❖ GROUPS AND WORK TEAMS

A **group** is two or more people having a unifying relationship, such as common objectives or physical proximity. Although group members generally share certain similarities, each member may have personal reasons for joining the group. People join groups for many reasons, including security, affiliation, esteem, power, and goal accomplishment. Basically, individuals choose group membership to achieve an outcome that requires their association with other people.

Everyone belongs to many groups—at work, in the community, and even at home (the family is a group). There are formal work groups, of course, made up of managers and subordinates. To a certain degree the line between managers

Everyone belongs to many groups at work, in the community, and even at home (the family is a group). Business teams throughout Honeywell help make the company more competitive, according to a company official. Kathryn Ybarra (center) is shown with part of her 30-person engineering team at Honeywell's Air Transport Systems Division in Phoenix. (Source: Photograph courtesy of Honeywell, Inc.)

and subordinates is becoming blurred at some companies. To increase individual and group job performance, managers need to understand the kinds of groups that exist both within and outside the organization.

Groups are categorized in a number of ways. Understanding the characteristics of each type of group can affect a manager's expectations of relationships among group members. Initially, managers need to appreciate the difference between primary and secondary groups. **Primary groups** are small groups characterized by relatively close associations among members. As might be expected, the closeness of these associations directly influences the behaviors of individuals in the group. In contrast, **secondary groups** are larger and less intimate than primary groups. Relationships tend to be more impersonal and frequently are formalized.

Everyone participates in both types of groups. Primary groups exert a greater influence on individuals' day-to-day activities through the presence of other group members and their ability to reinforce member behavior. Secondary groups rely instead on sanctions imposed through control systems (rules, regulations, policies) or exercised by designated individuals, such as group leaders. Groups also can be classified according to their function or the circumstances under which they are formed. Four types of groups commonly encountered in organizations are task (or functional) groups, work teams, project groups, and informal groups.

Task (Functional) Groups

Groups determined by prescribed job requirements are **task,** or **functional, groups.** The workers in the quality control department of a company would be considered a task group. They are brought together for the purpose of insuring the quality of their product. Functional group members usually interact with one another on a daily basis, and they are often organized into departments or work teams to facilitate the accomplishment of organizational objectives.

Work Teams

A **work team** is an "officially sanctioned collection of individuals who have been charged with completing a mission by an organization and who must depend upon one another for successful completion of work."[2] A work team is a fully functioning group whose focus is to accomplish specific tasks to enable the firm to complete its mission. Joseph C. Day, CEO of Freudenberg-NOK, a German-Japanese joint venture with 14 U.S. plants, believes in teams. To bring his plants up to speed he established *GROWTH* teams. GROWTH stands for "Get Rid of Waste Through Team Harmony," and Day hopes GROWTH will help the company more than double sales by the year 2000, without adding people or factory space.[3] As companies carve layers out of their organizations in an attempt to be contenders in the highly competitive international environment firms presently confront, many have formed work teams to deal with the issue. In the future, group membership will be required of more and more employees in many organizations. Companies such as Boeing, Caterpillar, Digital Equipment, Ford, and General Electric are already making work teams part of their push toward greater productivity.[4] Remember that at Volvo's Kalmar plant, 15 or 20 people are grouped into teams that build cars without a moving assembly line.

Project Groups

As discussed in Chapter 7, projects are formal, but temporary, assignments to committees, and special projects. All organizations have some activities requiring cooperation across functional lines—for example, a committee made up of members from several departments. After a project has been completed, project members return to their routine work activities or go to another temporary project. Examples of project groups include research and development teams and internal consultant groups.

Informal Groups

An **informal group** consists of two or more persons associated with one another in ways not prescribed by the formal organization. Such groups are very common. In some cases, they arise because people find themselves in a common location. They can also result from the need to solve organizational problems or achieve formal objectives. Thus, similarities or differences within formal groups can lead to informal activities in organizations. Informal groups can also take the form of two or three people who belong to the same church or baseball team, or who play racquetball or have parties together.

❖ ❖ FORMATION OF EFFECTIVE GROUPS AND TEAMS

People join groups for a multitude of reasons. As previously mentioned, they may spontaneously form informal groups in an organization or within a formal group, such as a network of professionals. They may also be placed in *formal groups,* which in some cases are referred to as *work teams*—those officially sanctioned and organized by managerial or other authority to accomplish organizational objectives.

As Figure 13.1 shows, groups form when individuals exhibit one or more of the following:

1. **Common interests.** Engineers employed by different companies often join the same professional groups.

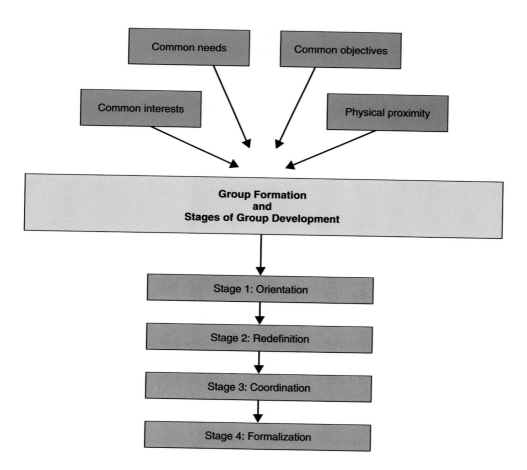

❖ **Figure 13.1**
Stages of group and team development

2. **Common needs.** Food cooperatives may be formed because individuals want to satisfy their basic needs for food at a low cost.

3. **Common objectives.** A board of directors of a company is formed to help the company reach its objectives.

4. **Physical proximity.** Employees in the same work area often join together as a social group.[5]

The reason for forming a group influences the nature and quality of the group's functioning. Studying the causes of group formation, then, helps predict and anticipate the ways a group is likely to act. To be really productive, the group must evolve into an effective collective unit through the process of team development, as is the case with General Motor's Saturn plant.

❖ ❖ DEVELOPMENT OF GROUPS INTO TEAMS

Once a group forms, it must resolve a variety of issues before it can function effectively. Tracing the development of groups provides one perspective for assessing a group's performance. There are essentially four stages of development—orientation, redefinition, coordination, and formalization (see Figure 13.1).

Orientation

The orientation stage occurs when the group views the task and determines acceptable interpersonal behaviors. At this stage, the group members gather information about the nature of the group's task. They also discover acceptable behaviors. Organizations that emphasize the team approach are becoming more and more sensitive to employee behavior, particularly the behavior of executives, on

---

Team Saturn

Team Saturn, the revolutionary approach to car manufacturing that has resulted in the Saturn automobile being named by J. D. Powers & Associates as the best built car in the United States, is based upon the concept of teamwork. Unlike other General Motors plants, Saturn is really a team effort, not just an exercise in lip service. Line worker

Deborah Wikaryasz couldn't believe the difference between teamwork at Saturn and at the Cadillac plant where she had worked previously. Wikaryasz is very impressed with the environment at Saturn, stating that "We don't have the backstabbing and the yelling." Her team not only assembles fixtures on the left side of each Saturn, but they also hire workers, approve parts from suppliers, and handle administrative

matters such as the budget. Wikaryasz is proud that her team "keeps down costs and passes the savings along to customers." This plant was started from scratch, with a team approach and all team members being selected from the best GM had to offer. At Saturn, teams were kept small and were composed of people with complementary skills who were committed to the common purpose of not compromising quality.[6]

ETHICAL DILEMMA

You are an up-and-coming manager who has been employed by a major tobacco company for six years. Managers in the company have a fairly consistent path up the corporate ladder to senior-level management positions by supporting the goals of the organization and working well in committees. You are placed on the committee that handles clients claiming that they or their loved ones got cancer from smoking cigarettes. Initially, this committee reviews the merits of each case and takes actions to limit the financial and public relations impact on the company. You have finished reviewing documents used in a case against the Liggett Group, Inc. A Liggett scientist apparently duplicated the experiments that suggested that the tar in cigarettes caused cancerous tumors to grow in mice. You have also read similar memos used as evidence against R. J. Reynolds. The memos also state that the research department has come up with a new, safer cigarette, but that marketing the cigarette might support the contention that the company recognizes that conventional cigarettes are unsafe. You confront the chairman of the committee with the memos and express your disgust at company executives for choosing not to market a safer cigarette. You are told to forget what you have seen and fall in line or to forget your career, and your job.

What would you do?

---

and off the job. At an Aetna Life & Casualty golfing party, four executives vented their resentment of female managers' presence at what had traditionally been an all-male event. Their mildest offense was calling women executives "sluts." In response, Aetna demoted two of the men and asked the two others to resign.[7] Such sensitivity to executive behavior is becoming more the norm than the exception, and is essential for effective work team development.

Redefinition

The redefinition stage occurs when the group redefines the task, tries to agree on its objectives and strategy, and develops group structure. In a work team, redefinition is essential because the team is always self-managing to a certain degree, which requires agreement on all of these issues and more. Conflict may result at this stage as the group members determine whether they like the task and their degree of commitment to it. In a work team all members must be committed or the team will not function well. Differences in members' reactions to the demands of the task often lead to conflict. Members may differ in the amount of time they are willing to devote to a particular task, the priority they assign to the task, or the means they believe will best accomplish it. The sharper the differences, the greater the intragroup (within the group) conflict.

Coordination

During the coordination stage, which is often the longest one, the group collects information and interprets it in order to facilitate the accomplishment of group objectives. Arguments over interpretation frequently take place. Here, discussions about the nature of the task, different emotional responses to it, alternatives, and possible action take place. A group's discussion about the types and quality of existing programs, as well as its members' participation in the process of developing a new program, illustrate the activities of this stage. The members resolve their differences after an open exchange of relevant interpretations and opinions and begin to act as a group. Often, groups do not reach this stage and therefore disintegrate. Because teams are becoming more common, companies are carefully selecting team members and defining aspects of work such as the nature of the task to limit coordination problems. Once the company is committed to the team approach, it cannot afford for the group to disintegrate. Saturn is a perfect example of a plant that is committed to work teams and has been successful in their utilization.

Formalization

The group specifies the final version of the decision in the formalization stage. It is at this stage that the choice and implementation of task activities occur. At this time, too, roles that match the group's needs for leadership and expertise, as well as the members' abilities and attitudes, are assigned. Only after successfully passing through these stages can a group be considered to be an effective team.

Moving Through the Developmental Stages

A group may recycle through the four stages of development, particularly as changes in its membership, its task, or the environment occur. For example, if a new member is added to the group, the group begins its development anew. In the case of teams, it is vitally important that new team members be carefully selected to limit team disruption. Of course, movement through the stages may occur more rapidly the second time. For example, orientation of a new member may require ten minutes rather than two hours. Instead of receiving new members, a group may change its objectives. The extent and uniqueness of the membership, task, or environmental changes will influence the speed with which the group moves through stages after the first time.

Some groups remain at one stage by failing to resolve the issues associated with it. Typically, the orientation stage is the shortest, followed in length by the redefinition and formalization stages; the coordination stage is longest. Groups experiencing difficulties tend to have a longer formation stage. Failure to move beyond redefinition signals a group's lack of conflict resolution mechanisms. Occasionally, groups remain stuck at other stages. Remaining at the orientation stage suggests that the group lacks the skill to screen out irrelevant information and behavior. Inability to move beyond coordination often reflects a group with poor information, which hinders effective interpretation. Frequently, such dilemmas can remain unresolved when a group lacks clear objectives or when individual members have incompatible objectives.

❖ ❖ FACTORS INFLUENCING GROUP AND TEAM EFFECTIVENESS

An effective group or team can attain, or make acceptable progress toward, its objectives or the objectives of its members. In an organization, this may mean getting a job done, providing members with a sense of belonging, or successfully competing with another group. As Figure 13.2 suggests, many factors influence group and team effectiveness. Among them are individual roles, group norms, conformity, leadership, group cohesiveness, group size, and synergism.

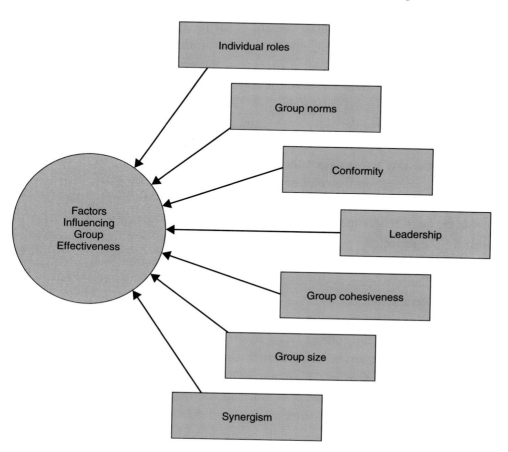

❖ **Figure 13.2**
Factors influencing group and team effectiveness

The Mediation of Role-Related Diversity Problems Through Role Playing

An individual's role includes more than the official content of the job description, and can be complicated by diversity issues. Failure to conform to the expected roles of those in a team may result in a member being cast out of the informal group, and this could have devastating consequences on work team effectiveness.

On the other hand, managers who appreciate the value of diversity may be able to create a team that is more productive than a nondiverse group. To help prevent problems related to roles in a diverse environment, many companies are establishing seminars to foster a better understanding of differences that could cause problems. These seminars help managers better anticipate role-related problems, and even to value diversity, as does Levi Strauss. At many companies like Johnson & Johnson, role-playing exercises are being utilized to help traditional white male senior managers gain a better understanding of probable role-related problems that are likely in a diverse team environment. Basically, these role-playing exercises help these managers "walk in the other person's shoes." Managers who realize that diversity is a way to get more productivity out of a team will be more successful in the global economy.[8]

Individual Roles

The concept of role is broader than that of its counterpart in the formal organization—the job. A **role** is the total pattern of expected behavior of an individual. It includes the official content of the job description, but goes beyond it. If a person is officially designated a supervisor, that person may be pressured to dress, talk, and act like other managers in the organization. If members of a work team typically dress formally, the team member who fails to do so may not be fulfilling the expected role. Roles that team members play are vitally important and are often regulated by other team members.

Individuals who are members of an informal group also are presented with roles to act out. Whether or not the informal group is supportive of management has a major impact on the roles of the group members. If the group decides not to support a decision made by top management, the pattern of members' behavior (role) may reflect indifference or slowing down on the job. Failure to conform to the expected role may result in a member's being cast out of the informal group. This may harm the formal organization as well as the individual. On the other hand, managers can usually work through informal group leaders to maximize productivity.

A person may have many roles to play. For instance, when working toward a doctorate, one of the authors was a student, a teacher, a consultant, and a military officer in the reserves. The failure to change roles immediately at the proper time sometimes resulted in difficulties. Being a military officer with considerable authority on the weekend and a humble doctoral student on Monday morning was sometimes not easy. Students who go back to school part time while working as supervisors often encounter the same difficulties.

Norms

Underlying group development and implicit in group functioning are expectations that guide behavior. A **norm** is a standard of behavior expected of informal group members. A student, for example, is expected to attend classes, prepare homework, and take examinations. A worker is expected to be at work on time, miss work only in case of illness, and put in a good day's work for a good day's pay. These unwritten expectations develop through the interaction of group members and the reinforcement of behaviors by the group. Generally, the expectations are in line with group objectives, which in turn are helpful in accomplishing organizational objectives.

Group members may act to encourage certain behaviors—for example, by reinforcing a specific level of production. Members may also discourage certain behaviors by responding negatively to their occurrence. A group may, for example, reject very low or very high performance.

There are norms about attendance, performance, interpersonal interactions, and dress, but not all norms apply to everyone. Different norms exist for managers and nonmanagerial employees, for professionals and nonprofessionals, for men and women. They might differ in the extent to which people are expected to be innovative on the job, follow organizational rules and regulations, or demonstrate loyalty to a specific department or supervisor. Members who are expected to demonstrate loyalty to their department might try to provide a larger role for that department than would individuals with more organizational loyalty.

Conformity

Once norms are established, the issue of conformity necessarily becomes a matter of concern. The anticipation of acceptance or rejection by the group for following or violating norms is usually enough to ensure that members conform to the group's expectations. Conformity offers the advantage of maintaining a predictable pattern of work, nurturing teamwork, and defending individual and group interests. When an individual does not conform to group norms, other group members will, at least initially, try to persuade the deviant to conform. In some groups, the nonconformist may even be physically harassed.

Conformity clearly has its negative side. It can stifle innovation and initiative, reduce performance, and even encourage undesirable actions. Solomon Asch demonstrated the power of small groups to pressure individuals into yielding to the majority opinion, even when that opinion is clearly false. Asch showed a group of people a card with lines of varying lengths and asked each person to determine which line was the same length as the line on a comparison card. Asch planted all but one of the people in the group, and the plants deliberately gave the wrong answers. About 35 percent of the subjects also gave the wrong answer. Asch found, however, that if just one of the individuals planted in the group gave the right answer, violating the unanimous judgment of the group, the tendency of the subject to conform was lessened considerably. Just one ally was often enough to encourage independent judgment on the subject's part.[9]

Leadership

In the formal organization, leaders are managers; they are placed in their positions of authority by top management. An entirely different process occurs in selecting a leader for the informal organization. The informal leader is usually chosen in one of two ways. First, people may appoint themselves informal leaders. A leadership vacuum may exist, and the first person who takes charge may be automatically followed. Second, the informal leader may be chosen through consensus. In this case, the person whose behavior is closest to the norms of the group often becomes the leader.

Although the informal leader may have no formal title, this person is the one who is looked to for guidance in achieving the group's objectives. If the leader begins to deviate from group norms, a group member whose behavior is closer to the group norms may take the leader's place.

Group Cohesiveness

Cohesiveness is the degree of attraction the group has for each of its members. Important to both the formal and the informal organization, cohesiveness is identified by attitudes such as loyalty to the group, friendliness and congeniality, a feeling of responsibility for group efforts, and a willingness to defend the group against outside attack. Cohesive informal work groups are powerful instruments; they can work for or against the formal organization. For instance, a highly cohesive group whose goals are in agreement with organizational objectives can use its strength to help the firm increase productivity. On the other hand, a highly cohesive group whose goals are not in agreement with organizational objectives can have an extremely negative effect on the accomplishment of the firm's objectives. Because of this potential problem, some managers attempt to reduce cohesiveness in order to maintain control.

Several factors will affect the degree of cohesiveness group members have for each other (see Figure 13.3). First, a group that is exposed to danger or to threats often develops great cohesiveness. For example, a manager who is seen as a threat to workers can cause the workers to band together in opposition. Second, frequency of contact has an effect. Groups whose members seldom see each other are not likely to be cohesive. Third, homogeneous groups are likely to be more cohesive than heterogeneous groups. For example, workers of one sex, race, or age are usually more cohesive than are mixed groups. Fourth, if being a mem-

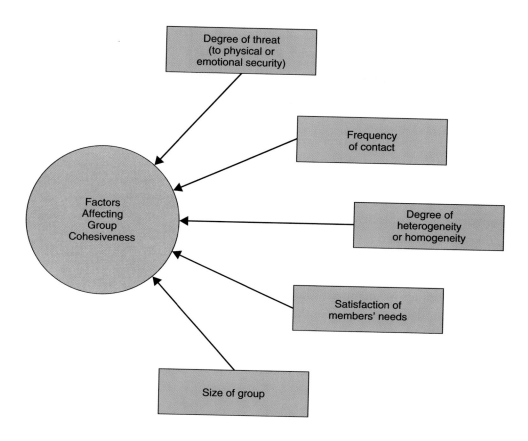

ber of the group satisfies members' needs, they will have a stronger desire to stay with the group. Finally, smaller groups tend to be more cohesive. Large groups have so many different relationships that cohesiveness is reduced.

Some managers oppose the existence of cohesive informal groups because they know they will have to implement unpopular decisions sooner or later. However, even for small companies—perhaps especially for them—a clear understanding of informal group characteristics such as cohesiveness can make implementing unpopular decisions easier.

Group Size

The informal group tends to be small so that its members may interact frequently. But when groups get too small, difficulties arise. The *dyad*, or two-person group, provides a perfect example. When a decision is required and there is no consensus, one group member must lose.

Considerable research has been devoted to determining the most effective group size. This research has led to the following conclusions:

• When the quality of a complex group decision is important, the use of seven to 12 members under a formal leader is most appropriate.

- When consensus in a conflict situation is important, the use of three to five members with no formal leader will ensure that each member's view will be discussed.
- When both quality and consensus are important, five to seven members seems most appropriate.[10]

There tends to be greater group conflict in even-sized groups, and there is more conflict in groups of two and four members than there is in groups of six members. In seating arrangements, members who sit across from each other tend to engage in more frequent, and often more argumentative, communication. If consensus is the objective, members with any potential conflict should be seated alongside each other.

Thus, managers dealing with the subject of effective work groups should be concerned primarily that they be small ones. Obviously, many organizations consist of thousands of members. The initial approach to organizing must therefore be formal in nature, resulting in the design of official units, jobs, and formal relationships of authority, responsibility, and accountability. Within this formal organization, a limitless number of small, informal work groups will be spontaneously established. It is hoped, of course, that they will be aligned with overall organizational objectives.

Synergism

Synergism is the cooperative action of two or more persons working together to accomplish more than they could working separately. Managers need to recognize that greater effect may be achieved when two workers are placed together.

Synergism may also allow the organization to attain a special advantage with regard to cost, market power, technology, or management skill. One of the prime reasons for acquiring certain organizations is the synergistic advantages the right pairing of organizations can provide.

The concept of synergism has implications for both formal and informal groups. However, through the synergistic effect, the informal group may become more powerful. People in groups often have much more influence than the same number of individuals working alone. In addition, group members themselves can also significantly influence group effectiveness.

❖ ❖ INCREASING TEAM EFFECTIVENESS

Teams are collections of people who must rely on group collaboration if each member, and the team as a whole, is to experience the optimum of success and objective achievement.[11] Team effectiveness is usually judged by the productivity of the team as a whole, not merely by the effectiveness of its members as individuals. They generally have specific projects with specified (short- or long-term) duration. Management groups, committees, task forces, and other work units strive to act as teams because they recognize the importance of concerted effort in accomplishing objectives.

J. Richard Hackman and Charles Morris note that team members can enhance the effectiveness of their team by increasing the following three variables:

1. The level of effort the team applies to carrying out its task.
2. The adequacy of the task performance strategies used by the team carrying out the task.
3. The level and appropriateness of the knowledge and skills brought to bear on the task by team members.

Organizational members can then manipulate (1) behavioral norms, (2) task design, or (3) team composition as ways of increasing these three variables.[12]

Changing existing norms is one of the most promising ways of increasing the effort of team members. The team or its representative can require regular attendance at meetings, extensive time—three to five hours, say—preparing for them, or extension of the length of meetings until a particular objective is reached.

Teams are collections of people who must rely on group collaboration for objective achievement. (Source: © John Coletti)

Redesigning the task is the most promising way to improve task performance strategies. The team might introduce greater specialization of responsibilities or increase the amount of job enrichment. Each member could be given responsibility for a single, integral part of the task, the part that best fits the person's expertise or experience.

❖ ❖ CHARACTERISTICS OF EFFECTIVE TEAMS

Table 13.1 summarizes one view of the characteristics of an effective work team. A team-building program must begin when a new team is formed or when an existing team stops functioning as effectively as possible. In forming a new team, members should ideally follow four steps:

1. Each member must determine the priority she or he attaches to participating in the team's activities and must assess the personal importance of these activities.
2. The members must share their expectations about working on the team.
3. The members must clarify the team's objectives.

TABLE 13.1 Characteristics of an Effective Work Team

- Objectives are clear to all and shared by all, and all care about and feel involved in the goals.
- All members participate and are listened to.
- Members freely express themselves and receive empathic responses.
- When problems arise, the situation is carefully diagnosed before action is proposed; remedies attack basic causes.
- As needs for leadership arise, various members meet them; anyone feels free to volunteer as he or she sees a group need.
- Consensus is sought and tested; decisions, when made, are fully supported.
- Members trust one another; they reveal to the group what they would be reluctant to expose to others; they respect and use the responses they get; they can freely express negative reactions without fearing reprisal.
- The group is flexible and seeks new and better ways of acting; individuals change and grow; they are creative.

(Source: Adapted from Edgar Schein, *Process Consultation* [Reading, MA: Addison-Wesley Publishing Co., Inc., 1969], pp. 42–43. Reprinted with permission.)

4. The team must formulate operating guidelines about the process of decision making, basic work methods, the extent and nature of member participation in discussion, ways of resolving differences, ways of ensuring that work is completed, and ways of changing nonproductive activities.[13]

As may be evident from these four steps, teams are intended to act as one unit to effect the goals of the organization.

❖ ❖ STRATEGIES FOR TEAM BUILDING

To improve the performance of work teams, managers (or outside consultants) may prescribe a variety of team-building activities. Data collection is one essential activity. Managers, team members, or outside parties may use group process observation as one means of data collection.[14] The observer collects data about the communication, decision making, and leadership in a team. The observer acquires information about group norms and roles by tabulating who talks to whom, how frequently, and about what topics, then feeds this information back to team members. A team process consultant may also be called in to help set agendas, coach the group or its individual members in effective interpersonal processes, and offer recommendations for more effective performance.

For effective team building to occur:

1. The primary objective of a team development meeting must be explicit and well articulated.
2. This objective must be held by the team or the team's representative and must be understood and agreed to by the work team members.

3. The objective should be the condition under which third parties (consultants) work. That is, the primary purpose is defined by the team representative, who sets the agenda and activities of the meeting.

4. If the consultants are working with the team directly, they should help their representative explicitly define and share the primary purpose with team members.[15]

Even though every effort may be made to foster effective team building, conflict may still exist. Conflict may be disruptive to team effectiveness, and therefore must be dealt with quickly and decisively.

❖ ❖ SELF-MANAGED TEAMS

One of the current rages in the field of organizational development is self-directed work teams, also known *as autonomous work teams, self-managed work teams, semiautonomous work groups, superteams,* and *leaderless work teams.*[16] **Self-managed work teams** are groups of workers who are given administrative responsibility to accomplish certain assigned tasks. Essentially, team members act as their own supervisor and perform such activities as planning, staffing, scheduling, and controlling the process. Self-managed teams may well be the wave of the future. The case study involving Volvo at the beginning of the chapter provides an example of self-managed teams.

As one might expect, all managers have not greeted the self-managed team concept with excitement because many of the traditional managerial rights are taken away. Managers cannot take a hands-on management approach with self-managed teams. They can really only provide direction, facilitate, and then let the team determine the means for goal accomplishment. For a traditionalist manager, this is often quite difficult. However, this is not the case for the CEO of IBM, Louis V. Gerstner, who believes that teams must be built around a corporate culture reflecting expectations of performance, not simply rules of behavior. Whatever enhances team performance is good for the company. "If everybody in the IBM lab in Austin decides they want to come to work in jeans and sandals, God bless 'em."[17]

❖ ❖ CONFLICT IN ORGANIZATIONS

When individuals and groups interact, there is always the potential for conflict. **Conflict** is antagonism or opposition between or among persons. It occurs when there is competition or mutual interference among people. Whenever individuals are brought together in a highly structured environment, the potential for con-

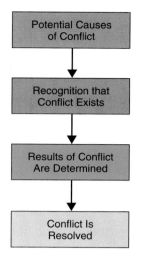

❖ **Figure 13.4**
Conflict resolution sequence

flict exists. As more companies implement the team approach, specifically in a diverse environment, the occurrence of conflict may also increase.

Conflict usually follows a pattern, as Figure 13.4 shows. First, conflict does not just happen; there must be causes. Second, even though the potential for conflict exists, it cannot be managed until it becomes apparent. Third, the results of conflict must be determined, since they may help or hurt the organization. Finally, the conflict is eventually resolved, sometimes to the benefit of the participants and the organization. At other times, the resolution of conflict harms one or more of the conflicting parties or the organization.

❖ ❖ POTENTIAL CAUSES OF CONFLICT

Since conflict results from the normal interactions of people, no organization is completely without it. Although conflict is not necessarily harmful, its potential cost is so great that it cannot be ignored. It is imperative that managers be familiar with the following categories of causes: objective interference, competition for scarce resources, personality differences, perception set differences, change, and failure to communicate.

Objective Interference

In many situations, the achievement of one person's objectives blocks the achievement of another's objectives. Both people may have the same objective, but only one may attain it. Suppose, for instance, a new office becomes available. Two supervisors want the office, but only one can get it. Another example of objective interference might be the manager who wants to produce as much as possible without worrying about quality versus the quality control person who concentrates primarily on quality. This kind of conflict can also result from a worker who wants to make as much as possible while the boss wants to maintain a balance in the pay structure.

Competition for Scarce Resources

No matter how much of a resource there is, there never seems to be quite enough to go around. For example, at budget time, managers seldom get all they want. There is only so much money available. Giving one manager more money usually means giving someone else less.

Logic seldom prevails when people compete for resources. It is human nature to want more. Sometimes, this competition becomes a way of keeping score with regard to status. A substantial budget increase implies influence with upper management. Telling people that your department received a budget cut may not be as pleasant.

Personality Differences

We all have different personalities, and each of us thinks and acts differently. It would be a boring world if this were not so. But personality differences among workers create the potential for conflict. An extrovert may find it difficult to work with an introvert, and vice versa. A highly disciplined person may find it impos-

---

MANAGEMENT IN PRACTICE

A Skill-Building Exercise: Jerry Sharplin eagerly drove his new company pickup onto the construction site. He had just been assigned by his employer, Lurgi-Knost Construction Company, to supervise a crew of 16 equipment operators, oilers, and mechanics. This was the first unionized crew Jerry had supervised. As he approached his work area, he noticed one of the "cherry pickers" (a type of mobile crane with an extendable boom) standing idle with the operator beside it. Jerry pulled up beside the operator and said, "What's going on here?"

"Out of gas," the operator said.

"Well, go and get some," Jerry said.

The operator reached to get his thermos jug out of the tool box on the side of the crane and said, "The oiler's on break right now, but he'll be back in a few minutes."

Jerry remembered that he had a five-gallon can of gasoline in the back of his pickup. So he quickly got the gasoline, climbed onto the cherry picker, and started to pour the gas into the tank. As he did, he heard the other machines shutting down in unison. He looked around and saw all the other operators climbing down from their equipment and standing to watch him pour the gasoline. A moment later, he saw the union steward approaching.

How might this conflict be resolved?

sible to work with a free spirit. Some people care about social relationships, and others do not. All of these instances hold the possibility of conflict.

Differences in Perception Sets

A **perception set** is a fixed tendency to interpret information in a certain way. Life experiences and objectives strongly influence the way things are seen. Differences in perception sets are a major source of conflict. For instance, a person who grew up in a racially segregated environment might be unfavorably disposed toward blacks, particularly black managers. Men who grew up in an environment where women rarely worked outside the home might experience conflict with a woman supervisor. A worker who grew up in a strong union community might be antagonistic toward anyone in management. The list could go on and on. Many potential conflict situations are caused by differences in perception sets.

Change

Moving from a known to an unknown is **change.** We live in a world where change is occurring at an ever-faster pace. When we are confronted with change, most of us feel insecure, even if the change is good for us. This insecurity often causes us to resist change, thereby creating conflict between us and whoever is imposing the change.

Organizations are usually in a constant state of change. Some changes are minor and others are major. It is human nature to enjoy doing things the way they have always been done. But change will occur, and the resulting conflict must be resolved.

In most instances, if a change is justified, people will accept it even if they do not like it. However, what might appear to be completely reasonable to the company might not appear so to the workers. Suppose, for instance, that a group of machine operators has to be moved to a new work area with new machines. A study by the company has shown that this is necessary to maintain efficiency and protect jobs. The new work area is also cleaner and safer than the old one. Still, workers may tend to resist the change unless management carefully presents the reason for it.

Failure to Communicate

Communication was defined earlier as the transfer of information, ideas, understanding, or feelings among people. In many instances, communication is not complete because it does not result in understanding. The words are heard, but the meaning is not transmitted. For instance, a supervisor might say, "Turn off the word processor!" One worker might interpret the message to mean he did something wrong and might therefore become defensive, creating the potential for conflict. Another worker might hear the message as a simple order to turn the word processor off. In this case, no conflict is likely.

Even when a manger communicates clearly, failure to communicate to everyone involved can cause conflict. For example, a supervisor might tell some workers that it will be necessary to work overtime for two days next week. Conflict could arise when the other workers who were not told are suddenly required to work overtime.

Communication also breaks down when the supervisor fails to obtain accurate information from the workers. Perhaps the workers fail to communicate honestly and openly or the supervisor fails to listen. For example, a worker may be dissatisfied with a certain machine assignment. He may be experiencing trouble, although the boss is not aware of it. The conflict may surface when the worker talks back to the boss about something completely unrelated to machine assignments. The classic case of inaccurate worker communication can be found in the reasons people give for quitting their jobs. Workers often mention higher pay in the new job as the reason for leaving, when, in actuality, conflict in the old job is the real cause. A worker may not have been able to get along with the boss or with a co-worker, for example. But the real reason may never be known.

❖ ❖ CONFLICT BECOMES APPARENT

Until a conflict becomes apparent, nothing can be done about it. One or both parties must recognize that conflict exists in order to resolve it. Conflict exists to the extent that it is felt, or perceived. The degree of conflict perceived may be different for each of the involved parties, as Figure 13.5 illustrates. Conflict is high for Joe but virtually nonexistent for Bill. The conflict might have arisen when Bill told Joe how to accomplish a task in a better way. To Bill, there was nothing negative about his training efforts. But Joe apparently saw them as a reprimand. He

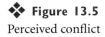
❖ Figure 13.5
Perceived conflict

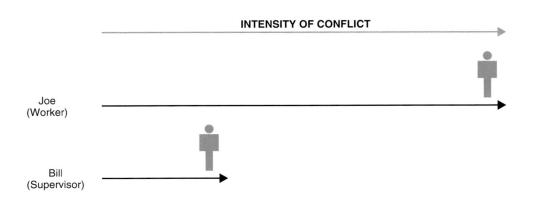

was heard saying to other co-workers: "Who does Bill think he is? He just walks around looking for chances to get on to someone."

At some point, conflict becomes noticeable. It is out in the open, and at least one party knows it exists. When conflict becomes apparent, a key point to consider is its impact on productivity. Conflict can sometimes be beneficial, leading to even higher productivity. But when productivity is lowered, the conflict must be resolved. It cannot be permitted to continue when it hurts the overall effectiveness of the organization.

❖ ❖ INTERPERSONAL CONFLICT MANAGEMENT

There are numerous techniques for dealing with conflict between two or more individuals. They range from the use of force to a problem-solving approach. Among the techniques are overpowering the other party, using outside force, planning a delay, ignoring the conflict, giving in, withdrawing, smoothing, compromising, using mediation and arbitration, having superordinate objectives, and problem solving.

Overpowering the Other Party

At times, one of the parties to a conflict will simply overpower the other in order to resolve the conflict. Confrontation occurs, and the result is that one party clearly wins and the other party clearly loses. At times, this form of conflict resolution is used to settle once and for all who is "boss." Some have compared this form of conflict resolution to the ways cowboys used to "break" horses. The wild horse and the cowboy were certainly in conflict when the cowboy got into the saddle. Conflict ended when the horse realized he could not get rid of the rider.

As humans, we are not horses to be broken. The person who has lost will often experience increased, though hidden, conflict. Grudges may be held. The losing party may find some way to sabotage the winner in the future. For this reason, overpowering the other party is not recommended as a usual practice for resolving conflict.

Using Outside Force

At times, a person in authority will step in to resolve conflict. For instance, two supervisors may be in conflict over who will be assigned a terrific new worker. Arguments may break out about it. Their boss may impose a decision on the supervisors. Since neither supervisor was forced to give in to the other, the loss of ego was slight. Resolution of conflict by an outside force may sometimes be best because it provides a face-saving means for the conflicting parties.

Planning a Delay

The planned delay creates a cooling-off period for conflicting parties. Although few managers readily confess to using this approach, practically all have used it at some time. For example, when an angry worker comes to the supervisor about something that has just happened, the supervisor might say: "I know that this is really important. But right now I have to go to a meeting. Let's get together the first thing tomorrow and talk about it." This allows time for the worker to think through the matter and to settle down. As a result, the discussion is often less emotional then it would have been earlier.

Ignoring the Conflict

Another technique is for the manager to pretend the conflict does not exist. A supervisor may sense that someone is angry and may even know the cause of the anger. Rather than bring it out into the open, however, and create a confrontation, the manager may choose to ignore it. Such a reaction may be appropriate if the cause of the conflict is beyond the supervisor's control, particularly if the supervisor has confidence in the general goodwill of the angry party. However, management must monitor the condition of the angry party to assure that the anger doesn't become destructive to either the individual or the organization.

Giving In

When one of the conflicting parties is clearly in error, that person should give in. Giving in also may be a useful tactic in at least two other circumstances. First, when the matter that is causing the conflict is a minor one, winning may not be as important as maintaining the goodwill of the other party. Sometimes, winning the conflict can cause major problems in the future, whereas giving in might be viewed as a favor. Second, it is often best to give in when the issue at conflict is a lost cause. It is better to lose gracefully than to pursue a lost cause doggedly. Others, including the boss, will appreciate the person who has both the common sense to know when to quit and the maturity to do it.

A supervisor should not give in simply to avoid conflict, however. If the supervisor is right about an important matter and there is a reasonable chance of winning, the supervisor should stand firm. Giving in may not resolve the conflict. In fact, conflict could be even greater, although hidden. In addition, the winner may see the supervisor as a weak person who can be taken advantage of. Giving in when one is right can diminish future influence.

Withdrawing

Although withdrawal may appear to be quite similar to giving in, it is actually quite different. This approach involves pulling back from a previously announced position. A problem often has several equally good solutions. However, one solution might create more conflict than another. The manager may tentatively decide to take one approach and see that considerable conflict is developing. The manager may then withdraw and decide to tackle the problem from another position. The situation that caused the conflict may never be mentioned again. This is the reason administrators, especially government officials, often send up "trial balloons." If the trial balloon raises too much conflict, it is allowed to float away.

Smoothing

A manager who uses a smoothing approach is attempting to provide a semblance of peaceful cooperation by presenting an image such as "we're one big happy family." With this approach, problems are rarely permitted to come to the surface, but the potential for conflict remains.

Compromising

Neither party gets all it wants in a compromise. This is the most typical way of dealing with labor-management conflict. For example, management may offer to increase wages by four percent, while the union may be seeking eight. A compromise figure of six percent may result in a reasonable settlement of the conflict.

Using Arbitration and Mediation

Both arbitration and mediation call for outside neutral parties to enter the situation to assist in resolving the conflict. In **arbitration,** a dispute between two parties is submitted to a third party to make a binding decision. Arbitration is frequently used in union-management conflicts. The arbitrator is given the authority to act as a judge. The decision rendered is usually final because both union and management agree in advance that it will be.

Mediation is the process in which a third party enters a dispute between two parties for the purpose of assisting them in reaching an agreement. A mediator can only suggest, recommend, and attempt to keep the two parties talking in hopes of reaching a solution.

Having Superordinate Objectives

At times, the opposing factions may encounter an objective that overshadows their own interests. For example, if a firm is in danger of going out of business, both union and management have been known to put aside minor conflicts and work toward the common objective of survival. There have been instances where union members have taken a decrease in pay and benefits in order to assist in the survival of the firm. Union members and management personnel at Chrysler, General Motors, and other large firms have cooperatively worked together to ensure the survival of their firms.

Both arbitration and mediation call for outside neutral parties to enter the situation to assist in resolving the conflict. When arbitration is used to settle formal employee grievances, as in the situation shown here, the arbitrator's decision is usually final because both parties have agreed in advance that it will be.
(Source: © Jim Pickerell)

Problem Solving

A recommended approach to conflict management is problem solving. Ideally, problem solving is characterized by an open and trusting exchange of views. Building trust is vital to resolving conflict. Managers who have established an environment of mutual trust are better able than others to resolve conflict situations. With the problem-solving approach, both parties can realize that conflict is caused by relationships among people and is not within one person. An individual can disagree with your ideas and still remain your friend. Problem solving is a healthy approach in that it recognizes that usually neither person is completely right or wrong. Granting a concession is not seen as a sign of weakness. Neither party feels that it has to win every battle to maintain self-respect.

A certain amount of conflict is healthy when the problem-solving approach is taken. If a difference of opinion exists between two individuals and they openly discuss their difficulties, a superior solution often results. With problem solving, a person is encouraged to bring difficulties into the open without fear of reprisal. When this occurs, a situation that initially appeared to be a major problem may become only a minor one, which is easily resolved.

❖ ❖ STRUCTURAL CONFLICT MANAGEMENT

Conflict can often be managed by a change in procedures, organizational structure, or physical layout.

Procedural Changes

Conflict can occur because a procedure is illogically sequenced. When a credit manager and a sales manager were both about to be fired because of an irreconcilable personality conflict, it was discovered that the processing of credit applications too late in the credit procedure was the cause of their difficulty. The credit manager was forced to cancel too many deals already made. When the credit check was placed earlier in the procedure, most of the conflict disappeared. In another instance, the personnel director and the production manager were in continuous disagreement. At times, the conflict almost caused them to come to blows. Then it was discovered that the production manager was not being permitted to review applications at an early stage of the hiring sequence and to make comments. When the procedure was changed, many of the difficulties were resolved.

Organizational Structure Changes

Some degree of conflict is often desirable. This is the case, for example, where the quality control department must inspect the work of the production department. Conflict between quality control and production could probably be minimized if the quality control director reported to the production manager. However, the quality control department would then lose its independence. This is why the quality control director typically reports to someone at a high level in the organization. The potential conflict is justified by the quality improvement that results from such a structure.

In other cases, conflict between departments is unplanned and undesirable. In some firms, sales and distribution are in separate departments, each reporting to a senior manager. This division often creates conflict. Individuals in sales expect quick delivery in response to customer requests. But the distribution department, in an effort to keep costs down, wants to make deliveries in full trucks and at scheduled intervals. To resolve this kind of conflict, it may be desirable to combine the two departments under a marketing manager who has experience in both sales and distribution. A marketing manager is likely to ensure that the organization's needs take priority over the preferences of sales and distribution personnel.

Physical Layout Changes

Changes in the design of the physical workplace have been used effectively to reduce or eliminate conflict. Office space can be designed either to force interaction or to make it difficult. People can use desks as barriers and buffers. Some offices have dividers to separate workers. However, if a manager wants to stimulate a problem-solving atmosphere, a more open office arrangement may be permitted. When known antagonists are seated in conference directly across from each other, the amount of conflict increases. When they are seated side by side,

A GLOBAL PERSPECTIVE

Productivity and Problem Solving Through Team Utilization

Competitors globally are certainly aware of the so-called Japanese marvels. Two of these so-called marvels are the top-quality products Japanese companies make and their loyal and dedicated workforces. However, even more amazing is the fact that the Japanese can export their methods and create such products and workforces wherever they choose to do so. It is no simple matter to import the Japanese system to the United States and put it in place with the effectiveness that such systems enjoy in Japan. Whatever arrives on the shores of the United States must be "Americanized" to some degree, especially those aspects of work that require group cooperation, tolerance, and understanding. Like most Japanese companies, Mazda, the Japanese automaker, uses work teams in its assembly plants. Mazda management tailored its work process plan and created a work team system it

believed would be effective in America. This work team system involves a work group for each department at the plant as well as a central work group that monitors, controls, and coordinates the activities of the departmental work groups. To make its first U.S. assembly plant in Flat Rock, Michigan, successful, Mazda recognized that such a work team system would require employees to be carefully selected and developed. They went to unprecedented lengths to find just the right kinds of people and then properly trained them. Mazda management realized that not everyone is suited for such a work environment, so it was essential that the staffing and development process be effective. Similar teams were setup at GM's Saturn plant, where only the best were selected from the GM ranks.[18]

Teams have been very effective at increasing productivity, and they have also been very valuable for solving organizational problems. In fact, some problems are so people-centered that the best so-

lution probably lies in team resolution. McDermott International, Inc. was paying $25 to $30 million in supplemental mid-year premiums to its insurance company each year before the compensation team solved its problems. The team has been so successful that McDermott now gets credits from its insurer.[19] Propery developed teams are essential for global success. Mazda and GM are two global competitors that appreciate the importance of tailoring the process to the characteristics of the work to be accomplished, and to further take into account the characteristics of those who will accomplish the work. The desire to tailor their methods will surely pay off in big dividends in America, as it has in Japan, and will certainly serve them well in other countries around the globe. Other global players may well benefit from these examples. Basically, tailoring the process often translates into success regardless of where in the world the company is doing business.

the conflict tends to decrease. These principles can be applied in arranging work spaces.

A detrimental conflict involving physical layout existed between two groups of workers in a truck assembly plant. Working at different phases of production on the assembly line, the two groups came into conflict because both had to obtain parts from the same shelving unit. Each group believed the other was deliberately rearranging its supply of parts, which sometimes resulted in fights. The conflict was resolved by moving the shelving unit between the two groups so as to set up a barrier between them. Thus, each group had its own supply area. As a result of this change, mistakes were reduced by 50 percent within two days.[20]

✗ Management Tips ✗

Guidelines for Dealing with Group Performance, Team Building, and Conflict

1. **Recognize that the goals of the informal group may not always be in line with management.** Some work groups insist that their members maintain a certain, often suboptimal, production level.
2. **Do not expect absolute conformity.** It can stifle innovation and initiative, reduce performance, and even encourage undesirable actions.
3. **Do not fight upper managers.** Such conflicts are seldom good for your career or the organization.
4. **Try to use existing conflicts to accomplish goals.** In some circumstances, conflict can be beneficial.
5. **Do not let conflict get out of hand.** Know how to resolve it, and take action at the proper time.
6. **Try to determine the real causes of conflict.** These may be different from the "obvious" causes.
7. **Give in if you are wrong.** Do not let pride stand in your way.
8. **Accept a certain amount of conflict as natural.** Do not feel that you have to solve every problem that arises.
9. **When you impose change, even change for the better, expect a certain amount of conflict.** Make sure your subordinates understand the reasons for the change.
10. **Recognize that building trust is vital to resolving conflict.** Managers who have established an environment of mutual trust are better able than others to resolve conflict situations.

SUMMARY

Groups—two or more people having a unifying relationship—are often categorized by size, function, or other criteria. Four types of groups commonly encountered in organizations are task (or functional) groups, project groups, work teams, and informal groups. Task (functional) groups are determined by job requirements, and project groups are formal, but temporary, assignments to groups, committees, and special projects. A work team is an officially sanctioned collection of individuals who have been charged with completing a mission by an organization and who must depend upon one another for successful completion of work. An informal group is two or more persons associated in ways not prescribed by the formal organization. Groups form when individuals exhibit common interests, common needs, common objectives, or physical proximity, which influence the nature and quality of the group's functioning. Once a group forms, a variety of issues must be resolved before the group can function effectively. Tracing the development of groups provides one perspective for assessing a group's performance. There are essentially four stages of development: orientation, redefinition, coordination, and formalization. Individual roles, group norms, conformity, leadership, group cohesiveness, group size, and synergism all influence group effectiveness.

Group members can enhance the effectiveness of their group by increasing the following variables: (1) the level of effort the group applies to carrying out its task, (2) the adequacy of the task performance strategies used by the group carrying out the task, and (3) the level and appropriateness of the knowledge and skills brought to bear on the task by group members. Organizational members can then manipulate behavioral norms, task design, or group composition as ways of increasing these three variables.

Teams are collections of people who must rely on group collaboration if each member, and the team as a

KEY TERMS

Group 408
Primary groups 409
Secondary groups 409
Task (functional) groups 409
Work team 410
Informal group 410
Role 416
Norm 417

Cohesiveness 418
Synergism 420
Self-managed work teams 424
Conflict 424
Perception set 427
Change 427
Arbitration 431
Mediation 431

REVIEW QUESTIONS

1. Define <u>group</u> and describe the various types of groups.
2. What are the reasons that groups form?
3. Describe the typical stages leading to group and team development.
4. Define the following terms:
   a. role
   b. norm
   c. cohesiveness
   d. synergism
5. List ways of increasing team effectiveness.
6. What are self-managed teams?
7. Define <u>conflict</u>. What are some of the potential causes of conflict?
8. How may managers become better at managing interpersonal conflict?
9. What are the means by which managers can overcome structural conflict?

whole, is to experience the optimum of success and objective achievement. A team-building program must begin when a new team is formed and when an existing team stops functioning as effectively as possible. Management groups, committees, task forces, and other work units strive to act as teams because they recognize the importance of concerted effort in accomplishing group objectives.

When individuals and groups interact, there is always the potential for conflict—antagonism or opposition between or among persons. Conflict occurs when there is competition or mutual interference among people. Whenever individuals are brought together in a highly structured environment, the potential for conflict exists.

Conflict usually follows a pattern. First, it does not just happen; there must be causes. Second, even though the potential for conflict exists, it cannot be managed until it becomes apparent. Third, the results of conflict must be determined, since they may help or hurt the organization. Finally, the conflict is eventually resolved, sometimes to the benefit of the participants and the organization.

Potential causes of conflict include objective interference, competition for scarce resources, personality differences, perception set differences, change, and failure to communicate. There are numerous techniques for dealing with conflict between two or more individuals. They range from the use of force to a problem-solving approach.

CASE STUDIES

CASE 13.1 "I Don't Really Have a Chance"

As James Mitchell approached the table where Betty Fuller was seated, he asked, "Mind if I sit here?"

"Of course not," said Betty. "I've been wanting to talk to you anyway." James placed his tray on the table and sat down.

"James," Betty said, "have you heard that Dave is being transferred?"

"Yes," said James, "I think he'll be leaving next month and going to the Jackson plant."

"Well," said Betty, "I've decided to apply for the job. I don't really have much hope, though. A woman doesn't have much chance for promotion, no matter how hard she works. Even if a woman did get promoted, she would probably be paid less."

"You have the same chance that everyone else does," James said. "I think I'm going to apply for that job myself."

"Well, that pretty well settles it," said Betty. "I don't really have a chance. But I am still going to apply."

"Don't you think that's a little unfair, Betty? Now, if you don't get promoted, you are going to think that it's because you're a woman."

"Well," said Betty, "don't you think it will be?"

"Of course not," James said. "I don't think you're so obviously superior to me. Of course, if you make a big issue of this sex thing, they might promote you just to show how open-minded they are."

"Look, James," said Betty, "I've earned everything I've gotten. Not only have I worked hard here and made a real effort to get along with everybody, I also went to night school and got my degree."

"Having a degree in management doesn't make you a manager, Betty. Anyway, I think I'm about to lose my temper. I'd just as soon not talk about this anymore." James took his half-eaten lunch and moved across the lunchroom to another table.

QUESTIONS

1. What is the main cause of this conflict situation? Discuss.
2. What means of resolving the conflict would you recommend? Explain.

CASE 13.2 No Cause for Concern

Springfield Products Company in Springfield, Missouri, is a medium-sized manufacturer of small outboard motors. The motors are supplied to major retailing chains, which sell them under their own brand names. For the past few years, sales at Springfield Products had been falling. The decline was industrywide. In fact, Springfield was faring better than its competitors and had actually been able to increase its share of the market slightly. Although forecasts indicated that the demand for the company's outboards would improve in the future, Anne Goddard, the company's president, believed that something needed to be done immediately to help the company maintain its financial health through this temporary slump. As a first step, she employed a consulting firm to determine if a reorganization might be helpful.

A team of three consultants arrived at the firm. They told Goddard that they had to gain a thorough understanding of the current situation before making any recommendations for action. After informing the consultants that the company was open to them, Goddard told the company's supervisors to not inform anyone of the purpose of the investigation because this might cause employees to act differently.

The grapevine was full of rumors from the day the consulting group arrived. Some employees heard that the company might be shut down, others heard that massive transfers were possible, and still others heard that forced retirements were probable. The work groups at Springfield Products Company were very close-knit, and the rumors upset virtually everyone. Matters were made even worse when workers received no explanation from their supervisors. The climate quickly changed from one of concern to one of fear. Rather than being concerned about their daily work, employees worried about what was going to happen to the company and their jobs. Productivity dropped drastically as a result.

Three weeks after the consultants left, a memorandum was circulated through the company. It stated that the consultants had recommended a slight modification in the top levels of the organization. No one would be fired, and any reductions in staff would be the result of normal attrition. However, by this time, some of the best workers had already found other jobs, and company operations were severely disrupted for several months.

QUESTIONS

1. What part did the informal group play in what happened at Springfield Products?
2. Describe in terms of cohesiveness the conditions that existed before the consultants arrived and after they left.

NOTES

1. This case is a composite of a number of accounts, among them: Jonathan Kapstein and John Hoerr, "Volvo's Radical New Plant: 'The Death of the Assembly Line?'" *Business Week* (August 28, 1989): 92–93; David Bartal, "Volvo's Back-to-the-Future Factory," *U.S. News & World Report* 107 (August 21, 1989): 42; Leigh Bruce and Jack Burton, "Strained Alliances," *International Management* 45 (May 1990): 29; and Patricia Sellers, "The Best Way to Reach Your Buyers," *Fortune* 128 (Autumn/Winter 1993): 14–17.
2. Clayton P. Alderfer, "An Intergroup Perspective on Group Dynamics," in *Handbook of Organizational Behavior*, ed. Jay W. Lorsch (Englewood Cliffs, NJ: Prentice-Hall, 1987) p. 211.
3. James B. Treece, "Improving the Soul of an Old Machine," *Business Week* (October 25, 1993): 134–136.
4. Work in America Institute, in John Hoerr, "The Payoff from Teamwork," *Business Week* (July 10, 1989): 56–62.
5. R. W. Napier and M. K. Gershenfeld, *Groups: Theory and Experience*, 2d ed. (Boston: Houghton Mifflin, 1981).
6. David Woodruff, James B. Treece, Sunita Wadekar

Bhargava, and Karen Lowry Miller, "Saturn," *Business Week* (August 17, 1992): 88.

7. Anne B. Fisher, "Sexual Harassment: What to Do," *Fortune* 127 (August 23, 1993): 84–88.

8. Alice Cuneo, "Diversity by Design," *Business Week* (Reinventing America 1992): 72.

9. Solomon E. Asch, "Effects of Group Pressure on the Modification and Distortion of Judgments," in *Groups, Leaders, and Men,* ed. H. Guetzkow (Pittsburgh: Carnegie Press, 1951).

10. L. L. Commings, George P. Huber, and Eugene Arendt, "Effects of Size and Spatial Arrangements in Group Decision Making," *Academy of Management Journal* 17 (September 1974): 473.

11. W. G. Dyer, *Team Building: Issues and Alternatives* (Reading, MA: Addison-Wesley, 1979).

12. J. R. Hackman and C. G. Morris, "Improving Group Performance Effectiveness," in *Advances in Experimental Social Psychology,* ed. L. Berkowitz (New York: Academic Press, 1975): 8, 345.

13. *Ibid.*

14. E. H. Schein, *Process Consultation* (Reading, MA: Addison-Wesley, 1969).

15. Adapted from R. Beckhard, "Optimizing Team Building Effort," *Journal of Contemporary Business* 1 (Summer 1972): 23–32.

16. Robert J. Doyle, "Caution: Self-Directed Work Teams," *HRMagazine* 37 (June 1992): 153.

17. Judith Dobrzynski, "Rethinking IBM," *Business Week* (October 4, 1993): 86–97.

18. "How Does Japan Pick Its American Workers," *Business Week* (October 3, 1988): 84–88; Louis Kraar, "Japan's Gung-Ho U.S. Car Plants," *Business Week* (January 30, 1989): 98–108.

19. Seth Lubove, "Produce—Or Else," *Forbes* 151 (May 10, 1993): 86–87.

20. H. Kenneth Bobele and Peter J. Buchanan, "Building a More Productive Environment," *Management World* 8 (January 1979): 8.

14 Power, Organizational Politics, and Stress

LEARNING OBJECTIVES

After completing this chapter students should be able to

✘ Define *power* and give reasons for exerting power.

✘ Describe the sources of power, how managers can increase their power, power configurations, and power differences.

✘ Explain the strategies for obtaining power, the significance of power to the manager, and means of resisting intimidation.

✘ Describe political action in organizations.

✘ Describe stress in organizations.

✘ Explain the concept of burnout.

America's Most Famous Billionaire Power Broker: Ross Perot

Self-made billionaire Ross Perot is a power broker extraordinaire. So powerful, in fact, that according to Democratic consultant Bob Beckel, "All (President) Clinton's people are afraid of him (Perot)." The mythical Perot is a person who as a boy delivered newspapers in a Texarkana, Texas, ghetto and who as a young salesman for IBM met his annual sales quota in January. Beyond the myth, he definitely is the man who started Electronic Data Systems, Inc. (EDS), the most antibureaucratic company in American history, after reading Thoreau's famous line, "The mass of men lead lives of quiet desperation." Perot is often portrayed as a "David bedeviling Goliath," and he is definitely a man who would relish the challenge of exerting his power over such a force.

Perot's power-centered personality is probably best illustrated by a remark he often quotes from Winston Churchill, which has become his credo. "Never give in. Never give in. Never. Never. Never." Power can be a highly effective instrument for good, or it can be an instrument of evil. Perot's power is so intimidating because "When right, he is an incomparable ally; when wrong, he is a fearsome foe." However, whatever course Perot selects, he is always utterly convinced that he is right, and those who disagree with him become the enemy, including the President of the United States, Bill Clinton. Being Perot's enemy is not a comfortable position to be in, because Perot will never give in; he will always exert the maximum power needed to win.

Perot definitely has the ability to influence behavior. The instances of Perot wielding his power are many. When a competitor outbid EDS for a $2 billion Texas data-processing contract, Perot declared a "scorched earth" campaign to discredit the competitor. After his campaign and some political arm-twisting, EDS regained the contract. When Perot was in the midst of a conflict with General Motors, the unions hailed him as a hero. But in the 1960s, Perot waged open war on organized labor. When one EDS facility in California voted to organize, Perot shut the facility down rather than tolerate a union at EDS.

When Perot took on General Motors, he was uncompromising, and he refused to budge, threatening to declare "World War III." Perot's power was so intimidating that GM management decided to buy his stock for a premium price of $742 million. After the buy-out was complete, Perot publicly denounced GM for the outrageous expenditure at a time when GM was closing plants.

Ross Perot has immense power, and he is willing to exercise it to get his way. For Perot, power is indispensable. The exercise of power and the utilization of political alliances are inherent in his life. Perot is a master at influencing the behavior of others, always perceiving his actions as righteous. Even lawmakers in Congress on both sides of the aisle are continually seeking his blessings before going ahead with legislation.[1]

Many effective managers work within the political system of the organization. Others confront "the system" at every opportunity. It is natural for people to struggle for power and to exercise it to accomplish objectives. It is also natural to fear, and sometimes admire, people like Ross Perot who possess extraordinary personal power.

Much of a manager's power can come from political alliances. Managers who play politics well are often able to gain the cooperation and assistance of their peers and superiors. The more powerful a manager's political alliances, the more able that person is to "work" the system. Also, developing political connections may help managers achieve personal goals. Perot plays all angles to assure that he has enough power to exert his will.

In this chapter, we will first define *power* and give reasons for exerting power. Then, we will discuss sources of power, how managers can increase their power, power configurations, and power differences. We will follow the discussion with sections on strategies for obtaining power, the significance of power to the manager, resisting intimidation, and political actions in organizations. In the final portions of the chapter, we will present a global perspective on politics, and discuss stress and burnout in organizations.

❖ ❖ POWER DEFINED

Power is the ability to influence behavior. Power covers a wide range, from outright domination to the gentlest persuasion. But the popular concept of power leans toward the harsh side. Whether exercised compassionately or ruthlessly, power is necessary to get things done the way a manager wants them done. However, the improper exercise of power is inappropriate and often costly. Sexual harassment is an improper exercise of power, and it's a costly abuse of power. Research by Freada Klein Associates, a workplace-diversity consulting firm, shows that 90 percent of *Fortune* 500 companies have dealt with power abuses that resulted in sexual harassment complaints. Klein estimates that this abuse of power costs the average large corporation $6.7 million a year.[2]

Power is an emotion-laden term, particularly in cultures that emphasize individuality and equality. To call a manager a power seeker is to cast doubt on that manager's motives and actions. Some of these negative views are from older analyses that suggest power is evil and corrupts people and that the amount of it available is fixed. Certainly, modern corporations constitute major concentrations of economic power. These concentrations have materially improved the standard of living of millions of people; but when they lead to abuse, control rather than elimination would appear to be the more desirable course of action.

Power can be a highly effective instrument for good, or it can be an instrument of evil. Frequently, there is disagreement regarding the exact nature of power. Ross Perot, founder of Electronic Data Systems (EDS), had loyal followers at EDS who respected the man and his actions; and from their high regard for him came his power over them.

Different individuals and groups within and outside the organization can exert power. Top and middle managers, technical analysts and specialists, support staff, and other workers can influence the actions an organization takes to reach its objectives. Formal groups of employees—including departments, work teams, management councils, and task forces, as well as informal groups of people with offices near one another or people who see one another socially—can similarly exercise power. In addition to individuals or groups within the organization, non-employees may try to influence the behavior of an organization and its members. Owners, suppliers, clients, competitors, employee associations (including unions and professional associations), the general public, and directors of the organization may all exert power.[3] Power is an inescapable part of a well-functioning organization and a definite result of human interaction. Therefore, it must be carefully managed to benefit everyone involved.

MANAGEMENT IN PRACTICE

A Skill-Building Exercise: Fredda Flint, the vice-president of Just-in-Time Manufacturing, called Barney Rubble in human resources to ask a favor. "Barney, I have a friend whose daughter needs a job. I'd like you to consider her for the new human resource position. I would really like to help out my friend and would appreciate anything you could do."

"Tell me about the person," said Barney.

"Well, she just graduated from the state university with a degree in history. She has no work experience, but I'm sure she'll learn quickly. Like I said before, her mother is a real good friend of mine, and I sure would like to help her out."

How would you respond?

❖ ❖ REASONS FOR EXERTING POWER

Why do individuals in an organization initiate acts of power? The reasons for developing a power base and then applying that power vary. In the case of job-related dependence—how dependent a person's position is on other positions—an individual's exercise of power may be a job-related necessity. In other cases, the basic needs of individuals may motivate them to exert power. Power and dependence relationships and individual needs for power are two of the more common reasons for exerting power.

Power and Dependence

Power usually involves exchange processes, through which a person who commands services needed by others exchanges them for compliance or obedience.[4] A supervisor may exchange time off for high-quality performance by workers. In such a relationship, power has also been viewed as a function of the ties of dependence.[5] For example, supervisors often have power because subordinates depend on them for rewards. In the same way, subordinates may have power if their supervisor's performance is linked to their own.

According to marketing researcher John Kotter, individuals engage in power-oriented behavior to reduce their dependence on others.[6] In such situations, individuals may seek to increase the size of their power bases in order to decrease their dependence on current power holders. A technician who must rely on the supervisor for pay increases may reduce dependence by acquiring expertise in an area that no one else in the firm has. As the number of job-related dependencies increases, the manager or other employee increases the time and energy devoted to power-oriented behavior as a way of coping with the dependencies.[7] Alternatively, a manager generates power over others by creating in them a sense of obligation, building their belief in the manager's expertise, encouraging others to identify with the manager, and making others feel—or in fact be—dependent on the manager for resources.[8] By creating such a dependence situation, managers can weave a web of control that will result in an enhanced degree of power.

Consider other people to whom power is typically attributed: the President of the United States, for example, or the head of a large corporation. The President of the United States is viewed as extremely powerful, but he can be severely stifled by uncooperative individuals in Congress. In order to limit such occurrences, the President often builds a power base of support, first among people in his own party, then among those who share his views in the other party, and finally among those who need his support to accomplish their political agendas.

This type of dependence analysis essentially derives from the association of power with mutual dependence in social relationships.

Individual Needs for Power

As was noted in Chapter 10, David McClelland and his associates have identified the *need for power* as a motivator that causes a person to wield power.[9] Individuals with a high need for power try to influence and control others; seek leadership positions in groups; enjoy persuading others; and are perceived by others as outspoken, forceful, and demanding.[10] Often, politicians, top managers, and informal leaders are perceived as having a high need for power. Most observers would probably assume that Ross Perot is an individual who has a high need for power.

David McClelland identified two types of men that demonstrate this need (although the research did not include women, realistically either sex could be either type):

1. The first type strives for dominance. He is the impulsive tough guy. He may be rude, fight with others, boast of sexual conquest, and try to exploit women. Such men tend to reject institutional responsibility and hate to join organizations.[11] These individuals influence subordinates to be responsible to them personally.

2. The second type, in contrast, is more successful at creating a good climate for regular work. His subordinates have both a sense of responsibility and a clear knowledge of the organization. Loyal to the organization, they are less defensive and more willing to seek expert advice in personal matters when they need it. They collect fewer status symbols.[12] This kind of maturity improves their performance from the organization's viewpoint.

Studying the specific types of individuals in an organization may allow a manager to predict their power behavior and its consequences for organizational performance. Such preparation could be beneficial for the person who must manage subordinates with different needs for power. The manager could predict, for example, that individuals high in the need for power would be more likely to look for opportunities to exert power than would individuals high in other needs. For example, one study of first-line supervisors showed that the need for affiliation, not power, related to favorable job performance and favorable attitudes of subordinates.[13]

Power is not limited to individuals, of course. Organizational units such as departments or work teams can also exercise power. The power of these units can be analyzed the same way as the power of individuals. For both, the sources of power are also the same.

❖ ❖ SOURCES OF POWER

The sources of power are many and varied, and not all of them are under the control of management. A listing of the sources of power, popularized by John French and Bertram Raven, is presented in Figure 14.1.[14] Legitimate, reward, and coercive power can be given to a person by a company, but expert and referent power must be earned.

Legitimate Power

Legitimate power results from a person being placed in a formal position of authority. Subordinates feel obligated to do as their legitimate superior says; they obey the superior's rules or orders because they view them as coming legitimately from the position the superior holds. Legitimate power exists regardless of the performance level of the person holding the position.

Reward Power

Reward power is derived from a person's ability to reward another individual. This power may be formal or informal. An individual who has control over orga-

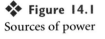
❖ **Figure 14.1**
Sources of power

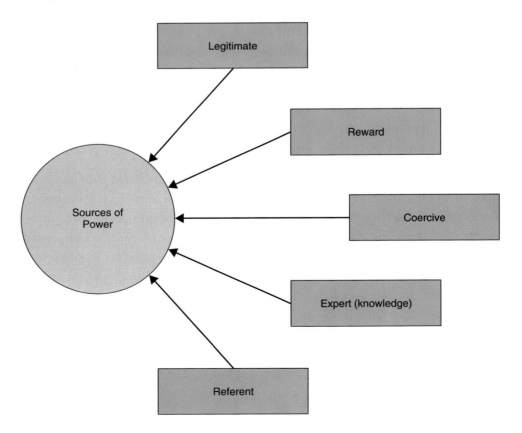

Ross Perot, founder of Electronic Data Systems, is viewed as a powerful businessperson who loves to win and knows how to use his power.
(Source: © Shelly Katz/ Gamma-Liaison)

nizational rewards, including pay raises, status, desirable work assignments, as well as praise, recognition, or group sanctions, may use them to encourage others' compliance with desired behaviors or goals. A manager can use this power effectively if subordinates believe that complying with the manager's request will result in their receiving some type of reward. Rewards are best used to reinforce the desired actions of subordinates, rather than as bribes for carrying out assigned tasks.

Ross Perot has the power to reward or deny rewards to any of his employees. However, even individuals without legitimate power may possess reward power. For example, a worker who has influence with upper management might informally put in a good word regarding a co-worker who has been cooperative. Or a worker with information desired by other workers may reward another worker by sharing this information when a favor is granted.

Coercive Power

Coercive power is derived from the ability to punish or to recommend punishment. A manager can exert this type of power over workers who fear punishment for violation of a rule or policy. The manager can force individuals to behave in certain ways by demoting or dismissing them or by increasing the direction provided to them.

Coercive power must be used with extreme caution. Misapplied, it can negate the manager's effectiveness. However, as with reward power, individuals do not have to possess legitimate power to possess coercive power. For example, one worker might punish an uncooperative co-worker by withholding informa-tion from him or her.

Expert Power

Expert, or **knowledge, power** is possessed by a person who has special knowl-edge or skills. It is considered by some to be the most effective type of power. Even if an individual has limited formal authority, expertise in a particular area will give that person considerable influence. "Red" Adair, the famed oil well fire-fighting expert, is well known by roughnecks (oil field workers) the world over for his knowledge of how to put out oil well fires. This expertise gives him the ability to go aboard an oil-drilling platform anywhere in the world and immedi-ately issue orders that will be obeyed without question.

Expert power possessed by subordinates is often difficult for managers to accept. For example, if a computer programmer becomes so knowledgeable and competent as to be considered indispensable to the organization, the manager may feel unable to even reprimand the programmer for fear that person will quit or sabotage the manager.

This brings to light a potential problem with line and staff organizations: The line has the legitimate power, whereas the staff depends on expert power. The formal right to manage a firm remains with line managers, but the capacity to manage it is spread among a number of experts.

Access to information or resources provides a source of influence by help-ing individuals or organizational units cope with uncertainty. An employee who has obtained information that others do not possess, but do desire, has a certain degree of power. For example, the first individual to learn how to operate a new software package has the power to share or not share the information. If other workers also have to learn how to use the software, this individual has the power to reduce their uncertainty.

Referent Power

Referent power is based on a liking for, or a desire to be liked by, the power holder. In the opinion of some, referent power is frequently stronger than expert power because the referent base is helped by perceived or imagined expertise on the part of those being influenced. The personality and characteristics of an indi-vidual affect the degree to which other people wish to identify and be associated with that person. President John F. Kennedy possessed referent power to a remarkable degree. His admonition "Ask not what your country can do for you but what you can do for your country" resulted in thousands of volunteers for the Peace Corps.

❖ ❖ HOW MANAGERS CAN INCREASE THEIR POWER

The concept of power extends far beyond the legitimate power normally associated with managers. A person's total power can be represented by the formula in Table 14.1, which shows that total power is the sum of all five types of power. The main power given by the manager's position in the organization is legitimate power. The formula shows that total power can be strengthened or weakened by reward, coercive, expert, and referent power. That is the reason for the plus or minus signs. For instance, a supervisor with little legitimate power might still be quite powerful by virtue of being an expert in the field. On the other hand, a manager with considerable legitimate power might be almost powerless because of a lack of job knowledge.[15]

Before Clarence Thomas was appointed as a justice of the Supreme Court, he probably already had great expert and referent power. After his appointment, this power was supplemented by extreme legitimate power, based on the respect people have for his position, and reward and coercive power, resulting from his ability to determine benefits and penalties in important cases.

❖ ❖ POWER CONFIGURATIONS

Until now, we have addressed the concept of power as if it were absolute. However, there are various configurations of power. Henry Mintzberg has identified eight configurations based on the nature of influence either inside or outside the organization.[16] He has described the external influencers as *dominated,* where one individual or group has the most power; *divided,* where a few competing groups or individuals share power; and *passive,* where no one outside the organization tries to exert power. The influence of those inside the organization is of five types: *personalized,* where the leader relies on personal control; *bureaucratic,* where formal standards are key; *ideologic,* where the norms created by the organization's ideology dominate; *professional,* where technical skills and knowledge are used; and *politicized,* where the political system is the key system.

TABLE 14.1 Determining a Person's Total Power

Total power	=	Legitimate power	±	Reward power	±	Coercive power	±	Expert power	±	Referent power

By appreciating the nature of the power configurations, mangers are better able to understand and appreciate the nature of organizational power. It is also important that managers know about the impact of power differences on organizational effectiveness. When interacting groups experience performance difficulties, power differences are frequently the source of the problem.

❖ ❖ POWER DIFFERENCES

Performance difficulties occur when interacting groups differ in the power they have. These power differences can create managerial problems, and managers must be prepared to deal with the differences effectively. Three major causes of power differences are perceptions of substitutability, the ability to cope with uncertainty, and the control of resources.

Perceptions of Substitutability

If the activities of a group are viewed as replaceable or if another group can perform the same work, the group is considered substitutable. The less a group performs substitutable tasks, the more power it possesses. Top managers often have unique knowledge and experience, which reduces their substitutability and results in greater power. Those with technical knowledge in companies that have a computerized operation may be perceived by the less technically knowledgeable as essential to the organization's functioning, and therefore they may have greater power than the less technically able employees. Basically, as the degree of substitutability increases, the degree of power a group possesses decreases, and vice versa.

Ability to Cope with Uncertainty

How well a group can deal with, and compensate for, a rapidly changing environment influences its power. It might be hypothesized that physicians can cope with a changing, complex environment and its demands better than nurses because physicians have a wider range of knowledge and experience to draw on. As nurses increase their professional training, however, this power difference is reduced. Essentially, as the ability to cope with uncertainty increases, so does the degree of power a group possesses, and vice versa.

Control of Resources

The amount of money, people, and time a group controls influences its power. The greater the amount of these resources the group controls, the more power the group has. Managers who control budgets often have greater power than those who do not. Similarly, managers of line functions may have greater power than managers of staff functions. Further, when two groups must divide resources, disagreements often arise about their optimal allocation, creating conflict between them. Communication between groups can increase or reduce these differences. Basically, however, as a group's control of resources increases, so does the degree of power the group possesses, and vice versa.

❖ ❖ STRATEGIES FOR OBTAINING POWER

Power is an inescapable element of management. When properly used, it enhances a manager's ability to attain organizational objectives. Because of the usefulness of power, individuals and groups constantly seek more favorable power positions in organizations. There are numerous means by which a manager may secure power. Among the most common are networking, coalescing, co-opting, and accepting the right projects.

Networking

Anyone who has worked in an organization for any length of time has likely heard the expression, "It's not what you know but who you know." At times, there is more than a smattering of truth to this statement. **Networking** is the cultivating of relationships with the right people for the purpose of obtaining power. As an example, a lower-level manager may meet an upper-level manager at the golf course. A friendship may develop as they build a social relationship at the golf club. This friendship may enhance the lower-level manager's personal power at

Networking is the cultivating of relationships with the right people for the purpose of obtaining power. A lower-level manager may build social relationships with upper-level managers through participation in sports such as golf or racquetball.
(Source: © Lafayette Photography)

the company. Networking relationships, however, do not necessarily involve upper-level management. They may also involve powerful peers and even subordinates. Influential peers and competent subordinates can enhance an individual's personal power, thereby facilitating the person's ability to perform.

Research has shown that informal influence among peers in a work unit and formal influence up the chain of command correlate positively with positional and personal bases of power.[17] For example, the informal network may result in the transfer of legitimate authority from a supervisor to an influential subordinate. Thus, the informal network can be used to build a power base.

Coalescing

Coalescing is the process of individuals or groups combining their resources to pursue common objectives. The purpose of individuals or groups creating such alliances is to increase the ability to influence others and to secure greater control over resources. Labor union leaders and members have long recognized the value of coalescing. "If I don't get a raise, I'll quit" will provoke little or no action on the part of management unless all the workers issue the same statement in unison. By coalescing, the group has considerably more influence with management. Even competing companies may coalesce to lobby for or against proposed legislation. Normally, the greater the influence of the individuals or groups combining their resources to pursue common objectives, the more significant the coalescing effort. Many organizations understand the concept of coalescing and use it to gain a business advantage.

Companies Coalesce for Paramount

In the 1990s, groups of companies will probably continue to combine their resources to pursue common objectives. Bidders for Paramount Communications Inc., clustered into strategic alliances to take over Paramount. The two major bidders, Viacom Inc., and QVC Networks Inc., formed strategic alliances to purchase Paramount. Both suitors offered to share the bounty with companies in each of the two strategic alliances. Although this battle is over, strategic alliances continue to transform the media and communications business. Since 1991, telephone companies, cable companies, and computer hardware and software companies have been forming strategic alliances. Strategic alliances were somewhat rare at one time, but in the global environment correctly structured alliances are seen as essential. The overall goal of those in the industry is to be at the forefront of the digital revolution that will bring text, video, voice, and graphics into the home via an *interactive electronic superhighway*. In fact, most alliances are the result of painstaking negotiations, but trying to snare Paramount has resulted in the creation of *shotgun strategic alliances*, formed quickly for the purpose of capturing one of the few remaining publicly traded entertainment and publishing companies. Shotgun alliances are by no means a trend for the future, but well crafted strategic alliances definitely are. Who will get Paramount is not really the issue; the issue is that the formation of strategic alliances based upon *commonality of interest* is a trend whose time has come.[18]

Co-Opting

Co-opting is the method of increasing power and creating alliances in which individuals or groups whose support is needed are absorbed into another group. The purpose of co-opting is to eliminate or reduce threats and opposition to the individual's or group's power base. Suppose, for instance, that a manager wants to implement a particular project but another manager of similar status has reservations about the project. The manager with the reservations may be invited to participate on the team responsible for implementing the project. If the invitation is accepted, it is likely that the resistance will be neutralized.

Accepting the Right Projects

Individuals can obtain power in organizations by engaging in activities that are highly visible, extraordinary, and related to accomplishing organizational objectives. For example, a faculty member may request and obtain the task of developing an important accreditation report. In obtaining data for the report, the person must work with the president, vice-presidents, deans, department heads, and other administrators across campus. If the faculty member accomplishes the task in an exceptional manner and accreditation results, then the person has obtained significant power. As might be expected, of course, risk is involved. If the project fails, everyone on campus will know who was in charge, and the faculty member may be left with less power than before.

Since power is an inescapable element of management, those with substantial power often have an edge in accomplishing organizational objectives. In fact, only those with a reasonable degree of power may be able to operate effectively. To maximize their effectiveness, therefore, managers should first obtain a reasonable power base.

❖ ❖ SIGNIFICANCE OF POWER TO THE MANAGER

Research has indicated that most managers want to acquire and use power. The famous power researcher David McClelland found that over 70 percent of the managers he studied had a higher need for power than did the general population.[19] Among better managers, McClelland said, the need for power was stronger than the need to be liked by others. The need for power is not normally a desire to be dictatorial, nor is it necessarily a drive for personal enhancement. Rather, it may simply reflect a manager's concern for influencing others on behalf of the organization.

Better managers probably have a need for power to get the job done rather than a need for personal power. Managers who feel a greater need to be liked than to influence others tend to be less effective.

The control of situational factors, both inside and outside the organization, is of significant concern to modern managers. It has been noted that when organizations grow so large and complex that no single individual has the capacity to manage all of the interdependencies, a dominant managing group will develop. Normally, however, it is not actually so recorded on a formal organizational chart. If the president of the firm depends heavily on the vice-president of finance to develop crucial programs, that vice-president will likely be a member of the dominant coalition and therefore will have power in excess of what the official chart suggests. Within the organization, smaller and sometimes more temporary coalitions are formed to execute tasks involving significant interdependencies.

❖ ❖ RESISTING INTIMIDATION

One reason power is often viewed negatively is that we feel intimidated when we deal with powerful people. Certainly, any average person would feel intimidated in a confrontation with Ross Perot. **Intimidation** occurs when a person fails to take action because of fear. For example, a manager may be intimidated by subordinates, peers, or other managers. A new or young supervisor who is managing more senior or older workers may be afraid of them. Often, a manager fails to discipline a worker because the manager thinks the worker knows a powerful person in the firm. Or the manager may fear that disciplining one worker will cause others to rebel.

Fear of peers can also intimidate. Perhaps a supervisor in another department is sending a supervisor too many defective parts and the receiver is afraid to reject them. If the sender is older or gives the impression of being mean and tough, that could be intimidating.

Intimidation by one's superior can cause major problems. Managers intimidated by their superiors cannot represent subordinates well or perform other aspects of their jobs well. When faulty instructions are passed down, the manager may be afraid to question them. This hurts both the subordinates and the organization. It is also likely that the workers will recognize such errors and the reason for them. Their future performance and their opinion of the manager may suffer.

At one time or another, everyone has been intimidated. But managers can take steps to keep intimidation from affecting their job performance. First, they can make themselves indispensable by being good at their job. It is difficult to intimidate a competent person. Second, they can view powerful people as simply other human beings. Most upper-level managers do not want subordinates to fear them. Third, they can show confidence. It is difficult to intimidate a confident person. A confident manager knows what action to take and is decisive in taking it. Finally, they can directly confront anyone who attempts intimidation.

❖ ❖ POLITICAL ACTION IN ORGANIZATIONS

Government-level politicians often receive low marks of approval from the general public. Political scandals regularly hit the front pages of daily newspapers. But politics and politicians exist in all forms of organized society, not just government. And political action can be positive when it promotes cooperation among individuals and groups with different interests and objectives.

Politics is a "network of interactions by which power is acquired, transferred, and exercised on others."[20] Individuals and organizational units use power to take political action. Politicians work with and through many people (hence the term *networking*). Thus, politics transcends traditional organizational boundaries. Power is the medium of exchange in politics, just as the dollar is a medium of exchange in economics. Shrewd politicians acquire power and transfer it to others when it can purchase something of value. Just like a banker, a politician can keep a balance sheet. When power is transferred, something is expected in return. To the politician, a favor given now is often power to be extracted in the future.

The degree of politicking a manager does is limited not only by formal organizational restrictions but also by the manager's personal code of ethics. The fact

ETHICAL DILEMMA

You are a successful salesperson who has just been rewarded by being appointed the regional sales manager for the company's most successful region. This operation is in a mid-sized city, whose close-knit community places a high value on local basketball. In fact, you soon realize that to most people local basketball is much more important than the Super Bowl. While watching a local game with a buyer who purchases almost 40 percent of your yearly volume, you learn that the star on the team may be leaving town because his father was laid off. The buyer has heard that you have an opening for a sales manager, and he asks you to hire the boy's father. You tell him that you will be glad to review the man's resume, but you have already found an extremely qualified person. The next day, the woman you are replacing explains that in this town people do each other favors, and that is how they build trust. She also tells you that if the boy's father is not hired, you may lose all of the buyer's business. You receive the individual's resume and soon realize that the man has no sales experience. You can either hire the extremely qualified person or capitulate to the demand of your primary buyer.

What would you do?

that at times politics might be unethical should not preclude studying the subject, and politicking cannot be condemned per se.

It is apparent that some degree of politicking is a fact of organized life, regardless of the caliber of people involved or the degree of formalization of organizational rules and regulations. No doubt, some political maneuvering can make contributions toward an organization's effectiveness. Where there is head-on conflict, and where interdependencies make some degree of cooperation essential, concessions worked out between parties often involve some bending or reinterpretation of rules. On many occasions, the conflicting interests are all legitimate and rest on solid ground.

Means of Influence

As discussed in the section on power configurations, individuals can exert influence in a variety of ways. Society or individuals outside the organization attempt to influence organizational behavior by using existing or developing social norms, imposing formal constraints on the organization, conducting pressure campaigns, instituting direct controls on the organization, or obtaining membership on the board of directors. Those inside the organization, in contrast, use authority, ideology, expertise, or politics, among others, to influence.[21] The legitimacy of each type of influence might be argued, but each can affect decision making.

Most attempts at influencing in an organization are oriented downward. Managers, for example, can give direct orders to subordinates, establish guidelines for their decision making, approve or reject their decisions, and allocate resources to them.[22]

Individuals in an organization can also exert upward influence, typically to promote or protect their self-interest. They can control the type of information passed to superiors, and they may consciously withhold information they think is detrimental to themselves. Occasionally, workers punish or reward their superiors—by withholding or providing a quality work effort, for example. Managing the boss effectively requires understanding and responding to the boss's needs.

People who identify and use resources implement their political influence along one of three dimensions: (1) internal-external, (2) vertical-lateral, or (3) legitimate-illegitimate.[23] On the internal-external dimension, they may rely on resources internal to the organization, exchanging favors or forming networks with other employees. When internal resources fail or become inadequate, they may turn to outside resources by joining professional organizations or forming alliances elsewhere. On the vertical-lateral dimension, individuals exert influence by relating either to superiors and subordinates or to peers. Mentor-protege activities occur vertically; coalition formation occurs laterally. On the legitimate-illegitimate dimension, normal and extreme behavior are contrasted. For example, most organizational members view forming coalitions as legitimate and sabotaging production as illegitimate.

Means of Improving Political Action

Exchange theories discuss power in terms of bargaining and negotiations, rather than in terms of social networks.[24] Labor negotiations, in particular, often involve acts of power that significantly influence bargaining outcomes. Coalitions often are formed as a way of increasing an individual's or group's power in a bargaining situation; that is, members of coalitions frequently muster sufficient resources to resolve a negotiating problem.

In the political arena, bargaining and negotiations are particularly important. Interest groups and political parties use power to influence authorities to give them what they want. A party will choose among the strategies of inaction, problem solving, yielding, and contending, depending on its level of concern for

---

A GLOBAL PERSPECTIVE

Power and Politicking: Global Necessities

Global managers must recognize and be prepared to deal with the political forces affecting their organizations. The degree of politicking a global manager does is limited not only by formal organizational restrictions and the manager's personal code of ethics and conscience, but also by the global environment the manager is operating in. At times, politics in a multinational environment may appear unethical from the American perspective. For example, many multinationals attempting to enter the Mexican market simply pay mordita (a "little bite"), a bribe of sorts. Some politically based accommodations are constructive, and others are destructive. But either way, politics is a reality of operating in

the global environment. Managers used to internal politics should be prepared to deal with global politics, since some political maneuvering can make a significant contribution toward an organization's effectiveness.

When entering a foreign market it is often necessary for companies to wield power when politicking and local lobbying is ineffective. Often to enter markets global companies like Campbell Soup must exercise their considerable power to assure global market growth. Entering new markets will often mean upsetting the business norms of the country. When Campbell Soup decided to buy Australia's Arnotts Ltd. to enter the Australian market, they seemed to be a natural fit. They needed Campbell's marketing savvy, and Campbell needed new and broader

markets. However, Arnotts's management fought the takeover, and the press vilified Campbell Soup CEO David W. Johnson and the Campbell Soup company. The company and Johnson were painted as "ugly Americans" that should not be allowed to control Australia's Arnotts Ltd. Johnson persisted and got a controlling interest in the company, a necessary purchase since he wants no less than half of Campbell's revenues to come from outside the United States by the year 2000.[25] Campbell Soup was simply doing what others must do to prosper in the future—that is, capture greater worldwide market share, which at times will require the wielding of corporate clout and power.

its own and another party's outcomes. A party with low concern for both its own and the other's outcome will not act (the inaction strategy). A party with high concern for both parties' outcomes will take a problem-solving approach. A party with low concern for its own outcomes and high concern for the other's will yield to the other party. It will not yield (but will contend) if concern for its own outcomes is high and concern for the other's is low.[26] An effective negotiator is aware of negotiation tightropes, avoids the need to impress others, develops interpersonal sensitivity, helps induce the other party's sense of negotiating competence, avoids commitments to irreconcilable positions, and is sensitive to conflict intensity and necessary coping strategies.[27]

Conflict is often created by the exercise of political power. To reduce conflict, formal leaders of both private and public organizations frequently seek ways to exert power without generating conflict, to limit power, and to restore an organization to equilibrium after the exercise of power.[28]

❖ ❖ STRESS IN ORGANIZATIONS

Hans Selye first used the term stress to apply to humans (rather than to animals) in the 1930s.[29] **Stress** is the body's reaction to any demand made on it. It is a psychological and physiological state that results when certain features of an individual's environment—including noise, pressures, job promotions, monotony, or the general climate—impinge on that person. Both positive and negative occurrences can give rise to stress.

As Figure 14.2 shows, individuals in stressful situations generally go through three stages: (1) alarm, (2) resistance, and (3) exhaustion.[30] In the alarm stage, they experience a stressor that causes a rise in adrenaline and anxiety. If the stres-

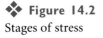
❖ Figure 14.2
Stages of stress

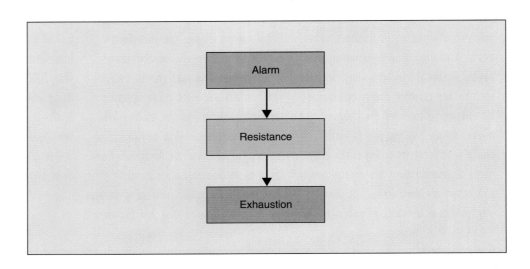

sor persists, they respond to it during the resistance stage. They may attack the stressor directly, adopt a previously successful coping behavior, deny the stressor, withdraw physically or psychologically from the situation, or persist in responding whether or not the response is effective.[31] When a stressor persists to the point of physiological or psychological damage, exhaustion has occurred.

Some respond to stress by becoming more productive and creative. Have you ever heard a friend or co-worker say, "I work best when I have a deadline in sight; I can't do anything productive unless I feel some pressure"? This person likely uses the stress resulting from the time pressure to increase productivity. Others respond to stress by experiencing gastrointestinal, glandular, or cardiovascular disorders or by overeating, drinking excessively, or taking tranquilizers.[32] Still others become impatient, detached, or despairing. Such physiological and psychological reactions can decrease creativity and productivity, which in turn often increases the level of stress, thereby causing a further decrease in effectiveness. Stress causes American workers to miss an average of 16 days on the job each year.[33]

Causes of Stress

Stress has become increasingly common in organizations, largely because of greater job complexity and economic pressure on individuals. Individuals at the beginning of their careers who are trying to establish themselves often experience stress. The midcareer crisis is virtually synonymous with stress. And facing the changes of retirement creates significant stress. Table 14.2 lists the major life stress

Stress is a psychological and physiological state that results when certain features of an individual's environment, including noise and job pressures, impinge on that person.
(Source: © John Coletti)

TABLE 14.2 Life Stress Events

Complete the scale by circling the mean value figure to the right of each item if it has occurred to you during the past year. To figure your total score, add all the mean values circled (if an event occurred more than once, increase the value by the number of items). Life stress event totals of 150 or less indicate generally good health, scores of 150 to 300 indicate a 35–50 percent probability of stress-related illness, and scores of 300+ indicate an 80 percent probability.

LIFE EVENT	MEAN VALUE	LIFE EVENT	MEAN VALUE
1. Death of spouse	100	22. Major change in responsibilities at work	29
2. Divorce	73	23. Son or daughter leaving home	29
3. Marital separation from mate	65	24. In-law troubles	29
4. Detention in jail or other institution	63	25. Outstanding personal achievement	28
5. Death of a close family member	63	26. Spouse beginning or ceasing work outside the home	26
6. Major personal injury or illness	53	27. Beginning or ceasing formal schooling	26
7. Marriage	50	28. Major change in living conditions	25
8. Being fired at work	47	29. Revision of personal habits	24
9. Marital reconciliation with mate	45	30. Troubles with the boss	23
10. Retirement from work	45	31. Major change in working hours or conditions	20
11. Major change in the health or behavior of a family member	44	32. Change in residence	20
12. Pregnancy	40	33. Changing to a new school	20
13. Sexual difficulties	39	34. Major change in usual type and/or amount of recreation	19
14. Gaining a new family member	39	35. Major change in church activities	19
15. Major business readjustment	39	36. Major change in social activities	18
16. Major change in financial state	38	37. Taking out a mortgage or loan for a lesser purchase	17
17. Death of a close friend	37	38. Major change in sleeping habits	16
18. Changing to a different line of work	36	39. Major change in number of family get-togethers	15
19. Major change in the number of arguments with spouse	35	40. Major change in eating habits	15
20. Taking out a mortgage or loan for a major purchase	31	41. Vacation	13
		42. Christmas	12
21. Foreclosure on a mortgage or loan	30	43. Minor violations of the law	11

(Source: Thomas H. Holmes, "Social Readjustment Rating Scale," *Journal of Psychosomatic Research 11*, Pergamon Press, pp. 213–218. Copyright 1967. Reprinted with permission.)

POWER, ORGANIZATIONAL POLITICS, AND STRESS 461

events and provides a way of calculating the probability of experiencing stress-related illness.

Interpersonal variables such as leadership style and extent of group cohesiveness and participation also contribute to stress both in and outside the workplace. Where the personalities of leaders and followers conflict, such as when an extroverted employee is supervised by an introverted manager, stress often occurs. Thus, the relationship between stressors and stress may be affected by personality, culture, or the nonwork environment. Professional women at times experience unique stressors: discrimination, stereotyping, conflicting demands of work and family, and feelings of isolation—all of which can dramatically affect performance and health.[34]

The Federal government's National Institute for Occupational Safety and Health (NIOSH) has studied stress as it relates to work. Its research indicates that some jobs are inherently more stressful than others. The 12 most stressful jobs are listed in Table 14.3.

TABLE 14.3 Stressful Jobs

TWELVE JOBS WITH THE MOST STRESS

1. Laborer	5. Office manager	9. Machine operator
2. Secretary	6. Foreman	10. Farm owner
3. Inspector	7. Manager/administrator	11. Miner
4. Clinical lab technician	8. Waitress/waiter	12. Painter

OTHER HIGH-STRESS JOBS (IN ALPHABETICAL ORDER)

■ Bank teller	■ Machinist	■ Railroad switchperson
■ Clergy	■ Meatcutter	■ Registered nurse
■ Computer programmer	■ Mechanic	■ Sales manager
■ Dental assistant	■ Musician	■ Sales representative
■ Electrician	■ Nurse's aide	■ Social worker
■ Firefighter	■ Plumber	■ Structural-metal worker
■ Guard/watchperson	■ Policeperson	■ Teacher's aide
■ Hairdresser	■ Practical nurse	■ Telephone operator
■ Health aide	■ Public relations person	■ Warehouse worker
■ Health technician		

(Source: From a ranking of 130 occupations by the National Institute for Occupational Safety and Health.)

The Stress Audit

In many organizations today, managers find they must be sensitive to potential stressors in order to maintain the productivity and involvement of employees. At the same time, employees often opt for minimizing stress, sometimes at the expense of promotions or significant pay increases. Managers and employees should recognize, however, that a certain amount of stress may be necessary for creative and productive work. Very little stress in the workplace can sometimes result in complacency.

Predicting the level of stress in situations can be difficult, however, largely because stress is often person-specific. Frequently, job features intuitively rated as stressful—such as the mental demands on and responsibilities of air traffic controllers or the life-and-death situations faced by the police—are neither disliked nor experienced as stressful by the job holders.[35] Alternatively, simple requests for overtime or revisions of completed work may cause stress. Any aspect of work that increases stress or fatigue will result in decreased productivity, and therefore stress abatement techniques could be quite useful.

The extent of dysfunctional stress in the work situation can be evaluated with a **stress audit,** a review that helps identify the symptoms and causes of stress. An audit includes managers' questions, such as the following:

1. Do any individuals demonstrate cardiovascular, allergy-respiratory, gastrointestinal, or emotional distress irregularities?
2. Is job satisfaction low? Is job tension, turnover, absenteeism, or accident proneness high?

Stress Abatement Through Ergonomics

Ergonomics, the science of how people interact with their work environment, is now more than a simple buzzword. Managers are beginning to realize that tailoring the office to the human physiology can enhance productivity and help avoid health problems and some types of work-related stress. What should managers do to assure an ergonomically sound workplace that will help enhance productivity?

Experts believe that the place to start is with chairs. A good ergonomic chair lets you sit with your thighs parallel to the floor and your feet flat on the floor. Computers are the alleged cause of numerous repetitive stress injuries; the position and accessibility of the computer are critical. The top of the monitor should be at, or slightly below, eye level so that employees are not continually tilting their heads to read the top of the screen. The keyboard should ideally be at elbow level. Light is the final major factor

in the world of office ergonomics. The ideal lighting arrangement is a combination of soft indirect overhead light that doesn't cause glare, and task lights that provide strong direct light for immediate work. The most common lighting problem is that the office is too bright. Also, each computer screen should be positioned so that no light falls directly on the screen. Basically, to maximize productivity and limit stress, an ergonomic office must be designed and employees must be given frequent breaks.[36]

3. Does the organization's design contribute to the symptoms?
4. Do interpersonal relations contribute to the symptoms?
5. Do career development variables contribute to the symptoms?
6. What effects do personality, sociocultural influences, and the nonwork environment have on the relationship between stressors—individual careers, interpersonal relations, and organizational design—and stress?[37]

To answer questions 1 and 2 completely and accurately requires a thorough description of the situation. To answer questions 3 through 6 requires an understanding of issues discussed in various chapters of this book.

Employees at Chevron Information Technology Company (CITC) certainly experienced some degree of stress when all 2,300 of its technology workers were informed that their positions were obsolete. From general managers down to programmers, no one was exempt. Chevron was going to get their technology house immaculate. Even the lucky ones to whom Chevron decided to give a chance had to prove they would be able to handle the revolutionary technical changes Chevron had planned for the 1990s. Mainframe knowledge was out of style, and many of these leading-edge skills were scarce within the CITC. Some longtime Chevron workers who resubmitted resumes in hopes of remaining employed knew they wouldn't make the cut, and they were all extremely stressed.[38]

❖ ❖ BURNOUT

The state of fatigue or frustration that stems from devotion to a cause, a way of life, or a relationship that does not provide the expected reward is **burnout.**[39] In essence, burnout is the perception that an individual is giving more than he or she is receiving—whether it is money, satisfaction, or praise. It is often associated with a midlife or midcareer crisis, but it can happen at different times to different people. Individuals in the helping professions, such as teachers and counselors, seem to be susceptible to burnout because of their jobs, whereas others may be vulnerable because of their upbringing, expectations, or personalities. Burnout is frequently associated with people whose jobs require close relationships with others under stressful and tension-filled conditions. While any employee may experience this condition, perhaps ten percent of managers and executives are so affected.[40] A study by Northwestern National Life Insurance Company found that burnout occurs at higher levels in firms that had substantially cut employee benefits, changed ownership, required overtime, or reduced the workforce.[41]

The dangerous part of burnout is that it is contagious. A highly cynical and pessimistic burnout victim can quickly transform an entire group into burnouts.

Therefore, it is important that the problem be dealt with quickly. Once it has begun, it is difficult to stop. Some of the symptoms of burnout are (1) chronic fatigue; (2) anger at those making demands; (3) self-criticism for putting up with demands; (4) cynicism, negativism, and irritability; (5) a sense of being besieged; and (6) hair-trigger displays of emotion.[42] The burnout victim is often unable to maintain an even keel emotionally; for example, unwarranted hostility may occur in totally inappropriate situations. Another possible symptom is recurring health problems, such as ulcers, back pain, or frequent headaches. Burnout is harmful to the individual's mental and physical health and results in performance problems for both the individual and the organization.

✘ Management Tips ✘

Guidelines for Dealing with Power, Organizational Politics, and Stress

1. **Do not be ashamed to use alliances, obligations, and debts.** They can help you protect yourself or do a better job.

2. **Use your influence.** Let workers know of the influence you have, both inside and outside the organization.

3. **Know your job.** Frequently, the most effective basis of power is expert power.

4. **Save up chips (power) and use them when they count the most.** Use your power for things that mean something.

5. **Tolerate individual differences.** Your stress level may be reduced if you accept people for what they are.

6. **Put stressful activities in perspective.** Ask yourself, "What is the worst that can happen?"

7. **Stay physically active.** If your job does not keep you in shape, develop an exercise program.

8. **Have at least one person you can confide in.** Do not keep everything bottled up inside.

9. **Recognize the fact that better managers probably have a need for power to get the job done rather than for personal power.** Managers who feel a greater need to be liked than to influence others tend to be less effective.

10. **Resist intimidation.** Managers can take steps to keep intimidation from affecting their job performance.

SUMMARY

Power is the ability to influence behavior. Why do individuals initiate an act of power? The reasons vary. In the case of job-related dependence, an individual's exercise of power may be a job-related necessity. In other cases, the basic needs of individuals may motivate them to exert power. Power and dependence relationships and individual needs for power are two of the more common reasons for exerting power.

The sources of power are many and varied, and not all are under the control of management. Legitimate power results from a person being placed in a formal position of authority. Reward power is derived from a person's ability to reward another individual. Coercive power is derived from the ability to punish or to recommend punishment. Expert (knowledge) power comes from a person possessing special knowledge or skills. Referent power is based on a liking for, or a desire to be liked by, the power holder. A person's total power is the sum of all of these forms of power.

Three major causes of power differences are perceptions of substitutability, the ability to cope with uncertainty, and the control of resources. If the activities of a group are replaceable or if another group can perform the same work, the group is considered sub-stitutable. The less a group performs substitutable tasks, the more power it possesses. How well a group can deal with and compensate for a rapidly changing environment (coping with uncertainty) influences its power. The amount of money, people, and time a group controls (the control of resources) also influences its power. The greater these resources, the more power the group has. There are numerous means by which a manager may secure power. Among the most common are networking, coalescing, co-opting, and accepting the right projects. Research has indicated that most managers want to acquire and use power.

One reason power is often viewed negatively is that we feel intimidated when we deal with powerful people. Intimidation occurs when a person fails to take action because of fear. At one time or another, everyone has been intimidated. But managers can take steps to keep intimidation from affecting their job performance.

Politics is a network of interactions by which power

KEY TERMS

Power 442

Legitimate power 446

Reward power 446

Coercive power 447

Expert (knowledge) power 448

Referent power 448

Networking 451

Coalescing 452

Co-opting 453

Intimidation 454

Politics 455

Stress 458

Stress audit 462

Burnout 463

REVIEW QUESTIONS

1. Define power.
2. Briefly describe each of the sources of power.
3. How can managers increase their power?
4. Briefly discuss each of the major causes of power differences.
5. What are the most common strategies for obtaining power?
6. What is the significance of power to a manager?
7. Define politics. What is the importance of an understanding of politics to a manager?
8. Define burnout. What are some symptoms of burnout?

is acquired, transferred, and exercised on others. Individuals and organizational units use power to take political action. Individuals can exert influence in a variety of ways. Exchange theories discuss power in terms of bargaining and negotiations, rather than in terms of social networks.

Stress is the body's reaction to any demand made on it. It is a psychological and physiological state that results when certain features of an individual's environment—including noise, pressures, job promotions, monotony, or the general climate—impinge on that person. Both positive and negative occurrences can give rise to stress. The stages of stress are alarm, resistance, and exhaustion. A stress audit can help identify the symptoms and causes of stress.

Burnout is the state of fatigue or frustration that stems from devotion to a cause, a way of life, or a relationship that does not provide the expected reward. Burnout is frequently associated with people whose jobs require close relationships with others under stressful and tension-filled conditions.

CASE STUDIES

CASE 14.1 Threatened by a Superstar

When Doug Self came to work in the accounting department at Ritger Paper Products Company, James Norris considered it a personal victory. Doug had been the top business school graduate at nearby Wichita State College the previous year. For two years, he had been president of the Student Government Association, and he had been active in every aspect of campus life.

James was the comptroller at Ritger. He supervised nine accountants and clerks. He was pleased to have attracted such an outstanding young man, and he made sure his superiors knew of the excellent recruiting job he had done.

Within a short while, it became clear to everyone in the department that Doug was not only friendly, outgoing, and easy to talk to but also well informed about accounting. Before long, Doug had made friends with everyone in the office, and James noticed that a number of the accountants began to take their questions and problems to Doug. He always seemed to have the right answer and to enjoy taking time to help. He also did an excellent job on all his own work.

Doug's presence in the accounting department made James's job easier. Only when a decision was required from outside the department would James be consulted. In a way, James was pleased with the way things were turning out. But two things bothered him. First, the accountants and clerks began to consult with Doug even about personal matters. James was 20 years older than Doug, and he felt more qualified in that regard. Second, Doug had developed a number of friendships outside the department, especially with two of the company's senior officials. James felt very insecure about this. He thought it was only a matter of time until Doug began to bypass him on official matters.

James decided to take action. Although he was not really sure how to handle the situation, he began to look for chances to criticize Doug in front of his peers. Anyone who took a problem or question to Doug was reminded that James was their direct superior, and he looked for ways to change or disparage the advice Doug had given. It was not long before the other employees got the signal. Ultimately James's strategy worked; Doug quit. But within a week, three others of James's best accountants turned in their resignations, and the department was thrown into confusion.

QUESTIONS

1. What sources of power did Doug possess? What sources of power did James possess?
2. To what extent was Doug a threat to James? Explain your answer in relation to power differences.

CASE 14.2 Power, Anyone?

Jim Perry was the director of special projects at the Main Street Bank and Trust Company, reporting directly to the bank president. Jim was assigned responsibility to initiate partnership banking at Main Street. This had become the "hot product" in the banking industry. In partnership banking, each customer is assigned a "partner" at the bank. The partner coordinates services and acts as an advocate for that customer.

Jim was assigned a "partnership task force" of five people, each selected by a different department head. The five were (1) Paul Goodman, an administrative assistant to the vice-president of operations; (2) Jenny Jackson, a newly appointed senior loan officer; (3) Michael Tracy, a recently promoted branch manager of a suburban branch; (4) Anne Richards, a marketing staff member; and (5) Jeffrey Wilson, a management trainee working for the president. The task force was to meet weekly with Jim to help him plan and implement the partnership program.

At the first meeting, Jim outlined his objectives for the project and set a tentative timetable. There was little discussion, and the meeting was quickly adjourned. At the second meeting, Anne presented a list of ideas she had garnered from an article in the *Journal of Commercial Bank Lending*. Michael offered several biting remarks about Anne's suggestions, to which Anne responded in kind. Otherwise, there was little interest in any particular suggestion.

Subsequent meetings followed a similar pattern. Either Jim offered suggestions, ideas, and comments, with little discussion, or discussions were reduced to verbal battles between Michael and Anne. Occasionally, task force members seemed to agree that they had identified some viable components of the new program. However, no one worked on the project outside the group meeting time; and at the start of each meeting, previous progress was ignored.

Jim expressed considerable frustration over the slow progress. He believed the task force members were not working as a team and that individual agendas were surfacing too frequently. After two months of weekly meetings, Jim told the president he thought the group should be reconstituted if partnership banking were ever to be successful at Main Street Bank and Trust.

QUESTIONS

1. From this case, identify any power positions that have developed or are developing.
2. Could politics be used to assist in this situation? Discuss.

NOTES

1. This case is a composite of a number of published accounts, among them: Steven Emerson, "Perot and the Politics of Power," *U.S. News & World Report* 104 (June 20, 1988): 28; Keith F. Girard, "Profiles in Power," *Business Month* 133 (May 1989): 28–37; Peter Elkind, "Perot and Con," *The Washington Monthly* (November 1990): 51–53; Todd Mason, "Will the Real Ross Perot Please Stand Up?" *Business Week* (May 21, 1990): 22–23, 26; and Mark M. Colodny, "Ross Perot on His Good Luck," *Fortune* (June 3, 1991): 211; Wendy Zellner and Richard S. Dunham, "What Does Ross Perot Want?" *Business Week* (April 19, 1993): 34.

2. Anne B. Fisher, "Sexual Harassment: What to Do," *Fortune* 128 (August 23, 1993): 84–88.

3. H. Mintzberg, *Power in and Around Organizations* (Englewood Cliffs, NJ: Prentice-Hall, 1983).

4. P. M. Balu, *Exchange and Power in Social Life* (New York: Wiley, 1964).

5. R. M. Emerson, "Power-Dependence Relations," *American Sociological Review* 27 (February 1962): 31–41.

6. J. P. Kotter, "Power, Dependence, and Effective Management," *Harvard Business Review* 55 (July 1977): 125–136.

7. *Ibid.*

8. J. P. Kotter, "Power, Success, and Organizational Effectiveness," *Organizational Dynamics* 6 (Winter 1978): 27–40.

9. D. McClelland and D. H. Burnham, "Power Driven Managers: Good Guys Make Bum Bosses," *Psychology Today* 9 (December 1975): 69–71.

10. R. M. Steers and L. W. Porter, *Motivation and Work Behavior* (New York: McGraw-Hill, 1979).

11. McClelland and Burnham, "Power Driven Managers: Good Guys Make Bum Bosses."

12. *Ibid.*

13. E. T. Cornelius III and F. B. Lane, "The Power Motive and Managerial Success in a Professionally Oriented Service Industry Organization," *Journal of Applied Psychology* 69 (February 1984): 32–39.

14. John French and Bertram Raven, "The Basis of Social Power," in *Studies in Social Power,* ed. Dorwin Cartwright (Ann Arbor: University of Michigan Press, 1959), pp. 150–167.

15. R. Wayne Mondy and Shane R. Premeaux, "Power, Politics, and the First-Line Supervisor," *Supervisory Management* 31 (January 1986): 36–39.

16. H. Mintzberg, "Power and Organization Life Cycles," *Academy of Management Review* 9 (April 1984): 207–224; Mintzberg, *Power in and Around Organizations.*

17. A. Cobb, "Informal Influence in the Formal Organization: Perceived Sources of Power Among Work Unit Peers," *Academy of Management Journal* 23 (March 1980): 155–161.

18. Laura Landro, "Instant Alliances Coalesce During Fight for Paramount," *The Wall Street Journal* XCII (October 13, 1993): B1.

19. David C. McClelland and David H. Burnham, "Power Is the Great Motivator," *Harvard Business Review* 54 (March–April 1976): 102.

20. John M. Pfiffner and Frank P. Sherwood, *Administrative Organization* (Englewood Cliffs, NJ: Prentice-Hall, 1960) p. 311.

21. Mintzberg, "Power and Organization Life Cycles."

22. *Ibid.*

23. D. Farrell and J. C. Petersen, "Patterns of Political Behavior in Organizations," *Academy of Management Review* 7 (July 1982): 402–412.

24. D. Kipnis, *The Powerholders* (Chicago: University of Chicago Press, 1976).

25. Joseph Weber, Gail Schares, Stephen Hutcheon, and Ian Katz, "Campbell: Now It's M-M-Global," *Business Week* (March 15, 1993): 52–54.

26. D. G. Pruitt, "Strategic Choice in Negotiation," *American Behavioral Scientist* 27 (November–December 1983): 167–194.

27. J. Z. Rubin, "Negotiation," *American Behavioral Scientist* 27 (November–December 1983): 136–148.

28. R. L. Kahn and E. Boulding, *Power and Conflict in Organizations* (New York: Basic Books, 1964).

29. H. Selye, *The Stress of Life* (New York: McGraw-Hill, 1956).

30. H. Selye, *The Stress of Life,* 2d ed. (New York: McGraw-Hill, 1976).

31. C. N. Cofer and M. H. Appley, *Motivation: Theory and Research* (New York: Wiley, 1964).

32. D. R. Frew, *Management of Stress* (Chicago: Nelson Hall, 1977), p. xix; see also A. P. Brief, R. S. Schuler, and M. Van Sell, *Managing Job Stress* (Boston: Little, Brown, 1982).

33. Janice Somerville, "Stress Treatment Costing Billions," *American Medical News* 32 (November 1989): 17.

34. D. L. Nelson and J. C. Quick, "Professional Women: Are Distress and Disease Inevitable?" *Academy of Management Review* 10 (January 1985): 206–218; G. L. Cooper and M. J. Davidson, "The High Cost of Stress on Women Managers," *Organizational Dynamics* 10 (Winter 1982): 44–53.

35. S. V. Kasl, "Epidemiological Contributions to the Study of Work Stress," in *Stress at Work,* ed. G. L. Cooper and R. Payne (New York: Wiley, 1978).

36. Pam Black, "A Home Office That's Easier on the Eyes—And the Back," *Business Week* (August 17, 1992): 112–113.

37. M. Kets de Vries, "Organizational Stress: A Call for Management Action," *Sloan Management Review* 21 (Fall 1979): 3–14.

38. Alice LaPlante, "Rightsizing Angst," *Forbes* 151 (June 7, 1993): 94–104.

39. Herbert J. Freudenberger, *Burnout: The High Cost of High Achievement* (Garden City, NY: Anchor Press, Doubleday and Company, 1980): 13.

40. Beverly Norman, "Career Burnout" *Black Enterprise* 12 (July 1981): 45.

41. Ron Zemke, "Workplace Stress Revisited," *Training* 28 (November 1991): 35–39.

42. Harry Levinson, "When Executives Burn Out," *Harvard Business Review* 59 (May–June 1981): 76.

15 Corporate Culture, Change, and Development

LEARNING OBJECTIVES

After completing this chapter students should be able to

✘ Define *corporate culture*, describe the factors that influence it, and explain the evidence of culture.

✘ Distinguish between a participative and a nonparticipative culture.

✘ Describe the change sequence.

✘ Identify sources of resistance to change, the approaches that can be used in reducing resistance to change, and diversity training.

✘ Describe the organizational development techniques that are available to implement change and team building.

Apple's New Corporate Culture, Directed by a True Believer: Michael H. Spindler

The Apple computer story is all too familiar now. Apple was founded by Steve Jobs and Steve Wozniak in 1976, after they built a few personal computers in Jobs's garage and sold them to friends. Through the mid-1980s the company was known for its counterculture-type organization, as well as its innovative product offerings and marketing savvy. Blue jeans, long hair, and yogurt were common at the informal gatherings that passed for management meetings in those days. A coat and tie, a Cadillac, a clear, direct order, or an organization chart would have seemed out of place. Wozniak left after a few years, and Jobs led Apple through nearly a decade of rapid growth, until 1984 when Apple dropped to number two, behind IBM. In 1985, John Sculley took over from Jobs. Under Sculley, the company nearly tripled in sales to $5.3 billion a year. Each year saw new highs in both sales and profits. Apple computers had evolved during those years toward compatibility with other brands. But Apple's success again began to fade in 1992 under Sculley, and Apple faced its most difficult challenges in the company's 17-year history. Sculley was a visionary, but what the Apple board wanted was a money and people manager. The board's solution was Michael H. Spindler, a stout 50-year-old German who is a press-shy, hands-on manager.

Sculley brought in Michael H. Spindler to head Apple's USA division to replace the conservative authoritarian, Allan Z. Loren, who helped reorganize Apple in 1989. As part of the reorganization, the organizational structure was tightened and Apple's "California mystique" was eliminated. Loren got the reorganization job done, but he scared the hell out of people in the process. When the reorganization was complete, Loren was replaced because Apple employees closed ranks against him.

Spindler, who had made himself a hero by nearly tripling Apple's European sales to $1.2 billion in two years, replaced Loren. Spindler emphasized teamwork and dramatically altered the corporate culture of the Apple corporation.

According to Spindler, "There will be no more prima donnas at Apple." Insiders say that this may be the most important change of all. However, some of the other changes will also affect the culture at Apple. Apple no longer depends on a few brilliant key people, but rather on more of an organized research methodology. Apple now assigns product-development teams with the challenge of "finding value in the inevitable mistakes, half steps and dead ends." Planning is now more of a discipline than a fantasy. Changes such as eliminating lavish spending are marshalling in a new way of life at Apple. Some insiders believe that Spindler's success was hampered by Sculley's visionary style. Spindler blends better with the new Apple corporate culture. Unlike Sculley, he is warm and approachable. He visits everyone at all levels and easily establishes rapport with them. Spindler enjoys roaming the halls and saying hello. Under his direction, the corporate culture he helped establish will run from the top down. Many experts believe that if Apple can return to its past glory, Spindler and his corporate culture can do it.[1]

The "loose and free" corporate culture at Apple was a reflection of the philosophies of Steve Jobs and his California friends. Things changed when Sculley took over. But now it appears that Apple's culture will return to one that more closely resembles the one that Jobs established. Spindler, however, will blend the new, more relaxed corporate culture with planning, teamwork, and the elimination of prima donnas to increase Apple's market share. Every organization has a distinct culture whether or not it has an influential chief executive.

Business scholars often treat the corporate culture as a constraint within which the management job is accomplished. However, it is desirable—and to some degree possible—to modify the corporate culture to help accomplish company objectives. Sculley was doing that at Apple, and now Spindler is changing it again. Culture can foster commitment to the organization and provide an identity for organization members. Managers need to understand the cultures that exist in their firms, whether or not they seek to change them. This is all the more important as Western countries try to match the Japanese devotion to quality and output.

In this chapter, we first define *corporate culture* and discuss the factors that influence it. Then, we offer evidence of culture, discuss participative versus nonparticipative cultures, and provide a global perspective related to corporate culture. Next, we present a model of the change sequence. Then, we explore the sources of resistance to change, ways to overcome it, and diversity training. In the final section of the chapter, we address organizational development and team building.

❖ ❖ CORPORATE CULTURE DEFINED

Corporate Culture is the system of shared values, beliefs, and habits within an organization that interacts with the formal structure to produce behavioral norms. Corporate culture embodies the values and standards that guide peoples' behavior. It determines the organization's overall direction. Culture governs what the company stands for, its allocation of resources, its organizational structure, the systems it uses, the people it hires, the fit between jobs and people, the results it recognizes and rewards, what it defines as problems and opportunities, and how it deals with them.[2] When mergers occur, different corporate cultures attempt to integrate, often causing problems.

When Bell Atlantic bought TCI and its cable-programming sister, Liberty Media Corporation, two different cultures merged. If conflicts do result, they could run deep, since the merging companies have highly divergent corporate cultures. Philadelphia-based Bell Atlantic is steeped in the tradition of the highly regulated, cautious Bell System, whereas TCI, based near Denver, epitomizes the freewheeling, cowboy opportunism of the cable industry.[3] Diversity is one factor that will have a major impact on corporate culture in the future.

Writing in 1967, Anthony Jay stated: "It has been known for some time that corporations are social institutions with customs and taboos, status groups and pecking orders, and many sociologists and social scientists have studied and written about them as such. But they are also political institutions, autocratic and democratic, peaceful and warlike, liberal and paternalistic."[4] What Jay was writing about, although the term had not then achieved broad usage, was corporate culture.

The Impact of Growing Diversity on Corporate Culture

Diversity is expected to alter the corporate culture of many corporations. Companies such as Colgate-Palmolive, Corning Inc., and Quaker Oats have accepted that diversity is a part of the organizational environment, and will in all likelihood continue to grow and impact corporate cultures. But what exactly is the nature of diversity in the United States? In actuality, the U.S. population grew 9.8 percent in the eighties to a total of 248,709,873, but minorities grew by 30.9 percent. According to *American Demographics*, the fastest growing county for blacks was Jefferson County, New York; for Hispanics it was Osceola County, Florida; and for Asians it was Kalawao County, Hawaii. Interestingly enough, only five counties had populations where non-Hispanic whites, non-Hispanic blacks, Hispanics, and non-Hispanic other races were nearly equal. Queens County, New York, San Francisco County, California, Los Angeles, California, Kings County, New York, and Alameda County, California were the most diversified counties. The point is that although the U.S. workforce is more diverse than in the past, with a concerted effort businesses throughout the U.S. do have time to welcome in workplace diversity.[5]

Just as physical climate is described by such variables as temperature, humidity, and precipitation, corporate culture is composed of such factors as friendliness, supportiveness, and risk taking. The culture existing within a firm influences the employees' degree of satisfaction with the job as well as the level and quality of their performance. The late Sam Walton said, "The customer is the boss," at Wal-Mart. At each store, customers are met at the door by "People Greeters." (Source: Photograph courtesy of Wal-Mart, Inc.)

Culture gives people a sense of how to behave and what they ought to be doing. It is similar in concept to meteorological climate. Just as the weather is described by such variables as temperature, humidity, and precipitation, corporate culture is described by such variables as friendliness, supportiveness, and risk taking. For instance, the weather of the southwestern United States may be described as "warm and pleasant," and the employees of an organization may characterize their organization as being "open and supportive." Such perceptions are gradually formed by each individual over a period of time as the person performs assigned activities under the general guidance of a superior and a set of organizational policies.

The culture existing within a firm influences the employees' degree of satisfaction with the job as well as the level and quality of their performance. The assessment of how desirable the organization's culture is may differ for each employee. One person may perceive the environment as bad, and another may see the same environment as good. An employee may actually leave an organization in the hope of finding a more compatible culture.

The late Ray Kroc, founder of McDonald's Corporation, was straightforward in what he expected in his corporate culture. He created a direct, people-oriented corporate culture. According to Kroc, "If you got time to lean, you got time to clean." In relation to company expansion, "When you're green, you grow; when you're ripe, you rot."[6] When Mike Quinlan became McDonald's new CEO, he pledged that McDonald's culture would remain unchanged under his leadership. McDonald's has no formal staff hierarchy. The annual report lists the company officers alphabetically instead of by rank, and no employee has an office door. Corporate culture is an integral part of the organization and has important implications for managerial action. However, corporate culture cannot transform a company unless cultural changes are tied directly into corporate strategy. According to Joseph L. Galarneau, executive-education director at AT&T, "You probably can't turn a culture around with an educational program alone, but when a program is tied directly to strategy, it does make a difference."[7] Apple CEO, Spindler, is determined to tie strategy and corporate culture together to help assure Apple is successful in the global marketplace.

❖ ❖ FACTORS THAT INFLUENCE CORPORATE CULTURE

The purpose of transforming corporate culture is simple: "To increase productivity by converting worker apathy into corporate allegiance."[8] Basically, this statement means that an organization should change its personality unless it is supporting the accomplishment of organizational objectives. Firms such as IBM and AT&T have been successful with the same corporate cultures for many decades, but their cultures no longer allow the firms to be as successful as they could be in the current global business climate.

MANAGEMENT IN PRACTICE

A Skill-Building Exercise: You are general manager of Clean-Care Janitorial Service, which was recently acquired by Super-Clean of North America (SCNA). SCNA is a nationwide commercial cleaning service that specializes in large office buildings. Its price schedules are fixed, and its cleaning and maintenance procedures are standardized. You have met some of the company's crew leaders, and you were surprised to find they were aggressive and well-spoken young management types.

Clean-Care does mainly residences, although the company accepts some commercial subcontracts. Clean-Care accepts residential calls on short notice. Much of its business is overflow from larger cleaning firms that have mostly commercial clients. Your workforce is basically unskilled and uneducated, and your supervisors are people who consistently did a good job as workers.

SCNA has just informed you that it will impose its participative management approach on Clean-Care. You are to establish formal procedures to make sure employees really help in solving problems and participate in decisions that affect them.

What would you do?

To change or maintain a corporate culture, managers should understand the factors that influence it. Among those factors are work groups, managers' and supervisors' leadership style, organizational characteristics, and administrative processes (see Figure 15.1). As in most management situations, the external environment also influences corporate culture.

❖ **Figure 15.1**
Factors that influence corporate culture

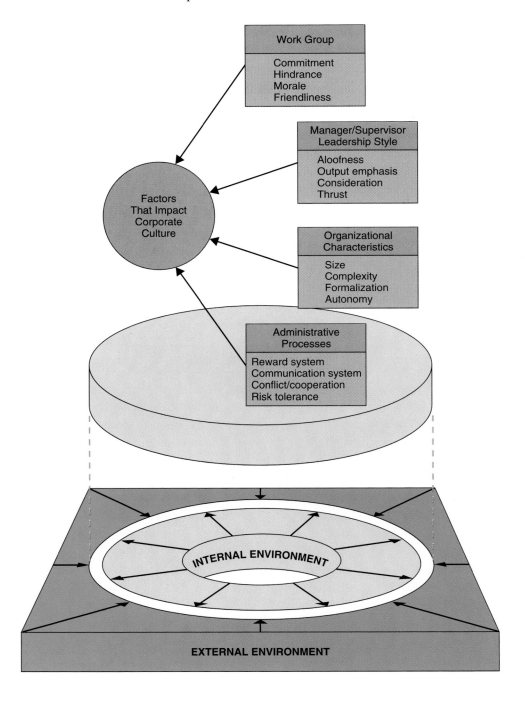

Work Group

The character of the immediate work group will affect one's perception of the nature of corporate culture. For example, commitment to the mission of the work group directly influences cultural perceptions. Commitment refers to whether or not the group is really working. If people in the work group are just going through the motions of work, it is difficult for an individual member to obtain high levels of output and satisfaction. Hindrance may also occur when individuals work together as a group. Hindrance is concerned with the degree of busywork (work of doubtful value) given to the group. Morale and friendliness within the group also affect the environment of the work group and the perceived nature of the corporate culture.

Manager/Supervisor Leadership Style

The leadership style of the immediate supervisor will have a considerable effect on the culture of the group, and vice versa. If the manager is aloof and distant in dealing with subordinates, this attitude could have a negative influence on the organization. If the supervisor is always pushing for output, this too alters the environment. Consideration is a desirable leadership characteristic that can positively influence group effectiveness. Thrust—managerial behavior characterized by hard work and example setting—is also a positive influence on the group.

ETHICAL DILEMMA

Your company recently adopted the Mead Corporation approach to ethics, and the newly appointed CEO made clear his determination to be the ethical leader in the industry. Mead Corporation has incorporated ethics into the total corporate culture as an effective and enforceable control for workplace behavior. Mead encourages line managers and other workers to spot problem areas and initiate appropriate responsible policies. One of the key aspects of this program is Project Hotline, a telephone hotline used to report unethical behavior, in lieu of employees reporting the behavior to a supervisor.[9] You are aware that the company that disposes of your plant waste is not following Environmental Protection Agency guidelines. The less toxic waste is being dumped at night in a closed landfill six miles from the plant. To make matters worse, the waste disposal company is operated by your brother-in-law. You have already warned him once, and you have just learned that he is still illegally dumping. You confront him, telling him that you are going to use the hotline to report him if he illegally dumps waste one more time, but he threatens to implicate you if you blow the whistle. You can either call and report your brother-in law, or you can let him continue to dump illegally.

What would you do?

Organizational Characteristics

The type of culture that develops can also be affected by organizational characteristics. Organizations vary on such attributes as size and complexity, for example. Large organizations tend toward higher degrees of specialization and impersonalization. Labor unions often find that large firms are easier to organize than smaller ones because smaller firms tend to be closer and have more informal relationships among employees and management. Complex organizations tend to employ a greater number of professionals and specialists, which alters the general approach to solving problems. Organizations also vary in the degree to which they write things down and attempt to program behavior through rules, procedures, and regulations. They can be distinguished, too, on the basis of the degree of decentralization of decision-making authority, which affects the degree of autonomy and employee freedom.

Administrative Processes

Corporate culture may be affected by administrative processes. Firms that can develop direct links between performance and rewards tend to create cultures that are conducive to achievement. Communication systems that are open and free-flowing tend to promote participation and creative atmospheres. The general attitudes that exist toward the tolerance of conflict and the handling of risk have considerable influence on teamwork. They also affect the amount of innovation and creativity.

From these and other factors, organization members develop a subjective impression of what kind of place the organization is to work in. This impression will affect performance, satisfaction, creativity, and commitment to the organization.

Classification of Cultures

Within most large organizations, both a dominant culture and many subcultures exist. The **dominant culture** is the corporate culture that expresses the shared views of the majority of the organization's members. **Subcultures** are corporate cultures characteristic of various units in an organization. For instance, the marketing department may have a culture that is different from that of the production department. Although members from both departments share the dominant culture, they may also develop other cultural aspects unique to their particular unit.

Cultures are also classified as strong or weak. The dominant corporate culture that is widely and ardently adhered to by members of the organization is a **strong corporate culture.** Many Japanese firms seem to have strong corporate cultures. Apple USA has a strong corporate culture, but this culture appears to be hindering needed changes, which is why Spindler was given the job of changing the culture.

EVIDENCE OF CULTURE

Determining exactly what type of culture exists in an organization can be difficult, but there are means available. The evidence of an organization's culture can be found in many places, particularly in status symbols, traditions, history, rituals, jargon, and the physical environment (see Figure 15.2).

Status Symbols

A visible, external sign of one's social position is a **status symbol.** A stranger who is aware of status hierarchies can enter an organization and obtain a social fix quickly by reading the various symbols. Status symbols vary from firm to firm. For example, one would usually expect higher-status positions to be accompanied by newer office furnishings. In one organization, however, the high-status managers were given antique roll-top desks, and the lower-level managers received new, shiny, modern furniture. Some typical status symbols in business are the following:

- Title.
- Pay.
- Bonus and stock plans.
- Size and location of desk or office.
- Location of parking space or reserved parking.
- Type of company car assigned.
- Secretaries.

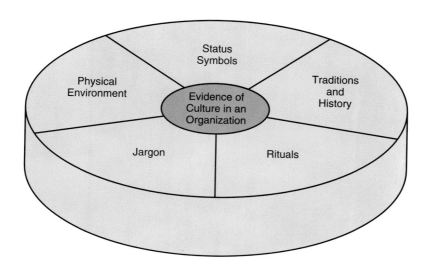

❖ **Figure 15.2**
Evidence of an organization's culture

- Privacy.
- Use of executive clubs.
- Cocktail party invitations.
- Furnishings, including rugs, pictures, and tables.
- Posted certificates.
- Privileges, including the freedom to move about, to not punch a time clock, to set one's own working hours, and to regulate one's own coffee breaks.
- Number of windows in an office.

In addition, status symbols tend to be different for different professionals. For example, research scientists and engineers often regard the importance or size of their projects as a status symbol.

Many status symbols are not controlled by management and may be the basis of unwarranted preoccupation. Executives have gotten down on their hands and knees to measure the comparative size of their offices. Windows are counted, steps from the president's office are paced off, parking space is fought for, and company cars are wrangled. In some organizations, having an office with windows is a major status symbol.

Traditions and History

Organizational traditions tend to distinguish one firm from another. Even firms that produce essentially the same product will be somewhat different because of

There are certain organizational traditions that tend to distinguish one firm from another. Even firms that produce essentially the same product will be somewhat different because of certain traditions. (Source: © Ron Chapple 1993/FPG International)

certain traditions. Workers act and react on a daily basis because of past events that have become traditional. Typically, their actions are unconscious. They just know what is expected of them in certain situations. In the past, IBM had a tradition of conservative dress, incentive-type compensation, and internal competition among employees. Apple USA's traditions were much different, but since have become more conservative.

Rituals

Closely related to traditions and history are company rituals. Many Japanese firms have their employees begin the day by doing exercises. The Mary Kay Cosmetics Company provides high-profile and embellished meetings, during which salespersons are awarded gold and diamond pins, furs stoles, and the use of pink Cadillacs. These awards are presented in an environment easily reminiscent of a Miss America pageant. There is a cheering audience in a large auditorium, and all the participants are dressed glamorously.

Jargon

Jargon is the special language that group members use in their daily interactions. The jargon used in one firm is often quite different from that of another. Sales representatives are keenly aware of this, and they train themselves to recognize the sales jargon of competing firms. Then, when they call on a new prospect, they can recognize which other sales representatives have already visited the prospect through the terminology the prospect uses when asking questions. Even in a single firm, jargon separates one group or unit from another. Accountants may use one jargon and sales representatives another.

The Physical Environment

The firm's physical environment often makes a statement about its type of culture. Office areas with few common locations for organization members to meet create an image of a closed form of culture. An office building with open offices and considerable common areas for employee interaction indicates a different culture. Whether office doors are consistently open or closed is a clue to the level of formality that exists in an organization. Even the type of furniture used can tell much about an organization's culture. For instance, round tables suggest more equality than do long ones.

❖ ❖ PARTICIPATIVE VERSUS NONPARTICIPATIVE CULTURES

Culture is often viewed in terms of the level of participation within the organization. Management participation is key in the effort to instill in executives a sense of total commitment, and when the top executive educates executives in the nature of participation it becomes more effective. According to William Wiggen-horn, president of Motorola University, "When you have to teach, you are forced to learn the greater nuances and details of the changes you are asking people to make." When the boss teaches others how to participate, the lesson is bound to have more weight than a seminar led by a consultant.[10] Because Apple's Spindler is warm and approachable, he will in all likelihood encourage participation from the executive level on down. On a continuum, involvement may range from highly participative to completely nonparticipative, with many degrees in between. An open and participative culture is characterized by such attributes as the following:

- Trust in subordinates.
- Openness in communications.
- Considerate and supportive leadership.
- Group problem solving.
- Worker autonomy.
- Information sharing.
- High-output objectives.

Some behaviorists contend that this type of culture is the only viable one for all situations.

The opposite of the open and participative culture is the closed and auto-cratic one. Both may be characterized by high-output objectives, but in a closed culture, such objectives are more likely to be declared and imposed on the orga-nization by autocratic and threatening leaders. There is greater rigidity in this cul-ture, resulting from strict adherence to the formal chain of command, short spans of management, and strict individual accountability. The emphasis is on the indi-vidual rather than on teamwork. Workers often simply go through the motions of work, doing as they are told.

Despite behaviorists' criticism of traditional corporate cultures, a more par-ticipative philosophy may not always work. In an instance involving the packag-ing of low-priced china, low productivity of the work group was caused by exces-sive and unnecessary interaction between employees during working hours. Management found that the threat of dismissal did not solve the problem. Management finally solved it by redesigning the space allocated to the china-packaging process. A cubicle constructed of soundproofing material was built for each worker. The cubicles virtually eliminated the unproductive conversation between workers. As a result, productivity increased substantially.[11]

Developing a Participative Culture

The managerial approach in most organizations has been characterized as highly structured. Consequently, most attempts to alter organizational culture have been directed toward creating a more open and participative culture. As Chapter 10 indicated, the theme of participation developed by Douglas McGregor, Frederick Herzberg, and Abraham Maslow, among others, relates primarily to self-actualization, motivator factors, consultative and democratic leadership, and job enrichment.

Benefits of Participation

The possible values of involving more people in the decision-making process relate primarily to morale. Increases in the levels of morale and job satisfaction when cultures are made more open and participative result in the following:

- Increased acceptability of management's ideas.
- Increased cooperation between management and staff.
- Reduced turnover.
- Reduced absenteeism.
- Fewer complaints and grievances.
- Greater acceptance of changes.
- Improved attitudes toward the job and the organization.

The development of greater employee participation may have a direct and immediate effect on employee morale. Employees are likely to take a greater interest in the job and the organization. They will tend to accept and sometimes initiate change, not only because they understand the necessity for change but also because knowing more about the change reduces their insecurity.

Though there is some question about the relationship between degree of participation and productivity, most experience and research indicate a positive relationship between employee participation and measures of morale, turnover, and absenteeism—which are all related to job satisfaction. However, there has been little evidence of a positive relationship between job satisfaction and productivity. Still, if productivity is not harmed by participation, these benefits should make participative management worthwhile. If management finds that productivity is actually decreased in a particular situation, then serious decisions will have to be made concerning the trade-off between organizational needs and human needs.

Limitations of Participation

Despite the value of a participative approach to management, there are some limitations. The requirements for greater participation in decision making are (1) sufficient time, (2) adequate ability and interest on the part of the participants, and (3) freedom to do the job.

If immediate decisions are required, time may not be available for group participation. The manager frequently decides what to do and issues orders accordingly. Also, if management decides to switch from a practice of autocracy to one of increased participation, some time for adjustment on the part of both managers and subordinates will be required. Participation calls for the ability to govern oneself and may therefore require the time for subordinates to learn how to handle this newfound freedom—and for supervisors to learn to trust their subordinates.

❖ **Figure 15.3**

Limits to participative freedom

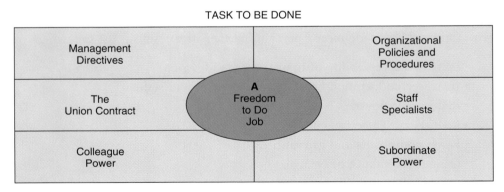

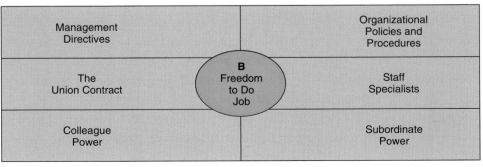

Whether or not greater involvement in decision making can be developed depends largely on the ability and interest of the participants, both subordinates and managers. This is not an easy concept to implement. Obviously, if a subordinate has neither knowledge of nor interest in a subject, there is little need to consult that person. Not all employees are desirous of participation. Managers should face the fact that some workers do not seek more responsibility and involvement in their job.

Finally, as Figure 15.3 indicates, the area of job freedom left to the individual may be quite restricted, but it can be expanded. An individual's task may be governed by management directives, organizational policies and procedures, the union contract, staff specialists, and colleague and subordinate power. The greater the area in the "Freedom to Do Job" section of the figure, the greater the degree of participative freedom. In the figure, employee A would have more freedom to accomplish the job than would employee B. Upper-level management may permit substantial latitude in decision making for employee A and less for employee B.

Measuring the Participation Level: Likert's Systems of Management

Rensis Likert, former director of the Institute for Social Research at the University of Michigan, developed a management systems theory that keyed in on a continuum of management styles ranging from autocratic to participative. Likert's theory calls for four systems of management: System I, exploitative autocratic; System II, benevolent autocratic; System III, consultative; and System IV, participative team. According to Likert, the last style is the best in the long run for all situations.[12]

System I—Exploitative Autocratic Managers make all decisions in the exploitative autocratic system. They decide what is to be done, who will do it, and how and when it is to be accomplished. Failure to complete work as assigned results in threats or punishment. Under this system, management exhibits little confidence or trust in employees. A typical managerial response is: "You do it my way or you're fired." According to Likert, there is a low level of trust and confidence between management and employees.

System II—Benevolent Autocratic Managers who are benevolent autocrats make the decisions, but their employees have some degree of freedom and flexibility in performing their jobs so long as they conform to specific procedures. Under the benevolent autocratic system, managers take a paternalistic attitude— "I'll take care of you if you perform well." This system offers a fairly low level of trust between management and employees, which causes employees to use caution when dealing with management.

System III—Consultative Managers in the consultative system consult with employees prior to establishing objectives and making decisions about work. This system is used by Wal-Mart Stores, whose employees are encouraged to make suggestions for improvements and changes, which are forwarded to Wal-Mart headquarters weekly. Wal-Mart management also includes employees in corporate decision making.[13] In the consultative system, employees have a considerable degree of freedom in deciding how to do their work. A manager using this system might say to an employee, "I'd like your opinion on this before I make the decision." Management also tends to rely on rewards rather than punishments to motivate employees. The level of trust between employees and management is also fairly high. This creates a culture in which employees feel relatively free to openly discuss work-related matters with management.

System IV—Participative Team Likert's recommended system is the participative team. The emphasis of this system is on group participation, with full involvement of the employees in the process of establishing objectives and making job-related decisions. Employees involved in a participative team system feel free to discuss matters with their manager, who is supportive rather than condescending or threatening. Likert contends that entire organizations should be designed along the lines of participative teams, with work being performed by a

A GLOBAL PERSPECTIVE

Profiting Through a Globally Compatible Corporate Culture

Corporate culture is the system of shared values, beliefs, and habits within an organization that interacts with the formal structure to produce behavioral norms. Corporate culture embodies the values and standards that guide people's behavior and determines the organization's overall direction. Long-term success means having a corporate culture that supports the goals of the organization and effectively deals with the business environment. As a firm becomes more

and more global in nature, it becomes more difficult to have a supportive corporate culture. Citicorp has operations that span the globe, which is good because of the overwhelming opportunities throughout the world, but it is often difficult from the standpoint of control.

The corporate culture of Citicorp has always "overprized vision and undervalued hands-on, day-to-day management, which to many Citibankers has looked an awful lot like work." Citi's corporate culture did not focus on making money, but rather it has been run for growth and revenue generation. Citi's corporate

culture has changed, and now the focus is on profits; no longer can Citi survive with the cultural attitude that they "could buy everything, fix anything, and do it all at once." Globally, no corporation has that much money, including Citicorp.[14] Citicorp discovered what other successful global companies are aware of, that profits are essential for global success. Combining an effective corporate culture that keys on effectively coping with the global environment and at the same time being profitable is what all global companies must strive for.

series of overlapping groups. The leader provides a link between the group and other units at higher levels in the organization. This concept is often referred to as the *linking-pin theory*. Decision making is widespread throughout the enterprise, with the power of knowledge usually taking precedence over the power of authority.

In the Likert framework, measurement of the type of management style is usually accomplished by having the employees assess the organizational culture and management system on a Likert scale (See Figure 15.4). For example, when the statement "Extent to which superior willingly shares information with subordinates" is made, the employee can respond on the continuum from "Provides minimum of information" all the way to "Seeks to give subordinates all relevant information and all information they want" (see item 3.c.2 in Figure 15.4). It has been found that the positions on these scales can be significantly altered through organizational and management development programs.

❖ **Figure 15.4**

Sample statements on the Likert Scale relating to communications within the organization (Source: Rensis Likert, *The Human Organization* [New York: McGraw-Hill, 1967]. Copyright by McGraw-Hill Book Company. Used with permission.)

3. Character of communication process				
a. Amount of interaction and communication aimed at achieving organization's objectives	Very little	Little	Quite a bit	Much with both individuals and groups
				13
b. Direction of information flow	Downward	Mostly downward	Down and up	Down, up, and with peers
				14
c. Downward communication 1. Where initiated	Initiated at all levels	Patterned on communication from top but with some initiative at lower levels	Primarily at top or patterned on communication from top	At top of organization or to implement top directive
				15
2. Extent to which superior willingly shares information with subordinates	Provides minimum of information	Gives subordinates only information superior feels they need	Gives information needed and answers most questions	Seeks to give subordinates all relevant information and all information they want
				16
3. Extent to which communications are accepted by subordinates	Generally accepted, but if not, openly and candidly questioned	Often accepted but, if not, may or may not be openly questioned	Some accepted and some viewed with suspicion	Viewed with great suspicion
				17

❖ ❖ THE CHANGE SEQUENCE

Change may affect individuals, groups, or even or entire organization. All organizations will experience change at one time or another. This is especially the case in Eastern Europe.

Among the most prominent changes occurring today in business are:

- Changes in organizational structure caused by downsizing and restructuring.
- Changes in technology and the way people work.
- A diverse workforce.

Change will require a sequence of events to occur in the organization. The sequence of events that is needed to bring about change in an organization is the **change sequence.** Whether the intended change is from a less participative to a more participative corporate culture or along some other dimension, the process tends to follow a certain pattern. The sequence of events, which was identified by social psychologist Kurt Lewin, is as follows (see Figure 15.5): Management should first recognize a need for change. Then, the specific change method should be identified. Finally, the following steps should be carried out: (1) unfreezing the status quo, (2) moving to a new condition, and (3) refreezing to create a new status quo. Feedback is provided to determine if the change has occurred or if further change is needed.

Recognizing the Need for Change

Perhaps the most important question to ask about change is: Is this change necessary? Some people unwisely believe that changes should be made merely for the

---

The Changing Face of Eastern Europe

Among the most prominent changes in Eastern Europe are those needed to make the countries efficient producers. One of the main problems confronting those charged with the makeover of Eastern Europe is overcoming the Eastern European corporate culture. The culture has been socialistic for so long that many experts fear that work ethic differences will be very difficult to overcome. Eastern bloc managers are unaccustomed to profit accountability, having survived so long in socialism. Unmotivated workers may resist having to work harder to be competitive. Almost everything produced in Eastern Europe is inferior to what is made in the West, and narrowing this gap will be difficult. Poland's own premier called his nation "the kingdom of shoddy goods." A Czechoslovakian Institute of Management survey showed that nearly half of all the factory managers consider quality of marginal importance. Even within Eastern Europe there are great differences in culture and work habits. Poles tend to be cooperative, while Romanians are adversarial and highly individualistic. However, Eastern Europeans should not be totally pessimistic, since it took the Japanese just 20 years to be extremely competitive with the United States and the Europeans.[15]

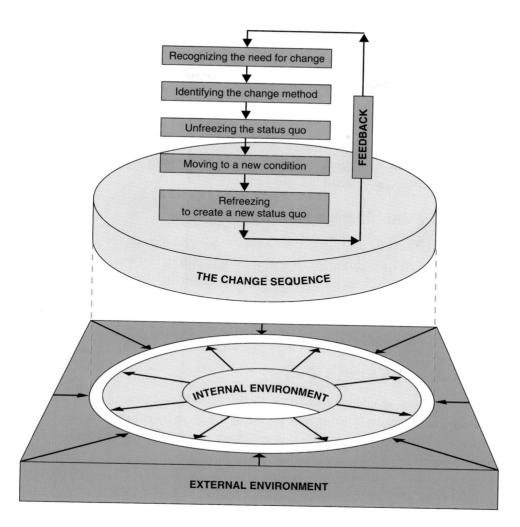

sake of change. Managers who make a change merely to satisfy a desire for change may disrupt their section. Organizations and people want some degree of stability in order to accomplish their assigned tasks. Yet there are times when changes are necessary, and the failure to be quick and decisive can have disastrous effects.

A number of major companies, particularly in the fast-moving computer industry, have found that cultural change is not only feasible but necessary. Apple used to be noted for a corporate culture that emphasized blue jeans and tennis shoes, video games outside the executive offices, free thinking, and a flexible organization structure. IBM, on the other hand, traditionally emphasized white shirts, gray suits, and conservative thinking. But IBM is changing too. Its new strategy appears to be aimed at making the company more like Apple, whereas Apple is becoming somewhat more like IBM. Some other companies that have accomplished large-scale cultural change are AT&T, PepsiCo, Chase Manhattan Bank, and Twentieth Century Fox.

Gordon Donaldson and Jay Lorsch argue that at times, companies may need to change their culture or go out of business.[16] There are five possible reasons for imposing rapid cultural change:

1. If your company has strong values that don't fit a changing environment.
2. If the industry is very competitive and moves with lightning speed.
3. If your company is mediocre or worse.
4. If your company is about to join the ranks of the very largest companies.
5. If your company is small but growing rapidly.[17]

Identifying the Change Method

Management has at its disposal numerous methods and techniques for organizational change and development. Some specific techniques (which will be discussed later in the chapter) are survey feedback, sensitivity training, management by objectives, the Grid approach, and team building. The technique a firm chooses should meet its needs in reacting to the external environment and identifying the type of culture that will provide the greatest productivity.

Unfreezing the Status Quo

If individuals are to change their present attitudes, their current beliefs need to be altered, or unfrozen.[18] Resistance to change needs to be eliminated or reduced if a change is to be effective. Reducing resistance to change may be accomplished by building trust and confidence, developing open communication, and encouraging employee participation. Once resistance is reduced, the manager is in a position to implement the desired change. Sources of resistance to change and some approaches to reducing resistance are discussed later in the chapter.

Unfreezing often generates self-doubt, but it also provides a means of overcoming it. Employees should be made to feel that ineffectiveness is undesirable but that it can be remedied. If organization members are to be receptive to change, they should feel that they can change.

Moving to a New Condition

The initiation of a change can come from an order, a recommendation, or a self-directed impetus. A manager with authority can command that a change be made and can enforce its implementation by threats, punishments, and close supervision. If this path of implementing change is taken, the manager will likely find that the change has to be constantly monitored. Change is more permanent and substantial if people truly want and feel a need to change.

The most effective approach to initiating change is developing a two-way relationship between the person who is attempting to implement the change and those who will be changed. The person implementing the change should make

The information revolution has forced change even in formerly staid agribusiness firms. Here, a state of the art computer system at Archer Daniels Midland Company's vegetable oil refinery in Des Moines controls the highly automated facility. Gauges at individual pieces of equipment have been replaced with sensors tied in to the computer system, and many hand-operated valves have been replaced with automatic ones. This has reduced cost as well as improved product consistency. (Source: Photograph courtesy of Archer Daniels Midland Company.)

suggestions, and those who will be changed should be encouraged to contribute and participate. The initiators should respond to suggestions, either by reformulating the change or by explaining why the suggestions cannot be incorporated.

Refreezing to Create a New Status Quo

If a person changes to a new set of work habits for a week and then reverts to former practices, the change has not been effective. Too often, changes that are introduced do not stick. If the change is to be permanent, people need to be convinced that the change is in their own and the organization's best interest. One of the best ways to accomplish this is to collect objective evidence of the success of the change. A manager who sees production increase because of a change in leadership style has excellent evidence of the success of the change.

People should feel competent about and take pleasure in using the new behavior. But the change will be completely accepted only if the reward system of the organization is geared to the new form of behavior. If the administrators of a university state that all its faculty should publish, and there is no reward attached to publishing, it is likely that few faculty members will be motivated to make this change. An employee's job may be substantially enriched in terms of content and self-supervision, but if the change is not accomplished by properly enriched pay and status symbols, dissatisfaction is likely to result. People tend to repeat behavior that they find rewarding.

SOURCES OF RESISTANCE TO CHANGE

A change may cause some loss to the person or organization affected by it. Attachments to old and familiar habits, places, and people must be given up. In major and unexpected changes, employees, groups, and even divisions often experience daze, shock, recoil, and turmoil. Some of the many sources of resistance to change are shown in Figure 15.6 and are discussed in the next several sections.

Insecurity

Once people have operated in a particular environment for a long time, they begin to feel comfortable. A change of environment often brings about uncertainty; people no longer know exactly what to expect. Almost everyone feels insecure during the transition from high school to college. The same sense of insecurity continues as the move is made from undergraduate to graduate work or from one job to another or to a new city.

Possible Social Loss

Change has the potential to bring about social loss. The informal work group may be extremely powerful, but if change causes individuals in the group to be transferred, the power of the group is likely to be diminished. A change may also cause established status symbols to be destroyed or low-status individuals to be awarded high-status symbols.

The effect a change can have on the social environment was vividly illus-

❖ **Figure 15.6**
Sources of resistance to change

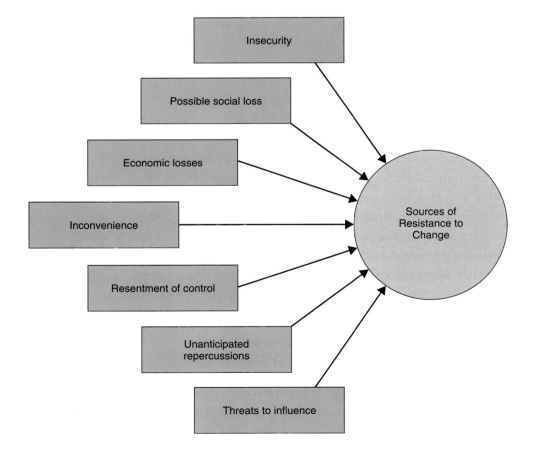

trated when one of the authors was doing a consulting job for a regional medical center. The hospital had been a small, local, 100-bed hospital. But because industry was moving rapidly into the area, the board of directors decided to expand the hospital to 300 beds. In one department, all the employees reported directly to the department head, and a close rapport had developed among the department members. Staff members on rotating shifts sometimes had to work the evening and night shift, but they could still maintain close contact with the other department members.

Because of the great increase in workload, the workforce was expanded, and a decision was made to have three shifts with a shift supervisor for each. The department head now had only three people reporting directly to him, and it was believed that the work could be performed much more efficiently. But the social loss was drastic. Subordinates no longer had a close relationship with the department head. Some rarely even saw him because they were on a different shift. This created a tremendous social loss, resulting in several workers quitting in a six-month period.

Economic Losses

New technology may enable a company to produce the same amount of output with fewer workers. While most companies make an honest attempt to transfer or retain employees affected by the change, the fear of being laid off remains. When the computer was first introduced, the number of clerical workers needed was often drastically reduced. Firms attempted to lessen employees' fear of losing their jobs by claiming that the number of jobs needed had actually increased through the use of the computer. This explanation did not help employees who were capable only of handling clerical work. For them, the new technology caused a major economic loss.

Inconvenience

Even when a change is not associated with a social or economic loss, new procedures and techniques may have to be learned. Physical and mental energy need to be expended, and for some people this is not enjoyable. When a new telephone system was installed at a university, there were many complaints. Time and effort had to be expended in learning how to use the system. It took approximately a year for the system to be accepted by a majority of the faculty and staff.

Resentment of Control

When employees are told that a change is to take place, they are made to realize that they do not have control over their destiny. Although the change may be for the better, a certain amount of resentment may develop. IBM's founder, Thomas J. Watson, was convinced that conservative dress would help sustain the company's image and, indirectly, increase profitability. Some within the company, however, resented being told how to dress. This might be true even for persons who normally dress conservatively.

Unanticipated Repercussions

Because the organization is a system, a change in one part is likely to have unforeseen repercussions in another. For example, a newly enriched job is likely to demand a change in supervisory behavior. Supervisors may resist this change even if they initially supported the concept of job enrichment.

Threats to Influence

At times, a change will reduce the power base of a group, department, or division. Even when the change is best for the organization as a whole, resistance may persist. This scene has often been enacted as state boards of education attempt to reduce the duplication of programs. If a university gives up a program, its personal influence in the total system is diminished. Calls are made to alumni and supporters throughout the state to keep this event from occurring, even though a reduction in program duplication would improve the overall quality of the state's educational program.

❖ ❖ APPROACHES FOR REDUCING RESISTANCE TO CHANGE

Change is often necessary, despite the resistance that might arise. During downsizing, companies can minimize resistance by communicating the need for new strategies; treating people who are laid off with respect and kindness; and letting key people know that the company, and the people, will be around for a long time. Then a grieving process will be needed to help everyone who remains with the organization move on with the change.[19] Some of the approaches designed to reduce resistance to change are shown in Figure 15.7 and discussed in the following sections.

Provide Information in Advance

Whenever possible, managers should provide the reasons for the upcoming change, its nature, its planned timing, and the possible effects on the organization and its personnel. Managers should avoid, if possible, withholding information that could seriously affect the lives and futures of particular individuals. A firm that is secretive about a change will have difficulty making future changes. There are, however, occasions when competitive survival requires that information be closely held until shortly before the change is to occur. In these cases, the information should be provided on an "as required" basis.

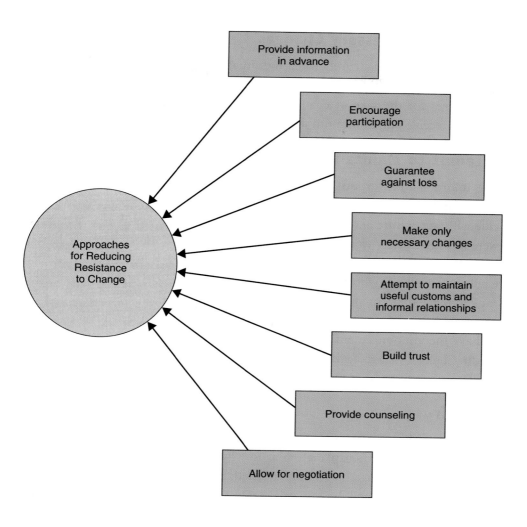

Encourage Participation

When possible, subordinates should be encouraged to participate in establishing the change. A person who is involved in implementing change procedures will likely be more supportive of the change. As mentioned in Chapter 10, Theory Y assumes that the abilities are widespread in the population. Thus, many valuable ideas may be gained by permitting employees to participate in implementing the change.

Guarantee Against Loss

To promote acceptance of changes, some organizations guarantee no layoffs as a result of such changes. In cases of changes in methods and output standards, employees are often guaranteed retention of their present level of earnings during the learning period.

Make Only Necessary Changes

Changes should be made only when the situation demands them, not because of a whim on the part of a manager. A manager who gains a reputation for making changes for the sake of change will discover that any change, beneficial or not, will receive only minimum acceptance.

Attempt to Maintain Useful Customs and Informal Norms

The informal work group has real value from the standpoint of interpersonal understanding and cooperation. When possible, changes should be made to coincide with the culture and informal norms of the organization. When safety shoes were introduced, few would wear them willingly because of their unusual appearance. When they were redesigned to resemble normal shoes, resistance faded. Civilian consultants who are to work with military personnel are granted fictional rank to make their integration into ongoing operations more understandable and acceptable. A staff expert who wants a change introduced may find it advisable to have the announcement made by a line executive, with some sharing of the credit. Changes that go against established customs and informal norms will likely create resistance and have little chance of being readily accepted.

Build Trust

If a manager has a reputation for providing reliable and timely information to employees, the person's explanation as to why a change is to be made will likely be believed. The change may still be resisted; but if the manager is trusted by the employees, problems will be minimized. On the other hand, managers who have gained a reputation for providing incomplete or inaccurate information will often have difficulty convincing employees that a proposed change is good for them.

Provide Counseling

At times, some form of nonthreatening discussion and counseling may not only prevent rebellion but also may stimulate voluntary adoption of a change. Nondirective counseling has been used effectively in many change situations. The approach rests on the belief that people have the ability to solve their own problems with the aid of a sympathetic listener. The role of the counselor is one of understanding and perhaps advising rather than passing judgment. This requires a somewhat permissive, friendly atmosphere, with actions and statements that exhibit continuing interest but not judgment. In most instances, managers with authority are unable to establish this type of atmosphere.

To be successful, nondirective counseling usually should be undertaken by staff psychologists. What the manager can do is to permit subordinates to ventilate some of their feelings, particularly those of frustration and anger. Just talking about the "good old days" will assist in the transition process. Discovering that others have similar feelings and doubts will often make the transition less painful.

Allow for Negotiation

Resistance to change can be reduced by the process of negotiation. Negotiation is the primary method used by labor unions to effect modification of proposed managerial changes.

❖ ❖ DIVERSITY TRAINING

As was previously discussed, one of the most prominent changes occurring today is that the workforce is becoming more diverse. It was not too many years ago that the primary component of the workforce was white males. This is certainly not true today, and the workforce of tomorrow will be even more diverse. In order for this new workforce to work effectively together, many firms are finding that diversity training is needed.

Diversity training often involves having employees and managers participate in role-playing activities. Members of the workshop typically consist of a diverse group and are asked to describe their own backgrounds and beliefs. Through this form of training, employees are made aware of the values and lifestyles of different cultures. They also become aware of their own prejudices.[20]

❖ ❖ ORGANIZATIONAL DEVELOPMENT

Change efforts that affect the entire organization involve techniques of organizational development. **Organizational development (OD)** is planned and systematic attempts to change the organization, typically to a more behavioral environment. OD education and training strategies are designed to develop a more open, productive, and compatible workplace despite differences in personalities, culture, or technologies.[21] The organizational development movement has been strongly advocated by such researchers as Chris Argyris and Warren Bennis.

Change Agents

The person or group responsible for ensuring that the planned change in organizational development is properly implemented is called the **change agent.** This individual or group may be either an external or an internal consultant. Change agents have knowledge in the OD techniques described in the following sections. They use this knowledge to assist in organizational change.

When an organization first attempts to change, outside consultants are often used. They may bring objectivity to the situation and be better able than outsiders to obtain the acceptance and trust of the organization's members. With

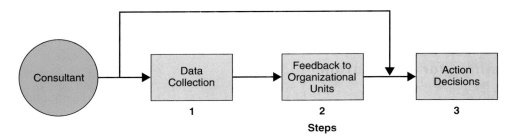

time, internal consultants may move into the role of change agent. It is important to understand and appreciate the following techniques for implementing
change: the survey feedback method, management by objectives, sensitivity training, the Grid approach to OD, and management development programs. Team
building as an approach to OD will be discussed in a later section.

The Survey Feedback Method

The organizational development method of basing change efforts on the systematic collection and measurement of subordinates' attitudes through anonymous
questionnaires is the **survey feedback method.** The three basic steps in the
process are shown in Figure 15.8. First, a consultant collects data from members
of the organization. Survey questions typically require either objective multiple-
choice responses (see Table 15.1) or scaled responses that suggest agreement or
disagreement with a particular question (see Figure 15.9). If truthful information
about attitudes is to be obtained, employees should feel comfortable, secure, and
confident in responding; hence the need for anonymity.

In the second step, the results of the study are presented to concerned organizational units. In the final step of the process, the data are analyzed and decisions are made. The means by which the data may be compared and analyzed
include the following:

- Scores for the entire organization now and in the past.
- Scores for each department now and in the past.

Considering all aspects of your job, evaluate your compensation with regard to your contributions to the needs of the organization. Circle the number that best describes how you feel.				
Pay Too Low	*Pay Low*	*Pay Average*	*Pay Above Average*	*Pay Too High*
1 2	3 4	5 6	7 8	9 10

What are your feelings about overtime work requirements? Circle the number that best indicates how you feel.		
Unnecessary	*Necessary on Occasion*	*Necessary*
1 2 3	4 5 6 7	8 9 10

TABLE 15.1 Examples of Multiple-Choice Responses to Survey Questions

Why did you decide to do what you are now doing?

a. Desire to aid or assist others.

b. Influenced by another person or situation.

c. Always wanted to be in this vocation.

d. Lack of opportunity or interest in other vocational fields.

e. Opportunities provided by this vocation.

f. Personal satisfaction from doing this work.

What do you like least about your job?

a. Nothing.

b. Pay.

c. Supervisor relations.

d. Problems with fellow workers.

e. Facilities.

f. Paperwork and reports.

(Source: Reprinted by permission from R. Wayne Mondy and Robert M. Noe III, *Human Resource Management,* 5th ed. [Boston: Allyn and Bacon, 1993], p. 718.)

• Scores by organizational level.
• Scores by seniority.
• Relative scores on each question.
• Scores for each question for each category of personnel cited above.

The decisions are directed at improving relationships in the organization. This is accomplished by revealing problem areas and dealing with them through straightforward discussion.

Sensitivity Training

The organizational development technique that uses leaderless discussion groups to develop awareness of and sensitivity to oneself and others is **sensitivity training** (also called *T-group training* and *laboratory training*).[22] The objectives of sensitivity training include the following:

• Increased openness with others.
• Greater concern for the needs of others.
• Increased tolerance for individual differences.
• Less ethnic prejudice.

- Awareness and understanding of group processes.
- Enhanced listening skills.
- Greater appreciation of the complexities of behaving competently.
- Establishment of more realistic personal standards of behavior.

Sensitivity training is not widely used today as an organizational development technique. It has been labeled psychotherapy rather than proper business training, and leaders of T-groups have been criticized for having an insufficient background in psychology. Detractors suggest that individuals' defense mechanisms—built up to preserve the personality over a period of years—may be destroyed, with little help provided in replacing them with more satisfactory behavioral patterns. It is contended that one cannot exist without ego defense mechanisms.

Management by Objectives

As described in Chapter 5, management by objectives (MBO) is the philosophy of management that emphasizes the setting of agreed-on objectives by managers and their subordinates and the use of those objectives as the primary bases of motivation, evaluation, and control efforts. It is a systematic approach to change that facilitates the achievement of results by directing efforts toward attainable objectives. MBO encourages managers to plan for the future. It is considered a philosophy of management because it emphasizes participative management. In this context, MBO is an important method of organizational development. The participation of individuals in setting objectives and the emphasis on self-control promote not only individual development but also the development of the entire organization.

The Grid Approach to OD

One organizational development approach is the Leadership Grid developed by Robert Blake and Jane Mouton. As Chapter 11 noted, the Grid approach suggests that the most effective leadership style is the one that stresses maximum concern for both output and people. The Grid approach provides a systematic method for analyzing leadership styles and helping the organization move to the best style.

Management Development Programs

Organizational development techniques are designed to change the entire organization. **Management development programs** are formal efforts to improve the skills and attitudes of present and prospective managers. In these programs, managers learn effective approaches for managing people and other resources. Specific areas identified as possible organizational weaknesses are included. These areas might entail, among others, leadership style, motivation approaches, and communication effectiveness.

The programs are administered by either in-house or outside consultants. The intent of such programs is not only to teach new methods and techniques but also to develop an inquisitive thought process. Too often, employees become so accustomed to performing the same task day after day that they forget how to think. A properly designed management development program puts people in a frame of mind to analyze problems. It is often used to provide the foundation for a change.

❖ ❖ TEAM BUILDING

One of the major techniques in the arsenal of the organizational development consultant is **team building**—a conscious effort by management to develop effective work teams throughout the organization. Team building utilizes self-directed teams composed of a small group of employees responsible for an entire work process or segment. Team members work together to improve their operation or product, plan and control their work, and handle day-to-day problems. They may even become involved in broader companywide issues such as vendor quality, safety, or business planning.[23] Team building is becoming one of the more popular approaches to OD.[24]

Frequently, work groups focus on solving actual problems to build efficient management teams. The team-building process begins when the team leader defines a problem that requires organizational change. Next, the group analyzes the problem to determine its underlying causes. These causes may be in such areas as communication, role clarification, leadership style, organization structure, and interpersonal relations. The next step is to propose several solutions and then to select the most appropriate one. Through this process, the participants are likely to be committed to the solution, and interpersonal support and trust are developed. The support and trust of group members enhance the implementation of the change.

The American Society for Training and Development (ASTD) recently conducted a survey that asked for the areas most improved through the use of trained self-directed teams. The factors that had significantly improved were:

- Productivity (77 percent of responding firms).
- Quality (72 percent).
- Job satisfaction (65 percent).
- Customer service (57 percent).
- Waste reduction (55 percent).[25]

✘ Management Tips ✘

Guidelines for Dealing with Corporate Culture, Change, and Development

1. **Realize that organizations continually evolve.** If the organization is to maintain its competitive edge and be a force in the globalization of business, it should have an appropriate corporate culture.

2. **Understand that change may be resisted.** Despite the certain resistance to change, managers should realize that without change, an appropriate corporate culture cannot be developed.

3. **Maintain open and effective lines of communication.** Clearly communicate the need for new strategies.

4. **Be honest and straightforward regarding the need for change.** Explain the need for change in terms that everyone can understand.

5. **Let your people know how the change will influence them.** The organization is, in large part, only as good as the people who work for it.

6. **Establish trust.** If the organization is ever to be as productive as it could be, trust needs to be established between management and employees.

7. **Recognize the status symbols at work in your organization.** Much can be learned by doing this.

8. **Encourage subordinate participation in establishing the change, when possible.** Employees who are involved in the change are more likely to support it.

9. **Do not make changes for the sake of change.** Changes should be made only when they better facilitate the accomplishment of your objectives.

10. **Attempt to maintain useful customs and informal norms.** The informal work group has real value from the standpoint of interpersonal understanding and cooperation.

SUMMARY

Corporate culture is the system of shared values, beliefs, and habits within an organization that interacts with the formal structure to produce behavioral norms. It influences employees' degree of job satisfaction and the level and quality of their performance. The assessment of how good or poor the corporate culture is may differ for each employee. Work groups, managers' and supervisors' leadership style, organizational characteristics, and administrative processes affect corporate culture.

Within most large organizations, both a dominant culture and many subcultures exist. Dominant cultures are those that express the shared views of the majority of the organization's members. Subcultures are cultures characteristic of the various units of an organization.

Most attempts to change organizations have been directed toward creating a more open and participative culture. Involving more people in the decision-making process improves productivity and morale. Still, there are some limitations. Rensis Likert developed a management systems theory that uses a continuum of management styles ranging from autocratic to participative. System IV, participative team, was deemed best in the long run for all situations.

No matter what the intended change, the change process tends to follow a pattern. Management first recognizes a need for change and then identifies a specific change method. Finally, the following steps are carried out: (1) unfreezing the status quo, (2) moving to the new condition, and (3) refreezing to create a new status quo. A change may cause a social or economic loss to the person affected by it. Despite the resistance that might arise, change is often necessary.

A change may cause some loss to the person or organization affected by it. Attachments to old and familiar habits, places, and people need to be given up. In major and unexpected changes, employees, groups, and even divisions often experience daze, shock, recoil, and turmoil. Some of the many sources of resistance to change include insecurity, possible social loss, economic losses, inconvenience, resentment of control, unanticipated repercussions, and threats to influence.

Diversity training often involves having employees and managers participate in role-playing activities. Members of the workshop typically consist of a diverse group and are asked to describe their own backgrounds and beliefs. Through this form of training, employees are made aware of the values and lifestyles of different cultures. They also become aware of their own prejudices.

Organizational development (OD) is planned and systematic attempts to change the organization, typically to a more behavioral environment. The person responsible for ensuring that the planned change is properly implemented is the change agent. A major technique in the arsenal of the organizational development consultant is team building, a conscious effort to develop effective work groups throughout the organization. Other OD techniques include survey feedback, sensitivity training, management by objectives, and the Grid approach to OD. Management development programs are formal efforts to improve the skills and attitudes of present and prospective managers. In these programs, managers learn effective approaches for managing people and other resources.

KEY TERMS

Corporate culture 473
Dominant culture 478
Subcultures 478
Strong corporate culture 478
Status symbol 479
Jargon 481
Change sequence 488
Organizational development (OD) 497

Change agent 497
Survey feedback method 498
Sensitivity training 499
Management development programs 500
Team building 501

REVIEW QUESTIONS

1. Define corporate culture. What are the factors that influence it?
2. Identify the benefits and limitations of a participative culture.
3. List and describe the elements of the change sequence.
4. What are the sources of resistance to change?
5. Describe the approaches that may be used in reducing resistance to change.
6. Define each of the following terms:
   a. organizational development
   b. sensitivity training
   c. team building

CASE STUDIES

CASE 15.1 Breaking Up the Team

Wayne, Don, and Robert were supervisors with a small chain of 15 convenience stores in north Dallas. Each had responsibility for five stores and reported directly to the company president; but actually they all just worked as a team. Wayne coordinated the scheduling of clerks at all 15 stores, Don took care of inventory control and purchasing, and Robert took responsibility for recruiting and hiring. Otherwise, they each just did whatever needed to be done.

Things changed markedly within just a year. The president, wishing to relieve himself of daily details, promoted Robert to vice president. Another supervisor, Phillip, was hired to manage Robert's five stores. At first, everything went well. But soon Robert, who was much more involved in store management than the president had been, told the three supervisors he wanted each of them to take care of his own five stores.

Wayne, Don, and Phillip initially resisted Robert's frequent orders and demands. After a few "chewing outs," though, the men decided to do as Robert wanted. They rarely saw one another, and each took care of all aspects of store operations, as well as filling in for clerks who were late or sick. There were frequent problems, however. Robert accused the three supervisors of working against him and threatened them with dismissal if operations did not get better. Wayne, Don, and Phillip saved him the trouble; they quit within days of one another. The president fired Robert a few days later.

QUESTIONS

1. What different organizational environment was created as a result of Robert's promotion to vice-president?
2. How do you think this situation could have been avoided? Discuss the use of the participative approach in this instance.

CASE 15.2 Fears of Layoffs at Duncan Electric

Donna Garcia was a supervisor for Duncan Electric Corporation, a manufacturer of high-quality electrical parts. Donna has been with the firm for five years and had one of the best teams in the plant. Donna had picked the majority of these employees and was proud of the reputation they had earned. But a problem was brewing that she felt could destroy her team.

For weeks, there had been rumors of a reduction in force at Duncan. Donna heard her workers talking about it, she heard it from other supervisors, and a local newspaper story even mentioned the possibility. The corporate office had said nothing about it, but the rumors persisted. The only basis for the fears that Donna could identify was a temporary cutback in production, which had soon been restored. Donna was able to refute the rumors for a while because her people trusted her. But soon she began to have doubts herself. Donna checked with her superior, who claimed he knew nothing of any possible reduction. She asked one of her most trusted workers why he thought there might be a layoff and he said, "I just hear it around the plant."

On Friday, Bob Phillips and Henry Barham, two of Donna's best workers, told her that they had taken jobs with one of Duncan Electric's competitors. This was what Donna feared. The most qualified workers were leaving, and it was due to rumors. Instead of having one of the best crews at Duncan Electric, she might very well end up with the worst.

QUESTIONS

1. To what extent did the rumors of the anticipated change in the workforce affect the morale of the employees?
2. What should management do to reduce the fear of the anticipated change?
3. What should Donna do in this situation?

NOTES

1. This case is a composite of a number of published accounts, among them: Brian O'Reilly, "Apple Computer's Risky Revolution," *Fortune* 124 (May 8, 1989): 75–83; "Apple Reshuffles Its Corps," *Business Week* (September 5, 1988): 34; Maria Shao, "Allan Loren," *1989 Business Week Top 1,000*, p. 158; Maria Shao, "Apple Turns from Revolution to Evolution," *Business Week* (January 23, 1989): 90–92; Lawrence M. Fisher, "Apple's Stock Falls $3; Estimates of Profit Cut," *The New York Times* (June 17, 1989): 33; Pascal Zachary, "Apple Computer Net Rose by 5.3% in Its 3rd Quarter," *The Wall Street Journal* (July 19, 1989): B4; Stephen Kindel, "Water into Wine," *Financial World* 158 (May 30, 1989): 32–35; Richard Brandt, Thane Peterson, and Deidre A. Depke, "The Toughest Job in the Computer Business," *Business Week* (March 19, 1990): 118–122; Barbara Buell, Jonathan B. Levine, and Neil Gross, "Apple Cover Story," *Business Week* (October 15, 1990): 87–96; Catherine Arnst, "The Unsung Hero of Apple's Success," *Business Week* (July 5, 1993): 26; Kathy Rebello, Russell Mitchell, and Evan I. Schwartz, "Apple's Future: Can CEO Michael Spindler Bring Back the Glory Days?" *Business Week* (July 5, 1993): 22–28, and other articles from *The Wall Street Journal*.

2. Frank Petrock, "Corporate Culture Enhances Profits," *HRMagazine* 35 (November 1990): 64–66.

3. Mark Landler, Bart Ziegler, Mark Lewyn, and Leah Nathans Spiro, "Bell-Ringer: How Bell Atlantic and TCI Hooked Up—And What It Means for the Information Age!" *Business Week* (October 25, 1993): 32–36.

4. Anthony Jay, *Management and Machiavelli* (New York: Holt, Rinehart and Winston, 1967).

5. "What the 1990 Census Reveals About Population Growth, Blacks, Hispanics, Asians, Ethnic Diversity, and Children—And What It Means to You," *American Diversity* (Ithaca, New York), Desk Reference Series, No. 1.

6. Robert Johnson, "McDonald's Combines a Dead Man's Advice with Lively Strategy," *The Wall Street Journal* (December 18, 1987): 1.

7. Lori Bongiorno, "Corporate America's New Lesson Plan," *Business Week* (October 25, 1993): 102–104.

8. Peter Waldman, "Motivate or Alienate? Firms Hire Gurus to Change Their 'Cultures,'" *The Wall Street Journal* (July 24, 1987): 19.

9. Barbara Jean Gray, "Taking a Stand on Ethics," *Human Resource Executive* 2 (May 1988): 34–35.

10. Lori Bongiorno, "Corporate America's New Lesson Plan," pp. 102–104.

11. H. Kenneth Bobele and Peter J. Buchanan, "Building a More Productive Environment," *Management World* 1 (January 1979): 8.

12. Rensis Likert, *The Human Organization* (New York: McGraw-Hill, 1967).

13. Thomas J. Murry, "Wal-Mart Penny Wise," *Business Month* (December 1988): 42.

14. Carol J. Loomis, "The Reed that Citicorp Leans On," *Fortune*, 128 (July 12, 1993): 90–93.

15. M. Maruyama, "Some Management Considerations in the Economic Reorganization of Eastern Europe," *Academic of Management Executive*, 2, 4 (1990): 90–91; "Crash Course in Capitalism for Ivan the Globe-Trotter," *Business Week* (May 28, 1990): 42–44.

16. Gordon Donaldson and Jay Lorsch, *Decision Making at the Top* (New York: Basic Books, 1983).

17. Bro Uttal, "The Corporate Culture Vultures," *Fortune* 108 (October 17, 1983): 66–72.

18. Kurt Lewin, *Field Theory and Social Science* (New York: Harper & Row, 1964), chapters 9, 10.

19. Anne B. Fisher, "The Downside of Downsizing," *Fortune* 123 (May 23, 1988): 42–52.

20. Melissa Lee, "Diversity Training Brings Unity to Small Companies," *The Wall Street Journal* (September 2, 1993): B2.

21. R. Wayne Mondy and Robert M. Noe III, *Human Resource Management*, 5th ed. (Boston: Allyn and Bacon, 1993): 330–351.

22. P. B. Smith, "Control Studies on the Outcome of Sensitivity Training," *Psychological Bulletin* 82 (July 1975): 597–622.

23. Richard Wellins and Jill George, "The Key to Self-Directed Teams," *Training and Development Journal* 45 (April 1991): 27.

24. Bert A. Spector, "From Bogged Down to Fired Up: Inspiring Organizational Change," *Sloan Management Review* 30 (Summer 1989): 31.

25. Wellins and George, "The Key to Self-Directed Teams," p. 27.

What Kind of Leader Are You?

Although there is no single best leadership style, it is important for you to appreciate the nature of your leadership style. Since an appropriate leadership style is crucial to the effectiveness of managers, you should assess your leadership style by taking the self-assessment exercise "What Is Your Leadership Style?" Then, turn to page 674 to evaluate yourself.

INSTRUCTIONS: Circle whether you would be likely to behave in the described way:

Always	= A			Seldom	= S
Frequently	= F	Occasionally	= O	Never	= N

A F O S N   IF I WERE THE LEADER OF A WORK GROUP . . .

❏ ❏ ❏ ❏ ❏ 1. I would most likely act as the spokesperson of the group.

❏ ❏ ❏ ❏ ❏ 2. I would encourage overtime work.

❏ ❏ ❏ ❏ ❏ 3. I would allow members complete freedom in their work.

❏ ❏ ❏ ❏ ❏ 4. I would encourage the use of uniform procedures.

❏ ❏ ❏ ❏ ❏ 5. I would permit the members to use their own judgment in solving problems.

❏ ❏ ❏ ❏ ❏ 6. I would stress being ahead of competing groups.

❏ ❏ ❏ ❏ ❏ 7. I would speak as a representative of the group.

❏ ❏ ❏ ❏ ❏ 8. I would needle members for greater effort.

❏ ❏ ❏ ❏ ❏ 9. I would try out my ideas in the group.

❏ ❏ ❏ ❏ ❏ 10. I would let the members do their work the way they think is best.

❏ ❏ ❏ ❏ ❏ 11. I would be working hard for a promotion.

❏ ❏ ❏ ❏ ❏ 12. I would be able to tolerate postponement and uncertainty.

❏ ❏ ❏ ❏ ❏ 13. I would speak for the group when visitors were present.

❏ ❏ ❏ ❏ ❏ 14. I would keep the work moving at a rapid pace.

❏ ❏ ❏ ❏ ❏ 15. I would turn the members loose on a job and let them go to it.

❏ ❏ ❏ ❏ ❏ 16. I would settle conflicts when they occur in the group.

(continued on next page)

A	F	O	S	N	IF I WERE THE LEADER OF A WORK GROUP . . .
❑	❑	❑	❑	❑	17. I would get swamped by details.
❑	❑	❑	❑	❑	18. I would represent the group at outside meetings.
❑	❑	❑	❑	❑	19. I would be reluctant to allow the members any freedom of action.
❑	❑	❑	❑	❑	20. I would decide what shall be done and how it shall be done.
❑	❑	❑	❑	❑	21. I would push for increased production.
❑	❑	❑	❑	❑	22. I would let some members have authority that I could keep.
❑	❑	❑	❑	❑	23. Things would usually turn out as I predict.
❑	❑	❑	❑	❑	24. I would allow the group a high degree of initiative.
❑	❑	❑	❑	❑	25. I would assign group members to particular tasks.
❑	❑	❑	❑	❑	26. I would be willing to make changes.
❑	❑	❑	❑	❑	27. I would ask the members to work harder.
❑	❑	❑	❑	❑	28. I would trust the group members to exercise good judgment.
❑	❑	❑	❑	❑	29. I would schedule the work to be done.
❑	❑	❑	❑	❑	30. I would refuse to explain my actions.
❑	❑	❑	❑	❑	31. I would persuade others that my ideas are to their advantage.
❑	❑	❑	❑	❑	32. I would permit the group to set its own pace.
❑	❑	❑	❑	❑	33. I would urge the group to beat its previous record.
❑	❑	❑	❑	❑	34. I would act without consulting the group.
❑	❑	❑	❑	❑	35. I would ask that group members follow standard rules and regulations.

P (Participative) Score: _____

A (Autocratic) Score: _____

Source: Reprinted from J. William Pfeiffer and John E. Jones, eds., *A Handbook of Structured Experiences for Human Relations Training*, vol. 1 (San Diego, CA.: University Associates, 1974). Used with permission. Originally from *American Educational Research Journal* 6 (January 1969): 62–79. Copyright 1969 by the American Educational Research Association. Reprinted by permission of the publisher.

16 The Controlling Processes and Techniques

LEARNING OBJECTIVES

After completing this chapter students should be able to

✗ Explain why controlling is necessary and describe the controlling process.

✗ Describe controlling and the business system and the importance of establishing strategic control points.

✗ Describe ways of overcoming negative reactions to controls.

✗ Explain the importance of disciplinary action and describe approaches to such action.

✗ Describe the various types of budgetary controls.

✗ Explain quality control, describe the evolution of international quality standards, and state the usefulness of control charts.

✗ Describe the importance of inventory control and explain various methods of inventory control.

✗ Explain network models and describe how PERT can assist in both planning and control.

McDonald's Remains Number One Through Consistency

In 1993, McDonald's sold enough hamburgers (95 billion—not counting their nonbeef sandwiches) to have fed nearly every human being born since the dawn of time. One hundred seventy-one McDonald's hamburgers leave the grill every second, enough to feed every living person on earth—5.3 billion. McDonald's worldwide brand recognition is second only to Coke, and McDonald's average domestic annual sales is far greater than Burger King's or Wendy's. Basically, McDonald's success is based on "Doing whatever it takes to make a customer happy," and delivering consistent quality.

Of course, creative merchandising helps keep McDonald's successful. So does a "single-minded determination" to do whatever is necessary to stay ahead of the competition. For example, when the recession chewed up profit margins, McDonald's introduced their "extra value" menu that knocked 20 percent off the price of sandwiches. McDonald's made up revenues lost with high-markups on fries and drinks. Beyond creative merchandising and focusing on the consumer, analysts believe that consistency, speed, and quality are paramount to McDonald's success. "McDonald's best weapon against upstart rivals remains the consistency of its operations." Such consistency grows out of an unmatched system of control.

Most McDonald's are franchised, so control of speed and quality starts with selection and training of franchisees. McDonald's owner-operators must work from before daybreak into the night seven days a week, and must "conform and become part of the system and do what they're told." After surviving the initial barrage of applications, credit checks, and interviews, aspirant franchisees spend most of the first two years working 20 hours a week at an existing McDonald's, for no pay. They must do it all—counter, kitchen, bathrooms, and book work. Trainees must also attend classes at regional offices, study a four-volume guide, and cram for periodic tests. A two-week stint at Hamburger University, in Oakbrook, Illinois, winds up the training, but franchise approval is still often a year or more away.

McDonald's administrative system tightly monitors the quality of food and service as well as the safety, cleanliness, and appearance of each restaurant. Precisely uniform raw materials—precut potatoes, breaded chicken nuggets, hamburger patties, paper goods—are supplied through a sophisticated system that provides just-in-time delivery. Every new product involves new training, for managers and workers. McDonald's "manufacturing system" including the grills, deep fryers, toasters, drink dispensers, coffee makers, and coolers are designed to minimize errors. Temperature and speed controls are automatic, and buzzers indicate when critical actions are required. All system components, from the juice dispensers to the belt-mounted radios, are standardized, supplied, and maintained under carefully administered contracts.

The system is tough, but "Do(ing) whatever it takes to make a customer happy," has created many wealthy and successful McDonald's franchisees. Undoubtedly, McDonald's will continue to look to new technology to make the operating system more flexible, while assuring speed, quality, and consistency.[1]

At McDonald's the control function is a vital part of the management process. A properly designed control system has allowed McDonald's to cut cost and enhance customer service. The effective control system that is presently in place at McDonald's is constantly being refined.

This chapter first describes why controlling is necessary. Next, the controlling process is described, followed by a discussion of controlling and the business system. Then, procedures for establishing strategic control points are described. This is followed by a discussion of how negative reactions to controls may be overcome, and a section on disciplinary action. Budgetary control, quality control, the evolution of international quality standards, and the usefulness of control charts will then be discussed. Next, the importance of inventory control and the various methods of inventory control will be addressed. The final section is devoted to a discussion of network models and a global perspective.

❖ ❖ WHY IS CONTROLLING NECESSARY?

Controlling is the process of comparing actual performance with standards and taking any necessary corrective action. A good control system is designed to keep things from going wrong, not just to correct them afterwards. Most managers are aware of the need for control. Some are farsighted enough to avoid many problem situations. For example, in selecting an appropriate location for a factory, there are many issues to consider, such as the quality of the workforce, the overall quality of life for managers and employees, and the availability of good schools and city services.

Controlling is the process of comparing actual performance with standards and taking any necessary corrective action. A good control system is designed to keep things from going wrong, not just to correct them afterward. Honeywell installed its TDC 3000 System to control digester operations at a bleach plant at the James River Corporation, a paper producer. (Source: Photograph courtesy of Honeywell, Inc.)

Managers often control activities too strictly, which can hurt morale and productivity. However, mistakes are more often made in the other direction. Among the symptoms that might indicate that the control process is not working are the following:

- Declining output or declining levels of service.
- Excessive machine breakdowns.
- An increase in absenteeism or tardiness.
- Increasing employee turnover.
- Declining product quality.
- Increasing customer complaints.
- Declining morale.
- Excessive labor, material, or energy costs.
- Too many accidents.
- Failure to meet objectives.
- Disorderliness.

Managers can use this list to help identify the critical symptoms in their units. However, the symptoms may be somewhat different for every department and organization. And if the symptoms of a problem are ignored, the problem is likely to worsen. It is vital that managers maintain control, in part because the price of regaining control may be high.

❖ ❖ THE CONTROLLING PROCESS

The controlling process has three steps: (1) establish standards, (2) evaluate performance, and (3) take corrective action. Figure 16.1 illustrates these steps. Notice

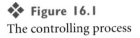

❖ Figure 16.1
The controlling process

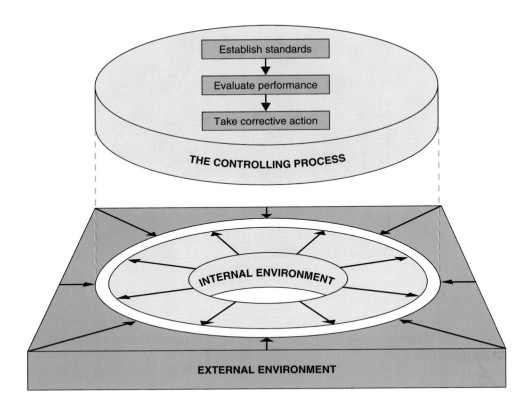

that like the other management functions, the controlling function is subject to environmental influences.

Establish Standards

Workers must know what is expected before the control process can be implemented. **Standards** are established levels of quality or quantity used to guide performance. For example, a shaft might have a standard diameter, and the machinist must try to cut the shaft to that size. Standards are sometimes viewed as objectives.

Wherever possible, standards should be expressed numerically to reduce subjectivity. Following are the most frequently used types of standards:

1. *Time standards.* Time standards state the length of time it should take to make a certain good or perform a certain service. An airline pilot has a standard time span in which to make a certain trip. Most organizations have a standard lunch time.
2. *Productivity standards.* Standards of productivity are based on the output of goods or services during a set time period. For instance, a productivity standard might be to complete ten units or to serve 150 customers per hour.
3. *Cost standards.* Cost standards are based on the cost associated with producing the goods or services. For example, the material cost might be $10

per unit. Cost standards are usually set in the expense budget for the supervisor's unit.

4. *Quality standards.* Standards of quality are based on the level of perfection desired. For instance, no more than a certain percentage of impurities may be allowed in a chemical, or a valve may have to hold pressure for ten minutes in order to pass inspection.

5. *Behavioral standards.* Standards of behavior are based on the type of behavior desired of workers in the organization. Expressing these standards precisely is difficult.

Although standards may be clear, control tolerances also need to be established. **Control tolerances** are specifications of how much deviation will be permitted before corrective action is taken. For instance, a standard size for a particular part may be 3.1 inches, but a tolerance of ±0.05 inch may be permitted. If a part is produced within the range of 3.05 to 3.15 inches, it is accepted. If it falls outside this range, it is rejected. As another example, a company might allow only two unexcused absences per month. A standard workday might be eight hours, but most managers have a certain control tolerance of lateness, perhaps five minutes. Whether the standard relates to a good, a service, or behavior, it is important to communicate both the standard and the control tolerances to workers. If this is done, many workers will control themselves.

Evaluate Performance

Evaluating performance consists of checking for deviations from standards and determining if the deviations exceed control tolerances. Basically, this evaluation process involves observing and measuring performance. Evaluation requires accurate measurement of what is taking place and an effective means of comparison with standards. Managers must realize that both problems and opportunities can be discovered during this phase.

When the process being controlled is a mechanical one, measurement and comparison may be quite simple. For example, a quality control inspector may use a micrometer or other instrument to measure a part. Other processes, especially behavioral ones, are more difficult to measure. Managers should be careful to measure accurately before taking corrective action. They should also keep in mind that the evaluation of performance must be taken into account in developing future standards.

Take Corrective Action

The manager must consider what action to take to correct performance when deviations occur. Often, the cause of the deviation must be found before corrective action can be taken. Assume that the number of allowable defects produced

Evaluating performance consists of checking for deviation from standard and determining if those deviations exceed control tolerances. When the process being controlled is a mechanical one, measurement and comparison may be quite simple. But the job is more complex for nonmechanical processes, as in the chicken hatchery shown here. (Source: © Jim Pickerell)

by a certain machine exceeds standard. The cause may be a faulty machine, or it may be a careless operator. Clearly, proper corrective action depends on which one is the cause.

Problems associated with taking corrective action may also be compounded by various top managers trying to protect their own turf at the expense of the entire organization. For example, AT&T was turned around when the upper management group of 27 executives, who were intent on controlling their own departments, met at a Cape Cod golf resort and agreed to compromise for the common good of the company, thereby allowing overall controls to be placed on the company, even to the point where they violated the traditional turf of different departments.[2]

Not all deviations from standard justify corrective action; and in some cases, personal judgment is necessary. Suppose that a worker is 15 minutes late for work (a deviation from the standard of being on time), but you realize the lateness was unavoidable. As manager, you may decide to take no action, even though a deviation has occurred.

Corrective action may be either immediate or permanent. Immediate corrective action is often aimed at correcting *symptoms*. Permanent corrective action is aimed at correcting the *cause* of the symptoms or problem. Most frequently, corrective action is of the immediate type; it is done right away to correct the situation. For example, a particular project is a week behind schedule. If the delay is not corrected, other projects will be seriously affected. The first thing to do is to get the project back on schedule rather than worrying about who or what caused the difficulty. Depending on the authority of the manager, the following immediate corrective actions may be ordered: (1) overtime hours may be authorized; (2) additional workers and equipment may be assigned; (3) a full-time director may be assigned to push the project through; (4) extra effort may be asked from all employees; or (5) if all these fail, the schedule may have to be readjusted, requiring changes all along the line.

After the degree of urgency has diminished, attention can be devoted to more permanent corrective action. Just how and why did events stray from their planned course? What can be done to prevent a recurrence of this type of difficulty? It is at this phase that many managers fail. Too often they find themselves "putting out fires," and they never discover the actual cause of the problem. For instance, managers may find themselves constantly having to interview and hire new people to replace those who quit. A manager may be working 12 hours a day locating new employees. However, the high turnover problem is not solved merely by this type of immediate corrective action. Some type of permanent corrective action must be taken once managers determine what is causing the high turnover. A supervisor may be extremely difficult to work with, or the pay scale may not be competitive for the area. Whatever the problem, it must be identified and corrected, or high turnover will likely continue. Permanent corrective action must be taken for the sake of economical and effective operations in the future.

❖ ❖ CONTROLLING AND THE BUSINESS SYSTEM

Recall from Chapter 2 that in the business system, inputs are converted to outputs through a transformation process. As Figure 16.2 shows, the controlling efforts by management may concentrate on inputs, on the process itself, or on outputs.

Controlling Inputs

With input controls, managers attempt to monitor the resources—materials and personnel—that come into the organization to ensure that they can be used effectively to achieve organizational objectives. The quality of inputs is vital to the quality of outputs.

Material Controls The material resources an organization requires must meet specified quality standards and be available when needed by the firm. If Ethan Allen, a major furniture manufacturer, purchased low-quality wood with which to manufacture furniture, the company would not maintain its reputation for producing excellent furniture. Statistical sampling is often used to assist in material control. With statistical sampling, a portion of the items received by the firm are checked to estimate the quality of the entire lot. For instance, Ethan Allen might examine five percent of the lumber it receives. In many situations, however, failure of even a small percentage of the incoming items could create difficulty. Components for commercial aircraft engines are an example. Statistical

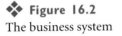

❖ **Figure 16.2**
The business system

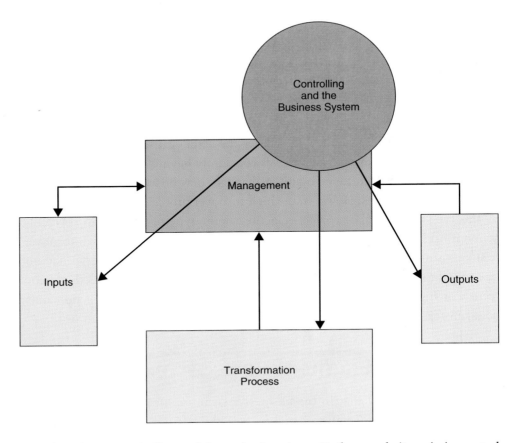

sampling is not typically used in such situations. Rather, each item is inspected individually.

Personnel Selection Controls If a firm is to remain stable or grow, it continually needs new workers, because of factors such as death, retirement, and loss of employees to other organizations. In order to obtain new workers capable of sustaining the organization, certain controls must be established regarding their selection. The skill requirements of each job must be determined, and new employees should meet or exceed these requirements before they are employed.

Controlling the Process

Overseeing the process of producing goods and services offers an opportunity to correct problems before outputs have been affected. Most of the time of a typical lower-level manager is spent overseeing the process. Effective lower-level managers usually become familiar with the sights and sounds of the workplace and can often tell when something unusual is occurring. A wide range of possible signals is available to the manager. A noisy bearing on a bolt machine might warn the manager that the machine will begin to make defective bolts. Before a single faulty bolt has been produced, the bearing can be replaced.

Perhaps the most important aspect of this kind of control is observation and correction of employee behavior. An observant supervisor may notice a worker looking around or behaving carelessly and will take action before output has been affected. Observing workers, managers, and machines in the process of doing the organization's work is a tool of management at every level.

Controlling Outputs

The ultimate purpose of controlling focuses on the quality and quantity of outputs produced. In fact, most people think of controlling as simply checking what has occurred and taking corrective action. In the business system, controlling output consists of quality and quantity controls, financial controls, and evaluation of employee performance on the basis of output. According to Manuel Werner, author of the *Great Paradox: Responsibility Without Empowerment,* "Hierarchies are designed to control organizational outputs, ensuring quality and consistency do not become random events."[3]

Quality and Quantity Controls The purpose of quality control is to ensure that a certain level of excellence is attained. Quality has received renewed emphasis in recent years. Quality control must also be concerned with the costs of increasing quality. Therefore, it is important that the quality necessary to meet company objectives be determined in the planning stage. Trade-offs are necessary between the quality level one might prefer and the cost of achieving that level.

A common approach to evaluating quality is to make comparisons with other organizations or units. Figure 16.3 shows how three shift crews compare in

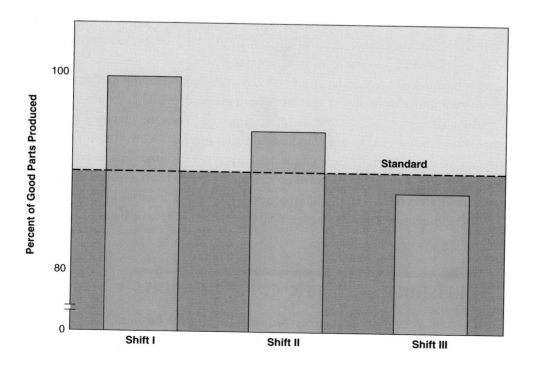

❖ **Figure 16.3**
Monthly quality comparison report, by shifts

terms of the acceptable parts they produce. The supervisor for shift III should see that the third shift is deficient in comparison to the other two and should take corrective action.

Productivity is normally thought of in terms of the quantity of output. Most companies also expect a certain amount of production from each individual or organizational unit, often expressed in terms of a quota. Sales quotas specify the amount of sales an individual, district, or region is expected to meet. Production quotas specify the amount or number of an item that needs to be produced. Control of quotas at every level is important if the organization is to achieve its objectives.

Financial Controls The ultimate output that most companies desire is profit. The quality and quantity of goods and services are often seen as means to this end. Financial statements provide valuable information about whether a company, department, or unit is effectively using its resources. Intelligent interpretation of financial data provides an excellent means by which management can control its overall welfare.

Budgetary controls (discussed in the next section) also offer a way of ensuring that the company is performing well financially. Plans are made for certain levels of revenues and expenses. If at any time the company is not on track toward achieving those levels, a good budgeting system will initiate corrective action.

Evaluation of Employee Performance As described in Chapter 9, performance appraisal is the formal and systematic measurement and evaluation of job performance.[4] An effective performance appraisal system is a means of control through which individuals learn of their strengths and weaknesses and are told what they should do to overcome deficiencies. The overall objective of such systems is to improve the organization's effectiveness by developing and communicating vital information about the firm's human resources. This requires providing feedback to employees about their performance. When the manager evaluates employees against established standards on the appraisal form, the manager is involved in controlling. At General Electric, teams of employees participate in job design and evaluate their own team members. Since this team approach has been in effect at General Electric, employee productivity has increased on an annual basis.[5] A unique approach to monitoring behavior that is now being used is the "Active Badge."

❖ ❖ ESTABLISHING STRATEGIC CONTROL POINTS

Management is centrally concerned with controlling the business system, which consists of inputs, processes, and outputs. A frequent problem is determining

The Active Badge Monitors Employee Performance

An evaluation of job performance involves tracking employee performance and evaluating how efficient and effective employees have been over a specific period of time. The "Active Badge" allows employers to track employees to maximize their efficiency. The employee-tracking data base can track the actions of any employee wearing the badge. The badge can determine where in the facility the employee is, who the employee is meeting with, and at what time; in addition, it tracks the employee's daily scheduled activities and compares them with a preset standard. The "active badge" is a clip-on ID badge that sends out infrared signals that are read by sensors placed throughout the office building. The sensors are wired to computers that collect the information and distribute it into the network. But, as the "Active Badge" system spreads, the employees' right to privacy must be balanced with corporate desires for efficiency and control. Even the patent holder, Olivetti, admits that "It's a great technology in the right hands. But if you've got a bad manager, he's going to make your life hell." The system doesn't use expensive technology, and Olivetti of Italy is currently selling the badges. According to the company spokesperson, "Everybody will be wearing Active Badges in five or ten years."[6]

what part of the system to monitor. Ideally, every resource, processing activity, and output should be measured, reported on, and compared to a standard. This can be extremely costly and time-consuming. A manager must determine what activity to measure and when to measure it.

The critical points selected for monitoring in the process of producing goods or services are **strategic control points.** These points should have a number of basic characteristics (see Figure 16.4).

First, strategic control points should relate to key operations or events. If a difficulty occurs at a vital point, the entire operation may grind to a halt. The problem created by poor quality equipment may have a detrimental impact on the company's sales even if the production personnel and sales force are of exceptional quality.

A second important characteristic of strategic control points is that they must be set up so that problems can be identified before serious damage occurs. If the control point is properly located, action can be taken to stop or alter a defective process before major harm is done. Testing for defects early in the process typically cuts costs and improves both production and quality. It does little good to discover that a million defective parts have been produced. The control point should be located in such a way that deviations can be quickly identified and corrected.

One of the authors, in the early days of his career, had the opportunity to observe how the improper selection of strategic control points almost caused a major tire manufacturer to be forced to cease operation. In the manufacture of a tire, four basic phases are required: mixing, tread shaping, tire building, and tire molding (see Figure 16.5). The mixing department obtains the proper blend of rubber for the type of tire that is being produced. The tread is then shaped, with

❖ **Figure 16.4**
Characteristics of effec-
tive strategic control
points

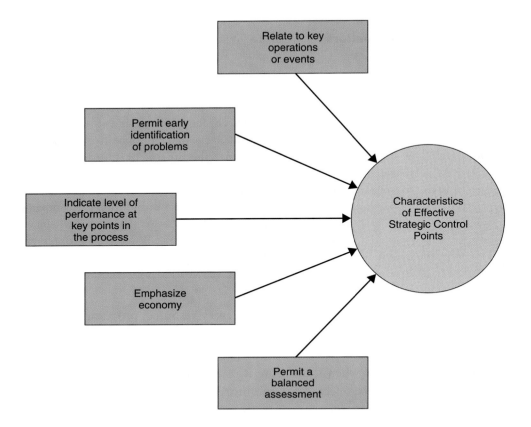

attention being given to length, width, and thickness. The next phase, building, entails placing the various components—such as the tread, steel belting, and white walls—together. In the molding department, the tires are heated and shaped into final form.

A major problem forced the tire company to reevaluate its entire control procedure. In the old system of control, a tire was inspected only after it had been molded. At that stage, there was already a large investment in the tire, and it would have to have a major defect before it would be rejected. The deficiency in the control process was recognized when the tire manufacturing firm delivered a several-million-dollar order to a company that purchased tires and sold them at retail outlets under its own brand name. The retail chain, after careful inspection of the tires, rejected the order and demanded that the entire batch be redone. The tire manufacturing firm nearly went out of business because of the large investment tied up in rejected inventory. The firm had to go heavily into debt to remake the order.

After this experience, major changes were made in the control process. A separate quality control department, reporting directly to the president, was established. Quality control inspectors were hired and given authority to stop

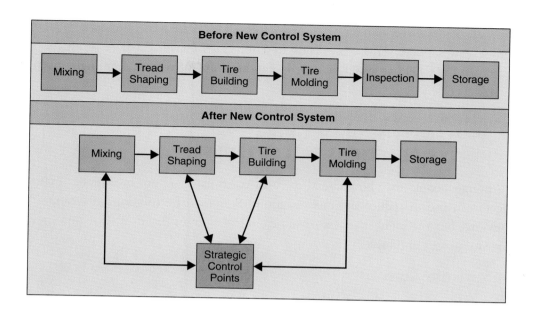

Example of placement of strategic control points

operations, even over the advice of the production superintendent. Strategic control points were located in each major department (see Figure 16.5). If a problem occurred in the mixing department, it would be discovered before the tire progressed to the other stages. Because of this intensive effort to improve quality, the firm was able to survive and prosper.

A third consideration in selecting strategic control points is that together they should indicate the level of performance for a broad spectrum of key events. At times, comprehensiveness conflicts with the need for proper timing. Profit, for example, is a comprehensive strategic control point, indicating the progress of the entire enterprise. Yet, if one waits until the end of the regular accounting period to obtain this figure, one loses control of the immediate future. It does little good to recognize that the firm is now bankrupt; managers need to have accounting figures ahead of time so that corrective action may be taken.

Economy is the fourth consideration in the choice of proper control points. With computers and management information systems (discussed in Chapter 20) readily available, there is a strong temptation to demand every conceivable bit of information. But an executive can effectively use only a limited amount of information. With so much available, critical information may be lost in the masses of data. Simply stated, you can't see the forest for the trees.

Finally, the selection of various strategic control points should be balanced. If only credit losses are watched and controlled, for example, sales may suffer because of an overly stringent policy in accepting credit risks. If sales are emphasized too strongly, credit losses will mount. There is a tendency to place tight control over tangible functions, such as production and sales, while maintaining limited control over intangible functions, such as employee development and other staff services. This often leads to a state of imbalance where production executives are held to exact standards and staff executives are seemingly given blank checks.

❖ ❖ HOW MANAGERS OVERCOME NEGATIVE REACTIONS TO CONTROLS

Although people may be inclined to resist controls, there are means that managers can use to reduce negative reactions. Some of the solutions may appear obvious, but the ineffectiveness of some control systems makes it clear that they are not always employed.

Justifiable Controls

A control system will have higher acceptability if the reason for the control appears justifiable to those who must comply with it. For instance, the firm may have to increase the quality of its product in order to obtain future contracts. These contracts may mean not only profit for the firm but job stability for the employees.

Understandable Expectations

Employees who know exactly what is expected of them with regard to a control system tend to exhibit less resistance. For instance, a statement by a manager that quality should increase does not clearly convey what is expected. A requirement that the percentage of defective parts should decrease by ten percent is precise and understandable. When workers do not understand what is expected of them, frustration and resentment can result.

Realistic Standards

A realistic control system involves standards that are attainable by the employees who work within the control system. At times, it may appear that controls are established merely to harass the worker. Standards that are higher than needed to accomplish the purpose of the organization are not only expensive but may well be resisted by company employees. Although Chase Manhattan Bank, for example, may desire to have zero loan losses, such an expectation is unrealistic. Banks typically have to decide what degree of risk is acceptable.

Timely Communication of Findings

For a control system to be effective, information about deviations should be communicated to employees as quickly as is practical. It does little good to tell workers that their performance was below standard three weeks ago. If a problem is to be corrected, it must receive timely attention.

Accurate Findings

Nothing could be worse than to have a control system that provides inaccurate information. If information feedback has proved incorrect in the past, employees may not trust the control system. If workers consistently find errors made by supervisors, all management input may be questioned. In such a case, for example, an employee who receives a low performance evaluation may have reason to suspect the evaluation is inaccurate even if it is not.

❖ ❖ DISCIPLINARY ACTION

The state of employee self-control and orderly conduct present in an organization is **discipline.** A necessary, but often trying, aspect of control is taking disciplinary action. **Disciplinary action** is action taken to correct unacceptable behavior. In spite of a firm's desire to solve its employee problems in a positive way, at times this is not possible. A major purpose of disciplinary action is to ensure that employee behavior is consistent with the firm's objectives. Rules are established to assist the organization in accomplishing these objectives. When a rule is violated, the effectiveness of the organization is diminished to some degree, depending on the severity of the infraction. For instance, if a worker reports late to work, the loss to the firm may be minimal. However, if a worker fails to use the safety guard on a machine and is severely injured, the loss may be substantial. Managers must realize that disciplinary action can be a positive force for the company. The firm benefits from developing and implementing effective disciplinary action policies. Without a healthy state of discipline, or the threat of disciplinary action, the firm's effectiveness may be severely limited.

The Disciplinary Action Process

The disciplinary action process is dynamic and ongoing. One person's actions can affect others in the group. For instance, if a worker receives disciplinary action, it is likely that this action will influence other workers when they learn that such mistakes will not be tolerated.

The disciplinary action process is shown in Figure 16.6. The external environment affects the process, as it does with all management activities. Laws that affect company policies are constantly changing. For instance, the Occupational Safety and Health Administration has caused many firms to establish new safety rules. Unions are another external factor. Specific punishments for rule violations are subject to negotiation. For instance, a union may negotiate three written

❖ **Figure 16.6**
The disciplinary action process
(Source: Reprinted by permission from R. Wayne Mondy and Robert M. Noe III, *Human Resource Management,* 5th ed. [Boston: Allyn and Bacon, 1993], p. 672.)

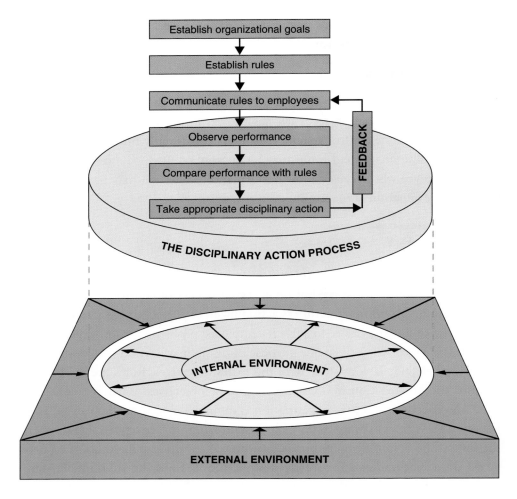

warnings for tardiness instead of the two warnings a present contract might require.

Changes in the internal environment of the firm can also alter the disciplinary action process. Through organizational development, the firm may alter its culture. This change may result in first-line supervisors handling disciplinary action in a more positive manner. Organization policies can also have an impact on the disciplinary action process. Seeing employees as mature adults rather than as irresponsible children could significantly affect the process.

The disciplinary action process deals largely with infractions of rules. Rules—specific and detailed guides to action—are created to facilitate the accomplishment of organizational objectives. The do's and don't's associated with accomplishing tasks are highly inflexible. A company rule may require wearing hard hats in hazardous areas. And, of course, after rules have been established, they must be communicated to the affected employees. Individuals cannot obey a rule if they do not know it exists. As long as employee behavior does not vary from acceptable practices, there will be no need for disciplinary action. But when an employee's behavior violates a rule, corrective action may be taken. The purpose of this action is to alter behaviors that can have a negative impact on achievement of organizational objectives.

Note that Figure 16.6 shows a feedback loop from "take appropriate disciplinary action" to "communicate rules to employees." Some employees find out that a rule is being enforced only when a peer receives disciplinary action. Employees will then conform to the rule to avoid similar disciplinary action.

Approaches to Disciplinary Action

Several concepts regarding the administration of disciplinary action have been developed. Two of these concepts are progressive discipline and discipline without punishment.

Progressive discipline is the disciplinary action approach designed to ensure that the minimum penalty appropriate to the offense is imposed. It involves answering a series of questions about the severity of the offense (see Figure 16.7). If the improper behavior is minor and has not previously occurred, perhaps an oral warning will be sufficient. Or an individual may receive several written warnings before a violation warrants more than another written warning. The manager does not consider termination until each lower-level question has been answered "yes." However, major violations, such as hitting a supervisor, may justify the immediate dismissal of the employee.

Discipline without punishment gives the worker time off with pay to think about whether he or she really wants to follow the rules and continue working for the company. When an employee violates a rule, the manager issues an "oral reminder." Repetition brings a "written reminder." The third violation results in the worker having to take one, two, or three days off (with pay) to think about the situation. During the first two steps, the manager tries to encourage the employee to solve the problem.[7] If the third step is taken, after the time-off period, the worker and supervisor meet to agree that the employee will not violate the rule again or that the employee will leave the firm. When discipline without

❖ **Figure 16.7**
The progressive discipline approach (Source: Reprinted by permission from R. Wayne Mondy and Robert M. Noe III, *Human Resource Management,* 5th ed. [Boston: Allyn and Bacon, 1993], p. 675.)

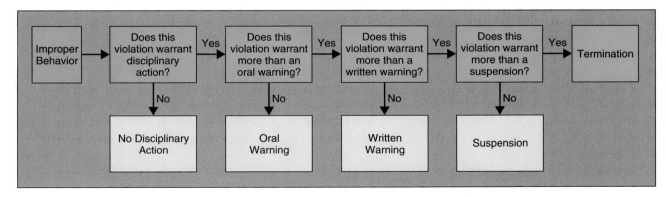

TABLE 16.1 Guidelines for Disciplinary Action

- The manager should assume that all employees desire to conform to reasonable organizational requirements.
- The act, rather than the person, should be condemned.
- Future desired behavior should be described.
- Reasonable promptness is important, so the employee can connect the penalty to the violation.
- A managerial listening role is highly essential to effect greater understanding of the reasons for the act and to prevent hasty decisions that may lead to unjustified penalties.
- Negative disciplinary action should be administered in private.
- Definite, but tactful, follow-up should occur to determine the degree of success of the disciplinary action.
- Consistency and flexibility, though apparently contradictory, are both desirable elements of a good program of disciplinary action.

punishment is used, it is especially important that all rules be explicitly stated in writing. At the time of orientation, new workers should be told that repeated violations of different rules will be viewed as several violations of the same rule. This keeps workers from taking undue advantage of the process.

The main purpose of disciplinary action is not to punish or fire employees, but to improve their contribution to the organization. Rehabilitation achieves this objective more often than termination. Table 16.1 lists guidelines for handling disciplinary action cases, whether or not managers explicitly practice the progressive disciplinary action approach.

MANAGEMENT IN PRACTICE

A Skill-Building Exercise: "I think I might have messed up this morning" said the maintenance supervisor, Carl Martin, to Doug Williams, the industrial relations manager. "One of the workers in my section wasn't doing the job exactly to specs and I told him rather forcefully how to do it correctly. He told me, rather sarcastically, 'to take it easy.' Then, he said 'Don't worry, be happy.' I blew up and fired him. Five minutes later, the union steward was in the office reading me the riot act. She said situations such as this one are covered in our contract and that I was violating it. I had never spoken to the worker before about that particular offense, and the steward said the contract called for both oral and written warnings before dismissal. Also, several of the worker's friends were around when I fired him. What are we going to do?"
How would you respond?

❖ ❖ ❖ BUDGETARY CONTROL

The most basic and widely used quantitative controlling technique is the budget. A **budget** is a statement of planned allocation of resources expressed in financial or numerical terms. Budgetary control is concerned with the comparison of actual and planned expenditures. Most areas of operation in a business enterprise—marketing, production, materials, labor, manufacturing expense, capital expenditures, and cash—have budgets. The operating budget for a McDonald's restaurant includes a specific allowance for every major activity.

In order to make a profit, a corporation must keep all of its operations within budgetary guidelines. If an operation cannot control its expenses through appropriate budgetary controls, then profit objectives may be difficult, or impossible, to achieve.

Types of Budgets

Often, the budget is the most important document a manager uses in planning and controlling operations. There are basically two broad categories of budgets: capital budgets and operating budgets. A **capital budget** is a statement of planned expenditures of funds for facilities and equipment. It therefore typically extends over several years. When it is first known that a new or replacement machine will be needed, the capital budget is modified to include the expected expenditure.

An **operating budget** is a statement of the planned income and expenses of a business or unit. It includes allowances for utilities, maintenance, and all other recurring expense items. For a unit of a large organization, the planned "income" is the allocation of funds from headquarters.

The most basic and widely used quantitative controlling technique is the budget. Budgetary control is concerned with the comparison of actual to planned expenditures. Variances are individually noted and usually must be justified. (Source: Jon Riley/ © Tony Stone Images)

Benefits of the Budgeting Process

Most organizations—profit or nonprofit—operate within the framework of budgets. Budgeting is a significant part of both the planning and the controlling processes. Budgets are widely used by managers to plan, monitor, and control various activities and operations at every level of an organization. Some of the benefits of the budgeting process are as follows:

1. *Provides standards against which actual performance can be measured.* Budgets are quantified plans that allow management to measure and control performance objectively. If, for instance, a department manager knows that the budgeted expenditure for supplies is $1,000 per month, the manager is in a position to monitor and control the expenses for supplies.

2. *Provides managers with additional insight into organizational objectives.* The allocation of funds more often than not is the true test of a firm's dedication to a particular objective. For instance, suppose that two firms of relatively equal size have a stated policy of being innovative with regard to research and development. Firm A allocates $1 million a year to R&D programs, and Firm B budgets only $100,000. We can conclude that Firm A has a much stronger commitment to R&D than Firm B.

3. *Tends to be a positive influence on the motivation of workers.* People typically like to know what is expected of them, and budgets often clarify specific performance standards.

4. *Causes managers to divert some of their attention from current operations to future operations.* To some extent, a budget encourages managers to anticipate and forecast changes in the external environment. For example, an increase in transportation costs created by higher-priced petroleum might force a firm to seek an alternate transportation or distribution system.

5. *Improves top management's ability to coordinate the overall operation of the organization.* Budgets are blueprints of the company's plans for the coming year. They greatly aid top management in coordinating the operations of each division or department.

6. *Enables management to recognize or anticipate problems in time to take the necessary corrective action.* For example, production costs substantially higher than the budgeted amount will alert management to make changes to realign actual costs with the budget. Not only are overall departmental costs monitored, but the costs of individual activities are isolated and controlled. Long before departmental expenditures can get out of control, corrective action can begin.

7. *Facilitates communication throughout the organization.* The budget significantly improves management's ability to communicate the objectives, plans, and standards of performance important to the organization. Budgets are

especially helpful to lower-level managers. They let them know how their operations relate to other units or departments in the organization. Also, budgets tend to pinpoint managers' responsibility and improve their understanding of the organization's objectives. This usually results in increased morale and commitment on the part of managers.

8. *Helps managers recognize when change is needed.* The budgeting process requires managers to review the company's operations carefully and critically to determine if resources are being allocated to the right activities and programs. The process causes management to focus on such questions as: Which products appear to have the greatest demand? Which markets appear to offer the best potential? What business are we in? Which business should we be in?[8]

Limitations of the Budgeting Process

Although numerous benefits can be attributed to the use of budgets, problems may arise. If the budgetary process is to achieve maximum effectiveness, these problems must be recognized, and attempts must be made to solve them. Some of the major problems are as follows:

• *Some managers believe that all funds allocated in a budget must be spent.* This attitude may work against the intent of the budgeting process. Often, managers learn from experience that if they do not spend the funds that have been budgeted, their budget will be reduced the following year. They have found that such conscientious cost-effectiveness can hurt their departments. A manager who operates in this type of environment may make an extraordinary effort to spend extra funds for reasons that may be marginal at best.

• *A budget may be so restrictive that supervisors are permitted little discretion in managing their resources.* Actual amounts that can be spent for items may be specified, and funds may not be transferable from one account to another. This sometimes results in seemingly ludicrous situations. For example, there may be funds to purchase personal computers but no money for printer ribbons.

• *In evaluating a manager, the main criterion may be conformity to the budget, rather than what the manager has actually accomplished.* If this philosophy is prevalent in a firm, poor managers may be viewed as superior because they met the budget and good managers may be reprimanded for failing to follow exact budgetary guidelines. This state of affairs can severely reduce the amount of risk a manager will be willing to take. Managers may spend a majority of their time ensuring that they are in compliance with the budget, when their time might be better spent developing new ideas.

Zero Base Budgeting

Originally developed by Texas Instruments, **zero base budgeting (ZBB)** is the system of budgeting that requires management to take a fresh look at all programs and activities each year, rather than merely building on last year's budget. In other words, last year's budget allocations are not considered a basis for this year's budget. Each program, or "decision package," must be justified on the basis of cost-benefit analysis. The three main features of zero base budgeting are as follows:

1. The activities of individual departments are divided into decision packages, which provide information to management so that management can compare the costs and benefits of each program or activity.
2. Each decision package is first evaluated and then ranked in order of decreasing importance to the organization. Thus, priorities are established for each program and activity. Each of these is evaluated by top management, which arrives at a final ranking.
3. Resources are allocated according to top management's final ranking of the programs and activities. As a rule, decisions to allocate resources for high-priority items are made quickly. Closer scrutiny is given lower-priority programs or activities.[9]

Zero base budgeting is not a panacea for all the problems associated with the budgeting process. Organizations may experience problems in implementing the system. Most managers are reluctant to admit that not all of their activities are of the highest priority, and they don't like submitting their programs to close scrutiny.

Nonetheless, under ZBB, a system is established in which an organization's resources can be allocated to higher-priority programs, and programs of lower-priority can be reduced or eliminated. Thus, the benefits of zero base budgeting appear to outweigh the costs.

❖ ❖ QUALITY CONTROL

Quality is a concern of most Americans. But what exactly is meant by the term? **Quality** is the degree of excellence of a good or service. Quality control is the means by which a firm makes sure that its goods or services will serve the purposes for which they are intended. Quality standards are determined by the company's objectives. McDonald's Corporation CEO Mike Quinlan seems dedicated to maintaining the standard of excellence instilled in the company by its founder, Ray Kroc. Kroc said: "Don't compromise. Use the best ingredients, the best equipment."[10] If a company wishes to gain a reputation for high-quality products, standards will have to be high, and the company must have a rigid quality control

Quality standards are determined by the company's objectives. (Source: © John Coletti)

program to help it meet those high standards. Although increased quality generally results in higher costs, it also allows for higher prices. On the other hand, some firms may sell to market segments that desire lower prices and will accept lower quality. Certain standards remain, but they are not as high as the standards of quality-oriented firms.

There are numerous ways to maintain product quality. A company could decide on 100 percent inspection of all items manufactured. Even so, some defects might not be discovered. When the human element is made part of the quality control environment, it is inevitable that mistakes will occasionally be made. Some good items may be rejected, and some bad items may be accepted.

In most instances, it is not feasible or desirable to have 100 percent inspection. For instance, if the standard for the life of a light bulb were 200 hours, the bulb would have to be burned for that many hours to determine if it met the standard. Naturally, there would be no product to sell after the inspection. Tire manufacturing provides a similar example. Companies set standards for their tires that specify the number of miles they can be safely driven. If each tire were placed on a machine to run the assigned number of miles, there would be no product to market. In still other instances, the costs involved in 100 percent inspection would be prohibitive. If each nail in a keg were inspected separately, for example, the cost of inspection might be higher than the price of the nails.

The technique used to overcome these deficiencies is statistical quality control. In *statistical quality control,* a portion of the total number of items is checked. For instance, inspectors might select five items out of 100 and estimate the characteristics of the other 95. Some degree of error exists, of course. For instance, if only five out of 100 items are defective, it is conceivable that all five defective items might be selected for testing and the entire lot might therefore be rejected. On the other hand, there might be only five good parts. These five good parts might be the ones drawn. Then the entire batch would be accepted. Statistical quality control involves risk, but usually the benefits justify the risk.

Acceptance Sampling

Acceptance sampling is the inspection of a portion of the output or input of a process to determine acceptability. Assume that it has been statistically determined that taking a sample of 15 items from each batch of 100 and limiting allowable defective units to one will result in the desired quality. In this case, if two or more items are defective, the entire lot will be rejected. When an entire lot is rejected, every item in it may have to be inspected. Or the lot may have to be returned to the supplier, who must evaluate the problem.

There are two basic approaches to acceptance sampling: sampling by variables and sampling by attributes. Each method is used under different circumstances.

Sampling by Variables A plan developed for sampling by variables consists of determining how closely an item conforms to an established standard. In essence, degrees of goodness and degrees of badness are permitted. For instance, a stereo speaker is designed to project a certain tone quality. But not all speakers will behave the same way. Some speakers will perform above the standard and some below it. The variance does not necessarily mean that the speaker will be rejected. It will be rejected only when the quality is outside a certain range.

Sampling by Attributes With sampling by variables, degrees of conformity are considered. The product is either good or bad; there are no degrees of conformity to consider. For example, if an engine block has a hole in the side of any cylinder, it is rejected.

Control Charts

A **control chart** is a graphic record of how closely samples of a good or service conform to standards over time. An example of a control chart is shown in Figure 16.8. The chart is used with both variable and attribute sampling, although the statistical procedures for developing the chart are different for each type of sampling. In both instances, though, the standard is first determined. A variable sampling plan in the manufacture of tire treads might have standards that test thickness, weight, length, and width. If the average thickness of a certain tire tread is expected to be .87 inch, this becomes the standard.

Once the standard has been established, the acceptable amount of deviation must be determined. The maximum level that will be allowed is referred to as the

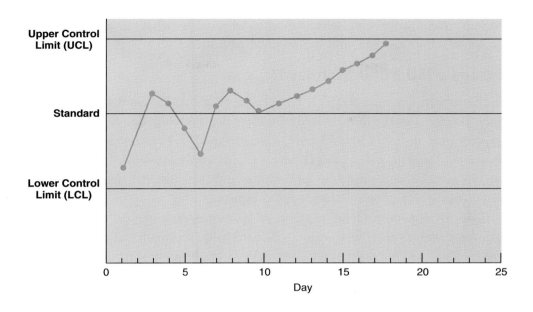

❖ **Figure 16.8**
An example of a control chart

upper control limit (UCL), and the minimum level is called the lower control limit (LCL). In the tire tread example, the UCL might be .89 inch and the LCL might be .85 inch. If the thickness of a tread being evaluated falls within the two extremes, it will be accepted. If it falls outside the limits, it will be rejected.

Another benefit of control charts is that potential problems may be recognized prior to their actual occurrence. Figure 16.8 shows that from day 10 until day 17, the quality of the product progressively worsened. The item is still within the limits of acceptability, but if the problem is not corrected, the deviation may soon go above the upper control limit. When managers see this pattern developing, they are in a position to take corrective action. Control charts are a basic tool of Total Quality Management, which is discussed in Chapter 17.

❖ ❖ INTERNATIONAL QUALITY STANDARDS

The emphasis on quality has evolved to such a point that international standards are being developed, with more standards surely to follow.[11]

Japan's Industrial Standard

The Japanese have developed a specification for quality that is published in Japan as *Industrial Stand Z8101-1981*. The standard states, "Implementing quality control effectively necessitates the cooperation of all people in the company, involving top management, managers, supervisors, and workers in all areas of corporate activities such as market research, research and development, product planning design, preparations for production, purchasing, vendor management, manufacturing, inspection, sales, and after-services, as well as financial control, personnel administration, and training and education."

Europe's ISO 9000 Standard

The European Community (EC) has developed a quality standard called *ISO 9000*. The focus of the EC standard is to force the establishment of quality management procedures on firms doing business in the EC. The three required components of the standard are to: (1) have a quality control manual that meets ISO guidelines, (2) document quality procedures, and (3) ensure written job instructions. Third-party auditors must verify compliance.

Several factors make ISO 9000 the subject of intense interest in the United States and worldwide. These include (1) worldwide acceptance as a quality system standard, (2) the reality that the standards will be applied to some products made or imported to the EC in 1993, and (3) the possible requirement that firms comply with ISO 9000 for product certification.

❖ ❖ INVENTORY CONTROL

Inventory is the goods or materials available for use by a business. Concern with inventory is almost continuous. A car dealer with excessive inventory will offer a special deal to sell a car. A furniture dealer provides a similar offer. Although there may be a bit of sales promotion in these offerings, inventory does represent a cost that must be controlled. A product in inventory constitutes a valuable, although

---

ETHICAL DILEMMA

The most difficult aspect of cost controls is controlling the people component of the process. The managerial component is probably the most difficult to effectively evaluate because many aspects of a manager's job are somewhat abstract. The ultimate managerial control would result if actual performance were accurately measured, and then reasonable performance levels established and implemented. Accurate tracking of all individuals who perform similar jobs would result in less abstract standards and more equitable evaluations. The "Active Badge" device allows employers to track employees and maximize their efficiency.

The employee-tracking data base can monitor the actions of any employee wearing the badge.[12] Some view the use of such badges as unethical because it signals that the company does not trust its employees. Also, as the "Active Badge" system spreads, the employee's right to privacy could be compromised because of the corporate desire for efficiency and control. Your assignment is to enhance managerial productivity. You are aware of the potential problems of the "Active Badge" system, but you have the option to use it.

What would you do?

idle, resource. Many of the resources of many major companies is inventory, so failure to control inventory can mean the difference between profit and loss.

Purposes of Inventory

Inventory permits the relative independence of operations between two activities. For instance, if machine A makes a product that will be used by machine B, and machine A breaks down, machine B will have to cease operations unless an inventory of the product has been built up.

Inventory also provides for continuous operations when demand for the product is not consistent. Electric razors are sold primarily during the Christmas holiday season, but a manufacturer of electric razors typically keeps production going through the entire year. That way, a skilled workforce can be maintained and equipment usage can be kept at an optimal level.

Another purpose of inventory is to allow the filling of orders quickly, thereby maintaining customer satisfaction. If orders come in at a constant rate, there may be no need to maintain inventory. But if five orders come in this month and 100 next month, a company without product inventory might be hard pressed to fill the 100 requests.

Economic Order Quantity Method of Inventory Control

The **economic order quantity (EOQ) inventory control method** is the procedure for balancing ordering costs and carrying costs so as to minimize total inventory costs. The economic order quantity (EOQ) is the amount of an inventory item that should be purchased to minimize total inventory cost. **Ordering costs** are administrative, clerical, and other expenses incurred in obtaining inventory items and placing them in storage. **Carrying costs** are the expenses associated with maintaining and storing products before they are sold or used. Taxes, insurance, interest on capital invested, storage, electricity, and spoilage are some of the carrying costs. The total inventory costs associated with a particular order are represented by the following general formula:

Total inventory costs = Ordering costs + Carrying costs

If orders are made less frequently, ordering costs go down but carrying costs go up. If frequent orders are submitted, ordering costs go up but carrying costs are reduced. This is graphically illustrated in Figure 16.9. The optimal number of items to order at any one time—the economic order quantity—is represented by the lowest point on the total cost curve. This is where the carrying costs and ordering costs lines intersect.

Managers need to identify the two primary costs: carrying (C) and ordering costs (O). The EOQ formula is determined from the total cost equation. The basic equation for EOQ is presented in Table 16.2.

TABLE 16.2 Basic Equation for EOQ

$$EOQ = \sqrt{\frac{2\binom{\text{ordering}}{\text{cost}}\binom{\text{annual}}{\text{demand}}}{\text{carrying costs}}} = \sqrt{\frac{2(O) \times (D)}{C}}$$

If the assumption is made that ordering costs are \$4, annual demand is 1,000 units, and carrying costs are \$2 per unit, the economic order quantity is as follows:

$$EOQ = \sqrt{\frac{2(\$4 \times 1,000)}{\$2}} = \sqrt{\frac{\$8,000}{\$2}} = \sqrt{\$4,000} = 63.25$$

which is rounded to 63. No other order quantity would lower the total cost. This model is one of the simplest to develop. The sophistication level of the model a manager will use depends on the needs of the company.

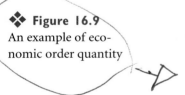

❖ **Figure 16.9**
An example of economic order quantity

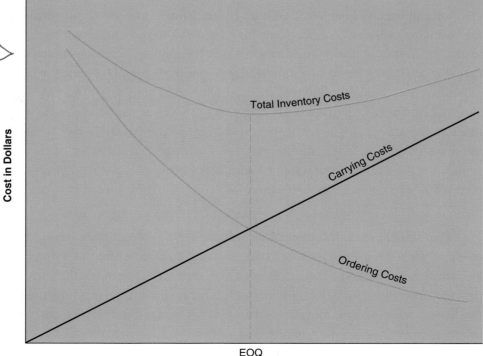

ABC Inventory Method

Sometimes, it is impractical to monitor every item in inventory with the same degree of intensity. In such cases, it is useful to categorize the items in inventory according to the degree of control needed. The **ABC inventory method** is the classification of inventory items, for control purposes, into three categories, according to unit costs and number of items kept on hand. The usual categories are as follows:

- *Category A.* Items in this group account for 70 percent of the dollar value of the inventory used. They represent a small number of items but high unit cost. They receive frequent, even daily, attention.
- *Category B.* Items in this group represent the next 20 percent of the dollar value of the inventory used. These items are not as important as category A items, but they do represent a substantial investment and should receive moderate attention.
- *Category C.* Items in this group are less expensive and may be used less often and therefore require less frequent attention.

To determine an item's classification, multiply the cost of the item by how often the item is used in a specific period. Then, list all items in order of total dollar amounts. Items representing 70 percent of the total dollars constitute the A group, items constituting the next 20 percent are the B group, and the remainder are the C group.

A manager using the ABC method should carefully monitor A items. This category might include automobiles, machinery, and tractors. B items, such as tables and chairs, require less vigorous control. C items might not even be formally controlled, especially if the cost associated with monitoring them is prohibitive, as may be the case for pencils and paper.

Just-in-Time Inventory Method

The **just-in-time (JIT) inventory method** is the practice of having inputs to the production process delivered precisely when they are needed, thereby assigning to suppliers the responsibility for keeping inventories to a minimum. McDonald's uses a system of just-in-time delivery for its raw materials, such as hamburger patties and paper goods. More and more companies, like the United States automakers, are using the just-in-time method to reduce inventories considerably.

Automobile makers are not alone in efforts to improve inventory control. To win back customers in the apparel market, America's textile companies are mounting a just-in-time delivery campaign. Each morning, Swift Textiles Inc.

JIT: No Longer Just for Japanese Manufacturers

Chrysler and General Motors (GM) are keenly aware of JIT's value. The near failure of Chrysler in 1980 was due in part to the high cost of inventory. In Chrysler factories, large stocks of components had to be kept on hand in case of strikes and other work stoppages in the plants of suppliers. Chrysler's comeback meant that they would quit producing cars for inventory, and Chrysler management mandated the use of JIT. Inventory problems are now the problem of Chrysler's suppliers and not Chrysler's manufacturing divisions. When GM moved to become a more competitive automaker, it also turned to just-in-time inventory management. At General Motors' Buick plant in Flint, Michigan, a number of suppliers placed their facilities within walking distance of the assembly line. Buick gave them complete responsibility for quality, inventory, and delivery of the items they supplied. When GM conducted its grand experiment, called Saturn, they implemented "one of the tightest just-in-time inventory systems in North America." Just-in-time inventory systems are a great savings for manufacturers, and will surely be part of any manufacturing system throughout the 1990s.[13]

ships just enough denim for a day's production at the nearby Levi Strauss plant in Valdosta, Georgia. With Swift certifying the quality of the denim, Levi closed its warehouse and quality testing lab and gained a competitive advantage.[14]

❖ ❖ NETWORK MODELS

The many complex tasks involved in building a skyscraper or a dam are almost impossible for the average person to comprehend. When a one-time project is large and complex and involves multiple organizations, two primary tools are available for coordinating the complicated network of interdependencies.

The two tools are the program evaluation and review technique (PERT) and the critical path method (CPM). PERT was developed under the Navy Special Projects Office to assist in the rapid development of the Polaris submarine program. During approximately the same time period, researchers for E. I. du Pont de Nemours and Company and computer specialists from Remington Rand's Univac division combined their talents to develop CPM. The initial purpose of CPM was to schedule and control all activities involved in constructing chemical plants.

Both PERT and CPM have received widespread acceptance. PERT and CPM are used primarily for construction projects. But some firms, such as 3M Corporation, use the techniques to assist in the development of new products. Firms that do major construction work for the government are often required by their contracts to use PERT. Because of the similarity of PERT and CPM, only PERT will be discussed in detail. The primary difference between the two is that, in CPM, time and cost are known factors. In PERT, time must be estimated and costs determined.

The **program evaluation and review technique (PERT)** involves the display of a complex project as a network of events and activities, with three time estimates used to calculate the expected time for each activity. An event is the beginning or completion of a step. It does not consume time or resources, and it is represented by a circle, or node, in the network. An activity is a time-consuming element of the program, and it is represented by an arrow.

PERT may serve as both a planning and a control tool. In planning, it forces the manager to think through the project and identify the tasks that must be accomplished and how they interrelate. PERT facilitates control mainly by highlighting the critical path.

Improvements in information-processing capabilities have expanded the inclusion of cost considerations in PERT analysis referred to as the PERT/Cost analysis. The purpose of PERT/Cost is to reduce the entire project completion time by a certain amount at the least cost. Reducing completion time might be

---

A GLOBAL PERSPECTIVE

Global Success Through Internal and External Controls

Multinational managers must be concerned with maintaining control, often through applying various controlling techniques globally. According to W. Edwards Deming, the man who is given credit for much of Japan's manufacturing preeminence, certain controlling techniques for improving quality can be effective globally. Deming recommends (1) that managers not rely on mass inspection; (2) that they drive out fear by encouraging open, two-way communication; (3) that they teach statistical techniques; and (4) that they make maximum use of the statistical knowledge and talent in their companies. In addition, the control systems that are imposed must support and encourage employees, not constrain them. Deming also claims that a company can improve quality by controlling its purchasing system. He recommends that management work with fewer vendors—by finding one good supplier, and then looking for more. He also recommends that management insist on evidence of quality through control charts from every vendor. Just as the Deming system worked in Japan, it is working in America.

Controlling also involves assuring that organizational goals are met, and that there is a market for outputs. It is vitally important that the long-term profit objectives of the organization be met, and that competitive forces be controlled. Philip Morris CEO Michael Miles protected the market for the company's cigarettes by starting and winning a price war with the RJR Nabisco Holding Company. Miles cut the price of their premier brand, Marlboro, and gained market share of both discount and premium brands from RJR, thereby protecting future profits and further insulating Philip Morris from anticipated tax increases. Philip Morris realized that the best internal controls are of little value unless there is a certain degree of control over the market share for their products. The worst thing that can happen to a company is the loss of market share, so controls in this area are essential.[15] American firms will have to maintain a competitive level of quality, at an appropriate price, and guard market share to be successful globally.

especially important to a company that faces costly penalties for being late with a project. Also, there may be very high fixed costs for every day of the project.

The **critical path method (CPM)** involves the display of a complex project as a network, with one time estimate used for each step in the project. The developers of CPM were dealing with projects for which the times and costs of tasks

---

✗ Management Tips ✗

Guidelines for Dealing with the Controlling Process

1. **Make the controls objective-oriented.** Base the control system on the objectives of the department, not on the personal preferences of the manager.

2. **Keep it simple.** Controls that are stated in simple language are more likely to be understood.

3. **Be practical.** Do not set standards beyond the ability of the average worker.

4. **Use controls to improve performance, not to punish.** Controls imposed after improper action has occurred are usually seen as punishment. Controlling while the action is still occurring may be accepted as guidance and assistance.

5. **Be accurate.** If the manager is known to measure performance inaccurately, workers may automatically reject corrective action.

6. **Do not procrastinate.** The longer a person waits to take corrective action, the better the chances are that the situation will get out of control. This can cause a small problem to grow into a catastrophe.

7. **Quantify standards.** It is easiest to measure performance against numerical standards. It is very difficult to control quality when, for example, the standard is only, "to keep defects down."

8. **Set a good example.** Through the example you set for your workers, you are telling them what is acceptable. Consistently breaking a rule yourself tells workers that the rule is unimportant.

9. **Consider the human element.** Remember that there is a natural resistance to controls. Minimize them. If the control is not useful in accomplishing goals, why have it?

10. **Do not over-control.** Establishing excessive controls is not helpful and often does more harm than good.

(activities) required to complete the project were known. In CPM, the points, or nodes, of the network represent activities, rather than the events represented in PERT. In PERT, three time estimates are used. In CPM, there is only one time estimate, because CPM was designed to accommodate situations in which sets of standardized activities are required for the completion of a complex project. Time for completion of a task is relatively easy to determine accurately. Because there is only one time estimate, probabilities for completing the project on time cannot be computed. With these exceptions, PERT and CPM are very similar.

SUMMARY

Controlling is the process of comparing actual performance with standards and taking any necessary corrective action. The controlling process has three steps: (1) establish standards, (2) evaluate performance, and (3) take corrective action. Standards are established levels of quality or quantity used to guide performance. Although standards may be clear, control tolerances may also need to be established. Control tolerances are specifications of how much deviation will be permitted before corrective action is taken. Evaluating performance consists of checking for deviations from standards and determining if the deviations exceed control tolerances. The manager must consider what action to take to correct performance when deviations occur. Immediate corrective action corrects symptoms. Permanent corrective action corrects the cause of the symptoms or problem.

With input controls, attempts are made to monitor the resources—materials and personnel—that come into the organization to ensure that they are used effectively to achieve organizational objectives. Overseeing the process of producing goods and services offers an opportunity to correct problems before outputs have been affected. The ultimate purpose of controlling focuses on the quality and quantity of output produced. In monitoring the process of producing goods or services, critical points called *strategic control points* are selected. Despite the importance of controls to effective management, employees often view them in a negative way because controls take away a certain amount of individual freedom. However, there are means that managers can use to assist in reducing negative reactions.

Discipline is the state of employee self-control and orderly conduct present in an organization. It indicates the potential for genuine teamwork. Disciplinary

KEY TERMS

Controlling 512	Acceptance sampling 534
Standards 514	Control chart 534
Control tolerances 515	Inventory 536
Strategic control points 521	Economic order quantity (EOQ) inventory control method 537
Discipline 525	Ordering costs 537
Disciplinary action 525	
Progressive discipline 527	Carrying costs 537
Discipline without punishment 527	ABC inventory method 539
	Just-in-time (JIT) inventory method 539
Budget 529	
Capital budget 529	Program evaluation and review technique (PERT) 541
Operating budget 529	
Zero base budgeting (ZBB) 532	
Quality 532	Critical path method (CPM) 542

action is action taken to correct unacceptable behavior. Progressive discipline ensures that the minimum penalty appropriate to the offense is imposed. In discipline without punishment, workers are given time off with pay to determine if they really want to follow the rules and continue working for the company.

A budget is a statement of planned allocation of resources expressed in financial or numerical terms. Budgetary control is concerned with the comparison of actual and planned expenditures. There are basically two broad categories of budgets: capital budgets and operating budgets. A capital budget is a statement of planned expenditures of funds for facilities and equipment. An operating budget is a statement of the planned income and expenses of a business or unit. Although there are numerous benefits in the use of budgets, problems may arise, and these problems must be recognized and solved. Zero base budgeting is the system of budgeting that requires management to take a fresh look at all programs and activities each year, rather than merely building on last year's budget.

Quality control, the means by which firms make sure their goods or services will serve the purposes for which they are intended, involves quality standards derived from company objectives. Inspection may involve acceptance sampling, either sampling by variables or sampling by attributes. The emphasis on quality has evolved to such a point that international standards are being developed. The Japanese have developed a specification for quality that is published in Japan as Industrial Stand Z8101-1981. The European Community (EC) has developed a quality standard called ISO 9000. The focus of the EC standard is to force the establishment of quality management procedures on firms doing business in the EC. Control charts show how closely samples conform to standards over time.

Inventory is the goods or materials available for use by a business. It permits independence of operations between two activities, provides for continuous operations when demand is not consistent, and allows orders to be filled quickly. One method of inventory control is the economic order quantity (EOQ)

method, which balances ordering costs and carrying costs to minimize total inventory costs. The ABC inventory control method classifies items into three categories, according to unit costs and number of items kept on hand. The just-in-time (JIT) method of inventory control ensures that inputs to the production process are delivered precisely when they are

REVIEW QUESTIONS

1. Define <u>controlling</u>. What are the steps in the controlling process?

2. What are the most frequently used types of standards? Briefly discuss each.

3. What are the specific means of controlling inputs and outputs? Briefly describe each.

4. What factors should a manager consider in establishing strategic control points?

5. What are the ways of overcoming negative reactions to controls?

6. Define <u>disciplinary action</u> and <u>progressive discipline</u>. What guidelines should a manager follow when disciplinary action must be taken?

7. Define <u>budget</u>. What are the two broad categories of budgets?

8. What are the benefits and limitations of the budgeting process?

9. What is zero base budgeting?

10. Define <u>quality</u>.

11. Describe the two basic approaches to acceptance sampling. How are control charts used?

12. What is the ISO 9000 standard?

13. Explain the purposes of inventory. What is the economic order quantity (EOQ) method of inventory control?

14. Distinguish between PERT and CPM.

needed, thereby assigning to suppliers the responsibility for keeping inventories to a minimum.

Network models are used in planning and controlling large, complex projects, usually construction projects. The program evaluation and review technique (PERT) involves the display of a complex project as a network of events and activities, with three time estimates used to calculate the expected time for each activity. The purpose of PERT/Cost is to reduce the entire project completion time by a certain amount at the least cost. The critical path method (CPM) also involves the display of a complex project as a network, but with one time estimate used for each step in the project.

CASE STUDIES

CASE 16.1 Controlling 10,000 7-Eleven Stores

The Southland Corporation operates more than 10,000 7-Eleven convenience stores. Most of the stores are in the United States and Canada, although hundreds are scattered all over the globe. Southland sales more than double those of second-place Circle K. For over 20 years the company's sales grew steadily, recently exceeding $8 billion. Yearly gains of 15 and 20 percent were not unusual.

But the company assumed $4 billion in debt in 1987 and converted to private ownership through a leveraged buyout. This put extreme pressure on the Southland organization in 1988–1989, as the company tried to service its new debt. Losses totaled $207 million in 1988 alone. Southland quickly started to adjust. Over 1,000 7-Eleven stores were sold, both the advertising and capital budgets were slashed, and controls were tightened throughout the company. By mid-1989, the cash situation was improving, and Southland began its most aggressive—and expensive—ad campaign ever.

The quick response to distress can be credited to the firm's well-known system of tight control and disciplined management. To make sure its small, 2,400-square-foot stores are successful, Southland studies potential sites extensively and uses computer programs to forecast a proposed store's sales for the first five years. A store that does not measure up to standards is often closed.

7-Eleven has been a leader in the computerization of store operations. Five automated distribution centers supply 7-Eleven stores in the United States. Specially made trucks deliver prepriced items, along computer-designed routes, to individual stores. Careful analysis is made of which items sell best in which stores. Even shelf location is the subject of careful computerized evaluation. When trends change, items that no longer sell well are replaced by others, which are being continually tested in a few strategically located stores. A product that appears to be a rapid seller is tried nationwide.

Because of the limited floor space and wide array of merchandise, inventories must be tightly controlled. Using central computers in Dallas, Southland is able to determine which items to stock and what prices to charge. In addition, it is possible to analyze the operations of each store in the system in terms of profitability, inventory turnover, and so forth.

Even before the recent crisis, the ability of the Southland Corporation to respond to changing conditions had been proven by the company's experience with gasoline marketing. In 1972, only 200 7-Eleven stores sold gasoline; but by the mid-1970s, when gasoline prices skyrocketed due to the Arab oil embargo, the self-service pumps at 7-Eleven stores had become very popular. The company began to relocate a few stores from the traditional midblock location to corners, a proven marketing technique for gasoline stations. The corner locations produced 50 percent extra sales. Of several thousand stores added since the mid-

1970s, almost all sell gasoline and almost all are on corners. Although gasoline produces a very small profit margin for 7-Eleven, gasoline customers must come inside to pay, and many make purchases other than gasoline.

QUESTIONS

1. What controlling techniques are used at 7-Eleven stores?
2. How have environmental factors affected the controlling process at 7-Eleven?

CASE 16.2 A Problem of Shrinkage

Martha Young is the supervisor of ten stores in a convenience store chain. Each of these small stores has a day manager and two assistant managers who work the evening and midnight shifts. These "managers" are mistitled; they have no subordinates reporting directly to them. The day manager is typically the senior person, and thus has chosen the day shift.

Mark McCall is the day manager of one of the stores. He has worked at the store for three months, and sales have been increasing steadily. Mark maintains his store in good order, and the first two monthly inventory checks have been satisfactory. But as Martha reads the inventory report for this month, she becomes quite disturbed. Inventory is $1,000 short over the previous month (anything over $200 is considered out of the ordinary). Such a discrepancy is called *shrinkage*.

Martha realizes that this report is extremely serious. Other managers have been dismissed for inventory shortages of this amount. She likes Mark, but something must be done to keep this situation from occurring in the future. Martha sits down and reviews the store's situation. The following points come to mind:

- The store is located close to a school. When Mark took control of the store, school was not in session. There might be some shoplifting occurring.
- One of the assistant managers has been with the store only a month. There is a possibility of internal theft.
- The other assistant manager broke up with his girlfriend last month. It is possible that he has not been paying close attention to his job.

QUESTIONS

1. What type of controls, if any, should Martha initiate?
2. If the inventory is short next month, what do you think Martha should do?

NOTES

1. This case is a composite of a number of published accounts, among them: Barbara Marsh, "Going for the Golden Arches," *The Wall Street Journal* (May 1, 1989): B1; Leon E. Wynter, "How Two Black Franchisees Owe Success to McDonald's," *The Wall Street Journal* (July 25, 1989): B1, B2; Brian Bremner, "Two Big Macs, Large Fries—and a Pepperoni Pizza, Please," *Business Week* (August 7, 1989): 33; Brian Bremner, "The Burger Wars Were Just a Warmup for McDonald's," *Business Week* (May 8, 1989): 67–70; Peter Pae, "Salad Bar Is Poised to Make Fast Exit from Fast Food," *The Wall Street Journal* (March 24, 1989): B1, B3; John A. Byrne, "Is Your Company Too Big?" *Business Week* (March 27, 1989): 84–94; Debi Sue Edmund, "The Secret Behind the Big Mac? It's Simple!" *Management Review* 79 (May 1990): 32–33; Lois Therrien, "McRisky," *Business Week* (October 21, 1991): 114–122; Standard and Poor's Corp., "McDonald's Corp.," *Standard NYSE Stock Reports* 56 (May 10, 1989), sec. 22; and Joan Goldwasser, "McDonald's: 95 Billion Burgers Served and a Lot More to Come," *Kiplinger's Personal Finance Magazine* 47 (January 1993): 32.
2. Aaron Bernstein, "AT&T: The Making of a Comeback," *Business Week* (January 18, 1988): 56–62.

3. Manuel Werner, "Great Paradox: Responsibility Without Empowerment," *Business Horizons* 35 (September–October 1992): 55–58.

4. R. Wayne Mondy, Robert M. Noe III, and Robert E. Edwards, "What the Staffing Function Entails," *Personnel* 63 (April 1986): 55.

5. Jill Andresky Fraser, "Women, Power, and the New GE," *Working Women* 17 (December 1992): 58–63.

6. Peter Coy, "Big Brother, Pinned to Your Chest," *Business Week* (August 17, 1992): 38.

7. David N. Campbell, R. L. Fleming, and Richard C. Grote, "Discipline Without Punishment—At Last," *Harvard Business Review* 63 (July–August 1985): 168.

8. Robert N. Anthony and Regina E. Herzlinger, *Management Control in Nonprofit Organizations* (Homewood, IL: Irwin, 1975) pp. 222–226.

9. Gordon Shillinglaw, *Managerial Cost Accounting: Analysis and Control,* 4th ed. (Homewood, IL: Irwin, 1977) pp. 142–143.

10. Penny Moser, "The McDonald's Mystique," *Fortune* 123 (July 4, 1988): 112–116.

11. The following section was adapted from Jay Heizer and Barry Render, *Production and Operations Management: Strategies and Tactics* 3d ed. (Boston: Allyn and Bacon, 1993): 745.

12. Peter Coy, "Big Brother, Pinned to Your Chest," 38.

13. David Woodruff, James B. Treece, Sunita Wadekar Bhargava, and Karen Lowry Miller, "Saturn," *Business Week* (August 17, 1992): 89; "Buick City Places Suppliers in Backyard," *Purchasing* 10 (November 1983): 15.

14. Otis Port, "The Push for Quality," *Business Week* (June 8, 1989): 134.

15. Subrata N. Chakravarty and Amy Feldman, "Don't Underestimate the Champ," *Forbes* 151 (May 10, 1993): 106–110.

17 Total Quality Management

LEARNING OBJECTIVES

After completing this chapter students should be able to

✘ Explain the history of Total Quality Management (TQM).

✘ Describe the objectives of TQM.

✘ Explain the concept of quality and TQM, and discuss some tools for problem solving.

✘ Describe the approaches to implementing TQM.

✘ Discuss the components of TQM.

✘ Describe some managerial mistakes in implementing TQM.

Total Quality Management: Is It the Real Competitive Advantage?

Throughout the seventies, many American companies tried to increase their competitiveness by imitating the Japanese, but that effort fell short. In the eighties, many companies organized workers into quality circles "as a kind of magic solution," but this concept was ineffective because "companies didn't recognize that such concepts are simply one methodology within a much larger concept of quality." Today most major American companies have *total quality* programs that integrate every department from manufacturing to marketing and research in the effort to improve. This so-called system of Total Quality Management (TQM) has thus far been effective at allowing companies to gain a "Quality Edge."

In recognition of the quest for quality, two trophies stand out: America's Baldrige award and the Deming prize from Japan. To win either award, companies must sweat through long hours of mind-numbing paperwork to prove that they are more thorough, more profitable, and simply better companies, whose watchword is "Quality." In the late eighties major companies such as 3M, IBM, Xerox, and Motorola dominated the ranks of Baldrige National Quality Award winners.

However, in 1991 all three winners of the Malcolm Baldrige National Quality Award were not the giants that everyone recognizes, but rather were small or midsize companies with little public recognition: Marlow Industries, Solectron, and Zytec. Two more such companies won in 1992—Granite Rock Company and Ritz-Carlton Hotel Company. The reason for the increase in applicants from small and midsize companies is not only the recognized benefits of TQM, but also that large companies such as Motorola are pressuring suppliers to prove their quality credentials or risk being dropped.

It is possible that the TQM glow is starting to dim. In a recent survey of 500 manufacturing and service companies that use TQM, only 36 percent believed that TQM was significantly improving their competitiveness. Many respondents also believed that TQM failure was often due to improper implementation. With TQM all aspects including quality must be linked to the bottom line. Just implementing quality techniques, empowering employees, and benchmarking strategies will not guarantee success. Careful planning must take place ahead of time for TQM to succeed. Examples of the acceptance of TQM in the United States abound, but what remains to be seen is whether a company can really survive in the nineties without embracing the concepts of TQM or whether TQM is just another passing trend.[1]

What has occurred at 3M, IBM, Xerox, and Motorola is happening in organizations throughout the United States, and indeed the world. It is quite possible that organizations that fail to pick up the quality baton and run with it now stand a good chance of becoming second-class players in our rapidly changing global environment.

In this chapter, we will first cover the essence of Total Quality Management. Then, the history of TQM will be addressed, followed by a discussion of the objectives of TQM. Next, the focal point of TQM, quality, will be reviewed and tools for problem solving discussed. Approaches to implementing TQM will be explored, followed by a discussion of the components of TQM. Finally, an example of TQM is provided to help explain the concept in practice and some managerial mistakes in implementing TQM are described. The chapter closes with a global perspective regarding TQM.

Total Quality Management (TQM) is a commitment to excellence by everyone in an organization that emphasizes excellence achieved by teamwork and a process of continuous improvement. Today most companies have "total quality" programs that integrate every department from manufacturing to marketing and research in the effort to improve. Implied in the concept is a commitment to be the best and to provide the highest quality products and services that meet or exceed the hopes of the customer. Businesses are making many changes to stay competitive. They are constantly seeking ways to improve quality, increase speed of operations, and adopt a customer orientation. These changes are so fundamental that they must take root in a company's very essence, which means in its culture. George Fisher, CEO, believes Motorola can compete effectively with AT&T by focusing on total quality. "We've got the fundamentals much more in place now than ever in the history of the company to compete around the world. The fundamentals of TQM are pretty simple, but Motorola has really focused on those in the last many years: quality, product manufacturing cycle time, product leadership, the ability to produce at the lowest cost."[2] Putting the TQM culture into place at Motorola meant changing the attitudes of management and employees toward teamwork and participative management.

TQM often involves major cultural changes, such as those that took place at Motorola. It requires a new way of thinking and strong leadership at all levels. Individuals throughout the organization must be inspired to do things differently. They must understand what needs to be done and why, and this takes strong leadership. Motorola management increased quality with the implementation of a TQM system, which paid off for them in a big way.

❖ ❖ HISTORY OF TOTAL QUALITY MANAGEMENT

TQM had its beginning in the 1930s with the pioneering work of Walter A. Shewart, who acted as a mentor to W. Edwards Deming. The concept really got a lift in World War II when the Allied cause was suffering. Shewart's method made quality a science. It also replaced traditional end-line inspection with an "on-line" awareness of variation. This process proved key to the war effort—so much so that at one point the techniques became military secrets. Basically, America's defense needs gave birth to a highly guarded and valuable "body of knowledge." When the war ended, the files were opened to the public, but by that time the interest in quality was fading in the United States. However, the country it had just defeated would soon embrace the concept of quality.[3]

Deming took his message to Japan in the 1950s and is credited with being instrumental in turning Japanese industry into an economic world power. He said, "Improve quality and you automatically improve productivity. You capture the market with lower prices and better quality. You stay in business and you produce jobs. It's so simple."[4] Deming applied Shewart's principles of statistical process control in Japan and convinced the Japanese to do more than merely monitor the quality level of their manufacturing systems. He worked with their scientists, engineers, and managers to identify and remove the causes of variation. As we know, the Japanese were able to improve quality and productivity, capture world market share, add jobs, and improve the standard of living in their country. In a matter of 40 years, the Japanese rose from the ashes of World War II and became a powerful economic force throughout the world. As you might expect, Deming is a hero in Japan. Today Deming, who is over 90 years of age, remains the dean of Total Quality Management.[5]

J. M. Juran arrived in Japan shortly after Deming and built an equally impressive record around quality planning, quality control, and quality improvement. Although Juran and Deming appear to have mutual respect for one another, Juran believes that Deming is basically a statistician "a bit out of place talking about management."[6] However, both leaders in TQM have had a major influence in championing quality. The basic message of both is essentially the same:

- Commit to quality improvement throughout your organization.
- Attack the processes, not the employees.
- Strip down the process to find and eliminate problems that diminish quality.
- Identify your customers and satisfy their requirements.
- Instill teamwork and create an atmosphere for innovation and permanent quality improvement.[7]

Both Deming and Juran had been promoting TQM for many years before Philip B. Crosby entered the field in 1979. Since that time, Crosby has had amazing success in the United States, Europe, and even Japan. His approach is based on four concepts:

- Quality means conformance to requirements.
- Defect prevention—not inspection—is the way to achieve quality.
- The only acceptable quality standard is one that tolerates zero defects.
- The cost of poor quality—in warranty payments, excess inventory, engineering errors, and other money eaters—can amount to 25 percent of sales at manufacturing companies and up to 40 percent of operating costs at service companies.[8]

Although highly successful, some have criticized Crosby for lacking substance, being more inspirational than practical, and being more of a public relations person than a quality control advocate.[9]

❖ ❖ THE OBJECTIVES OF TQM

As world market share shifted away from U.S. producers, forward-thinking American managers recognized the necessity for change. Since 1960, more than half of the world market share had been lost to other international producers in a number of product lines. These lines included athletic equipment, automobiles, cameras, computer chips, industrial robots, medical equipment, optical equipment, radial tires, stereos, and television sets. Something had to be done, so TQM was employed.

The ultimate goal of TQM is to alter the process by improving customer satisfaction. Instead of being content with the status quo, employees at all levels continually seek alternative methods or technologies that will improve existing processes. TQM provides a strategy for reducing the causes of poor quality and thereby increases productivity.

The increased employee participation required by TQM creates a new role for all organizational members. (Source: © John Coletti)

TQM is a process of continuously improving quality over the long run. In the short run, once each of the linked processes within a firm is operating at or above a desired level of quality, reliance on costly inspection practices can be reduced or eliminated altogether. Attention can then be turned to monitoring the overall process to determine the sources of variation still present. If these sources are also eliminated, then the process can be more precise and fewer defects or errors produced. In the customer's view, quality will have exceeded the expected level. The customer, more than satisfied, will probably remain a customer. Motorola has been so successful with TQM in Japan that they are taking market share from the Japanese.

The increased employee participation required by TQM creates a new role for all organizational members. Top management, middle managers, first-level supervisors, and all workers must embrace the philosophy and work to ensure its acceptance throughout the organization.

Quality is a universally acknowledged factor in successful businesses. According to Allen F. Jacobsen, chairman of the board and chief executive officer of 3M, "I'm convinced that the winners of the 1990s will be companies that make quality and customer service an obsession in every single market [in which] they operate."[10] Operative employees are consulted for assistance in determining and analyzing sources of process variation, and they are relied on to develop proposals for reducing or eliminating them.

Cultural change must precede or accompany the introduction of total quality management. And the organizational culture required to support the concepts of TQM is not likely to be changed quickly. Five to ten years is generally needed for such changes in the top management value system to permeate the organization. TQM is not a body of regulations, and it cannot be forced on employees. Since a company's culture is largely a product of positively reinforced behavior, the route to change is almost always through education and training.[11] In addition to training and development activities, employee selection practices will be a central component in implementing the TQM philosophy.

Several factors favor the growth of TQM in the United States. First, and perhaps most important, is the success of companies who embrace TQM. They are capturing world market share from traditionally managed organizations. Second, consumers are no longer satisfied with lower quality levels even if the products or services are labeled "Made in America." Third, national trade policy is decidedly against imposing trade restrictions of any kind to protect U.S. producers from international competitors, so American companies must actually compete. The passage of NAFTA further reinforced this competition-centered policy.

A fourth factor is the support and encouragement of the U.S. government for the TQM movement. In 1987, Congress created the Malcolm Baldrige National Quality Award. This award recognizes outstanding firms in both the manufacturing and service sectors for their quality management programs. In addition, the federal government is now requiring contractors bidding on federal jobs to provide evidence of the statistical control of their processes. These contractors are requiring similar evidence from their subcontractors. Finally, as was mentioned in the opening vignette, many large companies such as Motorola are pressuring suppliers to prove their quality credentials or risk being dropped.

The TQM movement began over a decade ago in this country. However, many firms, including 3M, IBM, Xerox, Motorola, Ford Motor Company, Florida Power and Light, and Federal Express, have demonstrated a long history of commitment toward improving quality. These firms have been recognized both in the United States and abroad for their efforts. As Robert Costello, former undersecretary of defense for acquisition, stated, "The ultimate goal is to ingrain basic cultural change to a depth where the slogan TQM will fade and, in its wake, the principles and practices of TQM will remain as a permanent, normal way of conducting business in the United States."[12] A summary of the differences between TQM and traditional management may be seen in Table 17.1.

❖ ❖ QUALITY AND TQM

The concept of quality in a TQM environment is based on the customer being served to the maximum degree possible. Quality means the product meets all requirements. At one time, Xerox lacked an understanding of what its customers

TABLE 17.1 The Differences Between TQM and Traditional Management

TQM	TRADITIONAL MANAGEMENT
Customer focus	Management focus
Quality first	Profits first
Multiple quality dimensions	Single quality dimension
Management and worker involvement	No worker involvement
Process-oriented	Results-oriented

(Source: Laurence M. Tobin, "The New Quality Landscape: Total Quality Management," *Journal of Systems Management* 41 [November 1990]: 13.)

really needed, not just wanted. To best satisfy consumers, Xerox turned to a full commitment to TQM and thereby regained its competitive advantage.

Adherence to the concepts of TQM means that before any product is produced, the producer must first know precisely the requirements the product must meet. Only those products that meet all of the conditions are produced and delivered to the customer. A product that meets 99 out of 100 requirements is defective and should not be shipped to the customer.

The concept of quality differs with the type of company involved. For example, the definition of quality would be different at McDonald's than it would be at the Ritz in Paris. The seller must understand the customer. Even a perfect product cannot do more than it was designed to do. A Chevy should not outperform a Rolls even if both are perfect. However, the customer should be able to get what he or she is willing to pay for, and maybe a little more.

With TQM, how a process is implemented is as important as what the process includes. Many organizations still work under a departmentalized approach in which some employees plan improvements, others carry out the work, and still others inspect to see if procedures and results are correct. With TQM, all employees are committed to improving the quality of their product or service so that customers' needs are not only met but exceeded. Under Motorola's "Six Sigma" quality program, everyone in the company is working together toward defect-free manufacturing that would lead to an unheard-of degree of consumer satisfaction.[13]

Until recently, many efforts to improve and gain a competitive advantage were delayed by the mistaken belief that better quality costs more.[14] Dean Cassell, vice-president for Product Integrity at Geuman Corporation, disagrees. Cassell believes that speed and quality are not tradeoffs, but rather speed is a component of quality. According to Cassell, many customers require a faster response time, and that means speed is important.[15] The historical approach was to add more inspection steps. In an inspection-oriented plant, more than half of all workers are somehow involved in finding and reworking rejects.[16] A company using TQM should inspect a product in the design phase. The product is engineered in the manufacturing process to be stable and reliable. As Genichi Taguchi, one of Japan's masters said, "To improve quality, you need to look upstream in the design stage. At the customer level, it's too late."[17]

TQM accomplishes just what Taguchi suggested. Under a system of TQM, managers are looking upstream to improve quality by focusing on the design stage, before the product reaches the customer level. When TQM is used, firms design quality into the product. Less emphasis is given to inspection and more emphasis is given to "front-end" planning and design. Certainly TQM does not advocate elimination of all inspection. Eliminating the cause of a defect is more important than continuing to reject defective parts. Josh Hammond, president of the American Quality Foundation, responded to a study in which more than half the U.S. companies reported that executive pay will soon be pegged in part to quality.[18] At Texaco, salaries are already pegged to performance; the result has been a resurgence of the company.

❖ ❖ TOOLS FOR PROBLEM SOLVING

A TQM culture encourages more employee participation in problem solving and decision making. TQM will not work unless each and every employee is trained to use problem-solving tools. A culture of continuous improvement is synonymous with a problem-solving culture. Any problem-solving procedure begins, obviously, with a problem. But where does the recognition of this problem come from? Historically, problems are brought to light by means such as control charts, and by customers, inspectors, managers, and sometimes workers. In the TQM environment, it is best if workers call attention to a problem. However, workers traditionally are not trained to solve problems. As those working closest to the problems, they must be trained to use basic problem-solving tools such as team building, brainstorming, process analysis, cause-and-effect diagrams, and Pareto analysis. Team building and brainstorming have already received considerable attention and will not be discussed further here.

Process Analysis

One goal of TQM is to reduce variation. A method of reducing variation is to standardize procedures. Often three people doing the same job will have developed three different procedures with three different outputs.

It will not be possible to improve any TQM process until that process is fully understood and standardized to some degree. After the team has broken down the process into all of its component steps, possible causes for the problem can be identified at each step. Then, possible solutions can be discussed and tested before being put into place. Several graphic methods that are used to understand the process are discussed in Chapter 19.

Cause-and-Effect Diagram

The **cause-and-effect diagram**—sometimes called the **Ishikawa diagram,** after one of the leading Japanese contributors to TQM—is used to classify and present the ideas from brainstorming in a manner more likely to lead to solving the problem at hand. A common form of the cause-and-effect diagram is the fishbone diagram. In a fishbone diagram, the problem is placed at the "head," a "spine" is drawn, and all the causes branch off the spine. The problem with the fishbone diagram is that it fails to classify the causes in any way. In TQM, the four primary causes of variation are human resource power, methods, materials, and machines. It is more valuable to alter the fishbone diagram to reflect each of these causes.

Pareto Analysis

Of the numerous things that can go wrong in a process, many cannot be fixed or prevented because of time and budget limitations. **Pareto analysis** is based on the Pareto distribution, which in its original analysis says that five percent of the people control 50 percent of the wealth, or that 20 percent control 80 percent of the wealth—this type of analysis is used to help decide which problems are most important to study. The ABC classification system presented in Chapter 16 was a form of Pareto analysis.

In TQM, where the focus is on problems, all of the problems identified during brainstorming and listed on the cause-and-effect diagram will not occur with equal frequency. It turns out that their rate of occurrence follows the Pareto distribution, most commonly stated in the form of the 20-80 rule.

A Pareto analysis consists of four steps:

Step 1. List all of the potential causes.
Step 2. Monitor the process for an appropriate time period to see how often each cause occurs.
Step 3. Rank the causes from greatest to least importance.
Step 4. Draw the Pareto chart, a bar chart showing frequency of occurrence.

A Pareto chart is shown in Figure 17.1. It should be obvious that having inadequate parts—represented by the tallest bar—is the problem most urgently in

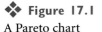

❖ **Figure 17.1**

A Pareto chart

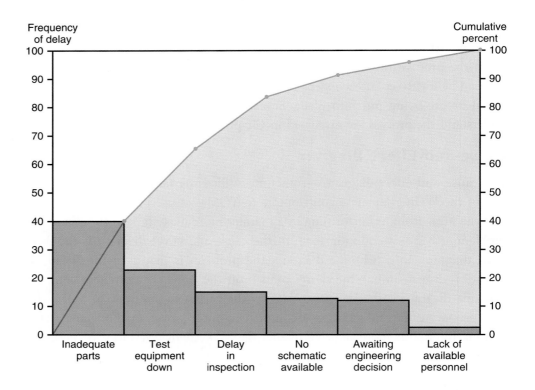

need of a solution. The Pareto chart goes beyond selecting the one problem to concentrate on in the near term. The sequence of problems on the chart provides a longer-term basis for planning process improvement.[19]

❖ ❖ APPROACHES TO IMPLEMENTING TQM

There are several approaches to implementing TQM, and all have been used successfully. The approaches to TQM that are discussed here include the TQM Element Approach, the Guru Approach, the Industrial Company Model Approach, and Next Generation.

The TQM Element Approach

This approach was used primarily in the early 1980s and employs elements of quality improvement programs such as quality circles and statistical process control, rather than full implementation of TQM.

Quality Circles Quality circles (QCs) are small groups of employees who get together on company time to develop ways to improve the quality and quantity of work. Quality circles encourage workers to use their energy and creativity to solve the company's—and the workers'—problems. The concept of quality cir-

ETHICAL DILEMMA

Total Quality Management (TQM) dictates that everyone in an organization accept working in teams and that these individuals accept a process of continuous quality improvement. When the Saturn company developed its revolutionary approach to car manufacturing, all of the General Motors employees selected were considered to be quite adaptable, able to work in teams, and in command of excellent communication skills. Additionally, only those perceived as committed to "Quality" were selected.[20] In an environment where total quality dictates, and in times where personnel cutbacks are a reality of business, this approach raises several ethical and employee responsibility issues. Are managers really capable of judging who has the desired characteristics? Also, since old line employees make more money and are usually considered to be less flexible in terms of retrenchment, will these individuals naturally be cut as a twofold cost-savings measure? Immediate savings are found in keeping both less highly paid employees and those who are more likely to readily accept retraining. You are in charge of selecting employees for a new plant where TQM will rule. Your boss has strongly implied that the lower-paid younger employees are probably the best choice for the new workforce. She has also stated that the more costly higher-paid employees who survive must be more productive in the new environment to justify their higher wages. Furthermore, according to her, you will be responsible for assuring the enhanced productivity.

What would you do?

cles is as relevant today as it was in the early 1980s. Even though this approach has proven effective, it has yet to be accepted by those in the service industries, which account for more than 70 percent of the employees in the United States.[21]

Statistical Process Control (SPC) One technique for meeting manufacturing standards is called statistical process control, or SPC. Basically, **statistical process control** gauges the performance of the manufacturing process by carefully monitoring changes in whatever is being produced. The goal is to detect potential defects before they result in off-quality products, then pinpoint the reason for the deviation and adjust the process to make it more stable. AT&T, Corning Glass, du Pont, Ford, Hewlett-Packard, IBM, Kodak, and Westinghouse are frequently cited as leaders in management by quality.

While statistical process control is not new in the United States, its focus had been to monitor rather than improve manufacturing systems. It had become normal to expect and even accept a certain percentage of defective products. This attitude necessitated conducting extensive inspection testing in order to identify the defects and either remove or rework them. All of this added to manufacturing costs, did little to improve quality, and lessened America's competitive position in world markets. Managers incorrectly perceived that the quality was satisfactory if products were not being returned, if complaints were not received, and if the price/performance ratio for the customer was improved.[22] Dissatisfaction with the element approach has led many firms to move to the guru approach.

The Guru Approach

This approach uses the writings of a guru such as Deming, Juran, or Crosby as a benchmark to determine what the organization lacks, and then uses the guru's system to make changes. Deming's 14-point model is one example of a guru's approach that has been widely embraced in America as well as in Japan.

1. Create constancy of purpose for improvement of product and service.
2. Adopt the new philosophy.
3. Cease dependence on mass inspection.
4. End the practice of awarding business on price tag alone.
5. Improve constantly and forever the system of production and service.
6. Institute training.
7. Institute leadership.
8. Drive out fear.
9. Break down barriers between staff areas.
10. Eliminate slogans, exhortations, and targets for the workforce.
11. Eliminate numerical quotas.
12. Remove barriers to pride of workmanship.

Quality circles are small groups of employees who get together on company time to develop ways to improve the quality and quantity of work.
(Source: © John Coletti)

MANAGEMENT IN PRACTICE

A Skill-Building Exercise: "Our fully integrated operations ensure exacting control over every phase of engineering, testing, and production—everything right down to final inspection," read the annual report of Stratton Corporation. Stratton had been continuously profitable for decades. Declared vice president Lonnie Phelps, "We will consider automation wherever possible, practical, and economical; but if you are talking about one of those unmanned factories, you'll never see our operation all automated like that."

Stratton made small gasoline engines, up to 18 horsepower. Almost all parts—engine castings, starters, alternators, ignition coils, and carburetors—were made in the Stratton factory. Unlike manufacturers who use components supplied by subcontractors, Stratton had to absorb the impact of any sales decline in-house. Far from throwing in the towel, Stratton quadrupled the advertising budget. Phelps promised, "We are not going to let the Japanese take this market from us."
What would be your response?

13. Institute a vigorous program of education and retraining.
14. Take action to accomplish the transformation.[23]

Organizations using this method focus on the Japanese Deming prize winners as a way to develop an implementation master plan. Japan's Deming prize symbolizes the excellence of Japanese quality. The prize, named after W. Edwards Deming, was established when Deming started donating lecture fees to the Union of Japanese Scientists and Engineers (JUSE) in 1951. They decided to use the funds to establish the prize. JUSE offered its first seminar in English in 1988 to such companies as Motorola, Volvo, Rolls-Royce, Dow Chemical, and Xerox.

With this approach, corporations try to duplicate the basics of Japanese quality management, popularly known as *total quality control.* Total quality control was first mentioned in an article published by Armand Feigenbaum entitled "Total Quality Control." Feigenbaum echoes the essence of TQM: "Quality is everybody's job." This approach focuses on fine-tuning an entire firm to make it as adaptable to changes in customer demands and market conditions as possible. A firm's management must continually analyze its strengths and weaknesses to allow improvement in processes. Although the prize is popular in nature, some companies have decided not to pursue it because of its strict guidelines.

Other lesser-known quality gurus who contributed in various ways to TQM and who have been briefly mentioned are Armand Feigenbaum, Kaoru Ishikawa, and Genichi Taguchi. Armand Feigenbaum recognized that statistics provided a "body of knowledge" for quality. As mentioned previously, he is responsible for adding a new concept to the idea of quality, in his article entitled "Total Quality Control." Feigenbaum also believed that design and material control departments had a responsibility to see what was producible on the shop floor. He also pointed out that quality is a technology that can be systemized and taught.

Kaoru Ishikawa strongly believed that every top manager's business is quality. He simplified the statistical methods of Deming into "Seven Tools," charts that any factory worker could use. These tools, such as Pareto charts, histograms, and scatter diagrams, are now part of America's TQM resources. According to Ishikawa, 95 percent of the problems that surface can be solved by utilizing these resources.

Genichi Taguchi focused mainly on the design stage of the process. Taguchi referred to his practice as "quality engineering." He was primarily concerned with the "losses" a product imparts to society from the time it is shipped to the consumer. To limit losses, quality must be designed into each product.

The Industrial Company Model Approach

This approach requires individuals to visit a U.S. industrial company that uses TQM, identify its successes, and integrate this information with their own ideas to create a customized approach. This method was used in the late 1980s by many of the Baldrige National Quality Award winners.

With the Baldrige approach, an organization uses criteria for the Malcolm Baldrige National Quality Award to identify areas of improvement. To apply for the award, a company must document, in no more than 75 data-filled pages, general statements such as the following:

• Top executives incorporate quality values into day-to-day management.

Winners of the Baldrige Award have a clear commitment to ultimate quality. These companies embrace the idea of total quality management because they want a competitive advantage.

- The company is working with suppliers to improve the quality of their products or services.
- The company trains workers in quality techniques and has systems in place to ensure that products are high quality.
- Their products are as good as or better than those of their competitors.
- Customer needs and wants are being met, and customer satisfaction ratings are as good as or better than those of competitors.
- The quality system yields concrete results, such as gains in market share and reduction in product-cycle time.

Once an application is submitted, examiners award points for accomplishments in the award criteria. Top scorers receive site visits by senior examiners, who then make recommendations to a panel of judges. As many as two winners each may be picked from the categories of manufacturing, services, and small business. 3M, Xerox, and Motorola are three such winners.

In 1991, all three winners of the Malcolm Baldrige National Quality Award were small or midsize companies: Marlow Industries, Solectron, and Zytec. Two more won in 1992—Granite Rock Company and Ritz-Carlton Hotel Company. The reason for the increase in applicants from small and midsize companies is that large companies such as Motorola are pressuring suppliers to prove their quality credentials or risk being dropped.[24] Regardless of the techniques utilized, the success of TQM is dependent upon a commitment to excellence by everyone in an organization. TQM also requires teamwork and a process of continuous improvement.

3M, Xerox, and Motorola Are Committed to Total Quality Management

3M, Xerox, and Motorola have all won America's number one award for quality, the Baldrige award. Besides being winners of the Baldrige National Quality Award for excellence in the area of Total Quality Management, 3M, Xerox, and Motorola have a strong sense that TQM is the best competitive tool available. These companies embrace the idea of TQM because they want a competitive advantage. 3M turned to TQM to achieve "uniform quality across the whole system." 3M's approach to TQM is so successful that it is being marketed to other corporations. George M. C. Fisher, chairman of Motorola Inc., used TQM to overtake the Japanese in the cellular-phone/pager market, plus other communication equipment. Xerox manufacturing costs were too high, its overhead was too large, and the organization was too complicated; then Xerox turned to TQM and regained its competitive edge. Today, few U.S. companies can match Motorola's devotion to quality, and the results of its commitment to TQM have been overwhelming. Examples of the acceptance of TQM in the United States abound, but what remains to be seen is whether a company can really survive in the nineties *without* embracing the concepts of TQM.[25]

❖ ❖ COMPONENTS OF TQM[26]

TQM is a structural system for creating organization-wide participation in planning and implementing a continuous improvement process that *exceeds* the expectations of the customer or client. It is built on the assumption that 90 percent of our problems are process problems, not employee problems. However, it is important that the ten percent related to human problems is not ignored because this could have a negative impact on the components of TQM. The three major components of TQM that address process problems are breakthrough planning, daily management, and cross-functional management.

Breakthrough Planning

Breakthrough planning is an extension of strategic planning (see Figure 17.2). It has the following purposes:

- Clarify a vision of where the organization wants to go in the next five or ten years.

❖ **Figure 17.2**
Breakthrough planning (Source: L. Edwin Coate, *Implementing Total Quality Management in a University Setting* [Oregon State University Press, July 1990], p. 5. Used with permission.)

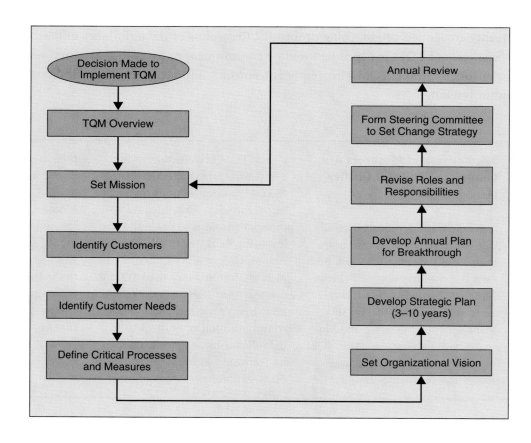

- Identify objectives that move the organization toward its vision.
- Identify critical processes that must deliver the product or services provided to clients in a way that exceeds their expectations.
- Select a few (no more than four) breakthrough items that can help the organization reach its vision quickly.
- Communicate this vision and the methods by which it will be met to all employees.
- Provide a structure for monitoring progress toward the vision.

Daily Management

This system shows people what they personally must do, and what they must measure and control, to keep the organization running smoothly. It helps them define and understand the processes they use in producing goods and services to meet customers' needs and expectations. Once these processes are understood, individuals and departments can continuously improve them, then standardize the improvements to ensure that gains are maintained.

This continuous improvement is achieved by problem-solving teams who engage in identifying customer problems, finding solutions, and then providing ongoing control of the improved process. Use of several basic quality control tests and statistical methods helps people manage with facts, not opinions, and solve the real problems, not just the symptoms. Problem solving requires the collective efforts of everyone in the organization.

Daily management is the most revolutionary of the three components of TQM. It empowers employees at all levels of the organization and focuses management improvement efforts on process problems.

Cross-Functional Management

This is the integration of team activities across divisions or departments to achieve organizational objectives. It is the vehicle for breaking down departmental and divisional barriers. Through cross-functional management, top-level managers can ensure that all groups in the organization are working together for the good of the institution. This system leads the organization to listen to the "voice of the customer," identify customer needs, and incorporate those needs into every phase of the firm's operation.

❖ ❖ ❖ TQM: AN EXAMPLE[27]

Early in 1990, Oregon State University set out to find its own answer to a question being asked by a growing number of colleges and universities across the

United States: How adaptable are the quality management methods of W. Edwards Deming, J. M. Juran, and Philip Crosby to higher education?

It is obvious that manufacturing processes are far more predictable and controllable than the learning process. As OSU's top management explored Total Quality Management, they realized that TQM principles should not be applied without a period of research, adaptation, training, and pilot testing in the actual university setting. It was decided that testing could best be conducted in OSU's service areas, many of which have counterparts in industry. Administrative units such as physical plant, business affairs, and printing and mailing could more readily adapt techniques of quality improvement to their processes. What they learned from their experience could be applied to the more complex issues of adapting TQM to the university's academic side.

The Pilot Program

During breakthrough planning, an initial step in implementing TQM, OSU's top management identified the 12 critical processes basic to carrying out the university's mission. The vice-president and the division directors for finance and

❖ **Figure 17.3**
OSU's critical processes: Finance and administration detail (Source: L. Edwin Coate, *An Analysis of Oregon State University's Total Quality Management Pilot Program* [Oregon State University Press, November 1990], p. 3. Used with permission.)

Vice President for Finance & Administration: Critical Processes

Fiscal Services | Information Services | Workforce Hiring & Development | Long-Range Planning | Budgeting | Community Relations | Facilities Management | Law Enforcement | Safety

Business Affairs
*Accounting
Property Control
Travel & Transport
*Fiscal Services
Telecommunications
Purchasing
Contracting
Risk Management

Computing Service
Maintaining Hardware
Computer Purchasing
*Networking
Training
Developing Standards

Printing & Mailing
Accounting
*Printing
Quick Copy
U.S. Mailing Services
Blank Paper Sales

Human Resources
Hiring
Labor Relations
Staff Development
Position Classification
Personnel Reporting
*Benefits
Administration
Workers' Comp.
    Claims Management

Radiation Center
Teaching
Research
*Technical Services

Facilities
*Maintenance
  & Repair
*Remodeling
  & Construction
Delivery Service

Facilities Planning
Campus Planning
Facilities Allocation
Capital Construction

University Police
Criminal Law
  Enforcement
Traffic Law
  Enforcement

Security
*Security
Parking

Environmental
Health & Safety
Information
  Dissemination
Compliance
  Monitoring
Technical Services

Budget & Planning
Long-Range Planning
Archiving/Records
  Management
Data Analysis
Budgeting
Policy Communication

Institutional Research
  and Planning
Information Gathering
Information
  Dissemination
Long-Range Planning

* Denotes Pilot Team

administration followed the same method to identify critical processes for their unit and for each division. These processes became the basis for the work of the pilot TQM study teams (see Figure 17.3).

Pilot TQM Teams OSU's early exploration of TQM had convinced management that teams are the very heart of TQM.[28] Better solutions emerge, are implemented faster, and last longer when the people affected help develop them.

TQM Study Teams Study teams are composed of people who normally work together on the process being reviewed. They are led by someone from the natural work group, typically the supervisor, and are assisted by a facilitator.

Teams usually work with processes that can be improved with resources they control. Teams are kept small (no more than ten), and each has a sponsor, usually the group's division director. The sponsor ensures that the team's work is linked to the university's critical process and moves the university toward its vision.

Ten Teams Formed The divisions of finance and administration formed ten pilot TQM teams (see Figure 17.4). Each sponsor assigned the team a study issue or problem related to one of his or her division's critical processes.

Leaders and facilitators of the teams received about 18 hours' training in TQM from a consultant. The consultant and the university's staff development officer then served as "coaches," providing "just-in-time" training to team members as they moved through TQM problem-solving steps.

Ten-Step Problem-Solving Process

OSU teams used a ten-step TQM problem-solving model to guide their study (see Figure 17.5). The process begins with the customer, focuses on root causes of problems, and ensures that decisions and actions are based on real data.

> **Step One. At the sponsor level,** opportunities for improvement that relate to the team's critical process are identified and team members who have ownership in that process are selected.
> **Step Two. Key customers** are surveyed to find out which services provided by the process are not meeting their expectations.
> **Step Three. The most important** customer issue or problem is selected and a clear issue statement is prepared.
> **Step Four. A flow diagram** is prepared, showing the process as it is now.
> **Step Five. A process performance measure** is established to track progress in meeting or exceeding customer expectations.
> **Step Six. Probable causes** of the problem are identified.

❖ **Figure 17.4**
Pilot TQM teams in finance and administration (Source: L. Edwin Coate, *An Analysis of Oregon State University's Total Quality Management Pilot Program* [Oregon State University Press, November 1990], p. 4. Used with permission.)

Team, Division		Critical Process	Issue Statement
1A	Physical Plant	Facilities Management	Reduce the amount of time it takes to complete the remodeling process.
1B	Physical Plant	Facilities Management	Improve servicing of fixed equipment.
2	Printing	Information Services	Reduce the amount of time in the prepress stage of the printing process.
3	Budgets and Planning	Budgeting	Increase the timeliness of the Budget-Status-at-a-Glance report development process.
4	Computing Services	Information Services	Increase the timeliness and consistent delivery of network information.
5A	Business Affairs	Fiscal Services	Increase the availability of information provided by Business Affairs for the monitoring of 050 income and expense projections.
5B	Business Affairs	Fiscal Services	Reduce the time expended in processing grant and contract documents within Business Affairs.
6	Public Safety	Safety	Decrease response time for requests for service.
7	Radiation Center	(President's critical processes: teaching, research, service delivery)	Increase customer demand for the Center's products and streamline response process.
8	Human Resources	Workforce Hiring & Development	Increase the speed of initial response in the information dissemination process.

Step Seven. Real-time data on the probable causes are gathered to establish a benchmark against which to measure future progress.

Step Eight. The data are analyzed and shown in "pictures"—charts and graphs.

Step Nine. Solutions to problems are developed through brainstorming. Each solution is measured against criteria that reflect customer needs. The best solutions are then implemented, their performance monitored, and they are adopted if they are successful.

Step Ten. If the problem is solved, improvements are standardized as normal operating procedures.

Case Example: The Business Affairs Team

The following section analyzes one of the ten TQM teams at OSU—the Business Affairs Team.

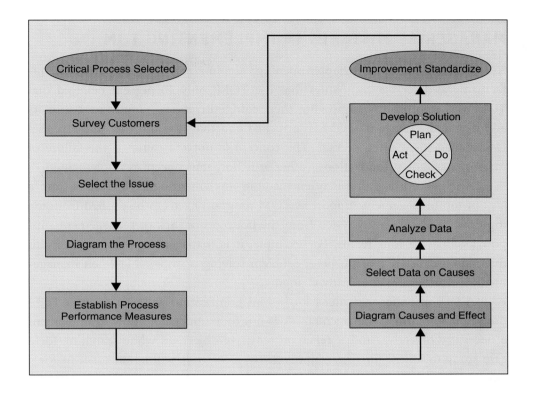

❖ **Figure 17.5**
Ten-step problem-solving process (Source: L. Edwin Coate, *An Analysis of Oregon State University's Total Quality Management Pilot Program* [Oregon State University Press, November 1990], p. 5. Used with permission.)

The Problem The number of erroneous journal vouchers returned to departments must be decreased.

Causes When the team began measuring journal voucher errors, they found a one-month total of 200 errors out of 7,971 vouchers processed, a rate of three percent. Of these, more than half, 103, were returned to the originating department for correction, a time-wasting process loop.

Solutions The team tested two solutions:

- Based on a better understanding of what customers wanted, the journal vouchers specialist called the originating departments and corrected most errors over the phone.
- To help departments complete their journal vouchers correctly at the outset, the specialist prepared a checklist based on data about common customer errors and sent it to all departments. The team helped with suggestions and reviews.

Results The journal vouchers error rate dropped from three percent to two percent, and the number of journal vouchers returned to departments dropped dramatically from 103 to four (see Figure 17.6).

❖ ❖ MANAGERIAL MISTAKES IN IMPLEMENTING TQM

As was mentioned in the chapter opening case, in a recent survey of 500 manufacturing and service companies that use TQM, only 36 percent believed that TQM was significantly improving their competitiveness.[29] Many practitioners admit that the image of TQM is tarnished and that it is not the quick fix that U.S. management often seeks.[30] The concept is not the cause of the failure of many management innovations; rather, it is how the concept is implemented.

A major mistake that is often made in implementing TQM results from a lack of top management support. A TQM program needs to be pushed from the top down and constantly tested from the bottom up. Lack of management support assumes various forms. For example, it is management's responsibility to maintain a constancy of purpose; problem solving is impossible when management's priorities are constantly changing.

A lack of patience or need for instant gratification will also doom a TQM program. Sometimes, management does not fully understand how to implement a necessary objective, and it relies on tentative objectives while searching for a case study to follow for firm objectives. No case study will be an exact fit for a particular company's needs. Each situation requires its own set of objectives. In some cases, management tries to legislate TQM. Such attempts to force improvement on the system will not work, in large part because they encourage the perception that TQM is yet another soon-to-be-discredited *magic solution*. Manage-

❖ **Figure 17.6**
Before and after
(Source: L. Edwin
Coate, *An Analysis of
Oregon State University's Total Quality
Management Pilot Program* [Oregon State
University Press, November 1990], p. 12.
Used with permission.)

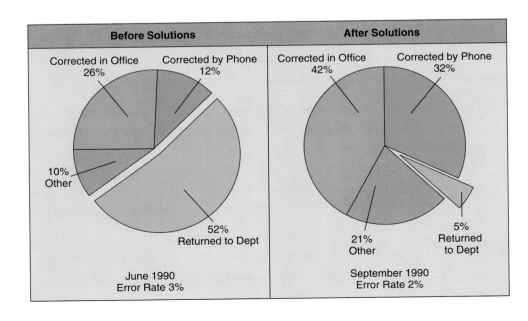

ment must change its style before the rest of the organization can be expected to respond.

There will always be bias when management evaluates its own corporate culture, usually resulting in an overly optimistic view of the quality of the environment. Failure to actively address this at all levels will shut off the flow of ideas and the problem-solving activities. In the chain of command, it only takes one individual or one level to ruin the system. Most often, this occurs at the supervisory level. Bias can be even more dangerous, however, if it occurs at higher levels in the organization.

There is also the tendency by management to take shortcuts, especially with employee training. Workers typically can be taught how to fill in control charts in less than four hours. It takes far longer to ground workers in the overall philosophy, and to provide them with the statistical knowledge they need to understand and interpret the charts. Since computers can be used to complete the control charts, managers often use automation as the excuse for failing to train workers properly. Another common shortcut is dispensing with problem-solving teams. Many managers view them as unproductive and a waste of time, especially when it is already the responsibility of designated employees to solve problems. Bypassing problem-solving teams results in many barriers to TQM remaining.[31]

TQM: More than a Dying Fad?

Management trends come and go, and what is a miracle today may be nothing tomorrow. As with all management movements, TQM has its critics. However, even most of the critics agree that the principles of TQM can still deliver big payoffs when they are properly applied. Still, TQM does not have all the answers, it does not turn lead to gold, and it is not the fail-safe solution to all management problems. Surveys show that two-thirds of American managers think TQM has failed companies. Even the number of companies vying for the Holy Grail of TQM, the Malcomb Baldrige National Quality Award, has fallen off sharply. Well then, what of TQM, is it a miracle or a disaster? It is neither. TQM is not simply a focus on quality at the expense of all else. It is not something that can be badly executed, and it cannot be imported in a cookie-cutter fashion. According to Ray Stata, CEO of integrated-circuit-maker Analog Devices, "Total quality essentially involves attention to process, commitment to the customer, involvement of employees, and benchmarking of best practices. It is hard to believe you cannot benefit from that." In fact, those who properly apply TQM do benefit, but what are the keys to making TQM work? (1) The CEO must be visibly behind TQM; (2) management must always ask what change does for the customers; (3) the organization must be limited to a few critical goals; (4) changes must be linked to clear financial paybacks; and (5) the program must be unique, not an off-the-shelf quality program.[32] This will make TQM pay off for the majority.

✘ Management Tips ✘

Guidelines for Working with Total Quality Management

1. **Recognize that TQM is a commitment to excellence by everyone in an organization that emphasizes excellence achieved by teamwork and a process of continuous improvement.** It is quite possible that organizations that fail to pick up the quality baton and run with it will become second-class players in our rapidly changing global environment.

2. **Constantly seek ways to improve quality, increase speed of operations, and adopt a customer orientation.** These changes are so fundamental that they must take root in a company's very essence, which means in its culture.

3. **Continuously improve quality over the long run.** In the short run, once each of the linked processes within a firm is operating at or above a desired level of quality, reliance on costly inspection practices can be reduced or eliminated altogether.

4. **Recognize that the increased employee participation required by TQM creates a new role for all organizational members.** Top management, middle managers, first-level supervisors, and all workers must embrace the philosophy and work to ensure its acceptance throughout the organization.

5. **Remember that TQM is not a body of regulations and cannot be forced on employees.** Since a company's culture is largely a product of positively reinforced behavior, the route to change is almost always through education and training.

6. **Accept the fact that the concept of quality in a TQM environment is based on the customer being served to the maximum degree possible.** Quality means the product meets all requirements.

7. **Recognize that the concept of quality differs with the type of company involved.** You must understand your customer.

8. **Remember that a TQM culture encourages more employee participation in problem solving and decision making.** TQM will not work unless all employees are trained to use the tools.

9. **Realize that TQM is a continuous journey toward quality.** There is no end toward this search for quality.

10. **Recognize that departmental and divisional barriers must be broken down.** TQM integrates team activities across divisions or departments to achieve organizational objectives.

A GLOBAL PERSPECTIVE

Global Quality and Value Through TQM

The global outlook for Total Quality Management (TQM) still appears promising. First, the United States used it to help win World War II. Then, the United States abandoned it to "enjoy the war's legacy of consumer prosperity" without an interest in quality. On the road to recovery, Japan embraced the concept of TQM. On July 13, 1950, W. Edwards Deming addressed the presidents of Japan's leading companies, telling them that quality was essential to their survival. "They saw quality as precepts and practices permeating every level of the enterprise, from the board room to the factory floor. The effort toward quality was, in a word, total."[33] From their humble beginnings, Japanese manufacturers have become the envy of the world. This level of success has come about primarily because of the conviction and discipline with which Japanese managers, over the last 40 years, have embraced various concepts of TQM.[34]

American automobile manufacturers are now using TQM to their best advantage and the American share of the automobile market continues to increase. Yes, the soaring value of the yen forced the Japanese to hike the prices of their cars substantially, thereby hurting sales, but the other aspect of American success is the resurgence of American quality. Adherence to TQM has resulted in "higher-quality competitive products with styling flash not seen since the fifties."

The biggest Japanese advantage in the past was quality. Today the quality difference between Japanese and American products is shrinking, and since American prices are substantially lower, customers are offered more value. Adherence to the mandates of TQM has allowed American manufacturers to be competitive not only in the United States, but also globally. The global word for success is still Quality, but it is also value.[35] Started in the United States, first embraced by Japanese companies after World War II, reintroduced and currently accepted by U.S. companies, Total Quality Management may well serve American firms throughout the world.

SUMMARY

Total Quality Management (TQM) is a commitment to excellence by everyone in an organization that emphasizes excellence achieved by teamwork and a process of continuous improvement. The ultimate goal of TQM is to alter the process by improving customer satisfaction. Instead of being content with the status quo, employees at all levels continually seek alternative methods or technologies that will improve existing processes. The concept of quality is based on the customer being served to the maximum degree possible.

In the TQM environment, it is best if workers call attention to a problem. However, workers traditionally are not trained to solve problems. As those working closest to the problems, they must be trained to

KEY TERMS

Total quality management (TQM) 550

Cause-and-effect diagram 557

Pareto analysis 557

Quality circles 558

Statistical process control 559

use basic problem-solving tools such as team building, brainstorming, process analysis, cause-and-effect diagrams, and Pareto analysis.

The approaches to TQM that are discussed include the TQM Element Approach, the Guru Approach, and the Industrial Company Model Approach. The TQM Element Approach was used primarily in the early 1980s and employs elements of quality improvement programs such as quality circles and statistical process control, rather than full implementation of TQM. The Guru Approach uses the writings of a guru such as Deming, Juran, Feigenbaum, Ishikawa, Taguchi, or Crosby as a benchmark to determine what the organization lacks; then it uses the guru's system to make changes. The Industrial Company Model Approach requires individuals to visit a U.S. industrial company that uses TQM, identify its successes, and integrate this information with their own ideas to create a customized approach.

TQM is a structural system for creating organization-wide participation in planning and implementing a continuous improvement process that exceeds the expectations of the customer or client. It is built on the assumption that 90 percent of our problems are process problems, not employee problems. The three major components of TQM are breakthrough planning, daily management, and cross-functional management. Breakthrough planning is an extension of strategic planning. Daily management shows people what they personally must do, and what they must measure and control, to keep the organization running smoothly. Finally, cross-functional management is the integration of team activities across divisions or departments to achieve organizational objectives.

Implementation problems caused the failure of many past management innovations, and TQM failures can often be traced to such problems. A major mistake that is often made in implementing TQM results from a lack of top management support. A lack of patience or the need for instant gratification will also doom a TQM program. There is also the tendency by management to take shortcuts, especially with employee training.

REVIEW QUESTIONS

1. Define Total Quality Management.
2. What is the history of Total Quality Management?
3. Explain the basic message of both Deming and Juran.
4. What factors favor the growth of TQM in the United States?
5. In relation to TQM, what is quality?
6. What are some tools for problem solving in TQM?
7. Describe the approaches to implementing TQM.
8. What are the components of TQM? Describe each.
9. Describe some managerial mistakes in implementing TQM.

CASE STUDIES

CASE 17.1 What Happened at Pontiac?

A 35-year veteran autoworker at General Motors' Pontiac engine plant number 18 in Detroit describes how it was in the old days when he found a tool was going bad. "I'd tell the supervisor and he'd say 'Leave it for the second shift.' The second shift would leave it for the third shift, and the third shift would leave it for me in the morning. Then my supervisor would say, 'Leave it for the weekend.' Well, now we've got only the day shift left, and if we didn't do better, there just wouldn't be a day shift."

Today worker participation and training are the rule rather than the exception at plant 18. Recently, workers and union officials even helped design a new production line; years earlier, that would have been left to the process engineers. Every worker takes a four-week course and leaves with a magnifying glass (to help see defects in the tools), a pocket calculator, and a good understanding of statistical controls. With many new quantitative controls in effect, workers find frequent uses for what they have learned.

The output of the plant shows the changes that have occurred. Pontiac struggled for years to improve the quality of its engines. Now improvements happen every day. Plant 18 had trouble with threads on the connecting-rod bolts it bought from four suppliers. As it turned out, practically all the defective bolts came from one supplier. When that supplier was dropped, the failures stopped. In another example, a certain camshaft gear has to be accurate within a few ten-thousandths of an inch. If the gear does not meet the standard, the engine has to be pulled and the gear replaced, at a cost of over $1,000. After it was discovered that checking three successive gears once an hour kept the boring from going out of kilter, failures dropped from 38 engines requiring the costly repair job one year, to six the next, to none last year.

What accounts for the change? The main factor is Dr. W. Edwards Deming, the statistician who is given credit for much of Japan's manufacturing preeminence, and for whom two of that country's national productivity prizes are named. Deming was invited to the Pontiac plant after General Manager William Hogland saw an NBC documentary, *If Japan Can, . . . Why Can't We?* Deming was already back in the United States at Nashua Corporation, when Hogland invited him to come to plant 18.

Hogland had no idea what a difference Deming would make. "His message shook the foundations of our approach to quality," says Hogland. Workers and managers alike at plant 18 view Deming with awe. Many have memorized his "14 points to improve quality." The new concern for qualitative controls applies not only to product quality, but to costs as well.

Thus, budgeting has taken on a new importance at plant 18.[36]

QUESTIONS

1. Evaluate the work environment at Pontiac plant 18 before and after implementing TQM.
2. What training took place to assist in the new focus on quality?

CASE 17.2 The Faulty Cues

"This is the third batch of sticks we've gotten back from Brunswick this quarter," said Jerry Hodges, "and it has been different problems each time." Along with the returned pool sticks, Brunswick had provided a checklist of defects, and Jerry and his shop manager, John Kenner, were looking it over. The sticks had been made by Jerry's company, Hodges Woodworks. Brunswick is a major distributor of recreation equipment of all kinds, and Hodges had contracted to provide the company with 5,000 pool sticks per month during 1994.

There were 200 defective sticks in the returned batch. Defects ranged from misaligned leather tips, to thread defects where the sticks screwed together in the middle, to an incomplete covering of varnish. Altogether, 16 types of defects were noted in the batch.

"The costs are just too high to inspect every piece of every stick," said Jerry.

"Yeah, I know," replied John, "but it's not as expensive as having to rework an entire batch. Anyway, Brunswick uses 100 percent inspection. Why shouldn't we?"

Jerry replied, "We may have to do that. But if the number of defects is below two percent, Brunswick will accept the batch. Let's see if we can figure out a cheaper way to accomplish that."

The manufacturing process for pool sticks is complex. The wood parts are cut from solid maple and machined to shape on numerically controlled lathes. Then they are drilled and shaped on other machines to fit plastic, metal, and rubber parts purchased from other manufacturers. After being assembled, the pool cues are varnished in batches of 20 with a spray gun. Because of the small volume, most of the assembly work is done by hand.

After some discussion, John and Jerry determined that except for the varnish problem, all of the defects in the present batch resulted from parts purchased from others. "Obviously," said Jerry, "we should do the same thing to our suppliers that Brunswick is doing to us: Check the parts when we get them, and return them if they are defective."

QUESTIONS

1. Could TQM assist in this situation? Explain.

NOTES

1. This case is a composite of a number of published accounts, among them: Robert Neff, "Going for the Glory," *Business Week* (October 25, 1991): 60; Mary T. Koska, "Case Study: Quality Improvement in a Diversified Health Center," *Hospitals* 64 (December 5, 1990): 19–20; David Kearns, "Quality in Copiers, Computers, and Floor Cleaning," *Management Review* 78 (February 1989): 61–63; Curt W. Reimann, "Winning Strategies for Quality Improvement," *Business America* 112 (March 25, 1991): 8; Thane Peterson, Kevin Kelly, Joseph Weber, and Neil Gross, "Top Products for Less than Top Dollar," *Business Week* (October 25, 1991): 66; Kevin Kelly, "Motorola Wants to Light Up Another Market," *Business Week* (October 14, 1991): 50; Alison L. Sprout, "America's Most Admired Corporations," *Fortune* 126 (February 11, 1991): 57–58; Otis Port, John Carey, Kevin Kelly, and Stephanie Anderson Forest, "Quality," *Business Week* (November 30, 1992): 67–68.

2. Gary Slutsker, "The Company that Likes to Obsolete Itself," *Forbes* 152 (September 13, 1993): 139–144.

3. Ellis Pines, "The Gurus of TQM," *Aviation Week and Space Technology* 121 (May 21, 1990): S34.

4. W. Edwards Deming, *Out of the Crisis* (Cambridge, MA: Massachusetts Institute of Technology Center for Advanced Engineering Study, 1986): Chap. 2.

5. Pines, "The Gurus of TQM," p. S29.

6. Jeremy Main, "Under the Spell of the Quality Gurus," *Fortune* 121 (August 18, 1986): 30.

7. Joseph Oberle, "Quality Gurus, the Men and Their Message," *Training* 27 (January 1990): 47.

8. Jaclyn Fierman, "Why Enrollment Is Up at Quality College," *Fortune* 120 (April 29, 1985): 170.

9. Main, "Under the Spell of the Quality Gurus," p. 30.

10. Thomas F. Rienzo, "Planning Deming Management for Service Organizations," *Business Horizons* 36 (May–June 1993): 19–29.

11. Ellis Pines, "TQM Training: A New Culture Sparks Change at Every Level," *Aviation Week and Space Technology* 132 (May 21, 1990): S38.

12. Ellis Pines, "From Top Secret to Top Priority: The Story of TQM," *Aviation Week and Space Technology* 132 (May 21, 1990): S24.

13. B. G. Yovovich, "Motorola's Quest for Quality," *Business Marketing* 76 (September 1991): 14–29.

14. Otis Port and John Carey, "Questing for the Best," *Business Week Bonus Issue, The Quality Imperative* (October 11, 1991): 10.

15. Joseph Blackburn, "Time Based Competition JIT as a Weapon," *APICS* (July 1991): 30–34.

16. *Ibid.*

17. Karen Lowry Miller and David Woodruff, "A Design Master's End Run Around Trial and Error," *Business Week Bonus Issue, The Quality Imperative* (October 25, 1991): 24; Pines, "The Gurus of TQM," p. S36.

18. Port and Carey, "Questing for the Best," p. 14.

19. Adapted from Howard J. Weiss and Mark E. Gershon, *Production and Operations Management* 2d ed. (Needham Heights, MA: Allyn & Bacon, 1993): 763–770.

20. David Woodruff, James B. Treece, Sunita Wadekar Bhargava, and Karen Lowry Miller, "Saturn," *Business Week* (August 17, 1992): 88.

21. John Hoerr, "The Payoff from Teamwork," *Business Week* (July 10, 1989): 56–62.

22. Fred G. Steingraber, "Total Quality Management," *Vital Speeches of the Day* 57 (April 15, 1991): 415.

23. Mary Walton, *The Deming Management Method* (New York: Perigee Books, Putnam Publishing Group, 1986).

24. Port, Carey, Kelly, and Forest, "Quality," p. 67.

25. This case is a composite of a number of published accounts, among them: Robert Neff, "Going for the Glory," *Business Week* (October 25, 1991): 60; Mary T. Koska, "Case Study: Quality Improvement in a Diversified Health Center," *Hospitals* 64 (December 5, 1990): 19–20; David Kearns, "Quality in Copiers, Computers, and Floor Cleaning," *Management Review* 78 (February 1989): 61–63; Curt W. Reimann, "Winning Strategies for Quality Improvement," *Business America* 112 (March 25, 1991): 8; Thane Peterson, Kevin Kelly, Joseph Weber, and Neil Gross, "Top Products for Less than Top Dollar," *Business Week* (October 25, 1991): 66; Kevin Kelly, "Motorola Wants to Light up Another Market," *Business Week* (October 14, 1991): 50; Alison L. Sprout, "America's Most Admired Corporations," *Fortune* 126 (February 11, 1991): 57–58.

26. This section is based on the work of L. Edwin Coate, *Implementing Total Quality Management in a University Setting* (Corvallis, OR: Oregon State University Press 1990): 5–6. Used with permission.

27. This example was adapted from L. Edwin Coate, *An Analysis of Oregon State University's Total Quality Management Pilot Program* (Corvallis, OR: Oregon State University Press, 1990): 4–24.

28. Coate, *Implementing Total Quality Management in a University Setting*, p. 2.

29. Port, Carey, Kelly, and Forest, "Quality," p. 68.

30. "TQM Worth It," *HRMagazine* 38 (August 1993): 30.

31. Adapted from Howard J. Weiss and Mark E. Gershon *Production and Operations Management* 2d ed, pp. 783–784.

32. Rahul Jacob, "TQM More than A Dying Fad?," *Fortune* 128 (October 18, 1993): 66–69.

33. Pines, "The Gurus of TQM," pp. S5–S8.

34. William H. Oliver, "The Quality Revolution," *Vital Speeches of the Day* 56 (August, 1990): 625–628.

35. William J. Cook and Warren Cohen, "Sparking a Revival," *U.S. News & World Report* 114 (June 14, 1993): 69, 71–73.

36. This story is a composite from a number of sources, including: "Dr. Deming Shows Pontiac the Way," *Fortune* 118 (April 1983): 19–36; and Daniel W. Gottlieb, "Purchasing's Part in the Push for Quality," *Purchasing* 10 (September 1981): 75–78.

Do You Manage Time Effectively?

Since effective managers must properly control their time, it is essential that you develop solid time management skills before entering management. To assess how well you currently manage your time, take the self-assessment exercise "Do You Manage Time Effectively?" Then, turn to page 675 to evaluate yourself.

INSTRUCTIONS: Check the box or boxes that are most appropriate to your usual behavior.

❑   **1. I am a hard worker, and as such, try to do every job with total commitment. Even though I am frequently tired at the end of the day, I feel a great sense of accomplishment.**

❑   **2. If asked to take on an extra assignment, I will consent. Even if this new responsibility makes it nearly impossible for me to finish current projects on schedule, it is hard for me to refuse.**

❑   **3. Most people consider me a workaholic. I am usually involved in several projects at once. No one can make an appointment to see me without having to wait at least two weeks. I'd like to exercise more, but cannot seem to fit such a program into my heavy schedule.**

❑   **4. I pride myself on the ability to anticipate most problems before they occur. To me, the work schedule is sacred. Therefore, I rarely deviate from it. Interruptions must be discouraged. As much as possible, I limit phone calls and prolonged conversations.**

❑   **5. The top and inside of my desk are covered with papers. A collector, I save telephone messages, reports, relevant newspaper articles, schedules, and letters. In fact, my filing system is so well organized that I can pull out a year-old memo at a moment's notice. Colleagues kid me about my tendency to store so many items, but I am sure that this is an asset.**

❑   **6. I tend to pay considerable attention to small details. I am an expert at catching even the tiniest mistake, whether in typing, grammar, or figures. Although most assignments take me hours to complete, I am known for my thoroughness and dedication. If necessary, I will take work home, to ensure that a job is finished on schedule.**

(continued on next page)

❑   **7. Large projects are not my forte. I find them too overwhelming and confusing. I much prefer to be given more routine tasks. It is generally difficult for me to focus on too many details at once. I enjoy the involvement and sense of accomplishment that results from a small job brought to completion.**

Source: Dorri Jacobs, "Your Time Management Profile," *Manage* 36 (May 1983): 4. With permission.

18 Management in the Multinational Environment

LEARNING OBJECTIVES

After completing this chapter students should be able to

✖ Explain the history and development of multinationals.

✖ Describe the multinational environment.

✖ Explain management in a multinational environment.

✖ Describe human resources in a multinational environment.

Dow: Trying to Overtake Number One DuPont

Dow Chemical is the world's second largest chemical company, behind DuPont, with over half of its sales, and even more of its operating income, coming from foreign operations. Third quarter sales increased at a rate of over six percent and operating income increased nine percent, without an increase in shares outstanding. Dow "sets strategies globally, as well as R&D priorities." Basically, all the things that drive the business long-term are done globally. Dow has six worldwide "commercial" divisions (e.g., Dow Europe), making it "[o]ne of the most balanced companies in the world." Dow has an excellent balance between its overseas and domestic markets, but Dow's foreign operations are continually more profitable than its domestic ones.

The mainstay of Dow's international business, industrial chemicals, were subject to unpredictable swings because of overseas market changes. Dow's overseas ventures, such as the joint venture Dow entered into with China's Zhejiang Pacific Chemical Corporation, illustrates Dow's global aggressiveness, but Europe is the region of the world with the best growth potential. Dow's business in Europe remains strong, and another record year is expected.

Dow's executive team is still mostly American, but it is becoming more and more internationalized. According to Dow's human resources vice president, "We consider each overseas move to be unique because each situation is different." Prospective expatriates, and those moving from one overseas assignment to another, are briefed and given an information packet on their destination. "An adviser—normally the spouse of a recently returned expatriate—will visit the transferee and his or her spouse to explain what sort of emotional issues they are likely to face in the early stages of the move."

A "godfather" is also assigned to each expatriate manager at Dow to assure "a relationship of mutual trust and interest." Basically, the expatriate keeps the godfather up to date on his or her activities, and the godfather keeps track of the expatriate's career while he or she is overseas. Expatriate managers are guaranteed that they can come back to jobs at the same level as the ones they left. The godfather is expected to arrange this transition. Upon repatriation, managers are encouraged to form support groups to discuss common overseas experiences.

Dow's division president is proud of Dow's ability to "'execute geographically.' There are those who've said that, using astronomical terms, there's a 'red shift,' a 'big bang,' with things getting further apart and Dow Chemical becoming a big holding company. I don't think that's the correct vision of Dow. I believe we'll be interlinked, intertwined, rather than continuing with the big bang." The globally oriented system at Dow appears to be sound, and Dow's quest for number one will continue.[1]

A company such as Dow engages in international business typically because of significant opportunities beyond the home country's borders. These opportunities are usually partly offset by the well-known problems of international business: cultural differences, legal restrictions, language barriers, monetary effects, and the distances over which information and materials must travel.

In the 1980s, the need for adapting business practices to different national environments was not fully appreciated. Today, if exports and imports were combined, they would total almost 25 percent of the U.S. economy. That is up from only 16 percent just ten years ago.[2] Thus, global corporations affect the lives of many U.S. citizens.

This chapter begins by describing the history and development of multinational corporations. Then, environmental factors confronting multinationals are described. Next, management in a multinational environment is addressed. The final section of the chapter focuses on human resources in the multinational environment and closes with an interesting global perspective on international management consulting.

❖ ❖ HISTORY AND DEVELOPMENT OF MULTINATIONALS

A **multinational company (MNC)** is a firm that is based in one country (the parent, or home, country) and produces goods or provides services in one or more foreign countries (host countries). The headquarters of the multinational corporation is located in the **parent country**. The operational unit of the multinational corporation resides in the **host country**.

The first MNC established with a global orientation grew out of a merger in 1929 between Margarine Unie, a Dutch firm, and Lever Brothers, a British company. The company became Unilever, and it has since become one of the largest companies in the world, with approximately 500 subsidiaries operating in about 60 nations. Unilever has two headquarters units, one located in Rotterdam and the other in London. Today, it is important for most companies to enter the

In recent years, there has been a rapid growth of direct investment by multinational firms averaging about ten percent a year. MNCs based in the United States account for more than half of this worldwide investment. This McDonald's restaurant is located in Tokyo, Japan.
(Source: ©1994 Jeffrey Aaronson/Network Aspen)

multinational market if they are to survive. With operations in many countries, Dow is clearly an MNC.

The economic output of MNCs is a significant portion of the total economic output of the world. Some economists have estimated that by the year 2000, about 200 to 300 multinationals will account for one-half of the world's total output of goods and services. In recent years, there has been a rapid growth of direct investment by multinational firms. This trend is expected to continue as majority-owned foreign affiliates of U.S. companies plan to increase capital expenditures to $61.2 billion, a six percent increase.[3] There tend to be some common characteristics among successful large American global companies, and these characteristics are worth noting.

The Face of the Global U.S. Competitor

Many large American global companies have common characteristics, such as their "willingness to experiment and improvise," that give many U.S. companies an open door to the global marketplace. Boeing is the world's largest aircraft maker, and it is the number one exporter in the United States. Boeing's success is primarily based on its concern for satisfying consumers worldwide and on its endless testing of new designs and materials. Even the Japanese purchase $2 billion worth of planes and related products and services annually. Rival allies, Ford and Mazda have had a partnership for over 13 years. With Mazda's help, Ford sells some 72,000 units in Japan annually, and with marketing assistance from Ford, Mazda sells 343,000 units annually in the United States. Other large American global companies are successful because of the inherent demand from customers in the global marketplace. Coca-Cola is the world's thirst quencher. European intellectuals call segments of their population the "Coca-Cola Culture," but there may actually be a Global Coca-Cola Culture because 80 percent of Coke's annual sales comes from outside the United States. Coke sells its product in the same way everywhere, with upbeat, energetic, and casually friendly people. In Tokyo, Levi jeans, tight T-shirts, and American music are all the rage, and a profitable rage it is. Going global is the reality of the 1990s and beyond.[4]

U.S. companies must also have a global presence if they are to expand. For example, the 100 largest U.S.-based multinationals experienced a decline in domestic sales of 1.6 percent after adjusting for inflation. But, foreign sales increased 15 percent. Of the total revenue of these firms, approximately 40 percent comes from foreign sales.[5] Recently, the top ten exporters from the United States included Exxon, IBM, General Motors, Ford Motor, Mobil, Citicorp, Texaco, E. I. du Pont de Nemours, ITT, and Philip Morris. A firm had to generate foreign revenue in excess of $1.8 billion to rank in the 100 largest U.S. multinationals.[6] The worldwide impact of these companies is significant. Their operations create interrelationships between countries and cultures as well as between economic and political systems.

Other companies not among the top ten exporters saw hefty gains in foreign revenues. Compaq Computer doubled its exports. Ethyl Corporation saw a 48 percent jump, mainly on the strength of sales of bromine as a flame retardant. And Alcoa's sales of aluminum products to foreigners shot up 75 percent. All together, export sales for the top 50 exporters grew 22 percent, to $97 billion.

In recent years many internationalists have distinguished between multinational companies and evolving transnational companies. A **transnational company** is a firm that views the world as one market, conducts operations in many countries, and makes decisions as if national boundaries did not exist. Thus a transnational manufacturing firm buys supplies, raises capital, conducts research and development, and manufactures its products wherever in the world it can do so most effectively and efficiently. It does not distinguish between its home and host countries; its headquarters can be in any country. It seeks to develop and maintain a single worldwide identity. Its executives are of various nationalities, and they are global managers. We will use international companies in the rest of the chapter when there is no need to distinguish between multinational and transnational firms.

❖ ❖ THE DIVERSE MULTINATIONAL ENVIRONMENT

Global competition, air travel, and satellite communication technology have made doing business abroad both necessary and feasible, and companies have responded by establishing operations overseas. A survey by McKinsey and Company of mid-sized companies doing business abroad shows that companies expect their international sales to jump 15 to 20 percent a year for at least the next five years.[7] In addition, 95 percent of the world's population lies outside the United States, and it's growing 70 percent faster.[8] Clearly, the majority of business opportunities in the future will be outside the United States.

Unfortunately, historically, some American managers have tended to fall back on their own limited experiences, treating an assignment in Hong Kong, Sydney, or Paris much like a stint in Dallas or Atlanta. Global managers must become effective in each of the host countries where they operate. One person constantly dealing with the complexities involved in operating in the global environment is Louis Hughes, the vibrant president of General Motors Europe. Hughes is in charge of the most efficient and profitable of Europe's automakers, but he wants more. Operating out of Germany, he radiates intensity, conviction, and drive, and he has even immersed himself in the German language for six months and is forcing colleagues to use it in meetings with him. Now, to illustrate his commitment to the country, he uses German even in conversation with English-speaking Germans.[9] Hughes realizes that when operating overseas, domestic managers must be adaptive and appreciate the nature of the environment in which they are operating.

American managers have recognized that the challenge of engaging in multinational operations is not easily met. This is especially true with regard to the challenges of management. In Chapter 2, the discussion was primarily focused on environmental factors of organizations located in the United States. However, the external environment that confronts multinational enterprises is even more diverse and complex than that confronted by domestic firms.

As is illustrated in Figure 18.1, working in a multinational climate adds another layer to the external environment (described in Chapter 2) that management must contend with. Although the basic tasks associated with management remain essentially the same, the manner in which the tasks are accomplished may be altered substantially by the multinational's external environment. As Figure 18.1 suggests, the MNC must deal with the environment not only of the parent country, but of the host country as well.

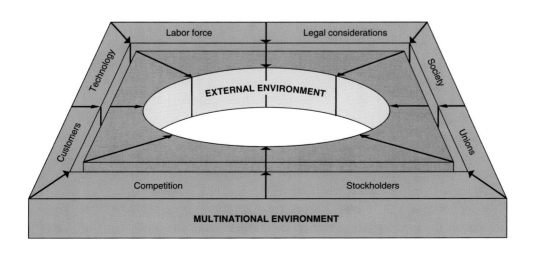

❖ **Figure 18.1**
The external environment of a multinational corporation

Legal Considerations

Multinational Corporations must obey the laws of the host country. In addition, some multinationals are under pressure to adhere to federal, state, and even local legislation of the parent country. However, there is no comprehensive system of international law or courts. Therefore, a multinational organization needs to understand in detail the laws of each host country. The United States, England, Canada, Australia, and New Zealand have developed their legal requirements by means of English common law. Under English common law, judges and courts are extremely important, for they are guided by principles declared in previous cases. In most of continental Europe, Asia, and Africa, the approach is one of civil law. Judges play a lesser role because the legal requirements are codified. The civil servant or bureaucrat has greater power under civil law than under the common law.

Although the United States is a highly legalistic country, and American MNCs tend to carry U.S. law with them, managers must realize that the legal systems of other countries can differ considerably. For instance, the Japanese dislike laws, lawyers, and litigation. Consider this example: "A Japanese contract is so vague it's unenforceable in U.S. courts. It says, well, the two of us will get together, and we think we're going to do this product, but if that doesn't work for us, then we'll have to change the terms of the agreement, because why would we want to go ahead with it and do it if it was killing us."[10] In France, lawyers are prohibited from serving on boards of directors by codes of the legal profession. The vastness and sheer complexity of various legal systems throughout the world

---

ETHICAL DILEMMA

Doing business in other countries is often quite different from doing business in the United states. Other cultures have different norms and social habits that often dictate the need for greater cultural sensitivity. However, often the norms of a country border on unethical and possibly even illegal acts from a U.S. perspective. Managers must be cautious in their actions, especially when entering a country for the first time. Your company, Empire Southwest, a distributor of Caterpillar equipment in Phoenix, wants to trade in the Mexican market where cash under the table——mordita (a "little bit")——is part of doing business. This payoff practice is so ingrained in the Mexican culture that a business virtually cannot open a Mexican operation without going along. You have observed many companies that did not pay and that failed to enter the Mexican market, as well as those that paid and entered the market and, overall, did fairly well.[11] You can continue to raise your stature with mining companies, farmers, and contractors, and encourage them to lobby the government to freely open the market, or you can pay the bribe.

What would you do?

demonstrate clearly the intricate and demanding legal environment of the MNCs. In order to function in a manner consistent with the host country, managers should become familiar with its legal considerations. Failure to carefully consider legal considerations could have a drastic effect on multinational success.

Multinational corporations headquartered in the United States must obey the laws of the host country. When operating in the multinational environment, U.S.-based firms often find their human resource policies in conflict with the laws and accepted norms of the host country. For instance, the influence of Title VII of the Civil Rights Act of 1964, as amended, has been felt by virtually all firms operating in the United States. But most countries in the world do not have such laws prohibiting discrimination. In fact, some countries practice overt discrimination against certain groups that would be protected if they were employed in the United States. The Civil Rights Act of 1991 extended the coverage of the Civil Rights Act of 1964 to extraterritorial employment. However, the Act does not apply to United States companies operating in another country if it would violate the law of the foreign country.

Labor Force

In filling key managerial, technical, or professional positions abroad, multinationals can choose among three basic types of employees: (1) parent country nationals (PCN), (2) host country nationals (HCN), and (3) third country nationals (TCN). Initially, it was common for MNCs to fill foreign key posts with trusted and experienced employees from the parent company. Using workers from the parent nation of the multinational ensures a greater degree of consistency and control in the firm's operations around the world. However, this approach is not without its costs, because these workers may experience considerable difficulty in understanding cultural differences and adapting to life in the host country. In addition, the common practice of frequent rotation of key employees intensifies the problem of understanding and adapting to local cultures. However, using PCNs facilitates communications with headquarters because both parties are of the same culture.

Utilizing workers from the host country in key positions will usually improve the MNC's relations with the host country government. It will also enable a quicker and more accurate adaptation to the requirements of the host country. Disadvantages include a lessened degree of centralized control and increased communication problems with headquarters. In addition, if the HCNs perceive that the opportunity for higher-level positions is blocked for ethnic reasons, they will use the MNC to gain experience and then transfer to higher positions in local national firms. Properly balancing the type of key employees stationed in the host country is often a complex and difficult task, but one that is critical to the success of the MNC.

Using workers from the parent nation of the multinational company ensures a greater degree of consistency and control in the firm's operations around the world. However, this approach is not without its costs, because these workers may experience considerable difficulty in understanding cultural differences and adapting to life in the host country. Here, a worker in Sweden transmits a facsimile message to her employer's U.S. headquarters. (Source: © Jim Pickerell)

The trend toward using large numbers of parent country nationals appears to be changing. In 1991, Resources Counselors, Inc. discovered that the number of U.S. parent country nationals per company is decreasing.[12] More and more firms are employing host country nationals and third country nationals. Apparently nationality is not as important a factor as the number of global managers.

MANAGEMENT IN PRACTICE

A Skill-Building Exercise: You have been managing in Japan for over 17 years. The new general manager of marketing has been transferred from an eight-year assignment in Britain. He came in and had to select four new marketing representatives. These individuals deal directly with the executives of major Japanese corporations. They are the company liaisons who make sure that the customer is satisfied with the products and services offered by the company. This position also requires the representative to frequently socialize with the client. The new general manager has decided that there aren't enough women in responsible positions in the Japanese operation, so he has decided to promote women to fill all four marketing representative positions. He has told you to notify them of their promotions. You quickly realize that he is making a mistake, so you inform him that the promotions would not be a good move. He tells you he is running the show now and will have a representative portion of management positions filled by women. **What would you do or say?**

Society

It is apparent that the significant societal considerations of one nation will differ to some extent from those of other countries. Customs, beliefs, values, and habits of each society will vary. If the multinational corporation is to operate in many nations, it will be required to adapt some of its managerial practices to the specific and unique expectations and situations of each nation. Attitudes will differ concerning such subjects as work, risk taking, change introduction, time authority, and material gain. It is dangerous for managers to assume that the attitudes within the parent country will be similar in all other countries. However, it is sometimes possible for successful multinationals to change the way those in the parent countries do business.

Lack of cultural sensitivity has limited the transfer of successful U.S. management practices to European countries and to Asia. For example, when Dow builds plants in foreign countries, they have to adapt somewhat to that culture. The same is true for some foreign MNCs doing business in the United States. A matter of concern to many Western managers is the demand for bribes in developing countries.

In certain societies, authority is viewed as a natural right and is not questioned by subordinates. In other cultures, authority must be earned and is provided to those who have demonstrated their ability to lead. In some cultures, work is good and moral; in others it is to be avoided. David McClelland discovered that the fundamental attitude toward achievement is somewhat correlated with rates of economic development. If a nation's citizens are willing to commit themselves to the accomplishment of tasks deemed worthwhile and difficult, a country will benefit economically. McClelland contends that one's sense of ability to influence his or her future will have a definite impact on the behavior of a country's workforce.[13] If the basic belief is one of fatalism—what will be, will be—then the importance of planning and organizing for the future is downgraded.

Societies also vary as to interclass mobility and sources of status. If there is little hope of moving up to higher classes in a society, then fatalism and absence of a drive for achievement are likely. In many instances, the MNC will have to adapt and conform to the societal requirements of the host country in order to successfully operate as a global corporation. Obviously, management is directly impacted by societal concerns; therefore, such concerns must be carefully considered by MNC managers.

Unions

Surprisingly, the future of unionism abroad seems much brighter than domestic unionism. According to economist Richard Freeman, unionism fell in some countries in the 1980s, but no country suffered the consistent abrupt drop experienced by U.S. unions. While unionism has waned in the United States, it is maintaining its strength abroad. Unions in all countries have been under increasing pressure in recent decades because of slowing productivity and economic growth, rapid technological change, and a shift toward a free market system, but unionism in the United States has suffered the most.[14]

Freeman and fellow economist David Blanchflower believe that the critical difference between U.S. unions and their overseas counterparts is that U.S. unions have managed to win much higher wages than those received by nonunion workers. That gap is 20 to 25 percent in the United States compared with ten percent or less abroad. This pronounced gap gives U.S. employers a major incentive to oppose unions and establish nonunion operations. In addition, foreign unions are generally less adversarial with management and are also less focused on wage gains, keying instead on worker councils and participative decision making.[15]

Before doing business in another country or entering into an international alliance, companies must understand the characteristics of the industrial relations system in the other country and in each partner firm. For example, contrast the following two situations: In the first situation, a German firm (where roughly 40 percent of the workforce is represented by unions domestically) forms an alliance with a Swedish firm (where roughly 93 percent of the workforce is represented by a union domestically).[16] Both partners are quite sympathetic to the desires of the workers to be represented collectively, in association with national or international unions. In the second situation, a Japanese firm (whose U.S. plant is nonunionized) forms an alliance with a U.S. company whose workers are members of a union. When asked for their most important concern about the partnership, the plant managers cited the fact that their alliance called for two companies with different industrial relations systems to work together.[17]

Obviously, the industrial relations issues that managers must address in these two situations are quite different. Understanding the implications of, and agreeing to abide by, a particular type of industrial relations system before consummating an international alliance are critically important issues. Regardless of the union or nonunion status of the country or alliance, it is imperative that the industrial relations issues that could decrease the productivity of the workforce be addressed prior to entering a country or forming an international alliance.[18]

Stockholders

Stockholders must be satisfied with their return on investment or they will seek other investment opportunities. An MNC seeks to produce and distribute products and services throughout the world in return for a satisfactory return on its invested capital. A multinational corporation survives, grows, and remains attractive to stockholders by maintaining its technological advantages and minimizing risks.

Competition

Competition impacting firms operating in a multinational environment typically comes from many directions. In the past, U.S. firms had the luxury of viewing the competition as primarily American. This is no longer true, however. Now these same firms find themselves competing with corporations in many countries. Furthermore, companies may now find themselves competing with other multinationals and host country firms for the same personnel. This situation compounds the problems associated with management and creates a need for greater emphasis on the importance of managers in multinational corporations.

Customers

In this new environment, customers may exist in any country in the world. Philip Knight, Nike CEO and founder, has made conquering foreign markets and cultivating customers his top priority. Knight believes that "Most of the growth for Nike over the next two or three years will take place outside the United States." Nike's goal is to boost global sales to more than half of the company's $6 billion in projected revenues for 1996.[19] Cultivating these potential customers often requires new, and sometimes innovative, management approaches. For example, fundamental selling skills transcend cultural barriers. However, the perception of the salesperson differs from country to country, and the manner in which the sale is culminated often differs.[20] Subsequently, it is the proper preparation of the sales force that could mean the difference between success and failure. Therefore, managers must make every attempt to ensure that critical personnel who directly influence customers are properly prepared to represent the MNC.

Technology

In the multinational arena, countries are quick to transfer changes in production machinery and technology across national borders.[21] Technology is borrowed and stolen constantly. Often the receiving country even improves on the product. For example, Toyota in Japan took the assembly line and made it radically better with the just-in-time parts delivery system.[22] Since copyright laws usually do not cross national boundaries, it is often easy to purchase a product with a given technology and then improve on it. Taizo Takushiji, a professor of international relations at Saitama University, said, "U.S. manufacturers are not studying their overseas competitors carefully enough."[23] Many U.S. companies are developing international joint ventures to get access to new technology. For instance, Boeing joined with Kawasaki and Fuji to obtain help in manufacturing the 767 airplanes, which seat as many as 260 passengers and can fly 7,000 miles nonstop.[24]

The Economy

The economy of the world and of various countries of the world is a major environmental factor affecting a manager's job in the global environment. Further complicating this is the fact that one country may be experiencing a downturn, another a slow recovery, and another a boom.

❖ ❖ MANAGEMENT IN A MULTINATIONAL ENVIRONMENT

Each of the management functions is quite important in the multinational environment. It is also quite important for a global firm entering a country to exercise patience. For UNUM Life Insurance Company, global expansion occurred when the firm acquired a Canadian life insurance company. According to Robert C. Cornett, second vice president of human resources and related businesses groups for UNUM, "We tried not to rush into things from market and business and also personnel perspectives. The company refers to its strategy as 'the patient road to international expansion.' "[25] Beyond patience, in order to effectively manage a multinational firm, proper utilization of each of the management functions is essential. However, some differences should be recognized when planning, organizing, influencing, and controlling in the multinational environment (see Figure 18.2). Small businesses are even going multinational to help assure future survival.

❖ **Figure 18.2**
Management in a
multinational
environment

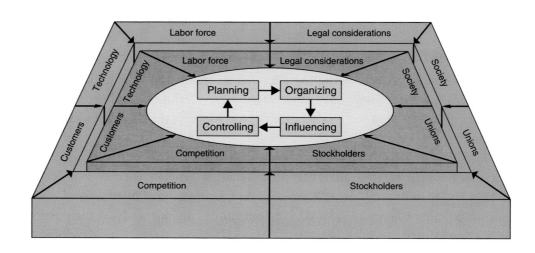

Small Businesses Shape Up by Shipping Out

More and more small businesses are coming to the stark realization that going global is necessary for many. Hackney & Sons, a maker of roll-up doors for beverage trucks, had a 50 percent market share in the United States, but as the economy slowed, market shares dwindled. At that point, Hackney & Sons viewed going global as the "only way to grow." They were assisted by two of their major customers, Coca-Cola Company and PepsiCo, and soon were providing doors to overseas bottlers.

Hackney & Sons president, Jay Troger, firmly believes "If you want to grow, exporting is a necessity." According to David L. Blond, "If you look at the kinds of products fueling the export boom, they've been many of the products produced by smaller, fast-moving companies." A recent *Business Week*/Harris Executive Poll discovered that only about 18 percent of small-business executives did any exporting. The reasons are quite obvious. Going overseas is a slow process, requiring a sizable investment of time, money, and effort, but probably the biggest problem for most small businesses is

lining up export financing. The Export/Import Bank in Washington, D.C., helps small businesses get loans from commercial banks by providing loan guarantees and insurance. Normally, financing is necessary so small businesses can build enough inventory to go overseas. Going global is often difficult and time consuming, but the rewards of going global are many, including extreme growth potential. Today's global economy is making not only mid- and large-size companies go global, but is also offering a lot to the little guy.[26]

Planning

At first glance, the objectives of MNCs may not appear to be any different from the objectives of businesses operating exclusively within the United States. The typical MNC objectives of survival, profit, and growth are indeed similar to those of companies operating in the United States. However, there is a major difference: The objectives of the MNC may clash with the objectives of the economic and political systems of the various countries within which they operate. Some of the objectives of countries may coincide with those of the MNC, and some may not. Most countries want improved standards of living for their people, and such objectives as a trained labor force, full employment, reasonable price stability, a favorable balance of payments, and steady economic growth are also fairly common.

In achieving some of these objectives, therefore, there is an overlapping of interests between the MNC and the host country. For example, a new MNC in a country will usually create jobs, thereby contributing to a higher level of employment, increased income, and economic growth. By doing so, MNCs often reduce the pressure on those political leaders who have high unemployment rates in their countries. Although the MNC usually contributes to the accomplishment of such objectives, it may not do so at the rate expected by the host country, and this can create problems.

One method of achieving a strategy of swift globalization is through the development of partnerships. Roland Smith, chairman of British Aerospace—which joined with counterparts from France, Germany, and Spain to form the aircraft manufacturer, Airbus Industries—said, "A partnership is one of the quickest and cheapest ways to develop a global strategy." Recent partnerships include Texas Instruments and Japan's Kobe Steel (for a semiconductor plant in Japan) and DuPont and Korea's Han Yang Chemical (for a chemical plant in Korea).[27] Even firms that have a history of going it alone, such as AT&T and IBM, are forming partnerships in order to achieve their strategic plans.[28]

Organizing

The organizational structure of a multinational firm must be designed to meet the needs of the international environment. Typically, the first effort of a firm to become a multinational is the creation of an export unit in the domestic marketing department. At some point, the firm may perceive a need to locate manufacturing units abroad, and after a time, these various foreign units are grouped into an international division.

The international division becomes a centralized profit center, equal in status to other major domestic divisions. It is typically headed by a vice-president and operates on a fairly autonomous basis, independent of domestic operations. The reasons for this approach are (1) the necessity of obtaining managerial and technical expertise in the diverse environments of many countries and (2) the reduction of control from the often larger domestic divisions. The disadvantage is the decreased coordination and cohesion of the international division with the rest of the company.

As the international division grows, it usually becomes organized on either a geographical or product base of specialization. In giant MNCs, the international division is often a transitional stage in moving toward a worldwide structure that discounts the importance of national boundaries. Any such global structure requires a careful balance of three types of specialization: functional, area (geographical), and product. When the primary base is any one of the three, the other two must be present in the form of specialized staff experts or coordinators. A clear-cut decision heavily in favor of any one base is usually inappropriate.

In a global functional organizational structure for a multinational, the executive in charge of the production function has worldwide responsibility. Together with the presidents and executives in charge of sales and finance, a small group of managers enables worldwide centralized control of the MNC to be maintained.

MNCs with widely diversified lines of products requiring a high level of technology to produce and distribute tend to use the area base in their global structures. General Electric moved from the international division form to the global area structure. Primary responsibility for worldwide operations was assigned to the 50 to 60 general managers in charge of product divisions. International specialists, formerly in the international division, were reassigned to the various product divisions, to aid them in adapting to a multitude of national environments. To ensure that the product orientation did not dominate to the exclusion of area emphasis, four regional managers were established in Europe, Canada, Latin America, and the rest of the world. These executives were General Electric's eyes and ears in the countries to which they were assigned.

They advised product executives on the most suitable approach in each country, identified potential partners, and aided in establishing locally oriented personnel programs. The area executive might be given line authority when a product division had not yet gained sufficient skill in the region or when a subsidiary unit reported to many product divisions. Though the basic emphasis was on product, the addition of the geographical concept produced a type of matrix organizational structure.

Finally, when the range of products is somewhat limited, or when the product is highly standardized, MNCs tend to use the global product structure. Executives with true line authority are placed over major regions throughout the world. This type of structure is used by international oil companies (with a limited variety of products) and soft-drink producers (with a highly standardized product). As in other instances, some supporting staff is necessary in the product and functional areas.

In all forms of MNC structures, one makes sure (1) that the product is properly managed and coordinated throughout the world, (2) that the functional processes of production, sales, and finance are executed efficiently, and (3) that proper and efficient adaptations are made in response to the environments in the host country.

Influencing

Many aspects of the influencing function may be altered in a multinational environment. Of particular significance in the operation of a multinational firm are the topics of leadership, motivation, and communication.

Leadership Successful management of an MNC requires that the manager understand the needs, values, and problems of employees in the countries where the company operates. The requirements for effective leadership of personnel in the United States, Canada, Great Britain, Australia, or many of the Western European countries differ significantly from those for such countries as Turkey, Mexico, Malaysia, Taiwan, and Thailand, or certain African, Asian, or South American countries. The needs and values of people vary from nation to nation, often the result of differences in economic living standards or cultural or religious influences.

In selecting individuals for overseas assignments, management must recognize that no one style of leadership will be equally effective in all countries. People in various countries have widely divergent backgrounds, education, cultures, and religions, and live within a variety of social conditions and economic and political systems. Managers must consider all of these factors, because they all can have a rather dramatic effect on the working environment.

Much that is said concerning the appropriate management approach for international businesses must be based on common sense and informed conjecture. It seems reasonable that a successful international manager should possess the following qualities, among others:

- A knowledge of basic history, particularly in countries of old and homogenous cultures.
- A social background in basic economics and sociological concepts as they differ from country to country.
- An interest in the host country and a willingness to learn and practice the language.
- A genuine respect for different philosophical approaches.

Basically, individuals transferred overseas should have a desire to function as well as possible in the host country environment.

Motivation

Unsatisfied needs tend to motivate behavior. In the United States and other highly developed countries, people's basic needs—physiological and security—are fairly well satisfied. Research on the application of Maslow's hierarchy of needs theory of human behavior has shown considerable differences concerning the dominant needs of people in different countries. Thus, in some advanced countries, managers must try to satisfy the needs for esteem and self-actualization. In developing countries with lower standards of living, appeals to basic human needs may prove to be not only appropriate, but the primary means for motivating desired behavior.

Communication

Communication is the transfer of information, ideas, understanding, or feelings among people. In a multinational environment, a difficulty one often encounters is ineffective communication. Certainly, working in a host country where the language differs from that of the parent country creates the possibility of communication breakdowns. An American working in an Asian country may experience this difficulty. Even when the same language is used, problems may occur. The meanings of words may be understood as defined. However, their interpretation may elicit other meanings. Even a tone of voice may be misinterpreted when two different cultures attempt to communicate.

The changing global environment has forced the need for global communication networks to the forefront. It has been estimated that global telecommunication networks may be more important to coordinate global operations than they are to the coordination of the parent country environment. In such a system, electronic messages may be exchanged throughout the world by people who are tied into the network. The vast time-zone differences can be overcome through such a system.

Controlling

Controlling has been defined as the process of comparing actual performance with standards and taking any necessary corrective action. The more multinational a firm becomes, the more important is its control system. The need to effectively control inputs, processes, and outputs is certainly applicable in the multinational environment. However, certain aspects of controlling may not be the same as in the United States. For example, as a control mechanism, disciplinary action may take different forms in various countries.

Standards are established levels of quality and quantity used to guide performance. In establishing standards in the multinational environment, both corporate objectives and the local environment must be taken into consideration. Often host country managers need to be consulted with regard to the feasibility of a particular standard.

Evaluating performance is a critical but often more difficult task to accomplish when operating in a multinational environment. Often an extensive management information system is needed to provide managers in the parent country with the knowledge they need to make timely and proper decisions. At times, too much or too little information is fed into the system. This factor, combined with the distance factor, places increased pressure on evaluating the performance of a multinational organization.

❖ ❖ HUMAN RESOURCES IN THE MULTINATIONAL ENVIRONMENT

By and large, the success of a multinational corporation hinges on the human component of the organization. Recruitment and selection, orientation, and training and development needs are often quite different in the multinational climate. Career development of individuals may also be helped or hindered, depending on the internal and external factors affecting the multinational. Compensation, performance appraisal, and employee relations should reflect the unique culture of the host country as well as the needs of the multinational firm.

Recruitment and Selection

One of the most difficult management problems for the multinational organization is that of recruiting and selecting suitable people to be sent on foreign assignments. Inappropriate selections are often made, negatively impacting the multinational operation. As the globalization of the world economy intensifies, U.S. corporations have found it more difficult to assure the uninhibited flow of adequate human capital to the multinational organization. Recruiting individuals with appropriate qualifications and encouraging them to apply are essential for global success. The essence of global business success is finding and employing the best people. Once the global business strategy is outlined, management must develop a corresponding recruiting strategy. The sooner human resource professionals are consulted about recruitment and selection, the better. In fact, establishing the global business strategy and the recruiting and staffing strategies concurrently will often result in a more effective overall strategy.

Poor selection, coupled with the stress of living and working overseas, have been documented as contributing to mental breakdown, alcoholism, or divorce. There are three common reasons why U.S. workers sent overseas fail: (1) Their family is misjudged as being adaptive to a multinational assignment or is not considered at the time of selection; (2) managers are selected solely on the basis of their domestic track records; or (3) they lack adequate cross-cultural training.[29] Other factors such as the following are also needed:

- A real desire to work in a foreign country.
- Spouses and families who have actively encouraged the person to work overseas.
- Cultural sensitivity and flexibility.
- A sense for politics.

Several surveys of overseas managers have revealed that the spouse's opinion and attitude should be considered the most important screening factor. Cultural sensitivity is also essential, to avoid antagonizing host country nationals unnecessarily.

The selection process for the expatriate should focus on measurement and evaluation of the candidate's current levels of expertise. Psychological tests; stress tests; evaluations by the candidate's superiors, subordinates, peers, and acquaintances; and professional evaluations from licensed psychologists can all aid in ascertaining the candidate's level of ability in interpersonal and cross-cultural skills. The candidate's spouse and children should undergo modified versions of the selection process, since family members confront slightly different challenges overseas than do employees.

Orientation

Orientation for new employees to the company, the job, and the work group varies in its degree of complexity, but global orientation will almost certainly be more complex than any domestic program. Because of the extreme cost of global staffing and the staggering cost of failed expatriate assignments, global orientation takes on increased importance; orientation for new global employees is critical. It must incorporate an introduction to the organizational (and perhaps national) cultures of all parties that the individual is likely to encounter. Such an introduction should also include an overview of the history, traditions, and corporate values of any partners. Then, it should include a description of the new venture, its organization, and its management structure, followed by an introduction of the employee to the manager, department, and co-workers.

Orientation cannot be a sketchy overview of the basics. It should be an in-depth process, thoroughly planned in advance, taking a long-term approach with provisions for follow-ups and evaluation. The benefits of such programs are evident. Two years after developing such a system, Corning, Inc. showed a 69 percent reduction in voluntary turnover among new hires, an 8:1 benefit-to-cost ratio in the first year, and a 14:1 ratio annually thereafter.[30]

Training and Development

People regarded as superior employees in the parent country often fail overseas because they are ill equipped to cope with the complexities and dangers of intercultural management.[31] A review of the placement decisions of some American multinational companies found that the companies reported 30 percent of their placements to be mistakes—primarily due to the employees' failure to adjust properly to a new culture.[32] However, multinational corporations are beginning to study culture to determine how different cultures communicate and work with each other.[33]

A major objective of intercultural training is to help people cope with unexpected events in a new culture. Once an expatriate is selected, it is essential to ensure that the person chosen is suitable for cross-cultural work. Needed skills may not be present in the most senior person—or in the person with the most technical competence. An individual overwhelmed by a new culture will be unable to perform required work duties effectively. Further, an ill-prepared

Only a few multinational corporations offer formal training programs to prepare people to live and work overseas. Employees often fail because they are ill-equipped to cope with the complexities and dangers of intercultural managing. Imagine yourself as the American shown here making a presentation to his Japanese colleagues in a Tokyo affiliate company. (Source: © Jim Pickerell)

individual may inadvertently offend or alienate a foreign host and perhaps jeopardize the MNC's existing long-term relations with the host country. Training should be sufficient to permit the manager (and spouse) to understand the new culture and adapt to their anticipated roles.

Career Development

Foreign assignments have often been thought to provide career advancement opportunities. However, the relationship between expatriation and career development or advancement is often not clear. With varying results in terms of advancement, it appears there is no standard interpretation of the importance of an overseas assignment. The impetus for overseas staffing seems to be more to meet immediate human resource needs than to create an integrated career development strategy for future corporate executives.[34]

Whatever the case, without generous support during the overseas assignment, employees can become demoralized, frustrated, and anxious.[35] Despite a company's intention to provide career advancement opportunities, there is still some danger that skilled managers assigned to foreign operations will ultimately perceive that their career progress has suffered. Some managers have returned from foreign assignments to find no job available, or they are given jobs that do not utilize skills obtained overseas. To solve this problem, a godfather system is often set up. Before the person leaves on assignment, a specific executive is appointed as the "godfather" to look after the person's interests while he or she is in a foreign country and to assist the executive in achieving a smooth transition when returning home. A repatriation plan is worked out, including the duration of the assignment and to what job the appointee will return. Ordinarily, the godfather becomes the person's boss when the expatriate returns to the parent country. During the overseas assignment, the individual is kept informed of major events occurring in the unit to which this person will be assigned in the future. In this way, not only is there a logical career plan worked out, but there is no feeling of being lost in the vast international shuffle of the company.

Some repatriated managers report that the overseas assignment is a haphazard, ill-planned affair that is usually accompanied by vertical advancement. Upon return, many have difficulty in readjusting to domestic operations, experience lowered self-confidence in their domestic position, and on occasion find themselves without a job. Managers may be unaware of the challenges facing the repatriated employee; thus, career obstacles persist for the expatriate.

At Dow, a "godfather" is assigned to each expatriate manager to assure "a relationship of mutual trust and interest." Basically, the expatriate keeps the godfather up-to-date on his or her activities, and the godfather keeps track of the expatriate's career while he or she is overseas." Expatriate managers are guaranteed that they can come back to jobs at the same level as the ones they left. The godfather is expected to arrange this transition. Upon repatriation, managers are encouraged to form support groups to discuss common overseas experiences.

Performance Appraisal

A performance appraisal system mandates a formal periodic review and evaluation of an employee's job performance. The development of an appropriate global performance appraisal system is a complex process, but an effective global system is essential for credible employee evaluations. Valid performance appraisal is difficult enough to achieve in the United States, whereas valid evaluations for overseas employees make a normally complex problem nearly impossible. What normally works in one culture might not work in another. What is a strength in one culture might be considered a weakness in another. When performance appraisals are done overseas, the issue of what performance standards to use comes into question. Differences in performance appraisal practices are almost always necessary. An improper performance appraisal system can create a great deal of misunderstanding and personal offense.

Such problems can be partially avoided by taking the following actions. First, determine the purpose of the appraisal, whether it is to enhance administrative decision making or to enhance the personal development of the employee. Second, whenever possible, develop performance objectives for job assignments or tasks. Third, allow more time to achieve results in an overseas assignment. Finally, keep the objectives of the appraisal system flexible and responsive to potential markets and environmental contingencies. As with a domestic performance appraisal system, a global one should result in a realistic review and evaluation of the employee's job performance.

Financial Compensation

The issue of global compensation is extremely important for a successful international business venture. Compensation must be a motivator and must encourage employees to perform. The ideal compensation system will help assure that the best performers receive the greatest level of compensation. Several additional questions arise when considering compensation levels for global employees. In the case of alliances, should the compensation systems of the partners be linked or will they be synthesized into a common system? Will compensation rates be pegged to local markets or tied to similar jobs in the partner's home country? Often each partner in a venture has an established pay policy, but policies differ among partners. At the very least, partners in such ventures should reach an agreement on the broad objectives of a compensation program for employees.

Global compensation programs should be designed to establish and maintain a consistent relationship between the compensation of employees in all international alliances and to maintain compensation levels that are reasonable in relation to leading competitors. Failure to establish a uniform compensation policy can result in predictable adverse effects, especially for employees doing the same jobs. Such compensation systems will inevitably lead to low morale, motivational problems, and less productive employees.

Employee benefits often vary drastically from country to country or from industry to industry. In Europe, for instance, it is common for employees to receive added compensation in proportion to their number of family members or the degree of unpleasantness in their working conditions. In Japan, a supervisor whose weekly salary is only $500 may also receive benefits that include family income allowances, housing or housing loans, subsidized vacations, year-end bonuses that can equal three months' pay, and profit sharing.

Employee Relations

The need for good employee relations takes on even greater significance in the global arena. Remember what Dow's human resources vice president said: "We consider each overseas move to be unique because each situation is different." Prospective expatriates, and those moving from one overseas assignment to another, are briefed and given an information packet on their destination. An adviser—normally the spouse of a recently returned expatriate—will visit the transferee and his or her spouse to explain what sort of emotional issues they are likely to face in the early stages of the move. The key to maintaining good employee relations is for the company to be there when an expatriate employee needs help. Global human resource professionals have been called on to assist employees based abroad with a wide and often difficult range of problems. Some of these include medical emergencies, natural disasters, wars, revolutions, and other international crises.[36]

Medical emergencies occur fairly frequently. Ralph W. Stevens, vice president of personnel and employee relations for Hamilton Oil Corp., recalls the case of a high-ranking technical manager who suffered a stroke while on business in Korea, where the company maintains no office. Stevens managed to find a first-rate physician, set the employee up in a well-regarded hospital, and transfer sufficient funds to cover his medical bills, while comforting the manager's frantic family.[37]

Because of its extensive operations in Latin America, Ferro, a $1 billion international manufacturer, has long had contingency plans in place for another kind of emergency: terrorist kidnapping. Nothing adverse has ever happened, but

---

A GLOBAL PERSPECTIVE

The Firm Sprinkles Consulting "Holy Water" Globally

Global firms throughout the world need it, and the global leader in it is "The Firm." The Firm is not the law firm in the successful novel or the Tom Cruise movie; it is the general management consulting firm of McKinsey & Company. Regardless of where a company is located, where it does business, or what the company's industry ranking is, it will at one time or another need consulting assistance. Whether the company is Hewlett-Packard, Johnson & Johnson, PepsiCo, BritishAir, AT&T, GE, American Express, GM, IBM, or Sears does not matter. When global companies need consulting assistance, they contact McKinsey. McKinsey is truly a global consulting firm, with non-Americans controlling its shareholder committee; the real possibility of electing a non-American as managing director in the near future; 60 percent of its revenues coming from outside the United States; and contacts in Russia, Eastern Europe, China, and India.

What does McKinsey do for its rather astonishing $200,000 to $300,000 per month fee, plus expenses? Well, they evaluate the relative economic performance of each company operation, the relative economic performance of each product category, consumer perceptions of each operation and each product category, and the strengths and weaknesses of the company's major competitors; in addition, they define the different strategic options and possible supporting organizational structures. Except that their fees appear to be much too high, what do they do that is different from competitors? They regularly sprinkle their consulting "holy water" at half of the companies in the Fortune Global 500. What do they do that is better? According to clients, the quality of their work is unquestioned—by the client, by the client's competitors, and even by those providing financial support.[38]

the company still strives to maintain a politically neutral and noncontroversial image when it operates in potential international trouble spots. Various contingency plans, including means and methods to evacuate workers if necessary, are in place for most U.S. companies currently operating in the Persian Gulf. CPC International Inc., for example, has a food-processing plant in Saudi Arabia. "Naturally we have contingency procedures approved and ready, although we

✘ Management Tips ✘

Guidelines for Dealing with the Multinational Enterprise

1. **Recognize that managing in a multinational environment provides different challenges.** Even so, it is often worth the effort.

2. **Understand that managing in a multinational corporation is usually more complex.** This complexity must be taken into account when managing.

3. **Realize that the laws of the host country may be quite different from those in the United States.** There is no comprehensive system of international law or courts.

4. **Acknowledge that the significant societal considerations of one nation will differ to some extent from those of other countries.** These different societal considerations are important when making global business decisions.

5. **Design the organizational structure of a multinational firm to meet the needs of the international environment.** It may be quite different from that of a firm operating in the United States.

6. **Understand the needs, values, and problems of employees in the countries where the company operates.** These needs, values and problems may be quite dissimilar.

7. **Realize that no one style of leadership will be equally effective in all countries.** This is a mistake that many Americans make when operating in a multinational environment.

8. **Recognize the potential for communication breakdowns when operating in a multinational environment.** The meaning of words may be understood as defined, but their interpretation may elicit other meanings.

9. **Remember that certain aspects of controlling may not be the same as in the United States.** For example, as a control mechanism, disciplinary action may take different forms in various countries.

10. **Select individuals who can be effective in a multinational environment.** Inappropriate selections are often made that negatively impact the multinational operation.

would rather not discuss them," according to Richard P. Bergeman, the company's vice-president of human resources.[39]

During its more than 100-year history, Fluor Daniel has had to deal with almost every kind of international crisis. "Earthquakes, hurricanes, uprisings, we've probably had employees caught in all of them," says Tom Blackburn, the company's director of international administration. To Blackburn, more difficult and wrenching than politically induced crises are instances in which an expatriate employee dies abroad. He once had to coordinate the transport of a worker's coffin from an international site back to the United States, giving what solace he could to the man's grieving widow.[40] The ultimate test of the company's concern about positive employee relations comes in times of global crises.

SUMMARY

Multinational corporations (MNC) are organizations with extensive international operations in two or more countries simultaneously. Their operations create interrelationships between countries and cultures as well as between economic and political systems.

The external environment is extremely diverse and complex, and the manner in which managers' tasks are accomplished may be altered substantially. Additionally, organizational behavior considerations are much more complex. The MNC must deal with the environment of the parent country in which the headquarters is located, and the host country in which the operational unit resides.

The same management functions are important in the multinational environment. However, there are some differences. The MNC objectives differ from those of domestic firms because of their potential clash with the objectives of the economic and political systems of the host countries. Strategic plans tend to originate in the home office. Tactical plans tend to be delegated to the individual international branches. Further, the organizational structure of a multinational firm must be designed to meet the needs of the international environment.

Many aspects of the influencing function may be altered when operating in a multinational environment. Successful management of an MNC requires that managers understand the needs, values, and problems of employees in the host countries. In

KEY TERMS

Multinational company (MNC) 584

Parent country 584

Host country 584

Transnational company 586

REVIEW QUESTIONS

1. What is a multinational corporation?
2. Briefly describe the major environmental factors affecting the management of multinationals.
3. How are the management functions influenced by the multinational environment?
4. What types of organizational structures are used for multinational firms?
5. How are human resource needs different for multinational firms?

selecting individuals for overseas assignments, management must recognize that no one style of leadership will be equally effective in all countries. People's basic needs may differ, and there may be problems in communication. A firm's control system is extremely important the more the company expands globally.

By and large, the success of a multinational corporation hinges on the human component. Selection and training and development needs are often quite different. Career development may be helped or hindered, depending on internal and external factors. The process of performance appraisal should reflect the unique culture of the host country as well as the needs of the multinational firm.

CASE STUDIES

CASE 18.1 Mr. Tanaka's Plea for Respect

Throughout the eighties, the U.S. trade deficit with Japan grew worse. Especially in automobiles and electronics, the Japanese share of American markets steadily increased. The steadily growing stock of U.S. dollars in Japanese hands was used to buy up increasing shares of U.S. companies. Labor unions and politicians complained about the loss of American jobs. Citizens expressed fear that the Japanese would come to own too much of American industry. And corporations griped that they were shut out of potentially profitable foreign markets.

U.S. managers accused the Japanese of "dumping" products in the States (that is, selling items in the United States for less than the costs of production). Another frequent complaint was that the Japanese government erected every conceivable trade barrier to keep U.S. products out of Japan. At the same time, it was argued, U.S. markets were essentially open to Japanese companies.

But George Tanaka, senior vice president of Toyonoka Electronics, said the problems were the Americans' own fault. Tanaka described what he saw as the "real" source of U.S. trade balance problems:

"In a nutshell, in Japan we treat customers as God and you only say, 'The customer is king.' Let me explain. Toyonoka sells microwave ovens in the United States. I have been trying for over a year to find an American company to make some of the parts we need. We want to have the parts shipped to Japan for

installation in United States-bound ovens. That would improve your trade balance. It would also allow us to take advantage of present favorable exchange rates.

"But I cannot find anyone who will produce the quality we need to stay competitive. American managers tell me, 'This is as good as we can do. You will have to change your operation to make the parts work.' In Japan, of course, suppliers value contracts like this and do all they can to meet our specifications. I am under a great deal of pressure to buy American. But American firms just do not seem to care about our needs.

"The same kind of attitude surfaces when I ask about shipping schedules. In our factories, we practice 'just-in-time' inventory control. Japanese suppliers deliver the parts we need just when we need them—and in small quantities. I know United States companies have to ship long distances. So we are willing to accept larger shipments and be somewhat flexible about delivery dates. But no American firm I have talked to will guarantee even the *week* of delivery. They say there are too many variables involved—strikes, raw material shortages, shipping problems. In Japan, a supplier would not ask *me* to worry about those things. I am the customer.

"The language also presents a problem. United States firms will not bother to use Japanese. They refuse to even print installation instructions and invoices in any language but English. This is especially grating since we take the time to learn even the American dialect of English. Can any American imagine buying a Toyonoka stereo or a Mazda automobile with the owner's manual written in Japanese? We take care of those problems because Americans are our valued customers."

Mr. Tanaka went on to reemphasize that American companies could sell as much in Japan as Japan sells in the United States if they gave Japanese customers proper regard.

QUESTIONS

1. Does Mr. Tanaka's "ugly American" argument have some validity?
2. What are the cultural factors that may account for the difference in perspectives on the balance of trade issue?

CASE 18.2 Renault: The American Adventure

When the American Motors (AMC) Alliance was named Motor Trend's "Car of the Year" in 1983, it was a compliment not only to the car but to a much broader alliance—that between Renault and AMC. Renault had purchased almost 50 percent ownership in AMC beginning in 1978. At that time, AMC may have seemed an unlikely choice for the French automaker. Renault was the sixth largest car maker in the world, with plants in 11 countries. Under France's socialist government, Renault was accustomed to being propped up whenever the need arose.

AMC, on the other hand, was by far the smallest of the big four U.S. automakers. There had been no really successful AMC model in over 20 years. Despite its name, American Motors was not an American favorite, and there was little public concern over the company's decline—and no government support.

But AMC did have things Renault wanted. Renault had set a goal to sell 2.5 million cars by 1985. But the European car market was in the doldrums. AMC gave Renault entree to the fastest-growing auto market in the world. AMC's 2,000 dealers and three underutilized auto assembly plants were also major pluses. And AMC had Jeep, the perennially successful line of utility vehicles.

AMC also had solid name identification in the United States, and company executives understood the U.S. culture. This provided the capability of eliminating many of the barriers foreign companies face. AMC managers were respected marketers; past failures were thought to have resulted from deficiencies in engineering and technology, not marketing.

The marriage was not an immediate success, nor was it to last a lifetime. There were a number of threats by U.S. lawmakers trying to prevent Renault from "taking over" an important U.S. company. Other U.S. automakers complained that the subsidies France gave Renault would translate into an unfair advantage for American Motors. Unions complained that AMC cars would only be assembled in the United States—the parts, they said, would be made in France, at the cost of U.S. jobs.

But as 1987 began, no hot replacement for the Alliance was in sight, and AMC sales crashed. It became increasingly clear that Renault would have to give up on its effort to become a major United States automaker. And in March of that year, the deal was cut to sell AMC to Chrysler. Relieved of its U.S. burden, Renault reported profits for the first time in six years.

In 1989, Chrysler Corporation and Renault agreed to invest $500 million together and make a new minisport utility vehicle. Both companies would begin marketing the vehicle worldwide in 1992; however, Renault did not have the resources to complete the deal.

QUESTIONS

1. For what reason did Renault want to be involved with AMC?
2. Describe the differences between AMC and Renault with regard to governmental influence.

NOTES

1. This case is a composite of a number of published accounts, among them: Peter R. Savage and Peter Coombes, "Sustaining Growth at Dow," *Chemical Week* 144 (April 5, 1989): 25–27; Paul L. Blocklyn, "Developing the International Executive," *Personnel* 66 (March 1989): 44–47; "Dow Chemical Profit Forecast," *The Wall Street Journal* (May 12, 1989): B4; Catherine Brady, "Plastics Recycling Moves Ahead," *Chemical Week* 144 (March 29, 1989): 20–21; Gregory Stricharchuk, "Dow Chemical Gets a Victory on Sarabond," *The Wall Street Journal* (May 10, 1989): A4; Joseph B. White, "Dow Chemical Says Earnings May Disappoint," *The Wall Street Journal* (June 16, 1989): B5; "Dow in China Deal," *The New York Times* (April 5, 1989): D4; Douglas A. McIntyre, "Companies I'm Glad They Didn't LBO," *Financial World* 158 (January 24, 1989): 76; David Hunter, "Atochem Bets on CFC in 1990s," *Chemical Week* 144 (January 18, 1989): 20–21; Ellen Goldbaum, "An Ag Venture Is Born," *Chemical Week* (April 26, 1989): 9; "The Fortune 500 Largest U.S. Industrial Corporations," *Fortune* 124 (April 24, 1989): 354–399; Patricia L. Layman, "Chemical Company Execs Chart Progress Toward Global Industry," *Chemical & Engineering News* 67 (October 16, 1989): 15–17; Alison L. Sprout, "America's Most Admired Corporations," *Fortune* 123 (February 11, 1991): 68–69; Albert Richards, "Is BASF the Next Company to Watch in Europe?" *Chemical Week* 147 (August 1, 1990): 11; Standard and Poor's Corporation, "Dow Chemical," *Standard NYSE Stock Reports* 56, No. 125 (June 29, 1989): sec. 9; William J. Storck, "Earnings at Monsanto, Dow Fall; Other Firms Gain," *Chemical Engineering News* 70 (October 26, 1992): 5; and William J. Storck, "Chemical Company Earnings Continue to Elude Upturns," *Chemical Engineering News* 71 (May 17, 1993): 16–19.

2. Michael J. Mandell, Wendy Zeller, and Robert Hof, "Jobs, Jobs, Jobs," *Business Week* (February 22, 1993): 70.

3. Raymond J. Mataloni, Jr., "Capital Expenditures by Majority-Owned Foreign Affiliates of U.S. Companies, Latest Plans for 1991," *Survey of Current Business* 71 (March 1991): 26.

4. "The Face of the Global Economy," *Business Week* (Reinventing America 1992): 151–159.

5. "U.S. Corporations with the Biggest Foreign Revenues," *Forbes* 148 (July 2, 1991): 286.

6. *Ibid.*

7. Walter Kiechel, "Love, Don't Lose, the Newly Hired," *Fortune* 123 (June 6, 1988): 87.

8. *Ibid.*

9. Alex Taylor III, "Why GM Leads the Pack in Europe," *Fortune* 127 (May 17, 1993): 83–87.

10. Leonard Greenhalgh, "I Would Abandon Business Contracts," *Fortune* 121 (March 26, 1990): 49.

11. Adapted from a case presented in Karen Berney's article, "Finding the Ethical Edge," *Nation's Business* 75 (August 1987): 22.

12. Calvin Reynolds, "U.S. Expatriates' Numbers Continue to Decline," *HR News International HR* (March 1991): Sec. C, p. 2.

13. David D. McClelland, *The Achieving Society* (Princeton, New Jersey: Van Nostrand, 1961).

14. Gene Koretz, "Why Unions Thrive Abroad—But Wither in the U.S.," *Business Week* (September 10, 1990): 26.

15. *Ibid.*

16. Wayne F. Cascio and Manuel G. Serapio, Jr., "Human Resources Systems in an International Alliance: The Undoing of a Done Deal?" *Organizational Dynamics* 19 (Winter 1991): 72–73.

17. *Ibid.*

18. *Ibid.*, p. 73.

19. Jim Impoco and Warren Cohen, "Nike Goes to the Full-Court Press," *U.S. News & World Report* 114 (April 19, 1993): 49–50.

20. Brian H. Flynn, "The Challenge of Multinational Sales Training," *Training and Development Journal* 41 (November 1987): 54.

21. Jay Jaikumar, "The Boundaries of Business: The Impact of Technology," *Harvard Business Review* 69 (September–October 1991): 100.

22. Susan Moffat, "To Be a Leader in Technology, You Must Share It," *Fortune* 124 (January 14, 1991): 34.

23. *Ibid.*

24. Ruth Simon and Graham Button, "What I Learned in the Eighties," *Forbes* 145 (January 8, 1990): 101.

25. Stephenie Overman, "International Waters," *HRMagazine* 38 (September 1993): 46–49.

26. Suzanne Woolley, "Shaping Up by Shipping Out," *Business Week* (April 19, 1993): 119.

27. Patricia A. Langan, "The New Look of Globalization," *Fortune* 121 (April 23, 1990): 18, 20.

28. Jeremy Main, "Making Global Alliances Work," *Fortune* 125 (December 17, 1990): 121.

29. Allen L. Hixon, "Why Corporations Make Haphazard Overseas Staffing Decisions," *Personnel Administrator* 31 (March 1986): 91.

30. *Ibid.*

31. Michael Berger, "Building Bridges over the Cultural Rivers," *International Management* 42 (July–August 1987): 61.

32. Christopher Earley, "Intercultural Training for Managers: A Comparison of Documentary and Interpersonal Methods," *Academy of Management Journal* 30 (December 1987): 685.

33. Berger, "Building Bridges over the Cultural Rivers," p. 61.

34. Mark E. Mendenhall, Edward Dunbar, and Gary R. Odou, "Expatriate Selection, Training and Career-Pathing: A Review and Critique," *Human Resource Management* 26 (Fall 1987): 331.

35. Philip R. Harris, "Employees Abroad: Maintain the Corporate Connection," *Personnel Journal* 65 (August 1986): 108.

36. Ellen Brandt, "Global HR," *Personnel Journal* 70 (March 1991): 43.

37. *Ibid.*

38. John Huey, "How McKinsey Does It," *Fortune* 128 (November 1, 1993): 56–60, 62, 66, 68, 72–74, 79, 80.

39. Ellen Brandt, "Global HR," *Personnel Journal* 70 (March 1991): 43.

40. *Ibid.*

19

Production and Operations Management

LEARNING OBJECTIVES

After completing this chapter students should be able to

✘ Explain the evolution of production and operations management.

✘ Identify and describe some of the graphic methods used in production and operations methods analysis.

✘ Explain the primary labor measurement methods and describe site selection.

✘ State the basic approaches to physical facility layout and explain the concepts of maintenance control and learning curves.

✘ Explain some of the basic financial models that are especially useful in production and operations management.

✘ Describe simulation and explain how it can be used in business.

Motorola's "Six Sigma" Quest: A Must, Not a Myth

In January 1987, Motorola adopted the objective of Total Consumer Satisfaction (TCS), meeting every expectation of every customer. To assist in its TCS effort, Motorola adhered to the concept of Total Quality Management (TQM), specifically Six Sigma, defect-free quality. Motorola is a global corporation with facilities on every continent. Its principal products include two-way land mobile communications systems; paging systems; semiconductors, including integrated circuits and microprocessor units; modems, multiplexers, and network processors; electronic equipment for military and aerospace use; cellular phones; and computers. Domestic high-tech companies such as Motorola face fierce competition from abroad, particularly from the Japanese, but Motorola has successfully met Japanese competition.

Fourteen years ago, then chairman Robert Galvin elevated the company's quest for quality, and began plowing massive funds into research and development and capital improvements. Since 1987, Motorola doubled its research and development and capital expenditures, as well as doubling sales and share values. Motorola also spends tens of millions of dollars annually on employee training. By 1993, the result of this strategy was that overall product defects had been slashed to about 5.9 sigma, between five and seven parts per million, below the ultimate goal of 3.4 defects per million. Customers responded favorably, and Motorola's global sales continually increased.

Thus far, Motorola's success stems partly from a team atmosphere generated among employees who produce the highest-quality products possible. Motorola spends half a billion dollars annually to ensure that new technologies keep their plants efficient and productive. Continuous training ensures that employees learn to use these new technologies effectively. Motorola motivates employees to produce quality products by creating and monitoring a team atmosphere; employees set their own goals in terms of achieving quality and meeting delivery schedules. Simultaneous design and manufacturing involve teams from engineering, marketing, and manufacturing joining together to design the product. In this environment, "Everybody's business is everybody's business." Working closely together permitted the most critical element in efficiency: "simultaneous design and construction of the product and factory." Motorola embraces the concept, as the Japanese have for years. Rather than design the product and then test whether it can be manufactured, the process makes manufacturing seamless. Redesign work that would have taken three weeks elsewhere is done in only two days because everyone participates in product design meetings. Therefore, the staff simply meets and solves problems whenever they occur, and engineers meet to solve defects when they occur.

Motorola has not yet reached its goal of "Six Sigma" quality, but it is still committed to defect-free manufacturing. Motorola has disproved conventional wisdom that higher quality costs more. Motorola employees are not discouraged by not reaching their Six Sigma goal, but instead accept the premise that "nothing less than consistently perfect" is acceptable.[1]

Only a few years ago, production management was taught exclusively in relation to factory environments such as that of Motorola. Today, the expanded field of production and operations management applies to all organizations, including banks, hospitals, schools, and government agencies. **Production and operations** is the application of objective, especially quantitative, techniques to the design and operation of any system that transforms inputs into outputs. Even with the continual quest for quality that Motorola strives for, its production techniques remain remarkably similar to those of the recent past. Most production and operations techniques are equally applicable to manufacturing and service industries. **Operations management** is the management of the complex activities relating to planning production, organizing resources, directing operations and human resources, and monitoring system performance.

In this chapter, we will first discuss the evolution of production and operations management. Then, we will review a number of traditional techniques, including graphic methods, labor measurement, site selection, physical facility layout, maintenance control, and learning curves. Next, we will discuss financial planning techniques. In the final sections of the chapter, we will address simulation as it relates to production and operations management, and examine a global perspective of production.

❖ ❖ THE EVOLUTION OF PRODUCTION AND OPERATIONS MANAGEMENT

The quality and cost of a product are determined largely by the effectiveness and efficiency of the production system. In recent years, the quality of products has continued to increase, while the cost of enhanced quality has steadied or been reduced. A substantial body of knowledge has accumulated on the use of statistics, computers, engineering, and behavioral science techniques in manufacturing environments since the Industrial Revolution. But recent cost-cutting efforts by U.S. manufacturers have typically relied on such approaches as plant closings; downsizing (discussed in Chapter 7); laying off production workers; and selling off failing, unwanted, or unprofitable businesses.

Experts argue that American firms focus on capital investment as a means of reducing labor costs and consequently ignore the huge benefits to be gained from improving quality, reducing inventories, and tapping the hidden productivity of the labor force. Basically, American managers have been underutilizing their human capital—pouring hundreds of billions of dollars into equipment and technological advancements rather than keeping and retraining valuable employees and gearing their efforts to improve the relationship between work and productivity. When trimming costs was necessary at Toyota, the firm's new factory at Kyushu was designed to be employee centered. Unlike the recent assembly lines built by Japanese rivals Mazda and Nissan, Toyota's new plant put workers, and not computer-controlled robots, at the center of the production process. The new factory has saved millions of investment dollars by employing machinery that makes workers more efficient rather than costing them their jobs.[2] Opel Automobile Chairman, David Herman, agrees with employee-centered management. Herman believes that "It is clear now to everyone that the management of people is the key to productivity."[3]

U.S. companies are extending the Japanese method of worker involvement. Although the Japanese have a group-oriented culture, where workers help find

---

MANAGEMENT IN PRACTICE

A Skill-Building Exercise: You have a boss who simply will not listen. Last week, you hired the two technical operators who will run the new $600,000 laser micro-milling (cutting) machine. The machine must be attended at all times in order to keep it operating to the precise tolerances that the titanium nose cones require. For two of the six operating steps, the process requires both workers. However, those two processes take only 12 minutes of the 80-minute cutting time. Both employees have four-year technical degrees. Your boss, the departmental manager, has just told you that the two employees will be in charge of the machine on alternate days. On each one's off day, that one will assist the other worker during the critical 12-minute period. For the other 68 minutes, the idle employee will clean up around the shop floor and help load and unload trucks. You personally recruited both employees, and you realize that they won't like clean-up duty and loading and unloading trucks.

What would you do or say?

Fortunately, American managers are beginning to balance their capital and human investments to improve the production system. Motorola's flexible "factory of the future" in Boynton Beach, Florida, produces high-quality Bravo pages in minutes instead of several days. Programmable robots are controlled by an integrated computer network.
(Source: Photograph courtesy of Motorola, Inc.)

and solve problems, activities are directed by managers and engineers. In the United States, the evolution has gone beyond mere group decision making to a point of American teamwork. American teamwork involves team members in management activities such as determining the appropriate method of work or rating other team members' performance; some teams even have the authority to fire loafers.[4] Remember that Motorola motivates employees to produce quality products by creating and monitoring a team atmosphere in which employees set their own goals in terms of achieving quality and meeting delivery schedules. Louis Hughes, the president of General Motors Europe, is in charge of the most efficient and profitable of Europe's automakers, which he credits to his ongoing mission of knitting together its disparate operations into a production system equal to the best Japan has overseas.[5] Combining excellence in product design and uncompromising quality is essential to global success.

Fortunately, American managers are getting better at balancing their capital and human investments to improve the production system. Managers also are more interested in any suggestions that can improve the production process. Maytag Company was so committed to improving their production operation that they solicited suggestions from nonsupervisory personnel. A total of 6,346 suggestions were turned in, an average of three per employee. More than 2,700 of these ideas were actually implemented. Maytag management gave employees awards ranging up to $7,500 and totaling $200,322 for suggestions used.[6]

Other companies are approaching production problems by developing a new way to improve productivity. Traditional cost accounting methods are out at many firms such as Calcorp, Inc. Managers at Calcorp, a maker of graphic plotters, are making capital investment decisions in fresh and innovative ways. For example, instead of automating to cut costs, they invest in equipment to cut lead times, boost quality, reduce inventories, and increase flexibility. Management de-automated the shop by eliminating the traditional assembly line and using carts to push work around. The new system takes a fraction of the former space, and output has tripled. It appears that this approach to productivity can benefit corporations by providing both structural changes and innovative approaches to technology, thereby improving the effectiveness and efficiency of the production system. Because of the need to revitalize production systems, production and operations management has reemerged as a challenge to all organizations. Companies that are lean producers are those who have effective production and operations management systems, as is the case with Nucor Steel.

❖ ❖ GRAPHIC METHODS

Several graphic techniques have been developed to assist in production and operations methods analysis. The techniques in and of themselves do not improve the way a task is done. Instead, they permit a person with an inquiring mind and knowledge of the subject to improve the production process. Four of these techniques are the flow process chart, the operation chart, the worker-machine chart, and the activity chart.

Flow Process Chart

A **flow process chart** illustrates the activities involved in an entire process, showing the sequence in which they are performed. Standard symbols have been developed to serve as a type of shorthand in recording activities. Each task to be

---

World-Class Lean Producers

Nucor Steel is a prime example of a very lean producer. Nucor Steel is what world leaders in the steel industry talk about when they meet to discuss global competitiveness. Nucor does not follow the standards in the steel industry, but actually sets the standards in the steel industry. Nucor is innovative and totally concerned with satisfying customer demands. It is participative, it is profitable, and it produces steel at a fraction of the cost of most competitors. When Nucor does anything, it does so with an eye to the future of the steel industry. Another lean producer is Mars, a leader in the candy industry. Mars follows the customer closely to maintain its high market share. Mars has very high profitability and is so productive that the firm operates with 30 percent fewer employees than its closest competitor. One of the factors accounting for its high productivity is that equipment is valued at replacement cost so there is a built-in bias toward having the latest equipment. Even though Mars is obsessed with quality, no one has *quality* in his or her job title. Even so, everyone at Mars is concerned about quality. Nucor Steel and Mars are both lean, efficient producers that view quality as job one, and key on satisfying customers at a profit.[7]

accomplished is identified, along with the time it will take. A person can then study the sequence of tasks to determine if there is a better way to accomplish the job. Figure 19.1 is the flow process chart for the manufacture of a cylinder head (the top part of a gasoline engine), which is to be ground and inspected prior to its assembly onto a tractor engine. Only the activities related to the grinding department are shown.

Operation Chart

An **operation chart** shows an operator's activities while one operation in a process is performed. The chart might show the motions of the left hand and right hand of an operator. Its use is essential when the time from start to finish of an operation (the cycle time) is fairly short. Operations are usually broken down into smaller categories than those used with a flow process chart. A major benefit of an operations chart is that it permits a manager to view a task to see if it is being done the best way.

Worker-Machine Chart

A **worker-machine chart** shows if there is excessive idle time associated with either the worker or the machine. These charts are beneficial when both a worker and a machine are used to perform a particular task. An idle worker may be assigned an additional machine to control. On the other hand, if the machine is expensive and needs to be kept operating, this may justify the cost of an additional operator even though the idle time of the worker goes up.

Activity Chart

In both the manufacturing and the service industries, efficient accomplishment of objectives requires the use of teams. An activity chart, which is similar to a worker-machine chart, is useful for this purpose. An activity chart can show the

❖ **Figure 19.1**
Flow process chart

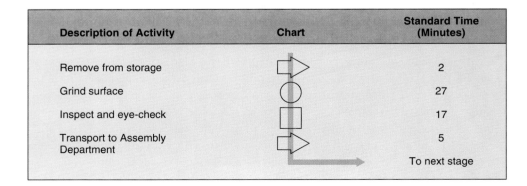

Description of Activity	Chart	Standard Time (Minutes)
Remove from storage		2
Grind surface		27
Inspect and eye-check		17
Transport to Assembly Department		5
		To next stage

interaction of members of the group in performing a task. For example, in a hospital, the activities of a surgical team in performing an emergency operation must be carefully controlled. If any member of the team fails to act correctly at the right time, the results could be disastrous. An activity chart allows the actions of each team member to be graphically displayed in relation to the actions of other members.

❖ ❖ LABOR MEASUREMENT

The most critical factor in the production process is labor. If management is to manage labor resources effectively, there must be some way of measuring their use. Labor standards specify the amount of time necessary to perform a certain task. Standards are used to set up incentive plans and to compare the performance of individuals doing similar tasks. They are also used in preparing bids on contracts and in estimating completion dates. There are three primary labor measurement methods: time study, predetermined time standards, and work sampling.

Time Study

Time study is the systematic measurement and analysis of the time required to do work. The most common approach to time study is patterned after the approach developed by Frederick W. Taylor in 1881. Under this procedure, a stopwatch is used to measure one worker's performance, and then the results become a standard for all workers. The following steps are normally included in a time study:

1. Describe the task to be performed.
2. Break the task down into a number of simple subtasks.
3. Measure the time required to perform each subtask and note operator performance. This should be done over a number of work cycles.
4. Compute the average time required to do the total task according to the following formula:

$$\text{Average time} = \frac{\text{Times recorded to perform all subtasks}}{\text{Number of cycles observed}}$$

5. Compute the normal time. The normal time is determined by computing a performance rating, that is, the percentage of reasonable working speed at which the observed worker is judged to be working. The formula for normal time is as follows:

$$\text{Normal time} = \text{Average performance time} \times \text{Rating factor}$$

6. Calculate the standard time according to the following formula:

$$\text{Standard time} = \frac{\text{Normal time}}{1 - \text{Allowance fraction}}$$

The allowance fraction adjusts for personal needs, unavoidable work delays, and worker fatigue, among other variables. Suppose, for example, that an average time of five minutes was determined for painting a tractor wheel hub and that the time study analyst decided the worker was moving at 90 percent of normal speed. Assume further that the work methods department of the firm has a standard allowance of 15 percent for this kind of work. The standard time is computed as follows:

$$\text{Normal time} = \text{Performance time} \times \text{Performance rating}$$
$$= 5.0 \times .9$$
$$= 4.5 \text{ minutes}$$

$$\text{Standard time} = \frac{\text{Normal time}}{1 - \text{Allowance}}$$
$$= \frac{4.5}{1 - .15}$$
$$= \frac{4.5}{.85}$$
$$= 5.3 \text{ minutes}$$

Although the worker is moving at only 90 percent of normal speed, standard time can still be computed.

Predetermined Time Standards

An alternative to the measurement of the actual time required to do work is the use of **predetermined time standards**—established estimates of the time that should be required to perform minute tasks. In order to estimate how long a certain task will take, the time factors for each element are added together.

The most widely known approach to using predetermined time standards was developed by Frank and Lillian Gilbreth and is called *methods time measurement* (MTM). The Gilbreths called the basic work elements *therbligs* (if you reverse the last two letters of the Gilbreths' name and then spell it backward, you get *therblig*). Therbligs included such activities as selecting, grasping, positioning, assembling, reaching, holding, resting, and inspecting. Time values for various therbligs are available from the MTM Association for Standards and Research.

The use of predetermined time standards has several advantages. First, the standards may be established in a laboratory environment, avoiding interruption of normal production activities. Second, the standards can be known before a task is done, and this knowledge can aid in planning. Finally, the method is widely accepted by unions, perhaps because the association that sets the standards is independent of management.

Work Sampling

A way of measuring work that does not use a stopwatch is called **work sampling**—the observation of a worker or workers at random times to determine the proportion of time that is being spent on various tasks. If employees can be shown how to better accomplish their work and how to add to the overall team effort, they will benefit themselves, their team, and the corporation. A detailed procedure for work sampling was developed by L. Tippet in the 1930s. Statistical sampling techniques are used to determine the number of observations needed to obtain the desired degree of reliability.

Suppose that we wish to determine how much of a word processor operator's time is involved in the preparation of correspondence. If we observe the operator at 100 randomly selected points and find that correspondence is being prepared at 30 of them, we can estimate that the operator works on correspondence 30 percent of the time.

❖ ❖ SITE SELECTION

Every firm has its own criteria for choosing a particular site for locating a new facility. In addition to cost considerations associated with purchasing and building a new site, many other factors must be evaluated, including the supply of skilled labor, union activities, quality of life, and local, state, and even international politics. For many reasons, a site that may be completely satisfactory for one company may be totally unacceptable for another.

A number of mathematical and computer-based techniques have been developed to assist in determining where to locate a physical facility. The most commonly used approach is to develop a set of criteria and rate each location on how well it meets the criteria. An example of this procedure is illustrated in Table 19.1. In this case, the most important factor for site selection is availability of skilled labor, so this factor is assigned a maximum score of 30. Availability of raw materials, with a maximum score of 20, is the next most important criterion. Third is access to transportation, with a top score of 15. In the example, three sites have been proposed and rated on each of the criteria. The total score for site 2 is significantly above the others, although site 2 ranks lowest on access to transportation. Often, there are many more factors than those shown in this simple illustration.

TABLE 19.1 Plant Location Scoring Model				
	MAXIMUM SCORE	SITE 1	SITE 2	SITE 3
Availability of skilled labor	30	18	25	15
Availability of raw materials	20	12	18	10
Access to transportation	15	10	5	10
Total score		40	48	35

❖ ❖ PHYSICAL FACILITY LAYOUTS

For virtually any type of operation, management must determine the most effective way to lay out the physical facilities. Among the more traditional approaches are process layouts, product layouts, and fixed-position layouts. In a factory environment, management might be concerned with the best placement for lathes and punch presses. Offices, desks, and computers might be of concern in an administrative setting. And in a hospital, the locations of operating rooms, laboratories, and nursing stations have a major impact on efficiency. The overriding objective of physical facility layout is to maximize efficiency and effectiveness, as is the case with Siemens.

Effective Layout Gives Siemens a Competitive Advantage

Germany's largest corporation, Siemens, is a world-class manufacturer of electronics. The Siemens process is built upon the concept of efficiency, getting the most out of every production dollar. At one plant, Siemens requires 20,000 different parts to manufacture its products, and as these parts enter the stockroom from the unloading docks, the majority go to Siemens's automated storage and retrieval system. This $3 million state-of-the-art manufacturing layout blends computers and robotics, and mechanically transports components from receiving to testing and from stocking to workstations. The system is a true marvel to view, somewhat like standing inside a huge vending machine that whirls and hums as machinery retrieves the selected items and presents them for assembly or further processing. The automated stockroom system frees 30,000 square feet of stockroom space, reduces the time needed to receive materials by 50 percent, and maintains accurate inventory. This semi-automated assembly line presents one circuit board at a time to an operator. Upon presentation, a light shines on the board to show the operator where to do the next assembly task, such as inserting an electronic component. This hybrid layout is a semi-automated assembly system that requires less tooling and is more flexible than a fixed line or even one driven totally by robots. The hybrid process is not a traditional assembly line layout, but it is definitely one that is quite effective in terms of producing quality products.[8]

The overriding objective of physical facility layout is to maximize efficiency and effectiveness. After winning certification for its all-composite Starship, Beech Aircraft, a subsidiary of Raytheon Corporation, rolled its first production aircraft off this assembly line. (Source: Photograph courtesy of Raytheon Company.)

Process Layouts

A wide variety of goods or services can be handled simultaneously when the process layout is used. A **process layout** is an arrangement of the processing components according to the functions they perform. A typical example of the use of the process layout is the job shop that produces different products, each by a different sequence of operations. Basically, there is no single best route through the system for all the goods or services produced. The product may be made one unit at a time or in batches (see Figure 19.2). The unit or batch moves from one department to another in a particular sequence.

A common example of the process layout is found in hospitals. Patients come to the hospital with a wide variety of problems. Depending on their ailment, they are routed through various departments—admissions, lab, x-ray, and so on. When the process layout is used, the objective is to arrange departments or work centers in the most economical manner. In most situations, an attempt is made to minimize material-handling costs.

A major advantage of the process layout is that it provides for flexibility in equipment and labor assignments. If one machine breaks down, for example, the entire process may not have to be stopped. Work can simply be rerouted. Another advantage is that the process layout permits the economical manufacture of goods and services in small batches. It also permits a wide variety of outputs in different sizes and forms.

❖ **Figure 19.2**
A process layout

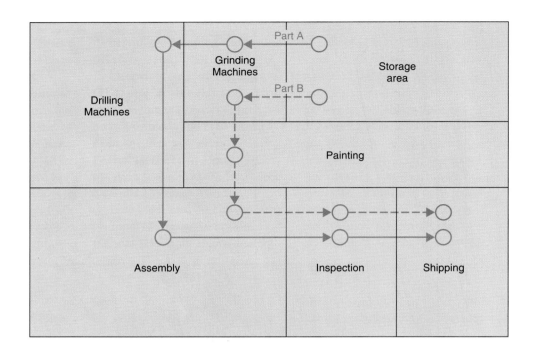

A disadvantage of the process layout is that it allows less specialized use of equipment and labor. Also, the items being processed require additional handling, since they must be moved to each process point. Finally, labor skill requirements are high, inventories must be large, and scheduling and coordination may present major problems.

Product Layouts

A **product layout** is the production arrangement that entails moving a product down an assembly line or conveyor and through a series of workstations until the product is completed. Automobiles, television sets, and soft drinks are produced in this manner. When the product layout is used, the objective is to create a smooth, continuous flow along the assembly line with a minimum of idle time at each workstation. The product layout presents a balancing problem. Time required at each workstation needs to be balanced so that it is nearly the same as at the following one.

The main advantage of a product layout is manufacturing efficiency when large numbers of essentially identical items are produced. This is partly because automated and specialized equipment is used. Also, material handling is lower, inventories are reduced, and workers can usually be more quickly trained.

Product layouts have weaknesses too. First, assembly lines typically require a large investment. Second, a breakdown at one point on the assembly line can require the entire line to be stopped. Finally, an assembly line typically cannot handle a wide variety of products.

Fixed-Position Layouts

A method used in manufacturing large or heavy products is the **fixed-position layout**—the production process in which the large or heavy product stays in one location, and people, tools, materials, and equipment are moved to the product as needed. Basically, the production process occurs around the product because it is too large or too heavy to move along a production line. A military aircraft carrier is a product that, at a certain stage, is too large and too heavy to make a standard production line feasible. In order to complete the product, it is necessary to move the process to the location of the carrier.

❖ ❖ MAINTENANCE CONTROL

In a typical organization, the breakdown of even one machine can have severe effects. Workers may be idled, and in some instances entire facilities may have to be closed. Consider what will happen if the air-conditioning system in a large, modern office building fails or if the central computer system at General Motors is out of order for even a day.

Maintenance is the sum of all activities involved in keeping a production system in working order. In most organizations, it represents a significant part of total costs. Routine inspection and other efforts aimed at preventing breakdowns and keeping equipment and facilities in good working order are known as **preventive maintenance**. If a company is not willing to bear the costs of preventive maintenance, breakdowns tend to occur. Such breakdowns typically must be repaired on an emergency or priority basis, often at considerable expense. The purpose of preventive maintenance is to identify potential problems and make

A balance must be struck between preventive and breakdown maintenance. At this automated van assembly line, where robotic arms weld van bodies, preventive maintenance is very important. (Source: © Tony Stone Worldwide/Andy Saeks)

❖ **Figure 19.3**

Preventive versus breakdown maintenance costs

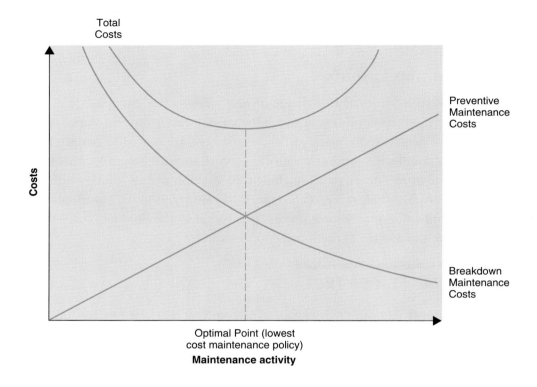

❖ **Figure 19.3**

Preventive versus breakdown maintenance costs

changes or repairs before breakdowns occur. For example, keeping a machine well oiled is a better alternative than replacing the machine because a bearing failure has caused it to break down.

A balance must be struck between preventive and breakdown maintenance. Notice in Figure 19.3 that as preventive maintenance costs rise, breakdown maintenance costs fall. The intersection of these two cost curves represents the lowest maintenance costs. Up to this point, putting more and more money into preventive maintenance will reduce total maintenance-related costs. Beyond this point, though, the firm will be better off waiting for breakdowns to occur and repairing them when they do.

❖ ❖ **LEARNING CURVES**

A **learning curve** is a graphic representation of the decreasing time required to do a particular task as that task is repeated by a certain person. Essentially, the more times a person does a particular job, the easier the task becomes. Two basic principles are involved. First, the more times a task is done by a particular person, the less time it will take. Assume, for example, that a technician has just begun assembling a number of identical small components. If she needs 20 minutes to complete the first unit, by the time she has done four units, the time may be down to 15 minutes. Second, the amount of time saved with each unit of experience normally decreases. The technician just mentioned has decreased the time required by five minutes in making just four units. Many additional repetitions may be needed to shave just one more minute off the time.

A mathematical relationship can be developed to determine how long it will take to produce any unit as a function of how many units have been produced before it. The implications of learning curve analysis are far-reaching. For instance, failure to consider the learning curve effect can result in running out of inventory and raw materials because the units produced are taking less and less time to finish. Also, considering the learning curve effect helps in labor planning and scheduling. It can keep managers from scheduling more time than is necessary for a project, thereby avoiding idleness or underemployment of workers.

❖ ❖ FINANCIAL PLANNING TECHNIQUES

One of the most valuable tools for a business planner is financial modeling. This tool is especially useful in making capital investment decisions. Factors related to profit and loss are so vital to the growth, and even survival, of a firm that it is advantageous for any planner to understand the available techniques. Some of the basic financial approaches are the payback method, break-even analysis, discounted cash flow, make/buy decisions, and purchase/lease decisions.

ETHICAL DILEMMA

For over ten years, American semiconductor makers have segregated production into on-shore and offshore operations. Highly skilled chores were accomplished in the domestic plants. Final work, which required a great deal of labor but less skill, was handled in overseas facilities, where wages were low. This scenario is changing because of automation. Machines now have the capacity to mount circuits onto metal frames, wire the circuits into place, and even test the finished product for flaws. They do all this, and at a quicker rate than humans. While a Southeast Asian worker can wire 120 integrated circuits to his frame in an hour, using manual equipment, an automated machine in the United States can wire 640 circuits in an hour. One worker is capable of monitoring eight machines at a time, and thus the output per person is an overwhelming 5,120 circuits an hour. For countries such as Malaysia, the Philippines, and Singapore, which have been heavily involved in electronics jobs, the impact could be devastating if technology replaces "final work" labor.[9] Would it be socially irresponsible for U.S. semiconductor makers to abandon these overseas labor pools and devastate the socioeconomic status of loyal, dedicated workers just to increase profits?

What would you do?

Payback Method

The most common and easiest method of financial analysis is the **payback method**—the method of financial analysis by which investments are ranked according to the payback period, the time it takes an investment to pay back the initial capital in profits. For example, if the initial investment is $1,000 and the return is $200 per year, the payback period is five years.

Although easy to understand, the payback method has major limitations. First, returns after the payback period are not considered. In the example, the investment might keep returning $200 for five more years. Second, the time value of money is not considered. A dollar today is not the same as a dollar ten years from now. To overcome the inaccuracy of this approach, many companies use it in a very conservative manner. For example, Lincoln Electric Company, the world's largest maker of arc welding products, has a maximum payback period of only two years for new projects. Thus, if a machine will not pay for itself during the first two years of operations, Lincoln will not buy it.

Break-Even Analysis

Break-even analysis is the financial analysis method used to determine the amount of a particular product that must be sold if a firm is to generate enough revenue to cover costs. Fixed and variable costs and total revenue (total income) are charted according to the number of units produced in order to determine the point at which revenue and costs are equal and the operation begins to make money. In order to progress in a break-even study, one must be capable of identifying the following elements:

- Fixed costs.
- Variable costs.
- Price of the item.

Fixed costs do not change with the level of output. Costs that normally are considered fixed are the salaries of top management, rent, property taxes, and other similar expenses. **Variable costs** are directly related to changes in output. Costs that might be included as variable costs are direct material and labor expenses incurred in manufacturing a particular product.

The distinction between fixed and variable costs is not always as clear-cut as we might like it to be. Often, there is a gray area in which some costs can be considered either fixed or variable.

The break-even point for selling a product is arrived at by dividing total fixed costs by price minus variable costs. To illustrate: Suppose a product is priced at $15, total fixed costs are $1,000, and variable costs are $10 per unit. Using the following formula to determine the break-even point in units of output, we have:

$$\text{Break-even point in units} = \frac{\text{Total fixed costs}}{\text{Price} - \text{Variable costs}}$$

$$= \frac{\$1,000}{\$15 - \$10} = 200$$

Thus, we would have to sell 200 units before we could begin making a profit.

Figure 19.4 shows graphically how break-even analysis is used. The vertical axis is costs and revenue, and the horizontal axis is units of output.

The $1,000 in fixed costs is represented on the graph by a straight line. Variable costs change with the level of production, so the variable cost line slopes upward. Variable costs are added to fixed costs to determine total cost, so the variable cost line starts at the point where the fixed cost line intercepts the vertical axis. The total revenue line is price times number of units sold. The break-even point of 200 units is at the intersection of the total revenue and total cost lines.

How reliable is break-even analysis? Would you bet your firm's survival on it? Probably not, but the benefits can be substantial if break-even analysis is used with full appreciation of its weaknesses. If you drew a bead on the break-even point with a shotgun and fired, the pattern of the shots would spread out around the break-even point. This is about as accurate as you might expect to be because of the difficulty of correctly identifying fixed and variable costs. But break-even

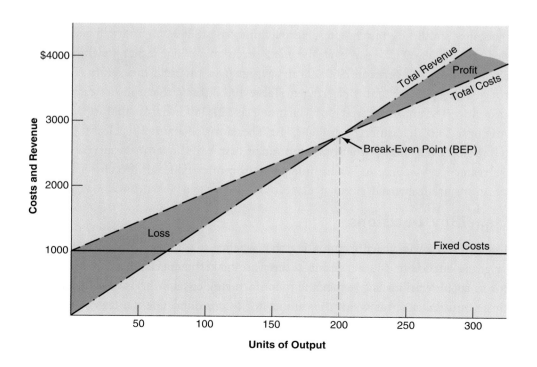

❖ **Figure 19.4**
Break-even analysis

analysis certainly forces a manager to plan. And an individual who plans is in a position to make better decisions than a nonplanner.

Regardless of the financial planning mechanism utilized, once a project is completed, dissembly and/or elimination of equipment is part of the cost of the project. Any way to save money related to used equipment would be quite desirable. Oil companies, in conjunction with several Gulf Coast states and environmental officials, are involved in the *Rigs to Reefs* program. Instead of removing used oil rigs one year after production has ceased, they are being toppled in place to create reefs that will last approximately 300 years, and save the oil company at least $150,000 per rig. These reefs attract 50 times more fish than other areas in the Gulf, making them ideal for the recreational and commercial fishing industry.[10]

Discounted Cash Flow

One of the disadvantages of the payback method is that it does not consider the time value of money. A common approach to considering the time value of money in business decision making is the **discounted cash flow technique**—the way of valuing an investment that uses an interest rate or discount rate to calculate the present value of the income the investment is expected to produce. Most of the uses of this technique involve capital investment decisions. Taking into consideration the time value of money can mean the difference between profit and loss.

Assume that the vice president of production must decide which of two machines should be purchased. One machine costs $200,000 and will generate a savings of $50,000 a year over the next seven years. The other machine costs $150,000 but will generate $60,000 in savings over the next four years. The discount rate is 15 percent. Referring to Table 19.2, notice that the net discounted cash flow (the amount saved) for Machine B is $21,360, whereas that for Machine A is only $8,050, a difference of $13,310. Therefore, Machine B is clearly the better choice, even though the total amount of cash saved over a seven-year period is greater for Machine A. When time value of money is taken into consideration, decisions are improved.

Make/Buy Decisions

Decisions concerned with evaluating the benefits of making a product in-house or going outside to another manufacturer are make/buy decisions. The main factor in such decisions is whether the manufacturing costs in-house are lower than those outside. But this is not the only factor to consider. The manager must also ask whether the space that will be used to manufacture the product in-house could be used more advantageously. If the space could be used to make more

TABLE 19.2 Purchase Decision

YEAR	SAVINGS PER YEAR MACHINE A	SAVINGS PER YEAR MACHINE B	PRESENT VALUE OF $1	PRESENT VALUE OF SAVINGS MACHINE A	PRESENT VALUE OF SAVINGS MACHINE B
1	$50,000	$60,000	0.870	$43,500	$52,200
2	50,000	60,000	.756	37,800	45,360
3	50,000	60,000	.658	32,900	39,480
4	50,000	60,000	.572	28,600	34,320
5	50,000		.497	24,850	
6	50,000		.432	21,600	
7	50,000		.376	18,000	
				208,050	171,360
		Less cost of equipment		200,000	150,000
		Net discounted cash flow		8,050	21,360
		Difference in net discounted cash flow		└─$13,310─┘	

Note: Machine A costs $200,000; Machine B costs $150,000.

money through manufacturing other things, the decision might be made to produce the product outside the firm.

Purchase/Lease Decisions

Another important financial decision is whether to purchase or lease (rent) equipment. Discounted cash flow methods are often used in making such decisions. In evaluating the purchase option, such items as interest expense, depreciation, and salvage value must be considered. However, leasing may involve only the lease payment.

❖ ❖ SIMULATION

Businesses have found simulation a valuable tool to use in the planning and decision-making process. **Simulation** is the technique for experimenting with a real-world situation through an artificial model that represents that situation. A model is an abstraction of the real world. Thus, a simulation model represents

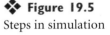

Figure 19.5

Steps in simulation

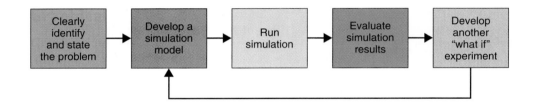

a real-world situation through mathematical logic in an attempt to predict what will occur in an actual situation. Its uses are many and widespread.

Simulation transcends the boundaries of many of the other quantitative techniques. As such, it is not a separate quantitative tool; rather, it is a procedure that has been used effectively in conjunction with other mathematical tools, such as inventory control and quality control. A manager who operates in an uncertain environment may consider simulation.

The general steps associated with developing a simulation model are presented in Figure 19.5. Once the problem has been identified, a simulation model is developed and run. The results are then analyzed. If the manager wants to ask other "what if" questions about the problem, they can be asked. The manager is in a position to ask many questions about the other factors that could affect the problem.

Railroads have found simulation particularly beneficial. Have you ever wondered why more trains don't arrive at the same time on a single track? Trains are different lengths and weights; they travel at different speeds and typically must share a common track to get from one place to another. At times there are two or more tracks that the cars could travel on, but the majority of the time there is only one. Simulation provides the manager with the ability to recognize the many variables that are involved with activities such as train scheduling and to ask questions regarding solutions to the problems.

Procter & Gamble utilizes simulation to assist in solving some unusual problems. P&G provides the following example of how the company uses simulation:

> Pulp forms the basic raw ingredient for manufacturing paper and can be made in a variety of grades that are dependent on the chemical processing and the blend of wood species. Procter & Gamble refines pulp from trees, and they use simulation to aid in the design of a wood yard, assuring maximum operating efficiency with a minimum of capital investment.
>
> A wood yard serves as a surge area for wood arriving from various sources by unscheduled railcars and trucks. The wood is in the form of short and long logs and must be stored until used in the pulp mill. Naturally, railcars require different unloading equipment than trucks, and the simulation helps determine the optimum number of unloading stations for both. Additionally, different equipment is needed to handle long logs

than short logs for both railcars and trucks. After long logs are unloaded, they are cut into short logs before they can be stored, an operation that requires other special equipment. Finally, the operation of the pulp mill needs a constant feed of a well-controlled blend of wood species to be efficient. Wood must be stockpiled sufficiently to assure a constant feed regardless of the weather, which can bring the tree-cutting operations to a standstill for a couple of weeks, or equipment failures in the wood yard. In net, the simulation of the flow of materials through the wood yard helps size equipment and stockpiles of logs to assure constant availability of the proper wood species for input to the pulp mill.

This example is only one of the ways simulation has been used effectively. If the risk of making a decision is great, the manager will need to evaluate many options before making a commitment to allocate resources. Simulation provides an excellent tool for evaluating alternatives and finding solutions to problems.

A GLOBAL PERSPECTIVE

Teams Reenergize Production Systems

The quality and cost of a product are determined largely by the effectiveness and efficiency of the production system. In order to be competitive globally, American firms must produce quality products at competitive prices. Manufacturing systems in the United States are now undergoing revitalization to assist American manufacturers in their attempt to be competitive in the global business environment of the next decade. Production systems that will allow American firms to be globally competitive will probably require adaptation to the most recent behavioral and technological changes.

American managers are beginning to balance their capital and human investments to improve their production systems. Managers also appear to be more interested in any suggestions that can improve the production process. Companies are beginning to follow, and extend, the Japanese method of worker involvement. American teamwork involves group members in management activities, such as determining the appropriate method of work and rating other group members' performance.[11] GM Europe is a perfect example of a company that is working in a team environment, where the production system evolves around the concept of teamwork. GM is already the most efficient and profitable automaker in Europe. GM recognizes that people working in a true team environment is the key to productivity, but the production system must evolve in such a manner to enhance overall productivity. The newest GM Europe car, the Corsa, embodies the latest production and people reforms. The car was designed, engineered, and brought to market in just 36 months. The Corsa contains 30 percent fewer parts than its predecessor, because suppliers are required to ship as much as possible preassembled. Such actions save GM and its customers money. The car is designed in such a way as to make it easier to assemble, improving quality and productivity. GM Europe is so successful because the focus is on teamwork and a production system that enhances the productivity of all concerned.[12] Because of the need to compete globally, American firms must reenergize production systems by balancing their capital and human investments and by using new approaches to production.

✗ Management Tips ✗

Guidelines for Dealing with Production and Operations Management

1. **Balance both your capital and human investments to improve the production system.** Both are important.

2. **Remember that operating in a service-producing industry as opposed to a goods-producing industry creates different problems.** But, they must be managed.

3. **Recognize and be able to use the production and operations management techniques.** This will allow you to improve the production process.

4. **Use the principles of motion economy to improve efficiency and reduce fatigue.** They can save your workers considerable time and effort.

5. **Remember that if you are to manage labor resources effectively you must have some way of measuring their use.** This is often a difficult but necessary task.

6. **Recognize the importance of proper site selection to a firm.** For many reasons, a site that may be completely satisfactory for one company may be totally unacceptable for another.

7. **Determine the most effective way to lay out the physical facilities.** The overriding goal of physical facility layout is to maximize efficiency and effectiveness.

8. **Remember that proper maintenance of equipment and facilities must be accomplished.** Failure to properly accomplish this task can be quite costly.

9. **Recognize that the more times a person does a particular job, the easier the task becomes.** When possible, you may want to permit workers to specialize in certain tasks.

10. **Realize that the factories of the future will likely be much different from what they are today.** You must learn to operate in this new environment.

SUMMARY

Several graphic techniques have been developed to assist in production and operations methods analysis. A flow process chart is an illustration of the activities involved in an entire process, showing the sequence in which they are performed. The operation chart shows an operator's activities while one operation in a process is performed. Through studying worker-machine charts, a manager is able to determine if there is excessive idle time associated with either the worker or the machine. An activity chart is useful to show the interaction of members of a group in performing a task.

There are three primary labor measurement methods: time studies, predetermined time standards, and work sampling. Time study is the systematic measurement and analysis of the time required to do work. Predetermined time standards are established estimates of the time that should be required to perform minute tasks. Work sampling is the observation of workers at random times to determine the proportion of time that is being spent on various tasks.

A number of mathematical and computer-based techniques have been developed to assist in determining where to locate a physical facility. However, the most commonly used approach is to develop a set of criteria and rate each location on how well it meets the criteria.

There are three basic approaches to arranging physical facilities: process layouts, product layouts, and fixed-position layouts. A process layout is an arrangement of the processing components according to the functions they perform. The production arrangement that entails moving a product down an assembly line or conveyor and through a series of work stations until the product is completed is a product layout. A fixed-position layout is the production process in which the large or heavy product stays in one location, and people, tools, materials, and equipment are moved to the product as needed.

Maintenance is the sum of all activities involved in keeping a production system in working order. A learning curve is a graphic representation of the decreasing time required to do a particular task as that task is repeated by a certain person.

The most commonly used and easiest method of financial analysis is the payback method, by which investments are ranked according to the time it takes an investment to pay back the initial capital in profits. The method used to determine the amount of a particular product that must be sold if a firm is to generate enough revenue to cover costs is break-even analysis. The discounted cash flow technique is the way of valuing an investment that uses an interest rate or discount rate to calculate the present value of the income the investment is expected to produce.

Simulation is the technique for experimenting with a real-world situation through an artificial model that represents that situation. Simulation transcends the boundaries of many of the other quantitative techniques of analysis.

KEY TERMS

Production and operations 614

Operations management 614

Flow process chart 617

Operation chart 618

Worker-machine chart 618

Time study 619

Predetermined time standards 620

Work sampling 621

Process layout 623

Product layout 624

Fixed-position layout 625

Maintenance 625

Preventive maintenance 625

Learning curve 626

Payback method 628

Break-even analysis 628

Fixed costs 628

Variable costs 628

Discounted cash flow technique 630

Simulation 631

REVIEW QUESTIONS

1. Define each of the following terms:
   a. flow process chart
   b. operation chart
   c. worker-machine chart
2. Distinguish between time studies and work sampling.
3. Describe a process layout, a product layout, and a fixed-position layout.
4. What is the purpose of preventive maintenance?
5. What are the basic principles associated with the learning curve?
6. What are the costs involved in break-even analysis? Define each.
7. Why might a manager want to use the discounted cash flow technique of evaluating investment decisions as opposed to the payback method?
8. Explain what is meant by this statement: Simulation transcends the boundaries of many of the other quantitative techniques.

CASE STUDIES

CASE 19.1 Materials Management at Newco

Tom Johnson, the new materials manager for the Newco Manufacturing Company, was concerned about the disorganization in his department. Newco had 250 employees and manufactured small electrical motors. Tom reported to the vice president of manufacturing, Charles McDowell. Tom's 15 subordinates performed such functions as stocking, receiving, inventory control, purchasing, and outside sales.

The previous materials manager had allowed the employees to do whatever job they thought necessary at the time. They had often shifted from job to job—working the parts-issue window while mechanics ordered parts, stocking the parts bin when time permitted, receiving parts when deliveries were made, and shipping orders to customers. The same employees answered the phone and handled outside sales as required. Employee complaints over matters such as inadequate pay, unclear work assignments, and lack of competent leadership had been frequent.

Charles gave Tom a detailed account of the past performance of the materials operation. He said the department performed very poorly, and he attributed this to a lack of overall direction, ineffective organization, and incompetent personnel. He said several of the employees were lazy and did as little work as possible. The turnover rate had been in excess of 200 percent per year for the past three years. Charles suggested that Tom "clean house" by firing most of the employees in the department and starting with a fresh crew.

Tom was shaken by what Charles had told him and by the complaints of the employees, and he considered finding a new position. He decided, however, to give the assignment his best effort for at least a few months.

QUESTIONS

1. Would a flow process chart assist Tom? Discuss.

2. How should Tom handle the human situation he faces? Justify your answer.

CASE 19.2 Briggs & Stratton

"Our fully integrated operations ensure exacting control over every phase of engineering, testing, production—everything right down to final inspection," reads the annual report of Briggs and Stratton Corporation (B&S), the dominant U.S. manufacturer of small gasoline engines. B&S is effective in managing its production system; the company has been continuously profitable, through recessions and economic upswings, for decades. With profits of $39.4 million on sales of $636 million, Briggs and Stratton recently ranked 44th in sales but 167th in total return to investors on the *Fortune* 500 list.

There is something particularly striking about Briggs & Stratton in today's world of robotized and flexible manufacturing systems; the company relies mainly on the most flexible manufacturing system of all—the human being.

Simply managing its complex operations, let alone maintaining its status as the world's lowest-cost producer of small engines, is a monumental task. A typical Briggs and Stratton engine has more than 500 parts, and almost everything—engine castings, starters, alternators, ignition coils, and carburetors, to name a few parts—is made in the B&S factory. The company proudly claims, "A Briggs and Stratton engine is Briggs and Stratton throughout."

Complicating the production management process is the company policy that engines are manufactured only to specific customer orders and according to individual specifications. Production is leveled through incentive discount plans to encourage customers to buy during the off season and contracts with customers who agree to buy evenly throughout the year. Still, B&S must stay on top of every aspect of factory operations. Unlike most other manufacturing concerns, which use components supplied by subcontractors, B&S must absorb any drop in quantities demanded in-house. The company also cannot close down a small factory here and there and thus minimize the impact of slowdowns. All 3,000,000 square feet of Briggs and Stratton's gasoline engine manufacturing facilities are located in the Milwaukee area, two-thirds of it in the Wauwatosa plant.

One thing Briggs and Stratton does not have to worry about is the motivation of its workforce. A formal employee-participation program reinforces quality control. A piecework incentive system motivates workers to be punctual and to produce as much as they can. And managers spend most of their time maintaining communication with workers.

There are some clouds on the horizon, however. Japan's Honda Motor Company has entered the U.S. market for small engines as a supplier to the Snapper power equipment unit of Fuqua Industries, Inc. Snapper has already taken part of the recreational generator business and claims that lawn mowers and generators will become its third major line behind autos and motorcycles.

Far from throwing in the towel, Briggs and Stratton quadrupled its advertising budget and introduced a number of product innovations, making its engines look better and run quieter and longer. The company also opened a new plant in Murray, Kentucky, where labor costs are expected to be lower.

QUESTIONS

1. To what do you attribute Briggs and Stratton having such a motivated workforce?
2. Which of the production and operations management techniques presented in this chapter do you believe B&S uses?

NOTES

1. This case is a composite of a number of published accounts, among them: Kevin Kelly, "Motorola Wants to Light Up Another Market," *Business Week* (October 14, 1991): 50; B. G. Yovovich, "Motorola's Quest for Quality," *Business Marketing* 76 (September 1991): 14–29; Jim Impoco, "Fighting Japan on Its Home Turf," *U.S. News & World Report* 110 (June 24, 1991): 50–52; and Kent Banning and Dick Wintermantel, "Motorola Turns Vision to Profits," *Personnel Journal* 70 (February 1991): 51–55; Bill Smith, "Six Sigma Quality, a Must Not a Myth," *Machine Design* 65 (February 12, 1993): 63–66.

2. Steven Butler and Warren Cohen, "Toyota Puts It on the Line," *U.S. News & World Report* 115 (August 23, 1993): 47–48.

3. Alex Taylor III, "Why GM Leads the Pack in Europe," *Fortune* 127 (May 17, 1993): 83–87.

4. John Hoerr, "The Payoff from Teamwork," *Business Week* (July 10, 1989): 56–62.

5. Taylor, "Why GM Leads the Pack in Europe," pp. 83–87.

6. S. Feinstein, "Labor Letter," *The Wall Street Journal* (March 15, 1988): 1.

7. "Quality Control from Mars," *The Wall Street Journal* (January 27, 1992): A10; *Fortune* 123 (September 26, 1988): 98–104.

8. Jay Heizer and Barry Render, *Production and Operations Management*, 3rd ed. (Boston: Allyn and Bacon, 1993), pp. 378–379.

9. Adapted from Steven P. Galante, "U.S. Semiconductor Makers Automate Cut Chip Production in Southeast Asia," *The Wall Street Journal* (August 21, 1985): 28; Robert D. Hof, Neil Gross, Otis Port, "Make It Fast— and Make It Right," *Business Week* (October 25, 1991): 76–79.

10. News report based on an NBC News Sunrise Program Feature Story, December 15, 1993.

11. Hoerr, "The Payoff from Teamwork," pp. 56–62.

12. Taylor, "Why GM Leads the Pack in Europe," pp. 83–86.

20 Management Information Systems

LEARNING OBJECTIVES

After completing this chapter students should be able to

✘ Explain the types of information needs firms have.

✘ Describe the characteristics of an effective MIS and explain the MIS at different organizational levels.

✘ Describe the steps involved in creating the MIS and offer guidelines for effective MIS design.

✘ Explain what is involved in the implementation of the MIS and the types of computers that are available for it.

✘ Describe the various types of information subsystems that are available for use by management and discuss the advantages of an integrated system.

✘ Describe major technology advancements and how they can affect productivity.

The Executive Support System (ESS) at Xerox

"I am not sure we have fewer meetings, but they are more productive," said Xerox president Paul Allaire. "We very rarely have a meeting at which we don't have enough information to make a decision." In 1985, Ken Soha, Xerox information systems director, began converting the company's top executives to computerized information management. The arrangement of work stations, networks, and software Soha designed was soon called the Executive Support System, or ESS. Currently, the top 100 managers and 400 other users at Xerox are tied into ESS. *Fortune* called the Xerox system "probably the most far-reaching in any company."

Allaire explained how ESS has improved meetings: "We had what's called the extended management committee meeting. When I was in Britain, I had to come to the United States for these meetings once a month. The reading material I had for the meeting was supposed to come a week in advance, but sometimes it was only three days. I still needed time to analyze it and comment on it, have my staff go over it. So I sometimes faced the prospect of reading it in a hotel room the night before the meeting, which was clearly ridiculous. Now, it's all on the ESS."

Allaire commissioned Soha to improve the effectiveness of the headquarters's staff and cut costs. Soha hired Jim Carlisle, managing director of Office of the Future Inc., to help. "Compared to people, technology is cheap," said Allaire. "I felt sure that technology could help reduce staff, the big expense item. But we realized we couldn't just present the system and say, 'Here's the answer to your prayers, and by the way, take a ten percent cut in your people.' You have to provide tools and let people decide how to use them most efficiently." He added, "But we had to start at the top."

Soha quickly ran into a problem created by nonstandardized reports and terminology. For example, two strategic business units might have different definitions for revenue. And the annual business plans were in varying formats, often depending on where the preparer previously worked or attended business school.

Working with Allaire and other executives, Soha designed a standard five-page business plan. Each business unit put its plan on ESS five days before the annual planning meeting. Security safeguards in the system limited access to executives with a "need to know." But Xerox managers all over the world could see the proposed plans immediately. Such information could be downloaded from ESS and called up on laptop computers even during airline flights.

ESS is central to execution of Xerox's overall strategic plan for the 1990s, and in serving customers. Former chief executive David Kearns was instrumental in turning the big marketer of document processing equipment into a customer-focused organization with "high expectations" of itself and "total quality control" (TQC). Kearns focused on reducing manufacturing costs and overhead and making the company less complicated. Kearns also keyed in on understanding what customers really needed—not just wanted—from Xerox. Among the elements of Kearns's plan were a "quality vice president" to act as change agent, "standards and measurements," training that would "cascade" down from senior managers, "recognition and rewards," and pervasive communication.

After putting the plan into effect, Xerox nearly doubled its return on assets and generated $1 billion in surplus cash. Effective communication and an emphasis on quality have become integral parts of the Xerox way of doing things, which may account for what appears to be a very bright future for the company. In fact, a main part of the executive support system is information concerning each of Xerox's customers. Xerox's policy of focusing on the total process and providing tools and letting people decide how to use them most efficiently has spread beyond the company to customers' companies. Xerox places great value on effective communication with customers and helping them enhance quality. Xerox employees actually listen to customers and help them rethink the way they work, so Xerox can better help customers be more productive. The executive support system at Xerox once again takes on new importance, as a customer satisfaction enhancement tool.[1]

The Xerox story illustrates how one leading company has progressed into the information processing age and taken its customers along with them. A multitude of similar stories may be told of businesses across the nation—in fact, the world is in the midst of both an information and a high-tech revolution. Information for use in business continues to expand rapidly. Managers now have various types of computers and technology that allow them to more effectively use this information. The high-tech revolution is creating unlimited possibilities for managers, and managers are now able to implement what had only been dreamed of before—an effective management information system. A survey of 203 chief executive and chief financial officers revealed that information systems should play a bigger, more powerful role in U.S. corporations, especially in boosting market position and profitability. According to John B. McCoy, chair of Banc One Corporation, a 63-bank holding company based in Columbus, Ohio, "The faster you go, the faster you want to go and the less forgiving you are when you're not going. Some of our deals are pure technology." The survey projected that in 1993, U.S. corporations would spend more than $200 billion on computers, telecommunications, and related services, making technology by far the largest capital expense for business. The poll found 81 percent of top executives regularly use PCs and/or terminals, nearly double the figure of four years ago.[2]

A **management information system (MIS)** is any organized approach for obtaining relevant and timely information on which to base management decisions. In all probability, no attribute of an organization so significantly affects decision making as does the management information system. An effective MIS typically employs computers and other sophisticated technologies to process data that reflect the day-to-day operations of a company, organized in the form of information to facilitate the decision-making process.

Because of the importance of the management information system, an entire chapter is needed to review the topic. This discussion begins with a presentation of the information needs of a firm and characteristics of an effective MIS. Then, the different roles of the MIS at various organizational levels are examined. This is followed by a discussion of the steps in creating the MIS. Guidelines for effective MIS design are then given. They are followed by a presentation on the implementation of the MIS. Computer selection and information subsystems available for use by management are next reviewed. Finally, MIS advancements are examined with regard to their effect on productivity, and a global perspective is provided.

❖ ❖ INFORMATION NEEDS OF A FIRM

As can be seen in Figure 20.1, both internal and external factors affect the organization, and therefore must be accounted for in the MIS. Each component of the internal and external environment creates information needs for managers. A properly designed MIS assists in satisfying these needs. Notice in Figure 20.1 that the MIS draws information from the various internal functional areas, such as marketing, production, and finance, and integrates this information with that of the external environment, resulting in the creation of an information system. Both types of information are needed if managers are to perform effectively. For example, the marketing function will probably not operate properly without knowledge of the types of customers the firm is attempting to serve. Certainly Xerox wants to know the types of customers that will ultimately purchase their

❖ **Figure 20.1**
Management information needs

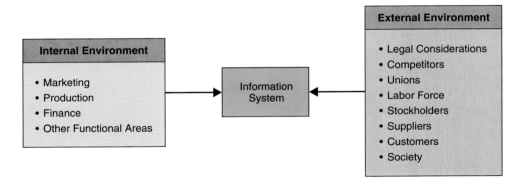

products, and their executive support system provides this information. And production may be hampered without an appreciation of the nature of the labor force available in certain areas. A multitude of internal and external interrelationships exist and must be reflected in the information system in order to satisfy the information needs of managers. For the MIS to provide maximum benefit, however, it must be designed in the manner that offers the most beneficial information possible.

❖ ❖ CHARACTERISTICS OF AN EFFECTIVE MIS

Any MIS, whether computerized or manual, should be designed to provide information with the following characteristics in order to afford managers the maximum utility from the information. Information should be

- **Timely—up-to-date**. Sound decisions cannot be based on outdated information. For example, a person desiring to invest in the stock market is at a severe disadvantage if decisions are made based on week-old or even day-old data.
- **Accurate—correct**. Managers must be able to rely on the accuracy of the information. Incorrect data probably will cause bad decisions to be made.
- **Concise—essential**. A manager can absorb only so much information during any one period. Therefore, the information should be limited to only the most necessary.
- **Relevant—what the manager needs to know**. Computers can provide managers with volumes of information. However, because only a small portion of available data is useful in a given situation, it is important to single out only the most relevant data to analyze.
- **Complete—everything that is needed**. Having no information is sometimes better than having partial information. A manager could draw false conclusions with incomplete information.

The absence of even one of these characteristics reduces the effectiveness of the MIS and complicates the decision-making process. Xerox's MIS has all of these characteristics, making it a highly effective executive support system.

❖ ❖ THE MIS AT DIFFERENT ORGANIZATIONAL LEVELS

An effective management information system is essential for managers to cope with the complex and competitive environment they face. Managers at each organizational level make particular demands on the MIS. Top-level managers often need information with which to make far-reaching decisions. Usually, they require extensive information relating to the external environment. For example, top-level managers at Xerox need to know about government legislation, economic trends and forecasts, and competitors' activities. On the other hand, Xerox's lower-level managers depend primarily on internal data. These managers typically need information in functional areas such as inventory reorder points and the number of workers to be assigned to a specific project. Top-level managers usually will want only product data that is summarized, perhaps by quarter. The Executive Support Systems (ESS) at Xerox is currently "empowering top executives to view critical information unfiltered by management layers, to communicate and coordinate in lightning speed with anyone in the organization, to analyze business scenarios as never before, like a master puppeteer, to control and shape decisions made in the far reaches of the corporation."[3] Lower-level managers are more likely to need production data on a daily or even hourly basis. Thus, each level of management benefits from information available from the MIS, but from different perspectives.

Whether used by top-, mid-, or lower-level managers, a successful MIS must produce several types of output that is related to business operations, such as the following:

- **Routine reports.** Routine reports include business data summarized on a scheduled basis. For example, weekly and monthly production reports may be sent to the general manager, whereas quarterly reports may be forwarded to upper-level managers.
- **Exception reports.** Exception reports highlight major variations requiring management's attention. An example is the quality exception report, which is completed when the number of defects increases beyond a predetermined maximum.
- **On-demand reports.** An on-demand or ad hoc report provides information in response to a specific request. The number of defects created by each worker in the plant is an example of an on-demand report that management could request.
- **Forecasts.** Forecasts report on the results of applying predictive models to

specific situations. Managers may want to forecast the number and types of employees needed to satisfy projected demand for a firm's product.

❖ ❖ CREATING THE MIS

In designing the MIS, managers must carefully consider four steps that will provide the needed output and conform to the MIS criteria discussed earlier. These steps (see Figure 20.2) are not separate and distinct; considerable overlapping exists. The development of the MIS is not merely a matter of properly designing the system. Without a major commitment from top management, it is virtually impossible for any MIS to become smoothly functional and operational.

Study the Present System

In assessing the existing information system, the following questions might be asked: (1) What is wanted from the new system, and what is the present flow of information? (2) How is the information used? (3) How valuable is this information in terms of decision making? There needs to be a thorough assessment of the organizational capabilities and strategic objectives and of any major external factors relevant to the organization's correct functioning. From this assessment, the determination of the informational, operational, and functional objectives can be realized, and the system can be designed to accomplish them.

At one stage in his career, one of the authors was a team member in charge of developing one of the first integrated state highway information systems. Detailed analysis was done of the information flows and uses. One of the agencies involved was the state highway patrol. In conversations with local troop members, the author discovered that a weekly report to headquarters caused special

❖ **Figure 20.2**
Creating the management information system

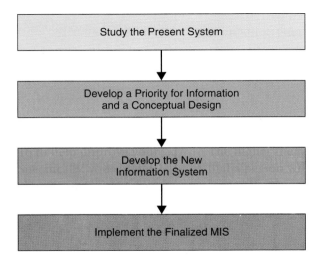

difficulty. For each troop (there were 13), it took one officer about four hours to prepare the report. The author went to headquarters to determine how the data were used in decision making. He found that the reports were neatly filed by a secretary and that the information was never used. When one of the reports was not submitted on time, however, the secretary was directed to prepare a letter of reprimand to the unit commander. Identifying this kind of deficiency is the reason for asking the third question in the assessment.

Develop a Priority for Information and a Conceptual Design

Once the current system is thoroughly understood, it is used to develop a priority for needed information. There is certain information a manager must have if proper decisions are to be made, but some is merely nice to have, not critical to the manager's job performance. The MIS design must ensure provision of high-priority information; data lower on the priority list should be generated only if their benefits exceed the costs of producing them. The weekly report just described should not have had the priority it was accorded. Once the information needs are determined, a conceptual design of the management information system is developed.

To set priorities for information needs, individual managers should develop their own priority lists, and the lists should be integrated into a single list for the entire organization. Certain departments may discover that the information they identify as top priority will be far down on the organization's list. The needs of the entire organization must be the controlling factor.

Develop the New Information System

The organization's priority list for information needs should govern the detailed design of the new MIS. A system of required reports should be developed and diagrammed. Treating the whole organization as a unit allows the elimination of duplicate information. At a certain point on the priority list, the information is not worth the cost of providing it and should not be included.

Once the exact needs are decided upon, a plan for the management information system can be established. Then, a model of the system is created, tested, and refined until it meets specified performance levels. This model should be capable of achieving the informational, operational, and functional objectives established in the first step of the MIS creation process.

After thoroughly studying the highway information system discussed earlier and setting priorities, the author prepared the diagram in Figure 20.3 to show how the system should function. The summary diagram was supported by many detailed reports and procedures. As can be seen, several types of input data are

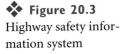

Figure 20.3

Highway safety information system

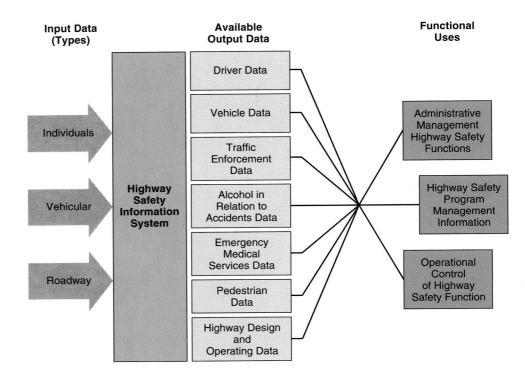

needed. For output, the system provides various types of information for both administration and operations. All departments are tied together. Data that come in from one department of the state can provide the information used in another department. If a person has a car wreck and is given a ticket, this information not only is used by law enforcement agencies but also becomes part of a database to identify high-accident locations. When the MIS is properly designed, the important information an organization needs in the decision-making process is available.

Implement the Finalized MIS

Once the formal model is finalized, the new management information system is ready to be implemented. At this point, the system must be made operational. Space allocations are made, computer equipment is selected, and all structural aspects of implementation are finalized. Once these decisions are made, the training program must commence. Software is completed or purchased, and the organization's data are entered into the system.

After all of this is completed and final checks are made, the management information system is ready for implementation. Naturally, once the system is in place and functioning, it must be maintained to ensure that continuous "enhancements and changes to the system" are made to keep the system effective.[4]

❖ ❖ **GUIDELINES FOR EFFECTIVE MIS DESIGN**

Designing an appropriate management information system is a long-term, complex, and often tedious project. It requires the skills of a variety of specialists and of managers responsible for the design, implementation, and eventual use of the system. MIS creation requires a major effort, often a team effort, by everyone involved over an extended period of two to four years. The first three steps in MIS creation relate to MIS design, which can most effectively be carried out by a focus on the following six guidelines:

1. *Form a design team of operating managers and system designers.* Operating managers must be involved because they best understand the information needs of various managerial levels. A system designed by such a team will probably satisfy the information needs of managers without burdening the managers with irrelevant information.

2. *Balance the value and cost of the system by designing and installing it on a cost-benefit basis.* This will help eliminate cost overruns. Designing to achieve the purposes of the MIS should always be the primary objective of everyone involved. Also, software must be appropriate to support the envisioned system. In order to limit cost overruns, seek out commercial software that can be adapted to the proposed system.[5] When Joe Michael Sanchez was the management information systems manager of the first U.S. office of Munich, Germany-based Bayerische Hypotheken-und Wechsel Bank, he wanted to use a specific PC security software package. His office paid $170 for each copy of the software package. When the bank's European subsidiaries also decided to use the same software, they found the price shot up to $450–500 per copy when going through a middleman. The parent company dealt directly with the software company and was able to get European versions shipped from New York at an affordable price without the use of a middleman.[6]

3. *Design a system that can provide relevant, high-quality information, rather than producing large quantities of information.* Providing high-quality information and limiting the quantity of information that has little value should increase the effectiveness of the management information system.

4. *Conduct a thorough pretest prior to final installation.* Make sure that omissions and errors in system design are detected, so such operational problems do not cause expensive changes in the final system.

5. *Provide adequate training and manuals for both users and operators of the system.* This is necessary to assure proper implementation of the system. It will

A Skill-Building Exercise: You have been appointed to the design team assigned the formidable task of developing the new management information system. A design engineer is in charge of the project, and she has the responsibility of developing the entire system. You were selected to be on the team because you have had some experience in designing a management information system for your previous employer. However, your current company is a manufacturing firm, and the one you were previously employed by was a service firm.

You have just reviewed the list of team members and found that you are the only manager on the team. Everyone else is either a systems analyst or an engineer. Also, the time frame for development and implementation of the system has been estimated to be only nine months. You mention that in the firm you worked for before, the team composition was totally different and the project took a lot longer than nine months. The design engineer tells you that you are not dealing with managers now and that technical people are much faster and better at management information system design.

What would you do or say?

also help make the system more effective. It should be made clear how the system will affect the organizational structure, the task responsibilities, and the jobs of each manager and employee.

6. *Make sure the management information system continually evolves, as the total business system does.* A management information system that fails to change will, in time, lose its effectiveness.

❖ ❖ IMPLEMENTATION OF THE MIS

Since today's management information systems are certain to utilize computers, the discussion of the implementation of these systems will assume that computers will be part of them. Although technical problems do occur in implementing any MIS, the concern here will be with the people problems associated with implementation. These are the problems that the majority of managers are likely to encounter. Basically, managers must be aware of the causes of resistance to MIS implementation and the means of overcoming this resistance.

Resistance to Implementation of the MIS

Five major factors can cause resistance to the implementation of a management information system:

1. *Disruption of established departmental boundaries.* Department members may resist changing how their department operates, and they may resent altering the work relationships that have been established over the years.

2. *Disruption of the informal system.* If the informal system is powerful and effective, those who are part of it may resist anything that would threaten their informal position.

3. *Specific individual characteristics.* People who know how to do their present job in a satisfactory manner frequently resist change to a new procedure.

4. *The existing organizational culture.* An organization that maintains open and honest communications and has a high-trust relationship with its employees will have a less difficult time with implementation, and vice versa.

5. *How the change is implemented.* Everyone involved in the change should have a say as to how the change will evolve. The less involved employees are, the greater the level of resistance that will normally be encountered.

Although employees at different levels of the organization are affected by implementation in different ways, most people are affected to some degree. When the inevitable resistance occurs, management must be prepared to overcome it.

Overcoming Resistance to Implementation of the MIS

No single approach will overcome all resistance to implementation of the management information system. Implementation problems can be limited, however, if managers observe the following guidelines:

1. Resistance is limited to some degree if the system is user-oriented. This is perhaps the most critical element in avoiding most of the resistance that is likely to occur.

Everyone involved in a major change should have some say in how the change will evolve. The less involved affected people are in decision making, the greater the level of resistance. Most companies have meeting rooms, such as the one shown here, and make these rooms available for meetings among managers from various departments. (Source: © Lawrence Migdale/Photo Researchers, Inc.)

2. If participation is encouraged and required of users, they must learn the system. Many of their fears will be alleviated when they become competent in using the system. Future users should be made part of the MIS team, so everyone who joins the firm immediately becomes oriented to the system.

3. Open and effective lines of communication should be established to make all users aware of the aims and characteristics of the system.

4. Individual performance measurements should be redefined to allow workers with changing roles to benefit as they gain new abilities and become adapted to changes caused by MIS implementation.

5. Everyone concerned with the system should know that the computer is a tool that can handle many boring and routine tasks. By allowing managers to access information quicker and more thoroughly, the system gives managers the opportunity to use information in more creative and productive ways.

❖ ❖ COMPUTER SELECTION

Because of the ever-expanding use of computers, it is becoming increasingly important for managers to be computer literate. Managers need not be technical experts, just as they need not be skilled accountants. Of course, they do need some accounting knowledge to understand and interpret financial reports, and they need to know what computers can and cannot do. Computers certainly should not be feared. Their presence is far too pervasive and their usefulness far too great.

If a computer is needed, the one chosen should provide the best capability of processing the needed data as accurately and quickly as possible. Therefore, users in the organization need to be involved in the computer selection decision. They must have an appreciation of the types of computers available to support their management information system. One of the major problems today in selecting hardware and software is the profusion of products available. Over 75,000 products are listed in one hardware/software directory, and that is only a partial listing.[7] Before choosing a computer, some managers have a systems analyst evaluate the choices with regard to how they can improve the management system. Computers are classified as supercomputers, mainframes, minicomputers, and microcomputers (see Figure 20.4). In many instances, a combination of these computers are used together as a total system called *client/server*.

Supercomputers

At the upper end of the spectrum are supercomputers that cost millions of dollars and are capable of handling vast amounts of numeric calculations at high speeds as well as supporting global networks. Included in this category are the

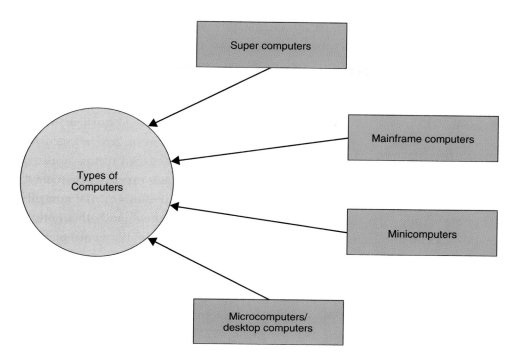

Cray, NEC, Fugitsu, and the CYBER computers. Depending on its configuration, a Cray may sell for up to $50 million.[8] The applications for supercomputers are varied also. Gilette used the supercomputer facilities at Los Alamos National Laboratory to model flow of human skin under an experimental razor.[9] IBM's Power Visualization System, a supercomputer designed for such projects as monitoring ozone data, was used at Boss Film Studios to create a breathtaking scene in which Sylvester Stallone scaled a jagged cliff while battling blowing snow and helicopters in the movie *Cliffhanger*.[10] But because of their cost and the availability of more applicable systems, these computers are not expected to be used extensively in the typical management information system.[11]

Mainframe Computers

Until recently, most of the data-processing work for large organizations was done on mainframe computers. Mainframes are normally housed in special rooms and are maintained by data-processing specialists. A data-processing manager is typically in charge of various computer specialists, such as systems analysts, programmers, and computer operators, who support the system. Because mainframes can support hundreds of individual terminals and wide-area as well as local-area networks, most large firms and many government agencies were equipped with them, but that is changing. The increased speed and capabilities of minicomputers and PCs have reduced the actual number of mainframes in use today. Some simulation, design, and engineering applications still require mainframe computers, but this is also changing. Mainframe computers are used to support very large volumes of transaction processing. For instance, Worldspan Travel Information Services, which serves about 11,600 travel agents worldwide and competes with AMR Corporation's Sabre, handles "up to 1,000 transactions per second on average and up to 'several thousand per thousand' during peak vacation and travel periods."[12] Prices for mainframes range from $500,000 to $10,000,000.[13]

Minicomputers

These medium-sized computers are smaller, slower, and less expensive than mainframes and do not require special power hookups or environmental controls. They are usually supplemented by a large number of terminals and other peripheral devices. A prime advantage of minicomputers is the ability to enlarge a system to meet the needs of a growing organization or to provide computing services for small organizations. Minicomputers are also used to support a PC network, and are becoming more and more powerful. Companies can link minicomputers in remote locations together using telecommunications media, giving users more control over their own processing.[14] Minicomputer prices range from $20,000 to $200,000 and well-known vendors include Digital Equipment Corporation (DEC), Prime, IBM, Hewlett-Packard (HP), and Wang.[15]

Microcomputers/Desktop Computers/
Personal Computers (PCs)

Microcomputers have gained widespread favor in research and development laboratories, on shop floors, and in office management operations, as well as in the executive suite. Microcomputers are easy to use, and hardware costs are low. Costs range from roughly $1,000 to just under $20,000.[16]

Is It the Twilight of Mainframe Computers for Big Blue and the Entire Industry?

For years the essence of computing throughout the world, and in the United States, was the mainframe computer. After 28 years, IBM's biggest profit-maker, the mainframe computer, is finally peaking, and may be on a permanent downward slide. The head of IBM's $14 billion mainframe processor business predicted that sales would run flat through 1994, if not longer. The ES/9000 that was shipped out the door by IBM in 1991 experienced only two years of good growth. The implications appear clear. The mainframe business, which is based on a design unveiled in 1964, is on the decline. Unfortunately, mainframes currently provide IBM with approximately 60 percent of its revenues. The investment firm, Smith Barney, Harris Upham & Company, changed its rating from "buy" to "hold" on IBM stock because it believes that the mainframe market has definitely peaked. The basic problem with the mainframe market is that large customers are using mainframes in fewer and fewer data centers, opting instead for minis or networks of micros. NCR is trying to remain profitable in the mainframe business with radically new mainframes that do much more and cost much less than current IBM models.[17]

Portable personal computers are becoming increasingly advanced. They now have better monitors and hard drives, improved battery life, and they are lighter and faster. Many executives, like the one shown here, use portable computers to stay in touch with headquarters and access their companies' mainframes. (Source: © B. Bachmann/The Image Works)

Microcomputers are not just for small businesses. Large corporations use thousands of them. Estimates of the number of personal computers shipped in 1993 ranged from 33–50 million units.[18] Because of their flexibility, micros simplify many aspects of management. The microcomputer, often called a PC (for personal computer), can be a stand-alone tool able to show financial trends, answer "what if" questions, and even maintain the executive's calendar. Some managers who previously wrote memorandums in longhand now zip them out on the keyboard. Compaq is also marketing a voice interactive computer that supplements keyboard interaction. Micros may interact with mainframes to give executives access to corporate databases or sophisticated programs.

Microcomputers are becoming even more versatile, with such additions as faxboards. Boise Cascade Office Products receives approximately 40 percent of its 20,000 orders each day by FAX. FAXs are received by a PC and translated and entered into a mainframe application. Boise Cascade found it could process 40 orders per hour using this system as opposed to 16 per hour manually.[19]

Mobile computing devices (portable, laptop, notebook, and subnotebook computers) are becoming more advanced. They now have better monitors, standard hard drives, longer battery life, and they are lighter and faster. With the addition of docking stations to hook them up to the primary microcomputer network in the office, portables, laptops, and notebooks are becoming even more useful. Portable computers weighing between four and seven pounds represent the notebook category.

Additional devices weighing less than four pounds are also being marketed.

Pocket organizers weigh less than one pound, and are basically used for organizational applications by mobile users who do not need communication capabilities. Handheld computers weigh less than one pound, and are used by field service personnel for data entry applications. Personal digital assistants weigh less than three pounds, and are easy-to-use, handheld communication-intensive devices used for two-way communication. Subnotebooks weigh less than four pounds, and are fully functional PCs with a reduced keypad and screen and no floppy drive. Pen-based devices weigh less than six pounds, and use an input stylus for data entry.[20] AT&T's Virtual Office Program, which began in 1991, equipped its commercial account executive with fax-modem equipped notebook computers, portable printers, telephone calling cards, and even some cellular phones. AT&T managed to eliminate assigned offices and lowered office space, cutting real estate costs by 25 percent.[21]

Microcomputerss are capable of acquiring data, taking measurements, and controlling all kinds of processes in ways that greatly simplify manufacturing and production. They can be used in remote locations such as offshore oil-well platforms. They also work well in adverse environments such as on ships and airplanes. Micros can automatically change the settings of valves and other control devices in response to changes in physical conditions such as pressures and temperatures. Industrial robots often depend on microcomputers to help them do factory assembly operations formerly too complex for mechanization.

Many engineering firms today specialize in computer-aided design and computer-aided manufacturing (CAD/CAM) systems. These systems permit designers and engineers to develop a product, test it, and then program the equipment that makes it. The cost of CAD/CAM has been greatly reduced through the use of powerful microcomputers, some of which even small engineering and machine shops can afford. Because of their application to each stage of the product development cycle, microcomputers have made major contributions toward meeting the productivity challenge.

In every kind of organization and at every level, microcomputers simplify the job of administration. Traditional office paperwork is created and processed with the help of computers. Because microcomputers can communicate with one another, many written reports and other types of written documentation have been eliminated. Word-processing software is available to assist in entering, arranging, correcting, retrieving, and printing all types of business information and correspondence.

It is obvious that more powerful microcomputers are gaining widespread favor, but managers should realize that computers are not a panacea for productivity problems. In addition to enhanced power, executives want more for their computing dollar. Citgo Petroleum Corp.'s CFO, Steve Berlin, believed there is a trend to "reduce and maximize computerization" and monitored employees-per-

PC as opposed to PCs-per-employee. Steering committees, long-range planning, and other efforts to better align information systems and business seem to be paying off. In a recent survey, 91 percent of the executives believed their company information system and business strategies were "very or somewhat" linked.[22]

Client/Server System

Client/server systems combine the strengths of various types of computers to split and deliver computer applications and data at reduced costs with greater reliability. These systems utilize networked personal computers (clients) and minicomputers or mainframe computers (servers).[23] Eli Lilly and Company handle payroll for 15,000 employees and 8,000 retirees on a client/server system.[24] Avis Rent-A-Car Systems, Inc., the $1.27 billion car rental agency, uses client/server computing to facilitate reservation processing. The system reduces processing time by 20 percent with such activities as accessing insurance regulations for the region where the driver will be traveling, using "quick" keys to pull up screens, and reducing new agent training by half.[25]

❖ ❖ POSSIBLE INFORMATION SUBSYSTEMS FOR MANAGERS

Management uses various information subsystems, including accounting information systems, office management systems, manufacturing systems, marketing systems, and human resource information systems. They are called *subsystems* here because, taken separately, they do not constitute a management information system. In addition, some firms may have only one or perhaps two of these subsystems.

Accounting Information Systems

The processing of accounting data is traditionally the first area to receive much attention. Accounting information systems provide managers with much of their control information. Accuracy and speed are stressed in the processing of profit-and-loss information, taxes, and a multitude of other accounting-related activities. Subsets of a typical accounting system include accounts payable, payroll, accounts receivable, sales and invoices, inventory control, and financial reporting. In addition, new uses are being developed daily.

Office Management Systems

Only a few years ago, the typical office management (or office automation) system involved filing cabinets; letters dictated to secretaries, who then typed and mailed them; and telephone messages placed on the manager's desk to be answered at a later time. The potential for totally restructuring these systems is

---

New Uses Can Always Be Found

Graceland, a division of Elvis Presley Enterprises, Inc., automated its ticket and reservation system for the first time in 1993. A database management system for ticket reservation and fund accounting management are used on a network to handle the nearly 700,000 visitors to Graceland each year. Revenues from each of the estate's attractions are tracked and the new system elimi-

nates workers stamping and sorting tickets by hand.[26]

Electronic data interchange (EDI) provides the electronic transfer of documents, such as purchase orders, invoices, and even payments, from one firm to another.[27] The Federal Home Loan Mortgage Corporation (Freddie Mac), the Federal National Mortgage Association (Fannie Mae), and the Government National Mortgage Association (Ginnie Mae) hold approximately

$1 trillion in outstanding residential loans. These agencies collaborate to standardize the flow of data in the mortgage industry. Together with the Mortgage Bankers Association of America, they work toward setting standards for the electronic data interchange (EDI) associated with creating, servicing, and selling mortgages. Plans have been made to develop artificial intelligence systems to allow faster mortgage evaluation.[28]

---

now a reality. Managers may now sit in front of their desktop computers and send messages to other company employees at distant points through electronic mail—messages that appear on the recipients' monitors.

Word processing has had a major impact on the modern office management system. Copies of correspondences that once filled a multitude of filing cabinets can now be conveniently stored on disks for rapid retrieval at a later date. Corrections, additions, and deletions can now be quickly accomplished without the need for a secretary to retype the document each time a change is made. Many managers have found it easy to learn word processing themselves. Often, they find it much quicker to type up correspondence themselves than to delegate this duty to others in the organization.

Family Practice Associates PC, in Liverpool, New York, was experiencing difficulty transcribing medical notes on approximately 250 patient visits per day. Records were sometimes as much as two weeks behind. They purchased DragonDictate-30K, a program that allows the doctors to dictate to their computer without a keyboard. The system produces notes that are immediately available in the patient's file and has eliminated errors in medication, dosages, and spelling.[29]

Manufacturing Systems

Not long ago, managers at an automobile assembly plant supervised long lines of workers attaching parts to each unfinished car as it passed separate work stations. Managers and workers using computer terminals can now determine the exact equipment configuration of each car as it passes by. The manufacturing process of production scheduling, inventory control, design, equipment control, and cost accounting is tied together through the use of computers. Computer innovations now provide even small firms with the capability of using modern production control and scheduling methods. Wagner Lighting in Sparta, Tennessee, uses a

Many managers realize the ease with which they can use computers. (Source: © John Coletti)

robotics inspection system to check component parts on the assembly line. The system measures components against the original drawing specifications and detects the slightest inaccuracies. Faulty products do not leave the factory.[30] Raychem, Inc., uses a paperless, automated production system to design and assemble aluminum adapters. The system accommodates purchase orders of as few as 15 units and cuts lead time from months to weeks. Orders are faxed to the system, and the computer-aided design system is initiated. The CAD system moves the job into a computer-aided manufacturing file and sends it to the shop floor. The order appears in an intelligent documentation form at a tooling presetting station, and a technician schedules the job.[31]

Marketing Systems

The purpose of marketing is to ensure that the proper product is offered to the customer at the right price and location and with the correct amount of promotion. In the past, the complexity of this task was often overwhelming. Tying together a marketing system consisting of product analysis and development, marketing research, place analysis, price analysis, promotional analysis, and sales was often difficult without the benefits of the computer. Through computerized marketing systems, information is made available to the marketing manager about such vital areas as product profitability and advertising effectiveness. Mervyn's department stores had the strategy to reduce inventory from $5 million to $3 million. They needed to have the right merchandise in each of their 275 stores in 15 states at the right time. Their solution was an inventory management system utilizing a minicomputer and a database as an intermediary between a network of PCs and the mainframe.[32]

Human Resource Information Systems

Whereas the accounting system was typically the first system to be installed in a firm, the human resource information system was often the last. Firms are now realizing that a properly developed human resource information system can provide tremendous benefits.

The human resource information system permits all human resource areas to be tied together into a single information system. Data from several input sources are integrated to provide needed output data. Information critical to the firm's human resource decision-making process is readily available when the system is properly designed. For instance, many firms are now studying historical trends to determine the best ways of securing qualified applicants. In addition, it would be difficult to comply with the many laws and government rules if not for these modern systems. As the human component of the firm gains greater importance, it is likely that we will see continued growth in human resource information systems.

❖ ❖ USING THE MIS

A true management information system has the capability of integrating the various subsystems in order to provide managers at all levels with better decision-making capabilities. For example, information from the human resource information system may provide the manager with knowledge about the feasibility of plant expansion in relation to specific human resource requirements. The accounting system may be consulted to determine if the anticipated plant expansion will be cost-effective. Rather than each subsystem acting as a separate entity, all are tied together in the MIS to give management an extra edge in making decisions.

Previous chapters identified the basic functions of management: planning, organizing, influencing, and controlling. The purpose of an effective and useful management information system is to help accomplish these functions, and each of the subsystems mentioned may assist in that effort. When all the subsystems are integrated into a total management information system, the power of the information available for decision making is greatly enhanced.

❖ ❖ TECHNOLOGY AFFECTING MANAGEMENT[34]

Technological advances in computer hardware and software occur virtually every day. These developments have the potential of improving management and raising employee productivity. It's impossible to foresee all the new uses for each technological breakthrough. The only certainty is that managers must be aware of these innovations and alert to their capabilities. Failure to keep up with developments in this rapidly changing area can threaten a firm's competitive position and possibly even its survival. We next discuss some of the uses of computer technology that most significantly affect management.

Application and Communication Software

Several types of existing software continue to impact management. This software includes data communication, word processing, computer graphics, image processing, spreadsheets, decision support systems, executive information systems, database management systems, and groupware. Finally, the legal issue of software piracy must be addressed.

Data Communication The sending of data produced by a computer over some form of communication medium, such as phone lines, is referred to as **data communication.** This form of communication is becoming pervasive throughout the business world. Managers can transmit documents or messages over phone lines and eliminate wasted time and possible misunderstandings, thereby facilitating decision making. For example, prior to a teleconference, it is often useful to transmit electronic mail so that everyone involved can become familiar with the exact nature of the discussion.

Electronic mail capabilities also include the ability to schedule a meeting for an entire work group, automatically sending messages to meeting attendees and even spell checking that message. MCA/Universal Studios provides remote local-area network access to provide e-mail to studio executives and to enable them to view financial information downloaded from the corporate minicomputer and mainframe.[35]

Word Processing A computer application that permits an operator to create and edit written material is referred to as **word processing.** Word processing allows simplified editing of manuscripts and correspondence. Managers, too, can use word processing. The manager types out the memo, edits it on the screen, and with a few commands, prints it out or routes it using electronic mail. Word processing also allows managers to develop sensitive documents, such as workforce reduction plans or performance appraisal reports, without risking a breech of security.

Computer Graphics "A picture is worth a thousand words." Managers can use computer programs to produce various kinds of graphs and charts in both black and white and color. These graphics represent a large amount of data reduced to a single image. Managers continually process data that can be graphically presented, thereby illustrating the message much more effectively than simple text could.

Image Processing Image processing systems enable companies to electronically capture, manipulate, and retrieve images that may include photographs, documents, numeric data, and handwriting.[36] By capturing the data's image, the need for rekeying the existing data is eliminated, thus reducing costs and eliminating possible data entry errors. The U.S. Customs Service developed an imaging system that enables agents to photograph smugglers in one airport and transmit the image to their central computer in Virginia. The digitized image is forwarded to the destination airport where the smuggling deal is completed, and both the smuggler and "pick-up" man are arrested. This system is integrated with the Service's primary database containing over 5,000,000 records.[37] Boston's Central Artery/Tunnel Project, an overhaul of a major traffic artery, undertaken by Bechtel Group, Inc., and Parsons Brinckerhoff, Inc., used a combination of computer-aided design, image processing, and three-dimensional modeling to facilitate construction. The project was further complicated by a tight budget and schedule, and the fact that it took place in a densely populated, historically significant area. Using automated mapping, engineers accessed more than 30,000 drawings. The 3-D modeling provided planners with a complete model of the project before a single brick was put into place.[38]

Spreadsheet Programs Spreadsheet programs provide a column-row matrix on which numbers or words can be entered and stored, and calculations performed on that data. Predefined statistical, financial, and mathematical functions make "what if" questions quickly and easily answered. Spreadsheet analysis is particularly beneficial in activities such as planning.

Decision Support Systems Often computer departments are backed up with demands for urgently needed information. To overcome this problem, many managers have acquired their own **decision support system (DSS),** an information system that allows users to quickly process and retrieve information. Normally DSSs are sophisticated database systems capable of retrieving, displaying, and processing a wide variety of information. Graphics, simulation, modeling, and quantitative analysis are also typically available through decision support systems. Obviously, DSSs can be very useful in planning and decision making.

Executive Information Systems (EIS) While decision support systems provide tools for the decision maker, an EIS provides the manager with up-to-date information to enable monitoring of critical efforts.[39] These systems are characterized as being easy to use, featuring graphics, and frequently using a touch screen or a mouse. Calvert's Inc., is a three-store off-price retailer whose executive information system is PC-based and has only two users. The system, however, enabled Calvert's to reduce inventories and increase profits, even while experiencing a slight drop in sales.[40] Xerox depends on its own version of EIS, its Executive Support System.

Database Management Information subsystems are commonly developed for accounting, office management, manufacturing, marketing, and human resources. Often the data and programs in these subsystems are considered separate and distinct, resulting in a tremendous amount of redundant data. For example, the accounting system would normally contain names and social security numbers of all employees—and so would the human resource files. The purpose of **database management** is to reduce such redundancies insofar as possible. The term thus refers to the integration of information subsystems in order to reduce the duplication of information, effort, and cost and to provide controlled access to this information.

Groupware Groupware is software that enables people to work together in groups and that assists in decision making, workflow, and work management. Decision-making groupware provides structure for discussing, analyzing, and problem solving by utilizing sophisticated applications of group theory and group dynamics. Activities supported include brainstorming, voting, and alternate evaluation and policy formulation. Examples of groupware include Group Systems V from Ventana Corporation and CM/1 from Corporate Memory Systems.

Workflow groupware assists in managing documents, processes, and information flows throughout an organization. This software enables users to set up routing systems and establish action and response rules with triggers that will release when particular events occur. Examples include Digital Equipment Corporation's TeamLinks and Reach Software's WorkMAN.

Work-management groupware assists individuals and teams in communicating (even to the extent of screening out junk e-mail), scheduling meetings, and managing tasks. Work-management groupware includes WordPerfect Corporation's Office, Microsoft's Mail, and Schedule+.[41]

Software Piracy Software is protected by federal copyright law, providing both civil and criminal penalties. Only the copying required to load onto a single machine and for backup and archival purposes is permitted.[42] In February, 1993, the third-largest electronic bulletin board in the United States, Rusty & Edie's, was raided by the Federal Bureau of Investigation. This was the first raid since Congress raised software piracy from a misdemeanor to a felony in October, 1992. The service has been shut down while the FBI and members of the Software Publishers Association search the service's files and documentation. The service had allegedly received more than 3.4 million calls since starting up in 1987.[43]

Teleconferencing

Partly because of the high cost of business travel, in terms of both time and money, teleconferencing is becoming increasingly popular. **Teleconferencing** is a method of conducting or participating in multiparty discussions by telephone or videophone. Teleconferencing may become a major means not only of improving managerial communication and productivity but also of lowering their cost. Such systems could allow managers to resolve many problems without ever meeting in person with other parties, thus saving both time and money. AT&T's Personal Video System provides a 3-inch by 3-inch window on computer screens to permit desktop videoconferencing characterized as "notes gone visual." While more expensive than electronic mail, John Hamilton of Midwest Power Systems in Des Moines, Iowa, justified the expense in travel payback alone.[44] It has been estimated that videoconferencing will replace 25 percent of all business travel by 2010.

Voice Mail

Voice mail is spoken messages transmitted electronically and stored for delivery to the recipient at a later time. When a voice mail system is used, an individual gains access by dialing a special number and providing a password and user identification number. The user may then listen to any new messages, replay old messages, eliminate messages, and/or record messages for others. Managers can place confidential information in the system and know that the message will be received in the exact manner that it was sent. Voice mail could prove useful when managers are dealing with sensitive matters, such as layoffs, and want to avoid phone communications that could be overheard.

Telecommuting

As previously mentioned in Chapter 13, many firms have turned to telecommuting as a way of meeting particular management needs. When workers at home or temporarily away from the office perform their work over telephone lines tied to a computer, as if they were at the office, the procedure is called **telecommuting.** Telecommuters generally are information workers. They perform jobs that require, for example, analysis, research, writing, budgeting, data entry, or computer programming.[45] Working at home is not for everyone, but certain people such as writers, reservation agents, researchers, and computer programmers can easily adapt to this style of work. One computer programmer quit his job in San Diego and moved to the island of St. John, agreeing to "help out" his former employer if needed. Within two weeks, the programmer had established a consulting firm and was working his own hours. Telecommuters often have more productive time since they do not drive to and from work. Also, handicapped people who cannot easily get to an office find telecommuting an excellent alternative.

Although the concept of telecommuting has many positive aspects, managers often have difficulty coping with it in practice. The question they often ask is, "How do I supervise a person that I never see?" And some workers dislike telecommuting because they miss the friendly association with co-workers. Pacific Bell has a systematic procedure for selecting the types of jobs and the types of people who would benefit from telecommuting. In 1993, an estimated 7.6 million people were working at home during normal business hours and approximately $4.7 billion was expended for telecommuter technology.[46] This represents a substantial increase over the 4.4 million people telecommuting in 1991. Managers must be prepared to deal with this alternative type of work.

Expert Systems

An **expert system** uses knowledge about a narrowly defined, complex area to act as a consultant to a human.[47] A prototype vehicle-tracking system in Birmingham, England, tells passengers how soon their bus will arrive at the stop. Navigational satellites track, calculate, and display arrival times and route numbers of the next three buses. Additional services presented using a Windows-based interface include querying best routes to destinations as well as fare and timetable information.[48]

Graphical User Interfaces

Graphical user interfaces (GUIs) represent a move to truly make software applications easy to use. Computer users touch or aim at graphic figures (icons) or framed written commands to communicate with the computer system. No longer are keys depressed on the keyboard. Popular GUIs include Microsoft's "Windows," the IBM/Microsoft "Presentation Manager," Open Software Foundation's "Motif," and the Macintosh GUI.[49] First National Bank of Chicago created First Window 2000, a Windows software package that provides corporate customers with funds-transfer and reporting functions for global payments.[50]

Multimedia

Multimedia is a computer application that produces presentations combining automation, stereo sound, full-motion video, and graphics. Because users are immediately drawn to these presentations, they are useful in sales presentations and in training and development. Lotus Development Corporation introduced a multimedia version of 1-2-3 that placed all of its program documentation on

A GLOBAL PERSPECTIVE

Defining Global Businesses Around Information

A global management information system is an organized approach for obtaining relevant and timely information on which to base management decisions. An ideal management information system exists when users are supplied with all the information they need when they need it. Such a utopian situation has not yet arrived for most companies, especially those with global operations. To help offset less effective global management information systems, companies are developing decision support systems that allow users to interact directly with a computer to get information quickly. A decision support system lets managers call up a menu of available programs. Normally, decision support systems are sophisticated database systems capable of retrieving, displaying, and processing information. Graphics, simulation, modeling, and quantitative analysis are also typically available through decision support systems.

7-Eleven Japan has defined its business around information. According to Richard Rawlinson, managing director of the Tokyo office of consultant Monitor Company, "No other retailer in the world has defined its business so tightly around information." At the heart of the information system is a custom-made NEC personal computer in each store. The system tracks the buying habits of customers by sex and approximate age. Naturally, the system is used to track inventory movement of the 3,000 items in each store. The system is extremely easy to use, with easy-to-follow graphics and coded keys. The information system also regulates store equipment and automatically contacts maintenance companies when a problem occurs. By adding a very powerful Hewlett-Packard system, 7-Eleven Japan can effectively staff stores, help manufacturers develop new products, and allow headquarters to monitor individual store sales, as well as aggregate sales. The system is a model for what a global information system should be; it is timely, accurate, useful, and easy to use by all concerned.[56]

disk, including interactive instructional "movies."[51] American Airlines uses it to train thousands of employees annually. Managers can incorporate photographs, voice, and document images into database files. The manager can access an employee's photograph, social security card, and signed year-end appraisals.[52] Electronic kiosks featuring touch-screen computers, colorful graphics, and sound are providing customer services while eliminating minimum-wage positions. Kiosks have been used to print sheet music, collect deli orders, and sell insurance policies.[53] In California, they are used to search job opportunities and order birth certificates. To ensure security, the machine reads the magnetic stripe on participants' driver's licenses.[54] Hallmark Cards provides electronic kiosks that enable customers to design and print customized greeting cards.[55]

✗ Management Tips ✗

Guidelines for Dealing with Information Systems

1. **Recognize that sound decisions cannot be based on outdated information.** You must have the most current information available to be effective.

2. **Realize that employees must be able to rely on the accuracy of the information provided to them.** Incorrect data probably will cause bad decisions to be made.

3. **Remember that workers can absorb only so much information during any one period.** Provide them with essential data only.

4. **Make sure that the information you provide employees is relevant.** This means providing them only with information that they need to know.

5. **Attempt to provide workers with complete information.** Having no information is sometimes better than having partial data.

6. **Realize that an MIS is useful to managers at all levels.** It is not merely useful to top-level managers.

7. **Remember that the MIS should be designed to assist in the accomplishment of the objectives of the organization.** The system should have no other purpose.

8. **Remember in designing an MIS that the most important information needs should be first considered.** Data lower on the priority list should be generated only if their benefits exceed the costs of producing them.

9. **Remember that the information needs of the firm are constantly changing.** Efforts should be made to ensure that the present system meets the information needs of users.

10. **Recognize that there may be some initial resistance to the implementation of an MIS.** Management should be prepared to overcome this resistance.

SUMMARY

A management information system (MIS) is any organized approach for obtaining relevant and timely information on which to base management decisions. An effective MIS typically employs computers and other sophisticated technologies. It draws information from various internal functional areas, such as marketing and finance, and integrates this information with that of the external environment. Both internal and external information is needed, and it should be timely, accurate, concise, relevant, and complete. If not, effectiveness is reduced, complicating the decision-making process.

Managers at each organizational level make unique demands on the MIS. Top-level managers need to make far-reaching decisions that usually require extensive information relating to the external environment. Lower-level managers depend primarily on internal data. In designing the MIS, all managers must carefully consider four recommended steps: study the present system, develop a priority for information and a conceptual design, develop the new information system, and implement the finalized MIS.

MIS design can most effectively be carried out by focusing on the following six guidelines: (1) Form a design team of operating managers and system designers; (2) balance the value and cost of the system by designing and installing it on a cost-benefit basis; (3) design a system that can provide relevant, high-quality information, rather than produce large quantities of information; (4) conduct a thorough pretest prior to final installation; (5) provide adequate training and manuals for both users and operators of the system; and (6) make sure the management information system continually evolves, as the total business system does. Managers must be aware of the causes of resis-

KEY TERMS

Management information system (MIS) 641

Client/server system 655

Electronic data interchange (EDI) 656

Data communication 659

Word processing 660

Image processing 660

Decision support system (DSS) 661

Database management 661

Groupware 661

Teleconferencing 662

Voice mail 662

Telecommuting 663

Expert system 663

Graphical user interfaces (GUIs) 664

Multimedia 664

REVIEW QUESTIONS

1. Define management information system. What are the information needs of a firm?
2. What are the basic characteristics required of the MIS?
3. Briefly describe the types of reports an effective MIS should produce.
4. Briefly describe the steps involved in creating the MIS.
5. List the guidelines for effective MIS design.
6. What are the factors that can interfere with implementation of the MIS?
7. Distinguish among the following general types of computers:
   a. supercomputers
   b. mainframes
   c. minicomputers
   d. microcomputers
8. Briefly describe the various information subsystems available to managers.
9. Briefly describe the new developments in computer hardware and software that can be used to enhance productivity.

tance to MIS implementation and the means of overcoming this resistance.

Because there are many types of computers and the capabilities of different types vary, users must review the possibilities and select the most beneficial computer. Before choosing a computer, some managers have a systems analyst evaluate the choices with regard to how they can improve the management system. Computers are classified as supercomputers, mainframes, minicomputers, microcomputers, and other smaller variations.

Management also uses various information subsystems, including accounting, office management, manufacturing, marketing, and human resource systems. A true MIS integrates these subsystems in order to provide managers at all levels with better decision-making information.

New developments in computer hardware and software occur virtually every day. Among them are data communication, word processing, computer graphics, spreadsheet programs, decision support systems, database management, teleconferencing, voice mail, telecommuting, expert systems, graphical user interfaces, image processing, and multimedia.

CASE STUDIES

CASE 20.1 "This Has Been a Fiasco"

David McNeil was CEO of the McNeil Company, which he had founded. The company was involved in three businesses. The medical division, Procare, offered extended care to the elderly through four facilities similar to nursing homes. Procare also operated two pharmacies. The second business was toys. McNeil had seven leased toy stores in malls. The third and biggest operation was shoes. McNeil ran ten shoe stores, mostly in malls, and 12 shoe departments in department stores. He was asked to tell of his recent experience with computerization.

He began: "When I bought the medical division five years ago, it had its own IBM mainframe computer system. John Seeger, previous owner and still president of Procare, is something of a computer whiz. So I asked him to help computerize Shoes and Toys and gave him a free rein about how to do it. Two years and $400,000 later, we had a Prime computer in the main office with point-of-sale terminals in all our stores. The system cranked out daily, weekly, and monthly reports on every topic imaginable. Procare was never hooked into the Prime since it already had a good system.

"The year before last, Procare got into financial trouble and John had to start spending all his time trying to get it back on track. However, his systems analyst, who had been with Procare for years, helped the people in Medical and Shoes when he could. Prime had no local office but quickly sent a maintenance person by plane when we called and was able to diagnose some problems through a modem hookup. Still, the system stayed down quite a bit after John went back to Procare.

"I soon realized that the stacks of computer paper on all my managers' desks were not being used. I don't know much about computers, but I do know how much useless paperwork costs. So I began to eliminate reports, waiting for someone to yell. No one ever yelled. Before long, the Prime was being used just for payroll, accounts receivable and payable, and general ledger. The point-of-sale terminals are still connected to the Prime, which costs a lot in phone charges, but the terminals are used just as cash registers. It's a good thing my managers kept their manual reporting and accounting system as a backup to the computer.

"This has been a fiasco," McNeil concluded. "We have all agreed that it will be a long time before we spend that much money and time again without knowing what we're doing."

QUESTIONS

1. Was McNeil's computerization effort doomed from the start? Explain.

2. What alternatives concerning his MIS did McNeil have after Procare got into financial trouble? What should he have done?

CASE 20.2 Fort Steel Products

"I don't know how we managed before we got our computer," said Martha Tolpin. Tolpin is the owner of Fort Steel Products, Inc., in Fort Collins, Colorado. Fort Steel makes a line of metal patio furniture that is marketed through lawn and garden stores and furniture stores in the Southwest. Selling is mainly done by telephone. Each Fort Steel salesperson has an interactive terminal that provides up-to-date information on inventory levels, prices of items, shipping availability and costs, customer credit status, and so forth. Of course, the system also performs all the usual accounting functions, such as payroll, accounts payable, and general ledger. Tolpin gets a single weekly report, which gives her summarized information for the week, the previous quarter, and the year to date.

Tolpin had decided early on that computers represented the wave of the future, but she shopped around several years before deciding on a system for Fort Steel. In the meantime, she became competent on an IBM PC she had bought, using it for word processing and for some spreadsheet calculations.

One of many computer salespeople who called on Fort Steel over the years was Ivan Pierson. Pierson was with Darkar, a consulting firm in New Orleans. After hearing Pierson's presentation and checking with several of his clients, Tolpin purchased a complete hardware and software package from Darkar. The system was designed especially for small manufacturers and cost $73,000, including 50 hours of programming and maintenance time. The initial price also included a three-day course on the system for Fort Steel's head bookkeeper and a clerk. Tolpin knew she could have bought the hardware locally for about $12,000. Spending the extra $60,000 or so just for software and support was a difficult decision.

Because she was "intrigued" with computers, as she put it, Tolpin went to New Orleans to sit through the course with her two employees. While she was in New Orleans, Pierson and his boss treated her to a Cajun dinner at K-Paul's Kitchen (owned by world-famous chef Paul Prudhomme) and a tour of Bourbon Street and the French Quarter.

During the two years since the system was installed, Tolpin has continued the friendship. She has recommended Darkar to several acquaintances, two of whom have made purchases. She also was instrumental in promoting the Darkar system through the Southwest division of the American Association of Manufacturers, a trade association to which Fort Steel belongs. Tolpin received no commission on the sales, but Darkar has improved the basic system markedly since she bought hers, and Pierson has ensured that each improvement was installed at Fort Steel at no charge. In fact, says Tolpin, "I haven't gotten any bill at all from Darkar in over a year."

QUESTIONS

1. Did Tolpin pay too much for her system? Justify your answer.
2. Discuss the human aspects of the case.

NOTES

1. This case is a composite of a number of published accounts, among them: David T. Kearns, "Xerox: Satisfying Customer Needs with a New Culture," *Management Review* 78 (February 1989): 61–63; Barbara Hetzer, "How Xerox Zapped the Japanese," *Business Month* 133 (June 1989): 81–82; Lou Wallis, "Power Computing at the Top," *Across the Board* 26 (January–February 1989): 42–51; James R. Norman, "Xerox Rethinks Itself—And This Could Be the Last Time," *Business Week* (February 13, 1989): 90–93; Jeremy Main, "At Last, Software CEOs Can Use," *Fortune* 124 (March 13, 1989): 77–83; Russell Mitchell, "How Top Brass Is Taking to the Keyboard at Xerox," *Business Week* (June 27, 1988): 86; James R. Norman, "Xerox on the Move," *Forbes* 150 (June 10, 1991): 70–71; Standard and Poor's Corporation, "Xerox Corporation," *Standard NYSE Stock Reports* 56, no. 128 (July 6, 1989): sec. 24; and Rahul Jacob, "Beyond Quality & Value," *Fortune* 128 (Autumn/Winter 1993): 8–11.

2. Joseph Maglitta, "Squeeze Play," *Computerworld* 27 (April 19, 1993): 86–91.

3. Gary K. Gulden and Douglas E. Ewers, "Is Your ESS Meeting the Need?" *Computerworld* 24 (July 10, 1989): 85.

4. Harry C. Benham, R. Leon Price, and Jennifer L. Wagner, "Comparison of Structured Development Methodologies," *Information Executive* 2 (Spring 1989): 19.

5. Michael Potter and Robin McNeill, "The New Programmer—The Next Wave of Computer Innovation in North American Business," *Business Quarterly* 48 (Winter 1983): 132–134.

6. Thomas Hoffman, "Here and There," *Computerworld* 27 (April 12, 1993): 81–82.

7. Dorothy Creswell, "Trends Emerge in Computer Industry," *Inside DPMA* 30 (December 1992): 6, 11.

8. James A. O'Brien, *Management Information Systems: A Managerial End User Perspective,* 2d ed. (Homewood, IL: Irwin, 1993), p. 119.

9. Gary H. Anthes, "A Labor of Labs," *Computerworld* 27 (July 19, 1993): 28.

10. James Daly, "Technology in Tinseltown," *Computerworld* 27 (May 10, 1993): 26.

11. Dave Evans, "An Old Idea Gets a New Twist," *Computerworld* 23 (May 29, 1989): 63.

12. Rosemary Cafasso, "Worldspan Travel's Plan for Single System Takes Flight," *Computerworld* 27 (June 28, 1993): 81.

13. Charles Parker and Thomas Case, *Management Information Systems: Strategy and Action,* 2d ed. (New York: Mitchell McGraw-Hill, 1993), p. 191.

14. James O. Hicks, Jr., *Management Information Systems: A User Perspective,* 3rd ed. (Minneapolis/St. Paul: West Publishing Company, 1993), pp. 228–229.

15. Parker and Case, *Management Information Systems: Strategy and Action,* pp. 189–190.

16. *Ibid.,* p. 185.

17. John W. Verity, "Twilight of the Mainframe," *Business Week* (August 17, 1992): 33.

18. Charles Babcock, "The Next PC Wave," *Computerworld* 27 (July 19, 1993): 37.

19. Lynda Radosevich, "Package Automatically Puts Faxed Data into Host Apps," *Computerworld* 27 (June 14, 1993): 74.

20. Keith Richard Aleshire, "Making Sense of Features," *Computerworld* 27 (June 28, 1993): 112–113.

21. Bryan Hastings, "Pioneers of the Information Age," *PC World* 30 (December, 1992): 265–266.

22. Maglitta, "Squeeze Play," pp. 86–91.

23. Elizabeth A. Regan and Bridget N. O'Connor, *End-User Information Systems* (New York: Macmillan Publishing Company, 1994), p. 52.

24. Kim Nash, "New Systems, New Business Practices," *Computerworld* 27 (May 24, 1993): 49.

25. Thomas Hoffman, "Avis Saves Time, Money with Mac Client/Server System," *Computerworld* 27 (May 24, 1993): 23.

26. Stephen P. Klett, Jr., "Graceland: Rockin' to the RS/6000," *Computerworld* 27 (May 10, 1993): 27.

27. Raymond McLeod, Jr., *Management Information Systems: A Study of Computer-based Information Systems,* 5th ed. (New York: Macmillan Publishing Co., 1993), p. 782.

28. Gary H. Anthes, "Rivals Team Up for EDI," *Computerworld* 27 (March 15, 1993): 64.

29. Stephen P. Klett, Jr., "Innovative Input," *Computerworld* 27 (August 23, 1993): 28.

30. Sall Cusack, "Robots Master Complexity with Machine Vision," *Computerworld* 25 (June 3, 1991): 20.

31. Maryfran Johnson, "Awards Praise the Human Touch: Manufacturing," *Computerworld* 25 (June 17, 1991): 90.

32. Mark Halper, "Department Store Tackles Inventory Stockpiles," *Computerworld* 27 (September 27, 1993): 79–80.

33. "Wings, Prayers, and Prudence," *Economist* 317 (December 1, 1990): 104; Christopher P. Fotos, "Task Force Outlines Fixes for Aging Douglas Fleet," *Aviation Week and Space Technology* 131 (September 18, 1989): 122–123; and Rick Wartzman, Asra Z. Nomani, Judith Valente, and John Koten, "Rough Air Ahead: Jetliner Crash in Iowa Seems Sure to Reopen Issue of DC-10 Safety," *The Wall Street Journal* (July 24, 1989): A1, A4.

34. This section written by Dr. Judy A. Mondy, Department of General Business, McNeese State University.

35. Stephen Rood, "Beyond the Notebook," *Computerworld* 27 (June 28, 1993): 110–111.

36. James A. O'Brien, *Management Information Systems: A Managerial End User Perspective* (Homewood, IL: Irwin, 1993), p. G–9.

37. Amy Bermar, "Custom Image," *Computerworld* 27 (July 5, 1993): 65–66.

38. Carol Hildebrand, "In Depth: High-Tech Heroes," *Computerworld* 25 (June 24, 1991): 99.

39. Robert Schultheis and Mary Sumner, *Management Information Systems: The Manager's View* (Homewood, IL: Irwin, 1992), p. 570.

40. Meghan O'Leary, "Selling Points," *CIO* 4 (November 15, 1991): 26–30.

41. Gary A. Egan, "Groupware: It's for All Companies," *Inside DPMA* 31 (October, 1993): 7.

42. Larry M. Zanger, "The Legal Risks in Copying PC Software," *Inside DPMA* 31 (August, 1993): 8, 11.

43. Kim Nash and Christopher Lindquist, "First Raid Tests Felony Law," *Computerworld* 27 (March 15, 1993): 43.

44. Joanie M. Wexler, "Face-to-face on the Desktop," *Computerworld* 27 (March 29, 1993): 2.

45. Michael Alexander, "Travel-Free Commuting," *Nation's Business* 78 (December 1990): 33.

46. Mitch Betts, "Telecommuter Quandary: Who Buys the PC?," *Computerworld* 27 (November 8, 1993): 41.

47. O'Brien, *Introduction to Information Systems in Business Management*, p. 325.

48. Elizabeth Heichler, "On-line at the Bus Stop," *Computerworld* 27 (June 28, 1993): 28.

49. William A. Newman and Floyd J. Brock, "Moving into the Graphical Decade: Graphical User Interfaces in the '90's," *Information Executive* 4 (Winter 1991): 28–32.

50. Anita Amirrezvani, "Of Mice and Yen," *Computerworld* 27 (May 24, 1993): 107.

51. "Issues and Trends: I Want My MPC," *Lotus* 8 (April 1992): 15.

52. Robert Sadarini, "The Art of Imagineering," *Information Executive* 4 (Summer 1991): 6–7.

53. Evan Schwartz, Paul Eng, S. Lynne Walker, and Alice Cuneo, "The Kiosks Are Coming, the Kiosks Are Coming," *Business Week* (June 22, 1992): 122.

54. Mitch Betts, "States Redefining Public Service," *Computerworld* 27 (April 19, 1993): 20.

55. James Daly, "Hallmark Offers Do-It-Yourself Cards," *Computerworld* 27 (June 14, 1993): 52.

56. Gale Eisenstodt, "Information Power," *Forbes* 151 (June 21, 1993): 44–45.

What Is the Makeup of Your Cultural Attitudes?

How well you would adapt and function in a multinational environment depends to some extent on the nature of your cultural makeup. If you are rather inflexible and insensitive in relation to other cultures, you may have problems adapting to new cultures. If you are to function effectively in the global economy, you will need to develop a certain degree of cultural sensitivity. To assess the makeup of your cultural attitudes, take the self-assessment exercise "What Is the Makeup of Your Cultural Attitudes?" Then, turn to page 676 to evaluate yourself.

INSTRUCTIONS: Indicate the extent to which you agree or disagree with each of the following statements. Answer each statement by checking the appropriate box; for example, if you strongly agree with a particular statement, you would check the "5" box next to that statement.

5 = Strongly Agree   3 = Neither Agree nor Disagree   2 = Disagree
4 = Agree   1 = Strongly Disagree

5 4 3 2 1   STATEMENT

❑ ❑ ❑ ❑ ❑   **1. It is important to have job requirements and instructions spelled out so people always know what they are expected to do.**

❑ ❑ ❑ ❑ ❑   **2. Managers expect workers to closely follow instructions and procedures.**

❑ ❑ ❑ ❑ ❑   **3. Rules and regulations are important because they inform workers what the organization expects of them.**

❑ ❑ ❑ ❑ ❑   **4. Standard operating procedures are helpful to workers on the job.**

❑ ❑ ❑ ❑ ❑   **5. Instructions for operations are important for workers on the job.**

❑ ❑ ❑ ❑ ❑   **6. Individual rewards are not as important as group welfare.**

❑ ❑ ❑ ❑ ❑   **7. Group success is more important than individual success.**

❑ ❑ ❑ ❑ ❑   **8. Being accepted by the group is more important than working on your own.**

❑ ❑ ❑ ❑ ❑   **9. An individual should not pursue his or her own objectives without considering the welfare of the group.**

❑ ❑ ❑ ❑ ❑   **10. It is important for a manager to encourage loyalty and a sense of duty to the group.**

❑ ❑ ❑ ❑ ❑   **11. Managers should make most decisions without consulting subordinates.**

(continued on next page)

5	4	3	2	1	STATEMENT
❏	❏	❏	❏	❏	**12. It is often necessary for a supervisor to emphasize his or her authority and power when dealing with subordinates.**
❏	❏	❏	❏	❏	**13. Managers should be careful not to ask the opinions of subordinates too frequently.**
❏	❏	❏	❏	❏	**14. A manager should avoid socializing with his or her subordinates off the job.**
❏	❏	❏	❏	❏	**15. Subordinates should not disagree with their manager's decisions.**
❏	❏	❏	❏	❏	**16. Managers should not delegate difficult and important tasks to their subordinates.**
❏	❏	❏	❏	❏	**17. Meetings are usually run more effectively when they are chaired by a man.**
❏	❏	❏	❏	❏	**18. It is more important for men to have a professional career than it is for women to have a professional career.**
❏	❏	❏	❏	❏	**19. Women do not value recognition and promotion in their work as much as men do.**
❏	❏	❏	❏	❏	**20. Women value working in a friendly atmosphere more than men do.**
❏	❏	❏	❏	❏	**21. Men usually solve problems with logical analysis; women usually solve problems with intuition.**
❏	❏	❏	❏	❏	**22. Solving organizational problems usually requires the active forcible approach, which is typical of men.**
❏	❏	❏	❏	❏	**23. It is preferable to have a man in a high-level position rather than a woman.**
❏	❏	❏	❏	❏	**24. There are some jobs in which a man can always do better than a woman.**
❏	❏	❏	❏	❏	**25. Women are more concerned with social aspects of their job than they are with getting ahead.**

Source: This questionnaire is part of a larger instrument currently under development by Professors Peter W. Dorfman and Jon P. Howell, both of New Mexico State University. Reprinted by permission of the authors.

Scoring and Interpretation of Management Skills

How Do Your Ethics Stack Up? (Part I) page 102.

Scoring Procedure

Strongly Agree:	3 points
Agree:	2 points
Disagree:	1 point
Strongly Disagree:	0 point

According to the author of the exercise, interpret the total score as follows:

0 point:	Prepare for canonization ceremony
1–5 points:	Bishop material
6–10 points:	High ethical values
11–15 points:	Good ethical values
16–25 points:	Average ethical values
26–35 points:	Need moral development
36–44 points:	Slipping fast
45 points:	Leave valuables with the warden

Recommendation to Improve Student Ethics

If you score at, or below, *average ethical values* (16 points or above), you are encouraged to carefully review Chapter 3, specifically the sections "A Model of Ethics" and "Business Ethics." Also, if you score in this range, you should carefully review the "Management Tips" section in Chapter 3.

Are You a Good Decision Maker? (Part II) page 197.

Scoring Procedure

Rating for Questions 4, 9, and 11:

Yes:	3 points
No:	1 point

Rating for the Remaining Questions:

No:	3 points
Yes:	1 point

The exercise should be interpreted on the basis of the total score, as follows:

Score of 32 and above:	Very good decision maker
Score of 23–30:	Average decision maker
Score of 22 or below:	Poor decision maker

Recommendation to Improve Student Decision-Making Ability

If you score at, or below, the level of an *average decision maker* (30 points or below), you are encouraged to carefully review Chapter 4, specifically the section "Decision-Making Requirements." Also, if you score in this range, you should carefully review the "Management Tips" section in Chapter 4.

How Well Would You Fit in a Bureaucracy? (Part III) page 302

Scoring Procedure

QUESTION NUMBER	RESPONSE	POINT VALUE
1.	Mostly Agree	2
2.	Mostly Agree	2
3.	Mostly Disagree	2
4.	Mostly Agree	2
5.	Mostly Disagree	2
6.	Mostly Disagree	2
7.	Mostly Agree	2
8.	Mostly Agree	2
9.	Mostly Disagree	2
10.	Mostly Agree	2
11.	Mostly Agree	2
12.	Mostly Disagree	2
13.	Mostly Disagree	2
14.	Mostly Agree	2
15.	Mostly Disagree	2
16.	Mostly Agree	2
17.	Mostly Disagree	2
18.	Mostly Agree	2
19.	Mostly Agree	2
20.	Mostly Disagree	2

The exercise should be interpreted on the basis of the total score, as follows:

Score of 30 and above: Very high bureaucratic orientation

Score between 29 and 10: Average bureaucratic orientation

Score of 9 and below: Very low bureaucratic orientation

As individual with a rating of *very high* will probably enjoy working in a bureaucratic environment. However, an individual with a rating of *very low* will probably be better off avoiding a bureaucratic environment. Individuals with an *average* rating may survive and thrive to a similar degree in either type of organization. But scoring at the higher range still indicates a greater bureaucratic orientation.

Recommendation to Refine Student Perceptions Regarding a Bureaucracy

If you score at, or below, an *average bureaucratic orientation* (29 points or below), you are encouraged to carefully review Chapter 8 to make sure that your perception of what a bureaucracy is all about is correct.

What Kind of Leader Are You? (Part IV) page 506

Scoring Procedure

In order to compute your leadership style, use the following guidelines:

1. Circle the item numbers for items 8, 12, 17, 18, 19, 30, 34, and 35.
2. Write a "1" in front of the *circled items* to which you responded S *(Seldom)* or N *(Never)*.
3. Write a "1" in front of *items not circled* to which you responded A *(Always)* or F *(Frequently)*.
4. Circle the "1's" you have written in front of the following items: 3, 5, 8, 10, 15, 18, 19, 22, 24, 26, 28, 30, 32, 34, and 35.
5. Count the circled "1's." This is your score for having a participation orientation. Record the score in the blank following the "P Score" at the end of the questionnaire.
6. Count the uncircled "1's." This is your score for having an autocratic orientation. Record

this number in the blank following the "A Score."

Interpretation of your scores: Three leadership categories will be addressed here:

Autocratic leadership
Participative leadership
Democratic/laissez-faire leadership

Autocratic Leadership: An *Autocratic leader* is a person who tells subordinates what to do and expects to be obeyed without questions.

Score of 16 and above:	Highly autocratic leader
Score of 10–15:	Somewhat autocratic leader
Score of 0–9:	Nonautocratic leader

Participative Leadership: A *participative leader* is a person who involves subordinates in decision making but may retain the final authority.

Score of 12–15:	Highly participative leader
Score of 9–11:	Participative leader
Score of 0–8:	Nonparticipative leader

Democratic/Laissez-Faire Leadership: A *democratic leader* is a person who tries to do what the majority of subordinates desire. A *laissez-faire leader* is a person who is uninvolved in the work of the unit.

A Score:	Score of 10–15:	Somewhat autocratic leader
P Score:	Score of 9–11:	Participative leader

Recommendation to Improve Student Leadership Ability

In Chapter 11, four basic leadership styles were identified: autocratic, participative, democratic, and laissez-faire (see Figure 11.1). You are encouraged to read Chapter 11 carefully, especially the sections dealing with these types of leadership. If you are rated as overly autocratic or overly participative, you are encouraged to carefully review and study the advantages and disadvantages of each type of behavior.

Do You Manage Time Effectively? (Part V) page 578

Scoring Procedure

All of these questions, 1–7, are evidence of ineffective time management.

The exercise should be interpreted on the basis of the total score, as follows:

1 or 2 boxes checked:	Average time management ability
3 boxes checked:	Below average time management ability
4 or more boxes checked:	Extremely poor time management ability

All of these questions illustrate the *extreme*, where time is out of the respondent's control. Each question illustrates some aspect of poor time management. Some comments regarding the seven questions are:

Question 1: A person who is continually tired probably is working improperly, is doing someone else's work, or is in the wrong line of work.

Question 2: It is not your responsibility to take on the work of others. Some people lack the ability to say no. When you are asked to do something, answer this question: If I accept, will this improve the productivity of my unit, help me in some way, or be of great service to others? In many instances, the answer will be no, so just say no.

Question 3: If work controls your life, you will probably not be as effective as you would be if you scheduled some time for recreation and some social activities.

Question 4: Although managers must adhere to a schedule, lack of flexibility can create productivity problems. Lack of organization wastes time, but rigidity may cause problems when unusual situations occur.

Question 5: Managers must be able to clear away work and set priorities. Don't allow yourself to put off work until you have so much to do that you do not do anything. It is best to complete both desirable and undesirable tasks as they come up rather than to continuously put them off. It may even be better to do the distasteful tasks first.

Question 6: Details are sometimes important, but managers must not get caught up in a web of details.

Question 7: Managers who do not delegate often achieve limited success and always feel overwhelmed.

Recommendation to Improve Student Time Management Ability

Basically, even if you are rated as *average* (one or two boxes checked), you probably have a time management problem. If you are rated *below average* or *extremely poor* you need to enhance your time management ability. You are encouraged to carefully review Chapter 16 to help improve your time management skills. Specifically, you should review the sections "How Managers Can Control Their Time Better" and "Management Tips."

What Is the Makeup of Your Cultural Attitudes? (Part VI) page 671

Scoring Procedure

Sum up items 1 through 5 and divide by 5. This is your mean **uncertainty avoidance** score.

Sum up items 6 through 10 and divide by 5. This is your mean individualism/collectivism score.

Sum up items 11 through 16, and divide by 6. This is your mean power distance score.

Sum up items 17 through 25 and divide by 9. This is your mean masculinity/femininity score.

The exercise should be interpreted on the basis of the mean scores, as follows:

1. **Uncertainty avoidance**—Defines the extent to which people in a culture feel threatened by uncertainty and ambiguous situations and try to avoid such situations. The higher the mean score (5 is the maximum mean score), the more likely the manager is to feel threatened in new cultures.

2. **Individualism/collectivism**—Individualism implies a loosely knit social framework in which people are supposed to take care of themselves (as opposed to collectivist cultures characterized by "individual groups" that are expected to take care of their members). The higher the mean score, the more likely a manager will be productive in a team or group environment.

3. **Power distance**—Defines the extent to which the less powerful person in a society accepts inequality in power and considers it normal. The higher the mean score, the more likely that a person will be power-oriented and may have difficulty working in an environment where power is distributed among many indi-

viduals or groups. This type of person may even be manipulative and over-emphasize control.

4. **Masculinity/femininity**—Defines the extent to which the dominant values of society are "masculine" (e.g., assertive and competitive) or feminine (e.g., less assertive and less competitive). The higher the mean score, the more likely that masculine traits are dominant. In a country such as present-day Japan, a feminine type may have trouble coping.

You can compare your scores with a sample of U.S. and Mexican students to see how well you would embrace their cultures. The closer your mean score is to their mean scores, the greater the likelihood that you would mesh with their culture.

DIMENSION	U.S. STUDENTS	MEXICAN STUDENTS
Uncertainty avoidance	3.41	4.15
Individualism/collectivism	2.19	3.33
Power distance	1.86	3.33
Masculinity/femininity	2.78	2.75

Recommendation to Improve Cultural Sensitivity

Basically, if you have a mean rating approaching 5, you probably are not very flexible and may find it difficult to adapt to new cultures. To enhance your skills in relation to cultural sensitivity, you should read Chapter 15 carefully. You should also read the section of Chapter 14 dealing with power.

Glossary

ABC inventory method: The classification of inventory items for control purposes into three categories, according to unit costs and number of items kept on hand.

Acceptance sampling: The inspection of a portion of the output or input of a process to determine acceptability.

Accountability: Any means of ensuring that the person who is supposed to perform a task actually performs it and does so correctly.

Action planning: The establishment of performance objectives and standards for individuals.

Affirmative action: Performance required to ensure that applicants are employed, and that employees are treated appropriately during employment, without regard to race, creed, color, or national origin.

Alternatives: Choices that the decision maker has to decide on.

Analyzer strategy: The business-level strategy of attempting to maintain a stable business while innovating on the fringe.

Arbitration: The process in which a dispute between two parties is submitted to a third party to make a binding decision.

Authority: The right to decide, to direct others to take action, or to perform certain duties in achieving organizational objectives.

Autocratic leader: A leader who tells subordinates what to do and who expects to be obeyed without question.

Backward integration: A company's taking control of any of the sources of its inputs, including raw materials and labor.

Body language: The nonverbal method of communication in which physical actions such as motions, gestures, and facial expressions convey thoughts and emotions.

Brainstorming: The idea-generating technique wherein a number of persons present alternatives without regard to questions of feasibility or practicality.

Break-even analysis: The financial analysis method used to determine the amount of a particular product that must be sold if a firm is to generate enough revenue to cover costs.

Budget: A statement of planned allocation of resources expressed in financial or numerical terms.

Burnout: The state of fatigue or frustration that stems from devotion to a cause, a way of life, or a relationship that does not provide the expected reward.

Business ethics: The application of ethical principles to business relationships and activities.

Business-level strategic planning: The planning process concerned with how to manage the interests and operations of a particular business.

Capital budget: A statement of planned expenditures of funds for facilities and equipment.

Carrying costs: The expenses associated with maintaining and storing products before they are sold or used.

Cause-and-effect diagram: Sometimes called the Ishikawa diagram, after one of the leading Japanese contributors to TQM—this diagram is used to classify and present the ideas from brainstorming in a manner more likely to lead to solving the problem at hand.

Centralization: The degree to which authority is retained by higher-level managers in an organization rather than being delegated.

Chain of command: The line along which authority flows from the top of the organization to any individual.

Change: Moving from a known to an unknown.

Change agent: The person or group responsible for ensuring that the planned change in organizational development is properly implemented.

Change sequence: The sequence of events that is needed to bring about change in an organization.

Client/server system: A system that combines the strengths of various types of computers to split and deliver computer applications and data at reduced costs with greater reliability.

Closed system: An organization or assemblage of things that neither affects nor is affected by outside events.

Coalescing: The process of individuals or groups combining their resources to pursue common objectives.

Coercive power: The power that is derived from the ability to punish or to recommend punishment.

Cohesiveness: The degree of attraction the group has for each of its members.

Committee: A group of people assigned to work together to do something not included in their regular jobs.

Communication: The transfer of information, ideas, understanding, or feelings among people.

Communication channels: The means by which information is transmitted in organizations.

Communication networks: The pathways through which messages between and among people in organizations flow.

Comparable worth: The concept that requires the value for dissimilar jobs to be compared under some form of job evaluation and pay rates to be assigned according to their evaluated worth.

Compensation: All rewards individuals receive as a result of their employment.

Compressed workweek: Any arrangement of work hours that permits employees to fulfill their work obligation in fewer days than the typical five-day workweek.

Concentric diversification: The development of businesses related to the firm's current businesses.

Conceptual skill: The ability to comprehend abstract or general ideas and apply them to specific situations.

Conflict: Antagonism or opposition between or among persons.

Conglomerate diversification: The development of businesses unrelated to the firm's current businesses.

Consideration: The extent to which leaders' relationships with subordinates are characterized by mutual trust and respect for employees' ideas and feelings.

Contact chart: A diagram showing various individuals in the organization and the number of interactions they have with others.

Contingency planning: The development of plans to be placed in effect if certain events occur.

Control chart: The graphic record of how closely samples of a good or service conform to standards over time.

Control tolerances: Specifications of how much deviation will be permitted before corrective action is taken.

Controlling: The process of comparing actual performance with standards and taking any necessary corrective action.

Co-opting: The method of increasing power and creating alliances in which individuals or groups whose support is needed are absorbed into another group.

Coordination: The process of ensuring that persons who perform interdependent activities work together in a way that contributes to overall objective attainment.

Corporate culture: The system of shared values, beliefs, and habits within an organization that interacts with the formal structure to produce behavioral norms.

Corporate-level strategic planning: The process of defining the overall character and purpose of the organization, the businesses it will enter and leave, and how resources will be distributed among those businesses.

Cost leadership strategy: The business-level strategy in which the organization aggressively seeks efficient facilities, pursues cost reductions, and uses tight cost controls to produce products more efficiently than competitors.

Creativity: The ability to generate ideas that are both innovative and functional.

Critical path method (CPM): The planning and control technique that involves the display of a complex project as a network, with one time estimate used for each step in the project.

Data communication: The sending of data produced by a computer over some form of communication medium, such as phone lines.

Database management: The exchange of information with people who are higher or lower in the organization but who are directly in the formal chain of command.

Decentralization: The condition that exists when a significant amount of authority is delegated to lower levels in the enterprise.

Decision making: The process of generating and evaluating alternatives and making choices among them.

Decision risk: Exposure to the probability that an incorrect decision will have an adverse effect on the organization.

Decision support system (DSS): An information system that allows users to quickly process and retrieve information.

Defender strategy: The business-level strategy that seeks to maintain current market share by holding on to current customers.

Delegation: The process of assigning responsibility along with the needed authority.

Delphi technique: The formal procedure for obtaining the consensus of a number of experts through the use of a series of questionnaires.

Democratic leader: A leader who tries to do what the majority of subordinates desires.

Departmentation: The process of grouping related work activities into manageable units.

Diagonal communication: The exchange of information with people who are higher or lower in the organization but who are not directly in the formal chain of command.

Differentiation strategy: The business-level strategy that involves an attempt to distinguish the firm's goods or services from others in the industry.

Directing: The process of telling a person what to do.

Disciplinary action: Action taken to correct unacceptable behavior.

Discipline: The state of employee self-control and orderly conduct present in an organization.

Discipline without punishment: A process whereby a worker is given time off with pay to think about whether he or she really wants to follow the rules and continue working for the company.

Discounted cash flow technique: The way of valuing an investment that uses an interest rate or discount rate to calculate the present value of the income the investment is expected to produce.

Diversification: Increasing the variety of goods or services made or sold.

Dominant culture: The corporate culture that expresses the shared views of the majority of the organization's members.

Downsizing: This procedure, also known as *restructuring* and *rightsizing,* is a one-time reduction in the size of the organization and the number of people who are employed by a firm.

Economic order quantity (EOQ) inventory control method: The procedure for balancing ordering costs and carrying costs so as to minimize total inventory costs.

Effectiveness: The capability of bringing about an effect or accomplishing a purpose, sometimes without regard to the quantity of resources consumed in the process.

Efficiency: The capability of producing desired results with a minimum of energy, time, money, materials, or other costly inputs.

Electronic data interchange (EDI): This method provides the electronic transfer of documents, such as purchase orders, invoices, even payments, from one firm to another.

Empathy: The ability to identify with the feelings and thoughts of another person.

Employee assistance program: A coordinated effort by an organization to help employees deal with special problems and needs.

Employee-centered work redesign: An innovative concept designed to link the mission of the company with the job satisfaction needs of employees.

Employee orientation: The formal process of helping new employees adjust to the organization, job, and work group.

Employment requisition: A form issued to activate the recruitment process, typically including such information as the job title, starting date, and pay scale and a brief summary of principal duties.

Equity theory: The motivation theory that people assess their performance and attitudes by comparing both their contribution to work and the benefits they derive from it to the contributions and benefits of "comparison others" whom they select—and who in reality may be like or unlike them.

Ethics: The discipline dealing with what is good and bad, or right and wrong, or with moral duty and obligation.

Executive Orders: Directives issued by the President that have the force and effect of laws enacted by Congress.

Expectancy theory: The approach to motivation that attempts to explain behavior in terms of an individual's objectives and choices and the expectations of achieving the objectives.

Expert (knowledge) power: The power that comes from a person's possessing special knowledge or skills.

Expert system: A system that uses knowledge about a narrowly defined, complex area to act as a consultant to a human.

External environment: Those factors that affect a firm from outside its organizational boundaries.

Extrinsic motivation: Motivation by factors outside the job, such as pay, job title, and tenure.

Fixed costs: Costs that do not change with the level of output.

Fixed-position layout: The production process in which the large or heavy product stays in one location, and people, tools, materials, and equipment are moved to the product as needed.

Flextime: The practice of permitting employees to choose, with certain limitations, their own working hours.

Flow process chart: A chart illustrating the activities involved in an entire process, showing the sequence in which they are performed.

Focus strategy: The business-level strategy in which the organization concentrates on a specific regional market, product line, or buyer group.

Formal communication channels: The communication channels that are officially recognized by the organization.

Forward integration: Integration toward the final users of a company's goods or services.

Function: A type of work activity that can be identified and distinguished from other work.

Functional authority: The right of staff specialists to issue orders in their own names in designated areas.

Functional authority organizations: Organizations whose staff departments have authority over line personnel in narrow areas of specialization (a modification of line and staff organizations).

Functional-level strategic planning: The process of determining policies and procedures for relatively narrow areas of activity that are critical to the success of the organization.

Glass ceiling: The invisible barrier in organizations that prevents many women from achieving top-level management positions.

Grapevine: The informal means by which information is transmitted in an organization.

Graphical User Interfaces (GUIs): These interfaces represent a move to truly make software applications easy to use. Computer users touch or aim at graphic figures (icons) or framed written commands to communicate with the computer program.

Grievance procedure: A systematic process through which employees complain about matters affecting them.

Group: Two or more people having a unifying relationship, such as common objectives or physical proximity.

Groupware: Software that enables people to work together in groups and assists in decision making, workflow, and work management.

Health: The condition of being physically and emotionally able to perform vital functions normally or properly.

Horizontal differentiation: The process of forming additional units at the same level in the organization.

Horizontal integration: Buying or taking control of competitors at the same level in the production and marketing process.

Host country: The country where an operational unit of a multinational company resides.

Human resource management (HRM): The wide range of organizational activities involved in staffing, training and development, compensation, health and safety, employee and labor relations, and human resource research.

Human resource planning (HRP): The development of strategies and tactics to ensure that the required numbers of employees with the required skills are on the job when they are needed.

Human skill: The ability to understand, motivate, and get along with other people.

Image processing: Systems that enable companies to electronically capture, manipulate, and retrieve images that may include photographs, documents, numeric data, and handwriting.

Influencing: The process of determining or affecting the behavior of others.

Informal communication channels: Ways of transmitting information within an organization that bypass formal channels.

Informal group: Two or more persons associated with one another in ways not prescribed by the formal organization.

Informal organization: The set of evolving relationships and patterns of human interaction within an organization that are not officially prescribed.

Information filtering: The process by which a message is altered through the elimination of certain data as the communication moves from person to person in the organization.

Information overload: The condition that exists when an individual is presented with too much information in too short a time.

Initiating structure: The extent to which leaders establish objectives and structure their roles and the roles of subordinates toward the attainment of the objectives.

Integration: The unified control of a number of successive or similar operations.

Internal environment: Those factors inside an organization that affect the organization's management.

Intimidation: Occurs when a person fails to take action because of fear.

Intrinsic motivation: Motivation by factors within the job, such as creativity, autonomy, and responsibility.

Inventory: The goods or materials available for use by a business.

Iron law of responsibility: The rule, first stated by Keith Davis, that "in the long run, those who do not use power in a manner society considers responsible will tend to lose it."

Jargon: The special language that group members use in their daily interactions.

Job analysis: The systematic process of determining the skills and knowledge required for performing jobs in the organization.

Job description: A document that describes the tasks and responsibilities of a job and its relationships to other jobs.

Job design: The process of determining the specific tasks to be performed, the methods used in performing these tasks, and how the job relates to other work in the organization.

Job enlargement: Changes in the scope of a job so as to provide greater variety for the worker.

Job enrichment: Basic changes in the content and level of responsibility of a job so as to provide greater challenge to the worker.

Job sharing: Two part-time people splitting the duties of one job in some agreed-on manner and being paid according to their contributions.

Job specification: A statement of the minimum acceptable qualifications a person should possess to perform a particular job.

Just-in-time (JIT) inventory method: The practice of having inputs to the production process delivered precisely when they are needed, thereby assigning to suppliers the responsibility for keeping inventories to a minimum.

Laissez-faire leader: A leader who is uninvolved in the work of the unit.

Lateral communication: Communication by managers at the same organizational level.

Leadership (leading): Influencing others to do what the leader wants them to do.

Leadership continuum: The graphical representation, developed by Robert Tannenbaum and Warren H. Schmidt, of the trade-off between a manager's use of authority and the freedom that subordinates experience as the leadership style varies from boss-centered to subordinate-centered.

Learning curve: A graphic representation of the decreasing time required to do a particular task as that task is repeated by a certain person.

Leased employees: Individuals provided by an outside firm at a fixed hourly rate, similar to a rental fee, often for extended periods.

Legitimate power: The power that results from a person's being placed in a formal position of authority.

Line and staff organizations: Organizations that have direct, vertical relationships between different levels and also specialists responsible for advising and assisting other managers.

Line departments: Departments directly involved in accomplishing the primary purpose of the organization.

Line organizations: Organizations that have only direct, vertical relationships between different levels in the firm.

Maintenance: The sum of all activities involved in keeping a production system in working order.

Management: The process of getting things done through the efforts of other people.

Management by objectives (MBO): The philosophy of management that emphasizes the setting of agreed-on objectives by managers and their subordinates and the use of these objectives as the primary bases of motivation, evaluation, and control efforts.

Management development programs: Formal efforts to improve the skills and attitudes of present and prospective managers.

Management information system (MIS): Any organized approach for obtaining relevant and timely information on which to base management decisions.

Managerial Grid: The two-dimensional matrix developed by Robert Blake and Jane Mouton that shows concern for people on the vertical axis and concern for production on the horizontal axis.

Managing diversity: Having an acute awareness of characteristics common to a culture, race, gender, age, or sexual preference, while at the same time managing employees with these characteristics as individuals.

Matrix departmentation: The form of departmentation that occurs when project departmentation takes on a permanent status designed to achieve specific results by using teams of specialists from different functional areas of the organization.

Matrix organization: A permanent organization designed to achieve specific results by using teams of specialists from different functional areas in the organization.

Mediation: The process in which a third party enters a dispute between two parties for the purpose of assisting them in reaching an agreement.

Middle managers: Managers above the supervisory level but subordinate to the firm's most senior executives.

Mission: A unit's continuing process, or reason for being.

Mission statement: A broadly stated definition of the basic purpose and scope of a unit.

Motivation: The desire to put forth effort in pursuit of organizational objectives.

Multimedia: A computer application that produces presentations combining automation, stereo sound, full-motion video, and graphics.

Multinational company (MNC): A firm that is based in one country (the parent, or home, country) and produces goods or provides services in one or more foreign countries (host countries).

Networking: The cultivating of relationships with the right people for the purpose of obtaining power.

Noise: Anything that interferes with the accurate transmission or reception of messages.

Nominal grouping: The approach to decision making that involves idea generation by group members, group interaction only to clarify ideas, member rankings of ideas presented, and alternative selection by summing up the rankings.

Nonroutine decisions: Decisions that are designed to deal with unusual problems or situations.

Norm: A standard of behavior expected of informal group members.

Objectives: The desired end results of any activity.

Ombudsperson: A complaint officer with access to top management who hears employee complaints, investigates, and recommends appropriate action.

Open-door policy: An established guideline that allows workers to bypass immediate supervisors in regard to substantive matters without fear of reprisal.

Open system: An organization or assemblage of things that affects and is affected by outside events.

Operating budget: A statement of the planned income and expenses of a business or unit.

Operation chart: A chart showing an operator's activities while one operation in a process is performed.

Operations management: The management of the complex activities relating to planning production, organizing resources, directing operations and human resources, and monitoring system performance.

Ordering costs: Administrative, clerical, and other expenses incurred in obtaining inventory items and placing them in storage.

Organization: Two or more people working together in a coordinated manner to achieve group results.

Organizational behavior modification: The application of B. F. Skinner's reinforcement theory to organizational change efforts.

Organizational constituency: Any identifiable group that organizational managers either have or acknowledge a responsibility to represent.

Organizational development (OD): Planned and systematic attempts to change the organization, typically to a more behavioral environment.

Organizational stakeholder: An individual or group whose interests are affected by organizational activities.

Organizational strategists: The people who spend a large portion of their time on matters of vital or far-ranging importance to the organization as a whole.

Organizational structure: The formal relationships among groups and individuals in the organization.

Organizing: The process of prescribing formal relationships among people and resources to accomplish objectives.

Parent country: The country where the headquarters of a multinational company is located.

Pareto analysis: This analysis is based on the Pareto distribution, which in its original analysis says that five percent of the people control 50 percent of the wealth, or that 20 percent control 80 percent of the wealth; it is used to help to decide which problems are most important to study.

Participative leader: A leader who involves subordinates in decision making but may retain the final authority.

Path-goal theory: The proposition that managers can facilitate job performance by showing employees how their performance directly affects their receiving desired rewards.

Payback method: The method of financial analysis by which investments are ranked according to the payback period, the time it takes an investment to pay back the initial capital in profits.

Payoff relationship: Alternatives are evaluated in terms of their potential benefits or costs.

Perception set: A fixed tendency to interpret information in a certain way.

Performance appraisal: The formal and systematic measurement and evaluation of job performance.

Planning: The process of determining in advance what should be accomplished and how it should be realized.

Plans: Statements of how objectives are to be accomplished.

Policy: A predetermined guide established to provide direction in decision making.

Political action committees (PACs): Tax-favored organizations formed by special interest groups to accept contributions and influence government action.

Politics: A network of interactions by which power is acquired, transferred, and exercised on others.

Portfolio strategy: The process of determining how an SBU will compete in a particular line of business, with a concentration on the mix of business units and product lines that fit together in a logical way to provide synergy and competitive advantage for the corporation.

Power: The ability to influence behavior.

Predetermined time standards: Established estimates of the time that should be required to perform minute tasks.

Preliminary interview: The type of interview used to eliminate any obviously unqualified job applicants.

Preventive maintenance: Routine inspection and other efforts aimed at preventing breakdowns and keeping equipment and facilities in good working order.

Primary groups: Small groups characterized by relatively close associations among members.

Proactive response: Taking action in anticipation of environmental changes.

Problem content: The environment in which the problem exists, the decision maker's knowledge of that environment, and the environment that will exist after a choice is made.

Procedure: A series of steps for the accomplishment of some specific project or endeavor.

Process layout: An arrangement of the processing components according to the functions they perform.

Product layout: The production arrangement that entails moving a product down an assembly line or conveyor and through a series of work stations until the product is completed.

Production and operations: The application of objective, especially quantitative, techniques to the design and operation of any system that transforms inputs into outputs.

Productivity: A measure of the relationship between inputs (labor, capital, natural resources, energy, and so forth) and the quality and quantity of outputs (goods and services).

Program evaluation and review technique (PERT): The planning and control technique that involves the display of a complex project as a network of events and activities with three time estimates used to calculate the expected time for each activity.

Progressive discipline: The disciplinary action approach designed to ensure that the minimum penalty appropriate to the offense is imposed.

Project organization: A temporary organization designed to achieve specific results by using teams of specialists from different functional areas in the organization.

Prospector strategy: The business-level strategy that involves innovation through seeking out new opportunities, taking risks, and expanding.

Quality: The degree of excellence of a good or service.

Quality circles: Small groups of employees who get together on company time to develop ways to improve the quality and quantity of work.

Reactive response: Responding to environmental changes after they occur.

Recruitment: The process of attracting individuals—in sufficient numbers and with appropriate qualifications—and encouraging them to apply for jobs with the organization.

Reengineering: The fundamental rethinking and radical redesign of business processes to achieve dramatic improvements in critical, contemporary measures of performance, such as cost, quality, service, and speed.

Referent power: The power that is based on a liking for, or a desire to be liked by, the power holder.

Reinforcement theory: The idea that human behavior can be explained in terms of the previous positive or negative outcomes of that behavior.

Responsibility: The obligation to perform work activities.

Retrenchment: The reduction of the size or scope of a firm's activities.

Reward power: The power that is derived from a person's ability to reward another individual.

Role: Total pattern of expected behavior of an individual.

Rule: A specific and detailed guide to action set up to direct or restrict action in a fairly narrow manner.

Safety: Freedom from danger.

Scalar principle: The philosophy that authority and responsibility should flow from top management downward in a clear, unbroken line.

Secondary groups: Groups that are larger and less intimate than primary groups.

Selection: The process of choosing from a group of applicants the individual best suited for a particular position.

Self-fulfilling prophecy: The idea that the manager's positive or negative expectations will have a significant influence on employee motivation and performance.

Sensitivity training: The organizational development technique that uses leaderless discussion groups to develop awareness of and sensitivity to oneself and others (also called *T-group training* and *laboratory training*).

Simulation: The technique for experimenting with a real-world situation through an artificial model that represents that situation.

Social audit: A systematic assessment of a company's activities in terms of their social impact.

Social contract: The set of written and unwritten rules and assumptions about acceptable interrelationships among the various elements of society.

Social responsibility: The implied, enforced, or felt obligation of managers, acting in their official capacity, to serve or protect the interests of groups other than themselves.

Source (sender): The person who has an idea or message to communicate to another person or persons.

Span of management (control): The number of direct subordinates reporting to any manager.

Specialization of labor: The division of a complex job into simpler tasks so that one person or group may carry out only identical or related activities.

Staff departments: Departments that provide line people with advice and assistance in specialized areas.

Staffing: The formal process of ensuring that the organization has qualified workers available at all levels to meet its short- and long-term business objectives.

Standard operating procedures (SOPs): The stable body of procedures, written and unwritten, that govern an organization.

Standards: Established levels of quality or quantity used to guide performance.

Standing plans: Plans that remain roughly the same for long periods of time.

States of nature: The various situations that could occur and the probability of each of them occurring.

Statistical process control: Gauging the performance of the manufacturing process by carefully monitoring changes in whatever is being produced.

Status symbol: A visible, external sign of one's social position.

Stockholders (shareholders): The owners of a corporation's stock.

Strategic business unit (SBU): Any part of a business organization that is treated separately for strategic planning purposes.

Strategic control points: The critical points selected for monitoring in the process of producing goods or services.

Strategic planning: The process by which top management determines overall organizational purposes and objectives and how they are to be achieved.

Strategic planning staff specialists: Specialists who assist and advise managers in strategic planning.

Stress: The body's reaction to any demand made on it.

Stress audit: A review that helps identify the symptoms and causes of stress.

Strong corporate culture: The dominant corporate culture that is widely and ardently adhered to by members of the organization.

Subcultures: Corporate cultures characteristic of various units in an organization.

Supervisory managers: The managers who directly oversee the efforts of those who actually perform the work.

Survey feedback method: The organizational development method of basing change efforts on the systematic collection and measurement of subordinates' attitudes through anonymous questionnaires.

Synergism: The cooperative action of two or more persons working together to accomplish more than they could working separately.

Systems approach: The viewing of any organization or entity as an arrangement of interrelated parts that interact in ways that can be specified and to some extent predicted.

Tactical plans: Plans designed to implement the strategic plans of top management.

Task (functional) groups: Groups determined by prescribed job requirements.

Team building: A conscious effort by management to develop effective work groups throughout the organization.

Technical skill: The ability to use specific knowledge, methods, and techniques in performing work.

Telecommuting: When workers at home or temporarily away from the office perform their work over telephone lines tied to a computer as if they were at the office.

Teleconferencing: A method of conducting or participating in multiparty discussions by telephone or videophone.

Theory X: The assumption that people dislike work and responsibility, lack ambition and creative ability, and mainly want security and money.

Theory Y: The assumption that expending physical and mental effort is natural, that people can be self-directed if achievement brings rewards, and that most can exercise imagination, ingenuity, and creativity and learn to seek responsibility.

Time study: The systematic measurement and analysis of the time required to do work.

Timing: The determination of when a message should be communicated.

Top managers: The organization's most senior executives.

Total quality management: A commitment to excellence by everyone in an organization that emphasizes excellence achieved by teamwork and a process of continuous improvement.

Training and development programs: Formal efforts to help employees learn new skills, improve existing skills, or otherwise improve their ability to perform in the organization.

Trait approach to leadership: The evaluation and selection of leaders on the basis of their physical, mental, social, and psychological characteristics.

Transformational leader: A person who has the special ability to lead an organization through major strategic change.

Transnational company: A firm that views the world as one market, conducts operations in many countries, and makes decisions as if national boundaries do not exist.

Tunnel vision: The extremely narrow viewpoint of people who have mental blinders, such as individual biases, that restrict the search for a solution to a narrow range of alternatives.

Type I ethics: The strength of the relationship between what an individual or an organization believes to be moral and correct and what available sources of guidance suggest is morally correct.

Type II ethics: The strength of the relationship between what one believes and how one behaves.

Union: A group of employees who have joined together for the purpose of dealing with their employer.

Unity of command principle: The belief that each person should answer to only one immediate superior.

Variable costs: Costs that are directly related to changes in output.

Vertical differentiation: The process of creating additional levels in the organization.

Voice mail: Spoken messages transmitted electronically and stored for delivery to the recipient at a later time.

Word processing: A computer application that permits an operator to create and edit written material.

Work sampling: The observation of a worker or workers at random times to determine the proportion of time that is being spent on various tasks.

Work team: An officially sanctioned collection of individuals who have been charged with completing a mission by an organization and who must depend upon one another for successful completion of work.

Worker-machine chart: A chart showing if there is excessive idle time associated with either the worker or the machine.

Worker participation: The process of involving workers in the decision-making process.

Zero base budgeting: The system of budgeting that requires management to take a fresh look at all programs and activities each year, rather than merely building on last year's budget.

References

Adler, Nancy J. "Women Managers in a Global Economy." *HRMagazine* 36 (September 1993): 52–55.

Adler, Paul S. "Managing Flexible Automation." *California Management Review* 30 (Spring 1988): 34–56.

Akers, John R. "Ethics and Competitiveness—Putting First Things First." *Sloan Management Review* 30 (Winter 1989): 69–71.

Albrecht, W. Steve, and David W. Schmoldt. "Employee Fraud." *Business Horizons* 31 (July–August 1988): 16–18.

Alderfer, Clayton P. *Existence, Relatedness, and Growth: Human Needs in Organizational Settings.* (New York: Free Press, 1972).

Aleshire, Keith Richard. "Making Sense of Features." *Computerworld* 27 (June 28, 1993): 112–113.

Alexander, John W. "Sharing the Vision." *Business Horizons* 32 (May–June 1989): 56–59.

Anderson, Joyce S. "Real Open-Door Communication." *Personnel Journal* 68 (May 1989): 32–37.

Anthes, Gary H. "Rivals Team Up for EDI." *Computerworld* 27 (March 15, 1993): 64.

————. "A Labor of Labs." *Computerworld* 27 (July 19, 1993): 28.

Applegate, Lynda A., James I. Cash, Jr., and D. Quinn Mills. "Information Technology and Tomorrow's Manager." *Harvard Business Review* 66 (November–December 1988): 128–136.

Aram, John D. "The Paradox of Interdependent Relations in the Field of Social Issues in Management." *The Academy of Management Review* 14 (April 1989): 266–283.

Attaran, Mohsen. "The Automated Factory: Justification and Implementation." *Business Horizons* 32 (May–June 1989): 80–86.

Axline, Larry L. "Business Ethics: Blackjack or Bust?" *Management Review* 79 (October 1990): 64.

————. "TQM: A Look in the Mirror." *Management Review* 80 (July 1991): 64.

Babcock, Charles. "The Next PC Wave." *Computerworld* 27 (July 19, 1993): 37.

Bahrami, Homa, and Stuart Evans. "Strategy Making in High-Technology Firms: The Empiricist Mode." *California Management Review* 31 (Winter 1989): 107–128.

Bales, R. F., and F. L. Strodtbeck. "Phases in Group Problem Solving." *Journal of Abnormal and Social Psychology* 46 (1951): 485–495.

Barnlund, Dean C. "Public and Private Self in Communicating with Japan." *Business Horizons* 32 (March–April 1989): 32–40.

Bavaria, Steve. "Corporate Ethics Should Start in the Boardroom." *Business Horizons* 34 (January–February 1991): 9–12.

Beilinson, Jerry. "Workforce 2000: Already Here?" *Personnel* 67 (October 1990): 3–4.

Bertrand, Kate. "Marketers Rush to Be First on the Bloc." *Business Marketing* 75 (October 1990): 20–23.

Bhide, Amar, and Howard H. Stevenson. "Why Be Honest if Honesty Doesn't Pay." *Harvard Business Review* 66 (September–October 1990): 121–129.

Blake, Robert B., and Jane S. Mouton, "Theory and Research for Developing a Science of Leadership." *Journal of Applied Behavioral Science* 18 (March 1982): 275–291.

Blake, Robert R., and Anne Adams McCanse. *Leadership Dilemmas—Grid Solutions* (Houston: Gulf Publishing Company, 1991).

Bongiorno, Lori. "Corporate America's New Lesson Plan." *Business Week* (October 25, 1993): 102–104.

Bowen, David E., Caren Siehl, and Benjamin Schneider. "A Framework for Analyzing Customer Service Orientations in Manufacturing." *The Academy of Management Review* 14 (January 1989): 75–95.

Burge, Benjamin D. "Producing a Quality Product." *Journal of Systems Management* 41 (November 1990): 7–9.

Butler, Steven, and Warren Cohen. "Toyota Puts It on the Line." *U.S. News & World Report* 115 (August 23, 1993): 47–48.

Byrne, John A. "Management's New Gurus." *Business Week* (August 31, 1992): 44–51.

————. "The Virtual Corporation." *Business Week* (July 8, 1993): 98–103.

Cafasso, Rosemary. "Worldspan Travel's Plan for Single System Takes Flight." *Computerworld* 27 (June 28, 1993): 81.

Carr, Clay. "Expert Support Environments." *Personnel Journal* 68 (April 1989): 117–126.

Caruth, Don. "Words: A Supervisor's Guide to Communications." *Management Solutions* 31 (June 1986): 34–35.

Chakravarty, Subrata N., and Amy Feldman. "Don't Underestimate The Champ." *Forbes* 151 (May 10, 1993): 106–110.

Coate, L. Edwin. *An Analysis of Oregon State University's Total Quality Management Pilot Program.* Oregon State University Press, 1990.

————. *Implementing Total Quality Management in a University Setting.* Oregon State University Press, 1990.

Coccari, Ronald L. "How Quantitative Business Techniques Are Being Used." *Business Horizons* 32 (July–August 1989): 70–74.

Cohen, Allan R, and David L. Bradford. "Influence Without Authority." *Organizational Dynamics* 17 (Winter 1989): 5–17.

————. "Organization Design: Beyond the 'Mafia' Model." *Organizational Dynamics* 17 (Winter 1989): 18–31.

Cohen, Warren. "Exporting Know-How." *U.S. News & World Report* (August 30/September 6, 1993): 53, 56–57.

Collins, Paul E., Jerald Hage, and Frank M. Hull. "Organizational and Technological Predictors of Change in Automaticity." *Academy of Management Journal* 31 (December 1988): 512–543.

Conger, Jay A. "Leadership: The Art of Empowering Others." *The Academy of Management Executive* 3 (February 1989): 17–24.

Conger, Jay A., and Rabindra N. Kanungo. "The Empowerment Process: Integrating Theory and Practice." *The Academy of Management Review* 13 (July 1988): 471–482.

Cook, William J., and Warren Cohen. "Sparking a Revival." *U.S. News & World Report* 114 (June 14, 1993): 69, 71–73.

Cooper, Robin. "You Need a New Cost System When . . . " *Harvard Business Review* 67 (January–February 1989): 77–82.

Cotton, John L., David A. Vollrath, Kirk L. Froggatt, Mark L. Lengnick-Hall, and Kenneth R. Jennings. "Employee Participation: Diverse Forms and Different Outcomes." *Academy of Management Review* 13 (January 1988): 8–22.

Coy, Peter. "Big Brother, Pinned to Your Chest." *Business Week* (August 17, 1992): 38.

Crandall, Lin P., and Mark I. Phelps. "Pay for a Global Work Force." *Personnel Journal* 70 (February 1991): 28–33.

Creswell, Dorothy. "Trends Emerge in Computer Industry." *Inside DPMA* 30 (December 1992): 6,11.

Cusumano, Michael A. "Manufacturing Innovation: Lessons from the Japanese Auto Industry." *Sloan Management Review* 39 (Fall 1988): 29–39.

d'Amboise, Gerald, and Marie Muldowney. "Management Theory for Small Business: Attempts and Requirements." *The Academy of Management Review* 13 (April 1988): 226–240.

Daly, James. "Technology in Tinseltown." *Computerworld* 27 (May 10, 1993): 26.

Davenport, Thomas H., Michael Hammer, and Tauino J. Metsisto. "How Executives Can Shape Their Company's Information Systems." *Harvard Business Review* 67 (March–April 1989): 130–134.

Dobrzynski, Judith. "Rethinking IBM." *Business Week* (October 4, 1993): 86–97.

Dolan, Shimon, and Aharon Tziner. "Implementing Computer-Based Automation in the Office: A Study of Experienced Stress." *Organizational Behavior Management* 9 (April 1988): 183–187.

Donovan, John J. "Beyond Chief Information Officer to Network Manager." *Harvard Business Review* 66 (September–October 1988): 134–143.

Doyle, Robert J. "Caution: Self-Directed Work Teams." *HRMagazine* 37 (June 1992): 153.

Drucker, Peter F. *Management: Tasks, Responsibilities and Practices.* New York: Harper, 1974.

————. "Management and the World's Work." *Harvard Business Review* 66 (September–October 1988): 65–76.

————. "The Coming of New Organization." *Harvard Business Review* 66 (January–February 1988): 45–53.

Duchessi, Peter, Charles M. Schaninger, and Don R. Hobbs. "Implementing a Manufacturing Planning and Control System." *California Management Review* 31 (Spring 1989): 75–90.

Dugan, Kathleen Watson. "Ability and Effort Attributions: Do They Affect How Managers Communicate Performance Feedback Information?" *Academy of Management Journal* 32 (March 1989): 87–114.

Duncan, W. Jack, Peter M. Ginter, Andrew C. Rucks, and T. Douglas Jacobs. "Intrapreneurship and the Reinvention of the Corporation." *Business Horizons* 31 (May–June 1988): 16–21.

Eckley, Robert S. "Caterpillar's Ordeal: Foreign Competition in Capital Goods." *Business Horizons* 32 (March–April 1989): 80–86.

Egan, Gary A. "Groupware: It's for All Companies." *Inside DPMA* 31 (October, 1993): 7.

Eisenhardt, Kathleen M., and L. J. Bourgeios III. "Politics of Strategic Decision Making in High-Velocity Environments: Toward a Midrange Theory." *Academy of Management Journal* 31 (December 1988): 737–770.

Eisenstodt, Gale. "Information Power." *Forbes* 151 (June 21, 1993): 44–45.

Etzioni, Amitai. "Normative-Affective Factors: Toward a New Decision-Making Model." *Journal of Economic Psychology* 9 (June 1988): 125–150.

Ewing, David W., and Pamela M. Banks. "Listening and Responding to Employees' Concerns." *Harvard Business Review* 58 (January–February 1980): 101–114.

"The Face of the Global Economy." *Business Week* (Reinventing America 1992): 151–159.

Feldman, Steven P. "How Organizational Culture Can Affect Innovation." *Organizational Dynamics* 17 (Summer 1988): 57–68.

Ferris, Rodney. "How Organizational Love Can Improve Leadership." *Organizational Dynamics* 16 (Spring 1988): 40–51.

Fiegenbaum, Avi, John McGee, and Howard Thomas. "Exploring the Linkage Between Strategic Groups and Competitive Strategy." *International Studies of Management & Organization* 18 (Spring 1988): 6–25.

Fierman, Jaclyn. "Beating the Midlife Career Crisis." *Fortune* 128 (September 6, 1993): 53.

Fiorelli, Joseph S. "Power in Work Groups: Team Members' Perspectives." *Human Relations* 11 (January 1988): 1–12.

Fisher, Anne B. "Sexual Harassment: What to Do." *Fortune* 128 (August 23, 1993): 84–88.

Fisher, K. Kim. "Managing in the High-Commitment Workplace." *Organizational Dynamics* 17 (Winter 1989): 31–50.

Fitzgerald, Thomas H. "Can Change in Organizational Culture Really be Managed?" *Organizational Dynamics* 16 (Autumn 1988): 4–15.

Folger, Robert, and Mary Konovsky. "Effects of Procedural and Distributive Justice on Reactions to Pay Raise Decisions." *Academy of Management Journal* 32 (March 1989): 115–131.

Fombrun, Charles J. "Structural Dynamics Within and Between Organizations." *Administrative Science Quarterly* 31 (September 1986): 103–121.

Fraser, Jill Andresky. "Women, Power, and the New GE." *Working Women* (December 1992): 58–63.

Fredericks, Peter, and N. Venkatraman. "The Rise of Strategy Support Systems." *Sloan Management Review* 29 (Summer 1988): 47–54.

Friedman, Milton. *Capitalism and Freedom.* Chicago: University of Chicago Press, 1962.

Fulks, Fred T. "Total Quality Management." *Food Technology* 45 (June 1991): 96–101.

Garsombke, Diane J. "Organizational Culture Dons the Mantle of Militarism." *Organizational Dynamics* 17 (Summer 1988): 46–56.

Garvin, David A. "Quality on the Line." *Harvard Business Review* (September–October 1983): 67.

———. "Quality Problems, Policies, and Attitudes in the United States and Japan: An Exploratory Study." *Academy of Management Journal* 29 (December 1986): 653–674.

Gellerman, Saul W. "Managing Ethics from the Top Down." *Sloan Management Review* 30 (Winter 1989): 73–79.

Gersick, Connie J. G. "Time and Transition in Work Teams: Toward a New Model of Group Development." *Academy of Management Journal* 31 (March 1988): 9–41.

———. "Marking Time: Predictable Transitions in Task Groups." *Academy of Management Journal* 32 (June 1989): 274–309.

Ghertman, Michel. "Foreign Subsidiary and Parents' Roles During Strategic Investment and Divestment Decisions." *Journal of International Business Studies* 19 (Spring 1988): 17–37.

Gist, Marilyn E., Edwin A. Locke, and M. Susan Taylor. "Organizational Behavior: Group Structure, Process, and Effectiveness." *Journal of Management* 13 (Summer 1987): 237–257.

Goddard, Robert W. "Effective Language." *Personnel Journal* 68 (April 1989): 32–37.

Gold, Bela. "Charting a Course to Superior Technology Evaluation." *Sloan Management Review* 39 (Fall 1988): 19–27.

Gold, Ben. "Computerization in Domestic and International Manufacturing." *California Management Review* 31 (Winter 1989): 129–143.

Goldstein, Jeffery. "A Far-from-Equilibrium Systems Approach to Resistance to Change." *Organizational Dynamics* 16 (Autumn 1988): 16–26.

Gomes-Casseres, Benjamin. "Joint Ventures in the Face of Global Competition." *Sloan Management Review* 30 (Fall 1988): 17–26.

Goodpaster, Kenneth E., and John B. Matthews, Jr. "Can a Corporation Have a Conscience?" *Harvard Business Review* 60 (January–February 1982): 132–141.

Gorry, G. Anthony, and Michael S. Scott Morton. "A Framework for Management Information Systems." *Sloan Management Review* 30 (Fall 1988): 49–61.

Graeff, C. L. "The Situational Leadership Theory: A Critical View." *Academy of Management Review* (April 1983): 285–291.

Grant, Rebecca A., Christopher A. Higgens, and Richard H. Irving. "Computerized Performance Monitors: Are They Costing You Customers?" *Sloan Management Review* 29 (Summer 1988): 39–45.

Green, Stephen G., and M. Ann Welsh. "Cybernetics and Dependence: Reframing the Control Concept." *The Academy of Management Review* 13 (April 1988): 287–301.

Greenfield, Sue, Robert C. Winder, and Gregory Williams. "The CEO and the External Environment." *Business Horizons* 31 (November–December 1988): 20–25.

Greiner, Ann Claire. "Quality Counts." *Technology Review* 93 (July 1990): 19–20.

Griffin, Ricky W. "Consequences of Quality Circles in an Industrial Setting: A Longitudinal Assessment." *Academy of Management Journal* 31 (June 1988): 338–358.

Griggs, Walter S., and Wallace R. Johnson. "Truth-in-Doors." *Management Solutions* (October 1988): 22–24.

Grinblatt, Mark, and Sheridan Titman. "Adverse Risk Incentives and the Design of Performance-Based Contracts." *Management Science* 35 (July 1989): 807–822.

Gross, Andrew C. "The Information Vending Machine." *Business Horizons* 31 (January–February 1988): 24–33.

Hahn, Chan K., Daniel J. Bragg, and Dongwook Shin. "Impact of the Setup Variable on Capacity and Inventory Decisions." *The Academy of Management Review* 13 (January 1988): 91–103.

Hambrick, Donald C. "The Top Management Team: Key to Strategic Success." *California Management Review* 30 (Fall 1987): 88–108.

Hammer, Michael, and James Champy. *Reengineering the Corporation: A Manifesto for Business Revolution.* New York: Harper Collins Publishers, Inc., 1993, p. 32.

Hampden-Turner, Charles. "The Boundaries of Business: The Cross-Cultural Quagmire." *Harvard Business Review* 69 (September–October 1991): p. 94.

Harper, Stephen C. "Now That the Dust Has Settled: Learning from Japanese Management." *Business Horizons* 31 (July–August 1988): 43–51.

————. "Intuition: What Separates Executives from Managers." *Business Horizons* 31 (September–October 1988): 13–19.

Harris, Robert G. "Telecommunications Policy in Japan: Lesson for the U.S." *California Management Review* 31 (Spring 1989): 113–131.

Haspeslagh, Philippe. "Portfolio Planning: Uses and Limits." *Harvard Business Review* 60 (January–February 1982): 58–73.

Hauser, John R., and Don Clausing. "The House of Quality." *Harvard Business Review* 66 (May–June 1988): 63–73.

Hawkins, Chuck, and Patrick Oster. "After a U-Turn, UPS Really Delivers." *Business Week* (May 31, 1993): 92–93.

Hax, Arnoldo C., and Nicolas S. Mailuf. "The Concept of Strategy and the Strategy Formation Process." *Interfaces* 18 (May–June 1988): 99–109.

Hayes, Robert H., and Ramchandran Jaikumar. "Manufacturing's Crisis: New Technologies, Obsolete Organizations." *Harvard Business Review* 66 (September–October 1988): 77–85.

Heiner, Ronald A. "Imperfect Decisions in Organizations: Toward a Theory of Internal Structure." *Journal of Economic Behavior & Organization* 9 (January 1988): 25–44.

Heizer, Jay, and Barry Render. *Production and Operations Management*, 3rd. ed. (Boston: Allyn and Bacon, 1993).

Hendricks, Charles F. "Rightsizing Remedy." *HRMagazine* 37 (June 1992): 13.

Heneman, Robert L., David B. Greenberger, and Chigozie Anonyuo. "Attributions and Exchanges: The Effects of Interpersonal Factors on the Diagnosis of Employee Performance." *Academy of Management Journal* 32 (June 1989): 466–476.

Hersey, Paul, and Kenneth H. Blanchard. *Management of Organizational Behavior*. 4th ed. Englewood Cliffs, NJ: Prentice-Hall, 1982.

Herzberg, Frederick. "Overcoming the Betrayals of the '80s." *Industry Week* 231 (July 13, 1987): 72.

————. "One More Time: How Do You Motivate Employees?" *Harvard Business Review* 65 (September–October 1987): 109–120.

Hill, Charles W. L. "Differentiation Versus Low Cost or Differentiation and Low Cost." *The Academy of Management Review* 13 (July 1988): 401–412.

Hiromoto, Toshiro. "Another Hidden Edge–Japanese Management Accounting." *Harvard Business Review* 66 (July–August 1988): 22–27.

Hirsch, Barry T., and David A. Macpherson. "Union Membership and Coverage Files from the Current Population Surveys: Note." *Industrial & Labor Relations Review* 46 (April 1993): 577.

Hoffman, Thomas. "Here and There." *Computerworld* 27 (April 12, 1993): 81–82.

Holland, Kelley. "Why the Chemistry Is Right at Chemical." *Business Week* (June 7, 1993): 90–93.

Holloway, Clark, and Herbert H. Hand. "Who's Running the Store, Anyway? Artificial Intelligence!!!" *Business Horizons* 31 (March–April 1988): 70–75.

Hornstein, Harvey A., et al. "Responding to Contingent Leadership Behavior." *Organizational Dynamics* 15 (Spring 1987): 56–65.

Hosmer, LaRue Tone. "Adding Ethics to the Business Curriculum." *Business Horizons* 31 (July–August 1988): 9–15.

House, Robert J. "A Path-Goal Theory of Leader Effectiveness." *Administrative Science Quarterly* 16 (1971): 321–338.

Howard, Patricia Digh. "World Shrink." *HRMagazine* 36 (January 1991): 42–43.

Howard, Robert. "The Designer Organization: Italy's GFT Goes Global." *Harvard Business Review* 69 (September–October 1991): 28–44.

Hudy, John J. "The Motivation Trap." *HRMagazine* 37 (December 1992): 63–67.

Huey, John. "How McKinsey Does It." *Fortune* 128 (November 1, 1993): 56–60, 62, 66, 68, 72–74, 79, 80.

Hunt, Bradley D., and Judith F. Vogt. "What Really Goes Wrong with Participative Work Groups?" *Training & Development Journal* 42 (May 1988): 96–100.

Hutheesing, Nikhil. "Games Companies Play." *Forbes* 152 (October 25, 1993): 68–69.

Hyman, Michael R. "Ethical Codes Are Not Enough." *Business Horizons* 33 (March–April 1990): 15–22.

Impoco, Jim, and Warren Cohen. "Nike Goes to The Full-Court Press." *U.S. News & World Report* (April 19, 1993): 48–50.

Ireland, Karin. "The Ethics Game." *Personnel Journal* 70 (March 1991): 72–75.

Isenberg, Daniel J. "Thinking and Managing: A Verbal Protocol Analysis of Managerial Problem Solving." *Academy of Management Journal* 29 (December 1986): 775–788.

———. "The Tactics of Strategic Opportunism." *Harvard Business Review* 65 (March–April 1987): 92–97.

Jacob, Rahul. "TQM More Than a Dying Fad?" *Fortune* 128 (October 18, 1993): 66–69.

Jacobs, Dorri. "Exploring Causes of Problem Performance." *Management Solutions* (December 1988): 10–17.

Jacobs, Raymond A., and Harvey M. Wagner. "Reducing Inventory System Costs by Using Robust Demand Estimators." *Management Science* 35 (July 1989): 771–787.

Jaikumar, Jay. "The Boundaries of Business: The Impact of Technology." *Harvard Business Review* 69 (September–October 1991): 100–101.

Jamson, W. A. "A Theory of Coalition Formation." *American Sociological Review* 26 (1961): 372–382.

Jordan, Paul C. "Effects of an Extrinsic Reward on Intrinsic Motivation: A Field Experiment." *Academy of Management Journal* 29 (June 1986): 405–412.

Joyce, William F. "Matrix Organization: A Social Experiment." *The Academy of Management Journal* 29 (September 1986): 537.

Juran, J. M., and Frank M. Gryna, and R. S. Bingham. *Quality Control Handbook.* McGraw-Hill Book Company: New York, 1974.

Kahn, R. L., and E. Boulding. *Power and Conflict in Organizations.* New York: Basic Books, 1964.

Kantrow, Alen M. "Why Read Peter Drucker?" *Harvard Business Review* 58 (January–February 1980): 74–83.

Kaplan, Robert S. "One Cost System Isn't Enough." *Harvard Business Review* 66 (January–February 1988): 61–66.

Katz, Jerome, and William B. Gartner. "Properties of Emerging Organizations." *The Academy of Management Review* 13 (July 1988): 429–441.

Keil, E. C. "Corporate Culture; Fashion or Fact?" *Colorado Business Magazine* 15 (May 1988): 105–109.

Keller, Robert T. "Cross-Cultural Influences on Work and Nonwork Contributors to Quality of Life." *Group & Organization Studies* 12 (September 1987): 304–318.

Kelly, Robert E. "In Praise of Followers." *Harvard Business Review* 66 (November–December 1988): 142–148.

Kerr, Jeffrey, and John W. Slocum, Jr. "Managing Corporate Culture Through Reward Systems." *The Academy of Management Executive* 1 (May 1987): 99–108.

Kester, W. Carl, and Robert A. Taggart, Jr. "Capital Allocation-Hurdle Rates, Budgets, or Both?" *Sloan Management Review* 30 (Fall 1988): 83–90.

Kets de Vries, Manfred F. R. "Leaders Who Self-Destruct." *Organizational Dynamics* 17 (Spring 1989): 5–11.

Kipnis, David. *The Powerholders.* Chicago: University of Chicago Press, 1976.

Kipnis, David, and Stuart M. Schmidt. "Upward-Influence Styles: Relationship with Performance Evaluation, Salary, and Stress." *Administrative Science Quarterly* 33 (December 1988): 528–541.

Kirkpatrick, David. "Lou Gerstner's First 30 Days." *Fortune* 127 (May 31, 1993): 57–62.

Klaas, Brian S. "Determinants of Grievance Activity and the Grievance System's Impact on Employee Behavior: An Integrative Perspective." *The Academy of Management Review* 14 (July 1989): 445–458.

Klein, Howard J. "An Integrated Control Theory Model of Work Motivation." *The Academy of Management Review* 14 (April 1989): 150–172.

Kleinman, Dan. "What to Look for in Tomorrow's Employee." *Personnel Journal* 66 (October 1987): 192–196.

Knotts, Rose. "Cross Cultural Management: Transformations and Adaptations." *Business Horizons* 32 (January–February 1989): 29–33.

Knowlton, Christopher. "The New Export Entrepreneurs." *Fortune* 123 (June 6, 1988): 87.

Krubasik, Edward G. "Customize Your Product Development." *Harvard Business Review* 66 (November–December 1988): 46–53.

Kuhlmann, Torsten M. "Adapting to Technical Change in the Workplace." *Personnel* 65 (August 1988): 67–69.

Kulik, Carol T. "The Effects of Job Categorization on Judgments of the Motivating Potential of Jobs." *Administrative Science Quarterly* 34 (March 1989): 68–90.

Laabs, Jennifer J. "The Global Talent Search." *Personnel Journal* 70 (August 1991): 38–44.

Landler, Mark, Ronald Grover, Bart Ziergler, and Chuck Hawkins. "Media Mania." *Business Week* (July 12, 1993): 110–119.

Landro, Laura. "Instant Alliances Coalesce During Fight for Paramount." *The Wall Street Journal* (October 13, 1993): B1.

Langowitz, Nan S. "Managing New Product Design and Factory Fit." *Business Horizons* 32 (May–June 1989): 76–79.

LaPlante, Alice. "Rightsizing Angst." *Forbes* 151 (June 7, 1993): 94–104.

Larsson, Rikard, and David W. Bowen. "Organization and Customer: Managing Design and Coordination of Services." *The Academy of Management Review* 14 (April 1989): 213–233.

Lawler, Edward E. III. "Substitutes for Hierarchy." *Organizational Dynamics* 17 (Summer 1988): 5–15.

———. "Choosing an Involvement Strategy." *The Academy of Management Executive* 2 (August 1988): 197–204.

———. "I Would Abandon Business Contracts." *Fortune* 121 (March 26, 1990): 49.

Lawrence, Barbara S. "New Wrinkles in the Theory of Age: Demography, Norms, and Performance Ratings." *Academy of Management Journal* 31 (June 1988): 309–337.

Lawrence, P. R. and J. W. Lorsch. *Organization and Environment.* Boston: Harvard University Graduate School of Business, Division of Research, 1967.

———. "Differentiation and Integration in Complex Organizations." *Administrative Science Quarterly* 12 (June 1967): 1–47.

Lederer, Albert L., and Aubrey L. Mendelow. "Information Systems Planning: Top Management Takes Control." *Business Horizons* 31 (May–June 1988): 73–78.

Lee, Dixie, and Richard Brostrom. "Managing the High-Tech Professional." *Personnel* 65 (June 1988): 12–17.

Lee, James A. "Changes in Managerial Values, 1985–1986." *Business Horizons* 31 (July–August 1988): 29–37.

Lee, Melissa. "Diversity Training Brings Unity to Small Companies." *The Wall Street Journal* (September 2, 1993): B2.

Lengel Robert H., and Richard L. Daft. "The Selection of Communication Media as an Executive Skill." *The Academy of Management Executive* 2 (August 1988): 225–234.

Lesly, Elizabeth, Zachary Schiller, Stephen Baker, and Geoffrey Smith. "CEOs with the Outside Edge." *Business Week* (October 11, 1993): 60–62.

Levine, Jonathan B. "For IBM Europe 'This Is the Year of Truth.'" *Business Week* (April 19, 1993): 45–46.

Levinthal, Daniel A., and Mark Fichman. "Dynamics of Interorganizational Attachments: Auditor-Client Relationships." *Administrative Science Quarterly* 33 (September 1988): 345–369.

Levitt, Barbara, and Clifford Nass. "The Lid on the Garbage Can: Institutional Constraints on Decision Making in the Technical Core of College-Text Publishers." *Administrative Science Quarterly* 34 (June 1989): 190–206.

Lieberman, S. "The Effects of Changes in Roles on the Attitudes of Role Occupants." *Human Relations* 9 (1956): 385–417.

Liebowitz, S. Jay, and Aubrey L. Mendelow. "Directions for Development; Long-Term Organizational Change Requires Corporate Vision and Patience." *Personnel Administrator* 33 (June 1988): 116–124.

Light, Larry. "The Job Engine Needs Fuel." *Business Week* (March 1, 1993): 78.

Longenecker, Justin G., Joseph A. McKinney, and Carlos W. Moore. "Ethics in Small Business." *Journal of Small Business Management* 27 (January 1989): 27–31.

Lubove, Seth. "Produce—Or Else." *Forbes* 151 (May 10, 1993): 86–87.

———. "Dow's Downer." *Forbes* 151 (June 21, 1993): 58–59, 64.

———. "We Have a Big Pond to Play In." *Forbes* 152 (September 13, 1993): 216–224.

Maddox, Robert C., and Douglas Short. "The Cultural Integrator." *Business Horizons* 31 (November–December 1988): 57–59.

Maglitta, Joseph. "Squeeze Play." *Computerworld* 27 (April 19, 1993): 86–91.

Magnus, Margaret. "Is Your Recruitment All It Can Be?" *Personnel Journal* 66 (February 1987): 54–63.

Mandell, Michael J., Wendy Zeller, and Robert Hof. "Jobs, Jobs." *Business Week* (February 22, 1993): 70.

Mann, Carl P. "Transformational Leadership in the Executive Office." *Public Relations Quarterly* 33 (Spring 1988): 19–23.

Mansfield, Edwin. "Technological Creativity: Japan and the United States." *Business Horizons* 32 (March–April 1989): 48–53.

Manz, Charles C., and Henry P. Sims, Jr. "Leading Workers to Lead Themselves: The External Leadership of Self-Managing Work Teams." *Administrative Science Quarterly* 32 (March 1987): 106–129.

Marash, Stanley A. "Blueprint for Quality." *Personnel Journal* 68 (March 1989): 120–123.

March, James G., and Martha S. Feldman. "Information in Organizations as Signal and Symbol." *Administrative Science Quarterly* 26 (June 1981): 171–186.

Marcus, Alfred A. "Responses to Externally Induced Innovation: Their Effects on Organizational Performance." *Strategic Management Journal* 9 (July–August 1988): 387–402.

Maremont, Mark, and Elizabeth Lesly. "Getting the Picture." *Business Week* (February 1, 1993): 24–26.

Martin, Robin, and Toby D. Wall. "Attentional Demand and Cost Responsibility as Stressors in Shopfloor Jobs." *Academy of Management Review* 31 (March 1989): 69–86.

Mascarenhas, Briance. "Strategic Group Dynamics." *Academy of Management Journal* 32 (June 1989): 333–352.

Maslow, Abraham H. *Motivation and Personality.* New York: Harper and Row, 1954.

McCullers, John C., Richard A. Fabes, and James D. Moran, III. "Does Intrinsic Motivation Theory Explain the Adverse Effects of Rewards on Immediate Task Performance?" *Journal of Personality and Social Psychology* 52 (May 1987): 1027–1033.

McFarland, Lynne Joy, Larry E. Senn, and John R. Childress. *21st Century Leadership.* New York: The Leadership Press, 1993, pp. 227–232.

McGregor, Douglas. *The Human Side of Enterprise.* New York: McGraw-Hill, 1961.

McGuire, Jean B., Alison Sundgren, and Thomas Schneeweis. "Corporate Social Responsibility and Firm Financial Performance." *Academy of Management Journal* 31 (December 1988): 854–872.

Meindl, James R. "Managing to Be Fair: An Exploration of Values, Motives, and Leadership." *Administrative Science Quarterly* 34 (June 1989): 252–276.

Mendenhall, Mark E., and Gary Oddou. "The Overseas Assignment: A Practical Look." *Business Horizons* 31 (September–October 1988): 78–84.

Meyer, Alan D. "Mingling Decision-Making Metaphors." *Academy of Management Review* 9 (January 1984): 6–17.

Meyer, Alan D., and James B. Goes. "Organizational Assimilation of Innovations: A Multilevel Contextual Analysis." *Academy of Management Journal* 31 (December 1988): 897–923.

Meyer, Marc H., and Edward B. Roberts. "Focusing Product Technology for Corporate Growth." *Sloan Management Review* 29 (Summer 1988): 7–16.

Michael, Steven R. "Feedforward Versus Feedback Controls in Planning." *Managerial Planning* 29 (November–December 1980): 34–38.

Middaugh, J. Kendall II. "Management Control in the Financial-Services Industry." *Business Horizons* 31 (May–June 1988): 79–86.

Miles, Carrie A., and Jean M. McCloskey. "People: The Key to Productivity" *HRMagazine* 38 (February 1993): 40–45.

Miles, Raymond E. "Adapting to Technology and Competition: A New Industrial Relations System for the 21st Century." *California Management Review* 31 (Winter 1989): 9–28.

Miner, Anne S. "Idiosyncratic Jobs in Formalized Organizations." *Administrative Quarterly* 32 (September 1987): 327–351.

Mintzberg, H. *The Structuring of Organizations.* Englewood Cliffs, NJ: Prentice-Hall, 1978.

———. *Power In and Around Organizations.* Englewood Cliffs, NJ: Prentice-Hall, 1983.

———. "The Strategy Concept I: Five Ps for Strategy." *California Management Review* 30 (Fall 1987): 11–24.

———. "The Strategy Concept II: Another Look at Why Organizations Need Strategies." *California Management Review* 30 (Fall 1987): 25–32.

Moad, Jeff. "Tools to Automate Quality Production." *Datamation* 37 (April 15, 1991): 63–66.

Moffat, Susan. "To Be a Leader in Technology, You Must Share It." *Fortune* 124 (January 14, 1991): 34–35.

Mondy, R. Wayne, and Robert M. Noe III. *Human Resource Management*, 5th ed. Boston: Allyn and Bacon, 1993.

Mondy, R. Wayne, Robert M. Noe III, and Robert E. Edwards. "What the Staffing Function Entails." *Personnel* 63 (April 1986): 55–58.

Mondy, R. Wayne, and Shane R. Premeaux. "Power, Politics, and the First-Line Supervisor." *Supervisory Management* 31 (January 1986): 36–39.

Mondy, R. Wayne, Shane R. Premeaux, and Arthur Sharplin. "Motivation in Practice." *Manage* 39, 2d Qtr (1986): 13, 22–23.

Moorhead, Gregory, and John R. Montanari. "An Empirical Investigation of the Groupthink Phenomenon." *Human Relations* 30 (May 1988): 300–311.

Morris, Barry G. "The Executive: A Pathfinder." *Organizational Dynamics* 16 (Spring 1988): 62–77.

Morrisey, George L. "Who Needs a Mission Statement? You Do." *Training and Development Journal* 42 (March 1988): 50–52.

Murphy, Patrick E. "Creating Ethical Corporate Structures." *Sloan Management Review* 30 (Winter 1989): 81–87.

Naisbitt, John. *Megatrends*. New York: Warner Books, 1982.

Nardone, Thomas. "Decline in Youth Population Does Not Lead to Lower Jobless Rates." *Monthly Labor Review* 110 (June 1987): 37–42.

Nardoni, Ren. "Integrated Staffing Systems." *Personnel Journal* 68 (May 1989): 106–110.

Nash, Kim. "New Systems, New Business Practices." *Computerworld* 27 (May 24, 1993): 49.

Nelson, Reed E. "The Strength of Strong Ties: Social Networks and Intergroup Conflict in Organizations." *Academy of Management Journal* 32 (June 1989): 377–401.

Nelton, Sharon. "Beyond Body Language." *Nation's Business* (June 1986): 73–74.

———. "Cultural Changes in a Family Firm." *Nation's Business* (January 1989): 62–65.

Nielsen, Richard P. "Changing Unethical Organizational Behavior." *The Academy of Management Executive* 2 (May 1989): 123–130.

Nitcoki, Joseph Z. "In Search of Sense in Common Sense Management." *Journal of Business Ethics* 6 (November 1987): 639–647.

Noble, Barbara Presley. "The Debate Over la Difference." *The New York Times* (August 15, 1993): B1.

O'Conner, John T. "The Well-Designed Office." *Harvard Business Review* 67 (March–April 1989): 125–129.

O'Donnell, Joseph. "The Creative-Rational Manager." *Manage* 10 (July 1988): 1–3.

O'Reilly, Charles A. III, David F. Caldwell, and William P. Barnett. "Work Group Demography, Social Integration, and Turnover." *Administrative Science Quarterly* 34 (March 1989): 21–37.

Ogilvis, John R., Michael F. Pohlen, and Louise H. Jones. "Organizational Information Processing and Productivity Improvement." *National Productivity Review* 7 (Summer 1988): 229–237.

Ohmae, Kenichi. "The Global Logic of Strategic Alliances." *Harvard Business Review* 67 (March–April 1989): 143–154.

———. "Managing in a Borderless World." *Harvard Business Review* 67 (May–June 1989): 152–161.

Olson, Philip D. "Entrepreneurship and Management." *Journal of Small Business Management* 25 (July 1987): 7–13.

Ono, Karou, and James H. Davis. "Individual Judgment and Group Interaction: A Variable Perspective Approach." *Organizational Behavior & Human Decision Processes* 11 (April 1988): 211–232.

Ordiorne, George S. "Uneasy Look at Motivation Theory." *Training and Development Journal* 34 (June 1980): 106–112.

Ornstein, Suzyn. "The Hidden Influences of Office Design." *The Academy of Management Executive* 2 (May 1989): 144–148.

Ouchi, William G. "Relationship Between Organizational Structure and Organizational Control." *Administrative Science Quarterly* 22 (March 1981): 95–113.

Overman, Stephenie. "A Measure of Success." *HRMagazine* 37 (December 1992): 38.

———. "International Waters." *HRMagazine* 38 (September 1993): 46–49.

Paquette, Laurence, and Kida, Thomas. "The Effect of Decision Strategy and Task Complexity on Decision

Performance." *Organizational Behavior & Human Decision Processes* 41 (February 1988): 128–142.

Pasewark, William R. "A New Approach to Quality Control for Auditors: Quality Circles." *The Practical Accountant* 24 (March 1991): 68–71.

Peters, Thomas J. "Facing Up to the Need for a Management Revolution." *California Management Review* 30 (Winter 1988): 7–38.

Peters, Thomas J., and Robert H. Waterman, Jr. *In Search of Excellence.* New York: Harper & Row, 1982.

————. "The Destruction of Hierarchy: The Information Revolution Is Killing Traditional Corporate Hierarchy." *Industry Week* 237 (August 15, 1988): 33–35.

Philbrick, Jane Hass, and Marsha E. Hass. "The New Management: Is It Legal?" *The Academy of Management Executive* 4 (November 1988): 325–330.

Port, Otis, John Carey, Kevin Kelly, and Stephanie Anderson Forest. "Quality." *Business Week* (November 30, 1992): 67–68.

Premeaux, Shane R., R. Wayne Mondy, and Art Bethke. "Decertification: Fulfilling Unions' Destiny?" *Personnel Journal* 66 (June 1987): 144–148.

Pryor, Austin K., and William K. Foster. "The Strategic Management of Innovation." *Journal of Business Strategy* 7 (Summer 1986): 38–42.

Quick, James Campbell, Debra L. Nelson, and Jonathon D. Quick. "Successful Executives: How Independent?" *The Academy of Management Executive* 1 (August 1987): 139–146.

Radosevich, Lynda. "Package Automatically Puts Faxed Data into Host Apps." *Computerworld* 27 (June 14, 1993): 74.

Ragozzino, Pat P. "IS Quality—What Is It?" *Journal of Systems Management* 41 (November 1990): 15–16.

Randolph, W. Alan., and Barry Z. Posner. "What Every Manager Needs to Know About Project Management." *Sloan Management Review* 29 (Summer 1988): 65–73.

Rapoport, Carla. "Mazda's Bold New Global Strategy." *Fortune* 123 (December 17, 1990): 109–113.

Rechner, Paula L. "Corporate Governance: Fact or Fiction?" *Business Horizons* 32 (July–August 1989): 11–15.

Regan, Mary Beth. "An Embarrassment of Clean Air." *Business Week* (May 31, 1993): 34.

Reilly, Bernard J. "Ethical Business and the Ethical Person." *Business Horizons* 33 (November–December 1990): 23–27.

Reimann, Bernard C., and Yoash Wiener. "Corporate Culture: Avoiding the Elitist Trap." *Business Horizons* (March–April 1988): 36–42.

Richman, Louis S. "Jobs that are Growing and Slowing." *Fortune* 128 (July 12, 1993): 53.

————. "When Will the Layoffs End?" *Fortune* 128 (September 20, 1993): 54.

Rienzo, Thomas F. "Planning Deming Management for Service Organizations." *Business Horizons* 36 (May–June 1993): 19–29.

Rigdon, Joan E. "Using Lateral Moves to Spur Employees." *The Wall Street Journal* (May 26, 1992): B1, B9.

Risman, Barbara J., and Donald Tomaskovic-Devey. "The Social Construction of Technology: Microcomputers and the Organization of Work." *Business Horizons* 32 (May–June 1989): 71–75.

Roberts, Nancy C., and Paula J. King. "The Stakeholder Audit Goes Public." *Organizational Dynamics* 17 (Winter 1989): 63–79.

Robin, Donald, Michael Giallourakis, Fred R. David, and Thomas E. Moritz. "A Different Look at Codes of Ethics." *Business Horizons* 32 (January–February 1989): 66–73.

Robin, Donald P., and Eric Reidenbach. "Balancing Corporate Profits and Ethics." *Business* 40 (October–November–December 1990): 11–14.

Rockart, John F. "The Line Takes the Leadership—IS Management in a Wired Society." *Sloan Management Review* 29 (Summer 1988): 57–64.

Rockart, John F., and James E. Short. "IT in the 1990s: Managing Organizational Interdependence." *Sloan Management Review* 30 (Winter 1989): 7–17.

Salwen, Kevin G. "Most Firms Fail to Warn Workers of Plant Closings." *The Wall Street Journal* (February 23, 1993): A2, A6.

Samuelson, Robert J. "R.I.P.: The Good Corporation." *Newsweek* 122 (July 5, 1993): 41.

Saporito, Bill. "Where the Global Action Is." *Fortune* 128 (Autumn/Winter 1993): 63–65.

Sass, C. Joseph, and Teresa A. Keefe. "MIS for Strategic Planning and a Competitive Edge." *Journal of Systems Management* 39 (June 1988): 14–17.

Schein, Edgar H. "Organizational Socialization and the Profession of Management." *Sloan Management Review* 30 (Fall 1988): 53–65.

Schemenner, Roger W. "Escaping the Black Holes of Cost Accounting." *Business Horizons* 31 (January–February 1988): 66–72.

Scheuing, Eberhard E. "How to Build a Quality-Conscious Team." *Supervisory Management* 35 (January 1990): 6.

Schiller, Zachary. "A Nervous P&G Picks Up the Cost-Cutting Ax." *Business Week* (April 19, 1993): 28.

Schmenner, Roger W. "The Merit of Making Things Fast." *Sloan Management Review* 30 (Fall 1988): 11–17.

Schroeder, Michael, and Joseph Weber. "Is Merck Ready for Marty Wygod?" *Business Week* (October 4, 1993): 80–84.

Sellers, Patricia, with David Kirkpatrick. "Can This Man Save IBM?" *Fortune* 127 (April 19, 1993): 63–67.

Seltzer, Joseph, and Rita E. Numerof. "Supervisory Leadership and Subordinate Burnout." *Academy of Management Journal* 31 (June 1988): 439–446.

Serwer, Andrew E. "America's 100 Fastest Growers." *Fortune* 128 (August 9, 1993): 40–56.

Sheehy, James W. "New Work Ethic Is Frightening." *Personnel Journal* 69 (June 1990): 28–36.

Sherman, Stratford. "The New Computer Revolution." *Fortune* 127 (June 14, 1993): 56–80.

Simon, Ruth, and Graham Button. "What I Learned in the Eighties." *Forbes* 145 (January 8, 1991): 100–114.

Sinetar, Marsha. "The Informal Discussion Group-A Powerful Agent for Change." *Sloan Management Review* 29 (Summer 1988): 61–65.

Skinner, B. F. *The Behavior of Organisms: An Experimental Approach*. New York: Appleton-Century, 1938.

Skinner, Wickham. "What Matters to Manufacturing." *Harvard Business Review* 66 (January–February 1988): 10–17.

Slutsker, Gary. "The Company that Likes to Obsolete Itself." *Forbes* 152 (September 13, 1993): 139–144.

Smart, Tim, Pete Engardio, and Geri Smith. "GE's Brave New World." *Business Week* (November 8, 1993): 64–70.

Smith, Gerald F. "Defining Managerial Problems: A Framework for Prescriptive Theorizing." *Management Science* 35 (August 1989): 963–981.

Smith, Harold Ivan. "Singles in the Workplace." *Personnel Administrator* 33 (February 1988): 76–81.

Smith, Kenwyn K. "The Movement of Conflict in Organizations: The Joint Dynamics of Splitting and Triangulation." *Administrative Science Quarterly* 34 (March 1989): 1–20.

Smith, Kenwyn K., and David N. Berg. "A Paradoxical Conception of Group Dynamics." *Human Relations* 10 (October 1987): 633–657.

Smith, Lee. "What the Boss Knows About You." *Fortune* 128 (August 9, 1993): 88–93.

Snyder, Neil H., Bernard A. Morin, and Marilyn A. Morgan. "Motivating People to Build Excellent Enterprises." *Business* 38 (April–June 1988): 14–19.

Spiers, Joseph. "An End to Efficiency?" *Fortune* 128 (September 6, 1993): 12.

Srivastva, Suresh, and Frank J. Barrett. "The Transforming Nature of Metaphors in Group Development: A Study in Group Theory." *Human Relations* 11 (January 1988): 31–63.

Steffy, Brian D., and Steven D. Maurer. "Conceptualizing and Measuring the Economic Effectiveness of Human Resource Activities." *The Academy of Management Review* 13 (April 1988): 271–286.

Steingraber, Fred G. "Total Quality Management: A New Look at a Basic Issue." *Vital Speeches of the Day* 57 (April 15, 1991): 415–416.

Strolle, Alfred. "Creating a Total Quality Management Culture Is Everyone's Business." *Research Technology Management* 34 (July –August 1991): 8–9.

Sullivan, Jeremiah J. "Three Roles of Language in Motivation Theory." *The Academy of Management Review* 13 (January 1988): 104–115.

Taylor, Alex, III. "Why GM Leads the Pack in Europe." *Fortune* 127 (May 17, 1993): 83–87.

Thibaut, J. W., and H. H. Kelley. *The Social Psychology of Groups*. New York: Wiley, 1959.

Thompson, J. D. *Organizations in Action*. New York: McGraw-Hill, 1967.

Tobin, Lawrence M. "The New Quality Landscape: Total Quality Management." *Journal of Systems Management* 41 (November 1990): 10–14.

Treece, James B. "Improving the Soul of an Old Machine." *Business Week* (October 25, 1993): 134–136.

Tully, Shawn. "The Modular Corporation." *Fortune* 128 (February 8, 1993): 106–115.

Tung, Rosalie L. "Career Issues in International Assignments." *The Academy of Management Executive* 2 (August 1988): 241–244.

Turney, Peter B. B., and Bruce Anderson. "Accounting for Continuous Improvement." *Sloan Management Review* 30 (Winter 1989): 37–47.

Ulrich David, and Margaret F. Wiersema. "Gaining Strategic and Organizational Behavior." *The Academy of Management Executive* 2 (May 1989): 115–122.

Venkatraman N. "The Concept of Fit in Strategy Research: Toward Verbal and Statistical Correspondence." *The Academy of Management Review* 14 (July 1989): 423–444.

Verity, John W. "Twilight of the Mainframe." *Business Week* (August 17, 1992): 33.

Victor, Bart, and John B. Cullen. "The Organizational Bases of Ethical Work Climates." *Administrative Science Quarterly* 33 (March 1988): 101–125.

Vroom, Victor H. *Work and Motivation*. New York: Wiley, 1964.

Walker, A. and J. Lorsch. "Organizational Choice: Product Versus Function." *Harvard Business Review* 46 (November–December 1968): 129–138.

Walsh, James P. "Selectivity and Selective Perception: An Investigation of Managers' Belief Structures and Information Processing." *Academy of Management Journal* 31 (December 1988): 873–896.

Walton, Mary. *The Deming Management Method*. New York: Perigee Books, Putnam Publishing Group, 1986.

Webber, Alan M. "Ricochet Change Across the Pacific." *Harvard Business Review* 66 (September–October 1988): 144–152.

Weber, Joseph, Gail Schares, Stephen Hutcheon, and Ian Katz. "Campbell: Now It's M-M-Global." *Business Week* (March 15, 1993): 52–54.

Weigelt, Keith, and Ian MacMillan. "An Interactive Strategic Analysis Framework." *Strategic Management Journal* 9 (Summer 1988): 27–40.

Weihrich, Heinz, and Diethard Buhler. "Training Managers for the Global Market." *Business* 40 (July–September 1990): 40–42.

Weiss, Alan. "Seven Reasons to Examine Work Place Ethics." *HRMagazine* 36 (March 1991): 69–74.

Weiss, Howard J., and Mark E. Gershon. *Production and Operations Management* 2d ed. Boston: Allyn and Bacon, 1993.

Welsh, M. Ann, and Gordon E. Dehler. "Political Legacy of Administrative Succession." *Academy of Management Journal* 31 (December 1988): 948–961.

Werner, Manuel. "Great Paradox: Responsibility Without Empowerment." *Business Horizons* (September–October 1992): 55–58.

Weston, Frederick C., Jr. "Computer Integrated Manufacturing Systems: Fact or Fantasy." *Business Horizons* 31 (July–August 1988): 64–68.

White, John A. "TQM: It's Time, Academia!" Paper based on a presentation given July 18, 1990, at the First National Symposium on the Role of Academia in National Competitiveness and Total Quality Management, hosted by West Virginia University.

Whitehill, Arthur M. "American Executives Through Foreign Eyes." *Business Horizons* 32 (May–June 1989): 42–48.

Whyte, Glen. "Groupthink Reconsidered." *The Academy of Management Review* 14 (January 1989): 40–56.

Woodruff, David, James B. Treece, Sunita Wadekar Bhargava, and Karen Lowry Miller. "Saturn." *Business Week* (August 17, 1992): 88.

Woolley, Suzanne. "Shaping Up By Shipping Out." *Business Week* (April 19, 1993): 119.

Wueste, Richard A. "A Matter of Inconsequence: Mastering the Art of Executive Triviality." *Management World* 17 (March–April 1988): 40–41.

Yasai-Ardekani, Masoud. "Effects of Environmental Scarcity and Munificence on the Relationship of Context to Organizational Structures." *Academy of Management Journal* 32 (March 1989): 131–156.

Zarembra, Alan. "Communicating Upward." *Personnel Journal* 68 (March 1989): 34–39.

Zauderer, Donald, and Joseph Fox. "Resiliency in the Face of Stress." *Management Solutions* (November 1988): 30–35.

Zeltmann, Steven M. "Communications Networks for Managing Global Operations." *Business Perspectives* 4 (Fall 1990): 20–22.

Zemke, Ron. "Workplace Stress Revisited." *Training* (November 1991): 35–39.

Zenger, Rodd R., and Barbara S. Lawrence. "Organizational Demography: The Differential Effects of Age and Tenure Distributions on Technical Communication." *Academy of Management Journal* 32 (June 1989): 353–376.

Index

Company Index

Subject Index